The Routledge Companion to Critical Management Studies

The scholarly field of Critical Management Studies (CMS) is in a state of flux. Against a backdrop of dramatic global shifts, CMS scholarship has lately taken a number of new and exciting directions and, at times, challenged older critical voices. Novel theoretical frameworks and diverse research interests mark the CMS field as never before. Interrogating conventional critiques of management and arguing for fresh approaches, *The Routledge Companion to Critical Management Studies* captures this intellectual ferment and new spirit of inquiry within CMS, and showcases the pluralistic generation of CMS scholars that has emerged in recent years.

Setting the scene for a crucial period for the discipline, this insightful volume covers new ground and essential areas grouped under the following themes:

* critique and its (dis-)contents
* difference, otherness, marginality
* knowledge at the crossroads
* history and discourse
* global predicaments

Drawing on the expertise of an international team of contributing scholars, *The Routledge Companion to Critical Management Studies* is a rich resource and the perfect reference tool for students and researchers of management and organization.

Anshuman Prasad is Professor of Management at the College of Business, University of New Haven, United States.

Pushkala Prasad is the Zankel Chair Professor of Management and Liberal Arts at Skidmore College, United States.

Albert J. Mills is Professor of Management at the Sobey School of Business, Saint Mary's University, Canada.

Jean Helms Mills is Professor of Management at the Sobey School of Business, Saint Mary's University, Canada.

Routledge companions in business, management and accounting

Routledge Companions in Business, Management and Accounting are prestige reference works providing an overview of a whole subject area or subdiscipline. These books survey the state of the discipline, including emerging and cutting edge areas. Providing a comprehensive, up-to-date, definitive work of reference, Routledge Companions can be cited as an authoritative source on the subject.

A key aspect of these Routledge Companions is their international scope and relevance. Edited by an array of highly regarded scholars, these volumes also benefit from teams of contributors that reflect an international range of perspectives.

Individually, Routledge Companions in Business, Management and Accounting provide an impactful one-stop-shop resource for each theme covered. Collectively, they represent a comprehensive learning and research resource for researchers, postgraduate students, and practitioners.

Published titles in this series include:

The Routledge Companion to Critical Management Studies

Edited by Anshuman Prasad, Pushkala Prasad,
Albert J. Mills and Jean Helms Mills

LONDON AND NEW YORK

First published 2016
by Routledge

2 Park Square, Milton Park, Abingdon, Oxfordshire OX14 4RN
711 Third Avenue, New York, NY 10017

Routledge is an imprint of the Taylor & Francis Group, an informa business

First issued in paperback 2018

British Library Cataloguing in Publication Data
A catalogue record for this book is available from the British Library

Library of Congress Cataloging-in-Publication Data
The Routledge companion to critical management studies / edited by
   Anshuman Prasad, Pushkala Prasad, Albert J. Mills and Jean Helms Mills.
      pages cm.—(Routledge companions in business, management and accounting)
   Includes bibliographical references and index.
   1. Management—Study and teaching.   2. Management.   3. Organizational
sociology.   4. Critical theory.   I. Prasad, Anshuman.
   HD30.4.R6836 2016
   658—dc23
   2015000491

ISBN: 978-0-415-50188-0 (hbk)
ISBN: 978-1-138-38620-4 (pbk)

Typeset in Bembo
by Apex CoVantage, LLC

To Larry Zacharias, our dear friend and teacher: with affection and enormous gratitude

— Anshu and Pushi

For Margaret Stark Somerville Beattie (1924–1948) the mother I knew only through stories

—Albert

In memory of my mother Sue Anne Helms (1929–2012) and my aunt Pauline Helms (1924–2013), two strong women who helped me become the person I am

—Jean

Contents

Contents

Acknowledgments

We would like to thank Terry Clague, Senior Commissioning Editor at Routledge, for supporting the idea for this book. Our thanks also to Terry, Nicola Cupit, Olivia Marsh and others at Routledge for patiently working with us on this project. Our grateful thanks to all the contributors for making the book possible.

Pushkala Prasad would like to thank Camila Mena for her diligent assistance in putting this volume together. She also sincerely thanks an incredibly supportive administration at Skidmore College – notably Paty Rubio (associate dean) and Beau Breslin (dean of the faculty) for their unfailing encouragement and appreciation of her scholarly pursuits.

Chapter 2 of the book was originally published as 'CMS: A Satirical Critique of Three Narrative Histories' in *Organization, 20*(1), pp. 117–129 and is reproduced here with permission from Sage.

Anshuman Prasad
Pushkala Prasad
Albert J. Mills
Jean Helms Mills

Notes on the contributors

Rafael Alcadipani is associate professor of organizational studies in the São Paulo School of Management of Getulio Vargas Foundation (EAESP-FGV) in Brazil. He is also visiting researcher at the Gothenburg Research Institute, is associate editor of *Critical Perspectives on International Business*, and has acted as a representative at large in the Academy of Management Critical Management Studies Division. He gained his PhD at Manchester Business School, U.K. His research interests are post-structuralism, ethnography, and postcolonialism in organizational studies.

Karen Lee Ashcraft is a professor of organizational communication at the University of Colorado, Boulder. Her research examines organizational forms and occupational identities, with a guiding interest in relations of power and difference, specifically gender, race, sexuality, and class. Her work appears in numerous management and communication journals – such as the *Academy of Management Journal, Administrative Science Quarterly, Academy of Management Review, Communication Theory*, and *Management Communication Quarterly* – and she coauthored the book *Reworking Gender: A Feminist Communicology of Organization* (Sage, 2004) with Dennis Mumby. Her recent empirical work investigates the historical and contemporary evolution of professional identities in the context of commercial aviation.

Emma Bell is professor of management and organization studies at Keele University, U.K. Her work focuses on organization studies and research methods in the context of critical management studies, where she has investigated issues such as gender, emotion, religion, spirituality, and organizational memory. A current project, with Nivedita Kothiyal, builds on her previous work on methodologies and methods in management research and focuses on the politics and practices of knowledge production in the Indian context.

Dr. Janet Borgerson works at the intersections of philosophy, business, and culture and is coauthor of *From Chinese Brand Culture to Global Brands* (Palgrave Macmillan, 2013). She earned a BA (philosophy) from the University of Michigan, Ann Arbor, and an MA and PhD (philosophy) from the University of Wisconsin, Madison, completing postdoctoral work at Brown University and receiving fellowships from the Cranbrook Institute and Harvard School of Public Health. She earned a docent degree in business administration from Stockholm University, where she was an associate professor of marketing. Her research has appeared in a broad range of business and philosophy journals, such as *Journal of Marketing Management* and *Philosophy Today*, in book chapters, and on the *Material World* blog. She has been a visiting professor at Walailak University, Thailand, and Shanghai Institute for Foreign Trade in China, and a research fellow at the Royal Institute of Technology, Stockholm. She serves on the editorial review board of *Consumption Markets and Culture* and on the board of trustees at Eastman House International Museum of

Photography and Film, for which she also does brand consulting. Currently a visiting scholar at Rochester Institute of Technology, she is working on two books, *Witnessing and Intersubjectivity* and *Designed for Hi-Fi Living*.

J. Michael Cavanaugh received his PhD from the University of Massachusetts, Amherst. He is an associate professor of management at the Dolan School of Business, Fairfield University, Connecticut. His classrooms explore the individual and communal power extended to those who take the provisional nature of management theorizing seriously. When he isn't out taking long bike trips, Dr. Cavanaugh is researching the implications of digital social media on "millennial" brain development and thinking what this might mean for management pedagogy and the Gutenberg ethos of the university.

Gabriela Coronado is a Mexican anthropologist with a PhD in social inquiry from the University of Western Sydney, Australia, and a senior lecturer in organizational studies in the School of Business at the University of Western Sydney. In Mexico, she has researched different aspects of Mexican culture, language, and identity, highlighting issues of intercultural communication and politics between Indigenous and non-Indigenous peoples. Adopting an interdisciplinary perspective, which incorporates ethnography, semiotics, critical discourse analysis, and critical management studies, her current work focuses on the politics of culture and its implications for social groups and organizations. This covers intercultural dialogues and the complexities of culture, society, and politics in the context of globalization, including transnational relationships and cultural impacts on the generation of new forms of organization. She is also interested in the complexities emerging along the interface between business and society, in particular the ideologies behind the discourses of business and management education.

Alexandre Faria is an associate professor at EBAPE, Fundação Getulio Vargas, Brazil. He is also a researcher of the Brazilian Research Council (CNPq) and acted as chair of the CMS Division at the Academy of Management from 2009 to 2014. His current research focuses on strategies for decolonizing management studies.

Jenna N. Hanchey is a doctoral student and William C. Powers Fellow in the Communication Studies Department at the University of Texas at Austin. Her work analyzes Western rhetorics of international aid and assistance, particularly focusing on organizations that work in and with sub-Saharan Africa. Integrating fieldwork and textual analysis, she also examines the way aid projects are received and responded to by local communities. She is a recent recipient of the Gerard A. Hauser Award from the Rhetoric Society of America, as well as support for dissertation research in Tanzania through the Jesse H. Jones Fellowship from the Moody College of Communication at the University of Texas at Austin.

Jeff Hearn is a professor of management and organization, Hanken School of Economics, Finland; guest research professor in the Faculty of Humanities and Social Sciences, based in gender studies, Örebro University, Sweden; professor of sociology, University of Huddersfield, U.K.; and a fellow of the U.K. Academy of Social Sciences. He has published very widely, for example, in *British Journal of Management*; *Equality, Diversity and Inclusion*; *Gender, Work and Organization*; *Human Relations*; *Leadership*; *Organization*; and *Organization Studies*. His latest books are *Rethinking Transnational Men*, edited with Marina Blagojević and Katherine Harrison (Routledge, 2013) and *Men of the World: Genders, Globalizations, Transnational Times* (Sage, 2015). He is managing co-editor of the *Routledge Advances in Feminist Studies and Intersectionality* book series, co-editor of *NORMA: International Journal of*

Masculinity Studies, and an associate editor of *Gender, Work and Organization*. His research focuses on gender, sexuality, violence, organizations, and transnational processes.

Jean Helms Mills is a professor of management at the Sobey School of Business at Saint Mary's University in Canada. She worked for 17 years as a reservations agent in the airline industry before returning to full-time education at the age of 34. She is a former co-chair of the Critical Management Studies (CMS) Division and currently is an associate editor of *Gender, Work and Organization*. Jean also serves on the editorial boards of several other journals. Her seven books include *Making Sense of Organizational Change* (Routledge, 2003), *Workplace Learning: A Critical Introduction* (Garamond Press, 2004), *Reading Organization Theory: A Critical Approach to the Study of Organizational Behaviour and Structure* (2005), and *Understanding Organizational Change* (Routledge, 2009).

Charlotte Holgersson is PhD and docent in gender, organization, and management at the Department of Industrial Economics and Management at KTH Royal Institute of Technology in Stockholm, Sweden. Her research is located at the intersection between organization and management studies and gender studies. One of her main empirical concerns has been the perpetuation of men's dominance at top positions in organizations. She defended her doctoral thesis on the recruitment of managing directors and the concept of homosociality in 2003 at the Stockholm School of Economics. Her research interest also includes issues related to sexuality in organizations, management careers, leadership, and processes of change. Several of her current research projects focus on gender equality, diversity, and inclusion practices in organizations.

Gavin Jack is a professor of management in the Business School, La Trobe University, Australia. His research interests include postcolonial theory and its application to the critical study of management and marketing, and gender and diversity in organizations. He has published in several journals, including *Sociology, Organization, Management International Review, Journal of Management Inquiry, British Journal of Management*, and the *Academy of Management Review*. He is currently chair of the Critical Management Studies Division of the Academy of Management.

Dr. Roy Jacques has a nearly 30-year history with gender and diversity research. After receiving his MBA and PhD from the University of Massachusetts, Amherst, he worked at several colleges and universities in the United States and New Zealand. Roy was the first chair of the Gender & Diversity Division of the Academy of Management after it changed its name and mandate from Women in Management. He is presently an independent practitioner in Phoenix, Arizona, where his primary interest is in mentoring and developing new first- and second-line managers, based on principles presented in the book *The Sergeant Major Syndrome* (iUniverse, 2011), which he coauthored.

Nimruji Jammulamadaka is an assistant professor at the Indian Institute of Management–Calcutta. A member of the Behavioural Sciences group, she teaches organization behavior and theory, corporate social responsibility, and research methods to graduate students. Her research interests are in the areas of corporate social responsibility, alternate forms of organizing, social sector, discourses of power, and the postcolonial condition.

Marjut Jyrkinen, PhD, docent (adjunct professor), is an acting professor in gender studies, University of Helsinki (2012–2015). She is also an affiliate researcher at the Department of

Management and Organisation, Hanken, and visiting scholar at the Centre for Research on Families and Relationships, University of Edinburgh, U.K. Jyrkinen co-convened, with Jeff Hearn, the Research Group on Gender Relations in Organizations, Management and Society at Hanken for over seven years. Her doctoral thesis ("The Organization of Policy Meets the Commercialisation of Sex: Global Linkages, Policies, Technologies," 2005) focused on the globalization of sex trade. She was funded in 2008–2010 by the Academy of Finland for her postdoctoral project on women managers, age, and gender. Jyrkinen's current research interests include intersectionality of age and gender; gender in organizations and management; organizational cultures and ethics in leadership; and gendered violence, justice, and policies.

Richard Marens is a professor of management at Sacramento State University. Marens graduated from the University of Washington with a JD/PhD, and over the last 15 years has published articles on the history of corporate social responsibility and business ethics, the shareholder activism of labor unions, the relevance of Marx's insights to organization studies, and the impact of employee stock ownership. He and his wife currently reside in Richmond, California, where they have become involved in new forms of local political activism.

Steve McKenna is full professor of global human resource management at York University in Toronto. He became a "serious" academic at 45 after an international life in the private and public sectors. He completed his PhD at the Industrial Relations Research Unit of the University of Warwick in 1988. His research interests include critical narrative analysis, critical approaches to global HRM, ethics and HRM, postcolonialism, global networks and mobility, and global elites. He has published in *Organization*, *British Journal of Management*, *Journal of Business Ethics*, and *Management International Review*, among others.

Susan Meriläinen is a professor of management at the University of Lapland, Finland. Her research on gendered organizational practices constitutes her main contribution to organization studies and qualitative research methods. Susan is an action–oriented feminist scholar, who has, for example, intervened in the gendered practices of her own work community. Detailed accounts of her joint interventionist work with Saija Katila have been published in *Gender, Work and Organization*. "Hegemonic Academic Practices: Experiences of Publishing from the Periphery," a journal article written together with Janne Tienari, Robyn Thomas. and Anette Davies is another good example of her interest in changing the taken-for-granted practices in academia. Susan's current projects relate to bodies and bodily practices (e.g., sleep) in organizations. Her aim is to advance research in the field of organization studies that take into account the materiality of the body as itself an active force.

Albert J. Mills left school at 15 and developed a critical stance through a series of unskilled jobs and involvement in various social movements for change that peppered the 1960s. He returned to full-time education at the age of 22 with a scholarship to Ruskin College, Oxford. Much to his father's surprise, Albert went on to become a university professor and is currently professor of management and director of the PhD program in the Sobey School of Business at Saint Mary's University, in Halifax, Nova Scotia, Canada. He is the co-chair of the International Board for Critical Management Studies (CMS) and has served as co-chair of the CMS Division of the Academy of Management. He is the author of nearly 40 books and edited collections that focus on the negative impact of capitalism and patriarchy on the lives and communities of people. His most recent books include *ANTi-History: Theorizing the Past, History, and Historiography in Management and Organizational Studies* (IAP, 2012); *Absent Aviators: Gender Issues in Aviation* (Ashgate,

2014); *The Routledge Companion to Management & Organizational History* (2015); and *The Oxford Handbook of Diversity in Organizations* (Oxford University Press, 2015).

Ali Mir is a professor of management in the College of Business at William Paterson University. He is currently working on issues related to migration/immigration and the international division of labor. He is on the board of directors of the Brecht Forum in New York City and serves on the editorial board of the journal *Organization*.

Raza Mir is a professor of management in the College of Business at William Paterson University. His research mainly concerns the transfer of knowledge across national boundaries in multinational corporations and issues relating to power and resistance in organizations.

Kiran Mirchandani is a professor in the Adult Education & Community Development Program at the University of Toronto. Her research and teaching focus on gendered and racialized processes in the workplace; critical perspectives on organizational development and learning; criminalization and welfare policy; and globalization and economic restructuring. She is the author of *Phone Clones: Authenticity Work in the Transnational Service Economy* (Cornell University Press, 2012), coauthor of *Criminalizing Race, Criminalizing Poverty: Welfare Fraud Enforcement in Canada* (Fernwood, 2007), and co-editor of *The Future of Lifelong Learning and Work: Critical Perspectives* (Sense, 2008).

Amanda Peticca-Harris is an Assistant Professor in the Department of People, Organizations, and Society at Grenoble Ecole de Management, France. She is currently in the final stages of completing her PhD in Human Resource Management at York University, Canada. Her research interests include contemporary careers and the meaning of work, working time and working conditions, and qualitative research methodology. Amanda has published in *Organization, Journal of Business Ethics* and *Journal of Management Development*.

Ajnesh Prasad is research professor and chair of the Entrepreneurship Research Group at EGADE Business School, Tecnológico de Monterrey in Mexico. His research interests broadly span the areas of entrepreneurship, gender, and diversity issues in organizations and interpretive research methods. His recent works have appeared in *Advances in Consumer Research, Business & Society, Critical Perspectives on Accounting, Human Relations, Industrial and Organizational Psychology, Journal of Business Ethics, Journal of Business Research, Management Learning, Organization, Scandinavian Journal of Management*, and elsewhere. He has guest edited special issues of the *Critical Perspectives on International Business* and the *Journal of Business Ethics*, and he currently serves on the editorial board of *Human Relations*. He was previously senior lecturer at UNSW's Australian School of Business and has held research fellowships at the Hebrew University of Jerusalem, Rutgers University, and Yale University. Ajnesh earned his PhD in Organization Studies from York University's Schulich School of Business in October 2012.

Anshuman Prasad is professor of management at the College of Business, University of New Haven. His current research mostly focuses on globalization and global shifts; workplace diversity and multiculturalism; and rethinking knowledge in an era of imperial decline. He is the editor of *Postcolonial Theory and Organizational Analysis: A Critical Engagement* (Palgrave Macmillan, 2003), and *Against the Grain: Advances in Postcolonial Organization Studies* (Copenhagen Business School Press, 2012), and a co-editor of *Managing the Organizational Melting Pot* (Sage, 1997). Before joining academia, he worked as a commercial bank executive for almost a decade.

Pushkala Prasad is the Zankel Chair Professor of Management and Liberal Arts at Skidmore College where she teaches in both the Business Department and the International Affairs Program. Her research interests are in the areas of organizational legitimacy, workplace diversity, and global capitalism. Her work has been published in a number of journals, including *Organization Science*, *Academy of Management Journal*, *Journal of Management Studies*, and *Organization*. She is the author of *Crafting Qualitative Research* (M. E. Sharpe, 2005) and co-editor of the *Handbook of Workplace Diversity* (Sage, 2006). Her research has been consistently funded by such bodies as the Social Science & Humanities Research Council of Canada and the Quality of Worklife Foundation in Sweden. Prior to coming to Skidmore College, she held faculty appointments at the University of Calgary, Lund University in Sweden, and the Helsinki School of Economics.

Adam Rostis obtained his PhD from Saint Mary's University in Halifax, Nova Scotia. His management research interests include humanitarianism, genealogy, critical management, organizational behavior, disaster and crisis in organizations, and how individuals and organizations perceive, construct, utilize, interpret, and remember these concepts. Adam's doctoral research involved the development of a genealogy of humanitarianism through a critical historical examination of the Red Cross and Doctors Without Borders. His work has been informed by his time as a delegate for the International Red Cross in Zimbabwe and as senior policy advisor for the Government of Nova Scotia's Emergency Management Office. Over the long term, he hopes to develop a critical mass of researchers with similar interests while maintaining a connection with those who experience disaster and crisis in government, communities, and business. Adam is currently completing his MD at Dalhousie University.

Maureen A. Scully is on the faculty in the College of Management at the University of Massachusetts, Boston. She is a faculty affiliate at the Center for Gender in Organizations at the Simmons School of Management. Her research focuses on the legitimation of inequality in workplace settings, particularly through persistent faith in meritocracy. She also studies how inequality is sometimes contested and redressed through local activist efforts inside workplaces, variously involving employee affinity groups, "tempered radicals," active bystanders, or unlikely activists from both the center and the margin. Two of her coauthored texts have been widely used in business school classrooms, hopefully to encourage bold future change agents: *Managing for the Future: Organizational Behavior and Processes* (Cengage, 2004) and the *Reader in Gender, Work, and Organization* (Wiley-Blackwell, 2003).

Sverre Spoelstra is an associate professor in organization studies at Lund University, Sweden. His research interests include academic labor, theological motives in leadership research, and philosophy of organization.

Peter Svensson is an associate professor at the Department of Business Administration, Lund University, Sweden. His research interests include organizational communication, organizational discourse analysis, workplace democracy and the language of financial communication.

Scott Taylor is a reader in leadership and organization studies at the University of Birmingham, in the English Midlands. He teaches leadership development and organizational behavior there and has recently been working on a co-edited leadership studies textbook: *Leadership: Contemporary Critical Perspectives* with Brigid Carroll and Jackie Ford (Sage, 2015). Scott's research is always qualitative and interpretive, often focuses on issues relating to the meaning of work, and has been published in a range of journals and edited collections. In 2012, he was elected to the Academy of Management Critical Management Studies division as co-chair with Emma Bell.

Janne Tienari is professor of organization and management at Aalto University, School of Business, Finland. He also works as guest professor at Stockholm Business School, Stockholm University, Sweden. Tienari's research and teaching interests include gender and diversity, managing multinational corporations, strategy work, and cross-cultural management and communication from a critical perspective. His latest passion is to understand management, new generations, and the future.

Terrance Weatherbee, for almost two decades, had worked in various managerial and leadership positions in a number of organizations in both the private and public sectors. After a particularly stressful year engaged with a major organizational restructuring and associated cultural change effort, he decided he needed a break; so he returned to university motivated by the thought of upgrading his education. It was during his MBA studies that he began to realize how much of management knowledge he had simply "taken for granted," had never deeply understood or ever questioned. Unsatisfied with this state of affairs, he went on to pursue a doctorate in management in order to correct these deficiencies. He has been "chasing" the knowledge(s) that underpin management ever since.

Foreword

Once upon a time, when the Frankfurt School of Critical Theory was in its ascendancy, being critical meant using a Marxist culture-critique of capitalist institutions to explain the lack of class-consciousness in the West. Of course, Marxism imploded both practically in the East and theoretically in the West, the latter probably best indicated by the publication of Laclau and Mouffe's (1986) *Hegemony and Socialist Strategy*. The historical subject of the western industrial working class was declining precipitously. Marcuse (1964), in *One Dimensional Man*, seeing the future from its Californian past, was well aware of this and sought new historical subjects amongst students and artists. In time, these subjects also proved less historical and more mundane than imagined. In an era when attending universities in many of the liberalized economies meant entering into increasingly expensive markets and where art became constructed with unmade beds and diamond encrusted skulls, these subjects were hardly ripe for action.

Out of the 1960s and the various protests that arose then, new, albeit more fragmented, historical subjects were constituted: from struggles over feminism and gender; over race, ethnic relations and civil rights; over sexualities and religiosities and other forms of identity differentiation, cleavage and affirmation; from the struggles for independence in the remains of both formal and informal empires and the search for postcolonial identities amongst their subjects thereafter; from the various diasporas of older ends of empire joined by those of the newer subjects of globalization; from the subjects imagined in new ideological discourses of consumption, privatization, deregulation, entrepreneurialism, anti-statism, anti-unionism, anti-welfareism, anti-socialism, hinging on conceptions developed through new forms of economic liberalism – from reflection on and practice in such sources of organizing have sprung the pages of this book.

The impacts of those practices glossed in the previous paragraph are many and varied; not only that, they are multi-causal and multi-variable, as well as non-essentialist in their provenance. Sometimes they overlap, but there is no universal subject at the back of them, no necessary shared continuity of interest. Interests are constituted and shaped in the various projects launched in and against the name of these new practices, identities and ideologies. Every one of them has organized, organizing and disorganizing impacts. Organized, in the shape of new social movements premised on claims to identity; organizing, in the sense of creating, mobilizing and contesting resources, slogans, visions and missions; disorganizing, as old identities of masculinity, labor, and their organization, wither under demographic, innovation and ideological pressures.

Critical Management Studies is born from these confusions. Unlike the older Critical Theory it defers to no search for the next historical subject nor pins its hopes for social transformations on any specific set of actors that will only let it down. Unlike more traditional management theory it does not assume that rationality overpowers history such that, for the future, managerially-approved subjects will managerially manage even those that are truculent, resistant even, to the thrust of rationality. In this volume the reader will find a wealth of topics, issues, studies and guides to this world of confusion for rationalists. Of course, it is also the case that they will find a great deal of realism as well, far removed from the more familiar orderly recipes, incantations and rituals of most modern management theory with its fetish for specific conceptions of order, system, consensus and methods.

Management, it may be said, is a persistent struggle to achieve order and predictability in the face of chaos, uncertainty, risk and events. To help in the task, management theory has produced a large number of smoothing tools, techniques and tendencies for flattening out the nature of the organizational-scapes necessarily encountered in seeking to impose order on its small worlds. Often, these devices have played both a legitimizing function and a generative function: they have glossed existing routines and ushered in new practices. All tools for smoothing meet resistance: with this volume explore the sources of dissonance, resistance and the innovations they offer.

The studies collected in this volume explore the fissures, stresses and less-charted areas in the organization-scapes of modern management theory. As such, they navigate the less chartered routes, the mysteries and myopias, of the modern society of organizations. Bringing news from the margins they offer re-imaginations of the center. Tracing the same old frames over and over grows increasingly wearisome, especially as more and more is occurring outside the frame. No doubt, some of the directions indicated in this volume will flourish more than others; some might perish, others will be reframed. Only hindsight will tell. The foresight of this volume is in providing a compendium of possibilities and imaginings for shaping the future field of management studies.

From little things big things grow: when, in 1977, imagining what might be *Critical Issues in Organizations*, one could not realize what the contributors and editors of this volume have made possible. For their vision we should be grateful.

Stewart R. Clegg

References

Clegg, S. R. & Dunkerley, D. (Eds.) (1977). *Critical issues in organizations*. London and Boston: Routledge and Kegan Paul. Reprinted as Clegg, S. R. and Dunkerley, D. (Eds.) (2013). *Critical issues in organizations*. London: Routledge Library Editions: Organization Theory & Behaviour Volume 8.

Laclau, E. & Mouffe, C. (1985). *Hegemony and socialist strategy*. London: Verso.

Marcuse, H. (1964). *One-dimensional man*. Boston: Beacon.

Part I
Introduction

Debating knowledge

Rethinking Critical Management Studies in a changing world

Anshuman Prasad, Pushkala Prasad,
Albert J. Mills and Jean Helms Mills

Globalization is creating . . . the conditions for 'barbarian theorizing': theorizing from/of the Third World (the expression used metaphorically here) for the . . . entire planet.
(Walter D. Mignolo, *Local Histories/Global Designs:*
Coloniality, Subaltern Knowledges, and Border Thinking)

Remember this: We be many and they be few. They need us more than we need them.
(Arundhati Roy, 'Confronting Empire')

In Hell there is a valley uniquely reserved for *ulama* who visit kings.
(Abu Hamid Muhammad al-Ghazali [1058–1111 CE],
quoted in Albert Hourani, *A History of the Arab Peoples*)

In the year 1627 of the common era (1036 AH), Mutribi al-Asamm al-Samarqandi – poet and scholar, and a courtier well versed in the refined etiquettes of the Persianate world which straddled large swathes of the Asia of his times – presented himself at the royal court of Emperor Nur-ud-Din Muhammad Jahangir, ruler of the mighty Mughal Empire in India, where he was received with due dignity and lavished with expensive gifts. The traveler from Samarqand stayed at the Mughal court for more than two months, during which time he and the Indian emperor developed a close relationship and held a number of extended conversations that provided the material for an account penned by the Central Asian visitor. In his account (generally known as *Khātirāt-i-Mutribī Samarqandī*),[1] Mutribi ranges over a variety of areas and, among other things, offers the reader several comparisons between Central Asia and Mughal India. As the historians Muzaffar Alam and Sanjay Subrahmanyam (2007) highlight in their commentary on the *Khātirāt*, Mutribi's account showers praise after praise on Emperor Jahangir – "one of the greatest rulers of the age," in Mutribi's words (p. 121) – and by means of a series of comparisons brings out "the wonders and the superiority" of India over Central Asia (p. 128). Indeed, observe Alam and Subrahmanyam (2007: 128), it seems that Mutribi's *Khātirāt* almost wishes to represent the Mughal emperor himself as one of the great wonders of India and virtually serves as a "vehicle for the expression of Jahangir's [and not only Mutribi's] opinions and prejudices."

Roughly a decade before Mutribi's visit to Jahangir, yet another visitor from distant lands had journeyed to India, in this instance for a rather more extended stay of close to three years (1616–1618) at the Mughal *darbar*. The visitor in question was Sir Thomas Roe, an ambassador dispatched jointly by James I, King of England, and the English East India Company to seek certain favors from Jahangir's court. Interestingly, it so happens that, somewhat similar to Mutribi, the English ambassador too has left for posterity his impressions of Emperor Jahangir and of the Mughal Empire more generally (see Subrahmanyam, 2005). However, if, as we saw above, Mutribi's impressions of India were exceedingly *positive*, Jahangir's empire seems to have left an overwhelmingly *negative* impression on the English ambassador. As Subrahmanyam (2005) points out, Thomas Roe's correspondence and journal relating to India often adopt a heavily denigrating tone that veers from the ironic to sneering and contemptuous, and his account of the Mughal Empire frequently tends to "drift towards the *topos* of Oriental Despotism: absence of laws, arbitrary royal power and a penchant for blood-lust, absence of private property" and so forth (p. 152). Indeed, so intense is Roe's aversion for some of the ceremonials of the Mughal court that when Jahangir honors the ambassador by organizing a dance for his entertainment, Roe can only refer to the dance disdainfully as: "some whoores[2] did sing and dance" (Thomas Roe quoted in Subrahmanyam, 2005: 155).

A reader of the accounts left by these two historical figures, who happened to have visited Jahangir's imperial court during roughly the same time period, would be justified in asking why the two authors offer such highly antithetical appraisals of early 17th-century India. Why, in other words, do the two writers *see and reconstruct* India so differently? Or, put differently, why the stark divergence between the *knowledge* about Mughal India being produced, on the one hand, by the Central Asian Mutribi Samarqandi and, on the other hand, by the Englishman Thomas Roe?

Before addressing these questions, it may be useful to point out that we have decided to open our introductory chapter to this volume by highlighting the question of (widely divergent forms of) knowledge because, as we discuss below, the *contestation* over knowledge is likely to be one of the most significant debates of the rapidly changing world of the 21st century, and, we believe, the scholarly field of Critical Management Studies (CMS) needs to be a full-scale participant in that important debate. Accordingly, critiques focusing upon different aspects of production and dissemination of knowledge constitute an important feature of the present *Routledge Companion to Critical Management Studies*. In addition, the contributors to this volume address a range of other issues that hold considerable significance in the context of today's transforming world. The remainder of this chapter is intended to outline the overall nature of this *Companion*, while also providing the reader with an understanding of the wider context in which the present volume's scholarly efforts are situated. We begin by going back to the question of the glaring difference between the knowledges being produced, respectively, by Mutribi Samarqandi and Thomas Roe. As we will see in the next section, a look at the differences that characterize those two knowledges is of considerable help in developing some important insights about the nature of *present-day* structures of knowledge.

Knowledge and xenology

Needless to say, the question as to why Mutribi Samarqandi and Thomas Roe have produced such extremely disparate knowledge about India is a complex one, and we would be well advised here to resist the temptation to come up with hasty and simplistic answers. For instance, although it is indeed the case that knowledge is often shaped by power, any attempt to explain Thomas Roe's contemptuous views of India on the basis of power differentials between England and India will quickly run into problems, because during the 17th century, England – at best "a medium-sized power from the [far] western end of Eurasia" (Subrahmanyam, 2005: 170) – was simply no match for the powerful Mughal Empire, whether economically, militarily, demographically, or in terms of other measures of state power (see, e.g. Madison, 2007).

Similarly, one needs to be somewhat wary also of explanations that seek to account for the nature of the writings under consideration simply on the basis of the Central Asian courtier's desire to ingratiate himself with the Mughal Emperor or, since Roe's embassy had largely failed in gaining the favors it sought from Jahangir, as merely reflecting the English ambassador's chagrin and his search for excuses for a failed embassy. Although factors like these may well have played a role in shaping the overall makeup of the writings in question, we propose to briefly explore here the idea that the stark difference in the knowledge being produced by Mutribi Samarqandi and Thomas Roe may be attributable, at least in part, to the differing *traditions of xenology* to which the two authors happened to belong. These two early modern traditions of xenology – one 'Indo-Persian' and the other 'Western' (Alam & Subrahmanyam, 2007; Subrahmanyam, 2005) – are complex and internally differentiated cultural/intellectual approaches for engaging with 'the outsider' and 'the foreign', and only a very rough outline of some of the differences that characterize the two can be offered here.[3]

The overall contours of the early modern Western[4] tradition of xenology seem to have been shaped, in particular, by two horrific calamities that unfolded during the course of the 15th, 16th, and 17th centuries: (a) the 'American Holocaust' (Stannard, 1992), i.e. the brutal European conquest of the so-called 'New World', and (b) the ferocious wars of religion in Europe. Importantly, the issue that lay at the heart of both of these catastrophic events was one of how to deal with 'difference': if the peoples of (what came to be called) 'the Americas' confronted Europe with the question of human difference, Europe's religious wars came to be waged in response to the 'problem' of difference involving modes of Christian worship and related doctrinal matters. As Inayatullah and Blaney (2004) have pointed out, the *unimaginable savagery* of the religious wars[5] produced deep "moral and psychic scars" on Europe (p. 29), and was accompanied by the consolidation of an intellectual and cultural way of being, thinking and seeing that came to regard 'difference' as leading to "disorder and degeneration" and "homogeneity [as productive of] . . . social order and stability" (p. 33). In sum, this cultural/intellectual mindset was *fearful* of 'difference' (because it believed that 'difference' led to a dangerous state of *disorder*), while also being *contemptuous* of 'difference' (because, according to this mindset, 'difference' produced *degeneration*).

Simultaneously, the European 'discovery' of the diverse peoples of the Americas (e.g. the Aztec, the Inca, the Maya, etc.) with their own unique cultural, political and religious practices, created new and added tensions for European Christianity's system of belief and led to major theological, legal and intellectual debates in Europe regarding "the degree of the humanity of the [American] Indians" (Mignolo, 2003: 428).[6] In the course of those debates, 'difference' once again was identified with degeneration, and, in a somewhat contradictory fashion, the American Indians came to be seen as civilizationally belonging to a *prior European age* (i.e. to the 'past' of Europeans of that time), while also representing *radical otherness* (Inayatullah & Blaney, 2004).

Thus, the early modern Western tradition of xenology may be viewed as an outcome of Europe's historical engagement with 'external' as well as 'internal' difference, and it seems to have produced a cultural and intellectual *mindset* – i.e. a combination of ethical as well as epistemological orientation (Spivak, 2008: 18) – that was, on the one hand, overwhelmingly inclined to *compare and rank* various cultural and political systems and, on the other hand, deeply committed to notions of Christian Europe's (religious/moral) superiority, as well as to a view of 'difference' as dangerous and degenerative. Once Thomas Roe is placed within such a tradition of xenology, his contemptuous assessment of India – in all its 'difference' and (to him) radical otherness – becomes more readily comprehensible.

It is important to emphasize here, moreover, that the orientation towards 'otherness' that manifests itself in the early modern Western tradition of xenology (of which the English ambassador appears to have been a fairly representative and faithful practitioner) does not seem to have completely left the cultural/intellectual world of 'the West' until this very day. As scholars have pointed out, over time, that orientation came to assume a highly systematized form in the West via the discourses of 'Occidentalism' (Mignolo, 2000, 2011) and 'Orientalism' (Said, 1978) and, in that process, became entrenched as one of the key organizing principles of much of modern Western knowledge. The selfsame orientation, we need to note, continues to animate significant sections of different social sciences (including organization and management studies) even today (Inayatullah & Blaney, 2004; Nederveen Pieterse, 2010; Westwood, 2004; Young, 1995).

In contrast to Thomas Roe's writing, however, Mutribi's account of Mughal India belongs to a stream in the Indo-Persian tradition of xenology that dates back to a time prior to the 15th century (Alam & Subrahmanyam, 2007; Subrahmanyam, 2005). Subscribing to such a perspective, Mutribi's organizing framework (for understanding and commenting upon India) is rooted not in notions of India as a radical other (which seems to have been the case with Thomas Roe), but in the idea of India as a "somewhat familiar" (Alam & Subrahmanyam, 2007: 295). As Subrahmanyam (2005) has pointed out, in travelling to India, Mutribi is entering a political/cultural/religious world which he considers, simultaneously, to be both different from, as well as similar to, his own Central Asian world. In other words, in Mughal India, Mutribi as a visitor/observer/author is both an 'outsider' as well as an 'insider'. Moreover, the Indo-Persian world of Mutribi's times was also a world in which there simply did not exist any *generally accepted* hierarchies across different peoples, cultures or regions. All in all, therefore, Mutribi seems to have subscribed to a xenological perspective informed by an element of hospitality to the cultural stranger, in which the nature of the relationship between the observer and the observed was markedly different from the characteristic features of that relationship in the Western xenological tradition. Hence, in part, the radical divergence that we find in the respective accounts of 17th-century India left by Mutribi Samarqandi and Thomas Roe.

The foregoing narrative about Mutribi Samarqandi and Thomas Roe brings us face-to-face with differing traditions of xenology and *different approaches to knowledge production*. Indeed, in some ways, this narrative is also a pointed reminder that, for most of human history, the world has been characterized by the simultaneous existence of a highly diverse range of knowledge systems in different regions of the planet. However, beginning perhaps in the late 15th century, when the project of modern Western colonialism came to be launched, 'the West' seems to have waged an ever intensifying war designed to eradicate the world's thriving heterogeneity of knowledge systems.[7] The *war on knowledge* served as one of the constitutive elements of the overall project of modern Western colonialism, and during the course of that war, the West's fear and contempt for 'difference' (noted earlier) was sought to be *globally* inscribed on the domain of 'Truth', epistemology and scholarly activities as well. Today, the results of that long Western war on the heterogeneity of knowledge systems are visible around the world in a variety of fields but most starkly so perhaps in institutions of learning and knowledge production, most of which tend to be rather uniformly organized around the 'disciplines' that emerged during the course of modern colonial and neocolonial encounters and which continue to largely subscribe to epistemologies and protocols of knowledge production that rose to prominence during the era of Western (neo-)colonial dominance.

Control of knowledge, thus, has long served as one of the key building blocks of the 'colonial matrix of power' that undergirds Western modernity and modern Western civilization (Mignolo, 2011). It needs to be emphasized, however, that even at a time when Western global power and colonial dominance were at their very peak (say, roughly during the years spanning the late 19th and early 20th centuries), the colonized *never* fully accepted the idea that, somehow, the Western colonizer held a monopoly of 'knowledge' and 'Truth'. Indeed, the history of the modern colonial encounter is marked by fierce contestations in the domain of knowledge. Moreover, as Walter Mignolo, among others, has pointed out, such disputes over knowledge are likely to become more and more intense in the changing world we inhabit now because, with the 21st century, "we . . . have entered an irreversible *polycentric world order* (2011: xiv; italics added). Hence, we tend to agree with Mignolo's perceptive observation that "the dispute for the control . . . of knowledge will be . . . [a major] battlefield of the twenty-first century" (2011: 67). In this battle over control of knowledge, Critical Management Studies as an ethico-political project cannot remain a disinterested bystander.

Our perspective in this matter has been significantly informed by the writings of a range of critical scholars in the field of knowledge and epistemology, who have repeatedly emphasized the ethical necessity of working towards a world of plural knowledges and multiple epistemologies (see, e.g. Harding, 1998, 2008; Lal, 2000; Nandy, 2000; Mignolo, 2000, 2011). From such a perspective, "the belief in one sustainable [and universal] system of knowledge [persistently and ruthlessly promoted by modern Western (neo-)colonialism] . . . is pernicious to the well-being of the human species and to the life of the planet" (Mignolo, 2011: xii). In our considered opinion, therefore, CMS in the 21st century needs to commit itself to, among other things, the project of plural knowledges and, as part of that project, steadfastly work towards subverting the current dominance of the modern Western regime of knowledge, while also creatively constructing new approaches for producing knowledge.

In this regard, while the project of plural knowledges[8] will necessarily proceed along a number of vectors, we believe that one of the important vectors of this enterprise will need to be involved also with a persistent interrogation and problematization of various *boundaries* that mark the existing terrain of knowledge (e.g. boundaries that separate different business fields like accounting, management, marketing, etc.; boundaries across various disciplines in the social sciences/humanities; boundaries that divide Western and non-Western knowledge systems; boundaries between elite and subaltern, as well as between academic and nonacademic knowledges; etc.). These and several other issues related to the project of 'rethinking CMS in a changing world' are briefly outlined in the rest of the chapter.

We begin, in the next section of the chapter, by asking the important question, 'What is CMS?' Or, put differently, 'How should we conceptualize (or map) CMS as a field of scholarly inquiry?' CMS, we may note, is an umbrella term that accommodates a variety of loosely gathered scholarly streams and groups of researchers. Hence, developing a map of CMS is useful for gaining an understanding of the different communities of critical organizational scholarship that may be found within the CMS field. Furthermore, we believe that an exercise aimed at mapping CMS is important also because some other attempts to map the field seem committed to a view of CMS that is unjustifiably narrow and restrictive.

Conceptualizing Critical Management Studies: Mapping a contested field of inquiry

It is not without some trepidation, however, that we embark on an exercise to map CMS as a field of inquiry by asking the question, 'What is CMS?' There is a long history and extensive oeuvre of scholarly works offering critical assessments of organizations, as well as of the wider contexts within which organizations operate, with the result that any attempt to map the CMS field must necessarily be partial and incomplete. In a somewhat related vein, moreover, attempts to answer the question 'What is CMS?' need to contend also with the caution issued by Derridean thinking, which regards all questions of the form 'What is X?' – and all statements in the form of 'X is Y' – as extremely problematic (see, e.g. Derrida, 1991, 1993; Royle, 2000; Wolfreys, 1998; see also Kamuf, 1991). Nevertheless, in view of the requirements of the task at hand, we would still like to pose this question about CMS, keeping it firmly in mind that all conclusions are impermanent and contested. Asking and addressing this question reminds us of various intellectual positions subsumed, excluded or marginalized by the CMS label and simultaneously helps us envision other possible futures for what we might call CMS. Furthermore, while asking this question – 'What is CMS?' – we need to keep in mind that CMS has emerged also via a process of academic consolidation and institutionalized actions of specific individuals, networks and organizations.

We are by no means the first to point to such institutionalized aspects of CMS or of any other academic grouping for that matter. In their Introduction to *Critical Management Studies: A Reader*, Grey and Willmott (2005a), for instance, also note some of the institutionalized features of the CMS field, even as they themselves produce a particular narrative designed to give a very specific direction to the ongoing institutionalization of CMS. The narrative offered by Grey and Willmott (2005a) seems to suggest that CMS may well be seen as 'starting' with a collection of essays edited by Mats Alvesson and Hugh Willmott in 1992, which presumably represents the first capitalized use of the term 'Critical Management Studies'. The publication of that collection, they further posit, "appears to have acted as a catalyst for work positioning itself under this label" (Grey & Willmott, 2005a: 3). Reference to such a putative 'starting point' for CMS is a recurring theme in a series of review articles and compendiums that seem to be aimed at engineering, among other things, a somewhat precise moment of 'beginning' for Critical Management Studies. Indeed, the Wikipedia discussion about CMS (accessed July 27, 2014) goes so far as to claim that '[i]t is *generally accepted* that CMS *began* with Mats Alvesson and Hugh Willmott's edited collection, *Critical Management Studies* (1992)" (emphasis added).

Some of us may be inclined to dispute this somewhat arbitrary (dare we say even unreflective) narrative about the 'origin' of CMS because of the existence of a much longer history of scholarly critiques of organizations, work and administrative practices. Clearly, such critiques were occurring during the 1970s and the 1980s in a range of disciplines and interdisciplinary programs, such as industrial relations, labor economics, sociology, public administration, management, women's studies, business history, organizational communication, anthropology and so forth, and critical works of that time were posing a variety of fundamental and difficult questions about the desirability and effectiveness of contemporary work and organizational arrangements. Here, one may think particularly of the contributions of Kenneth Benson (1977), Richard Harvey Brown (1978), Michael Burawoy (1979), Stewart Clegg (1979, 1989), Robert Denhardt (1981), Stuart Ewen (1976), Kathy Ferguson (1984), Peter Frost (1980), Steve Marglin (1974), Walter Nord (1978), Aihwa Ong (1987), Charles Perrow (1972), George W. Stocking (1985), Katherine Stone (1974), Michael Useem (1979), Maurice Zeitlin (1974) and others. These critical endeavors were wide-ranging in scope and method, covering such matters as worker exploitation and resistance, elite networks and control, the subjugation of specific identity groups, the limits of humanistic management, the ubiquitous reach of powerful business corporations into different walks of life and so on. These researchers made use of a variety of critical frameworks, with many of them drawing substantially on what Collins (1985) refers to as the *conflict tradition*, a scholarly tradition that is broadly (rather than literally or dogmatically) influenced by Marxian notions of class struggle and contestations over resources, and which employs frameworks of power as a central guiding principle in organizational analysis.

Similarly, during the 1980s and early 1990s, one witnesses also, for instance, a growing number of critical discussions focusing upon such themes as technocratic rationality of organizations (Adams & Ingersoll, 1990; Alvesson, 1987), the nature of organizations and organizational analysis in postmodernity (Clegg, 1990; Cooper & Burrell, 1988), the ideological functions performed by organizations (Czarniawska-Joerges, 1988; Du Gay, 1996; Rosen, 1988; Willmott, 1984), the communicative power that organizations exercise (Mumby, 1988; Steffy & Grimes, 1986) and the deep investment of organizations in notions of masculinity (Collinson, 1988; Mills 1988). We see also, among other things, an expanded critique of heightened consumption, consumer cultures and the corporate engineering of consumers' desires (Belk, 1994; Hirschman, 1990; Murray & Ozanne, 1991), as well as critical explorations of the role of accounting practices in protecting and legitimizing powerful corporations (Neu, 1992; Power & Laughlin, 1992). Works like these are accompanied by a fairly discernible shift in the direction of understanding the more 'subjective' dimensions of power, i.e. dimensions that are less obviously coercive and more insidiously hegemonic. In theoretical terms, this shift involved, among other things, a greater reliance upon neo-Marxian ideas (particularly Critical Theory) in the course of making scholarly arguments about the generally oppressive nature of both public as well as private organizations.

Generally speaking, these and similar other organizational critiques may be seen as extensions and reflections of wider intellectual developments occurring around roughly the same time period in the world of social sciences and humanities, particularly in fields like literary theory, history, political economy, sociology, anthropology, and women's studies. As academic conversations took a more linguistic turn, moreover, critics of organizations also began to pay greater attention to the discursive dimensions of organizations resulting, for instance, in scholarly explorations of the discursive constitution of such mundane and taken-for-granted concepts as corporate image (Mills, 1996), organizational leadership (Calás & Smircich, 1991), job enrichment (Waring, 1991), or the employee (Jacques, 1996). By the mid- to late 1990s, the imprint of postcolonial theory could also be seen in critical studies of organizations and institutions, notably in Harrison's (1997) study of transformation of museums, in Perera and Pugliese's (1998) work on urban spaces, and in Prasad's (1997a) examination of Western media's representations of OPEC (Organization of Petroleum Exporting Countries) and the oil shock. In short, what we find over a period of some three decades (1970s through the 1990s) is a large number of critical voices on the subject of work, administration and organization, whose theoretical and disciplinary affinities were characterized more by variation than uniformity.

The end of the 1990s and the early years of the new millennium also saw efforts to gather together such critical voices in institutionalized forums like the International Critical Management Studies (CMS) Conference in the United Kingdom, and the CMS Interest Group at the Academy of Management in the United States, the latter subsequently becoming a formal division of that academy. These newly institutionalized forums adopted a welcoming stance toward a *wide spectrum of critical approaches* given, among other things, their need to draw sufficient numbers of participants in order to be functionally viable.

A careful scrutiny of the period from the late 1990s into the first decade and beyond of the 21st century reveals several features worth mentioning. The first is an astounding number of vibrant voices in multiple scholarly disciplines critically commenting upon a variety of organizational practices and arrangements. The scope of this chapter prevents us from documenting in detail the broad oeuvre of critical scholarship (focusing upon organizations and a variety of phenomena that provide the overall context in which organizations function), which emerges at this time in academic disciplines located *outside* the world of business schools. We do, however, want to underscore the extent and heterogeneity of this scholarship and also to alert readers to the sheer range of phenomena being covered by it. Some examples of such scholarship would include works like Cooperman and Shechter's (2008) investigation of new consumer formations in the Middle East, Dauvergne's (1997) discussion of institutional politics and environmental resistance movements in the context of deforestation in Southeast Asia, Dobbin and Zorn's

(2005) critique of corporate malfeasance in the West, Appadurai's (1996) and Hannerz's (1996) explorations of the complexity of cultural flows under globalization, Kaplan's (2008) study of news agency reports of global disasters and the imagery created by such reporting, Sassen's (2008) analysis of novel labor supplies in new employment regimes, Schweder, Minow and Markus's (2002) scrutiny of multiculturalism in practice, Wallerstein's (2000) world-systemic assessment of globalization, Young's (1999) examination of Western transnational corporations in Africa and many, many more. What unites these different writers' varied analyses of organizations and institutions is a distinctly *critical* orientation involving, among other things, a recognition of and a focus upon the centrality of power, conflict and interests in organizational/institutional life, as well as a commitment to providing an ethico-politically engaged appraisal of their consequences.

A second discernible feature of the critical terrain at this time may be observed in some strenuously focused efforts to carve out, or even canonize (Hartman, 2014), an academic field labeled 'Critical Management Studies' (CMS) through the publication of weighty compendiums (e.g. readers, handbooks and other edited volumes) and review articles. What many of these texts may be seen as collectively attempting to achieve is the consolidation of the notion of a putative CMS *core* centering around a set of (so-called) 'classics' (Alvesson, 2011) and (allegedly) 'foundational' texts (Alvesson, Bridgman & Willmott, 2009; Grey & Willmott, 2005b), alongside a story of the 'origins' of CMS, which seeks to firmly locate the 'beginnings' of the field in the United Kingdom (Fournier & Grey, 2000) and to tie it securely to an academic network that some scholars have termed the 'Manchester School' (e.g. Wray-Bliss, 2005). For Wray-Bliss (2005: 409), the Manchester School broadly refers to a "loose community" of mainly Marxist and neo-Marxist writers (originating out of or connected to the University of Manchester in England) who increasingly also draw upon some poststructuralist ideas for certain purposes (e.g. while engaging with questions of subjectivity and identity in the workplace).

A closer scrutiny of this research network reveals some interesting dynamics relating to the categorization of certain texts as 'canonical' through an exercise in academic branding. We are by no means the first to note that various efforts to equate the much broader scholarly field of CMS with the rather narrow world of the Manchester School, and to demarcate CMS as a field strictly falling within the boundaries of Organization and Management Studies, strongly resemble the practice of branding (see, e.g. Thompson, 2005). Branding, as most marketers know, strives for product (in this case, academic field) recognition, an aura of distinctiveness, and a symbolic connection to particular objects, images, ideas or experiences. Brands not only attract consumers, aficionados and adherents but also secure a level of legitimacy for the product or profession they are associated with. However, branding a segment of organizational critique is trickier than branding a T-shirt and requires considerably greater exertion in the act of drawing and maintaining *boundaries* (Ashcraft, Muhr, Rennstam & Sullivan, 2012).

In this instance, it appears that some of the boundaries being constructed involve the drawing of various imaginary lines of demarcation in conceptual, geographical or institutional space. Thus, according to the Manchester School, the broad field of CMS derives its unique identity not only from (a) its theoretical attachment to specific strands of Marxism, neo-Marxism, poststructuralism and so forth but also from (b) its alleged geographical origins in the United Kingdom, as well as from (c) the purported location of its primary institutional base in the academic area of *management*. The geographic boundary erected by the Manchester School attempts to give the CMS field a somewhat ethno-national character that is substantially British (or broadly Northern European), while the institutional boundary seeks to place the *entire* field of CMS squarely within the world of business schools and to align it rather narrowly with the discipline of management.

It should come as no surprise, therefore, that despite repeated assertions by compendium editors and review essay writers (e.g. Alvesson, Bridgeman & Willmott, 2009; Grey & Willmott,

2005a) regarding the *heterogeneity* of the CMS field and their frequent declarations favoring a 'Big Tent' strategy for the field, only a relatively limited number of works and authors are repeatedly cited by this research network as setting the CMS tone, representing the CMS mandate or covering issues of relevance to CMS. Needless to say, these *chosen works* frequently have a relatively close fit with the Manchester School *brand* of CMS, which may very well explain why they are seen as 'fit to print' in readers and handbooks that claim to lay out the general terrain of CMS as a field of scholarship (see Ashcraft, Chapter 6 in this volume). In short, what we have here is a series of attempts by the Manchester School – a research network marked by its mostly British character, its opposition to what Thompson (2005) calls the 'bogeyman' of mainstream American management, its embeddedness in the world of business schools and its theoretical attachment to Critical Theory, neo-Marxism, Gramscian analysis and poststructuralism, with occasional nods in the direction of feminism, Queer Theory, postcolonialism, and the like – seeking to make the claim that, somehow, this narrow school (together with its unique *brand* of CMS) needs to be regarded as the 'core', or the 'essence', or the 'vanguard' of the much larger intellectual enterprise that is CMS.

Finally, our exercise of mapping CMS reveals also a large number of scholars who extensively engage in critical organizational research and who frequently place their own works explicitly under the CMS umbrella, but who generally *reject* the implicit and/or explicit boundaries to which the Manchester School appears to be committed. The work of these scholars is decidedly critical because of, for instance, its serious engagement with various forms of power relations and its ethico-political critique relating to the exercise of power and consequences thereof. These scholars tend to be influenced by a wide range of theoretical traditions, including actor network theory, critical race theory, cultural studies, critical realism, dramaturgy, dramatism, different genres of feminism, hermeneutics, institutional theory, neo-Marxism, participatory action research, postcolonialism, postmodernism, poststructuralism, praxeology, psychoanalysis, semiotics and many others, while always retaining a distinctly critical edge. They are located (institutionally and through personal self-identification) across a number of countries of the world – e.g. Australia, Brazil, Canada, Finland, Germany, India, Israel, the Netherlands, Sweden, the United Kingdom, the United States and others – and they generally maintain a variety of professional links with business academia and/or with different institutionalized forums using the CMS label (e.g. the CMS Division of the Academy of Management, the biannual International CMS conference, etc.) or with other formal assemblies like, for instance, the Standing Conference on Organizational Symbolism (SCOS), which provide a hospitable setting for discussions of critical organizational research. As a group, they are too numerous to be individually listed in this chapter. We would, however, like to draw attention to some of them in order to provide readers with a tangible sense of the work being produced by CMS scholars having a more elastic conception of CMS as a field of inquiry.

Without any claim of being a comprehensive listing, a sample of writers falling within this category might include, for example, Alcadipani and Caldas (2012), Bell and King (2010), Boje and Rosile (2003), Boussebaa, Sinha and Gabriel (2014), Bryman (2004), Case and Piñeiro (2006), Coronado (2012), Dar (2014), Driver (2009), Durepos, Helms Mills and Mills (2008), Faria (2013), Frenkel and Shenhav (2003), Gagnon (2008), Ganesh (2003), Hartt, Mills and Helms Mills (2012), Jacques (2006), Jammulamadaka (2013), Marens (2011), McKenna (2012), Mills (2006), Mir and Mir (2009), Mirchandani (2004), Mizruchi (2004, 2010), Mumby (2005), Özkazanç-Pan (2008), Prasad (2003a, 2012a), Prasad, Prasad and Mir (2012), Schroeder and Borgerson (2012), Scully and Segal (2002), Vaara and Tienari (2011), Westwood and Jack (2008) and several others.

We have already alluded to the extraordinary diversity of theoretical frameworks undergirding the scholarship of these researchers. A similar heterogeneity is evident in the sheer range of organizational phenomena being studied by them. Here we may find, for instance, studies focusing upon disastrous corporate scandals (Boje & Rosile, 2003), the complex identity dynamics within management development programs and nongovernmental organizations (NGOs) (Dar, 2014; Gagnon, 2008; Ganesh, 2003), 'Disneyization' as a central organizing principle (Bryman, 2004), workplace activism (Scully & Segal, 2002), the writing and rewriting of organizational histories (Durepos, Helms Mills & Mills, 2008), paradoxes in the management of workplace diversity (Prasad, Prasad & Mir, 2012), the emergence of business ethics as a field (Marens, 2011), the packaging of 'exotic' tourist destinations (Echtner & Prasad, 2003; Schroeder & Borgerson, 2012), the persistence of neocolonialism in different organizational sectors (Alcadipani & Caldas, 2012; Coronado, 2012; Frenkel & Shenhav, 2003; McKenna, 2012; Mir & Mir, 2009; Westwood & Jack, 2008), future prospects for CMS inquiry (Driver, 2009; Faria, 2013; Jammulamadaka, 2013) and so on and so forth. Aside from the aforementioned critical works, mention may also be made of Ashcraft's (2005) study of masculinity among commercial airline pilots, Davis' (2009) exploration of the takeover of the U.S. economy by financial capital, Gabriel's (2005) commentary on organizational images in postmodern times, Gopinath and Prasad's (2013) critical hermeneutic analysis of Western discourses on Coca-Cola's exit from India, Ibarra-Colado's (2006) discussion of epistemic coloniality in Latin America, Mirchandani's (2012) ethnography of authenticity work in Indian call centers, Prasad and Elmes' (2005) investigation of the discourse of pragmatism in environmental management and Westwood's (2006) critique of international business studies as a form of Orientalist discourse.

In addition to their theoretical diversity and focus upon a wide range of topics, many of the authors from this group display also considerable interest in studying *embodied identities* – i.e. identities relating to gender, race, nationality and linguistic communities (Gagnon, 2008; Prasad, Prasad & Mir, 2012; Schroeder & Borgerson, 2012), rather than those pertaining only to managerial, professional and occupational positions – and exhibit, moreover, a stronger interest in looking at organizations *outside* the West (e.g. Boussebaa, Sinha & Gabriel, 2014; Dar, 2014; McKenna, 2012; Mir & Mir, 2009; etc.). Furthermore, researchers in this group also draw extensively on the writings of a variety of prominent contemporary scholars in the social sciences and the humanities (e.g. Appadurai, 1996; Ahmed, 2004; Clifford, 1997; Goody, 2006; Gordon, 1995; Mignolo, 2000, 2011; Munasinghe, 2002; Nandy, 1983, 1995; Ong, 2003; Sassen, 2008; Spivak, 1999, 2008; etc.) whose works are resolutely critical of various aspects of organizations and/or their wider contexts, even if they may not always explicitly identify themselves as engaging in organizational critique.

In sum, as we look back at our brief exercise in mapping the field, three distinctive features of the overall scholarly landscape of organizational critique may be identified: (1) a large and growing corpus of critical studies of organizations/management (and/or their contexts) by authors located in a range of disciplinary and interdisciplinary sites – authors who generally do *not* maintain professional links with business academia or with various institutionalized forums that have sprung up in recent years around the CMS label; (2) an ever expanding group of critical organizational scholars with professional ties to business schools (and/or to one or more of the institutionalized bodies related to the CMS acronym or to other forums generally open to critical organizational research), who may often adopt the CMS nomenclature for their own work and who subscribe to a fairly elastic conception of CMS as a field of inquiry; and (3) the ongoing institutionalization of a rather narrow Manchester School brand of CMS along the lines discussed earlier in this section. Figure 1.1 provides a schematic outline of these features of the general terrain of critical organizational scholarship.[9]

According to our map, the overall CMS field (Circle B in Figure 1.1) may be viewed as constituted by (a) the second group of scholars identified above, together with (b) academics of

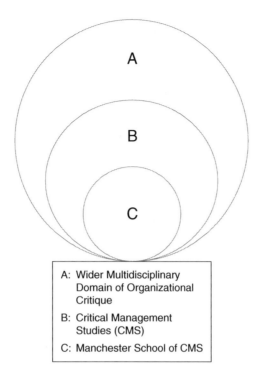

A: Wider Multidisciplinary
   Domain of Organizational
   Critique
B: Critical Management
   Studies (CMS)
C: Manchester School of CMS

Figure 1.1   Mapping Critical Management Studies

the Manchester School.[10] In terms of this map, researchers of the Manchester School (Circle C), representing a more bounded approach to organizational critique, are seen as forming a subset of the larger CMS group as a whole (Circle B). From the perspective of this map, the overall CMS field itself (Circle B) is seen as embedded in the wider multidisciplinary domain of organizational critique (Circle A). Moreover, our exercise in mapping the CMS field alerts us to the fact that the boundary separating many of the scholars in Circle B from those in Circle A is highly tenuous, often being a function mostly of researchers' professional/institutional linkages, and such linkages can change.

The next section of the chapter engages more closely with the complex scholarly terrain just mapped. In that process, the next section revisits some of the current debates and discussions about CMS,[11] challenges specific attempts to contain the field within a variety of arbitrary boundaries, and draws attention to the rich variety of theoretical frameworks and research themes that hold the potential to significantly energize and transform CMS as a scholarly field.

Engaging with CMS: Breaching boundaries and fostering intellectual heterogeneity

Over the past several years, a number of scholars have sought to provide well reasoned assessments of different aspects of critical research taking place in organization and management studies, with the result that there is no dearth within the discipline of writings that engage with CMS. These writings come in a variety of forms and range from the more thoughtful (Brewis & Wray-Bliss, 2008; Gabriel, 2001; Parker, 2005) and the somewhat wishful (Stookey, 2013; Tatli, 2012), to those that are of a fairly general nature (Ford, Harding & Learmonth, 2012; Spicer, Alvesson & Kärreman, 2009). These and other scholars express a host of concerns about CMS including, for instance, (what they see as) a growing distance between CMS and its original mission of praxis (Barros, 2010; Stookey, 2013; Voronov, 2008), its lack of serious attention to the ethics of the research process (Brewis & Wray-Bliss, 2008), its somewhat routine exclusion of various theoretical orientations (Ackroyd, 2004; Ferdinand, Muzio & O'Mahoney, 2003; Thompson, 2005), as well as different social identity groups, such as women, the disabled, non-Westerners and others (Cunliffe, 2008; Ford, Harding & Learmonth, 2012; Tatli, 2012), and its tendency to be distracted by presumably superficial postmodern notions (Parker, 1995; Thompson, 2005) leading to, among other things, its over-aestheticization (Gabriel, 2001).

Notwithstanding the diversity of such concerns, a common thread that seems to run through all these writings is that their critique is largely directed at the Manchester School brand of CMS research rather than at the CMS field as a whole. Indeed, such a focus on the Manchester School is not altogether surprising, given the recent barrage of handbooks, readers, multivolume sets and review essays brought out by the School (e.g. Alvesson, 2011; Alvesson, Bridgman & Willmott, 2009; Alvesson & Willmott, 2012; Grey & Willmott, 2005b; etc.), all of which claim to represent the entire CMS field, even though they mostly feature the work of just a handful of authors of this particular school. Generally speaking, not only are these works by the Manchester School somewhat limited in the scope of their critical imagination, but they are also startlingly repetitive. Volume after volume largely carries the same set of messages (mostly by the same group of authors), and increasingly, moreover, several of these volumes tend to merely offer *reprints* of articles/chapters already published during prior years. Indeed, the tendency of the Manchester School's publications to rework the same material was noted as early as 2003 by Ferdinand, Muzio and O'Mahoney in their scathing assessment of *Studying Management Critically*, a collection edited by Mats Alvesson and Hugh Willmott.

Despite Ferdinand, Muzio and O'Mahoney's (2003) critique, the flood of such compendiums continues unabated and shows no signs of letting up. It should be pointed out, however, that the publication of compendiums that endlessly repeat themselves may well serve some purpose in the context of current attempts to institutionalize the contested field of CMS. That is to say, while reflective voices might decry the meaninglessness of this kind of incessant and repetitive publication by the Manchester School, these edited tomes may also work in the service of institutionalizing the contours of something called CMS in accordance with the vision of those volumes' editors. In short, it should come as no surprise that even in the academic world, if something is proclaimed loudly and long enough, it might help consolidate a taken-for-granted reality that acquires the status of 'truth.' That being the case, a brief look at the scholarly efforts of the Manchester School might be in order.

We would like to begin by emphasizing that it is not our intention to suggest that the Manchester School has little of substance to offer or that the CMS field should ignore this School's research efforts. As a matter of fact, we fully recognize the contributions made by this school, especially its early work that has furthered our understanding of such phenomena as the ideological texture of organizations (Alvesson, 1987; Willmott, 1984), the less visible forms of control used by organizations (Deetz, 1992; Rosen, 1988) and so on. However, we do take serious issue with the Manchester School's tireless efforts to represent its limited genre of critical research as constituting the core, or the vanguard, of the entire scholarly field of CMS. Such claims are ill-founded and must be rejected.

It may be worth pointing out here that the present chapter is by no means the first to critique the curious tendency on the part of Manchester School to claim to be the core/vanguard of the CMS field as a whole. For instance, in a relatively pungent review of the edited collection

Studying Management Critically (Alvesson & Willmott, 2003), Ackroyd (2004) takes the collection's editors to task for trying to pass off their own and their immediate network's limited scholarly output as exemplifying an *entire field* of scholarship, when in actuality their research comprises only a small *segment* of the wider CMS field. In his own rather forceful language, Ackroyd (2004: 169) accuses the Manchester School of being little more than a "sect puffing itself up in order to persuade itself that it is actually a church." Somewhat similar concern has been expressed also in Prasad's (2008) review of *Critical Management Studies: A Reader* (an anthology of previously published writings brought together in 2005 by Chris Grey and Hugh Willmott as editors), drawing attention to the tension or ambivalence that marks that particular anthology's editors' "attempt to speak for an entire emergent area of scholarship with a view to institutionalizing the field" on the one hand and, on the other hand, their open admission of simply pulling together a set of readings that merely represent their own "fantasy" of what CMS might be (p. 283).

One cannot but feel that these and similar other criticisms have been failing to have the desired effect, given the unrelenting production by the Manchester School of various compendiums virtually claiming 'eminent domain' over the entire CMS field. CMS scholarship needs to persistently challenge this self-portrayal by the Manchester School, not only because of its obvious presumptuousness but also because it conveys a grossly inaccurate sense of the overall CMS field, with the distinct possibility of misleading first-time readers. Here we find ourselves in sympathy with the sentiments expressed by Willmott (2005) himself, who in the course of writing his response to Ferdinand, Muzio and O'Mahoney's (2003) excoriating critique of *Studying Management Critically* (Alvesson & Willmott, 2003), insists that informed correctives to unsubstantiated claims are especially necessary with a view to ensuring that curious readers less familiar with a particular area of research do not come away with unfounded notions about that scholarly area. We are equally concerned with ensuring also that doctoral students with an interest in critical organizational scholarship (who are more likely to consult handbooks, readers and the like) are given exposure to a fuller spectrum of scholarly possibilities than currently on offer in various compendiums brought out by the Manchester School.

Stated briefly, the Manchester School may be seen as representing an attempt to institutionalize a rather narrow program of critical research barricading itself behind a set of arbitrarily drawn *boundaries* that are more likely to limit rather than enhance the overall potential for critique in CMS. The previous section of the chapter has already alluded to such boundaries, and we will take a closer look at some of them here. To begin with, the Manchester School draws a boundary in institutional space and argues that only the research taking place within the walls of business schools may be regarded as genuinely belonging to the field of CMS (Fournier & Grey, 2000; Grey & Willmott, 2005a). In this regard, while – as a result of certain socio-historical factors – the last several decades have indeed witnessed further expansion of critical research in business schools, it is unclear as to why these particular institutions need to be designated as the fulcrum around which *all* critical studies of organization and management must necessarily revolve. As pointed out in the previous section, organizational critique has long existed both inside as well as outside business schools. Moreover, as discussed below, we anticipate some distinct problems with the central role given to business schools in the Manchester School's truncated conceptualization of CMS.

It is by no means a secret that, by and large, business schools tend to be relatively anti-intellectual places with rather limited interest in sophisticated scholarly work informed by learned social/ political/cultural theorizing (critical or otherwise). The Manchester School's attempts to impose a definition of CMS that encloses critical studies of management and organization narrowly within business schools will inevitably curtail conversation between CMS and critical (organizational) research taking place in a plethora of *non*-business disciplines, and engender, within CMS, a much greater reliance on business school–based critical research for new ideas, perspectives and other intellectual resources needed for scholarly sustenance and enrichment. In the professional world of business academia, we can see this already happening, to a varying degree, in doctoral workshops and journal publishing, where incipient CMS scholars are sometimes being nudged (by reviewers, editors and senior scholars) to narrowly consult or cite or draw upon only the Manchester School 'canon' currently being constructed by this school. The Manchester School's attempts to *contain* CMS within the boundaries of business schools, in other words, might be leading to a higher level of self-referentiality in the field (and a corresponding neglect, within CMS, of cutting-edge critical research being carried out by some of the world's leading thinkers institutionally located in a variety of non-business disciplines), and are hardly likely to be of help in creating an intellectual environment more conducive to producing exciting breakthroughs in future CMS scholarship.

Even within the institutional world of business schools, moreover, the Manchester School seems implicitly committed to various boundary lines that demarcate different functional areas of business (e.g. accounting, management, marketing, etc.) and, in addition, appears to regard *management* (loosely understood as organizational behavior/theory, human resource management and the like) as the *home base* of CMS. Indeed, notwithstanding the inclusion of voices from information systems and marketing in earlier texts that set the Manchester School agenda (e.g. Alvesson & Willmott, 1992), more recent collections brought out by this school seem less and less interested in academic areas outside management. We need to keep in mind that functional boundaries in business education emerged partly out of a pragmatic need to provide training to students in different functions. Holding onto (or fetishizing) these boundaries while trying to make *critical* sense of organizational processes and dynamics may be useful, perhaps, for certain forms of journal publishing and academic career building, but not necessarily for strengthening the broader scholarly project of critique focusing upon management and organizations. In other words, one may foresee that, parallel to the dynamic of increasing self-referentiality in research as a result of attempts aimed at enclosing CMS within the boundary of the business school (discussed above), attempts to define CMS as a scholarly enterprise primarily based in the academic area of management are also likely to render CMS research more narrowly self-referential and may considerably hamper future prospects of the broader critical project in CMS.

Furthermore, as critical reviewers have pointed out (see, e.g. Ferdinand, Muzio & O'Mahoney, 2003; Prasad, 2008), significant sections of the Manchester School tend to draw a boundary line through conceptual space as well and seem to subscribe to the notion that the theoretical perspectives needed to inform and inspire critical studies of organizational phenomena are to be found largely within different genres of (neo-)Marxism and postmodernism/poststructuralism. We briefly touch upon the implications of this boundary later in the section.

Similarly, in its (empirical) research, the Manchester School appears to focus attention mostly upon such matters as managerialism, managerial identity, managerial control, employee relations, the workplace, local organizational cultures and so on and mostly tends to ignore macro-level phenomena involving global and transnational issues and concerns. There is, of course, nothing wrong with this broadly micro- and/or meso-level focus per se, although we do need to take into account the important point being made by scholars like Wallerstein (1999) that even micro- or meso-level analyses cannot be done *meaningfully* unless due attention is paid to macro-level contextual factors.[12] More to the point, however, Manchester School's largely micro/meso focus does imply that, generally speaking, this school is confined to addressing only limited aspects of different organizational phenomena and therefore cannot but fall far short of adequately representing a more comprehensive critical management studies agenda.

Another problematic boundary drawn by the Manchester School is geographical in nature, attributing a broadly European (but mostly British) 'origin' to the field of CMS. This notion – first proposed, it seems, by Fournier and Grey (2000) as part of their attempt to construct a historical narrative about the 'emergence' of CMS – has over the past years come to be seen by some researchers as one of the defining hallmarks of CMS. Indeed, Fournier and Grey (2000) take considerable pains in making this claim, offering a variety of arguments that purportedly explain why the United Kingdom – and not the United States – emerged as the 'natural' home of CMS. In part, Fournier and Grey's claim rests on a set of beliefs concerning (a) the nature of the U.S. academia as a largely positivist (and anti-critical) space, (b) the relative isolation of business schools in the United States from the scholarly world of social sciences, and (c) the absence of a radical intellectual tradition in the United States (in contrast to the U.K. and Europe).

Unfortunately, these assertions by Fourier and Grey (2000) suggest a lack of familiarity with U.S. intellectual history and merely perpetuate an American straw (bogey) man that serves as a perfect foil for the seemingly 'natural' rise of CMS in the United Kingdom. Fournier and Grey's various assertions are easy enough to refute, but limitations of space prevent us from taking up each one of them individually. At this juncture, it might be sufficient merely to point to the existence of a long-standing and well established 'Left' tradition in the United States, which gathered considerable strength during the Progressive Era (1890s–1920s) and the period of the Great Depression and the New Deal (1930s–1940s). Indeed, the progressive ideas informing the New Deal left an imprint even on *business education*, especially in the area of business and society programs that were generally taught by labor economists, industrial relations specialists, economic historians and labor lawyers (see Marens, 2011, for a detailed discussion of these trends). Even more to the point, perhaps, our earlier exercise of mapping the CMS field should serve as a constant reminder of the wide variety of critical organizational research that has been taking place in the United States for a long time.

Our main objective here is not so much to depict the United States as a bastion of progressive critique or to suggest that a deep antipathy towards critical/radical ideas does not exist in the United States (it certainly does) but to point out that the geographical boundary erected by the Manchester School – a boundary which deeply informs this school's identity as well as its self-understanding of its own historical 'origins' – seems to perilously obscure its vision, rendering it virtually blind to a host of critical intellectual developments taking place not only in the United States but also in different parts of Africa, Asia and Latin America. This school's apparent conviction that a fertile and plenitudinous terrain for fully developing critical studies of management and organization is to be found primarily within the boundaries of Europe and the United Kingdom may well be responsible, arguably, for the Manchester School's obvious *provincialism* as regards the school's choice of intellectual sources that largely provide its theoretical inspiration, as well as its selection of empirical phenomena to be studied. With respect to sources of theoretical inspiration, there is, after all, a frequently repeated declaration in the Manchester School's writings that the school has been primarily influenced by critical theory, other genres of neo-Marxism and variants of poststructuralism/postmodernism, with a fringe section of the school drawing also upon critical realism and certain writers belonging to the 'post' tradition (e.g. Bourdieu, Deleuze, Žižek, etc.).

As a result, what we are faced with is a pervasive and unreflective Eurocentrism, which betrays rather strong parochial inclinations and seems to render the Manchester School's approach to CMS remarkably unfit for conducting meaningful research in a globalized world of unprecedented connectivity and interdependence, in which fully 88% of the planet's population dwells, works and organizes in the non-West, i.e. in the global South. We see a problem here not only with the (un)ethical dimension of such unrestrained Eurocentrism – a point that has previously been made quite eloquently by Brewis and Wray-Bliss (2008) as well – but at a more pragmatic level, we have serious concerns also about the adequacy of such a deeply Eurocentric scholarly approach for producing knowledge about a world in which the non-West has a far more urgent presence and greater influence than at any time during the past couple of hundred years or so.

When we look outside the limited world of the Manchester School, certain sections of CMS scholarship do seem to be somewhat less Eurocentric as regards the theoretical/philosophical resources they choose to draw upon. Nevertheless, it still appears to be the case that large parts of CMS remain distinctly Eurocentric in terms of their overall intellectual approach and apparatus. Over the last several decades, Eurocentrism has been subjected to intense criticism (see, e.g. Blaut, 1993, 2000; Mignolo, 2000; Prasad, 2012b; Shohat & Stam, 1994; etc.), and it is beyond the scope of this chapter to systematically go over this much treaded ground. We would, however, like to highlight a few limitations of Eurocentrism, which may work to seriously undermine the overall project of critique in (organizational) scholarship.

In brief, by positing that European culture and European/Western genres of knowledge occupy a privileged and universal (epistemological) center, Eurocentrism exerts relentless pressure on scholarship to attempt to understand all forms of being and organizing – Western as well as non-Western – solely in reference to Europe/the West and only by means of employing European/Western concepts and categories that barely even begin to capture the diversity and complexity of myriad forms of action and experience across the multiplicity of cultures that populate the planet. Eurocentrism is, arguably, also partly responsible for a widespread Western disinterest in non-Western phenomena, unless these phenomena can be analyzed with the help of conceptual frameworks rooted in Western philosophy and social theory. In sum, what we are faced with – even among CMS scholars who are explicitly committed to critique – is a conceptual and empirical laziness that breeds a reliance on familiar and comforting theoretical notions and a concomitant reluctance to engage seriously with a range of contemporary scholars – such as, to give only a few illustrative examples, Anzaldúa (1987), Mignolo (2000), Nandy (1983) and many others – who have persistently challenged Eurocentric scholarship and proposed alternative conceptual frameworks for critique.

One obvious problem with Eurocentric theories and philosophies lies in the way in which they deal with *difference*. In this connection, the reader may recall our earlier discussion highlighting the fact that large sections of modern Western knowledge/philosophy are predisposed to view 'difference' not only as inferior but also as dangerous and degenerative. To that we would like to add that when considering 'difference', many European critical traditions (with a few notable exceptions) primarily choose to focus upon *class* rather than on race, gender, ethnicity, religion, nationality, sexual orientation and similar other dimensions of difference. As feminists, critical race theorists, queer theorists, postcolonialists and other critical scholars have repeatedly emphasized, a major problem with this one-dimensional fixation with class (as the primary locus of difference) is that it tends to foster a blindness towards various other dimensions of difference that frequently intersect with class itself in significantly shaping a range of sociocultural, economic, political and other dynamics. Furthermore, even when such differences are taken into account by Eurocentric scholarship, they are often simply reinserted within an already imagined hierarchy (of race, culture, nation, etc.) that underwrites the work of major European thinkers not only of the olden days (such as G.W.F. Hegel, Immanuel Kant, Karl Marx or Max Weber), but even those belonging to our own times (such as Habermas, Hardt & Negri, and Žižek).

It is important to note here that a sophisticated incorporation of difference into social theorizing (one that not only goes beyond class but also interrogates Eurocentric approaches to difference) has long been taking place in a variety of disciplinary and interdisciplinary fields, and this genre of scholarship has significantly reoriented and reinvigorated the critical project in the social sciences and the humanities.[13] In this regard, one may point, in particular, to the writings of such celebrated scholars as, for instance, Gloria Anzaldúa (1987), Arjun Appadurai (2006), Kwame Anthony Appiah (2006), Homi Bhabha (1994), Dipesh Chakrabarty (1992, 2000), Kuan-Hsing Chen (2010), James Clifford (1997), Enrique Dussell (1998), Arturo Escobar (1995), Nestor Garcia Canclini (1995), Lewis Gordon (1995), Ranajit Guha (1997), Sandra Harding (2008), Koichi Iwabuchi (2002), Will Kymlicka (1995), Tomoko Masuzawa (2005), Walter Mignolo (2000), Trinh T. Minh-ha (1989), Timothy Mitchell (2005), V. Y. Mudimbe (1988), Ashish Nandy (1983), Gayatri Chakravorty Spivak (1999), Charles Taylor (1994), Michael Taussig (2009), Cornell West (1994) and others, who have been writing and theorizing for several decades about a wide spectrum of economic, social, political, cultural and other human/ecological processes and phenomena and who have inspired a generation or more of researchers engaged in critical scholarship. Regrettably, much of the CMS field has opted to remain relatively insulated from these vibrant intellectual conversations and is therefore at a considerable disadvantage in terms of producing knowledge that might hold greater *relevance* in a rapidly changing and globalizing world.[14]

The CMS field, we suggest, needs to give up this ostrich-like head-in-the-sand mindset and enter into deeper and more sustained conversations with leading critical scholars (like the ones just listed, for instance) with a view to expanding its own intellectual horizons, enriching its theoretical toolkit and initiating new debates that might be more relevant to the requirements of the rapidly transforming 21st-century world. It is only by entering into a persistent and in-depth engagement with the wider world of critical scholarship that the CMS field will be able to draw upon a host of sophisticated concepts and categories that are indispensable today for meaningfully examining various processes in contemporary organizations that are often deeply embedded in broader global dynamics and structures.

By way of example, some of the more powerful and influential concepts offered by leading critical scholars in the social sciences and the humanities might include such notions as 'subalternity' (Guha, 1982a,1982b, 1997), 'disjunctive cultural orders' (Appadurai, 1996), 'strategic essentialism' (Spivak, 1988), 'multicultural citizenship' (Kymlicka, 1995), 'cultural hybridity' (Bhabha, 1994; Garcia Canclini, 1995), 'borderlands' (Anzaldúa, 1987), 'flexible citizenship' (Ong, 1999), 'sanctioned ignorance' (Spivak, 1999), 'mimicry' (Bhabha, 1994), 'second colonization' (Nandy, 1983), 'cosmopolitanism' (Appiah, 2006), 'colonial matrix of power' (Mignolo, 2011), 'connected histories' (Subrahmanyam, 2005), 'cultural odor' (Iwabuchi, 2002) and so on. A number of contributions to the present volume do indeed draw upon the work of this wider group of prominent critical scholars with a view to offering new and unique insights about organizations, management and organizing in our interconnected world.

Apart from the problems of Eurocentrism and lack of attention to the issue of difference, it seems also that, at the broader level, large sections of CMS may be mostly oblivious to a multitude of exciting intellectual developments that have been taking place during the last several decades in scholarly disciplines like anthropology, comparative literature, critical legal studies, environmental studies, gender studies, geography, history, international affairs, media and communication studies, religious studies and so on. This can, perhaps, partly be explained (a) as a result of an overinvestment by CMS researchers in existing management theory of a broadly critical bent or (b) as an outcome of narrowly focused attention upon sociological traditions of a particular stripe that are mostly preoccupied with investigating employee relations, workplace or organizational culture, local resistance, discourses of professionalism, emotional work, identity formations and other similar phenomena that are part of micro- and/or meso-level dynamics in organizations.

Not only does this state of affairs result in a somewhat restricted theoretical repertoire for CMS, but it also seems to lead to a disappointing level of unawareness (among large sections of CMS researchers) of the global and/or colonial dimensions of contemporary organizations and institutions. One result of such unawareness of the global and the colonial is *almost* a complete absence (in the body of empirical CMS research) of studies focusing upon a host of phenomena that are in urgent need of critical investigation but that traditionally fall outside the purview of micro- and/or meso-level research in organization studies/sociology. The list of significant global-level phenomena needing in-depth critical attention might include, for instance, such topics as intellectual property rights (IPR) regimes, organ trafficking, the 2008 financial meltdown, drug money laundering and other acts of criminality by major Western (financial) institutions, corporate efforts aimed at gaining regulatory capture, the global arms trade, the new food security discourse, the rise in hydraulic fracturing ('fracking'), the pornography industry, illicit global trade in historical cultural artifacts looted from Third World countries, corporate links to geopolitics, the role of different organizations in global health epidemics (e.g. AIDS, SARS and Ebola), the consumption of religion and the growing backlash in Western media against members of the BRICS group of countries, to name a few.

In drawing this section to a close, hence, we would like to emphasize that if CMS is not to become simply another site for trivial scholarly pursuits, the field needs to (a) repeatedly breach a variety of self-imposed academic boundaries, (b) systematically resist Eurocentric theories and explanations, (c) develop deep linkages with cutting-edge intellectual developments taking place in various disciplinary and interdisciplinary domains, and (d) substantially expand the scope of its empirical research interests along the lines just suggested. This volume represents a step in that direction and may be seen as offering an example of critical organizational research that is of relatively greater *relevance* for our rapidly changing world.[15] The question of relevance of CMS research is taken up for more detailed consideration in the next section of the chapter.

Critical Management Studies and the question of 'relevance'

CMS scholarship, it may be noted, has long been concerned with the issue of its own 'relevance', with different researchers advocating different ways in which the field can make itself more 'relevant' (see Spoelstra & Svensson, Chapter 4 in this volume). For some researchers, the project of making CMS more relevant seems to be inseparably tied to gaining added influence for the field by deepening its institutionalization "within journals, funding bodies and other forums", in the hope of improving the field's "prospect of changing the theory and practice of management" (Grey & Willmott, 2005a: 12). Other researchers have proposed that CMS can become more relevant either by engaging in what may be called 'critical consulting' (namely, working closely with managers and offering them advice about how to make today's organizations more egalitarian and humane)[16] or by way of participating in activism aimed at promoting emancipation and/or empowerment of workers, women, racial/ethnic minorities and other marginalized groups. The issue is undoubtedly an important one, and precisely for that reason, we believe, there might be a need for a critical engagement with the notion of relevance. Our objective here, needless to say, is *not* to make the argument that CMS should not be relevant. Rather, in what follows, we first briefly highlight the complexity of the notion of relevance by drawing attention to certain issues that are often overlooked in current discussions of relevance and then offer some thoughts on making the *content* of CMS research more relevant for the 21st-century world.

It may perhaps be useful to note here that the idea that intellectuals need to be intimately involved with the world of *action* seems to be a somewhat unique product of relatively recent Western history, the notion having consolidated itself in the cultural consciousness of the West's (overwhelmingly male) scholarly classes mostly during the course of the latter half of the 18th and first half of 19th centuries (see Lears, 2012). In the Western cultural world of that time, 'man' represented the active principle, and 'action' was commonly viewed as one of the defining attributes of 'masculinity'. Not surprisingly, therefore, the yoking together of (male) intellectuals and the need for action was significantly mediated by certain Western cultural anxieties that regarded a man's lack of strenuous involvement with practical action as either a symptom or a cause of sterility, impotence and emasculation. Writing in 1837, for instance, the U.S. essayist Ralph Waldo Emerson gave voice to these anxieties by noting that "practical men sneer at speculative men . . . who are . . . [often] addressed as women . . . [because of their] mincing and diluted speech" (Emerson, quoted in Lears, 2012: 83). This voicing of cultural anxiety was followed by a stern Emersonian warning to the fellowship of scholars: "Action is with the scholar subordinate, but it is essential. Without it, he is not yet man" (Emerson, quoted in Lears, 2012: 83).

The privileged role that men like Emerson accorded to action in the (Western) world of scholarship was further deepened, during the course of the 19th and 20th centuries, with the growth of the more practically oriented social sciences and even more so, perhaps, following the creation of area studies and professional/applied social sciences (e.g. business administration) in the wake of the mid-20th-century decolonization of the world.[17] Hence, different CMS researchers' exhortations to establish close links between scholarship and 'action' – whether by means of 'critical consulting' or 'activism' – need to be seen as deeply enmeshed in a uniquely Western history of cultural anxieties, and there would appear to be a pressing need in future CMS research for in-depth examination of the complex implications of that enmeshment for scholarly calls that promote greater involvement with 'action' as a solution to the field's quest for enhanced relevance.

Apart from the vexing issue of this historico-cultural enmeshment, CMS scholars' desire for (being close to the scene of) 'action' raises some other difficult questions as well. For instance, a strong scholarly commitment to the idea of strenuous, hands-on engagement with the world of practice may sometimes lead to a belief that "doing something . . . [is] always better than doing nothing" (Lears, 2012: 105). Often enough, a result of such belief is considerable impatience with the more deliberate realm of ideas, abstraction and speculation, inasmuch as the holders of the said belief come to regard (what they see as) 'endless' speculation and 'empty' (so-called) abstraction as unnecessary impediments that needlessly delay (the excitement of) 'action'. Hence, the scholarly obsession with engagement with action may sometimes lead to somewhat hasty proposals for action that tend to obscure, in particular, the negative consequences of such action (see Lears, 2012).

In addition, action of the critical consulting variety (whether paid or unpaid) is faced with further dilemmas relating to the risk of being co-opted by existing structures of power. In this regard, the example of Reinhold Niebuhr – a Christian theologian and intellectual committed to active engagement with the political world of the United States during the middle of the 20th century – would seem to be instructive. As Lears describes it, Niebuhr "feared being exiled from the rush of events and becoming an ineffectual bystander" (2012: 86) and hence worked hard at cultivating close links with various networks of influence in the United States. When the United States dropped atomic bombs on the civilian populations of Hiroshima and Nagasaki, Niebuhr was among those who viewed such bombings as unethical and signed a protest to that effect. Before long, however, Niebuhr was approached by a major figure of the U.S. establishment, James Conant, president of Harvard University and "a key promoter of the Manhattan Project" responsible for developing the nuclear bomb (Lears, 2012: 105). Conant expressed displeasure at Niebuhr's ethical stance, and, following that, Niebuhr changed his position regarding the dropping of the atomic bombs on Japan and offered an apology.

Niebuhr's example, by no means the only one of its kind, ought to serve as a cautionary tale that scholarly search for relevance by engaging in action – especially action that takes scholars closer to the world of the mighty and the powerful – may sometimes 'lead to de facto acquiescence in established power' and considerably blunt the critical edge of our thinking and scholarship (Lears, 2012: 86). CMS researchers, hence, would do well to recognize the wisdom contained in the words of the great Arab thinker, al-Ghazali (quoted as one of the epigraphs at the top of this chapter), which caution scholars to maintain a healthy distance from domains of power. Needless to say, Ghazali's caution would appear to be equally relevant for those CMS scholars (for example, Grey & Willmott, 2005a) who seem inclined to believe that simply improving the field's chances for getting published in journals and/or winning grants from funding bodies would somehow improve its "prospect of [*critically*] changing the theory and practice of management" (p. 12).

CMS research, as we discussed earlier, aims to offer a persistent critique of a variety of organizations and a wide range of topics. In that process, researchers may bring critical focus to bear upon different types of companies, industries, institutions, (global) regimes of governance, issues of race/gender relations, natural environmental crises, methodological and epistemological concerns, matters of diversity and multiculturalism, control and resistance at the workplace and so on and so forth. As a result, the content of CMS research tends to be characterized by considerable diversity. Accordingly, by way of rounding out our discussion of the CMS field's search for greater relevance, we would now like to offer three quick suggestions for making the *content* of CMS research more relevant to the needs of a world that is being rapidly transformed.

The first of our suggestions derives largely from the present structure of global demographics. As Kishore Mahbubani (2008), the scholar-diplomat from Singapore, has pointed out, we inhabit what may be called an '88–12 world', i.e. a world in which 88% of global population lives in the non-West, while the West accounts for only 12% of the world's population. However, it is easy enough to see that most of CMS research continues to revolve around the needs and concerns of merely the Western 12% of global population. Hence, if CMS knowledge is to become more relevant to the 88% of the peoples of the world, CMS needs to switch gears and start focusing more and more on issues of greater relevance to the non-West. However, this is easier said than done because frequently non-Western issues cannot be adequately studied simply by *applying* Western theories/categories/epistemologies to the non-West. Rather, a proper study of non-Western issues and concerns often requires recourse to local categories as well as local epistemologies (see Anshuman Prasad, Chapter 10 in this volume).

Our second suggestion follows from Walter Mignolo's recent research that views today's polycentric global order as being marked by a range of "different and coexisting trajectories" or tendencies (2011: 33). Out of the various tendencies identified by Mignolo, we will briefly touch upon the following three here: (1) 'rewesternization', (2) 'dewesternization', and (3) decoloniality, or 'the decolonial option' (2011: 34). Without getting into the complexity of Mignolo's (2011: 27–74) detailed and sophisticated analysis of these and other tendencies, rewesternization may be seen as an attempt by the U.S.-led Western alliance to somehow turn back the clock and reestablish something approaching a relatively unchallenged Western dominance in the four mutually overlapping spheres of (a) global economy, (b) geopolitical power, (c) knowledge/epistemology and (d) culture/ideology/subjectivity.

Needless to say, the project of rewesternization faces serious difficulties today because, among other things, (a) in *relative* terms, Western 'hard' power (i.e. military and economic strength) seems to be steadily declining vis-à-vis many of the larger non-Western nations, while (b) Western 'soft' power (i.e. the ideological attraction of the Western 'model' for the rest of the world) continues to atrophy in the wake of long-drawn-out Western wars of dubious legitimacy, widespread violations of (international) law involved in Western practices like rendition and torture of 'enemy combatants' (prisoners of war), a massive financial meltdown precipitated by Western corruption and mismanagement, extreme levels of regulatory capture and huge bailouts to Big Business in several Western countries, repeated acts of fraud and criminality (including drug money laundering) by a host of 'prestigious' Western banks and financial services firms, escalating socio-economic inequality in the West, growing global discussions about the deeply racialized structuring of Western society/economy/culture/politics, the flood of damaging revelations (about the West) made by WikiLeaks, the tarnished image (and troubled future) of the project of European integration, and a variety of other developments that cast the West in a decidedly negative light.[18]

As distinct from rewesternization, the project of dewesternization seeks to consolidate the multipolar world that may be seen as progressively emerging in the four spheres previously identified, and, in so doing, this project aims to regain something the non-West came to lose during the period of colonialism, namely, the non-West's own status as a major actor/agent on the global stage. The BRICS countries (Brazil, Russia, India, China, and South Africa), for example, are often seen as belonging to the group of nations occupying the front ranks of this project.

Finally, decoloniality may be viewed as a project having considerable overlaps with that of dewesternization, the difference between the two being, perhaps, that decoloniality seems to devote greater attention to (a) the task of creating multiple alternatives to the currently dominant global economic system, as well as to (b) the 'decolonization of knowledge' and 'epistemic disobedience and epistemic delinking' (i.e. disobedience towards, and delinking from, Western epistemologies and structures of knowledge), with a view to working towards a world of multiple knowledges and epistemologies (Mignolo, 2011: 54).

The projects of dewesternization and decoloniality, needless to say, are allies that march arm in arm. It is important to note, moreover, that while these two projects are opposed to rewesternization, they are *not* anti-West. Once again, therefore, if the CMS field wants its own output of knowledge to resonate with the needs and aspirations of the overwhelming majority of the planet's population, it would need to adopt a research agenda that explicitly promotes dewesternization/decoloniality, while persistently challenging the project of rewesternization.

Our final suggestion (for producing CMS knowledge more in tune with the requirements of a rapidly transforming world) is linked to the host of crisis conditions that stare us in the face today (e.g. crises involving the natural environment, the growing militarization of the world, increasing disparities of income and wealth within and between countries, the vanishing welfare state etc.). In a nutshell, the CMS field can enhance its own relevance by increasingly choosing to produce knowledge that critically addresses these and other global crises. But there is a catch here. As a number of scholars have pointed out, the crises that threaten our world are deeply embedded in a way of being, thinking, seeing and acting that takes its paradigmatic form in modern/colonial Western knowledge and epistemology (see, e.g. Escobar, 1995; Harding, 2008, 2009; Nandy, 1983, 2000; Sachs, 1992; Spivak, 2003, 2008, 2012). In other words, the various crises that confront us today may be viewed as products of what Sandra Harding has called 'the epistemological crisis of the West' (2009: 411). Hence, our efforts aimed at finding solutions for these crises cannot remain confined within the boundaries of the selfsame modern/colonial Western epistemology that is largely responsible for having produced these crises in the first place. Such efforts, if they are to have any hope of success, must consistently and repeatedly *breach* those boundaries and, in so doing, work with 'infinite patience' (Spivak, 2012: 216) to produce alternative knowledges and alternative epistemologies (see also, Mignolo, 2011). Set against the preceding backdrop, the next section of the chapter offers a brief outline of the *Companion*.

Overview of the *Companion*

The present *Routledge Companion to Critical Management Studies* has been structured in six parts. Part I ('Introduction') consists of a single chapter, the current one. The remainder of the *Companion* is made up of five additional parts with the following headings: 'Critique and its (dis-)contents' (Part II), 'Difference, otherness, marginality' (Part III), 'Knowledge at the crossroads' (Part IV), 'History and discourse' (Part V), and 'Global predicaments' (Part VI). Short synopses of Chapters 2–24 follow.

Chapters 2–5, comprising Part II, adopt a variety of perspectives with a view to offering reflections on different aspects of CMS as an academic enterprise. Chapter 2 ('Critical management scholarship: A satirical critique of three narrative histories'), by Albert J. Mills and Jean Helms Mills, examines the role of the past and history in critical studies of management. The chapter does this through analysis of three selected accounts of how critical studies of management came into being as a field of study. Drawing on Hayden White's approach to history, Mills and Helms Mills analyze three histories of Critical Management Studies through a focus on their respective narrative form, choosing to privilege their own narrative as satirical critique. Thus, the chapter does double duty by reflecting on the development of critical studies of management, while providing an argument for the need for greater theorization of the past and history. In that process, the authors provide some clues to the development of the field of critical studies of management, problematize the associated notions of history and the past and make suggestions for future directions for what has become known as Critical Management Studies.

In Chapter 3 ('An ethic of care within Critical Management Studies?'), Emma Bell, Susan Meriläinen, Scott Taylor and Janne Tienari focus on the embodied and enacted practices that operate in the academic community of Critical Management Studies and explore the masculinist rationalities that inform them. Drawing on their own personal experiences and reflecting on how individuals contribute to the reproduction of these rationalities, Bell and colleagues explore moments of discontinuity whereby certain forms of criticality are inscribed upon our bodies. The chapter concludes by proposing an alternative mode of embodied critique, based on a moral practice of relationality and care for the self, as well as for others.

As noted earlier, there seems to be a growing anxiety among critical management researchers about the relevance (or lack thereof) of CMS: What if nobody listens? What if nobody cares? What if CMS research is not even produced to be listened to? In Chapter 4 ('Critical performativity: The happy end of Critical Management Studies?'), accordingly, Sverre Spoelstra and Peter Svensson identify Spicer et al.'s (2009) plea for critical performativity as a starting point in order to critically reflect upon the increasing concern for relevance within CMS. Spicer, Alvesson and Kärreman (2009), it may be noted, have proposed the notion of 'critical performativity' as a way of overcoming the purported lack of relevance of CMS. In this chapter, Spoelstra and Svensson problematize the notion of critical performativity by means of exploring the limits of the role and expertise of critical management scholars.

In Chapter 5, 'A rebel without a cause? (Re-)claiming the question of the 'political' in Critical Management Studies', Ajnesh Prasad contends that CMS, although it claims otherwise, is reflective of the mainstream academy – with all the problematic and hierarchical power systems embedded within the latter. Indeed, the author charges, CMS has the same types of celebrity adulation, wanton careerism and detachment from praxis that is to be found in mainstream circles. The chapter argues for the need to dispel the myth that the CMS community occupies a higher moral or intellectual ground vis-à-vis the mainstream because of purportedly being more reflexive, engaged, and conscientious.

Next, Part III (Chapters 6–9) examines a range of concerns relating to issues of 'difference', 'otherness' and 'marginality'. The opening chapter of this part – Chapter 6 ('Fringe benefits? Revisi(ti)ng the relationship between feminism and Critical Management Studies') by Karen Lee Ashcraft – argues that contrary to expectation, feminist theory, research and practice do not figure prominently in (the Manchester School brand of) CMS. Indeed, gender and many other matters of difference, much less feminist accounts of them, remain on the fringes. Her chapter first substantiates this claim, weaving personal experience with quantitative and qualitative evidence to render a nuanced portrait of the current relation between CMS and feminism. The chapter then demonstrates how feminism's peripheral status is perpetuated in routine discursive habits of scholarly practice. The chapter concludes by considering how we might go about revising this relation.

In Chapter 7 ('Humility and the challenge to decolonize the "critical" in Critical Management Studies'), Janet L. Borgerson contends that critical intentions will deliver and reveal nothing beyond the colonized other if theory, as mobilized by Critical Management Studies, fails to open up to the other's value creation role; and she interrogates the notion that relevant manifestations of the 'critical' emerging from European intellectual traditions are sufficient to decolonize the 'critical' in CMS. Following a growing tradition in Africana philosophies of existence, Borgerson argues for shifting the CMS 'geography of reason'. Hope for decolonizing the critical in CMS, she contends, resides in attending to the sociality of possible practices, focusing on the potential of perlocutionary performativity and continually abdicating a delusional arrogated perspective in favor of humility that opens to the humanity and contribution of others.

In Chapter 8 ('Sexualities and/in 'Critical' Management Studies'), Jeff Hearn, Charlotte Holgersson and Marjut Jyrkinen point out that, although sexuality(ies) and management, organizations, working life and labor processes are interconnected, sexualities and gender have gained surprisingly little research attention within Critical Management Studies. This chapter, accordingly, explores the different strands of focused literature on sexuality in management, organizations and work in the realms of (a) sexual harassment, (b) sexualization of work and 'The Other', (c) heteronormative and heterosexist work cultures, and (d) management change practices addressing sexuality. Themes for future research and how a focus on sexuality(ies) might revitalize the criticality of what has become the putative 'mainstream' of CMS are also discussed.

The next chapter, by Roy Jacques (Chapter 9, 'Power failure: The short life and premature death of critical "diversity" research'), asks, 'What meanings does the term 'diversity' signify? Does it describe practices for progressive change, or has it been co-opted into practices which reproduce privilege and marginality?' In order to answer questions like these, this chapter's 10-year, empirical topic study analyzes every submission to the Gender and Diversity in Organizations Division of the United States Academy of Management with a view to developing an empirical description of what diversity has, *de facto*, meant in the mainstream of management discourse in the United States. The chapter concludes that this signifier has functioned more to support than to challenge the status quo.

Part IV (Chapters 10–15) of the *Companion* consists of a series of critical considerations on different aspects of production and dissemination of knowledge. Chapter 10 ('Toward decolonizing modern Western structures of knowledge: A postcolonial interrogation of (Critical) Management Studies'), by Anshuman Prasad, offers a critique of management as an applied social science. Highlighting the significant part played by Western (neo-)colonialism in the emergence and growth of Western social science, the chapter examines a range of limitations of the social scientific approach to knowledge and discusses different ways in which postcolonial theory might be helpful in addressing those limitations and thereby giving a profoundly new orientation to management scholarship.

In Chapter 11 ('Debating Critical Management Studies and global management knowledge'), Gavin Jack focuses upon inequality in the current system of knowledge production about management and organization on a global scale. 'Global' management knowledge, he argues, is parochial and often ethnocentric and is constructed within highly limiting frontiers. His chapter first considers whether CMS may share some of these characteristics and concludes that the 'theory culture' of CMS is, in significant part, Eurocentric and relies almost exclusively upon guiding frameworks from the Global North. Building on extant (decolonial) critiques from within CMS, the chapter then goes on to explore the possibility of reconstructing multiple CMSs. To this end, the chapter draws on some of the works of comparative literary theorist Aamir Mufti and Australian sociologist Raewyn Connell, critically engaging with their respective concepts of global comparativism and Southern Theory.

Chapter 12 ('Rethinking market-ing orientation: A critical perspective from an emerging economy'), by Alexandre Faria, draws upon an 'emerging' economy perspective and offers a critique of what the chapter calls 'market-ing orientation', an orientation representing a powerful Euro-American project that has been transformed into a global project by means of a vast and complex array of Western neoliberal mechanisms, despite the project's well-known negative consequences in terms of inequality, injustice and other undesirable outcomes. Interestingly, it seems that this project has remained virtually invisible to both mainstream as well as critical researchers in fields like management studies, marketing and so on. This chapter calls for an interdisciplinary countermovement aimed at the co-construction of an international critical perspective that challenges the existing Anglo-American dominance of knowledge in marketing, management and other similar fields.

In Chapter 13 ('Social movements and organizations through a Critical Management Studies lens: Metaphor, mechanism, mobilization or more?'), Maureen Scully examines internal efforts to effect social change within organizations in the United States. These efforts are quite distinct from anti-corporate activism that is orchestrated primarily by external groups who are focused on increasing government regulations and reducing the power of corporations in society. Scholars looking at employer-driven change efforts have often connected social movement theories with organization theories to understand the dynamics of these internal changes efforts. Social movements in this literature are invariably treated as a metaphor or a mechanism that has mobilization as the ultimate objective. A critical lens rooted in a CMS tradition, however, is likely to offer us a sharper vision of this phenomenon, allowing us to see such elements as the rigidity of the status quo, the resistance of managerial elites to any change involving the redistribution of resources and the inherent riskiness of employee activism. The use of a critical lens also raises questions about the value of incrementalist approaches to organizational change, while simultaneously recognizing the need for stronger alliances across and outside corporations.

Chapter 14 ('The usual suspects? Putting plagiarism 2.0 in its place') by J. Michael Cavanaugh constitutes an attempt to loosen the grip of the largely judgmental discourse framing student plagiarism by offering a discussion about the landscape of plagiary and, not least, our own connection to it. Behind this chapter's effort lies a concern that, in the rush to finger the 'usual' student suspects, academic faculty risk undertheorizing student plagiarism *as a social practice*, alienating students in the process. In effect, emphatic and unreflexive efforts to shore up ratified notions of intellectual property (IP), the chapter argues, may produce as much irony as desired results because we, faculty, may not fully appreciate what we are up against. Mindful of the reputational and example-setting implications of tight-lipped countermeasures and locating students as one link in a chain of contingent events, the chapter hopes to provide readers with a more rounded and ambivalent appreciation of the social and institutional coordinates of e-student plagiarism within the academic workplace.

In Chapter 15 ('Teaching management critically: Classroom practices under rival paradigms'), Gabriela Coronado proposes that different social values in business practices have created paradigm differences between 'hegemonic' and 'Critical' Management Studies. Locating itself in a critical management education perspective, this chapter explores the tensions between the two paradigms, identifying several obstacles to teaching business students to become critical thinkers. The chapter explores some challenges of teaching management critically in view of different meanings of the notion of 'critical thinking' and reflects upon students' positive engagement with or resistance to the CMS forms of education. The chapter emphasizes the significance of subtle forms of critique of the hegemonic paradigm and the potential role of research assignments as drivers of critical social consciousness.

Part V (Chapters 16–19) of this volume looks at a host of complexities surrounding 'history' and 'discourse.' In Chapter 16 ('History of-in-and Critical Management Studies'), Terrance Weatherbee's contribution is a theoretical exploration of the scholarly activities associated with what has been coined the 'historic turn' currently unfolding in both Management and Organization Studies (MOS) and Critical Management Studies (CMS). The chapter presents a synthesis of the work which has taken place at the sites where history and MOS/CMS have intersected and interacted over the last two decades. Positioning historical considerations in research as a collective process rather than as a product or outcome of individual history-work, the chapter explores the potentials of the turn in order to identify implications for advancing future efforts at historiographical understanding in MOS/CMS.

The chapter by Richard Marens (Chapter 17, 'Let them eat ethics: Hiding behind corporate social responsibility in the age of financialization') is rooted in the paradox that in an era in which the need for corporate social responsibility (CSR) has won widespread acceptance, economic inequality is such a contentious issue. Understanding the historical evolution of CSR, Marens suggests, solves this mystery. CSR was first advanced a century ago to legitimize the autonomy of American industrial corporations in the face of opposition from both labor and economic traditionalists. Over more recent decades, acceptance of CSR has spread internationally along with globalization but with an important distinction from earlier versions. Issues of economic fairness are downplayed in contemporary formulations of CSR because satisfying employees is not nearly as essential within our globalized economy.

Next, Chapter 18 ('Towards a genealogy of humanitarianism: Revealing (neo-)colonialism in organizational practice'), by Adam Rostis, takes a critical approach to the humanitarian organization as a central but under-theorized element of the organization of work. The chapter uses genealogy to defamiliarize humanitarianism through an examination of the Nigerian Civil War of 1967–1972 and the involvement of the Red Cross in that war. In that process, the chapter explores the question of how humanitarianism has become a *taken-for-granted* social construction aimed at alleviating suffering.

In Chapter 19 ('Deconstructive criticism and Critical Management Studies'), Steve McKenna and Amanda Peticca-Harris pose a couple of intriguing questions, namely, 'What might be hidden in the way managers talk or write about their experiences as managers?' and 'What alternatives ways of managing and organizing might be contained in what they say or write?' The chapter approaches these questions by using three examples of written managerial narratives to investigate the alternative ways of managing and organizing that might be hidden in managers' experiences. Influenced by the work of Derrida and Bakhtin, the authors deconstruct those three managerial narratives and reveal how alternative approaches to managing and organizing are suppressed beneath a dominant discourse which influences the thoughts and material actions of managers.

Part VI (Chapters 20–24), serving as the final part of this volume, is concerned with investigating a variety of complex global issues. Chapter 20 ('The "iron" in the iron cage: Retheorizing the multinational corporation as a colonial space'), by Raza Mir and Ali Mir, argues that we increasingly inhabit a world where multinational corporations (MNCs) have become hegemonic. The size and scope of MNC operations have begun to lead to a great sense of unease in light of troubling signs that these corporations have begun to use their size and scope to operate in a zone that exists beyond the reach of institutional governance. In this chapter, the authors use their research from an MNC setting to draw certain conclusions about capability transfer. They contend that an MNC that has a more egalitarian (a less colonial) approach to capability is more sensitive of dialogic issues despite the existence of a power differential favorable to itself. When it achieves its ends through coercive means, it ends up being a loser despite potential short-term gains.

Chapter 21 ('"We're not talking to people, we're talking to a nation", Crossing borders in transnational customer service work'), by Kiran Mirchandani, explores the contributions of Critical Management Studies through an analysis of the experiences of transnational call center workers employed in India. Conceptualizing call center work in terms of its border crossings, rather than in terms of tasks required, pinpoints the relational nature of this work. Given the location of call center workers as intermediaries between organizations and their customers, much of the workers' job involves interpreting the needs and expectations of clients and managers, as well as performing their job in line with these expectations. In transnational call center work, these expectations are influenced by national histories and global inequalities.

Chapter 22 ('Microfinance: A neoliberal instrument or a site of the "other's" resistance and contestation?'), by Nimruji Jammulamadaka, questions the contemporary discourse of microfinance, which casts the poor regions/peoples of the world as the substratum on whom the tool of microfinance is 'operationalized'. By tracing the historical developments in the domain of microfinance both globally and in India, the chapter makes a case for looking at microfinance as a contested site – a site where neoliberal, local and native forces are simultaneously at play and where each is trying to realize its own agenda and satisfy its own interests. The chapter concludes by suggesting that the politics of microfinance in the Indian context can serve as an illustration of plural politics.

In Chapter 23 ('Exceptional opportunities: Hierarchies of race and nation in the United States Peace Corps recruitment'), Jenna N. Hanchey examines United States Peace Corps recruitment materials with a particular focus on the intersection of whiteness and neocolonialism. Arguing that both lenses are necessary to understand the complex dynamics of international volunteer organizations, the author demonstrates how image and text in those recruitment materials work to normalize the white volunteer over the 'exceptional' volunteer of color and construct the host country national as subordinate to the (white) volunteer. Drawing from Critical Management Studies and critical intercultural communication, this chapter invites future collaboration between the two fields, as well as further work on the Peace Corps.

Finally, in the volume's last chapter (Chapter 24, 'American soft imperialism and management education in Brazil: A postcolonial critique'), Rafael Alcadipani proposes the notion of 'soft imperialism' with a view to understanding the enormous influence of the U.S. business school model on management education in Brazil. This model, the author argues, performs clear ideological functions by constructing U.S. corporations and managerial practices as superior and desirable and thus becomes a central weapon in today's neo-imperial regime. Consequences for the wider Brazilian society are also discussed in the chapter.

Concluding thoughts: Looking to the future

As previous sections of the chapter have pointed out, the CMS field – like any other area of scholarship with its 'locus of enunciation' (Mignolo, 2000) primarily grounded in Western epistemological and representational frameworks – is an inheritor of the troubled legacies of modern Western traditions of xenology and the discourses of Occidentalism (Mignolo, 2000, 2003, 2011) and Orientalism (Said, 1978). Not surprisingly, therefore, the general oeuvre of CMS scholarship tends to be overwhelmingly Eurocentric and parochial. As we have seen, such tendencies of

Eurocentrism and parochialism manifest themselves (in one or more sections of CMS scholarship) in a variety of ways including, for instance, (a) a broad neglect of non-Western phenomena as topics of research, (b) a 'sanctioned ignorance'[19] (Spivak, 1999) of non-Western theories/ knowledges, as well as of the global and/or (neo-)colonial aspects of management and organizations, more generally, (c) an imperialist pretense that Western theories, concepts or categories are adequate for understanding non-Western subject matters, (d) a relative neglect of the issue of difference, and so on.

This state of affairs, we believe, is untenable in today's world owing to ethical as well as pragmatic reasons, and the CMS field needs to radically rethink its intellectual approach and scholarly trajectory. Toward that end, it has been suggested during the course of this chapter that, among other things, the CMS field needs to (a) systematically breach various boundaries that mark the field today, (b) deepen intellectual links with different disciplinary and interdisciplinary programs of critical research in the social sciences and the humanities, (c) significantly increase the effort currently being devoted to studying non-Western phenomena, (d) persistently critique the project of rewesternization, while promoting dewesternization and decoloniality, (e) focus considerably greater research attention on major global crises like rising inequality, growing militarization, the environmental crisis and so forth, (f) methodically resist Eurocentrism, (g) learn to use in research non-Western categories and knowledges for purposes of *producing* new CMS knowledge, and (h) become an active participant in the project of 'plural knowledges'. These and other suggestions for rethinking CMS in the 21st century raise a number of complex issues, and we will briefly touch upon some of them here.

In her critique of Hegel's (1835/1975) reading of the Indian sacred poem the *Srimadbhagvadagitā*, Gayatri Chakravorty Spivak (1999) notes that the famous German philosopher's 'ostensibly benevolent' and admiring remarks on the *Gitā* (p. 43) are found, upon closer examination, to be wholly given to making the point that the art and literature of India are not produced by the *Geist*, i.e. the Universal Spirit, that 'Indians cannot move history' and that hence India stands for *stasis* in world history (p. 48). Elaborating further, Spivak (1999) points out that, as someone who was 'well acquainted with contemporary German scholars of Sanskrit' (p. 48, n. 59), Hegel himself possessed – and, indeed, 'professed to possess' – the necessary 'knowledge of the Indian background' and the intellectual 'wherewithal' to offer a *different* reading of the *Gitā*, a reading not committed to viewing India as a civilization possessed of a *flawed* essence (p. 47). However, what such a different reading of the *Gitā* requires on Hegel's part is an 'absence of the *ideological motivation* to prove' that, in comparison with Europe/the West, India can occupy only a hierarchically inferior position in the now familiar schema of West/non-West binaries (Spivak, 1999: 47; italics added). As Spivak puts it, 'because Hegel . . . wants and needs to prove that "India" is the name for . . . [a] stop on the Spirit's . . . journey, he makes his "India" prove it for him' (1999: 47–48).

Spivak's critique of Hegel helps us draw at least two useful lessons in the context of this chapter's suggestion that the CMS field needs to devote considerably greater attention to studying non-Western phenomena. First, somewhat similar to Hegel – who took the time to do the necessary preparatory work on India before writing his remarks on the *Gitā* – CMS scholars desirous of conducting research on organizations located in a non-Western country must '(take) the trouble to do enough homework' (Spivak, 1999: 50) on the relevant non-Western country's culture, economy, politics, history and so forth and thereby attend to the necessary background preparation without which a *meaningful* analysis (critical or otherwise) of a country's organizations/institutions is simply impossible. Secondly, however, as Hegel's example itself clearly shows, such background preparation *alone* is not enough. Rather, learning from Hegel's ideological folly, CMS scholars need to exercise constant vigilance in the interest of ensuring that their writings on non-Western issues do not bear the imprint – explicit and/or implicit – of the infamous system of colonialist binaries and other elements of Eurocentrism. This second lesson, though, may be particularly difficult to put in practice, especially for First World[20] researchers who are deeply schooled in the hierarchizing cultural myth of European exceptionalism/universalism and whose very identity, often enough, is crucially dependent on that myth.

Perhaps even more difficult for First World researchers to implement might be the chapter's proposal that CMS in the 21st century needs to learn to view the Third World as a producer of sophisticated knowledge (not only as a source of 'data') and begin using non-Western epistemologies, categories and knowledges in the process of generating new CMS knowledge. The difficulty of implementing this suggestion is linked to a variety of factors including, for instance, the limited availability in Western languages of resources dealing with the epistemologies/knowledges/categories of Third World cultures, the widespread illiteracy of First World (CMS) scholars in Third World languages and so on. Faced with this situation (and lacking the motivation to put in the hard work required for earning fluency in a Third World language), a First World researcher interested in pursuing this kind of research might decide in favor of collaboration with Third World scholars. Needless to say, such collaborations are invariably complex exercises, especially so, moreover, in a hierarchically structured global system caught right now in the middle of a massive power shift. In addition, however, another word of caution to First World scholars contemplating such collaboration might be in order.

In some of her remarks on the difficulty of First World–Third World collaborations, Spivak has drawn attention to Jacques Derrida's observation that philosophical/cultural categories and 'concepts [cannot] transcend *idiomatic* differences' (Derrida, 1992: 54, quoted in Spivak, 2003: 10; emphasis added). This implies, says Spivak (2003: 10), that cross-cultural importations and transfers (or 'translations') of concepts and categories require an idiomatic – rather than merely a mechanical or 'objectifying' – understanding of the two languages/cultures involved in any instance of such 'translation'. But the problem facing a First World CMS academic who may lack even a mechanical understanding of the Third World language relevant for a given research project and who has hopes of filling the gap in her/his language skills by collaborating with a Third World researcher is particularly complex because, for the most part, such collaboration is likely to take place with members of a particular class of professionalized Third World researchers, many (though not all) of whom might have been educated either in the West or in Western-style institutions and who may frequently be 'out of touch with the idiomaticity of . . . [their own] languages' and/or of the languages of the poor and the subaltern within their societies (Spivak, 2003: 10). In other words, the mere fact of collaboration between First and Third World scholars is no guarantee of the idiomatic adequacy of cross-cultural transfers of categories/knowledges from the Third World to the West, although some collaborations may well be successful in achieving this goal.

These considerations pave the way for three preliminary conclusions. First, unless adequate translations are available, a Western CMS scholar interested in making use of epistemologies/concepts/categories from a Third World culture may have no choice, generally speaking, but to go through the laborious process of idiomatically learning the relevant language from that culture. Secondly, as we explain below, it seems to be highly unlikely over the next several years that significant numbers of First World CMS scholars might engage in research that draws upon Third World concepts and categories *if* such research requires the learning of Third World languages. Hence, finally, it would seem also that, for a number of years into the future, it is mostly (though not exclusively) Third World scholars with strong links to Third World languages/cultures who might be in a position to address the important task of importing Third World knowledges into the CMS field. It appears, therefore, that the future (shape) of CMS may crucially depend upon what this particular group of Third World scholars decides to do, a point we will return to presently.

First, however, we need to briefly go back to the question of why we believe that, during the next several years, First World CMS researchers are unlikely to undertake the kind of research being discussed here. While it is possible to suggest a variety of reasons for the First World CMS scholars' refusal to engage in such research, the following discussion restricts itself to only one such reason, namely the nature of the present-day CMS 'research industry' in First World countries. Without getting into great detail, we may think of this 'research industry' as organized around a set of practices (e.g. publishing/presenting papers in journals/conferences, training novice researchers in doctoral programs etc.), and a reward structure, i.e. a variety of rules and conventions that determine how those practices will be rewarded by way of, for example acceptance of manuscripts for publication in journals, academic tenure and promotion decisions, award of grants from funding bodies and so forth. It is easy enough to see that, in its current form, the First World CMS 'research industry' does not offer any *added incentive* for conducting research that might draw upon Third World epistemologies/concepts/categories, nor does the industry impose any costs on academics for *not* doing that kind of research. At the same time, moreover, certain *implicit disincentives* tend to dissuade scholars from undertaking research of this type. For instance, to keep it brief, why would any researcher run the risk of submitting to a First World CMS journal a manuscript discussing, say, the complexity of epistemological thinking in a largely unknown part of the Third World – largely unknown, that is, to the journal's editor/ readership – when that journal might not even be able to find enough reviewers with adequate interest or expertise in that subject?

The CMS field, thus, finds itself at a somewhat awkward moment in its history. On the one hand, as a result of various developments characterizing a world in the middle of a far-reaching systemic shift, the field is now being called upon to respond to a range of novel and urgent concerns and, in that process, to meaningfully re-form, decolonize and reorient itself. On the other hand, for a variety of reasons, the First World CMS 'research industry' – a factor of undoubted importance in the field of CMS today – is mostly unable (but perhaps also generally unwilling) to make large-scale contributions toward all the necessary aspects of this project of reforming and decolonizing the field. For instance, as already noted, some of the reforms of CMS being proposed in this chapter are unlikely to receive extensive *concrete* support over the next several years, either from significant numbers of First World CMS researchers or from the First World CMS journals. Hence, for the foreseeable future, many aspects of the overall project of seriously overhauling CMS may need to be carried out mostly by Third World scholars, and much indeed will depend upon whether or not Third World scholars decide to become significant contributors in those matters. If the Third World scholars do so decide, however, they can succeed in giving a fundamentally new and exciting direction to the CMS field as a whole.

It needs to be noted that, for CMS scholars from the Third World, the project of radically reorienting and decolonizing the CMS field comes wrapped in interesting challenges and opportunities.[21] Clearly, the project may be seen as having considerable affinities with Walter Mignolo's (2011:54) notion of 'epistemic delinking' alluded to earlier, which calls for delinking the production of new knowledge from Western epistemologies, concerns and structures of knowledge. In addition to epistemic delinking, however, the project of reforming/decolonizing CMS may also require considerable 'institutional delinking/relinking', comprising a variety of initiatives across different parts of the Third World.

Without getting into exhaustive details here, one important initiative in this regard, for instance, may need to address the task of developing new research outlets (e.g. workshops, conferences and conference proceedings, edited volumes/serials, working papers series, monographs, launching new journals and/or strengthening existing journals and so on, *as well as* creatively imagining other *novel avenues* for disseminating research) that may serve as *alternatives* to the existing First World CMS journals and other publication channels. Moreover, the creation of new research outlets will necessarily need to be accompanied by suitable changes in local academic reward structures, which may provide adequate incentives to scholars to publish their research in these newly developed Third World outlets. Similarly, another initiative in this regard may need to focus upon establishing new scholarly networks (and/or strengthening existing ones) not only within individual countries but also along international lines that promote greater South-South linkages (e.g. networks spanning scholars from countries belonging to different groupings like ASEAN (Association of South East Asian Nations), BIMSTEC (Bay of Bengal Initiative for Multi-Sectoral Technical and Economic Cooperation), BRICS (Brazil, Russia, India, China, and South Africa), IBSA (India-Brazil-South Africa Dialogue Forum), SAARC (South Asian Association for Regional Cooperation), SADC (South African Development Community), UNASUR (Union of South American Nations) and others). These and other epistemological/institutional initiatives launched in several regions stretching across the Global South may serve as pathways leading to a world of plural (CMS) knowledges mentioned earlier in the chapter.

In this regard, it might be useful to point out that, although one of the goals of the project of plural knowledges is indeed that of undermining the current dominance of modern Western knowledge, this project is driven neither by a desire to further deepen the West/non-West divide in the service of relativism nor by a commitment to cultural nativism. Indeed, instead of any commitment to nativism, it is rather the notion of cultural hybridity/hybridization that is taken seriously by this project. Among other things, this implies a recognition on the part of this project that what hybridization produces (for instance, in the course of West/non-West encounters in different parts of the world) is *not* uniformity but difference, and this for the simple reason that different cultural sites – serving as different 'loci of enunciation' (Mignolo, 2000, 2011) – invariably assimilate/appropriate outside influences in their own different ways. Not to recognize this aspect of hybridity is to deny agency to the 'recipients' (so-called) of external influences. Turning to Homi Bhabha, therefore, we could say that what hybridity produces is 'the difference of the same' (1994: 22). That is to say, hybrid productions that look similar across different cultures may be marked by profound differences, while things that appear different may well have significant similarities.[22]

The project of plural knowledges, therefore, aims to create (at multiple loci of enunciation around the world) the necessary conditions and the required infrastructure (epistemological and institutional) for promoting and facilitating the production of knowledges that are *hybrid* and (therefore) *different*. Hence, although different cultural sites of knowledge production may choose to reject one or more of the concepts of the Western social sciences, the project of plural knowledges does not necessarily require a complete rejection of all such concepts. Rather, what this project requires is making *use* of the needed social scientific concepts in a way that brings the *force* of locally embedded knowledges and epistemologies (elite *and* subaltern) to bear upon the existing concepts of the social sciences and, in that process, hybridizing those concepts, i.e. making those concepts 'strangers' to 'themselves'. In sum, therefore, the project of multiple forms of CMS being proposed here is intended to help develop, at different sites (or loci of enunciation) around the world, different kinds of CMS knowledges, each addressing those issues that might be of greater importance to a specific site, while using localized epistemologies and protocols of knowledge production and not feeling any need or desire to regard modern Western epistemology and the protocols of the First World CMS research industry as universal norms.

Scholarly discussions of the project of plural knowledges often raise the question of whether a world of diverse knowledges – or, as in our case, of multiple CMSs – represents 'a mosaic of distinct knowledge systems . . . all functioning independently' (Connell, *Southern Theory*, 2007: 223). In this regard, while Connell (2007: 223) herself has proposed that such a world is 'unrealistic',[23]

Ashis Nandy offers the view that a world of multiple knowledges is one in which only some (and not necessarily all) of the different coexisting knowledges of the planet might be 'in communication with each other' (2000: 81). In any event, it needs to be emphasized that the pattern of communication across different knowledges in such a world would involve significant South-South exchanges and would not be centered on the Western world of knowledge.

In many ways, one of the goals of the project of plural knowledges (and that of multiple forms of CMS) is to imaginatively recuperate the energy, sophistication and heterogeneity of the multitude of long-standing cultural traditions of thinking, being, seeing and acting that have suffered from the depredations of modern Western (neo-)colonialism. As already suggested, however, this does not imply an outright rejection of modern Western epistemology in its entirety. Indeed, for those of us who have been schooled in this epistemology, it is an *indispensable* tool in our critical endeavors. However, it is also a tool that is *inadequate* for our purposes. Indeed, as critical scholars like Dipesh Chakrabarty (2000) and Sanjay Seth (2007) have long been pointing out, modern Western knowledge/epistemology is inadequate not only for the needs of the Third World but even for those of the First World as well. Hence, this book is also an invitation to all critical scholars – those in the Third World and those in the First – to join us in imagining new ways of being and thinking that bring with them a promise of justice.

Notes

1 *Khātirāt-i-Mutribī Samarqandī* is often referred to as 'The Memoirs of Mutribi Samarqandi'.
2 "Whoores", i.e. 'whores' according to present-day spelling.
3 It needs to be noted that neither of these two xenological traditions was monolithic. Considerations of space prevent us from looking into the heterogeneity that marks the two traditions.
4 For the most part, this chapter uses terms like 'Western', 'the West', etc. as "figures of the imaginary" having "somewhat indeterminate geographical referents" (Chakrabarty, 1992: 1). Any deviation in the chapter from this meaning will occur in well-defined contexts where the different meaning of the terms will be readily discernible. The chapter, moreover, duly recognizes that these terms should not be viewed as referring to essentialist and/or monolithic entities. See, in this regard, Chakrabarty (1992), Prasad (1997a: 306, n. 4), Prasad (2003b: 34–35, n. 5), etc.
5 The European wars of religion were fought over a long period stretching broadly from the 1520s to the middle of the 17th century. The Thirty Years' War (which came to an exhausted end in 1648 with the Peace of Westphalia) may have been the most brutal phase of these religious wars with unspeakable acts of barbarity committed by all sides and is often regarded as not only the 'most destructive war in preindustrial Europe' (historian Hugh Trevor-Roper quoted in Inayatullah & Blaney, 2004: 29) but also as 'a total ideological war' and 'the greatest calamity to befall . . . [parts of Europe] in the period bounded by the Black Death [occurring during the middle of the 14th century] and World War II' (Inayatullah & Blaney, 2004: 29).
6 The most famous of these debates were the Valladolid Debates (1550–1551) between Bartolomé de Las Casas and Juan Ginés de Sepúlveda. The "principles of those debates . . . [were further refined] in the university of Salamanca" (Mignolo, 2003: 428).
7 In this context, we need to take note also of the extremely ferocious wars waged in Europe on the knowledge systems of the witches during a long period stretching from the 12th to 17th centuries (Barstow, 1994). Largely for reasons of space, however, we have decided not to take up that question in this chapter.
8 See, e.g. Anshuman Prasad (Chapter 10 in this volume) for further thoughts on the project of plural knowledges.
9 Needless to say, the lines demarcating different circles in Figure 1.1 represent porous boundaries rather than impermeable ones that may not be breached.
10 The authors of this chapter are themselves part of the CMS community. In that sense, this chapter's critique of CMS may be regarded as an 'internal' critique of the field. However, we hold a more elastic view of CMS than the one proposed by the Manchester School.
11 As we will see in the next section, current debates and discussions about CMS mostly focus only on one segment of the field (namely, the Manchester School of CMS), rather than on the CMS field in its entirety.

12 On this matter, Wallerstein deserves to be quoted at some length: "If I insist on . . . [global] analysis . . . it is certainly not because I am asking . . . [everyone] to look only at macro-phenomena. Far from it. It is because I do not believe one can make relevant, meaningful analyses of the data (at whatever level from which they are drawn) if one omits significant contextual . . . [factors] at the level of the . . . [global] system. . . . Groups of any size (from casual duos . . . to large-scale organizations, to state structures) operate within an evolving historical [global-level] system and can only be understood if carefully placed within that system" (1999: 260).

13 This genre of writings in the social sciences and the humanities, while occupying a location that is 'inside' the discourse of Western knowledge, functions at what scholars like Mignolo (2003) refer to as the 'exteriority' of the Western discourse and, as a result, exerts relentless pressure in the direction of *decolonizing* that discourse.

14 We address the question of relevance of CMS knowledge in the next section.

15 Note, however, that this volume does not advance any claim of being the one and only 'true' way forward for CMS. Other approaches and possibilities, needless to say, always exist. From our perspective, CMS as a scholarly field needs to keep itself open to new critical influences, always be intellectually on the move and resist systematization.

16 Note that, in our use, the term, 'critical consulting' holds a somewhat different meaning from the one in which this term has been used by Voronov (2008).

17 For a brief history of the transformation of business administration into an applied social science, see Anshuman Prasad (Chapter 10 in this volume).

18 There exists a huge literature addressing the ongoing decline in Western 'hard' as well as 'soft' power. For an overview, see e.g. Bacevich (2012), *Foreign Affairs* (2010), Kupchan (2012), Layne (2006), Mahbubani (2008), National Intelligence Council (2008, 2012), Packer (2013), PricewaterhouseCoopers (2013), Scahill (2013), Stiglitz (2012), Taibbi (2010, 2014), Wilson & Purushothaman (2003), World Bank (2011), Zakaria (2008), etc.

19 In brief, Spivak's (1999) concept of 'sanctioned ignorance' may be said to refer to the idea that Eurocentric knowledge *learns to ignore* (the challenge posed by) 'other' knowledges because of "the availability, within the Eurocentric tradition, of key texts [e.g. Kant, Hegel, Marx, Weber, etc.] that endorse and *sanction* such ignorance" (Prasad & Prasad, 2003: 288, italics in the original). We need to take note also of a fairly widespread habit of scholarship (in business academia in the West) that encourages researchers to mostly ignore international issues *beyond the Western group of countries.*

20 It needs to be emphasized that our use of expressions like 'First World' or 'Third World' does not subscribe to notions of hierarchical ordering that might be embedded in such expressions. Moreover, similar to Walter Mignolo's (2000) use of expressions like these (see this chapter's epigraph quoting Mignolo), our use of these expressions also is of a somewhat metaphorical nature.

21 For reasons already alluded to, the following discussion focuses only on Third World CMS researchers. However, *mutatis mutandis,* many of the challenges and opportunities being identified here are equally relevant for all CMS scholars (from any part of the world) who might be interested in the kind of reform under consideration.

22 Taking hybridity seriously involves a recognition also that the various characteristic elements and features that make up the modern West (e.g. modern Western philosophy, or the social sciences, etc.) are themselves hybrid productions. Consequently, different forms of modern Western knowledge, or the modern social sciences, which were once regarded as autonomous and internal products of the West, now come to be seen as resulting from colonial and neocolonial encounters.

23 However, Connell does accept the feasibility of the 'mosaic model' of multiple knowledges "as a rare limiting case" (2007: 224).

References

Ackroyd, S. (2004). Less bourgeois than thou? A critical review of *Studying management critically. Ephemera,* 4: 165–170.

Adams, G., & Ingersoll, V. H. (1990). Culture, technical rationality and organizational culture. *American Review of Public Administration, 20*: 285–302.

Ahmed, S. 2004. Affective Economics. *Social Text, 22*: 117–139.

Alam, M., & Subrahmanyam, S. (2007). *Indo-Persian travels in the age of discoveries 1400–1800.* New York: Cambridge University Press.

Alcadipani, R., & Caldas, M. (2012). Americanizing Brazilian management, *Critical Perspectives on International Business*, 8: 37–55.

Alvesson, M. (1987). *Organization theory and technocratic consciousness: Rationality, ideology and quality of work*. Berlin: Walter de Gruyter.

Alvesson, M. (Ed.). (2011). *Classics in critical management studies*. London: Edward Elgar.

Alvesson, M., Bridgman, T., & Willmott, H. (Eds.) (2009). *The Oxford handbook of critical management studies*. Oxford: Oxford University Press.

Alvesson, M., & Willmott, H. (Eds.). (2003). *Studying management critically*. London: Sage.

Alvesson, M., & Willmott, H. (Eds.). (2012). *Critical management studies* (4 vols.). London: Sage.

Anzaldúa, G. (1987). *Borderlands/la frontera: The new mestiza*. San Francisco: Aunt Lute Books.

Appadurai, A. (1996), *Modernity at large: Cultural dimensions of globalization*. Minneapolis: University of Minnesota Press.

Appadurai, A. (2006). *Fear of small numbers: An essay on the geography of anger*. Durham, NC: Duke University Press.

Appiah, K. A. (2006). *Cosmopolitanism: Ethics in a world of strangers*. New York: W. W. Norton.

Ashcraft, K. L. (2005). Resistance through consent? Occupational identity, organizational form and the maintenance of masculinity among commercial airline pilots. *Management Communication Quarterly*, *19*: 67–90.

Ashcraft, K. L., Muhr, S. L., Rennstam, J., & Sullivan, K. (2012). Professionalization as a branding activity: Occupational identity and the dialectic of inclusivity-exclusivity. *Gender, Work and Organization*, *19*: 467–488.

Bacevich, A. (Ed.). (2012). *The short American century: A postmortem*. Cambridge, MA: Harvard University Press.

Barros, M. (2010). Emancipatory management: The contradiction between practice and discourse. *Journal of Management Inquiry*, *19*: 166–184.

Barstow, A. L. (1994). *Witchcraze*. London: Pandora.

Belk, R. W. (1994). Carnival, control and corporate culture in contemporary Halloween ceremonies. In J. Santino (Ed.), *Halloween and other festivals of death and life*: 105–132. Knoxville: University of Tennessee Press.

Bell, E., & King, D. (2010). The elephant in the room: Critical management studies conferences as a site of body pedagogies. *Management Learning*, *41*(4): 429–442.

Benson, K. (1977). Organizations: A dialectical view. *Administrative Science Quarterly*, *22*: 1–21.

Bhabha, H. K. (Ed.). (1990). *Nation and narration*. London: Routledge.

Bhabha, H. K. (1994). *The location of culture*. London: Routledge.

Blaut, J. M. (1993). *The colonizer's model of the world*. New York: Guilford Press.

Blaut, J. M. (2000). *Eight Eurocentric historians*. New York: Guilford Press.

Boje, D., & Rosile, G. A. (2003). Life imitates art: ENRON's epic and tragic narration. *Management Communication Quarterly*, *17*: 85–125.

Boussebaa, M., Sinha, S., & Gabriel, Y. (2014). Englishization in offshore call centers: A postcolonial perspective. *International Journal of Business Studies*, *45*: 1152–1169.

Brewis, J., & Wray-Bliss, E. (2008). Re-searching ethics: Towards a more reflexive critical management studies. *Organization Studies*, *29*: 1521–1540.

Brown, R. H. (1978). Bureaucracy as praxis: Toward a political phenomenology of formal organizations. *Administrative Science Quarterly*, *23*: 365–382.

Bryman, A. (2004). *The Disneyization of society*. London: Sage Publications.

Burawoy, M. (1979). *Manufacturing consent: Changes in the labor process under monopoly capitalism*. Chicago: University of Chicago Press.

Calás, M., & Smircich, L. (1991). Voicing seduction to silence leadership. *Organization Studies*, *12*: 567–602.

Case, P., & Piñeiro, E. (2006). Aesthetics, performativity and resistance in the narratives of a computer programming community. *Human Relations*, *59*: 753–782.

Chakrabarty, D. (1992). Postcoloniality and the artifice of history. *Representations*, *37*: 1–26.

Chakrabarty, D. (2000). *Provincializing Europe: Postcolonial thought and historical difference*. Princeton, NJ: Princeton University Press.

Chen, K-H. (2010). *Asia as method: Toward deimperialization*. Durham, NC: Duke University Press.

Clegg, S. (1979). *The theory of power and organization*. London: Routledge and Kegan Paul.

Clegg, S. (1989). *Frameworks of power*. Thousand Oaks, CA: Sage.

Clegg, S. (1990). *Modern organizations: Organization studies in the postmodern world*. Thousand Oaks, CA: Sage.

Clifford, J. (1997). *Routes: Travel and translation in the late twentieth century*. Cambridge, MA: Harvard University Press.

Collins, R. (1985). *Three sociological traditions*. Oxford: Oxford University Press.

Collinson, D. (1988). Engineering humor: Masculinity, joking and conflict in shopfloor relations. *Organization Studies*, *9*: 181–199.

Connell, R. (2007). *Southern theory*. Cambridge: Polity.

Cooper, R., & Burrell, G. (1988). Modernism, postmodernism, and organizational analysis. *Organization Studies*, *9*: 91–112.

Cooperman, H., & Shechter, R. (2008). Branding the riders: 'Marlboro country' and the formation of a new middle class in Egypt, Saudi Arabia and Turkey. *New Global Studies*, *2*: 1–41.

Coronado, G. (2012). Constructing the 'neocolonial' manager: Orientalizing Latin America in the textbooks. In A. Prasad (Ed.), *Against the grain: Advances in postcolonial organization studies*: 155–176. Copenhagen: Copenhagen Business School Press/Liber.

Cunliffe, A. L. (2008). Will you still need me . . . When I am 64? The future of CMS. *Organization*, *15*: 936–938.

Czarniawska-Joerges, B. (1988). *Ideological control in non-ideological organizations*. New York: Praeger.

Dar, S. (2014). Hybrid accountabilities: When Western and non-Western accountabilities collide. *Human Relations*, *67*: 131–151.

Dauvergne, P. (1997). *Shadows in the forest: Japan and the politics of timber in Southeast Asia*. Cambridge, MA: MIT Press.

Davis, G. F. (2009). *Managed by the markets: How finance re-shaped America*. New York: Oxford University Press.

Deetz, S. (1992). *Democracy in an age of corporate colonization*. Albany: State University of New York Press.

Denhardt, R. B. (1981). *In the shadows of organization*. Lawrence, KS: Regents Press.

Derrida, J. (1991). Letter to a Japanese friend. In P. Kamuf (Ed.), *A Derrida reader*: 270–276. New York: Columbia University Press.

Derrida, J. (1992). *Given time: I. Counterfeit money*. Chicago: University of Chicago Press.

Derrida, J. (1993). *Aporias*. Stanford, CA: Stanford University Press.

Dobbin, F., & Zorn, D. (2005). Corporate malfeasance and the myth of shareholder value. *Political Power and Social Theory*, *17*: 179–198.

Driver, M. (2009). Encountering the arugula leaf: The failure of the imaginary and its implications for research on identity in organizations. *Organization*, *16*: 487–504.

DuGay, P. (1996). *Consumption and identity at work*. London: Sage.

Durepos, G., Helms Mills, J., & Mills, A. (2008). Flights of fancy: Myth, monopoly and the making of Pan American Airways. *Journal of Management History*, *14*: 116–127.

Dussel, E. (1998). Beyond Eurocentrism: The World System and the limits of modernity. In F. Jameson & M. Miyosagi (Eds.), *The cultures of globalization*: 3–31. Durham, NC: Duke University Press.

Echtner, C., & Prasad, P. (2003). The context of Third World tourism marketing. *Annals of Tourism Research*, *30*: 660–682.

Escobar, A. (1995). *Encountering development: The making and unmaking of the Third World*. Princeton, NJ: Princeton University Press.

Ewen, S. (1976). *Captains of consciousness: Advertising and the social roots of consumer culture*. New York: McGraw-Hill.

Faria, A. (2013). Border thinking in action: Should Critical Management Studies get anything done? In V. Malin, J. Murphy & M. Siltaoja (Eds.), *Dialogues in critical management studies*: 277–300. Bingley, UK: Emerald.

Ferdinand, J., Muzio, D., & O'Mahoney, J. (2003). Book review of *Studying management critically* edited by M. Alvesson & H. Willmott. *Organization Studies*, *25*: 1455–1465.

Ferguson, K. E. (1984). *The feminist case against bureaucracy*. Philadelphia: Temple University Press.

Ford, J., Harding, N., & Learmonth, M. (2010). Who is it that would make business schools more critical? Critical reflections on critical management studies. *British Journal of Management*, *21*: 571–581.

Foreign Affairs. (2010). Special Issue: The world ahead. *89*(6), November–December.

Fournier, V., & Grey, C. (2000). At the critical moment: Conditions and prospects for Critical Management Studies. *Human Relations*, *53*: 7–32.

Frenkel, M., & Shenhav, Y. (2003). From Americanization to colonization: The diffusion of productivity models revisited. *Organization Studies*, *24*: 1537–1561.

Frost, P.J. (1980). Toward a radical framework for practicing organizational science. *Academy of Management Review*, *5*: 501–507.

Gabriel, Y. (2001). The state of critique in organizational theory. *Human Relations*, *54*: 23–30.

Gabriel, Y. (2005). Glass cages and glass palaces: Images of organizations in image conscious times. *Organization*, *12*: 9–27.

Gagnon, S. (2008). Compelling identity: Selves and insecurity in global corporate management development. *Management Learning*, *39*: 375–391.

Ganesh, S. (2003). Organizational narcissism: Technology, legitimacy and identity in an Indian NGO. *Management Communication Quarterly*, *16*: 558–594.

Garcia Canclini, N. (1995). *Hybrid cultures: Strategies for entering and learning modernity.* Minneapolis: University of Minnesota Press.

Goody, J. (2006). *The theft of history.* Cambridge: Cambridge University Press.

Gopinath, C., & Prasad, A. (2013). Toward a critical framework for understanding MNE operations: Revisiting Coca-Cola's exit from India. *Organization*, *20*: 212–232.

Gordon, L.R. (1995). *Fanon and the crisis of European man.* London: Routledge.

Grey, C., & Willmott, H. (2005a). Introduction. In C. Grey & H. Willmott (Eds.), *Critical management studies: A reader*: 1–15. Oxford: Oxford University Press.

Grey, C., & Willmott, H. (Eds.). (2005b). *Critical management studies: A reader.* Oxford: Oxford University Press.

Guha, R. (1982a). Preface. In R. Guha (Ed.), *Subaltern studies I: Writings on South Asian history and society*: vii–viii. Delhi: Oxford University Press.

Guha, R. (1982b). On some aspects of historiography of colonial India. In R. Guha (Ed.), *Subaltern studies I: Writings on South Asian history and society*: 1–8. Delhi: Oxford University Press.

Guha, R. (Ed.). (1997). *A subaltern studies reader.* Minneapolis: University of Minnesota Press.

Hannerz, U. (1996). *Transnational connections.* New York: Routledge.

Harding, S. (1998). *Is science multicultural? Postcolonialisms, feminisms, and epistemologies.* Bloomington: Indiana University Press.

Harding, S. (2008). *Sciences from below: Feminisms, postcolonialities, and modernities.* Durham, NC: Duke University Press.

Harding, S. (2009). Postcolonial and feminist philosophies of science and technology. *Postcolonial Studies*, *12*(4), 401–421.

Harrison, J. (1997). Museums as agencies of neocolonialism in a postcolonial world. *Studies in Cultures, Organizations and Societies*, *3*: 41–65.

Hartmann, R. K. (2014). Subversive functionalism: For a less canonical critique in Critical Management Studies. *Human Relations*, *67*: 611–632.

Hartt, C. M., Mills, A. J., & Helms Mills, J. (2012). On the Cold War front: Dissent, misbehavior and discursive relations at Pan American Airways guided missiles divisions. In L. Taksa & A. Barnes (Eds.), *Rethinking misbehavior and resistance in organization*: 111–140. London: Emerald.

Hegel, G.W.F. (1975). *Aesthetics: Lectures on fine art* (trans. T. M. Knox, 2 vols.). Oxford: Clarendon Press.

Hirschman, E. (1990). Secular immortality and the American ideology of affluence. *Journal of Consumer Research*, *17*: 31–42.

Hourani, A. (1991). *A history of the Arab peoples.* New York: Faber & Faber.

Ibarra-Colado, E. (2006). Organization studies and epistemic coloniality in Latin America: Thinking otherness from the margins. *Organization*, *13*: 463–488.

Inayatullah, N., & Blaney, D. (2004). *International relations and the problem of difference.* New York: Routledge.

Iwabuchi, K. (2002). *Recentering globalization: Popular culture and Japanese transnationalism.* Durham, NC: Duke University Press.

Jacques, R. (1996). *Manufacturing the employee: Management knowledge from the 19th to the 21st centuries.* London: Sage Publications.

Jacques, R. (2006). History, historiography and organization studies. The challenge and the potential. *Management and Organizational History*, *1*: 31–49

Jammulamadaka, N. (2013). What to stop doing in order to get things done? A critical engagement with the discourse of Critical Management Studies. In V. Malin, J. Murphy & M. Siltaoja (Eds.), *Dialogues in critical management studies*: 225–243. Bingley, UK: Emerald.

Kamuf, P. (1991). Introduction: Reading between the blinds. In P. Kamuf (Ed.), *A Derrida reader*: xiii–xlii. New York: Columbia University Press.

Kaplan, A. E. (2008). Global trauma and public feelings: Viewing images of catastrophe. *Consumption, Markets and Culture, 11*: 3–24.

Kupchan, C. (2012). *No one's world: The West, the rising rest, and the coming global turn.* New York: Oxford University Press.

Kymlicka, W. (1995). *Multicultural citizenship: A liberal theory of minority rights.* Oxford: Clarendon Press.

Lal, V. (Ed.). (2000). *Dissenting knowledges, open futures.* Delhi: Oxford University Press.

Layne, C. (2006). The unipolar illusion revisited. *International Security, 31*(2): 7–41.

Lears, T. J. J. (2012). Pragmatic realism versus the American century. In A. Bacevich (Ed.), *The short American century: A postmortem*: 82–120. Cambridge, MA: Harvard University Press.

Madison, A. (2007). *Contours of the world economy 1–2030 AD.* New York: Oxford University Press.

Mahbubani, K. (2008). *The new Asian hemisphere: The irresistible shift of global power to the East.* New York: Public Affairs.

Marens, R. (2011). Speaking platitudes to power: Observing business ethics in an age of institutional turbulence. *Journal of Business Ethics, 94*: 239–253.

Marglin, S. (1974). What do bosses do? The origins and functions of hierarchy in capitalist production. *Review of Radical Political Economics, 6*: 24–52.

Masuzawa, T. (2005). *The invention of world religions.* Chicago: University of Chicago Press.

McKenna, S. (2012). A critical analysis of North American business leaders' neocolonialist discourse: Global fears and local consequences. *Organization, 18*: 387–406.

Mignolo, W. (2000). *Local histories/global designs: Coloniality, subaltern knowledges, and border thinking.* Princeton, NJ: Princeton University Press.

Mignolo, W. (2003). *The darker side of the Renaissance* (2nd Ed.). Princeton, NJ: Princeton University Press.

Mignolo, W. (2011). *The darker side of Western modernity.* Durham, NC: Duke University Press.

Mills, A. J. (1988). Organizations, gender and culture. *Organization Studies, 9*: 351–369.

Mills, A. J. (1996). Corporate image, gendered subjects and the company newsletter: The changing face of British Airways. In G. Palmer & S. Clegg (Eds.), *Constituting management: Market, meanings and identities*: 191–211. Berlin: de Gruyter.

Mills, A. J. (2006). *Sex, strategy and the stratosphere: The gendering of airline cultures.* London: Palgrave MacMillan.

Minh-ha, T. T. (1989). *Woman, native, other: Writing postcoloniality and feminism.* Bloomington: Indiana University Press.

Mir, R., & Mir, A. (2009). From the corporation to the colony: Studying knowledge transfer across international boundaries. *Group and Organization Management, 34*: 90–113.

Mirchandani, K. (2004). Practices of global capital: Gaps, cracks and ironies in transnational call centers in India. *Global Networks, 4*: 355–374.

Mirchandani, K. (2012). *Phone clones: Authenticity work in the transnational service economy.* Ithaca, NY: Cornell University Press.

Mitchell, T. (2005). The work of economics: How a discipline makes its world. *European Journal of Sociology, 46*: 297–320.

Mizruchi, M. S. (2004). Berle and Means revisited: The governance and power of large U.S. corporations. *Theory and Society, 33*: 579–617.

Mizruchi, M. S. (2010). The American corporate elite and the historical roots of the financial crisis of 2008. In M. Lounsbury & P. M. Hirsch (Eds.), *Markets on trial: The economic sociology of the U.S. financial crisis*: 405–442. Bingley, UK: Emerald.

Mudimbe, V. Y. (1988). *The invention of Africa: Gnosis, philosophy and the order of knowledge.* Bloomington: Indiana University Press.

Mumby, D. (1988). *Communication and power in organizations: Discourse, ideology, and domination.* Norwood, NJ: Ablex.

Mumby, D. (2005). Theorizing resistance in organization studies: A dialectical approach. *Management Communication Quarterly, 19*: 19–44.

Munasinghe, V. (2002). Nationalism in hybrid spaces: The production of impurity out of purity. *American Ethnologist, 29*: 663–692.

Murray, J. B., & Ozanne, J. L. (1991). The critical imagination: Emancipatory interests in consumer research. *Journal of Consumer Research, 18*: 129–144.

Nandy, A. (1983). *The intimate enemy.* Delhi: Oxford University Press.

Nandy, A. (1995). *The savage Freud and other essays on possible and retrievable selves.* Princeton, NJ: Princeton University Press.

Nandy, A. (2000). The defiance of defiance and liberation for the victims of history. In V. Lal (Ed.), *Dissenting knowledges, open futures*: 3–93. Delhi: Oxford University Press.

National Intelligence Council. (2008). *Global trends 2025: A transformed world.* Washington, DC: National Intelligence Council.

National Intelligence Council. (2012). *Global trends 2030: Alternative worlds.* Washington, DC: National Intelligence Council.

Nederveen Pieterse, J. (2010). *Development theory* (2nd Ed.). Thousand Oaks, CA: Sage.

Neu, D. (1992). Reading the regulatory text: Regulation and the new stock issue process. *Critical Perspective on Accounting, 3*: 359–388.

Nord, W. R. (1978). Dreams of humanization and realities of power. *Academy of Management Review, 3*: 674–678.

Ong, A. (1987). *Spirits of resistance and capitalist discipline: Factory women in Malaysia.* Albany: State University of New York Press.

Ong, A. (1999). *Flexible citizenship: The cultural logics of transnationality.* Durham, NC: Duke University Press.

Ong, A. (2003). *Buddha is hiding: Refugees, citizenship and the new America.* Berkeley: University of California Press.

Özkazanç-Pan, B. (2008). International management research meets "the rest of the world." *Academy of Management Review, 33*: 964–974.

Packer, G. (2013). *The unwinding: An inner history of the new America.* New York: Farrar, Straus and Giroux.

Parker, M. (1995). Critique in the name of what? Postmodernism and critical approaches to organization. *Organization Studies, 16*: 553–564.

Parker, M. (2005). Writing critical management studies. In C. Grey & H. Willmott (Eds.), *Critical management studies: A reader:* 353–363. Oxford: Oxford University Press.

Perera, S., & Pugliese, J. (1998). Parks, mines and tidy towns: Enviro-panopticism, 'post'colonialism and the politics of heritage in Australia. *Postcolonial Studies, 1*: 69–100.

Perrow, C. (1972). *Complex organizations: A critical essay.* New York: Random House.

Power, M,, & Laughlin, R. (1992). Critical theory and accounting. In M. Alvesson & H. Willmott (Eds.), *Critical Management Studies*: 113–135. London: Sage Publications.

Prasad, Anshuman. (1997a). The colonizing consciousness and representations of the other: A postcolonial critique of the discourse of oil. In P. Prasad, A. Mills, M. Elmes & Anshuman Prasad (Eds.), *Managing the organizational melting pot: Dilemmas of workplace diversity*: 285–311. Thousand Oaks, CA: Sage.

Prasad, Anshuman. (1997b). Provincializing Europe. *Culture and Organization, 3*: 91–117.

Prasad, Anshuman. (Ed.). (2003a). *Postcolonial theory and organizational analysis: A critical engagement.* New York: Palgrave Macmillan.

Prasad, Anshuman. (2003b). The gaze of the other. In Anshuman Prasad (Ed.), *Postcolonial theory and organizational analysis*: 3–43. New York: Palgrave Macmillan.

Prasad, Anshuman. (2008). Book review of *Critical Management Studies: A Reader* edited by C. Grey and H. Willmott. *Academy of Management Review, 33*: 278–283.

Prasad, Anshuman. (Ed.). (2012a). *Against the grain: Advances in postcolonial organization studies.* Copenhagen & Malmo: Copenhagen Business School/Liber.

Prasad, Anshuman. (2012b). Working against the grain: Beyond Eurocentrism in organization studies. In Anshuman Prasad (Ed.), *Against the grain: Advances in postcolonial organization studies*: 13–31. Copenhagen and Malmo: Copenhagen Business School/Liber.

Prasad, Anshuman, & Prasad, P. (2003). The postcolonial imagination. In Anshuman Prasad (Ed.), *Postcolonial theory and organizational analysis*: 283–295. New York: Palgrave Macmillan.

Prasad, Anshuman, Prasad, P., & Mir, R. (2011). 'One mirror in another': Managing diversity and the discourse of fashion. *Human Relations, 64*: 703–724.

Prasad, P., & Elmes, M. (2005). In the name of the practical: Unearthing the hegemony of pragmatism in the discourse of environmental management. *Journal of Management Studies, 42*: 845–867.

PricewaterhouseCoopers. (2013). *The world in 2050: The BRICs and beyond.* London: PricewaterhouseCoopers LLP.

Rosen, M. (1988). "You asked for it": Christmas at the boss's expense. *Journal of Management Studies, 25*: 463–80.

Roy, A. (2003). 'Confronting empire'. World Social Forum, Porto Alegre, Brazil, January 27, 2003.

Royle, N. (Ed.). (2000). *Deconstructions: A user's guide.* New York: Palgrave.

Sachs, W. (Ed.). (1992). *The development dictionary.* London: Zed Books.

Said, E. (1978). *Orientalism.* New York: Vintage Books.

Said, E. (1993). *Culture and imperialism.* New York: Alfred A. Knopf.

Sassen, S. (2008). Two stops in today's new global geographies: Shaping novel labor supplies and employment regimes. *American Behavioral Scientist, 52*: 457–496.

Scahill, J. (2013). *Dirty wars*. New York: Nation Books.

Schroeder, J. E., & Borgerson, J. L. (2012). Packaging paradise: Organizing representations of Hawaii. In A Prasad (Ed.), *Against the grain: Advances in postcolonial organization studies*: 32–53. Copenhagen: Liber.

Schweder, R. A., Minow, M., & Markus, H. R. (Eds.). (2002). *Engaging cultural differences*. New York: Russell Sage.

Scully, M,, & Segal, A. (2002). Passion with an umbrella: Grassroots activism in the workplace. *Research in the Sociology of Organizations, 19*: 125–168.

Seth, S. (2007).*Subject lessons: The Western education of colonial India*. Durham, NC: Duke University Press.

Shohat, E., & Stam, R. (1994). *Unthinking Eurocentrism*. New York: Routledge.

Spicer, A., Alvesson, M., & Kärreman, D. (2009). Critical performativity: The unfinished business of critical management studies. *Human Relations, 62*: 537–560.

Spivak, G. C. (1988). Subaltern studies: Deconstructing historiography. In R. Guha & G. C. Spivak (Eds.), *Selected subaltern studies*: 3–32. New York: Oxford University Press.

Spivak, G. C. (1999). *A critique of postcolonial reason: Toward a history of the vanishing present*. Cambridge, MA: Harvard University Press.

Spivak, G. C. (2003). *Death of a discipline*. New York: Columbia University Press.

Spivak, G. C. (2008). *Other Asias*. Malden, MA: Blackwell.

Spivak, G. C. (2012). *An aesthetic education in the era of globalization*. Cambridge, MA: Harvard University Press.

Stannard, D. E. (1992). *American holocaust: Columbus and the conquest of the New World*. New York: Oxford University Press.

Steffy, B. D., & Grimes, A. J. (1986). A critical theory of organization science. *Academy of Management Review, 11*: 322–336.

Stiglitz, J. (2012). *The price of inequality*. New York: W. W. Norton.

Stocking, G. W. (Ed.). (1985). *Objects and others: Essays on museums and material culture*. Madison: University of Wisconsin Press.

Stone, K. (1974). The origins of job structures in the steel industry. *Review of Radical Political Economics, 6*: 61–97.

Stookey, S. (2013). Getting (the wrong/right) things done: Problems and possibilities in U.S. business scholars. In J. Murphy, V. Malin & M. Siltaoja (Eds.), *Dialogues in critical management studies: Getting things done*: 73–90. Bingley, UK: Emerald.

Subrahmanyam, S. (2005). *Explorations in connected history: Mughals and Franks*. Delhi: Oxford University Press.

Taibbi, M. (2010). *Griftopia*. New York: Random House.

Taibbi, M. (2014). *The divide: American injustice in the age of the wealth gap*. New York: Random House.

Tatli, A. (2012). On the power and poverty of critical (self) reflection in critical management studies: A comment on Ford, Harding & Learmonth. *British Journal of Management, 23*: 22–30.

Taussig, M. (2009). *What color is the sacred?* Chicago: University of Chicago Press.

Taylor, C. (1994). The politics of recognition. In A. Gutman (Ed.), *Multiculturalism*. Princeton, NJ: Princeton University Press.

Thompson, P. (2005). Brands, boundaries and bandwagons: A critical reflection on Critical Management Studies. In C. Grey & H. Willmott (Eds.), *Critical Management Studies: A reader*: 364–382. Oxford: Oxford University Press.

Useem, M. (1979). The social organization of the American business elite and participation of corporate directors in the governance of American institutions. *American Sociological Review, 44*: 553–572.

Vaara, E., & Tienari, J. (2011). On the narrative construction of multinational corporations: An antinarrative analysis of legitimation and resistance in a cross-border merger. *Organization Science, 22*: 370–390.

Voronov, M. (2008). Toward engaged critical management studies. *Organization, 15*: 939–945.

Wallerstein, I. (1999). Afterword. In J. Abu-Lughod (Ed.), *Sociology for the twenty-first century*: 258–261. Chicago: University of Chicago Press.

Wallerstein, I. (2000). Globalization or the age of transition? A long term view of the trajectory of the world system. *International sociology, 15*: 249–265.

Waring, S. P. (1991). *Taylorism transformed: Scientific management theory since 1945*. Chapel Hill: University of North Carolina Press.

West, C. (1994). *Race matters*. New York: Random House.

Westwood, R. (2004). Towards a postcolonial research paradigm in international business and comparative management. In R. Marschan-Piekkari & C. Welch (Eds.), *Handbook of qualitative research methods for international business*: 56–83. Cheltenham, UK: Edward Elgar.

Westwood, R. I. (2006). International business and management studies as an orientalist discourse: A postcolonial critique. *Critical Perspectives on International Business*, 2: 91–113.

Westwood, R. I., & Jack, G. (2008). The U.S. commercial–military–political complex and the emergence of international business and management studies. *Critical Perspectives on International Business*, 4: 367–388.

Willmott, H. (1984). Images and ideals of managerial work. *Journal of Management Studies*, 21: 349–368.

Willmott, H. (2005). Muddling with CMS: Response to special book review of *Studying Management Critically*. *Organization Studies*, 26: 1711–1720.

Wilson, D., & Purushothaman, R. (2003). *Dreaming with the BRICs: The path to 2050*. New York: Goldman Sachs.

Wolfreys, J. (1998). *Deconstruction-Derrida*. New York: St. Martin's Press.

World Bank. (2011). *Global development horizons 2011: Multipolarity: The new global economy*. Washington, DC: World Bank.

Wray-Bliss, E. (2005). Abstract ethics, embodied ethics: The strange marriage of Foucault and positivism in Labor Process Theory. In C. Grey & H. Willmott (Eds.), *Critical Management Studies: A reader*: 383–417. Oxford: Oxford University Press.

Young, R. J.C. (1995). *Colonial desire*. London: Routledge.

Young, R. J.C. (1999). Dangerous and wrong: Shell, intervention and the politics of transnational companies. *Intervention*, 1: 439–464.

Zakaria, F. (2008). *The post-American world*. New York: W. W. Norton.

Zeitlin, M. (1974). Corporate ownership and control: The large corporations and the capitalist class. *American Journal of Sociology*, 79: 1073–1119.

Part II
Critique and its (dis-)contents

Critical management scholarship
A satirical critique of three narrative histories

Albert J. Mills and Jean Helms Mills

Introducing a cautionary tale

To be perfectly honest, this essay did not start off as it is now. Our initial intent was to understand the emergence of the field of critical studies of management (csm) through examination of "its condition of possibility" (Fairclough, 2010: 10). Drawing "strategically" (Ferguson, 1984), on the work of Foucault, we set out to examine the discursive space that preceded the establishment of the field (viz. csm) and its institutional incarnation – Critical Management Studies (CMS): the former referring to everyone contributing to critical management scholarship, the latter to those who associate themselves, through their identity work and affiliations, with the term 'CMS'. As we shall show, the distinction between csm and CMS is not always easy or meaningful. In any event, our aim was to gain a sense of the contextual influences that shaped the development of csm (Kieser, 1994; Booth and Rowlinson, 2006) in order to explain its viability as a field of scholarship. However, our attempts to gather insights into the history of the field confronted us with diverse accounts based on under-theorized notions and/or absence of reference to the problematic character of history and the past (Jenkins, 1994; Munslow, 2010). In the process, as we shall argue, such accounts end up privileging certain (Anglo-American and Eurocentric) voices, marginalizing others; grounding arguments in embedded factual claims (e.g., resting on "the past" as ontologically real – see Munslow, 2010); and failing to reveal the politics of the constructed historical account (Durepos and Mills, 2012b). In the end, we were more impressed by the narrative form of each account rather than what it had to tell us about the development of critical studies of management. It reminded us of Hayden White's (1973; 1984) analysis of history as more about narrative form than telling of facts. It is to White that we turned for analysis of three selected accounts.

Narrative forms and history: Three weddings and a funeral

The starting point for this study is three scholarly works published between 1994 and 2006. The choice of these works arose out of an extensive review of the literature in preparation for our original focus on the discursive conditions and the development of critical studies of management. In the process, we stumbled across two articles and a book chapter that are useful for illustrating different ways of conceptualizing the development of the field (including *Organization*). Each, in its own way, involves an attempt to reflect on the discursive space out of which the field emerged. As such, each contributes to a sense of the history of the field and the events that preceded its development. And each provides a strong and contrasting narrative to the other two. In our own efforts to analyse these works, we drew on White's (1973) notion of genres of historical writing.

White (1973) contends that history is not so much about capturing the "facts" of a situation (e.g., specific events that led to the establishment of csm) as about the way those "facts" are assembled into a narrative (e.g., a tale that pulls together selected events for its storyline on the development of csm). He argues that history is about "emplotment," achieved through the utilization of well established forms of expression, or tropes (White, 1985). Tropes include metaphor (metonymy, synecdoche, irony) and are linked to narrative forms that include *romance* ("a focus on the heroic qualities of an individual"); *tragedy* ("a focus on the impact of fate on events, usually with a bad ending"); *comedy* ("a focus on human beings as part of a greater organic whole, not subject to fate so much as resolving things through harmonious relations"); and *satire* (a focus on absurdity and a questioning of "such things as the role of individual attributes, the fates, and harmony in the resolve of organizational problems") (Bryman, Bell, Mills, & Yue 2011: 430–431). Our use of White is as much adaptive as adoptive to account for postmodernist (as well as modernist) ideological impulses and notions of the individual (Nord & Fox, 1996) that can be found embedded in narrative forms.

The three works we focus on are (1) "Why Organization? Why Now?" (Burrell, Reed, Calás, Smircich & Alvesson, 1994), written as the introduction to the launch of *Organization*; (2) "Critical Management Studies: Premises, Practices, Problems, and Prospects" (Adler, Forbes & Willmott, 2006), written for the *Annals of the Academy of Management* to introduce and explain to readers the philosophy of the CMS Interest Group of the Academy of Management; and (3) "From Labor Process Theory to Critical Management Studies"(Hassard, Hogan & Rowlinson, 2001), written as a reflection on the "intellectual trajectory" of CMS and its potential as a force for radical change. All three works provide historical "traces" (Jenkins, 1991) of the reflections of "founding" participants associated with the "conditions of [csm's] emergence" (Adler, Forbes & Willmott, 2006: 21); in the first case it is the founding editors of *Organization*; in the second case, it is a combination of organizers of the early CMS workshops at the Academy of Management (1998) and the first international CMS conference (1999); the third case involves three leading activists associated with CMS. We would note that the term 'traces' is far from unproblematic in its suggestion that real aspects of the past can be uncovered. We use the term more loosely to refer to examples of things said (or constructed) in a given period of time. We do not surface these examples as evidence of what *really* happened so much as indications of discursive thinking (Foucault, 1979).

What follows are three narratives based on our reading of the selected works. In each case, we try to identify a dominant narrative form and discuss the implications for understanding history and the past and their relationship to the field, in particular to *being* in CMS (the focus of two of the studies) and the future of *Organization*. In the two former cases, we have not tried to define CMS and its relationship to *Organization*, viewing the definitions (plural) as outcomes of processes of knowledge production (Latour, 2005) and, as such, more flexible than fixed definitions would imply. We are more interested in what the selected narratives have to say about csm in general and CMS in particular. This will allow us a greater grasp of the role of discursive thinking in the (re)production of something called CMS. While the first two accounts (along with our own critique) focus on the viability of CMS as a marriage of different critical communities, the latter account provides a more pessimistic view that envisions the eventual demise of CMS.

The writers' tale: Satirical critique

> *Satire* – a focus on absurdity and a questioning of "such things as the role of individual attributes, the fates, and harmony in the resolve of organizational problems."
>
> *Bryman, Bell, Mills & Yue 2011: 430–431*

Drawing on White (1973), we characterize our approach as satirical critique: critique because we adopt a critical stance to the analysis of different understandings of CMS and its history; satirical because it involves a strong sense of parody or caricature in the reduction of complex positions to fairly simple narratives. Through humor we hope to engage rather than close debate. Satire allows the authors (us!) some sense of distance from the object of humor while simultaneously including the authors in the joke (we have been associated at some point or other with each of the narratives critiqued).

Distancing is also attempted through an amodernist approach (Latour, 1993) where we understand CMS as the outcome of several communities of scholars – at once, and fleetingly, a unified community and, at once, a series of disparate knowledges about what constitutes CMS. In short, we have avoided the temptation to privilege unity over fragmentation, and modernist over postmodernist thinking by focusing on the relational aspects of knowledge production. Finally, following White (1984: 7), we view our approach to narrative "as simply one discursive 'code' among others, which might or might not be appropriate for the representation of 'reality,' depending only on the pragmatic aim in view of the speaker of the discourse." Ultimately, our critique is intended to reveal the problematic use of the role of history and the past not only by mainstream (Booth & Rowlinson, 2006) but also by critical management scholars. In that vein, we surely recognize that the authors associated with each narrative are not reducible to the narrative forms we highlight and that the thinking of the people involved is far more porous than we have suggested.

Tale one: Romantic fragmentationism

> *Romance* – "a focus on the heroic qualities of an individual"
>
> *Bryman, Bell, Mills & Yue, 2011: 430–431*

Narrative form: We have designated the first narrative (the 1994 introduction to *Organization*) as romantic fragmentationism. At first glance, this may seem misplaced. Strictly speaking, it is an account that lacks a focus on "heroic qualities," let alone on selected individuals. However, we argue that there is a sense throughout the piece that the fragmentary aspects of an emergent postmodernist world have opened the possibility of greater potential for human emancipation and that fragmentation (in a postmodernist sense) stands as the (individual) subject.

From the opening line we get a tremendous sense of the emancipatory potential of a new era: "The context in which *Organization* is launched is one which few academics could have envisaged a decade ago" (Burrell, Reed, Calás, Smircich & Alvesson, 1994: 5). It was a decade that saw the termination of the "bipolar balance of terror," the "demise of 19th-century God surrogates" (Gellner, 1993: 3, cited in Burrell, Reed, Calás, Smircich & Alvesson, 1994: 5), the destruction of "older ideological equilibriums and ingrained intellectual habits" and the "severe fragmentation and decay of 19th- and early 20th-century meta-narratives of liberation, freedom, progress, order, and control" (p. 5).

If not the causal force of the new era, fragmentation is referred to throughout as characterizing the various processes through which the modernist worldview is dissolving. This includes the fragmentation of the "supporting institutional base" of orthodoxy (p. 6) and with it "the field of organization studies" itself (p. 8). This somewhat flawed hero (fragmentationism) offers both a challenge but also a release. Fragmentation heralds uncertainties, contradictions (p.10) and "weaknesses leading to political insecurity" (p. 8). Nonetheless, it provides the spaces in which to "craft" new emancipatory agendas (p. 13) and a "return to a different 'original story,' where multiplicity and fragmentation – the road not taken by the 'founding fathers' – enrich organizational analysis" (p. 9).

CMS, history and the past: By asking, "Why Organization? Why Now?" Burrell, Reed, Calás, Smircich & Alvesson, (1994) draw on selected notions of the past to create a proto-history of CMS. The narrative form infuses the historical account, which is constructed in broad terms around the themes of modernity and postmodernity and the unity and fragmentation of ideas. Thus, the "context" in which *Organization* appears is portrayed as the interstices between the collapse of modernity and the emergence of postmodernity (p. 5): "[w]e are facing a new situation in which the old polarities of thought can no longer be applied, or at the very least require scrutiny. This clearly will be the central task of social thought during the coming years" (Gellner, 1993: 3, cited in Burrell, Reed, Calás, Smircich & Alvesson, 1994, p. 5). In this brief and fleeting "history of the present," the past is quickly passed over and left to hang like a dead weight (e.g., as remnants of a series of outmoded meta-narratives) that appears detached and suffused with the ghost of Hegel. It is detached insofar as it reflects on a past filled with "bipolar forces of terror" and "God surrogates" but fails to reflect on the engagement of people in overcoming those phenomena and helping to create the fragmentary spaces before us; people whose anticolonial struggles, peace activism, women's liberation, class warfare and the like may have served as impulses for the creation of critical studies of management. While the narrative encourages the idea of a fragmentation of history or multivocal versions of the past, the idea is indirect and unexplored, left open for anticipated debates in future issues of *Organization* (see, e.g., Calás, 1994). Nonetheless, this romantic narrative leaves us with the ambiguous idea that history (however understood) is in the past!

Implications for CMS: The narrative of romantic fragmentationism, we contend, placed an early postmodernist imprimatur[1] on the field that can be found in many, if not all, of the articles over the 20-year span of *Organization*[2] and, beyond that, some of the perceptions of those involved in or engaged with CMS (Rowlinson and Hassard, 2011; e.g., Ford, Harding & Learmonth, 2010; Tatli, 2012).

In terms of history and the past, almost one-third of all articles in *Organization* make reference to history, yet remarkably few are concerned with the socio-historical context of their research subject. Fewer still theoretically engage with issues of the past and history. For example, more by illustration than critique, Stokes and Gabriel (2010) utilize the idea of history to detail a number of discrete examples of genocide. They are not so much interested in socio-historical explanations of how or why such atrocities occurred so much as revealing the lessons involved for organization studies. In the process, history is referred to as a more or less factual accounting of the past (rather than, perhaps, a socially contrived narrative [Jenkins, 1991]), the implication being that a desired goal might be good, better, or more improved histories of the past – ones that account for genocide. This is somewhat surprising given the fact that the Introduction is centered on the "socio-historical" context (1994: 5), in which the journal was emergent, and the fact that a postmodernist imprimatur is associated with Lyotard and the deconstruction of meta-narratives (see, e.g., Lyotard, 1984) and the new historicism of Foucault (e.g., Foucault, 1979). Part of the explanation may lie in the fact that the Intro's use of historical context is fleeting and introduced in a way that problematizes the past while privileging the (potentially postmodernist) present.

Tale two: Comedic integrationism

Narrative form: A review of PPPP suggests elements of comedy in the classical Greek sense of stage plays with happy endings, with the play being constructed around the idea of a (more or less) unified body of scholarship.

We gain a sense of CMS as an integrated scholarly community from the opening paragraph, which announces an "overview of a *growing movement* in management studies" (p. 119; our emphasis). It quickly locates the development of the movement's critical agenda in "contemporary developments beyond academia" (p. 121). In tracing those developments, the paper refers to the fact that while "CMS has been strongest in the United Kingdom . . . [the] United States side of the CMS movement first became visible as a workshop at the 1998 Academy of Management meetings" (p. 123). CMS is described as "broadly 'leftist' in leaning" yet attracting those who might normally be considered in the mainstream of management whose boundaries are no longer "fixed but the subject of contestation" (p. 125). CMS also "*accommodates* diverse theoretical traditions, ranging from varieties of Marxism through pragmatism to poststructuralism" (p. 125; our emphasis). But the integration does not stop there. Critical theory is seen as "an influential strand in the development of CMS" (p. 125); feminism and environmentalism are "new social movements . . . [that] have considerably enriched" CMS thinking (p. 130); and the work of "pragmatist symbolic interactionism, actor-network theory" and those drawing on the theories of Giddens and Bourdieu "are all important" aspects of CMS engagement with social theory (p. 130).

The narrative ends by stating, "As the preceding discussion has made clear, CMS is a catchall term signifying a heterogeneous body of work, a body that shares some common themes but is neither internally consistent nor sharply differentiable from mainstream analysis" (p. 154). It also concedes that a "major tension within CMS has been between structural/materialist streams, which are often Marxist inspired, and postmodernist/poststructuralist streams which place greater emphasis upon agency, language, and contingency" (p. 155). Nonetheless, it is predicted that these divisions are "interwoven with personal political biographies" that are likely to disappear over time with the ascendancy of younger scholars "more at ease with a less orthodox, more eclectic approach that favours rich diversity over rigorous consistency" (p. 155).

A sense of the play's initial staging is glimpsed in the middle of the narrative, where it is stated that the "theoretical resources used by CMS can be usefully characterized using Burrell and Morgan's (1979) matrix of approaches" viewed as distinctions that "can be heuristically useful as a way to locate varieties of CMS and their theoretical roots" (p. 130). At first glance, this is a strange staging choice given the fact that Burrell and Morgan (1979) originally conceived a framework composed of incommensurable scholarly communities. However, the heuristic value of Burrell and Morgan's paradigms for staging an integrationist play becomes clearer as the plotting of the various cells becomes increasingly blurred. First, there are the addition of *new* (!) communities of scholars that include feminists and environmentalists. Second, recent years have seen the development of increasingly radical interpretivist strands of thought (including pragmatist symbolic interactionism). Third, "the line between order and change [has become] fuzzy insofar as CMS proponents leverage mainstream, regulation-oriented theories to critical, albeit reformist, purpose" (p. 130) – generating "radical core" and "reformist" variants of CMS.

In terms of the (potentially) global reach of CMS, the integrative approach, conceding that the core group of scholars originated largely in the UK, followed to a lesser extent by U.S. scholars, contends that "other geographic modes . . . have arisen too, notably in Canada, Australia, New Zealand, Scandinavia, and Brazil."

CMS, history and the past: The integrationist narrative is also evident in the construction of a history of CMS. The scene is set by reference to "the decline and fragmentation of the Left since around 1970," which is accompanied by the development of "new social movements [and] . . . new critical perspectives" (p. 121). What then follows is more a listing of events than the outlining of a social–historical context to explain CMS through "the conditions of its emergence" (p. 121). The list includes such things as the "broader liberalization of advanced capitalist societies and their universities" (p. 122); "some relaxation of the grip of positivism in the late 1960s and 1970s" (p. 122); the "expansion of the European Community and the rise of China, India, and other emergent economies" (p. 121); and several things associated with the era of "Post-September 11, 2001" (p. 121).

Unlike romantic fragmentationism, the integrative narrative casts the historical context of CMS's development in terms of changes due to "the cultural logic of late capitalism" (Jameson, 1984), in which "many certainties have been unsettled, even as others have been reinforced [and that a] succession of major and natural social crises has brought into sharp focus issues that previously may have seemed more peripheral, issues such as business ethics, environmentalism, and imperialism" (p. 121). In consequence, it is implied, there has been the rise of new forms of radicalism whose concerns are broader than those of the old "left" and have risen to meet new demands of a changing capitalist world. In the process, the blurring of capitalist lines of thought has the potential to build broader coalitions of critical thinkers, uniting the formerly radical left with conservative radicals or reformers (Perrow, 2008).

In delineating the core communities of scholars involved in the development of CMS, the integrative approach talks in terms of the additive effect of a growing movement that begins in large part with Labor Process Conference (LPC) and Standing Conference on Organizational Symbolism (SCOS) scholars in the early 1980s, where critical scholarship is honed with the move into the 1990s. Scholars from these (largely European) groups will eventually fuse with groups of U.S.-based scholars with the development of an Academy of Management CMS interest group. In the latter case, an interesting claim is made for pragmatism as "an important inspiration for CMS, especially US proponents" (p. 139). It is argued that "pragmatism plays a background role for much U.S. CMS similar to the role played by Marx for U.K. CMS work" (p. 139). The works of Sidney Hook and John Dewey are cited as important pathways for CMS in the U.S. This history, however, strangely leaves out of account the role of Hook and Dewey during the Cold War and their commitment to the American Committee for Cultural Freedom, a CIA-funded body that was associated with attacks on the left (Lasch, 1970): Hook went on to support the U.S. war in Vietnam and a number of other conservative political stances.

Implications for CMS: The comedic integrative narrative presents an interesting paradox. In seeking to explain the increasing institutionalization of CMS (Adler, 2008), it suggests several grounds of harmony across differing paradigms (Burrell and Morgan, 1979) and traditions (Prasad, 2005). In the process, it may well contribute to a strong sense of commitment from those who feel the need to be part of a dedicated critical management scholarship. Indeed, there are a number of examples where people express an emotional commitment to CMS. Cooke (2008: 913), for example, states that "people working within CMS have been one of the central pillars of comradeship and collegiality in my life." Cunliffe (2008: 936) states that during her time in academia "it was the CMS community . . . who frankly kept me sane." And Ford (Ford, Harding & Learmonth, 2010: s72) "found in critical management the language that allowed her to articulate the feelings of unease she had experienced when working as a manager." Thus, the idea of a harmonious CMS community, no matter how intellectually ridiculous or far-fetched, is attractive to many, and it may be that various efforts to stage that illusion serve to enroll participants and black box (Latour, 2005) the idea of Critical Management Studies. An allied part of the process can be seen in the 2008 issue of *Organization* on "Speaking Out on the Future of Critical Management Studies," where almost all of the participants argue for a broad, rather than a narrow, definition of what should constitute CMS: "I am uncomfortable with some representations of CMS as politically left wing and critical of the shortcomings of others. This can lead to a narrow view of critically-oriented work that might exclude scholars who don't see themselves as political activists [and those] managers and academics engaged in mainstream work" (Cunliffe, 2008: 937).

On the other hand, the enrollment process seems to be achieved not only by a blurring *of* the ideological lines (and history) of CMS but also by a philosophical commitment *to* blurred lines. This, if nothing else, has led to a series of reflections on CMS over the years, with participants repeating the oft used phrase that "we need to be clear about who are we, what we stand for and what resources we have" (Stookey, 2008: 923). Enter stage left Hassard, Hogan and Rowlinson (2001) and the narrative of tragic modernism!

Tale three: Tragic modernism

Narrative form: We have called the narrative in IT tragic modernism for three reasons. First, the various points of analysis throughout the piece reference and seem nostalgic for a time past (modernism), a time when being critical seemed to have a greater clarity than it does today. Second, discussion centers on the problematic nature of CMS, including a failure to clearly delineate its political agenda and a tendency to incorporate disparate forces that include scholars that are mainstream and reformist. Third, in the absence of a detailed historical account of the loss of certain modernist concerns from CMS (e.g., class struggle), we are left with the fates as an explanation.

The narrative quickly moves to explain the development of CMS (and its attendant problems) through an historical account that focuses on the "political context of the historical defeat of the Left since its high point in 1968" (p. 339) and the role of labor process theorists who played a role in that defeat and who constituted an important tributary of CMS in the period following. These two elements are immediately characterized as contributing to a failed project, as a move from (modernist) concerns with the revolutionary role of the working class to (postmodernist) deconstructions of Marxism as an outmoded meta-narrative: the "potential of the working class to fulfill its Marxist destiny to lead a revolutionary transformation of society [and] any such confidence in the second coming of communism has long since evaporated from critical management studies. Instead of adhering to Marx's or Braverman's historical visions critical management studies have increasingly turned to Foucault or critical theorists such as Adorno or Marcuse, who provide the basis for a deconstruction of Marxian eschatology" (Hassard, Hogan & Rowlinson, 2001: 339). Ultimately, the move from labor process theory to Critical Management Studies is seen not as "an intellectual progression" but rather as "a manifestation of the defeat of the Left and the need to temper our radicalism in the context of neo-liberal hegemony."

In the narrative that follows, we gain a growing sense of nostalgia for something preceding labor process theory (LPC). LPC is portrayed as rooted in forms of "managerialism," and the increasing managerialism of LPC is seen as somehow responsible for CMS's retreat from class politics: "As a consequence of his managerialism Braverman himself could be said to have opened the way for those labor process theorists . . . who began to evoke Foucault in the 1980s to argue that power rather than exploitation drives domination in the labor process" (p. 347). But at the heart of the managerialist turn in Critical Management Studies has been abandonment of the fundamental Marxist "law of the tendency of the rate of profit to fall, which predicts that economic crises are inevitable within capitalist economies" (p. 343): this abandonment is portrayed as having "inevitably [led] to reformist politics" (p. 343).

CMS, History and the Past: The modernist aspect of the narrative is achieved through a history dedicated to revealing the socio-political development of CMS. As such, it is the most historically engaged of the three narratives; that is, the emplotment is undertaken as a history. In the process, it provides a powerful trace of several of the important issues (e.g., class struggle) and debates (e.g., the revolutionary role of the working class) that informed many of the early adherents to CMS. Although it is far from a crude "historical commentary on the movement of leftist labor process theory into critical management studies" (p. 357), the narrative is accomplished through a mode of historical analysis that itself is rooted in modernist notions that tend to reify the past. The narrative ends with awareness that there are "problems with writing *such* history" and goes on to recognize that it includes "many omissions" (p. 357; our emphasis). Nonetheless, this continues to suggest that crafting a history involves an uncovering of facts (things that have happened in the past) rather than a construction of a particular narrative.

Like the comedic integrationist narrative, this account involves histories of the U.K. and U.S. contributions to CMS. However, while the former seeks out positive points of unity, the latter seeks to reveal the underlying reformist and managerialist philosophies across U.S.–U.K. scholarship that, while potentially unifying, threatens to undermine the idea of a critical project.

Implications for CMS: The narrative construction of a history of CMS may nonetheless provide the "alignment" (Crawford, 2004: 2) needed to fuel the identity work of those wanting to feel part of a critical *movement* (Adler, Forbes & Willmott, 2006: 119), rather than a "loose community that describes itself as 'critical management studies'"(Hassard, Hogan & Rowlinson, 2001: 340). In other words, a "strong" history of intellectual engagement across the supposed modern and postmodern divides may contribute to a stronger sense of CMS as an established body of scholarship. However, in this particular narrative, the sheer weight of tragedy threatens to overwhelm the possibilities of a united movement of critical scholars (comedic integrationism) and fail to convince those deeply suspicious of the role of history (romantic fragmentationism), where that threatens to anchor discursive analysis to modernist notions of historiography. The latter may help to explain why an intellectual history of the modernist roots of CMS is largely missing from current CMS debates.

Observations and conclusions

Following a satirical critique of three narratives, we offer the following observations and "conclusions."

First, CMS is not so much a "movement" or even a "loose community" as much as a contested actant (i.e., a strong idea that influences behavior; see Latour, 2005). Debates about the future of CMS (e.g., Adler, 2007; Cunliffe, 2008) should focus not simply on its *direction* but also its *translation* through specific narratives. It is a socio-political process rather than a theoretical debate! That this raises peculiar tensions between recognition of the discursive character of social activism and the need to engage others in processes of social change has long been identified (Calás and Smircich, 1992) but with little resolve. We can only repeat the suggestions of Calás and Smircich for critical researchers to engage in social struggles for change while recognizing the problems of developing new truth claims and meta-narratives. An understanding of the existence and significance of competing narratives and their rootedness in different communities may help to focus attention of where we (whoever we are) might form critical alliances and where, how and when (if at all) we might accept the notion of different communities to gain greater clarity within each.

Second, the process of translation crucially involves some attempt to historicize the notion of CMS, be it through problematization of the present (e.g., romantic fragmentationism), tales from the past (e.g., comedic integrationism) or modernist representation (e.g., tragic modernism). Yet, in an area of scholarship where almost each and every concept and theory is problematized and contested, ideas of history and the past slip through hardly unnoticed (Weatherbee, Durepos & Mills, et al., 2012; Durepos and Mills, 2012a). This has led some, specifically Rowlinson and his colleagues (Rowlinson, 2004; Clark and Rowlinson, 2004; Booth and Rowlinson, 2006), to call for a "historic turn" in management and organization studies through a thoroughgoing critique of historiography. Thus, we may not need to understand such things as the "political context of the historical defeat of the Left" (Hassard, Hogan & Rowlinson, 2001: 339) as much as the problem of history as a contested notion and how this contributes to the socially constructed nature and absence of "the Left" from current CMS debates.

Third is the level of confusion in the constitution of the different communities of critical management scholarship. In the various attempts to avoid a narrow and sectarian approach to the definition of CMS, people seem to have neglected the limits of a broad approach to the notion of "critical." As all three narratives suggest, Critical Management Studies embraces scholars from the radical left to the mainstream, including reformists and even, at times, those normally associated with conservative social theory. This, according to Hassard, Hogan and Rowlinson (2001: 339), is reflective of a situation of tempered "radicalism in the context of neo-liberal hegemony." We suspect that unless different communities of CMS scholars attempt to rein in the boundaries of critical (management) scholarship, the promise that is CMS will disappear as a *potential* force for change.

Fourth – and perhaps the most crucial issue – is that the various histories tend to reinforce the idea of CMS as an Anglo-American project. Clearly, romantic fragmentationism encourages a questioning of the whole project of modernity and with it issues of postcoloniality, but the latter is more implied than explored. Comedic integrationism also envisions a broader constituency that includes Brazil and potentially other national communities, but it is a broadening of the Anglo-American project. What are needed are postcolonialist analyses that not only deal with the core issues delineated by a supposed CMS project but that deconstruct the very character of the project itself. To that end, Ibarra-Colado (2008) offers a fifth narrative, a narrative of transdisciplinarity. As such, he starts off by questioning the absurdity of a project that does not locate its own knowledge generation in the context of colonialism, arguing, "It is essential to discuss the function of knowledge as a mechanism of colonization" (p. 932). This leads to the suggestion of a process of transdisciplinarity involving recognition and transcendence of the colonial condition. This ultimately "entails an encounter with a '*trans-discipline*,' understood as a corpus of knowledge that 'transcend[s] the discipline' because their knowledge is transversally built from one locale to another, considering different problems, experiences and solutions all over the world" (p. 934). In short, "the future of CMS must be imagined as a set of multiple dialogues and conversations . . . across different regions and cultures" (p. 934).

Notes

1 We use the term "postmodernism" as an umbrella term that includes "intellectual positions intended to offer a radical critique of the entire fabric of modern Western thinking" (Prasad, 2005), including poststructuralist accounts. Beyond that, we broadly agree with Prasad's (2005) distinction between postmodernism (pp. 219–237) and poststructuralism (pp. 238–261).

2 Analysis of the 87 articles published in *Organization* as of March 2012 indicates that at least one-quarter specifically adopt postmodernist (including poststructuralist) frameworks. That number climbs when you include articles that don't specifically refer to postmodernism (or poststructuralism) yet draw on so-called postmodernist theorists (e.g., Foucault, Derrida, Lyotard) to make sense of some aspect of social life. For example, Al-Amoudi (2007) engages with Foucault's work, albeit from a critical realist perspective, and Bardon and Josserand (2011) undertake a "Nietzschean reading of Foucauldian thinking." Indeed, works that utilize and otherwise engage with Foucauldian analysis account for a further 29% of all *Organization*

articles. By way of comparison, specifically feminist accounts can be found in roughly 18% of all articles, but more than a third of those adopt a postmodernist framework. Similarly, discussions of Marx and Marxism constitute about 9% of all articles, but a good half of those draw on/engage with postmodernist thought. Finally, the 9% of articles that are focused on postcolonialism constitute the more theoretically diverse group of papers, but even here a quarter of them (two articles!) take a poststructuralist position.

References

Adler, P. S. (2007). The future of critical management studies: A paleo-Marxist critique of labour process theory. *Organization Studies, 28*: 1313–1345.

Adler, P. S. (2008). CMS: Resist the three complacencies! *Organization, 15*: 925–926.

Adler, P. S., Forbes, L. C., & Willmott, H. (2006). Critical management studies: Premises, practices, problems, and prospects. *Annals of the Academy of Management, 1*(1): 119–179.

Al-Amoudi, I. (2007). Redrawing Foucault's social ontology. *Organization, 14*: 543–563.

Bardon, T., & Josserand, E. (2011). A Nietzschean reading of Foucauldian thinking: Constructing a project of the self within an ontology of becoming. *Organization, 18*: 497–515.

Booth, C., & Rowlinson, M. (2006). Management and organizational history: Prospects. *Management & Organizational History, 1*: 5–30.

Bryman, A., Bell, E., Mills, A. J., & Yue, A. R. (2011). *Business rresearch methods* (1st Canadian Ed.), Toronto: Oxford University Press.

Burrell, G., & Morgan, G. (1979). *Sociological paradigms and organizational analysis.* London: Heinemann.

Burrell, G., Reed, M. I., Calás, M. B., Smircich, L., & Alvesson, N. (1994). Why organization? Why now? *Organization, 1*: 5–17.

Calás, M. B. (1994). Minerva's owl? Introduction to a thematic section on globalization. *Organization, 1*: 243–248.

Calás, M. B., & Smircich, L. (1992). Using the "F" word: Feminist theories and the social consequences of organizational research. In A. J. Mills & P. Tancred (Eds.), *Gendering organizational analysis*: 222–234. Newbury Park, CA: Sage.

Clark, P., & Rowlinson, M. (2004). The treatment of history in organization studies: Toward an 'historic turn'? *Business History, 46*: 331–352.

Cooke, B. (2008). If Critical Management Studies is your problem . . . *Organization, 15*: 912–914.

Crawford, C. S. (2004). Actor network theory. In G. Ritzer (Ed.), *Encyclopedia of social theory*: 1–3. Thousand Oaks, CA: Sage.

Cunliffe, A. L. (2008). Will you still need me . . . when I'm 64? The future of CMS. *Organization, 15*: 936–938.

Durepos, G., & Mills, A. J. (2012a). *Anti-history: Theorizing the past, history, and historiography in management and organizational studies,* Charlotte, NC: Information Age.

Durepos, G., & Mills, A. J. (2012b). Actor network theory, ANTi-history, and critical organizational historiography. *Organization, 19*(6): 703–721.

Fairclough, N. (2010). *Critical discourse analysis. The critical study of language.* London: Pearson Education.

Ferguson, K. (1984). *The feminist case against bureaucracy,* Philadelphia: Temple University Press.

Ford, J., Harding, N., & Learmonth, M. (2010). Who is it that would make business schools more critical? Critical reflections on critical management studies. *British Journal of Management, 21*: s71–s81.

Foucault, M. (1979). *Discipline and punish: The birth of the prison.* New York: Vintage Books.

Gellner, E. (1993). What do we need now? Social anthropology and its new global context. *The Times Literary Supplement, 16* (July): 3–4.

Hassard, J., Hogan, J., & Rowlinson, M. (2001). From labor process theory to critical management studies. *Administrative Theory & Praxis, 23*: 339–362.

Ibarra-Colado, E. (2008). Is there any future for critical management studies in Latin America? Moving from epistemic coloniality to 'trans-discipline'. *Organization, 15*: 932–935.

Jameson, F. (1984). Postmodernism, or the cultural logic of late capitalism. *New Left Review, 146*: 53–93.

Jenkins, K. (1991). *Re-thinking history,* London & New York: Routledge.

Jenkins, K. (1994). *Re-thinking history,* London: Routledge.

Kieser, A. (1994). Why organizational theory needs historical analyses – and how this should be performed. *Organization Science, 5*: 608–620.

Lasch, C. (1970). *The agony of the American left,* London: Andre Deutsch.

Latour, B. (1993). *We have never been modern,* Hemel Hempstead: Harvester Wheatsheaf.

Latour, B. (2005). *Reassembling the social: An introduction to actor-network-theory,* Oxford: Oxford University Press.

Lyotard, J-F. (1984). *The postmodern condition: A report on knowledge,* Minneapolis: University of Minnesota Press.

Munslow, A. (2010). *The future of history,* London: Palgrave Macmillan.

Nord, W., & Fox, S. (1996). The individual in organizational studies: The great disappearing act? In S. R. Clegg, C. Hardy, & W. R. Nord (Eds.), *Handbook of organizational studies*: 148–175. Thousand Oaks, CA: Sage.

Perrow, C. (2008). Conservative radicalism. *Organization, 15*: 915–921.

Prasad, P. (2005). *Crafting qualitative research. Working in the postpositivist traditions,* Armonk, NY: M. E. Sharpe.

Rowlinson, M. (2004). Historical perspectives in organization studies: Factual, narrative, and archeo-genealogical. In D. E. Hodgson & C. Carter (Eds.), *Management knowledge and the new employee*: 8–20. Burlington, VT: Ashgate.

Rowlinson, M., & Hassard, J. (2011). How come the critters came to be teaching in business schools? Contradictions in the institutionalization of critical management studies. *Organization, 18*: 673–689.

Stokes, P., & Gabriel, Y. (2010). Engaging with genocide: The challenge for organization and management studies. *Organization, 17*: 461–480.

Stookey, S. (2008). The future of critical management studies: Populism and elitism. *Organization, 15*: 922–924.

Tatli, A. (2012). On the power and poverty of critical (self) reflection in critical management studies: A comment on Ford, Harding and Learmonth. *British Journal of Management, 23*: 22–30.

Weatherbee, T. G., Durepos, G., Mills, A. J., & Helms Mills, J. (2012). Theorizing the Past: Critical Engagements. *Management & Organizational History*, 7(3), 193–202.

White, H. (1973). *Metahistory: The historical imagination in nineteenth-century Europe,* Baltimore, MD: Johns Hopkins University Press.

White, H. (1984). The question of narrative in contemporary historical theory. *History and Theory, 23*: 1–33.

White, H. (1985). *Tropics of discourse. Essays in cultural criticism,* Baltimore, MD: Johns Hopkins University Press.

3

An ethic of care within Critical Management Studies?

Emma Bell, Susan Meriläinen, Scott Taylor and Janne Tienari

Introduction

As this book and others make clear, critical analyses of management constitute a wide field where researchers draw from different theoretical traditions. This variety notwithstanding, Alvesson & Deetz (2000) suggest that Critical Management Studies (CMS) is primarily concerned with the ways in which powerful actors contribute to freezing social reality for the benefit of certain sectional interests at the expense of others. Although the community of scholars who associate themselves with CMS is as broad as the theoretical range, a sense of social justice is perhaps something that unites them/us, especially when contrasted with their more managerialist colleagues. In addition, the reflexive recognition that knowledge has a politics brings together critical scholars, again, relative to their mainstream fellow academics (Parker & Thomas, 2011). Overall, this ethic of social justice and epistemological sensitivity can be seen as the central characteristics of critical management scholarship (Wray-Bliss, 2003).

As might be expected in a community founded in part on reflexivity, debating what CMS is and might be has become an academic discussion in its own right (Alvesson & Willmott, 1992; Fournier & Grey, 2000; Wray-Bliss, 2003; Grey, 2004; Grey & Willmott, 2005; Adler, Forbes & Willmott, 2007; Spicer, Alvesson & Karreman, 2009; Alvesson, Bridgman & Willmott, 2009; Rowlinson & Hassard, 2011; Tatli, 2011). For some, it is now fashionable to predict the demise of CMS and to think beyond it. Much of this discussion has been led by a handful of influential CMS scholars. It focuses on what being critical means and what CMS is as a theoretical and political project, rather than envisioning what it could be as a sociocultural community.

There have been attempts to rebalance this conversation by shifting attention towards reflection on the power relations associated with embodied academic practices, especially with regard to gender (Katila & Meriläinen, 2002; Maclaren, Miller, Parsons & Surman, 2009; Bell & King, 2010; Ford & Harding, 2010). For these writers and community members, CMS must be understood as an organization like any other, where processes of domination, subordination and resistance may be observed and critiqued. Despite the sensitivity of CMS scholars to analysis of power relations and dominant rationalities in the organizational contexts we study, and despite the increasing presence of reflexive accounts of the cultures of CMS, we still cannot help but feel that the CMS community does not always embody the principles it preaches.

For this reason, we explore here how ideas about what is expected of a CMS academic have become sedimented into a particular set of established rationalities that constitute the basis for a body of thought – and how these ideas have also become a means of determining which bodies can legitimately participate in academic work (Townley, 2008). Analysing how we as active critical management scholars take part in reproducing such rationalities, we focus on the intellectual and physical ways in which the ethics of being critical are constructed within the CMS project. In doing this, we are aiming, first, to bring the dominant embodied rationalities that characterize CMS as a social community (and are used to frame this intellectual and political project) into an analytical space; second, to analyse how the centre of CMS is constructed relative to its margins; and, third, to present some alternatives to this by introducing the possibility of enacting a feminist ethic of care (Held, 2006).

Our principal aim is to suggest that an ethic of care may be seen as a complement to the ethic of justice which has traditionally formed the *raison d'être* for CMS. Through this we explore the possibility of being different, as well as thinking and acting differently (Burrell, 2009). Our analysis can be read as an exploration of how self and social (Thomas, 2009) might be better aligned in a productive way, rather than providing yet another resigned contemplation of the 'horror of the tensions' (Burrell, 2009: 557) and contradictions involved in embodying CMS and its values. We realize that this might be considered naïve and idealistic and that parts of our account are dangerously close to whining or grumbling, but for us an inherent part of belonging to the CMS community involves contemplating the construction of not yet existing, yet closer to ideal worlds.

The chapter is organized as a conversation among the four authors, through which we highlight the importance of relationships in constructing community within CMS. This dialogue is grounded in sharing our experiences of participating in the knowledge production process from a variety of positions: journal editor, author, lecturer, PhD supervisor or examiner, reviewer, conference participant. The opportunity to write together about these issues came about when one of us was invited to contribute a chapter to this edited collection and subsequently invited the others to collaborate on it. Having agreed to write the chapter together, we undertook collectively to talk, think and write, with the aim of generating autoethnographic data based on our experiences within CMS (Parry & Boyle, 2009; Snyder-Young, 2011).

The inset sections come from dialogues between the authors. They are deliberately not attributed to any one individual. Although that has implications for the reader's ability to contextualize the experiences described, we would like the story to be considered as extracts from a single narrative that we have all contributed to. We present it as a 'story for consideration' (Sparkes, 2007) made up of, and from, moments that we have lived through, in our human bodies, over time and in various spaces. Having written this piece, we will now try to remain living in the story, reflecting and becoming, changing and being changed as we try to create meaning in and through our academic work.

Throughout the chapter, we write as 'we'. This means four scholars and teachers who share a belief in social justice but differ in terms of positions and interests as academics at the time of writing (Thomas, Tienari, Davies & Meriläinen, 2009). Emma was a happy, recently appointed professor at Keele University in the U.K., who had contributed to and drawn on CMS for most of her academic working life. Susan was a professor at the University of Lapland in Finland and feels a stronger sense of belonging to feminist communities than to Critical Management Studies. Scott had recently taken up the position of reader at University of Birmingham; he enjoys working at home and would be bereft if CMS disappeared. Janne was a professor at Aalto University in Finland. For him, the critical is about challenging the 'taken-for-granted' and self-evident, and he feels that CMS has provided great opportunities for doing so. We are very clear that, both independently and as a group of four, we take part in reproducing practices and conventions in the CMS field and do not imply that we are somehow beyond the issues that we reflect upon in this chapter. We are, as we all are, only human . . .

The emergence of dominant rationalities

> He [the ideal critical scholar] is well published and publishing more all the time, furiously active and mobile – always on the move to prove his theoretical elegance and up-to-date-and-beyond knowledge to significant other critical scholars. Talking, writing, publishing. A lot. This is how muscle is built: living up to the hyperactive 'ideal'. I'm whining again because I have problems with this, playing the role of that kind of 'ideal' critical scholar. My physique and mental capacity are not geared to constant fiery-eyed argumentation and elbowing those who come in my way. Moreover, I was raised in a society where the building of consensus and welfare for all was considered to be a smart idea, rather than pitting groups of people against each other.

This chapter began with the shared understanding that there is an ideal critical scholar, an academic star, whom we are unlikely, perhaps unable, definitely unwilling, to become. We believe that certain forms of reasoning have been constructed and inscribed as rational and reasonable within CMS and therefore see a need to examine how the community constructs itself as a rationalized field of knowledge production. In thinking about this, we returned to an analytical frame that we have found helpful in thinking about the organizations we study and teach about every day: Townley's (2008) argument that practical reasoning and rationality form the basis for the construction of knowledge. Townley (2008: 9) argues that what organizational members and analysts understand as rational 'needs to be examined for its power effects and power for its inscription in rationality'. She is interested in exploring the interstices generated when we practise rationalities, to question the assumption that rationality inheres in certain tools, policies or actions. Instead, she argues, reason is always ascribed so that anything we understand as rational qualifies as such only *in context*. In other words, rationalities can only be an active human production.

It seems to us, as active members of CMS, that axes of power (knowledge, discipline and subjectivity) regulate the organization of the community and are underpinned by dominant and suppressed rationalities. However, the practised embodiment of these rationalities in which 'the location of reason within the physical body of the reasoning subject . . . [and recognition of] the importance of the tacit, emotional and psychoanalytical as dimensions which inform the rational' (Townley, 2008: 15) is something that is conspicuous by its absence, both when we practise community and when we write about it. As the opening quote from our conversations indicates, the degree of embeddedness that we experience in relation to CMS 'has implications for how it constructs the individual and produces different subject positions from which to speak' (Townley, 2008: 207).

How much is enough?

> The big boys of "critical management studies" are big for a reason. They've developed muscles, and they know how to take care of themselves. I like to whine about this, but see some of the symptoms in myself. Perhaps I have become too preoccupied with getting stuff published . . . and I guess that part of my recent disappointments is that I realize that I don't carry any weight . . . I feel inadequate. I don't have muscle.

As we thought about the critical community, we returned again and again to the idea and practice of publishing. Putting ideas and arguments into print is surely the purest form of disembedded rationality within academic work (Townley, 2008). It is also a key means of satisfying performance measures that we are all subject to. For most of us, it involves constructing arguments based on Enlightenment rationalities to try to contribute to establishing universal truths about organizing and managing. In principle, we often also reason that we publish because we feel we have something to say, to make a contribution to problematizing existing inadequate knowledge, to create greater understanding or insight – reasoning from within our professional community ideals. In practice, it appears we publish as a result of a variety of economic, bureaucratic, or even technocratic rationalities that encourage reasoning from a disembedded object-oriented position.

The recognition and appreciation of fellow critical scholars is a central preoccupation for us because the community would not exist without public statements of position and difference. However, our conversations are woven through with doubts about the process of publishing, the effects its prominence has on career progress and personhood and the feelings of adequacy or inadequacy that publishing can produce. We read this preoccupation as a symptom of a deeply ingrained sense of what it means to be a convincing academic in the eyes of others. Although we sometimes like to think otherwise, there is no escape for critical *scholars* from an institutionalized preoccupation with publishing in the 'right' journals. In order to achieve in the eyes of our employers, to be legitimate in our community, it seems we are destined to reproduce ways of practising our profession that we say we despise. As we complain about the dominance of publishing in constructing community relations, as we recognize that these practices construct and reconstruct an ideal subject, which is at the same time attainable and elusive, something that can never be truly achieved – we strive to publish our work.

The metaphor of muscles that we used as we wrote this chapter was intended to signify the competitive, often masculine ethos that pervades contemporary academia. Our experience suggests that those who publish a lot gain a much higher degree of legitimacy to speak in the name of critical scholarship. In particular, agenda-setting and territorializing statements about CMS tend to be written by members of the community with 'big muscles' (or aspirations to develop them), publishing in the right places, time and again.

But as we all know, writing itself and working through the publishing process are extremely time-consuming. For those of us who publish three, four, five or even more pieces of work each year, sometimes all in 'high-level' journals, how does this work? Obviously we choose our orientation when we decide to do academic work; the traditional binary of 'teaching oriented' or 'research focused' can be complemented by a desire to do institutional labour as programme director, providing pastoral care for students or taking responsibility for accreditation.

Task orientation of this kind is, however, a choice with significant ethical implications. While the popular image of the lone scholar hunched over a desk may not be as valid today as in medieval times, publishing work remains a largely self-contained activity, even when pursued through collaboration. It excludes much other academic work simply in terms of time and effort required. As well as reducing the ability to contribute to institutional maintenance or student development, we think it also has implications for the enactment of an ethic of care.

The dominant rationality of publishing has a tendency to disembed us from everyday social norms of behaving humanely towards colleagues with whom we build our profession:

> I've been working on a journal paper with a colleague who is not 'REF-ready'. She has been funded by her university to develop this piece of work, on the understanding that it would result in a highly ranked journal paper. We submitted it to a 'good' journal, and ensured it would speak to the journal's readership. It went through two reviews and was then rejected by the editor . . . but the important thing was how we worked together during the process – my colleague seemed to be under a very high degree of pressure throughout, emailing and

phoning in ways to make me concerned about her. Oddly, since the paper was rejected, she's become much more calm and amiable.

We have come to think that a desire to be appreciated within our academic community in relation to publishing, through our publication, can produce feelings of insecurity, make us less calm and amiable. The audit cultures that many of us work within (Sparkes, 2007) and the practices of publishing inevitably encourage us to compete with each other – including, perhaps especially, our fellow critical scholars. We become each other's calculative enemies. To appreciate, support and help one another more, in whatever form that takes, would involve a lot of courage, especially if we think we are challenging a well-developed set of cultural norms.

As part of our multiple roles, we are also observing disembedded rationalities, ethics of un-care, from the other side of the publishing fence when acting as a reviewer:

> About a year ago I was asked by a critical journal to review a paper. I noticed from the document name when I downloaded it that the paper was at the third revision stage. I read the paper, didn't like it, thought about it, read it again, liked it even less, and thought some more. Finally I wrote a two-page review, structuring it by saying that I was going to recommend acceptance because I didn't think it was very ethical to recommend rejection of a paper at this stage, especially coming to the review process so late in the game. However, to satisfy my own feelings about the paper I wrote a very careful outline of why I disliked it and felt it should not be published.
>
> A few weeks later the editor's decision came to my inbox. The paper had been rejected. I felt pleased. There were three reviews – mine, another recommending acceptance with very minor revisions, and a third recommending rejection for many of the same reasons I had objected to the paper.
>
> Then an odd thing happened. I was looking for a paper that I wanted on the journal's early publication page. As I did [this], I found the paper I had reviewed and that had been rejected – this was around 4 months after the rejection. I read it; it was the same paper, a full paper, and it even incorporated some of the comments I had written, word for word in some cases. I was puzzled, a little unhappy, and curious – but what could I do? It was published. I was only a referee, and a minor referee at that. What would you do? I did nothing, for about 3 months. Then I decided to write to the associate editor and ask about it, offering the option not to respond. To his great credit, he replied at length. [It seems] the paper's authors had protested, perhaps loudly. This worries me. Especially as I now know who the paper's authors are – they have a reputation for . . . their approach to publishing, playing the game. The final irony? The paper is about reflexivity. I also feel that there's something else going on here, which relates to a desire to take up journal space.

None of us labors under the illusion that peer reviewing is a 'pure' process, and we benefit from our location within the community in being granted voice (as in this chapter). However, we are concerned if a willingness to exercise voice during the peer review process for journal publishing, on which our professional standing and positions depend, can become a route to presence in this way. At conferences or in seminars, we might be more accepting of this kind of vocalizing, even if we don't like it when the same people are given space to speak, again and again.

But what if those with voice are just as insecure and vulnerable as the rest of us? Perhaps they, too, feel pressured to publish all the time in a competitive space where yesterday's heroes are just that, gone and forgotten. When do they decide that they have done (or had) enough, that they are safe or secure? Perhaps when they publish a paper in every issue of every journal. . . .

Embodied masculinism

In trying to think through the ways our community practices giving and denying voice and the associated rationalities, we are confronted with the inevitable observation that both are closely bound together with modernist masculinities. Masculinism often materializes in assertive and aggressive behavior. Is it wrong—unreasonable—to note that this is a significant dynamic within the CMS community?

> There are many masculinities, of which informalism and careerism are two, as David Collinson and Jeff Hearn remind us. In my experience, these building blocks make up a powerful contemporary, apparently easy-going, but very competitive masculinity. And yes, we have witnessed that this can take a macho-critical form. Macho-critters . . . beat their chests in seminars and conferences, and through text as authors, editors and reviewers.

When apparently amiable critical scholars suddenly burst out in aggressive criticism of others' work, the experience is uncomfortable and scary. The feeling is very physical in seminars and conferences where presenters are humiliated in front of their peers; shoulders drop, faces and necks redden, sweat begins to appear. The same practice is reproduced, from a safe and anonymous distance, in texts such as reviewer statements. Young aspiring scholars learn the practice of humiliation from their more senior idols:

> Is masculinity necessarily contextual? Becoming part of the community, the in-group, the gang, is crucial for individuals in playing the critical management academic, like it is for any social group. And like in any social group, chieftains, medicine men, totems and rituals emerge over time, and start forming the context that then informs and affects the ways in which individuals think that they are expected to behave to be appreciated and to be able to climb the group hierarchy. A particular form of masculinity becomes part of the (re)production of the context as well as us, a self-fulfilling process, perhaps.

Animalistic competition and survival of the fittest become the name of the masculinist game. It seems that, despite all of our reflexivity and desire to promote social justice in other communities, we continue to act according to the rationality we feel that we somehow must embody:

> A couple of weeks ago [we] had a presentation in a doctoral seminar at [my colleague's] department. There were about 10–15 people present. Many of them were our colleagues (as well as good friends). We did the presentation in English because we knew that one of our friends was bringing her colleague from abroad to the seminar. Very soon after we had started (I guess it was when we showed our second slide, in which we described the aim of our study) one of our colleagues stopped us and said that she couldn't understand what we were doing. We tried to give her an answer, but again she interrupted us and said that she still didn't understand what we are doing and asked us to explain what we meant by sensorial cues, sensorial way of knowing, etc. We did our best to answer but she was still not satisfied. And this continued almost until the end of our presentation. I was very unhappy after the seminar. Perhaps this was because the situation reminded me of things that [I] wrote about in the mid-1990s, i.e. about the aggressive atmosphere in the doctoral seminars. When I told about my feelings to one of my female colleagues after the seminar she said that her interpretation of the situation was quite different. She thought that this was the way we always communicate with each other, calling into question each other's viewpoints, being

straightforward and even aggressive when expressing our own opinions. To be quite honest, many of the critical management scholars whom I know . . . are a bit like this. Their behaviour could be described as unfriendly. Of course this does not apply to everyone, but perhaps it is characteristic at least to some of the CMS scholars. Here I refer especially to conference behaviour and especially the ways in which they behave in the official situations like when commenting on others' presentations. I also paid attention to the bodily postures and facial expressions of my CMS friends during our seminar presentation. The facial expression of some of them signalled 'I couldn't care less' or 'how boring' or 'there is nothing new in what you are saying'. It is quite difficult to describe on which kind of bodily postures and facial expressions my interpretations are based, but let me try. Imagine a person sitting slightly aside, looking a bit grumpy (sour?) and arms across, or another person sitting in the second row, gaze wandering around and restless bodily movements.

Masculinism materializes in assertive and aggressive behaviour for women just as much as for men (as in this story). Humiliating others is a *practice*, and playing the intellectual sophistication game is one of its forms – often through professing a lack of understanding of what the speaker is trying to do. Critical scholars seem to have an urge to revert to their theoretical sophistication when they feel a need to question and challenge (and sometimes humiliate) others. But there is always someone who has read one more book than you.

At the same time as we are critical of others, our own behaviours are also open to the same interpretation:

> Both I and [a male colleague] served as pre-examiners in this process [of examining a PhD]. However, [my male colleague] was the one who was also invited to serve as the external examiner [in the viva]. I guess this was a bit of a surprise for both of us because we thought that a female examiner would be a more politically correct choice. When [we] talked about this we both had different explanations for such a choice. I thought that [he] was chosen because he comes from a much more prestigious university than I do. [My male colleague] in turn thought that it was because he is a milder (more tolerant/permissive) person than I am. To put it in another way, he thought that I might be thought of as a too-critical person and, thus, would ask too difficult questions of the doctoral student. I have to admit that for my taste [he] behaved far too gently [during the viva]. He did not ask any difficult questions directly. On the contrary, when he had a more difficult question in mind he talked about the issue for a while before asking the question, kind of softening the way for the doctoral student. And when the doctoral student was not answering soon enough, he either said 'I am not even expecting an answer to this question' or started to answer it himself. When reflecting on this now I realize that I kind of associate criticality to being straightforward, i.e. going straight to the point. One of the rituals in the [post-viva] is that the doctoral student gives a speech after the main course and everybody (s)he mentions in her/his speech is supposed to answer to this speech. I was a bit surprised when the doctoral student spoke to me (after first thanking the external examiner and the [main supervisor]) and said that for some reason she was a little bit afraid of receiving my assessment in the pre-examination phase. I thought, 'Oh my god! Am I that scary?'

Formality is an important aspect of academic work, critical or otherwise. We construct and maintain our communities through ritual, symbolism and beliefs. We might think that being critical would involve challenging such conventions, problematizing them, resisting them, perhaps through informality. This is certainly one way to work around damaging modernist rationalities, inasmuch as it provides more space for 'being nice' and embodying an ethic that provides an alternative to public humiliation and the creation of physically threatening conflict. However, an ethic of care does not simply involve being friendly or asking only easy questions of people; rather, it suggests a way of being that brings together human care with good thinking – care-full analysis, perhaps.

These forms of embodied masculinism run through our work in many contexts. Two of us presented the work in this chapter at an international conference. We received encouragement from some of the 10 or so people in the room:

> One person in the audience, who has recently got his PhD and is in his first [academic] post, said that he liked our writing because it drew attention to the normality of these experiences, enabling him to feel that he was not alone/abnormal; he saw this kind of confession as a form of resistance.

Following this, however, the conversation took a different turn:

> The comments were, I felt, mostly supportive and constructive – but I didn't enjoy the few minutes when [a prominent critical scholar] spoke; it seemed to be very directed and a little angry. Thinking about the comments now, and my physical and cognitive response to them (nervous and fearful, respectively), I could relate it to status within the community (I see this person as very status-ful) – or I could relate it to the way that the comments challenged the purpose of our analysis, in the 'where is this going?' question (I finally came up with a response to this, 2 days later – for me, it's going towards practice, in that I hope to be able to enact/embody an ethic of care) – or I could relate it to my realisation, stimulated by the overall theme of the session, that there are limits to my (desire for) reflexivity (and perhaps should be).
>
> Oh, and to the very belated realisation that we're all four writing about our marginality – three full professors/one reader working at good universities, two white men, four white people, two native English speakers and two Scandinavian English speakers, four people who are demonstrably successful in publishing and well regarded as teachers, four able-bodied people, one [until recently] editor of a very well regarded journal, two Academy CMS Division co-chairs. . . our individual and collective achievements are many! So I feel like anyone would be justified in saying 'Analyse that!' as the saying goes.

It is interesting to think, months after this discomfiting experience, that the comments made were helpful in developing our analysis further. However, the approach, the ethic enacted in the moment, still rankles for the person who made the presentation. The day came to a good end, though, when this happened:

> Later on that day, there was a session [about future possibilities for CMS]. It was a panel discussion involving [five men] as presenters; the room was full. I only caught the end of it but I gathered that there was some unhappiness in the audience about the extent to which the time had been used by presenters to talk and others had been able to contribute. A woman whom I recognised from our earlier session came up to me and said, 'You could use this as a story for your paper, it illustrates what you've been talking about perfectly'.

'Ideal' bodies

It has become clear to us, as we have told each other stories, talked and written together, that academic work provides a cultural setting for the development of security, insecurity, celebrity, obscurity and experiences of work that are sometimes bizarre but always meaningful in multiple ways. Although we have read many accounts of organization and work that analyse dynamics of embodiment, meaning or injustice, we remain surprised (and perhaps disturbed) that our own professional community is host to practices that we would condemn in other contexts. It seems that strength is power, size matters and bodies are simply carriers for the intellect.

We have returned again and again in our conversations to the idea of embodiment, in different variations. It is also present in Townley's (2008) categories of rationality; her third variety of reason's enactment rests on the notion that we all act, think and reason in and through our bodies. This can make some of us uncomfortable, especially if we aspire to an ideal type of disembodied scholarly practice. Despite this reluctance, in conversation we have gradually come to talk about embodiment, ours and others', and what we see as the ideal body of a CMS scholar. Someone like this:

> CMS is a man's game, I think, in terms of body counting and also in relation to modes of working, interaction, theory . . . I think it helps a lot to be tall, have a loud speaking voice, and an ability to put at least one, preferably three, obscure conceptual terms in each sentence. I wonder why I think of theory as masculine, though.

This ideal subject, (re)constructed in and through practices of conferencing and publishing, does not react with the body—at least in showing any weakness. However, the experience of academic work is always a bodily one. This was evident in the international conference where we presented our work:

> Anyways, after the session I did the usual things – went to the toilet, drank some water, wished I still smoked, wandered around – then I decided to go visit another part of the conference altogether.
>
> I woke up a couple of times the night after the presentation, with beautifully crafted elegant sentences on the tip of my tongue. During the presentation I mostly spoke in short, blunt sentences. I think I communicated the key issues of a) the need for cultural and ethical reflexivity, b) the need to think about our community in the ways we think about other social groups and organizations, and c) the need to consider the rationalities and ethics of care we practice. But I really don't know.

It seems that the ideal subject that is (re)constructed in the practices of conferencing, and publishing, and cannot show vulnerability in front of others. In this sense, critical scholars are probably no different from more mainstream colleagues. But perhaps the notion of an *'ideal critical body'* is specific to our community; it emerged from a thread in our conversation when we began to fantasize about an ideal business school context. Apart from being bodily different, it relates to the clothes we cover our bodies with:

> It seems that a person who is interested in business is condemned to be an ally with those in power. And it does not help at all if you are wearing clothes that are too stylish (clean-cut) to a critical scholar who should rather have a more casual (this applies especially to the faculty of social sciences of which management is part) or artistic outfit (this applies especially to the faculty of arts which is one of the four faculties at [my university]). I have had quite concrete experiences of how you are judged based on your clothing.

This can be especially striking at conferences when hundreds of self-identified critical scholars come together:

> [A] few years ago I noticed a trend about critical scholars wearing black clothes at conferences, perhaps as a marker of difference from the mainstream. When I asked colleagues about this I got some quite different answers. Several women spoke of how black work wear signified professionalism, career commitment, gravitas and also how for them it potentially hid, minimised or detracted attention away from the body which was sometimes a good thing for women in a professional context. This latter part I find interesting because it seems to confirm the mind/body dichotomy as alive and well in CMS, with the intellectual mind being of importance and the physical body as something to be hidden. When I asked critical male colleagues why they wore black, they claimed it was not significant as an identity marker.

Some do challenge the 'critical uniform', although in our experience this tends to be women rather than men:

> I went to Australia last year, to visit [a well-known critical female scholar]. When I met with her soon after I arrived she had been teaching and she was wearing a fitted sleeveless dress and high heel white pointed toe shoes. It was not what I expected, I guess in relation to her feminist/critical identity. I liked her for it though, because I felt she was saying 'this is me, my body and I am happy to draw attention to it!'

In these moments, many of the available possibilities for exclusion and participation come together, as cultural experience, gender, physicality and academic positionality intersect with the reflex of critical distance. We, like many others, attempt to respond to the ideal while simultaneously finding it problematic in its context of practice. In this respect, we do not see ourselves as outsiders; rather, we sometimes embody aspiration to the ideal (as far as we can), making use of what cultural, academic, and physical resources we have – but ultimately we fail, as we suspect all of us do.

An ethic of care within CMS?

> Should "critical" scholars somehow behave differently from others (whoever these others may be)? Should they act as if they were not greedy and vain?
>
> For me the dilemma is how to be critical about gendered power relations in a way which might keep the audience that you want to reach engaged. Whether that is in teaching or in research. So when I teach I try to avoid referring to gender or the 'f' word – feminism – in the lecture title. I try instead to work gender through all the content. However in research it is harder . . . [on one] occasion I presented a paper at a business ethics conference. There were lots of critical male scholars at the conference. The paper I presented had the word 'feminist' in the title. There were two tracks running simultaneously and virtually all the men attended the other paper session. In the room where I presented the audience was almost exclusively women.

We are conscious that here and elsewhere we have presented CMS as a relatively uncaring community, as a culture that is more individualistic than collective and that promotes a masculine ideal intellectually and physically. This is how we have experienced CMS, over more than a decade of writing, teaching, attending conferences and working to support or promote the community. The stories we have told each other reinforce this as we have considered our own actions and the behaviours of others in more detail. We have chosen, as Sparkes (2007) emphasises in his account of academic work in the U.K., a way of approaching the analysis of one's own working context that is best concluded by offering it as just one chapter in a continuing constructive narration of our working lives, and perhaps yours. However, we also want to raise one final possibility that has become more and more convincing to us as we have written this chapter: the feasibility of a community based on an ethic of care.

This idea is controversial within feminist thinking, where it originated, and in the wider academy. It is founded on the possibility of a morality that is based on relationality of care, rather than the impartial rationality entailed in theories of right action offered by Kantian and utilitarian moral philosophies; as one scholar put it, 'when justice is the guiding value, it requires that individual rights be respected' whereas care invites consideration of 'the relatedness that constitutes a social group and is needed to hold it together' (Held, 2006: 41–42). Thus, instead of being based on the notion of the autonomous, independent, rational, atomistic individual, 'an ethic of care focuses on attentiveness, trust, responsiveness to need, narrative nuance and cultivating caring relations' (Held, 2006: 15).

Drawing on aspects of feminist thought, an ethic of care further asserts that reason should not leave behind all that belongs to emotion and the body (Held, 2006: 60). Care also involves skill and requires work and energy on the part of the persons who are doing the caring. As a postpatriarchal ethic, care can be adopted by both men and women through the development of relationships in which carer and cared-for share an interest in their mutual well-being. This perspective moves us away from seeing care as a virtue that is the possession of the individual and towards a view of care as based on interdependence and careful attention to context. Consequently, it invites consideration of the values such as sensitivity, trust, mutual concern, attentiveness and the commitment to see issues from a variety of different perspectives. The challenges of trying to encourage this approach to working in the collective of CMS – of even thinking of the community as a collective – are illustrated in this ambivalent extract:

> I suppose being critical for me characterised a degree of uncertainty and separation and about being OK with that . . . Not disengaged and disconnected necessarily, but not really belonging to an organization that has a fixed identity. I don't really understand 'critters' who say that participating in critical events such as conferences is about belonging, which they don't feel when they are in the mainstream of the business school . . . I don't feel that belonging is really the basis of my criticality, even if that involves belonging to a critical community or group. It just feels a bit too comfortable somehow. Instead I feel that if I can create a balance between separation and connectedness, invisibility and visibility, I have a better chance of maintaining my criticality.

This perhaps is one possibility that is different from the current (as we see and experience it) somewhat damaging ethic that CMS embodies.

In conclusion

I think I'm starting to dislike reflexivity, in this very personalised way. I love it as a methodological approach; I like the philosophical basis of the practice; and I value what its practice encourages. But I'm not sure I want to write about it anymore in relation to my professional self and professional community. But . . . we still as a community do and tolerate crap stupid things, which should be written about. [I'm pretty tired so my everyday language is leaking into the academic bit of my brain. . . .]

In this chapter we have explored how ideas about what is expected of a CMS academic become cemented into a particular set of established rationalities (Townley, 2008) that constitute the basis for a body of thought and that can also become a means of determining which bodies can legitimately participate in academic work in the particular field. We have sought to practise the kind of reflexivity that some within CMS, we think rightly, encourage (Wray-Bliss, 2003). Reflexive writing encourages affective and emotive engagement with how we work, enabling empathy among members of a community rather than just sympathy (Parry & Boyle, 2009).

We have also tried to understand better the effects of our own practices through examining how we ourselves contribute to the construction of disciplined knowledge and embodied identity within CMS. Seeing ourselves, looking at ourselves, in this way enables interrogation of the social bases of knowledge, the ethical aspirations and political practices we engage in and the forms of otherness (Fawcett & Hearn, 2004) that norms of embodied participation generate. Although we might sometimes like to think of ourselves as marginal within CMS, between us we hold a significant amount of structural power and responsibility, for example through occupying relatively high-status positions within the academic career hierarchy and by taking on roles in editing journals, writing articles, reviewing others' work and organizing conferences.

As contributors to the social project that CMS was founded on, we have become acutely conscious of the gaps between the aspirations our writing and teaching promote and the cultural conditions in which we produce our knowledge. Is it too much to ask that members of this research community might become more conscious of the systems of power that are used to regulate our own organizational practice and become more sensitive and responsive to the embodied experiences of members? We have suggested drawing on a feminist ethic of care (Held, 2006) as an alternative moral basis through which we might think about the relationships between members of the community, as well as its moral structures, as a way of complementing the ethics of justice which has traditionally characterized CMS.

We feel that an ethic of care could provide a valuable complement to the ethics of justice and virtue which have traditionally dominated intellectual and political debates within CMS. This would enable CMS members/us to engage in the process of constituting a more diverse notion of academic subjectivity that more effectively includes marginalised groups, especially (but not limited to) women. It would also invite sensitivity to the development of caring relations and could be used to promote a model of community building as relational and interdependent. Emotional values of sympathy, empathy, sensitivity and responsiveness to others would be seen as feelings to be reflected on and educated with. This might entail reconfiguration of the traditional moral divide between the public and private spheres of community members, inasmuch as the latter as well as the former could also be seen as relevant to the development of morality within the community.

Finally, an ethic of care could also have implications for the theoretical and political development of CMS, as well as for the organization of the community, as the formation of caring relations between persons and imposing limits on the markets that undermine them could be seen as the basis for engagement with members of other, non-academic organizations. In so doing, an ethic of care could provide an alternative to the liberal individualism and rational self-interest that characterise normative engagement within academic communities and could open up spaces for different forms of organizing within CMS and beyond.

References

Adler, P., Forbes, L., & Willmott, H. (2007). Critical management studies. *Academy of Management Annals*, *1*: 119–179.

Alvesson, M., & Deetz, S. (2000). *Doing critical management research*. London: Sage.

Alvesson, M., Bridgman, T., & Willmott, H. (Eds.). (2009). *The Oxford handbook of critical management studies*. Oxford: Oxford University Press.

Alvesson, M., & Willmott, H. (1992). *Critical management studies*. London: Sage.

Bell, E., & King, D. (2010). The elephant in the room: Critical management studies conferences as a site of body pedagogics. *Management Learning, 41*(4): 429–442.

Burrell, G. (2009). Handbooks, swarms, and living dangerously. In M. Alvesson, T. Bridgman & H. Willmott (Eds.), *The Oxford handbook of critical management studies*; 551–562. Oxford: Oxford University Press.

Fawcett, B., & Hearn, J. (2004). Researching others. *International Journal of Social Research, 7*(3): 201–218.

Ford, J., & Harding, N. (2010). Get back into that kitchen, woman: Management conferences and the making of the female professional worker. *Gender, Work and Organization, 17*(5): 503–520.

Fournier, V., & Grey, C. (2000). At the critical moment: Conditions and prospects for critical management studies. *Human Relations, 53*(1): 7–32.

Glassner, B., & Hertz, R. (Eds.). (2003). *Our studies, ourselves: Sociologists' lives and work*. Oxford: Oxford University Press.

Grey, C. (2004). Reinventing business schools: The contribution of critical management education. *Academy of Management Learning & Education, 3*(2): 178–186.

Grey, C., & Willmott, H. (2005). *Critical management studies: A reader*. Oxford: Oxford University Press.

Held, V. (2006). *The ethic of care: Personal, political, and global*. Oxford: Oxford University Press.

Katila, S., & Meriläinen, S. (2002). Metamorphosis. *Gender, Work & Organization, 9*(3): 336–354.

Maclaren, P., Miller, C., Parsons, L., & Surman, E. (2009). Praxis or performance: Does critical marketing have a gender blind-spot? *Journal of Marketing Management, 25*(7–8): 713–728.

Parker, M., & Thomas, R. (2011). What is a critical journal? *Organization, 18*(4): 419–427.

Parry, K., & Boyle, M. 2009. Organizational autoethnography. In D. Buchanan & A. Bryman (Eds.), *The SAGE handbook of organizational research methods*: 690–702. London: Sage.

Rowlinson, M., & Hassard, J. (2011). How come the critters came to be teaching in business schools? Contradictions in the institutionalization of critical management studies. *Organization, 18*(5): 673–689.

Snyder-Young, D. (2011). Here to tell her story: Analyzing the autoethnographic performances of others. *Qualitative Inquiry, 17*(10): 943–951.

Sparkes, A. C. (2007). Embodiment, academics, and the audit culture. *Qualitative Research, 7*(4): 521–550.

Spicer, A., Alvesson, M., & Karreman, D. (2009). Critical performativity: The unfinished business of critical management studies. *Human Relations, 62*(4): 537–560.

Tatli, A. (2011). On the power and poverty of critical (self) reflection in Critical Management Studies: A comment on Ford, Harding and Learmonth. *British Journal of Management* forthcoming [doi: 10.1111/j.1467–8551.2011.00746.x].

Thomas, R. (2009). Critical management studies on identity: Mapping the terrain. In M. Alvesson, T. Bridgman & H. Willmott (Eds.), *The Oxford handbook of critical management studies*:166–185. Oxford: Oxford University Press.

Thomas, R., Tienari, J., Davies, A., & Meriläinen, S. (2009). Let's talk about 'us': A reflexive account of a cross-cultural research collaboration. *Journal of Management Inquiry, 18*(4): 313–324.

Townley, B. (2008). *Reason's neglect: Rationality and organizing*. Oxford: Oxford University Press.

Wray-Bliss, E. (2003). Research subjects/research subjections: Exploring the ethics and politics of critical research. *Organization, 10*: 307–325.

4

Critical performativity

The happy end of Critical Management Studies?

Sverre Spoelstra and Peter Svensson

Introduction

The aim of this chapter is to engage in the perennial debate concerning the relevance (or lack thereof) of Critical Management Studies (CMS) (see e.g. Parker, 2002; Spicer, Alvesson & Kärreman, 2009). There seems to be a growing – and perhaps well deserved – anxiety among researchers labeled or labeling themselves critical management scholars. In the early days of CMS, much of its legitimacy stemmed from its negation of established, or so-called mainstream, management research. Being something else—presenting a provocative alternative to the hegemony of positivist and realist management research and management guru discourse—rendered CMS fresh, interesting and relevant. But time passed, and CMS soon started to experience the academic equivalent of a midlife crisis. The field got more and more established, special journals were launched, professors were assigned and professors became rich and famous. Lurking beneath this success, however, was the doubt that CMS perhaps was not very useful for social change. What if people didn't care? What if nobody listened? What if our writings are not even worthy of being read?

Many attempts have been made to increase the relevance of Critical Management Studies. Some researchers have utilized the established channels within academia to increase the impact of CMS writings, e.g. publishing in highly ranked journals with relatively high impact factors or publishing in web journals that non-academics also have access to. Others have argued for the role of CMS as an activist or critical consultant.

In the midst of this plethora of alternatives, we think we recognize a growing desire to make CMS more positive, perhaps even 'positivist'. This, of course, does not mean that CMS has started to embrace the methods of (post-)positivist hypothetico-deductive testing. The desire for the positive that we are interested in stems from a growing fear of not being able to build something new. For CMS, this 'something' cannot be knowledge itself, given its skepticism toward the idea of steadily progressing social science, but it does increasingly put its faith in one of the buzzwords within contemporary academia: 'relevance'.

We will take Spicer and colleagues' (2009) plea for 'critical performativity' as an illustrative example of this trend. In particular, we will use their argument to critically reflect upon the growing concern with relevance within CMS. In this chapter, we wish to address some concerns about their proposal, which would raise the impact of CMS and regain its credibility and legitimacy. In contrast, we are afraid that critical performativity, if practiced, could signal the end of Critical Management Studies.

The chapter is structured as follows. In the first section, we discuss the increasing concern for relevance within CMS. We then critically discuss one recent contribution to this debate, which proposes the idea of 'critical performativity' as a way of overcoming the purported lack of relevance of CMS. In the next section, we problematize the idea of critical performativity by exploring the limits of the expertise and role of critical management scholars. In particular, we argue for the creation of problems rather than the contribution to solutions, the importance of uselessness and the importance of keeping a distance toward the actors that are being researched.

The relevance debate in CMS

The social sciences in general and the managerial sciences in particular are increasingly occupied with questions of relevance. This is partly motivated by larger discourses around the purported lack of relevance of the humanities and social sciences: the authority of the academic has waned considerably in popular opinion. Academics are increasingly portrayed as solipsistic people who spend taxpayers' money on their useless and self-fulfilling pet projects. Most scholars of management would probably nuance this picture but do speak of a gap between the so-called 'rigor' of the academic management journals and the 'relevance' for practitioners that management studies should be striving toward (e.g. Bennis & O'Toole, 2005; Gulati, 2007).

If there ever were a gap between mainstream management and Critical Management Studies, this gap seems to narrow fast. At least on the topic of relevance, the self-critique of critical management scholars is surprisingly similar to what goes on in management studies at large. CMS scholars are not so much concerned about the costs of 'rigor', which in the North American context is still predominantly associated with large survey-based datasets and hypothetico-deductive research, but they care just as much about the lack of relevance of their work as their 'mainstream' counterparts. The editors of the recent *Oxford Handbook of Critical Management Studies*, for example, express their concern about CMS scholars who have used CMS as a 'career platform' to pursue their 'esoteric' interests in 'cartoons, fictional literature, philosophy, etc.' (Alvesson, Bridgman & Willmott, 2009: 19–20). These interests, the editors suggest, are hardly legitimate, as they do not translate into something that is relevant for managers and organizations. Others have criticized critical management scholars for their exclusive focus on journal publications. Voronov (2008: 940), for example, observes that critical management scholars 'seek to conduct research that is publishable in top academic journals and consider such publication the ultimate destination of the research process'. Others have pointed at the dangers of 'journal-list fetishism' (Willmott, 2011) and 'game-playing' (Butler & Spoelstra, 2012) in Critical Management Studies. All these critiques point to a growing dissatisfaction with the present form and direction of CMS research.

Behind the critique of the purported lack of relevance of CMS lurks the question of its purpose. In self-presentations CMS is often portrayed as a scholarly community that opposes managerialism and its negative consequences, that fights for the emancipation of workers, women, minorities and so on, that offers alternative ways of organization, that unmasks bankers, accountants and other bad people who have caused the various crises of our times and that teaches managers how to make their workplace more humane and egalitarian.

While this picture has been created by critical management scholars, they are also the first to admit that there is little in reality that corresponds to this image. Self-reflections often make the argument that these ideals have not been realized: CMS has been accused of having no impact outside a small academic community, of writing in inaccessible ways, of being destructive rather than constructive, of being a career platform for researchers rather than an engaged form of scholarship and of being little more than a label or brand (e.g. Grey & Sinclair, 2006; Parker, 2002; Thompson, 2004). On the basis of these critiques, one could conclude that CMS has largely failed to fulfill its promise and that it is time for CMS scholars to reinvent their strategies and practices.

In our view, underneath the constant questioning of the purpose and success of CMS, answers to the question of where CMS happens have changed quite significantly. It seems to us that in the early years of CMS, it was thought to happen in the books and journals of our field, and the main critical questioning was directed at the accessibility, usefulness or audience of these publications. This was, for example, provocatively captured by Martin Parker's question: 'what Theory do you need to throw a brick through the window of a McDonald's?' (2002: 162). Parker's concern was that CMS had become a 'glass bead game' with no relevance for the outside world. In the last 10 years, CMS still revolves around these glass bead games (perhaps even more than before), but it also seems that most contributors to the debate on CMS have accepted the uselessness of journal publishing or are at least increasingly skeptical about it (Butler & Spoelstra, 2012, 2014; Willmott, 2011). As a consequence, the emphasis has shifted: from a concern on how to bridge the gap between theory and practice (e.g. how to make CMS research more accessible or more relevant to practitioners) to a concern on how to move from theory to practice or between theory and practice. In other words, the question has shifted from indirect relevance (communication and usefulness of CMS theory) to direct relevance (engagement with practice).

An early suggestion in this direction is Steffen Böhm's (2002) plea for a 'theoretical practice'. Böhm observes that much of the debate around the purpose and practice of CMS is based on an overly simplistic theory/practice dichotomy, where CMS is located on the theory side (it produces theoretical reflections *in its practices*) and where it dreams of being on the practice side (it dreams of emancipation, resistance, etc. *in its theorizations*). Instead, Böhm argues for a theoretically engaged form of practice, understood as 'theory that aims at interrogating and concretely effecting social organization and contributes to a project of radical change' (2002: 328). Similarly, Edward Barratt (2003: 1069) has argued for 'more practical and engaged forms of critical intellectual work'. Barratt finds inspiration in Foucault's idea of a critical attitude, which could find its way into CMS as an 'engaged scholarly practice' that bridges the intellectual and the practical by challenging the dangers of the present in the midst of power relations (Barratt, 2003: 1084).

We are sympathetic to this idea of a theoretical practice or engaged scholarly practice and agree that the separation between theory and practice tends to be too facile in debates about the (lack of) relevance of CMS. However, we find some recent articulations of this idea problematic as they are, in our view, in danger of being usurped by managerial university rhetoric. We are particularly skeptical toward Andre Spicer, Mats Alvesson and Dan Kärreman's (2009) plea for what they call 'critical performativity'. In our reading, they too easily succumb to a discourse of relevance that is increasingly pervasive within the university-based business school. In particular, we contest the idea that CMS becomes more relevant by seeking to meet managers and organizations on their own premises, by giving them advice on how to humanize their workplaces or improve work processes, for example. This, we argue in this chapter, is not the kind of theoretical practice that CMS scholars should be striving toward.

In what follows, we set off with Spicer and colleagues' argument, which has already become quite influential within management studies (at least in terms of citation count) despite the fact that it is a fairly recent publication. We see the article as paradigmatic for a broader concern about the (lack of) relevance of CMS, which is also reflected in other recent publications (e.g. Alvesson & Spicer, 2012; Grint & Jackson, 2010; Tourish, 2013; Voronov, 2008).

The idea of critical performativity

In their paper 'Critical performativity: The unfinished business of Critical Management Studies', Spicer, Alvesson and Kärreman (2009) argue against Fournier and Grey's (2000) proposition that CMS research is best characterized as non-performative. Loosely drawing upon Judith Butler's concept of performativity, the authors argue that Critical Management Studies, in its present form, is not 'socially influential' (2009: 540) and 'socially relevant' (2009: 549). Their claim is that CMS, as it is currently practiced, is essentially a negative or utopian[1] enterprise and as such is incapable of realizing anything of significance for management and organizations. They therefore argue that the negativity pervading CMS needs to be complemented by a more 'affirmative', 'caring', 'pragmatic', 'potentiality-oriented' and 'normative' stance (Spicer, Alvesson & Kärreman, 2009), which they see as the main components of a 'critical performativity' that would redeem Critical Management Studies from its present uselessness. The authors summarize their concern as being in line with Marx's concerns about philosophy: 'CMS might cease to merely interpret the world in a negative way and instead seek to actively change it' (p. 554).

The central use of the term 'performativity' in Spicer and colleagues' argument deserves further attention, as they use the term in at least three different ways. They start off positioning themselves against Fournier and Grey's (2000) characterization of CMS as being non-performative: 'We reject the idea that CMS is best characterized as non- or anti-performative' (Spicer, Alvesson & Kärreman, 2009: 538). For Fournier and Grey, performativity refers to the optimization between input and output, so it seems as if Spicer and colleagues make a plea for a more business-oriented CMS that takes efficiency and productivity as its guiding principles. But in what follows, they change the terms of the debate by drawing upon a very different concept of performativity, stemming from J. L. Austin's and, especially, Judith Butler's work.

Though Spicer and colleagues (2009) do not discuss Austin's work in detail, a few words on Austin's argument will be useful for presenting (and problematizing) their argument. Austin was interested in the way words not only describe but also act. In his lecture-based book *How to Do Things with Words* (1962), Austin makes a distinction between the illocutionary act of utterances and the perlocutionary act. The first effectuates what is said in the very moment of utterance, whereas the perlocutionary act refers to consequences after the moment of utterance. Utterances that exemplify the illocutionary force of utterances include 'I crown this ship the *Queen Elizabeth*' and 'This meeting is closed', where the said immediately realizes what it speaks of (e.g. the utterance 'this meeting is closed', if successful, actually closes the meeting).

For Austin, it was crucial, however, that the intention in an illocutionary act does not necessarily realize itself in its utterance. To effectively crown a ship *Queen Elizabeth* by saying 'I crown this ship the *Queen Elizabeth*', one must be authorized to do so. It is therefore crucial, Austin argues, to take the context of an illocutionary act into account, which explains why some performative utterances are 'happy' (they realize what they speak about) and others 'unhappy' (they have consequences, as all utterances do, but fail to instantly realize what they intend). The important point here is that the illocutionary force of an utterance is dependent on convention or authorization.

Austin's distinction between happy and unhappy performative utterances (or felicitous and infelicitous utterances, as Austin also puts it) has been picked up in two radically different ways. The first, as exemplified in the work of analytic philosophers such as Searle and (especially) Grice, takes the distinction as the starting point for a search for the conditions that make utterances happy, similar to the way (post-)positivism has tried to clarify the conditions for verifiable or falsifiable knowledge (Felman, 1983). The second, which is the route that Judith Butler follows (and also Jacques Derrida and Shoshana Felman), is to emphasize the importance and subversive potential of unhappy performatives. An example from Butler may serve as an example of this:

'When Rosa Parks sat in the front of the bus, she had no prior right to do so guaranteed by any of the segregationist conventions of the South' (Butler, 1997: 147). Performativity is here no longer simply a question of language use; even a silent body can make a performative 'utterance' by not moving, as this example illustrates. The capacity of utterances to 'misfire' gives them a scandalous or disruptive character (Felman, 1983: 84). On the basis of this we can distinguish between two different forms of the illocutionary act of performatives: those that actualize conventions (authorized utterances) and those that cause an event or scandal (authoritative utterances).

Let us now return to Spicer, Alvesson and Kärreman's argument and ask which of these two illocutionary acts they propose as a model for CMS. Given the centrality of Butler's work on the performative in the article, it seems self-evident that the authors see authoritative utterances as the model for CMS, rather than authorized utterances. Some statements in the text support this: '[i]f CMS was to think of itself as a performative enterprise, its central aim would be to actively and *subversively* intervene in managerial discourse and practices' (Spicer, Alvesson & Kärreman, 2009: 544; emphasis added). On this reading, CMS scholars should dare to be like Rosa Parks by affirming radical change in action, against the power relations produced by certain discourses.

This raises a difficult question in the context of CMS: what could be considered to be the CMS equivalent of Rosa Parks and drag queens, which have unsettled certain discourses?

Spicer, Alvesson and Kärreman do not answer this question directly, but they do hint at more concrete practices that they have in mind for the CMS scholar: they argue for a careful, affirmative, pragmatic and relevant engagement with people within organizations. In this, CMS avoids 'attacking organizational life from the outside' (Spicer, Alvesson & Kärreman, 2009: 547) by getting inside the organizations in order to meet the members on their own premises. The critical management scholar, they say, should follow the example of 'tempered radicals' (Meyerson, 2001), which roughly refers to leaders who incrementally change the system from within.

What we see here is a much less radical picture than Butler proposes. The picture that emerges as the paper develops seems rather far away from a scandalous, event-like intervention in organizational discourse. Instead of problematizing established discourse though a scandalous or authoritative performative utterance, the CMS scholar is invited to contribute to actual organizations by means of solving concrete problems that organizational members face in their daily working lives.

This also raises another question: how do CMS scholars enter these organizations? In other words, apart from the organizations they are already part of (e.g. the university), how do they become insiders so that they can offer their help and advice from within? At this point Spicer and colleagues propose a number of suggestions that correspond to well established literatures but that are not (yet) associated much with CMS. Critical performativity in practice, they propose, should take the form of action research (practitioners should be allowed to partly shape research), therapy (one should question managers and provide them with relevant feedback), normative guidance (advise managers how to act) and critical consultancy (a critical stance that is aligned with managerial or organizational interest). Together, they are best read as a plea for social relevance in the narrow sense of constructively helping to design new solutions to existing organizational problems.

As indicated, these are certainly not brand new ideas. Many attempts have been made to argue for more action-oriented or interventionist research strategies that not only analyze social change but also partake of it actively. The most famous attempts of this ilk are perhaps action research and participatory research (for a discussion of the different ideologies between the two, see Brown & Tandon, 1983). There are a number of takes on these approaches, but what seems to unite them all is the aspiration to intervene in organizational practice, e.g. organizational change, as a way of not only understanding what goes on in organizations but also as a way to contribute to the improvement of processes, routines and outcomes.

At this point in Spicer, Alvesson and Kärreman's argument, one may wonder what happened to the theme of performativity. Indeed, it is difficult to recognize anything that could link critical performativity, in the guise of action research or critical consultancy, to the illocutionary act of an utterance. If we do push for a link with performativity, we may even say that instead of taking the illocutionary act of an utterance as their model for CMS, Spicer and colleagues end up taking the perlocutionary act of an utterance as their model. Or, put in less technical terms, they propose that CMS scholars should say things that result in something relevant (doing A results in B), preferably for managers or other organizational members. At times, it also seems as if the critical performativity argument is rooted in an urge to control the ways in which performativity operates, similar to the ways in which analytic philosophers have built on Austin's work. Interestingly, and indeed paradoxically, this resembles the managerial anxiety of not being in control, of not being on top of things, of not being able to determine the destiny of one's actions.

So what is our problem? Is our problem merely that the notion of the performative is not taken seriously enough in Spicer, Alvesson and Kärreman's text? Well, that is certainly *part* of our problem: the slippery use of the concept of performativity makes it extremely difficult to understand what Spicer and colleagues are actually arguing for. The text could be interpreted as arguing for almost any activity within a 'real' organization, which may make it highly citable (given the widespread fear among CMS scholars that their work has little impact) but also hard to interpret. Our main concern, however, is not so much the conative contents of the text. What concerns us most of all is its illocutionary force.

Indeed, so far we have acted as if Spicer, Alvesson and Kärreman's text is (meant to be) a conative text (it speaks about a performative CMS but does not itself intend to be performative in an authorized, authoritative or perlocutionary fashion). But the text is (as all texts are) also performative, and it is at this point that we find the text most problematic. Instead of causing a scandal, we feel that the argument is in danger of confirming a managerial discourse of relevance that already dominates the university-based business school. In other words, while the text at times appears to argue for the authoritative illocutionary act of an utterance as a model for CMS and at other times for the perlocutionary act of an utterance, the text itself gives the impression of being an authorized article, in the sense that it seems to confirm rather than contest a managerial discourse of relevance. In short, Austin's happy performative, the one that realizes itself by being authorized, appears to be the model for CMS, if Spicer, Alvesson and Kärreman's article is itself measured on its (not so critical) performativity.

Thus, the problem is not necessarily the idea of striving for relevancy but actually the ways in which the 'relevant management critic' is constructed in Spicer and colleagues' article (and in similar calls). As Prasad and Elmes (2005) note in their analysis of environmental management discourse: 'By and large, being practical is equated with maintaining economic growth and success (for individual firms and societies), entering into alliances and agreements with specific stakeholders and ensuring low levels of societal confrontation' (p. 863). Precisely because Spicer, Alvesson and Kärreman are not very clear on what they have in mind for CMS, we fear that some of their recommendations are in danger of aligning the CMS scholar with such a discourse of relevance. This would be an unfortunate development in our view and could mark the end of CMS in the sense that it would no longer be distinguishable from other forms of research (such as action research). Hence, our argument is not targeted against action research per se but against the idea of transforming CMS in some form of action research or critical consultancy. The reason is straightforward: we consider CMS to be important in its own right (and believe that it can be even more important).

Rethinking relevancy critically

Against the background of this reading of Spicer, Alvesson and Kärreman's paper, we will seek to offer an account of CMS that goes against the sentiment that CMS should look for its relevance in its added value for organizations and in its capacity to find solutions to existing problems. In what follows, we will therefore offer a reconstruction, as it were, of the relevant critical management researcher that stands very much in opposition to the impression of critical performativity that Spicer, Alvesson and Kärreman leave us with. In particular, we argue against three ideas in Spicer, Alvesson and Kärreman's paper: (1) that CMS scholars should offer solutions, (2) that CMS should be useful and (3) that CMS research should be properly located within organizations.

The relevant CMS researcher opens the door but refrains from closing it

It seems to us that the kind of concerns expressed in Spicer, Alvesson and Kärreman (2009) is based upon an anxious fear of not being the one who comes up with the new solutions to the problems of contemporary capitalism. They, for instance, argue that it is important that CMS researchers not only contribute 'to the death of management' but also take responsibility for 'what is replacing it' (p. 541). One way of taking on such a responsibility would then be to 'seek to change management by making incremental incisions into particular processes' (p. 550) and to 'rearticulate and re-present new ways of managing and organizing' (p. 555).

To our mind, this fear of not delivering the solutions to social problems can lead CMS into a position in society from which it becomes difficult to address critique on a continuous basis. If solutions start to constitute the goal for CMS research, then critical diagnosis that does not translate into this goal is in danger of being disqualified as 'irrelevant'.

In contrast to this view, we would like to argue that a relevant CMS researcher is one who does not partake in the manufacturing, renovation, repair and adjustment of organizations but restricts him- or herself – in the role as a researcher – to the incessant critical scrutiny of the current state of affairs and the 'solutions' that continually are offered from politicians, consultants, activists, culture workers and so on and so forth. The role of the CMS researcher thus involves revealing, disclosing and illuminating the darkness of contemporary management practices, consumer society and capitalism without necessarily pointing out new solutions to what is conceived of as problems and malfunctions.

It might be crucial to make a distinction between the role of detecting or constructing problems (problematizing) and that of designing the solutions to such problems. One reason for this is that attempts to design solutions to social problems should be treated as one of the main *objects of study* for CMS. The world of management and business is full of solutions. Politicians formulate them, consultants sell them, management gurus promote them. What the world needs (indeed a question of relevancy) is perhaps not more solutions but problematizations and critical scrutiny of the industry of solutions already operating.

It should be noted at this juncture that we are not rejecting the idea (or dream) of the critical management researcher playing the role of an expert. The crux of the matter is rather the object of expertise, i.e. what the CMS scholar should be an expert in: creating problems or suggesting solutions? We would put our vote on the former area of expertise.

In that sense, the role of the critical management scholar is that of someone who *opens up* rather than closes down. The CMS researcher analyses rather than synthesizes, deconstructs rather than reconstructs, stresses contradictions and heterogeneity in society rather than suggesting models that reduce the complexity of social relations. The CMS researcher should open the door and leave it open for others to close. If the door is being closed again (which is going to happen), then the CMS researcher should try to open it again. And again. And again. This is the Sisyphus work of critique, the work that renders CMS relevant.

Relevant CMS research is outside and distant (not inside and close)

Spicer, Alvesson and Kärreman (2009) argue that critical management researchers need to be more engaged and intimate with the field, *within* the field. They suggest that 'a good strategy of critique may involve infestation from the inside rather than attack from the outside' (p. 548).

There are, however, good reasons for not coming too close to the field, for being distant in relation to the object of critical study. Being located too close to the object of study makes it cumbersome to question and challenge underlying assumptions and premises; they have, as it were, become a part of that which connects the close researcher to that which he or she studies critically.

Thus, 'at distance' is in fact the best place to be if critical analyses are to be delivered, and the role of the relevant CMS researcher is – once more in contrast to the idea of critical performativity – a *distant* role, one that does not operate *within* the world of management but outside it.

It is important, though, to clarify what we mean by 'distance' here. First, distance does not refer to a withdrawal from empirical fieldwork and a glorification of armchair critique (although a lot of insightful and meaningful critique is avowed in the armchair rather than in the field). Proximity to the field can often be very important in order to get empirical insights for critical analyses.

Secondly, neither does distance refer to being disengaged. Associating proximity with engagement is in fact a misguided thought. Quite to the contrary, being engaged as a critical researcher has to do with care and honesty rather than whether one is in a close relationship with the members of the empirical field. To engage oneself in the topic of research is, in other words, to reject pragmatism in favor of honest concern, not necessarily for individual managers, workers or consumers but for the circumstances under which these people lead their lives. From outside, at a distance, we can study the members of the field as *symptoms* of what the CMS scholar subjects to critical analysis, e.g. marketization, entrepreneurialism, neo-liberalization, leadership ideas, gender stereotypes, postcolonial discourse, relevance discourse among academics and so on and so forth. This is not, we argue, to reduce the importance of individual experiences and accounts but to engage in a critique of the *game* rather than the players, conceiving of the latter as products of the former. It might be worthwhile, therefore, to distinguish between critique of actors and critique of systems, contexts, structures and situations. Capitalist critique is not (necessarily) a critique of individual capitalists but rather a way of illuminating, e.g., the dysfunctionalities and oppressive effects of the capitalist way of organizing production and consumption. Paying attention to these effects is very much what critical engagement means.

Relevant CMS research is not (directly) useful

The hegemonic conception of what it means to be a responsible and meaningful human being today emphasizes the importance of making oneself useful in the market. We are, in the spirit of entrepreneurialism, increasingly requested to work on our employability and market value. One of the chief problems related to the plea for critical performativity is that it is all too easily aligned with this burgeoning call in society for relevant, useful and productive knowledge. Put differently, critical performativity fits very well with the dominant and established discourse of relevance that emphasizes usefulness and exchange value. According to the hegemonic discourse of relevance, useful knowledge corresponds to a (use-)demand out there, on the market. 'Useful' knowledge can be used for the accomplishment of valuable goals.

There is an increasing willingness among European universities to adopt a market/management language in both internal and external communication. Employing terms such as 'customers', 'competition', 'productivity', 'brand' and 'market demand' can be seen as an attempt to adopt rather than resist the marketized discourse on higher education. When CMS uncritically, without much of a struggle, subscribes to the prevalent idea of relevance or usefulness in society, it runs the risk of adding oil to the fire. A politically more interesting – and critically oriented – response to the call for relevant and usefulness would be to take control of (rather than adopting) the language used to evaluate knowledge and research. *Not* talking about CMS research in terms of relevance or usefulness then presents itself as an alternative way to go (*cf.* Kaulingfreks, 2005), especially if terms such as 'relevance' and 'usefulness' are notions that merit critical scrutiny in their own right. Maybe other terms do a better job to describe what CMS-research might accomplish in order to support social change, e.g. 'provocative', 'meaningful', 'remarkable', 'illuminating', 'important', 'interesting', 'mind-blowing', 'scandalous', 'eye-opening' and so forth. Or maybe we should try to interrupt the prevailing discourse of relevance by calling something irrelevant that is generally seen as relevant – or the other way around (as we have tried to do here).

Concluding discussion: Critical relevance as discursive interventions

The CMS dream of becoming relevant, as expressed in the idea of critical performativity, seems to be based upon a misguided premise: that relevance is first and foremost a question of responding to the surrounding environment's wishes and demand. The dream of being useful – being of use for someone else – very easily detracts attention from what, arguably, could be seen as the most crucial task for CMS, viz. to subject to critical study the contemporary *society* in which we live, particularly those sectors and spheres of society permeated by management-related ideology. Being relevant to *social actors* should not (uncritically) be confused with being relevant to *society*. Social actors are, in part, products (or symptoms) of society and should be treated as such. As a matter of fact, the dominant ideas of 'relevancy' are part of what CMS should subject to study rather than respond to.

Spicer, Alvesson and Kärreman's paper assumes a world where CMS research is either positive ('critical performativity') or negative (the alleged irrelevance of anti-performative CMS research), but in our view relevant CMS research cannot be located on either side. Hence we agree with Spicer and colleagues when they argue that CMS research should not aim to be negative only, in positioning itself 'against' (but who would argue this?), but we do not accept that 'positive' research is a good alternative or that it is the only alternative. In our view, CMS should not want to be positive by limiting its endeavors in research that results in something tenable. Instead, we contend that CMS should (and often does) challenge certain managerial or organizational practices by saying things that do not fit within dominant forms of thinking about management and organizations. Paradoxically, Parker's (2002) book *Against Management* may be seen as an example of this (rather than of a 'negative' critique), precisely because according to established discourse, it is not possible to be 'against management' (as Parker notes in the introduction). In contrast, yet another paper about the importance of organizational relevance for management research or yet another attempt to close the 'rigor-relevance gap' does not provide any intervention: it simply confirms what is already there.

Ironically, this is precisely one of the guiding ideas in Butler's work on performativity. The (authoritative) performative utterance, in the sense of Butler, is neither positive nor negative in relation to performative discourses: it neither confirms by means of the habitual repetition of discursive conventions (the happy performative) nor denies by offering a critique from the outside (of discourse). As noted, Spicer, Alvesson and Kärreman's article shows some awareness of this but quickly slips into a plea for positive outcomes that chimes well with a prevalent discourse of relevancy in research. When CMS researchers try to be relevant and useful, they have already subscribed to the hegemonic ideas of relevance and usefulness. When they try to be more relevant by means of becoming more performative through action research, moral advice and other forms of consultancy, they situate themselves within the logic or discourse of exchange value, efficiency (the relation between input and output) and productivity.

Part of the reason why Spicer, Alvesson and Kärreman locate CMS outside the academic journals and within 'actual' organizations is that they recognize the poor quality of many journal publications under the label of CMS. Indeed, so much of what is called CMS today are professionally crafted papers that are tailor-made for the 'leading' journals in the field but are hardly worth reading as they merely repeat a 'critical' cliché according to a pre-established formula, e.g.: a tiresome literature review (mainly meant to boost the citation index of the journal), followed by an introduction of some French thinker, a long method section, and then a few bits of empirical material that (allegedly) result in some theoretical novelty that no one is really interested in. We also consider this to be a serious problem in CMS (as well as in management studies at large), but an escape into critical consulting and the like does not make CMS more interesting.

We do not propose that the critical researcher should not intervene and should not be interested in changing the world (instead of just studying it). It is our conviction that CMS should take its social change aspirations seriously. However, the impression of critical performativity that Spicer, Alvesson and Kärreman's article leaves us with is the wrong path to choose. Maybe CMS researchers should not try so hard to act as reformers or revolutionaries – at least in their role as critical researchers. Given that the researcher is already working within a performative system of text production, performativity as the propeller of social change is what should be developed and refined. Thus, writing and talking and being read and listened to are part of the critical intervention in current state of affairs. In fact, it is hard not to intervene when working with performative tools (language and other kinds of symbol systems). What we need to reflect upon, though – which we have tried to do in this chapter – is whether such an intervention should operate through the creation of problems or the suggestion of solutions, through asking questions or formulating answers.

What we would argue for, then, is something that could be referred to as *discursive intervention*, which again brings us back to the Butlerian moments in Spicer, Alvesson and Kärreman's paper (i.e. the authoritative utterance as the model for CMS). Discursive intervention is an approach to relevancy and social change that differs from critical performativity in that it emphasizes the problematization of existing ideas as the primary means by way of which social change can be stimulated. Discursive interventions are accomplished through attempts to interrupt, negotiate, challenge, remake and/or deconstruct established ways of talking and writing about organizations, production, consumption, leadership, etc. That is, rather than adopting the established conceptions of 'relevancy' and 'usefulness', discursive interventions seek to turn these notions into objects of critical study and discussion.

In sum, discursive interventions are engaged with problems and questions rather than with solutions and answers, and the main point is not to offer alternatives to the current state of things. In fact, the alternative (to the current state of affairs) already resides in the questions and problems that the CMS researcher can offer. Hence, the task of CMS is not to respond to questions but to question the terms and conditions underpinning the established questions and problems in society today. The research task is not to solve problems but, through discursive interventions, to create new ones.

Note

1   There is an interesting paradox here: while Spicer, Alvesson and Kärreman (2009) argue against utopian research, is their own proposal for critical performativity not itself the formulation of (yet another) utopian picture of CMS? It could be argued that their alternative falls prey to what Ford, Harding and Learmonth (2010:S78) describe as the tendency within CMS to see itself as some kind of heroic savior: 'The academic as hero informed the intellectual self: a hero bringing knowledge and wisdom to current and future generations of managers' (p. S78)

References

Alvesson, A., Bridgeman, T., & Willmott, H. (2009). Introduction. In *The Oxford handbook of critical management studies*: 1–28. Oxford: Oxford University Press.

Alvesson, M., & Spicer, A. (2012). Critical leadership studies: The case for critical performativity. *Human Relations*, *65*(3): 367–390.

Austin, J. L. (1962). *How to do things with words*. Oxford: Oxford University Press.

Barratt, E. (2003). Foucault, HRM and the ethos of the critical management scholar, *Journal of Management Studies*, *40*(5): 1069–1087.

Bennis, W. G., & O'Toole, J. (2005). How business schools lost their way, *Harvard Business Review*, *85*(5): 96–104.

Böhm, S. (2002). Movements of theory and practice. *ephemera*, *2*(4): 328–351.

Brown, L. D., & Tandon, R. (1983). Ideology and political economy in inquiry: Action research and participatory research. *The Journal of Applied Behavioral Science*, *19*(3): 277–294.

Butler, J. (1997). *Excitable speech: A politics of the performative*. London: Routledge.

Butler, N., & Spoelstra, S. (2012). Your excellency. *Organization*, *19*(6), 891–903.

Butler, N., & Spoelstra, S. (2014). The regime of excellence and the erosion of ethos in critical management studies, *British Journal of Management*, *25*: 538–550.

Fairclough, N. (2003). 'Political correctness': The politics of culture and language. *Discourse & Society*, *14*(1), 17–28.

Felman, S. (1983). *The literary speech act: Don Juan with JL Austin, or seduction in two languages*. Ithaca, NY: Cornell University Press.

Ford, J., Harding, N., & Learmonth, M. (2010). Who is it that would make business schools more critical? Critical reflections on critical management studies. *British Journal of Management*, *21*: S71-S81.

Fournier, V., and Grey, C. (2000). At the critical moment: Conditions and prospects for critical management studies, human relations, *53*(1): 7–32.

Grey, C., and Sinclair, A. (2006). Writing differently, *Organization*, *13*(3): 443–453.

Grint, K., & Jackson, B. (2010). Toward 'socially constructive' social constructions of leadership. *Management Communication Quarterly*, *24*(2): 348–355.

Gulati, R. (2007). Tent poles, tribalism and boundary spanning: The rigor-relevance debate in management research. *Academy of Management Journal*, *50*(4): 775–782.

Kaulingfreks, R. (2005). On the uselessness of philosophy. In C. Jones & R. Ten Bos (Eds.), *Philosophy and organization*. London: Routledge.

Meyerson, D. (2005). *Tempered radicals: How people use difference to inspire change at work*. Boston: Harvard Business School Press.

Parker, M. (2002). *Against management: Organization in the age of managerialism*. Cambridge: Polity.

Prasad, P., & Elmes, M. (2005). In the name of the practical: Unearthing the hegemony of pragmatics in the discourse of environmental management. *Journal of Management Studies*, *42*(4), 845–867.

Spicer, A., Alvesson, M., & Kärreman, D. (2009). Critical performativity: The unfinished business of critical management studies, *Human Relations*, *62*(4): 537–560.

Thompson, P. (2004). Brands, boundaries and bandwagons: A critical reflection on critical management studies. In S. Fleetwood & S. Ackroyd (Eds.), *Critical realism in action in organization and management studies*: 54–70. London, Routledge.

Tourish, D. (2013). *The dark side of transformational leadership: A critical perspective*. London: Routledge.

Voronov, M. (2008). Towards engaged critical management studies. *Organization*, *15*(6): 939–945.

Willmott, H. (2011). Journal list fetishism and the perversion of scholarship: Reactivity and the ABS list. *Organization*, *18*(4): 429–442.

5

A rebel without a cause? (Re)claiming the question of the 'political' in Critical Management Studies

Ajnesh Prasad

What is the organizational imagination? It is the quality of mind that enables organizational researchers to make linkages between history, structures, and individual lives in the service of an intellectual and political purpose.

(Mir & Mir, 2002: 121)

Introduction

In the last couple of decades, Critical Management Studies (CMS) has exponentially grown in purchase. There are now conferences (the biennial International CMS Conference in Europe and the biennial CMS Research Workshop in North America), edited books (Alvesson, Bridgman & Willmott, 2009; Grey & Willmott, 2005; Wolfram Cox, LeTrent-Jones, Voronov & Weir, 2009), and special issues (Prasad & Mills, 2010) devoted to this academic domain. Given the proliferation of CMS scholarship that has emerged, there have been concerted efforts, in the last several years, to identify CMS's origins (Rowlinson & Hassard, 2011) and its underlying "pillars" (Adler, Forbes & Willmott, 2007; Fournier & Grey, 2000). Perhaps no other evidence of its growth – and its legitimacy – is greater than the fact that articles have emerged from non-CMS members of the academy appraising and critiquing this intellectual domain (Eden, 2003; Frenkel, 2009). Given its prolific growth, some scholars have observed that CMS is approaching a state of 'institutionalization' (Rowlinson & Hassard, 2011).

One pivotal effect of the institutionalization of CMS is that it is dangerously close to losing its political edge. Indeed, CMS scholarship appears to be increasingly moving against the contours of its original radical political orientation. This political orientation was, at one point in time, the defining feature of scholarship being conducted under the CMS label. As Cunliffe and colleagues (2002: 489) elucidated in their description of CMS: '[it is] a branch of management theory that critiques our intellectual and social practices, questions the "natural order" of institutional arrangements, and engages in actions that support challenges to prevailing systems of domination'. If CMS's radical political orientation is forsaken, then it becomes severely vulnerable to being subsumed by the wider academy – which does not share CMS's ontological affinities – or otherwise risks almost wholly failing to realize that which it was created to redress:

the rectification of the underlying problems caused by mainstream management theory and practice. Hence, at this juncture it may be timely to ask, 'Has CMS become the proverbial rebel without a cause?'

The intention of this chapter is to reclaim the question of the 'political' in CMS. I argue that research conducted within the loose domain of CMS ought to be explicitly motivated by a political agenda. This political agenda will, of course, vary depending on the nature and the scope of the research project; however, the point remains that CMS scholarship should be directed toward contributing to the actualization of social change through the careful enactment of, and engagement with, the question of the political (Prasad, 2014a). The specific aims underlying the political agenda would be located within the purview of what CMS, as a broad intellectual tradition, already advocates for in theory. One way by which to achieve this directive would require CMS scholars to engage with what Paulo Freire (1970) calls, in his writings on critical pedagogy, *objectification* – a trajectory by which subjects learn about themselves and the social world. As he explains, 'without objectification, man [and woman] would be limited to be *in* the world, lacking both self-knowledge and knowledge of the world' (Friere, 1970: 40; emphasis in original). Thus, objectification results in a level of *conscientization* – again I borrow here from Friere (1970) – which opens up paths for greater lucidity of the political aims underlying CMS scholarship (see Fotaki & Prasad, 2014). In sum, I contend that if CMS is to harness its full – and this certainly means its socially transformative – potential, then at the ideological crux of CMS scholarship ought to be the explicit consideration of the political and, by extension, an accounting for how it informs social change (Prasad & Mills, 2010).

At this point, it would be appropriate to provide a caveat. The aim of this chapter is not to denigrate or otherwise negate the important contributions that have been made by critical scholars who have sought to utilize their positions as members of the so-called intellectual elite to dismantle the structural systems of hegemony and domination that continues to subjugate various oppressed classes and, in the most extreme of cases, society's subaltern constituents (Prasad, 2009; Spivak, 1988). Indeed, as a relatively junior member of the academy, I remain in admiration of scholars who have thoroughly engaged with the political by having had the courage to confront the inequities in our society and to demand their proper destruction – the very inequities that have furnished undeserved privilege to one group at the direct disenfranchisement of another (on this point, see McIntosh, 1998). Bobby Banerjee's commitment to exposing the abject marginalization of indigenous communities through a plethora of neocolonial discourses (Banerjee, 2000; Banerjee & Linstead, 2004), Stella Nkomo's diligent efforts to constructively render visible those racialized minorities silenced in the writing of management research (Cox & Nkomo, 1990; Nkomo, 1992), and Karen Ashcraft's thoughtful endeavors to illuminate not only women's voices at the organizational margins but also the paradoxical fruitfulness of feminist organizational forms (Ashcraft, 1998; 2001) – these are but a few examples of those who have mobilized their scholarship (and themselves, in some instances) to move toward engendering productive social change. I will not even mention the contributions in this project for social change imparted by the editors of this volume as that would merit a chapter of its own. These scholars are nothing short of trailblazers for me and for many of my contemporaries, as they have taken the necessary personal and career risks to open up space from which to catalyze dialogue and to conduct research on phenomena that *substantively* matter. With that said, I believe that the amount of CMS research being conducted in the 'political' spirit underlying the works of the previously named authors is diminutive. As such, there remains a pertinent need for CMS scholars to partake in a more concerted effort to engage the question of the 'political' in their scholarship and in their practice.

The remainder of this chapter unfolds in three substantive sections. In the first section, I discuss how the current disposition of CMS as a paradigmatic – or perhaps to be less terse, as an intellectual – domain is a recursive illumination of the broader academic field of organization and management studies. This is especially the case in terms of how CMS centralizes certain scholars and relegates others to the periphery through the exercise of myriad systems of disciplinary power. I use academic conferences to describe one particular site at which this disciplinary power operates. In the second section, I further extend this discussion by elucidating the implications that emerge from the present disposition of CMS. My focus in this section is largely reserved for two related manifestations that I have witnessed: the sanitization of CMS's radical and ideological edge and, by extension, the ontological disjuncture in CMS praxis. Finally, in the third section, I contend that CMS would be better served if the scholars who work within it began to more explicitly, more provocatively and more unapologetically integrate a political agenda into the studies that they produce. To contextualize this point, I revisit the case of academic dismissal of Norman Finkelstein from DePaul University.

CMS (at conferences): A reified site of ordained power relations?

CMS – Are we any different?

There is a tendency among CMS scholars to stringently demarcate the research that they generate from the type of scholarship being produced by non-CMS members in the field (Voronov, 2008). This demarcation is predicated on the origins, the pillars and the undergirding conviction of CMS versus those of the mainstream academy (Fournier & Grey, 2000). Dov Eden's (2003) editorial in the *Academy of Management Journal* on his accidental encounter with the CMS community at an Academy of Management Annual Meeting elaborates on this point. As he observed:

> [T]he group comprised many disgruntled members who think the Academy runs a dull, one-sided show that takes an uncritical – almost unthinking – pro-management stand. They stressed their call for "critical" research and writing to get management scholars to question their assumptions and to analyze whose interests they are promoting with their research, at whose expense. Their agenda for a critical approach to management research includes positions on feminism, sexism, and ageism, but it goes far beyond these . . . When they say "critical," these people mean business. They correctly dub their approach "radical"; the word is derived from the Latin *radix,* which means root. It is appropriate because the critters seek to go deep in their quest to expose, understand, and change the underlying causes of managerial and organizational phenomena that others study more superficially.
>
> *(Eden, 2003: 390)*

It is precisely these characteristics that often serve as the basis for identity formation – and for pride – for constituents of the CMS community.

Retaining hierarchical power structures

Although there appear to be ontological and epistemological differences between the CMS and the mainstream communities, several scholars have noted that in some arenas, CMS reflects the same hierarchical power structures of the mainstream of the academy. One site where these dynamics play out most vividly is the academic conference.

Academic conferences have been the subject of critical inquiry from numerous CMS scholars of late (Bell & King, 2010; Ford & Harding, 2008; 2010; Learmonth & Humphreys, 2012; McLaren & Mills, 2008; O'Doherty, 2013; Parker & Weik, 2014; Spicer, 2005). While some observers have noted differences between academic conferences, as defined particularly by geographical boundaries (Learmonth & Humphreys, 2012), there remain many similarities. Andre Spicer's description of the academic conference aptly captures its defining features: 'Indifferent food. Petty controversy of the latest theory. Many glasses of the local liquor. Extramarital affairs. Verbal violence. Arrogant grunts. Closed circles. Dashed hopes. Petty promotionalism. Scholastic policing. Grinding headaches. Boredom. Body pain' (cf. Parker & Weik, 2014: 169). Given that the academic conference is a site that most academics must traverse in the process of circulating scholarly ideas, ascertaining feedback, professional networking and seeking first or new academic appointments, it functions as a location from which to analyze how CMS scholars engage in myriad forms of performativity. In particular, it allows for the understanding of the juxtaposition between what CMS scholarship advocates and how CMS scholars present themselves.

Among the most lucid (and poignant) description of the CMS conference comes from the auto-ethnographic experiences of Emma Bell and Daniel King (2010). As they write:

> Although certain superficial cultural practices distinguish CMS conferences from the mainstream – CMS is no place for the smart suit, well-polished CV or business card (Burrell, 1993) – we experienced the power relations that characterized CMS conferences as more competitive, aggressive and masculine than their mainstream equivalents. While these dynamics were most obvious at the main conference, we observed similar practices at other CMS events, including smaller seminars and tracks at other conferences.
>
> (Bell & King, 2010: 432)

In this account, Bell and King assert that CMS conferences in fact embody the 'competitive, aggressive and masculine' cultures, which CMS academics all too often loathe about their mainstream counterparts. This type of culture is consistent with incidents described by others. For instance, Marianna Fotaki (2013: 1262) recalls a story from one of her informants in a study on the experiences of women academics in the field: '[a]s a postdoctoral fellow and an attendee at an international critically orientated organizational studies conference, Joanna, a North American woman in her early 30s, describes an established middle-aged male professor "demolishing" a female PhD student's work at the conference'. Fotaki goes on to elaborate that '[t]he incident reported occurred during the doctoral consortium where the role of the professor was to provide developmental feedback. When questioned, the senior male professor explained, to her disbelief, that "he was not used to women doing theory"'. This is precisely the type of patterned behaviors that result in CMS reflecting the institutionalized power hierarchies that we often accuse the mainstream constituent of the academy of embodying. CMS scholars must be more self-reflexive of, and more active in deconstructing, such systems of power relations. Indeed, it is virtually impossible to ignore the power dynamics in the following conference scene described by O'Doherty (2013: 6), which is hardly impervious from CMS activities: 'The image of tenured professors swarming around the hotel pool surrounded by an entourage of pin-striped PhD students waving their CVs and publication list'.

Losing the political

In her book *Teaching to Transgress* (1994), bell hooks beautifully advocates for teaching to be used as a mechanism to subvert the systems of oppression that are laden in the communities in which the teaching occurs. Certainly, research has a similar potential. Yet when CMS comes to reflect the mainstream of the academy – and comes to adopt the mainstream's values – its radical potential is forsaken along the path of such things as careerism and game playing (Prasad, in press). Within this purview, research becomes apolitical. I am not trying to negate, here, that many CMS researchers are invested in advancing the good in some way, for instance, in attempting to recognize the voices and the positions of members of marginalized classes and seeking to identify appropriate forms of rectification. Nonetheless, there remains a salient disjuncture in CMS praxis – namely, a rift between theory and practice in CMS scholarship. Indeed, there exist few initiatives that conscientiously confound what phenomena we study (and how we study it) with the lived realities of the disenfranchised in such a way that our research cannot be demarcated from our political statement. CMS scholars are largely situated at a distance from the material conditions of those who suffer, those who are exploited, as a corollary of the organizations and the forms of organizing that prevail and that support contemporary power relations (on the concept of distance, see McCabe, 2015).

CMS research ought to be guided more explicitly by an engagement with the political. Mir and Mir (2002: 105) have articulated this point when commenting on social science research: 'Social science needs to recover its purpose as a tool of intellectual and political transformation and that avant garde scholarship that is bereft of a commitment to transform social institutions represents a failure of purpose, of politics, and of imagination'. One of the symptoms of the 'avant garde scholarship' which Mir and Mir decry is the field's fetishization of theory and theory advancement. Indeed, editors and reviewers (including those inflected by the CMS mandate) at 'career-making' journals will rarely consider publishing a manuscript that does not overtly advance theory, even if the paper covers important CMS phenomena (Tourish, 2011; also see Voronov, 2008). The field, including CMS, is now in a predicament where theory is being built on theory, and yet without any intervening empirical validation. This obsession with theory – not with the material conditions of lived realities – is indeed what Mir and Mir observe as 'a failure of purpose, of politics, and of imagination'. On this point, Paul Adler (2008: 926) states that '[e]ngagement with the practice of management means studying it from close up, not just from our office armchairs; it means working shoulder-to-shoulder with those struggling against oppression and exploitation to how management looks from their vantage point'. While some initiatives, such as the Getting Out workshops sponsored by the CMS division at the Academy of Management Annual Meetings, attempt to bridge the disjuncture in praxis, there remain too few of these endeavors.

Several scholars have prudently noted that political engagement with CMS is essential but must be duly balanced with other considerations (Stookey, 2008; Voronov, 2008). This includes consideration of our own careers – to maintain jobs that allow us to sustain ourselves and thereby permit us to engage with projects for social and political transformation (Stookey, 2008). Requirements for job security (i.e. tenured or continuing appointments) often require research output in the form of publications in the field's most coveted journals. As a result, there must be balance between what Sarah Stookey (2008) calls 'populism' and 'elitism'. However, in striking this balance, we should never lose sight of what our research is intended to achieve.

Reclaiming the political in CMS

The preceding discussion ultimately prompts the question, 'What ought to be done to save CMS from itself?' The short answer, which I am proposing in this chapter, is that CMS studies require a more explicit and a more conscious engagement with the political. This is to say that scholars working within CMS should be aware of the political project that underlies their studies. To contextualize this point, I will revisit a case revolving around a scholar from the humanities and social sciences: Norman Finkelstein.

The case of Norman Finkelstein

Norman Finkelstein was born in 1953 to parents Zacharias and Maryla Finkelstein. Both of his parents were Jewish and victims of the Nazi holocaust, having survived their confinement in several concentration camps and the Warsaw Ghetto. Finkelstein was raised in New York City. Following graduation from high school, he earned his undergraduate degree from Binghamton University in 1974 and subsequently completed his PhD in the Department of Politics at Princeton University in 1988. Perhaps informed by his own personal history – the experiences of his parents living under the brute conditions of the Final Solution in 1930s and 1940s Europe – Finkelstein's research focused on Zionism.

It was during his graduate student days at Princeton that Finkelstein had his first substantive brush with controversy as a consequence of his research pursuits. MIT professor emeritus and public intellectual Noam Chomsky (2002) describes the case in his essay 'The Fate of an Honest Intellectual'. In the process of researching for his dissertation, Finkelstein read Joan Peters' highly acclaimed book (at the time), *From Time Immemorial* (1984). In the book, Peters develops a detailed argument that essentially proclaims Palestinians to be recent immigrants to the land that is present-day Palestine and Israel. The thoroughly cited account served as dangerous ammunition for the Zionist project inasmuch as it offered academic validation to the belief that the region, until only recently, was barren land. This belief simultaneously negated the historical argument for the entitlement of Palestinians to their own lands and contended that the region was *destined* for Jewish settlement. As Chomsky (2002) describes, Finkelstein was perplexed by the claims of the book and elected to scrutinize its sources: '[h]e's [Finkelstein] a very careful student, and he started checking the references – and it turned out that the whole thing was a hoax, it was completely faked: probably it had been put together by some intelligence agency or something like that'. In response to the fraudulent claims found in *From Time Immemorial*, Finkelstein drafted a paper summarizing his findings and circulated it to some 30 scholars in the field (Chomsky, 2002), hoping to receive feedback. As Chomsky (2002) recounts:

> [H]e got back one answer, from me. I told him, yeah, I think it's an interesting topic, but I warned him, if you follow this, you're going to get in trouble – because you're going to expose the American intellectual community as a gang of frauds, and they are not going to like it, and they're going to destroy you. So I said: if you want to do it, go ahead, but be aware of what you're getting into. It's an important issue, it makes a big difference whether you eliminate the moral basis for driving out a population – it's preparing the basis for some real horrors – so a lot of people's lives could be at stake. But your life is at stake too, I told him, because if you pursue this, your career is going to be ruined.

Chomsky could see the proverbial writing on the wall. In debunking the text that reified the most insidious of myths that justify the ongoing systematic mistreatment of Palestinian subjects, Finkelstein became a pariah in his field. Chomsky (2002) recalls how Finkelstein's professors at Princeton refused to read drafts of his work, make appointments to see him or write letters of reference on his behalf; academics in the field applied pressure on him to suspend his line of scholarly inquiry, and editors refused to publish his research. During this time:

> He's [Finkelstein] living in a little apartment somewhere in New York City, and he's a part-time social worker working with teenage drop-outs. Very promising scholar – if he'd done what he was told, he would have gone on and right now he'd be a professor somewhere

at some big university. Instead he's working part-time with disturbed teenaged kids for a couple thousand dollars a year.

Not heeding Chomsky's warning about the backlash that he would encounter, Finkelstein continued with his stream of research. In 2000, Finkelstein published his provocative book, *The Holocaust Industry: Reflections on the Exploitation of Jewish Suffering*. In the book, Finkelstein offers an incisive critique against the Jewish community in the United States that promotes the Israeli agenda. He argued that Holocaust memories are ideologically invoked by certain unscrupulous constituents of the community for various political and monetary gains (for similar observations, see Berkowitz, 1997). *The Holocaust Industry* appeared around the same time that Finkelstein secured a tenure-track position in the Department of Political Science at DePaul University in Chicago, Illinois.

By the time that Finkelstein arrived at DePaul, his research had placed him in the crosshairs of the Israeli lobby in the United States (Klein, 2008–2009). Several commentators on the case have suggested that the initiative to delegitimize and derail Finkelstein's work was led by Harvard Law School chaired professor Alan Dershowitz (Abraham, 2011; Klein, 2008–2009). Abraham (2011: 184–185) recalls the campaign that Dershowitz lodged against Finkelstein:

> [I]n September 2003, Dershowitz began a personal campaign to drive Finkelstein out of the academy (see: Finkelstein, n.d.; Goodman, 2003). In 2004, Dershowitz contacted [DePaul University] President Dennis Holtschneider, attaching a manuscript entitled "Literary McCarthyism," arguing that DePaul should fire Finkelstein. In addition, Dershowitz contacted the chair of DePaul's political science department, Professor Patrick Callahan, as early as 2004, and again three months prior to the political science department's considering Finkelstein's tenure case (see: Dershowitz, 2006). There is also strong circumstantial evidence that Dershowitz sought to contact members of DePaul's Board of Trustees, specifically its chair, Mr. John Simon, about Finkelstein, who Dershowitz labeled "a full-time, malicious defamer" (see Jenner & Bloek, 2004).

In 2007, Finkelstein went up for tenure at DePaul. At the time of his tenure application, Finkelstein had published five books and was widely considered to be a leading commentator on the Palestinian–Israeli conflict. His teaching evaluations were also excellent. These credentials earned his tenure application the support from DePaul's Department of Political Science and the college personnel committee (Klein, 2008–2009). Even with the support that he received from the department and faculty levels, Finkelstein's bid for tenure was ultimately denied by DePaul's University Board on Promotion and Tenure (Cohen, 2007). One observer notes, 'There can be little doubt that Finkelstein was fired because of his criticisms of Israel's human rights violations against the Palestinian people and for his fact-based criticisms of the Israel lobby' (Klein, 2008–2009: 307). Reflecting on his rejection for tenure, Finkelstein commented that he refused to 'indulge in a bout of self-pity' and reflected on his parents' experience in Nazi concentration camps in an effort to contextualize his own circumstances. As he stated, '[t]hey survived . . . I'll survive' (Cohen, 2007).

Norman Finkelstein's case illuminates the importance of pursuing scholarship that socially and politically matters even when ideologically driven elements seek to thwart the research (and the researcher). For instance, in undoing the underlying argument found in *From Time Immemorial* and therein deconstructing the myth that propagates an 'empty' Palestine, Finkelstein's work demands that the Palestinian question be resolved while affording dignity and respect to groups that lived in the region prior to Jewish settlement. His research stands up for disenfranchised Palestinian constituents who increasingly must live under subaltern conditions (Spivak,

1988). His research equally demands that memories of the Holocaust not be exploited for self-interested, ideological objectives. In the process, unfortunately, Finkelstein found himself under attack, which engendered his dismissal from his academic post. Finkelstein could have played it safe and pursued a comfortable (and apolitical) academic career – which so many of us, including those with tenure, routinely do. While he was forewarned by Chomsky that his research would encounter severe hostility, Finkelstein had the courage – and took the necessary risks – to engage the political in the most provocative of ways.

I have sought to use Finkelstein as a source of inspiration to specifically inform my research on the Palestinian–Israeli conflict and, more generally, to posit the political into my scholarship. In a recent article on my experiences in conducting fieldwork in the region, I explicitly reflected on this point:

> Witnessing the conditions of the West Bank firsthand, I have made a concerted effort in framing my interpretation of the ongoing occupation in terms of neo-colonialism, hegemony, and oppression, rather than conforming to the dispassionate vernacular that defines much of the field of organization and management studies. This has meant that I not only unapologetically circulate the stories of the informants, but it further demands that I expose the reprehensible conditions of neo–colonial occupation. I understand that doing so may entail certain consequences to my career; however, I equally recognize that such an act also ensures that I am giving back substantively to those individuals who took the necessary risks to share their stories with me so honestly and openly.
>
> *(Prasad, 2014b: 250)*

In my own small way, I hope that the research that I am pursuing on the topic will make a constructive impact on the subjects and the communities that I have studied. It would be useful for scholars in the field of CMS to look at Finkelstein as a case, *par excellence*, for positing the political into academic inquiry.

The political in organization and management studies

Scholars in the field of organization and management studies have addressed the political in fruitful ways. My example here may seem curious at first as to capturing the question of the political in CMS studies. In 1998, Karen Ashcraft published an article in *Management Communication Quarterly* entitled, 'I Wouldn't Say I'm a *Feminist*, but. . .'. In the article, Ashcraft adopts a narrative perspective to illuminate the discursive tensions that emerge between adopting a *feminist* label and encountering mundane forms of gender-based inequities in organizational and familial settings. The political is located in her reflexive insights – at minimum, it can be found in the ways in which she conflates the personal and the political, thus capturing the spirit of the old feminist adage *the personal is the political*. Indeed, Ashcraft offers a contextualized understanding of how myriad micropractices create, maintain and reify gendered systems of everyday social life, which individuals should be aware of and which should be subject to deconstruction where necessary.

At around the same time that I first read Ashcraft's article, I was beginning to teach my own courses as a sessional instructor. Given my research interests in gender and diversity, I would introduce, to the students enrolled in the courses that I taught, issues pertaining to the specific challenges confronting women and minorities in the workplace. I was habitually taken aback by just how resolutely students would distance themselves from assuming the 'feminist' label, much akin to what Ashcraft describes. Often, women students appeared to more emphatically disassociate themselves from the feminist label than even the men students in class. Inasmuch as the feminist movement seeks to achieve substantive forms of gender egalitarianism, I was somewhat puzzled by the responses that I received from students. As such, in 2010, when I assumed a tenure track appointment at a business school, and I was assigned to teach an undergraduate course on the social organization of work, I elected to use Ashcraft's article as a required reading. Given the nonthreatening and intuitively interesting exposition of the article, I was curious to learn precisely how it would be received by students. It was apparent that her article resonated with members of the class (both women and men), who would explain how they had a new awareness and a different interpretation of how some of their own experiences – or the experiences that they were complicit in creating – represented micropractices of gendering or outright sexism. At the very least, the article prompted many students to engage in objectification and develop a new conscientization on the matter, as Friere articulates (1970).

On a final point, I believe that a conscientious and thorough consideration of the political will contribute to researchers avoiding what I would qualify as bad or socially irresponsible research. When I entered the doctoral program in the autumn of 2006, the *Journal of Organizational Behavior* had just published an article by Kingsley Browne (2006) entitled 'Evolved Sex Differences and Occupational Segregation'. In it, Browne adopted a neo-Darwinian perspective to explain occupational segregation by asserting the saliency of ontological sex differences. I was concerned with the argument presented by Browne inasmuch as it appeared to concurrently negate the social determinants of human behavior and naturalize the assumption that there is a biological basis of social phenomena, in this case why women are underrepresented in certain occupations. One implication that I could foresee emerging from this argument is that occupational segregation along the fault line of sex need not be rectified as it is the corollary of *naturalized* dispositional traits. Given that the article can serve as scholarly support for such a conclusion is, for me, an example of socially irresponsible scholarship *par excellence*. More than two decades ago, Alison Davis-Blake and Jeffrey Pfeffer (1989) predicted some of the outcomes of Browne's position. As they observed, a dispositional-based approach to management poses serious implications, and not least is that it 'tends to excuse individuals from confronting the consequences of their actions and, in particular, tends to allow organizational participants to escape responsibility for the systems they design'. Extending from Davis-Blake and Pfeffer's (1989) astute critique of dispositional research, scholars should consider the negative social implications that their work can potentially realize. Retaining the political at the forefront of CMS scholarship is, I believe, one way that the field moves toward avoiding the creation of bad or socially irresponsible research.

Concluding remarks

This chapter has sought to illustrate how one interpretation of the current status of CMS suggests that it is reflective of the mainstream academy – with all the problematic and hierarchical power systems embedded within it. Indeed, with only some exceptions, we have the same celebrity adulation, wanton careerism and detachment from praxis that is to be found in mainstream circles. Given this, we need to dispel the myth that I have encountered in so many CMS forums over the years – which, admittedly, I have accepted at various points – that we possess more moral or intellectual foresight vis-à-vis members of the academy who adopt a functionalist approach to research because we perceive ourselves as being more reflexive, engaged and conscientious. If my interpretation is to be afforded any veracity, and if the field continues on the trajectory that it has, we will meaningfully lose the ideological convictions that originally catalyzed the emergence of CMS. At that juncture, we will merely pay lip service to the ruins of these convictions. One avenue by which to address this predicament is to (re-)engage the question of the political in CMS scholarship. To do so would mean that scholars pursue impassioned research with ideological aims that are intended to subvert exploitative or otherwise harmful structures in society and to engender positive social change. This means capturing the 'organizational imagination' that Mir and Mir (2002) describe in the quote at the introduction of this chapter. A not so modest but worthy endeavor, I think.

References

Abraham, M. (2011). The question of Palestine and the subversion of academic freedom: DePaul's denial of tenure to Norman G. Finkelstein. *Arab Studies Quarterly*, *33*(3–4): 179–203.

Adler, P. S. (2008). CMS: Resist the three complacencies! *Organization*, *15*(6): 925–926.

Adler, P. S., Forbes, L. C., & Willmott, H. (2007). Critical management studies. In J. P. Walsh & A. P. Brief (Eds.), *Academy of Management Annals, Vol. 1*: 119–179. Mahwah, NJ: Lawrence Erlbaum.

Alvesson, M., Bridgman, T., & Willmott, H. (Eds.), (2009). *The Oxford handbook of critical management studies*. Oxford: Oxford University Press.

Ashcraft, K. L. (1998). 'I wouldn't say I'm a *feminist*, but. . .': Organizational micropractice and gender identity. *Management Communication Quarterly*, *11*(4): 587–597.

Ashcraft, K. L. (2001). Organized dissonance: Feminist bureaucracy as hybrid form. *Academy of Management Journal*, *44*(6): 1301–1322.

Banerjee, S. B. (2000). Whose land is it anyway? National interest, indigenous stakeholders, and colonial discourses: The case of the Jabiluka Uranium Mine. *Organization and Environment*, *13*(1): 3–38.

Banerjee, S. B., & Linstead, S. (2004). Masking subversion: Neocolonial embeddedness in anthropological accounts of indigenous management. *Human Relations*, *57*(2): 221–247.

Bell, E., & King, D. (2010). The elephant in the room: Critical management studies conference as a site of body pedagogics. *Management Learning*, *41*(4): 429–442.

Berkowitz, S. J. (1997). Empathy and the 'Other': Challenging U.S. Jewish ideology. *Communication Studies*, *48*(1): 1–18.

Browne, K. R. (2006). Evolved sex differences and occupational segregation. *Journal of Organizational Behavior*, *27*(2): 143–162.

Chomsky, N. (2002). The fate of an honest intellectual. Retrieved on June 6, 2013 from http://www.chomsky.info/books/power01.htm

Cohen, P. (2007). Outspoken political scientist denied tenure at DePaul. *New York Times* (June 11).

Cox, T., Jr., & Nkomo, S. M. (1990). Invisible men and women: A status report of race as a variable in organizational behavior research. *Journal of Organizational Behavior*, *11*(6): 419–431.

Cunliffe, A. L., Forray, J. M., & Knights, D. (2002). Considering management education: Insights from critical management studies. *Journal of Management Education*, *26*(5): 489–495.

Davis-Blake, A., & Pfeffer, J. (1989). Just a mirage: The search of dispositional effects in organizational research. *Academy of Management Review*, *14*(3): 385–400.

Eden, D. (2003). Critical management studies and the *Academy of Management Journal*: Challenge and counterchallenge. *Academy of Management Journal*, *46*(4): 390–394.

Finkelstein, N. (2000). *The holocaust industry: Reflections on the exploitation of Jewish suffering*. London: Verso.

Ford, J. & Harding, N. (2008). Fear and loathing in Harrogate, or a study of a conference. *Organization*, *15*(2): 233–250.

Ford, J., & Harding, N. (2010). Get back into the kitchen, woman: Management conferences and the making of the female professional worker. *Gender, Work and Organization*, *17*(5): 503–520.

Fotaki, M. (2013). No woman is like a man (in academia): The masculine symbolic order and the unwanted female body. *Organization Studies*, *34*(9): 1251–1275.

Fotaki, M., & Prasad, A. (2014). Social justice interrupted? Values, pedagogy and purpose of business school academics. *Management Learning*, *45*(1): 103–106 [doi: 10.1177/1350507613476617].

Fournier, V., & Grey, C. (2000). At the critical moment: Conditions and prospects for critical management studies. *Human Relations*, *53*(1): 7–32.

Frenkel, S. (2009). Critical reflections on labor process theory, work and management. In M. Alvesson, T. Bridgman & H. Willmott (Eds.), *The Oxford handbook of critical management studies*: 525–535. Oxford: Oxford University Press.

Friere, P. (1970) *Pedagogy of the oppressed.* New York: Continuum International.

Grey, C., & Willmott, H. (Eds.). (2005). *Critical management studies: A reader*. Oxford: Oxford University Press.

hooks, b. (1994). *Teaching to transgress.* New York: Routledge.

Klein, D. (2008–2009). Why is Norman Finkelstein not allowed to teach? *Work & Days, 26/27*(51–54): 307–322.

Learmonth, M., & Humphreys, M. (2012). Autoethnography and academic identity: Glimpsing business school doppelgängers. *Organization, 19*(1): 99–117.

McCabe, D. (2015). The tyranny of distance: Kafka and the problem of distance in bureaucratic organizations. *Organization, 22*(1): 58–77.

McIntosh, P. (1998). White privilege: Unpacking the invisible knapsack. In M. McGoldrick (Ed.), *Re-visioning family therapy: Race, culture, and gender in clinical practice*: 147–152. New York: Guilford Press.

McLaren, P. G., & Mills, A. J. (2008). 'I'd like to thank the academy': An analysis of the awards discourse at the Atlantic Schools of Business Conference. *Canadian Journal of Administrative Sciences, 25*(4): 307–316.

Mir, R., & Mir, A. (2002). The organizational imagination: From paradigm wars to praxis. *Organizational Research Methods, 5*(1): 105–125.

Nkomo, S. M. (1992). The emperor has no clothes: Rewriting 'race into organizations'. *Academy of Management Review, 17*(3): 487–513.

O'Doherty, D. (2013). Conferences: A critical management perspective. In *Critical Management Studies Newsletter* (June).

Parker, M., & Weik, E. (2014). Free spirits? The academic on the aeroplane. *Management Learning, 45*(2): 167–181.

Prasad, A. (2009). Contesting hegemony through genealogy: Foucault and cross cultural management research. *International Journal of Cross Cultural Management, 9*(3): 359–369.

Prasad, A. (2014a). Playing the game and trying not to lose myself: A doctoral student's perspective on the institutional pressures for research output. *Organization, 30*(4): 525–531.

Prasad, A. (2014b). You can't go home again: And other psychoanalytic lessons from crossing a neo-colonial border. *Human Relations, 67*(2): 233–257.

Prasad, A., & Mills, A. J. (Eds.). (2010). Critical management studies and business ethics. *Journal of Business Ethics, 94*(S2).

Rowlinson, M., & Hassard, J. (2011). How come the critters came to be teaching in business schools? Contradictions in the institutionalization of critical management studies. *Organization, 18*(5): 673–689.

Spicer, A. (2005). Conferences. In C. Jones and D. O'Doherty (Eds.), *Organize! Manifestos for the business schools for tomorrow*: 21–27. Abo: Dvalin.

Spivak, G. C. (1988). Can the subaltern speak? In C. Nelson & L. Grossberg (Eds.), *Marxism and the interpretation of culture*: 271–313. Urbana: University of Illinois Press.

Stookey, S. (2008). The future of critical management studies: Populism and elitism. *Organization, 15*(6): 922–924.

Tourish, D. (2011). Journal rankings, academic freedom and performativity: What is, or should be, the future of leadership? *Leadership, 7*(3): 367–381.

Voronov, M. (2008). Toward engaged critical management studies. *Organization, 15*(6): 939–945.

Wolfram Cox, J., LeTrent-Jones, T. G., Voronov, M., & Weir, D. (Eds.). (2009). *Critical management studies at work: Negotiating tensions between theory and practice.* Cheltenham: Edward Elgar.

Part III
Difference, otherness, marginality

6

Fringe benefits? Revisi(ti)ng the relationship between feminism and Critical Management Studies

Karen Lee Ashcraft

Scholars affiliated with Critical Management Studies (CMS) debate many things, but few would contest that concern for power at work distinguishes the enterprise. Most would likely concur that relations of power have long been configured and exercised around human difference – social identities like gender, race and class, for instance. In this respect, feminist scholarship is a natural ally of CMS. We might reasonably expect feminist theory to be among the major resources on which CMS scholars draw and to which they actively contribute. All the more so, since feminist scholars and activists have interrogated the political character of organizing for nearly 50 years and, in that time, have experimented extensively with alternative ways to enact power and participation (see Ferree & Martin, 1995).

Yet contrary to expectation, feminist theory, research, and practice do not figure so prominently in CMS. Indeed, gender and other matters of difference beyond class, as well as feminist accounts of them, remain on the fringes of CMS. In the first half of the chapter, I substantiate this argument, weaving personal experience with quantitative and qualitative evidence in order to characterize with more nuance the current relation between CMS and feminism. The second half demonstrates how feminism's peripheral status is accomplished in routine discursive habits. The chapter concludes by considering implications for how we might go about revising this relation.

Feminism on the fringe: Reviewing the evidence

Several caveats are in order first. Although I refer throughout to 'feminists,' 'feminism' and 'feminist scholarship' as recognizable entities, it is vital to acknowledge that feminist studies, like CMS, comprises multiple and competing philosophies (i.e., feminism*s*). Most of these place gender at the crux of analysis, and this chapter does the same. That said, many feminists urge us to examine gender as it is entangled with other social identities, such as sexuality, race, ethnicity, nation, class, age, ability and religion (e.g., Crenshaw, 1991; Fenstermaker & West, 2002). This call rightly holds us accountable to specify '*which* women and men' or 'what precise sort of gendered bodies,' '*whose* feminism' or 'feminism in the service of what particular interests?' Even as this chapter privileges gender, I do not mean to minimize such imperative questions. Indeed, the sort of criticism I conduct here can be applied to the chapter itself; for, in casting the spotlight on gender,

I effectively streamline the argument *and* commit some of the very sins of exclusion I seek to challenge. For example, the chapter normalizes Western relations and theories of gender and organization. Moreover, the marginalization of gender in CMS pales in comparison to that of race, sexuality, ability and, frankly, most other dimensions of difference.

Two final caveats follow from these observations. The first is that my intent is to stimulate an open, nuanced dialogue about the status of feminism in CMS, *not* to render a definitive portrait of their relation or to depict it as more pressing than other relations of power. Second, readers may note that I employ the term 'Critical Management Studies' to signal both broad and narrow meanings. In the former sense, it refers to a loose community of scholars and texts whose aims regarding organization may be fairly described as critical, radical, progressive, reformist, de- and reconstructive in some way – that is, focused on critique and revision of extant power relations toward enhanced equity or empowerment. Such a broad meaning includes authors and works aligned with these pursuits, even if they are not regularly or formally identified with the CMS moniker. In the narrow sense, CMS refers to a group of scholars and associated texts that not only explicitly identify with the acronym and related professional projects, associations and gatherings but that also support the making and maintenance of a CMS 'canon,' often serving custodial roles. This narrow group of CMS scholars is sometimes referred to as the Manchester School of CMS (see the introductory chapter in this volume by Prasad, Prasad, Mills & Helms Mills). The reflection and critique I undertake in this chapter are mostly addressed to the narrow sense of the term.

As these qualifiers suggest, I make a number of analytical 'slices' in aspiring to deliver a brief yet coherent case. However necessary, these inevitably cut the complexity endemic to the issues at hand. What follows is an admittedly vulnerable depiction. I welcome the chance to restore complexity as other voices join the conversation.

Starting at home: Sifting through personal experience

Because my own experience formed the impetus for this chapter, I begin with related context. For some 20 years, my work has entailed theorizing, researching and teaching about gender and organization. Like many feminist scholars of my generation, my conception of gender has expanded over time to include an array of intertwining differences. Of particular interest to me are the ways that gender, race, class and sexuality function simultaneously to organize our work lives, especially occupational identities and organizational forms.

Crucial to situating my analytic voice is that I do this work from the 'home field' of organizational *communication* studies. I came of age as a scholar when gender and feminism were just beginning to appear on the register of organization studies in both the communication and management disciplines. Several well-intentioned mentors discouraged me from studying 'tangential' topics; one proposed that I begin my career with a more established focus and turn to gender once my reputation was secure. When it came to the marginal status of gender and feminism, I suspect communication and management studies were not so different at that time.

In the communication discipline, however, my timing proved ripe with opportunity to participate in shaping a new area of inquiry. Burgeoning interest became an established arena, such that today, gender and feminist scholarship enjoys a comfortable home in organizational communication studies. In fact, interpretive, critical and feminist approaches are regarded by most as mainstream and by some as even dominating the field. In significant part, this occurred because several leading scholars actively embraced the rise of diverse approaches and institutionalized related conferences, thereby creating the discursive and material conditions wherein audience and legitimacy were readily negotiable. In any case, one would now be hard pressed to support a claim that feminism teeters on the margins of organizational communication; it is at least on par with other perspectives. This is the basis of comparison from which I encountered CMS.

One of the first ironies I observed, which continues to strike a chord in my experience of CMS, is that a field premised on the study of power and the pursuit of emancipation feels some-how ambivalent about gender equality. Not long after I began to engage with CMS, I encoun-tered a conversation that has since been repeated over time and space. This itinerant conversation typically arises among feminist-sympathetic scholars (often, though not always, women), and it concerns the status of gender and feminism across CMS endeavors, from published scholarship to event programming, from professional interaction to after-hours socializing. It was in this con-versation that I learned I am not alone (a) when I notice the many venues that still feature only white male experts, (b) when I am asked to recommend 'good women' worthy of such venues, (c) when I am charged to represent the 'special interest' of gender, (d) when I see brown women predictably tasked with serving up intersectional or postcolonial feminism, (e) when I heed the particular sort of masculine ethos that tends to script intellectual exchange and (f) when I squirm at the sexualized, (hetero)sexist banter that suffuses much social exchange, even as I liberally partake in it. Until hearing others' stories of similar encounters, I did not trust my own. After all, I know that I am complicit in these dynamics. I profit from them, to some extent, and could certainly resist with greater vigor. Of course, most work environments are riddled with similar practices. It may be a sense of hypocrisy that intensifies their sting in CMS: if only we did not claim to do otherwise, to be authorized critics of politics elsewhere, to be gender-conscious, on board with feminism.

For me, this hushed, evolving conversation came to a head with *The Oxford Handbook of Criti-cal Management Studies* (Willmott, Bridgman & Alvesson, 2009), for which I was invited to write *the* chapter on 'gender and diversity.' Even as I am still pleased to be part of the volume, it gnaws at me that such a hefty anthology does not contain a single chapter on feminist theory and only one on difference, charged with lumping together all such matters (i.e., '. . . and diversity'). In the chapter, I made a few veiled observations on this point and otherwise plodded through. None-theless, this was a final straw that prompted a more systematic investigation.

Fit to print: 'Counting' the published evidence

To determine whether the *Handbook* was idiosyncratic in its treatment of feminism, gender and difference – or if perhaps I had missed something by looking for devoted chapters – I first consulted five volumes widely regarded as major CMS works: (1) *Critical Management Studies* (Alvesson & Willmott, 1992); (2) an updated version of the original collection, *Studying Manage-ment Critically* (Alvesson & Willmott, 2003); (3) *Critical Management Studies: A Reader* (Grey & Willmott, 2005); (4) *Power and Organizations* (Clegg, Courpasson & Phillips, 2006); and (5) *The Oxford Handbook of Critical Management Studies* (Willmott, Bridgman & Alvesson, 2009). All but one are edited anthologies; *Power and Organizations* serves as an advanced textbook guide to major concepts and theories informing critical perspectives on power.

The original *CMS* (1992) barely nods to gender or feminism; only the chapter on pleasure seeks to weigh such matters. Change seems afoot in the *Studying* update ten years later, which includes a new chapter on feminism. Read more closely, however, this chapter confirms the peripheral standing of feminist theory in CMS and suggests potential points of alliance to be cultivated. Out of nearly 20 chapters, the *Reader* includes one on sexuality. Across nearly 400 pages of *Power and Organizations*, little if any mention of gender or feminist theory can be found, such that neither warrants an entry in the index. As noted earlier, *The Oxford Handbook* contains a single chapter on gender and diversity out of almost 30. Feminist theory does receive cursory mentions in Chapters 2, 7, 8, 13, 17 and 23. For example, Chapter 7, which theorizes power, is authored by one of the most prolific gender theorists in CMS. Initially, the chapter implies that feminist theory is central to critical conceptions of power, yet goes on to mention feminism only briefly, as it attests to strengths and limitations in Foucauldian analysis. References to feminism in the other listed chapters are as or more perfunctory.

Next, I searched the past decade (2000–2010) of works in six journals known to publish CMS scholarship: (1) *Organization Studies (OS)*, (2) *Human Relations (HR)*, (3) *Organization,* (4) *Culture & Organization,* (5) *Ephemera* and (6) *Tamara*. I sifted through all titles and abstracts and, where still uncertain, the actual text of articles to discern whether they featured gender as a focus and/or feminist theorizing as a perspective. As with the preceding books, my goal was to identify with greater clarity the relative amount of work occupied with gender and feminist issues, as well as any evident patterns in the publication of such work.[1]

Over a 10-year period, articles that emphasized gender accounted for 2–3% of *Organization Studies* content (i.e., 10 articles over 10 years, adjusted for shifting publication rate) and 4–5% of *Human Relations* content (i.e., 25 articles in 10 years, adjusted for higher, steady publication rate). Whereas most of the *OS* articles employ feminist perspectives, few of the *HR* pieces do. Articles in *HR* appear more likely to examine gender phenomena (e.g., wage difference) through other theoretical lenses. Both journals are loosely regarded as 'critical-friendly,' though this is, of course, a contested marker, but they are neither expressly nor exclusively so.

Turning to those journals that are avowedly critical, 6–8% of *Organization* content (i.e., 25 articles in 10 years, adjusted for several irregularities in publication rate) accentuated gender, and most of these works employed feminist perspectives. It is worth noting that the editors during this period were leading feminist scholars in the CMS community. Over the same decade, around 7% of *Culture & Organization* content highlighted gender and feminism; notably, however, this figure includes a special issue devoted to "gender and organization culture." Same with *Tamara* (7–8%), whose higher percentage is heavily influenced by a special issue on "critical feminism," which hosted over half of its total gender/feminist articles for the 10-year period. For *Ephemera*, the figure was back down to 4%, and few of these articles addressed feminist theory per se.

Finally, I combed these journals for symposia about CMS and identified three: (1) the August 2002 issue of *Organization*, (2) the September 2007 issue of *Organization Studies*, and (3) the November 2008 issue of *Organization*. The first presents Mayer Zald's keynote talk from the CMS workshop at the 2001 Academy of Management (AOM) conference, as well as several responses and a rejoinder. Zald's speech briefly mentions feminist theory in reference to critical developments in *other* professional (read 'not business') schools but does not cite feminism as part of the history, present or future of CMS. Only one other response (Adler, 2002) addresses feminist theory, and I return to this later.

The second symposium debates the "cleavage" in CMS between Marxist and poststructuralist orientations. It features all male authors, and none of the commentaries consider gender, much less how feminist theory contributes to the debate. In contrast, the third symposium demonstrates heightened consciousness of difference, motivated by the convener's "particular concerns . . . about class, affluence, locality, masculinity and age, and the way these play out in CMS career paths and practices" (Cooke, 2008: 912). This passage goes on to explain the inclusion of contributors beyond the usual CMS suspects. Some of these authors urge CMS to rectify a tendency to privilege voices that are overwhelmingly white, Western and/or Northern, and masculine. One of the more usual suspects in the exchange (Willmott, 2008) is the only contributor to discuss feminist theory, another instance to which I later return.

At least two other developments are worth noting for their potential influence on these overall findings. One is the rise of a new journal in 1994 – *Gender, Work, and Organization* – which supplies a separate, devoted space for gender and feminist organization and management scholarship. The concentration (ghettoization?) of such theory and research in an isolated, specialized journal merits further dialogue. We may dispute whether this is positive and/or negative, as well as how it reflects institutional and market forces and/or personal and collective preference. Either, both or some other way – the answer does not relieve us of questioning the condition. A second development is a decided shift in feminist theorizing from the GDO (Gender and Diversity in Organizations) to the CMS division of AOM. The history, politics and interaction of both developments are beyond the scope of this chapter, but they surely merit reflection in future dialogue.

Summarizing my findings of frequency and pattern, we can make three broad observations. First, major CMS volumes include gender and/or feminism in highly circumscribed ways or not at all, despite the canonizing function of such works. Second, overall journal coverage appears to hover around 5% for gender, less for feminist theory, albeit with variation among journals (e.g., slightly more in explicitly critical journals, particularly those with feminist editors and/or related special issues). Finally, CMS symposia barely nod to gender and feminist theory, if at all, although the most recent instance suggests rising attention to issues of difference more broadly. It seems safe to say that the marginal status of feminism is more than impression and anecdote. By multiple measures, feminism remains peripheral to the CMS core.

Lest this preliminary conclusion be misconstrued – to imply that a certain higher percentage of feminist inclusion would resolve the need for concern, for instance – I underscore now a point I elaborate later: I am arguing that feminism is among those voices that belong in the bustling hub of CMS conversation and that, despite common claims that it is already well integrated, this is not so. I am *not* arguing that feminism deserves a larger, fixed share of the CMS 'pie.' Such territorial claims evoke a zero-sum model of the CMS enterprise that is counterproductive and precisely what I argue against, as explained in the section on discursive device 2 later in this chapter.

Core and periphery: Hearing the critique

Of course, this is hardly the first criticism of marginality in CMS. As part of my investigation, I gathered reviews of the previously examined major volumes (e.g., Ackroyd, 2004; Costas, 2010; Ferdinand, Muzio & O'Mahoney, 2005; Prasad, 2008), as well as individual articles that primarily reflect upon CMS as a field (e.g., Brewis & Wray-Bliss, 2008; Fournier & Grey, 2000; Spicer, Alvesson & Kärreman, 2009; Wray-Bliss, 2004), much like the collective symposia considered earlier. Read together, these commentaries converge on two forms of exclusion: content and voice.

A first area of critique surrounds what counts in CMS as central topics and theoretical, epistemological and methodological lenses. Prasad (2008), for example, observes that the *Reader* is strikingly devoid of "race, ethnicity, workplace diversity, multiculturalism, (neo-)colonialism, imperialism, Eurocentrism, postcolonial theory, queer theory, subaltern, and so on" (p. 282). Likewise, but more generically, Ferdinand, Muzio and O'Mahoney's (2005) review of *Studying Management Critically* finds that the volume "ends up imposing, against its stated objectives, and artificial closure of criticalness. . . . A broader and more inclusive approach . . . would have provided a better foundation . . ." (pp. 1715–1716).

A second area of critique entails questions of voice or representation – namely, who is represented in and by CMS (i.e., who is it about/for, or what we might call the 'object' voice), and who is hosting these representations (i.e., who does CMS, or the 'subject' voice). Speaking to the former, Ackroyd's (2004) review of *Studying* notes the volume's narrow focus on a small selection of professionals:

What strikes one forcibly about this, of course, is the combination of a very limited purview, and the totalising claims that are made off the back of them. The powers often attributed to what are, after all, very limited sections of the professional and managerial class (to say nothing of the total working population), are extraordinary indeed . . . even taking all of the occupations considered in this book for the UK . . . the ideas of less than 5% of the working population of the country are considered.

(pp. 167–168)

Similarly, Ferdinand, Muzio and O'Mahoney (2005) critique *Studying* for addressing a limited set of profession(al)s and failing to acknowledge this focus as a defining aspect of the CMS project.

Turning to the dimension of subject voice, Prasad (2008) characterizes the *Reader* as a "restricted segment of scholarship – occurring primarily, though certainly not exclusively, within metropolitan Anglophone academic circles" (p. 279). Wray-Bliss (2004) and Brewis and Wray-Bliss (2008) critique the privileging of academic over non-academic voices, arguing for the extension of political consciousness and reflexivity into CMS empirical studies.

Of particular relevance to the present chapter, feminist critiques of CMS have begun to emerge as well, formalizing the roving conversation described earlier. Most of these efforts have so far occurred at conferences. I participated, for example, in a 2005 AOM session on the status of feminist theory in management studies. Although the session emphasized the major academy journals and the GDO division, concerns regarding relations with CMS surfaced as well. A CMS professional development workshop at the 2006 AOM meeting, entitled "The Uneasy Marriage of Feminism and CMS," explored these concerns in depth. The session interrogated gender relations within the CMS community, including specific trends noted earlier: for example, how feminist scholarship tends to take backstage to 'regular' critical scholarship, how it became isolated within specialized venues like *GWO*, how it shifted from GDO to CMS as a primary community of practice, and how CMS 'classics' and 'experts' continue to be aligned with a predictable form of white masculinity. I review these prior critiques because the ensuing analysis follows in their footsteps.

Left to our own discursive devices: How CMS claims feminism and keeps her in her 'rightful' place

Thus far, I have explored the contours of the CMS–feminism relation from three angles: personal experience and observations, relative volume of and patterns in published scholarship and extant criticisms of exclusivity and marginality. My goal has been to substantiate and explicate feminism's peripheral status in CMS. As just noted, feminist critics have begun to raise kindred questions, surfacing the tense relation between feminism and CMS, offering explanations as to why it occurs and recommending ways we might change it. In collaboration with their efforts, I take a somewhat different tack next.

Specifically, I apply my 'home' disciplinary training in communication analytics in order to illuminate *how*, rather than why, the feminism–CMS relation is discursively constituted and maintained as one of periphery to core. As I conducted the analysis for the first half of this chapter, what particularly caught my eye were the repetitive sleights of hand[2] whereby gender and feminism seemed to recede 'naturally' into the wings. Below, I identify five of these. To be clear, I am not interested in claims regarding individual or collective intention; rather, I situate the five 'tricks' as communal discursive practices that many of us (myself included) perpetrate and accept as a matter of reflex. My hope is that exercising an astute eye for these habits can help us to recognize and resist them in the routine moments of their operation and develop discursive countertactics. As you will see, some aspects of the five habits are gender and feminist specific, but many pertain to other forms of exclusion as well, such as those Prasad (2008) just enumerated.

1: Nominal inclusion negated by exclusionary narrations of history

In the discourse of CMS, gender and feminisms are regularly embraced as an integral part of the enterprise. Adler's (2002) response to the Zald symposium begins by quoting the CMS divisional mission: "We aim to foster critiques coming from labor, feminist, anti-racist, ecological . . ." (p. 387). Likewise, Fournier and Grey's (2000) touchstone article cites sexism as a motivating concern and lays claim to feminism as one of several philosophical positions characteristic of CMS. Yet the evolution of CMS charted in the essay treats neither sexism nor feminism as pivotal players. In their introduction, Spicer, Alvesson and Kärreman (2009) identify "feminist organization studies" as one among several key "attempts to question management," which "are now brought together under the banner of CMS" (p. 538). The subsequent history they chart, however, has nothing to do with feminist organization studies.

History is relevant in at least two ways here. The first entails whether gender and feminism are identified as part of the *catalyst* or impetus for the development of CMS, part of its 'conditions of possibility.' Rarely are discussions of how CMS came about linked to gender struggle, feminist activism, or feminist theoretical developments, much less to that surrounding other differences like race. If gender, race or other differences are mentioned, they are typically subsumed into the larger cultural milieu of political unrest that motivated CMS but *not* included as part of the subsequent core theory. Zald (2002), for example, mentions civil rights and antiwar movements as significant stimuli for the surge of CMS in the U.S. context, but he does not include critical race theory or peace studies as significant bodies of theory in CMS; nor does he mention gender and feminism, except for later reference to critical legal studies and other professional schools that faced pressure to make room for feminist critique.

As that suggests, a second way history is relevant involves whether gender and feminism are included in the *classics* or intellectual lineage of CMS. Rarely are feminist ideas, theories and theorists touted as influential in the development of CMS conceptions of power and resistance. For a quick taste of the partial historical narrative of CMS that is reproduced across major volumes, collective symposia and individual commentary articles, visit the Wikipedia entry for CMS, at least at the time of this writing.

2: Feminism framed as a specific subset or parallel track of CMS, which is framed as a general, encompassing enterprise

In the third CMS symposium just described, Willmott (2008) explains:

> Consider, for example, how feminist ideas and modes of organizing have been central to the UN world conferences on women and the Latin American Feminist encuentros and also to NGOs doing popular education around women's human rights . . . In a similar register *but on an even wider terrain*, it is possible to connect key elements in the CMS Domain Statement to the aspirations of the Global Justice Movement which emphasize the importance of self-determination as an alternative to continued dependence upon corporate patronage or marginalization.
>
> *(p. 928; emphasis added)*

99

This excerpt is useful for tracing the subtle ways in which feminism is both celebrated *and* relegated to a secondary seat, the concern of "women's human rights" (presumably narrow terrain because it does not apply to those for whom gender is not a problem – i.e., those privileged by gender?). Other forms of justice, it seems, are more universal in their reach, though presumably they, like feminism, seek to intervene in interdependent relations of advantage and disadvantage that touch us all. Similarly, Spicer, Alvesson and Kärreman (2009) say of Judith Butler's feminist/queer theoretical contributions: "Butler's *particular* concern is how discourses of gender and sexuality are made performative" (p. 544; emphasis added). They go on to apply Butler's performativity to an array of discourses that concern CMS, of which gender is one strand. Jacques (2006) puts the general–specific relation most bluntly: "Within the Academy of Management at the present time, feminist theorizing and critical systems of thought are not in opposition. Rather, the former is a more specific case, the latter a more general case, of the same problem – the discursive neutering of incommensurable difference."

I hasten to spell out what I am *not* claiming here: that gender and feminism should somehow take their rightful, permanent place on the CMS center stage. On the contrary, I *am* claiming that:

1   If we take the emancipatory aims of CMS seriously, we should be wary of a fixed center stage, or 'core';
2   There is no generic approach to power against which feminism is a special interest, unless you begin with the (antifeminist, or at least not so feminist) premise that it is viable to proceed as if there are nongendered subjects;
3   If we really wish to play the what-encompasses-what game (and we should not: it is futile and destructive), gender is as much an omnipresent feature of power relations as any, unless one erroneously reduces gender to the province of those categorized as women (even so, 51% of the population hardly seems 'narrow'?); and
4   The narrative of CMS history that currently masquerades as general or universal (exemplified on Wikipedia) is far from both; it simply fails to concede and interrogate its own partialities.

In sum, it is not that I seek a greater share of fixed territory for gender and feminism, which would succeed only in edging out other vital concerns. As noted earlier, a zero-sum image of the CMS 'pie' promotes a competition that ultimately helps no one. Rather, the problem I see is that foreground and background, core and periphery, general and specific, so rarely shift around, as confirmed by my earlier frequency findings. I do not recall ever reading or hearing that "neo-Marxist labour process theories represent the 'special interest' of class and furnish one narrow lens through which we might understand broader relations of gendered power at work" (she says facetiously). Instead, the steady CMS script depicts such labor process theories as 'our' home, 'our' genesis – as if 'we' share a common origin, as if that is a good or necessary thing. I am advocating, then, for a more genuine 'heterarchy'[3] of interests and influences – the sort we often evoke in our opening characterizations but negate in our expositions.

Elsewhere, Dennis Mumby and I (Ashcraft & Mumby, 2004) elaborate the problems with depicting feminism as derivative of CMS, as playing a specific, supporting role (i.e., the Eve to CMS's Adam). Such depictions punctuate temporal, spatial and intellectual boundaries in a way that ensures feminism will continue to appear subsidiary, 'naturally' second fiddle. These depictions eclipse how feminist organization scholarship responds to a history of its own, which gives it distinctive contours that are broadly, not narrowly useful.

A slight variation on this discursive device highlights another aspect of the general–specific relation. Here, feminism is framed as one of many parallel tracks on the broader path that is CMS.

This notion of CMS as an 'umbrella' for equivalent endeavors is evident, for example, in an earlier quote from Spicer, Alvesson and Kärreman (2009), who cast feminism as one of many "attempts to question management . . . now brought together under the banner of CMS" (p. 538). Under the heading, "In the Name of Whom," Adler (2002) reports his preference for treating "capitalist, market-based form of society" as the object of CMS critique, on behalf of "working people." Other "critters,"[4] he acknowledges, have different trajectories of concern. Feminists, for example, target patriarchy on behalf of gender interests; likewise, environmentalists have their agenda; and the list goes on. On the one hand, this characterization can be read as a commendable recognition that the dominant version of CMS, typically taken as *the* version (as previously demonstrated), is partial, one of many possible renditions. But, we must also ask, are not capitalism and "working people" gendered? Are gendered, capitalist formations not implicated in our relation with the natural environment? As feminist and other theorists have repeatedly pointed out, these are not parallel but intersecting tracks, so thoroughly interdependent that analysis in isolation is misguided. Adler acknowledges that "the debates here . . . are long-standing and difficult" yet critical to setting "common ground and basis for common action" (p. 390).

It is not enough, then, to say that there are specific renditions of CMS, each with its own concerns and classics, as if these can or should remain separate branches of shared emancipatory aims. Feminist and queer theories reveal how gender and sexuality are organizing principles of venerated CMS classics (e.g., Calás & Smircich, 1991), just as critical race and postcolonial theories reveal disturbing race-nation foundations embedded in much feminist theory (e.g., hooks, 1995). To stretch the metaphor, we do well when parallel tracks collide, rather than grant one another wide berth.

3: Appropriation and omission of feminist contributions

Spicer, Alvesson and Kärreman's (2009) rethinking of 'critical performativity' offers five strategies whereby CMS scholars enact social change in their work. The related discussion does not acknowledge the considerable debt owed to feminist (among other) traditions for these strategies; they are instead presented as if discovered by, or the distinctive products of, the CMS community. Yet consider a few of the strategies more closely: an ethic of care, an affirmative epistemological stance that preserves and honors participant voices[5] and pragmatism with particular regard to alternative organizational forms and practices. These commitments have been at the heart of much feminist theory for some time, and feminist theorists have contributed significantly to, and in some cases led, their development (see Fine, 1993). But the discussion mentions feminist praxis only by way of "tempered radicalism," drawing on a specific feminist project within CMS (Meyerson, 2001). As feminism is invoked only to illustrate approaches that pursue modest, incremental change, its deeply oppositional, revolutionary history of intervening in organization theory and practice – which spawned innovative pragmatic hybrids of form and from which CMS stands to learn a great deal – becomes obscured (see Ashcraft, 2006).

Similarly, we might ask why the considerable contributions of feminist theorists to debates surrounding Marxist and poststructuralist perspectives were not considered in the CMS "cleavage" symposium described earlier or why prominent CMS debates regarding discourse and materiality rarely include pertinent developments in feminist theory, such as feminist philosophy on the body and sexual difference, despite repeated calls from feminist CMS scholars to do so.

My argument, then, is that feminist scholarship is often absent from the critical discussions where it is most relevant and that this absence takes at least two forms: failing to adequately *consider* feminist contributions to the pivotal theoretical debates of CMS and failing to sufficiently *credit* feminism when its contributions are appropriated. In this sense, the third discursive device can be seen in part as a consequence of the second: the boundaries of CMS history are routinely drawn in such a way that it is difficult to imagine independent feminist trajectories that inform CMS philosophy and practice; moreover, one does not need to.

4: Selective representations of CMS identity simultaneously minimized as individual preference and authoritatively canonized

In his review of the *Reader*, Prasad (2008) captures an uneasy tension in the way such anthologies tend to be introduced, at once with reassuring openness and insistence on closure. In the *Reader's* case, the editors begin by acknowledging that CMS is a robustly contested terrain, couching the volume as their own "fantasy football team" and apologizing for the inevitable exclusions wrought by personal preference. Soon after, the editors proceed to embrace the contents of the volume as fairly reflecting the core of CMS, and they gesture to the vital institutionalizing function such a volume can perform, enabling the maintenance of healthy academic community.

My own reading of CMS volumes, symposia and commentaries strongly concurs with Prasad's assessment that this tension abounds in CMS discourse. As in the *Reader*, slippage from openness to closure, from provisional to certain, occurs within single paragraphs, much less single essays. The cumulative effect is admittedly disarming: if we openly confess our exclusions, are we really committing them? Do they really require accounting? Prasad (2008) summarizes the problem:

> Hence, in pointing to the exclusions, I do not object to the editors' leaving such issues out of their anthology; I merely draw attention to what the editors think is (un)important. However, it needs to be kept in mind that this anthology is also a part of the editors' declared project to institutionalize CMS – to draw boundaries that would define what is "inside" and/or "outside" this area of research – and, in so doing, to shape the future scholarly contours of this emerging genre. From a scholarly perspective, therefore, it would have been extremely useful had the book provided a cogent explanation as to why the editors believe their version of CMS (with its unique inclusions and exclusions) to be intellectually preferable to other possible versions that might *include* many of the themes and issues excluded from the *Reader*.
>
> (p. 282; original emphasis)

In short, the discursive tactic of individualistic transparency (e.g., "I freely admit this is just my view") supplants critical dialogue about what CMS might in-/exclude and why. It softens and sweetens the otherwise sharp edge of transforming a partial agenda into an institutionalized canon. It helps the medicine go down, so to speak.

5: Dominant CMS masculinity de-/recentered through focus on the plight of knowledge work/ers

As noted earlier, critics have observed that CMS emphasizes a narrow set of occupations and practitioners – specifically, the managerial and professional classes, or what are today often hailed as 'knowledge work/ers.' In their review of *Studying*, Ferdinand, Muzio and O'Mahoney (2005) urge CMS to engage more fully and explicitly with the professions literature, since that appears to be the population of interest. In response, Willmott (2005) clarifies that professionals are not the focus of the CMS project but rather management practices. Since formal managers and nearby professionals are typically tasked with the development and implementation of such practices, it is reasonable to highlight organizational dynamics among these groups. But the formation, maintenance and transformation of professions per se are beyond the central scope of CMS.

Whether or not this is an adequate response for the critique made, it is less so if we lean into the critique. As previous critics have hinted (e.g., Ackroyd, 2004; Ferdinand, Muzio & O'Mahoney, 2005), comparatively privileged knowledge workers – that is, mostly white, Western, Northern, male and/or masculine and heterosexual – are the lead characters of CMS: sometimes as protagonists (e.g., targets, victims and resistors of managerial imperatives), sometimes antagonists (e.g., perpetrators, though often unwitting), and sometimes both – but commanding the spotlight on a regular basis, nonetheless. In the spirit of productive provocation, allow me to climb out further on this limb: I suspect it is no coincidence that this lead character is fashioned in the image of, or at least sympathetic with, the dominant masculine ethos evident within the CMS community – a kind of disgruntled, disaffected, ironic, cynical (often lubricated/medicated) competitive intellectual jousting among relatively privileged professionals. Might this be an instance of scholarly narcissism or homosocial desire (see Roper, 1996)? Whatever the case, the self-proclaimed core of CMS appears rapt in its own reflection yet unable (unwilling?) to see itself – that is, the striking resemblance between the lead characters in our work and the image in the mirror. Or perhaps what is seen in the mirror is a 'universal' human struggle (returning to the second discursive device), when it is anything but.

A poignant example of this discursive habit emerged at a recent workshop I attended designed to showcase new perspectives from a few leading as well as up-and-coming CMS scholars. Three speakers in a row employed a generic vocabulary: "the nature of work and organizations today," "the contemporary workplace," "the situation faced by today's workers" and so forth. But which workers, what sort of work, in what kinds of organizations? Without exception, every example referenced a kind of so-called knowledge worker – management consultants, computer programmers and high-level technicians, to name a few – with no caveat about the particular and relatively privileged set of conditions associated with this work. Are such workers subjected to contemporary regimes of managerial discipline? No doubt. Do they encounter significant struggles worthy of investigation? Of course. Are they generic, representative or even primary – in a word, *the* – victims of contemporary work and organizational power relations? No.

It is not sufficient, therefore, to say that we need not contend with the professions literature because that is not our central project. A more self-reflexive question might be, if that is not our central project, and if the brunt of management practices are born on Other[6] backs, why are these our lead characters? Here, I mean to merge two lines of critique noted earlier. Whereas others have criticized the limited 'objects' or 'subjects' of CMS (i.e., who it is about and who does it, respectively), I seek dialogue about their apparent alignment – the ways in which the subjects allegedly served by CMS reflect the interests of who does it.

Conclusion

This chapter has argued chiefly that, despite claims to the contrary, feminist theory and research remain on the fringes of CMS scholarship and that this problematic relation is routinely remade and obscured through a number of discursive tactics. I analyzed five, though these are by no means exhaustive, and I welcome challenges, revisions and additions to those identified here. In a thoughtful take on an earlier version of this chapter, for instance, one respondent wondered to what extent feminism remains on the margins because many men in CMS continue to experience pressure to stay away from participation in feminist theorizing. Challenges to the legitimacy of their feminism, he observed, can stem from an ironic convergence of discursive forces, as when the policing of rigid masculinity norms becomes allied with guarding who can 'rightfully' do feminist theory. This is precisely the sort of dialogue I hope to provoke with this chapter.

Meanwhile, we could begin to cultivate a number of practices in an effort to redress these habits, in addition to honing our recognition of the moments when they are in play and of our own participation. We could, for example, proceed as if feminism and other (more excluded) perspectives are legitimate origins for CMS, as indeed they are. Many of us came to this work through other philosophical and practical trajectories, on which we can draw to articulate alternative histories of CMS. These could foster a fuller heterarchy of interests, toying with relations of general and specific, foreground and background, core and periphery, in creative, productive and even playful ways.

With more histories in circulation, we would also be better positioned as a community to direct due attention and credit to a wider range of influences on CMS theory and praxis. An example of the sort of multivocal work this could promote can be found in a noteworthy exception to the trends previously analyzed: in their analysis of research ethics, Brewis & Wray-Bliss (2008) consider Critical Theory,[7] feminism and postcolonialism as three major ways that CMS scholars have grappled with ethical dilemmas in the research process. Contrasted with the tendencies of omission and appropriation analyzed in this chapter, this work models what it can look like to honor a diversity of trajectories *and* put them into conversation with one another, rather than holding them apart as viable yet parallel tracks.

Pursuing such intersections is especially crucial to politicizing our own scholarly relations. As it stands, the Manchester School brand of CMS is rarely called to practice self-reflexivity – to see itself through Others' eyes, to explain canonical representations in vulnerable dialogue with those excluded from these depictions, to account for the resemblance of CMS 'objects' and 'subjects' and confront narcissistic desires at work in our own community. For feminist scholars and scholarship in particular, I seek a relation of mutual, sympathetic, productive agitation with the multiple constituents of CMS, wherein the very point of 'our' community is to enable such differences to collide, irritate and generate, among other things, rich comprehension of the intricate layers, tangles and 'workings' of organizational power. Such is how I understand and relate to the project of this book.

Notes

1 The phrase "identify with greater clarity" (as opposed to "resolve with absolute precision") is critical here. I happily concede the interpretive nature of my analytic process and the inevitable ambiguities that accompany it. First, the frequencies and patterns I found reflect a number of choices I made along the way – for example, journal selection, reliance on titles and abstracts, inclusion of only those works that explicitly invoke gender and/or feminism, judgments as to what distinguishes a "mention" from a "focus" (i.e., "intercoder reliability"), exclusion of book reviews and calculations of percentage based on the standard assumption of four or five articles per issue (e.g., 10 articles over 10 years, with 6 issues per year = 10 out of 240–300 articles, or 1 out of every 24–30 = 2–3%). Moreover, I adjusted my findings for journal variations. For example, most of the selected journals are published at different rates (e.g., monthly, bimonthly, quarterly, unevenly); and five out of six altered their publication rate during the decade in question. These changes and irregularities are factored into my calculations. In sum, I am confident that my findings reflect *both* the analytical choices I made *and* a reasonable correspondence with reality. They are, in other words, sufficiently accurate to support my claims *and* open to question. I welcome the productive debate that could follow comparison with similar analyses premised on different assumptions.

2 I do *not* make claims of intent here; I mean only to suggest a kind of "magical disappearance" whose subtlety takes at least some recognizable form and rhythm.

3 Here, I borrow a term from studies of feminist organization (e.g., Iannello, 1992): 'heterarchy' refers to shifting rather than fixed relations of power and priority, center and periphery, foreground and background.

4 For those less familiar, 'critters' is a term of endearment often used by CMS scholars and sometimes others to refer to members of the CMS community.

5   Obviously, many qualitative traditions have shared in the development of this epistemological commitment and related methodological practices.
6   The capitalization is intended here to signal that this generalized 'Other' hinges around many simultaneous forms of 'othering,' such as those of race, ethnicity, nation, gender, sexuality, ability, religion and so on.
7   Capitalization signals reference to the Frankfurt school and affiliated theorists.

References

Ackroyd, S. (2004). Less bourgeois than thou? A critical review of *Studying Management Critically*. *Ephemera*, *4*(2): 165–170.

Adler, P. (2002). Critical in the name of whom and what? *Organization*, *9*(3): 387–395.

Alvesson, M., & Willmott, H. (Eds.). (1992). *Critical management studies*. Newbury Park, CA: Sage.

Alvesson, M., & Willmott, H. (Eds.). (2003). *Studying management critically*. London: Sage.

Ashcraft, K. L. (2006). Feminist bureaucratic control and other adversarial allies: How hybrid organization subverts anti-bureaucratic discourse. *Communication Monographs*, *73*: 55–86.

Ashcraft, K. L., & Mumby, D. K. (2004). *Reworking gender: A feminist communicology of organization*. Thousand Oaks, CA: Sage.

Brewis, J., & Wray-Bliss, E. (2008). Re-searching ethics: Towards a more reflexive critical management studies. *Organization Studies*, *29*(12): 1521–1540.

Calás, M. B., & Smircich, L. (1991). Voicing seduction to silence leadership. *Organization Studies*, *12*: 567–602.

Clegg, S. R., Courpasson, D., & Phillips, N. (2006). *Power and organizations*. London: Sage.

Cooke, B. (2008). If Critical Management Studies is your problem . . . *Organization*, *15*(6): 912–914.

Costas, J. (2010). Book review: Unveiling the masks: Critical management studies: *The Oxford Handbook of Critical Management Studies*. *Organization*, *17*(6): 789–792.

Crenshaw, K. (1991). Mapping the margins: Intersectionality, identity politics, and violence against women of color. *Stanford Law Review*, *43*: 1241–1299.

Fenstermaker, S., & West, C. (Eds.). (2002). *Doing gender, doing difference: Inequality, power and institutional change*. New York: Routledge.

Ferdinand, J., Muzio, D., & O'Mahoney, J. (2005). Book review: Muddling with CMS: A reply. *Organization Studies*, *26*(11): 1714–1716.

Ferree, M. M., & Martin, P. (Eds.). (1995). *Feminist organizations: Harvest of the new women's movement*. Philadelphia: Temple University Press.

Fine, M. (1993). New voices in organizational communication: A feminist commentary and critique. In S. Bowen & N. Wyatt (Eds.), *Transforming visions: Feminist critiques in communication studies*: 125–166. Cresskill, NJ: Hampton Press.

Fournier, V., & Grey, C. (2000). At the critical moment: Conditions and prospects for critical management studies. *Human Relations*, *53*(1): 7–32.

Grey, C., & Willmott, H. (Eds.). (2005). *Critical management studies: A reader*. Oxford: Oxford University Press.

hooks, b. (1995). Black women: Shaping feminist theory. In B. Guy-Sheftall (Ed.), *Words of fire: An anthology of African-American feminist thought*: 270–282. New York: New Press.

Iannello, K. P. (1992). *Decisions without hierarchy: Feminist interventions in organizational theory and practice*. London: Routledge.

Jacques, R. S. (2006). Twelve-stepping Sid & Nancy: Never mind the bollocks, here's GDO & CMS. Paper presented at the Academy of Management, quotation from the CMS PDW proposal, "The uneasy marriage of feminism and CMS."

Meyerson, D. E. (2001). *Tempered radicals: How people use difference to inspire change at work*. Boston: Harvard Business School Press.

Prasad, A. (2008). Review of *Critical management studies: A reader*. *Academy of Management Review* (January): 278–283.

Roper, M. (1996). "Seduction and succession": Circuits of homosocial desire in management. In D. Collinson & J. Hearn (Eds.), *Men as managers, managers as men*: 210–226. Thousand Oaks, CA: Sage.

Spicer, A., Alvesson, M., & Kärreman, D. (2009). Critical performativity: The unfinished business of critical management studies. *Human Relations*, *62*(4): 537–560.

Willmott, H. (2005). Muddling with CMS: Response to special book review of *Studying Management Critically*. *Organization Studies*, *26*(11): 1711–1720.

Willmott, H. (2008). Critical management and global justice. *Organization, 15*(6): 927–931.

Willmott, H., Bridgman, T., & Alvesson, M. (Eds.). (2009). *The Oxford handbook of critical management studies.* Oxford: Oxford University Press.

Wray-Bliss, E. (2004). A right to respond? Monopolisation of 'voice' in CMS. *Ephemera, 4*(2): 101–120.

Zald, M. N. (2002). Spinning disciplines: Critical management studies in the context of the transformation of management education. *Organization, 9*(3): 365–385.

7

Humility and the challenge to decolonize the "critical" in Critical Management Studies

Janet L. Borgerson

In an essay written for *Al Jazeera* entitled, "Can Non-Europeans Think?," U.S.-based Iranian scholar Hamid Dabashi explored the possibility that, even as popular lists of important contemporary philosophers continue to include only European and U.S. names, the so-called West is slowly being forced to surrender the parochial view that the resources of Western versions of reason and the interpretative depth of the related vision are enough to make sense of the entire world (Dabashi, 2013). In other words, Dabashi's discussion exposes a *geography of reason*. As those who are attempting to "shift" this geography have shown, attributed and apparent distinctions between global hemispheres grant legitimacies to some societies, rather than others, as well as within societies (e.g., Comaroff, 2011; Gordon, 2006; Henry, 2005; Mignolo, 2013). Mapping geographies of reason offers insight into the particularities, potentialities and limitations of – as well as bias against – epistemic and logical forms that emerge from specific locations, eras and groups of people. Franz Fanon's observation that "when a black man enters the room it is as though reason walks out" provides a devastating example (Gordon, 1995a).

Attending to the geography of reason that animates Critical Management Studies (CMS) may reorient assumptions around the apparent neutrality of familiar theory (e.g., Connell, 2007) or genealogies of theory. Moreover, engaging theorists who are specifically attempting to "shift the geography of reason" may allow us to confront essentializing Eurocentrism that creates conceptual and theoretical worlds that fail to reflect upon and alter their own universalizing and generalizing tendencies – in effect, ironically distorting the potential of critical work.

This chapter adds to a stream of analytical research, interrogating the notion that relevant manifestations of the "critical" emerging from European intellectual traditions are capable of decolonizing the "critical" in CMS and arguing that approaching CMS via postcolonial conceptions can help shift the CMS geography of reason. I follow feminist critical theorist Drucilla Cornell's call to attend to black philosophies of existence, including the work of philosopher Lewis Gordon, regarding possibilities for decolonizing the "critical" in critical theory, which I argue has implications for Critical Management Studies. I develop Gordon's contributions, particularly in relation to a fundamental position for *humility* that Cornell finds in Gordon's thought.

I have drawn upon Gordon's work for over a decade, bringing his critical race theory and existential phenomenological reworkings of W.E.B. Du Bois, Frantz Fanon and Jean-Paul Sartre to bear on research in organization studies, critical marketing and business ethics (Borgerson, 2011;

Borgerson & Rehn, 2004; Borgerson & Schroeder, 2008). This research has included analyses of the "packaging of paradise" (Schroeder & Borgerson, 2012). "Packaging paradise" describes the ways in which the historical archive of marketing representations of Hawaii and Hawaii's indigenous people reveals the transformation of Hawaii and Hawaiian natives into geographical and human "exotic others," subordinated by advertising images' epistemic and ontological closures and consumed as "difference" by white Western viewers (Borgerson & Schroeder, 1997, 2002). Mobilizing Gordon's understandings of concepts such as "bad faith," "anonymity" and "typicality" helps us comprehend the ways in which these closures happen (Gordon, 1995a, 1995b, 1997, 2000).

In pursuing a path to shift the CMS geography of reason, I discuss Dabashi's essay on postcolonial realism and film that further contests notions around a universal Western aesthetic engagement. Dabashi emphasizes that the "decisive confrontation" with modern technological culture will take place not in the realm of art, as philosopher Martin Heidegger argued, but in the lived realities of the colonized (Dabashi, 2004). To further comprehend a CMS geography of reason, I explore an influential and oft cited rendition of the development of CMS (e.g., Alvesson, 2008), which included the call to avoid so-called performative research (Fournier & Grey, 2000). My own work on related understandings of performativity from philosopher Judith Butler suggests that this early directive was theoretically and practically shortsighted, yet resulted in more recent suggestions to think the performative "critically" (Spicer, Alvesson, & Kärreman, 2009; Borgerson, 2005; Butler, 2010), with the potential to impact management and organization practices, as well as aspects of management pedagogy, positively (Alder, 2002; Gabriel, 2009; Zald, 2002).

Accepting the contributions of black philosophies of existence

Critical intentions will deliver and reveal nothing beyond the colonized other if theory, as mobilized by CMS, fails to open up to the other's value creation role. In the context of what Gordon conceives of as *disciplinary decadence*, scholarly disciplines may become idealized, reified or cut off from the work and existence of others (Gordon, 2006). Some researchers in CMS have noted the weaknesses in their field created by Eurocentric perspectives (Jack & Westwood, 2006; Jack, Westwood, Srinivas & Sardar, 2011; Long & Mills, 2008; Mills & Mills, 1999; Peruvemba, 2001; for review see Prasad, 2012). *Eurocentrism* relates to theoretical lapses that include the universalizing of European reason, aesthetics and affect, as well as a tendency to generalize related individual human and societal concerns, desires and goals. Cornell (2008) points out that "it is not European ideas and culture that are being resisted in the battle against the dominance of Eurocentrism. Instead, it is a resistance against the attempt to turn an idealized Europe into the only cultural reality" (p. 132). Evading responsibility for the implications, outcomes and arrogance of universalizing – yet at the same time parochial – aspects of scholarly theory and attendant potential actions, continues the effortless colonizing of the very entities, environments and research subjects that CMS has sought to engage. As the colonizing agent takes up a sovereign perspective, or appropriates the God's-eye view of theory, what hope do the colonized have to be able to say, "Here I am in the world with you"?

CMS scholars should be interested, then, when Cornell (2008) argues that the critical in critical theory might be "decolonized" by attending to the challenge of black philosophies of existence (p. 105). Black philosophies of existence and related notions of Africana phenomenology make the moment of transcendental reflection, or reflection upon the conditions of possible experience, "the confrontation with the searing force of racism" and the "problem of blackness" rather, Cornell (2008) writes, "than in Husserl . . . the crisis of European reason" (p. 106). Gordon writes, "Whereas for Husserl there was a nightmare of disintegrated reason, for Fanon there was the nightmare of racist reason itself" (1995b: 8). This is a kind of reason that, in its relation to humanity, refuses human status and value creation to the racially othered.

Racist essentialism in critical work appears as a denial of sociality, even as critical work asserts superiority, as critically, socially concerned and aware. Rather than accepting the Other as part of who the Self becomes, there is an arrogance, a refusal to accept humbly one's place among others and a denial of the Other's crucial role in the existence and meaning of the Self. Denials of the Other's contribution to the Self and to intersubjective existence mark the need for a profound transformation of understanding and indeed a move from a substance-based to a relational metaphysics (Gordon, 2003). Mapping geographies of reason often unveils a narcissistic focus and fantasies of Self generation: moreover, an inconsequential, unrecognized or replaceable Other results in a lack of meaningful engagement or ethical context. Here, "ethical" invokes *not* moral notions of "should" or good but rather the notion of ethical as it pertains to modes of relation, cocreation, intersubjectivity and sociality. An essentialized, substance-based understanding of the Self tends to deny cocreative and, in this sense, ethical relations.

The Hawaii example mentioned earlier highlights contexts of image and meaning making. In Hawaii-focused marketing communications, conflicts emerged between picturing human potential and contingency and the contrasting oppressive repercussions of designating and picturing essentialized, or naturalized, qualities that carry negative meanings or designation of value in the context of racism. Gordon's work helps make sense of such instances: subordinating not only pictured individuals but the entire geographical location of the fiftieth state invoked a racializing, subordinating discourse that delivered up exotic islands and "natives" alike for marketing and consumption (Borgerson, 2011; Schroeder & Borgerson, 2012). Attending to designations of racial difference, Gordon (1995a) writes:

> [E]ventually, blackness and whiteness take on certain meanings that apply to certain groups of people in such a way that makes it difficult not to think of those people without certain affectively charged associations. Their blackness and their whiteness become regarded, by people who take their associations too seriously, as their essential features, as, in fact, material features of their being.
>
> *(p. 95)*

Bringing contingency into understandings of human existence disrupts essentialized associations and epistemological closures around possibility and potential that are particularly active in racist contexts. This is important as determining apparent differences from others becomes "a matter of evaluative determinations."

Gordon notes that from a Sartrean perspective we seek our own identity, our sense of Self, by way of negating, or "freezing," that of Others. An attempt to escape the freedom of human existence, crystallized in Sartre's analysis of bad faith, emerges in a solidifying of the other's nature, a completing of the Other's being, that makes the Other and sometimes Oneself into an object. Processes of epistemic and ontological closures – in other words, placing narcissistic limits around possibilities of knowing and being – lead to the belief that others are known or understood completely. This assumption of knowledge denies the other status as a human being – in that a human being escapes from complete and final definition – mutes the cocreative role of others in our lives and erases the possibility for human relationships (Borgerson, 2011: 230).

Indeed, these closures tend toward creation of a recognizable identity while knowing next to nothing "about the typical Other beyond her or his typicality" (Gordon, 1997: 81). Knowing the other as typical refers to an abstracting and condensing of characteristics that create a familiar identity or pattern for beings and occurrences of a kind. A further concern arises around a phenomenon of absence through presence, or appearing to be absent, or invisible, even when present, that is manifested as an *anonymity* through which anyone might stand in for anyone else of a certain kind or type (Gordon, 1997: 80).

In Gordon's reworking of bad faith, Cornell (2008) finds a way to begin thinking "of what kind of struggle we must take on if we are to actually change forms of oppression that are so pervasive that they almost become unnoticeable and, due to their pervasiveness, demand radical transformation of all of us in our day-to-day activities and the depth of our being" (p. 118). Gordon argues for a critical ontological role for the concept of bad faith, allowing for understandings of "human *beings* in the face of the rejection of human *nature* and a reductive view of history" (1995a: 136). Gordon attends to Sartre's denial "that there is a transcendent intersubjectivity: a beyond that is presupposed" (Cornell, 2008: 128), and Cornell attributes to Gordon a reintegrating of intersubjectivity as a basis for the possibility of experience in the world.

These are key points for Cornell (2008): Gordon's analysis of the "beyond of intersubjectivity" that Sartre apparently left behind and the reworking of phenomenological existentialism – "an exploration of 'the implications and the possibility of studying the phenomenon of beings that are capable of questioning their ways of being'" (p. 126, citing Gordon, 2000: 119). "Questioning their ways of being" here might mean accepting or denying various situations that make possible the world in which we live. Gordon places bad faith into an intersubjective context, or a context of sociality, wherein being in bad faith fails to acknowledge this context – that is, the reality of others and of all that is not Self, and their cocreation of our existence. In short, in a narcissistic gesture, bad faith denies the foundational context of sociality, reducing the role of others to cartoonish fantasies.

Such a denial demonstrates an arrogated perspective that veils the contribution of others and demonstrates a lack of *humility*. Cornell (2008) asserts that Gordon's work entails humility, or finding oneself "just another human being who must come to terms with other people as capable of transforming the world in accordance with their own perspective" (p. 129). Moreover, Gordon compels us to remain awake to the irreplaceability of the human and thus the irreplaceability of the experience of others in the world (Borgerson, 2008; Gordon, 2003). Such an approach inspires us to recognize "the ways in which we are enabled to act by a sociality that is beyond us" (Cornell, 2008: 129). Gordon's contribution allows us to highlight the roles that others play in our coming into being in the world. Moreover, there is an emphasis on our daily life, our actions and engagements with others, which include research and work, enabled by intersubjective contexts. In this sense, then, the conditions of intersubjectivity and the ethical relation enact human engagements that necessitate the collapse of the colonial project and its debilitating, devastating practices and outcomes.

What this analysis suggests is that the ethical is misappropriated through colonialism and the affiliated inhuman conditions and attitudes that continue to create contexts of being and knowing: "the very opening of the ethical will have to be reasserted against its fundamental violation by colonial conditions and obviously implicit racism" (Cornell, 2008: 107). In other words, with humility we might witness sociality as intrinsic to our human being. Where previously was anonymity, nothing, we find a point of view and a transformer of value and the world. The incompleteness, irreplaceability, and openness of the human thus appear in the black, in the non-European, in the colonized, in a position made to appear through struggle to become the Other and a limit in an ethical relation.

Cornell (2008) reminds us that in black philosophies of existence, reinterpretation of phenomenological "perspectives," black persons see "themselves being looked at but also develop a second sight where they, too, can envision how the whites are seeing them as less than human" (p. 105). To be positioned as white in these circumstances is also a denial of humanity. For both, then, there is the question of not only who or what one *is* but, as Gordon writes in his focus on liberation, "what we *ought* to become" (Cornell, 2008: 107). In this, intersubjectivity and sociality are foundational.

As might be expected – and regardless of Eurocentric narcissistic oversight – marginalized, "peripheral," and colonized populations have voiced critical responses to encounters with Western reason (Smith, 2012), which would include experiences with "management." Management practices and techniques manifested in conjunction with colonialist strategies of bureaucracy and audit that played out in Britain's central role in European colonial expansion (Connell, 2007: 45–47; Disks, 2006; Nechtman, 2010) and further as part of the East India Company – arguably one of the earliest organizations engaged in management rooted in colonialist practice – in the development of organizational structures (Litvin, 2004; Sen, 1998; Wild, 1999). These populations' often invisible and inaudible – but also simply unperceived, unread and uncited – contributions provide the conditions of possibility for Critical Management Studies and serve as provocations for decolonizing the "critical" in CMS. Does CMS perceive, acknowledge and abide by the value-creating role of the Other in a world that emerges through cocreated social existence? Can the challenge to decolonize the critical in CMS inspire an attitude of humility as, rather than move to appropriation, we accept the Other's value as an epistemological and ontological limit?

Postcolonial realism: Remapping the "decisive confrontation"

During a recent visit to a university in Southern Thailand, I was asked to lead a conference workshop on publishing in international journals. I faced my Thai colleagues and the Thai graduate students who had come from around Southern Thailand to participate in the day's events and felt the geography of reason's full force. Some of the faculty present had returned to Thailand after earning PhD degrees in the U.K.: they had published articles that I highly valued in English language journals, yet their expertise was not being highlighted. A short seminar earlier in the day made clear that most of the university's PhD students were far from fluent in English. Nevertheless, all successful careers were said to depend upon writing dissertations in English, as well as publishing in relentlessly ranked journals from the Euro-American world, even while the lack of viable English language support networks seemed insurmountable. These are impossible demands, and the impossibility becomes clearer, there, in the context of the realities of these geopolitical locations.

A program of unveiling realities as lived has seemed important particularly in cases to which attention might be brought in order to dwell with those whose invisibility maintains suffering and ossifies their future possibilities. Drawing upon an illustrative example of contesting a Eurocentrist perspective with the resources of postcolonial realism does offer insights into the ways in which CMS might shift its "geography of reason." Dabashi's (2004) attention to philosopher Martin Heidegger in this section does not intend to suggest that Heidegger stands in for all instances of the colonizing "critical." However, acting upon the realities of intersubjectivity – as well as valuing often denied points of view, agencies and thought in the world – suggests a way to address the continued colonizing potential of the "critical" in CMS.

Critical Realism as a theoretical approach may contest both positivist and purely subjectivist approaches to questions of what we can know and what is, as well as emphasize an understanding of social relations and structures and a "transformational conception of social activity" (Bhaskar, 2011: 2–3). Critical Realist approaches to management and organization studies have addressed ontological assumptions that maintain an unsustainable capture of reality, or the Real (Contu & Willmott, 2005). Attempts to remain reflective upon understandings of existence – and the apparent foundations of that which is said to exist – offer a challenge in coherent management research, whereas realism in film has long been treasured and censured as a way of showing conditions that might otherwise remain hidden, sometimes intentionally.

For example, in an essay on Iranian cinema and technological modernity, Dabashi argues that realism in cinema offers access to change, and Dabashi illustrates this. He traces transformation in Iranian filmmaker Mohsen Makhmalbaf from self-colonizing Islamist ideologue to one who attends to *realities* "that in both their enduring miseries and their hope of redemption have the ring of truth that no ideological movement in contemporary Iran has addressed, let alone changed" (Dabashi, 2004: 142). In lieu of empty, abstract platitudes or mystification, attention to the realities of domestic conditions, daily experiences and the individual lives of colonial subjects provides the impetus for "real" art.

As theoretical orientation, Dabashi takes the "colonized perspective" on Heidegger's understanding of technology as dehumanizing. Dabashi places colonized subjects "where we are, at the receiving end of the project, at the colonial site of Capitalist Modernity, at the tropical outposts of the polar centers of the European Enlightenment" (Dabashi, 2004: 118). Here the relevance of Self/Other relations, particularly in the form of colonizer and colonized, comes to the fore, where colonizing is understood as a Self-raising/Other-lowering project, and the European particular becomes the reigning global universal. "Colonialism *is* the essence of technology," Dabashi argues, the site of the human reduced to use value. He writes, "For us, technology did not come from the Greek *technê* but out of the long and extended barrels of European vernacular guns" (p. 117). Dabashi rejects Heidegger's Eurocentric notion that "essential reflection" upon technology and "decisive confrontation" with it must happen in a realm of *art* (p. 119). The decisive confrontation takes place in "the sub-Saharan continents of colonial catastrophes that Technological Modernity entailed" (p. 119).

Drawing upon these insights, Dabashi marks Makhmalbaf's transformation – the "exorcising of his demons" through film – from "Manichean determinism in the bifurcation of Good and Evil" to realism, as crucial to creating his later, truly great work (Dabashi, 2004: 132). Dabashi sees this transformation as important not simply because Makhmalbaf made better movies but because Islamism as a form of resistance to colonialism and technological modernity "is itself the most effective form of self-colonization" (p. 122). In other words, "an anti-colonial ideology *is* a colonial ideology" (p. 123), which sheds doubt on Islamism as an effective source of resistance to subordination and other undermining processes and practices. Focusing on "a solid material base in Iranian realities that defies the counter/colonial constitution of all revolutionary ideologies," Makhmalbaf brings out the true "danger" of the (post-)colonial artist, as he moves away from "mystical" abstractions and the "psychopathological impotence to face the real," especially in explicating the lives of women after the revolution (Dabashi, 2004: 141). Dabashi argues that the theorized exclusive European access to various aesthetic ideals kept aspects such as the *sublime* at a distance. Art at the site of (post-)colonial contexts raised the possibility of "creative revolt." In short, Dabashi calls for a geographical shift in understandings of the decisive confrontation. "Europe, except in its moments of crisis, is *not* that site; the serious site can only be the colonial realm, its categorical denial, its civilizational Other" (p. 119). The challenge put forward here requires denizens of Eurocentrism to become aware of denials, exclusions and convenient but delusional universalizing.

Echoing the phenomenological insights more generally, Gordon (1995b) has argued that it is crucial to pose "the question of the questioner: the very investigation is possible only by virtue of a being that can not only question its own being, but may also deny its involvement in the questioning" (p. 16). The problem of bad faith, or fleeing from the conditions of involvement, suggests the danger in the continued failure in CMS to take on the cocreative responsibility and task of decolonizing the critical. It may be interesting, then, to follow a narrative of Critical

Management Studies' contextualized emergence from the United Kingdom's soil and soul, allowing reflection upon aspects of the geography of reason. As we shall see in the next section, there has been a call for a move from criticism of, and disdain for, "performative intent" to practices of implementation in line with potential alternatives and disruptions that have managerial implications – or, in other words, a move toward the possibility that CMS would help create better management, less devastating work environments and a more just world.

Becoming CMS

Management always has been as much a colonialist practice as anything else, and perhaps it should not have taken the New Right in the U.K. to reveal this aspect to, and trigger response from, critically minded U.K. business academics, even if some were newly transferring their attentions from other social science disciplines. In an early influential reflection on the development of CMS, Valerie Fournier and Chris Grey (2000) outline the conditions within the U.K. that made an emergence of CMS possible. They argued that shifting management styles and techniques demonstrated varying contexts and perspectives that went beyond singular, or universal, approaches in management science. That CMS was born from such anti-universalizing insights bodes well for a decolonizing project; however, the conditions of emergence are not the same as the research approaches and perspectives that then engaged the CMS field: indeed, one might note the idealization and universalizing of the CMS project itself in the years that followed.

Articulating conditions of possibility for CMS, Fournier and Grey argued that management gained new status in the U.K. in the 1990s, legitimated upon ontological, epistemological and moral grounds relevant to a particular situatedness of that era's social and political shifts. Managers and managerialization attempted to bring forth the "real world," offer "input knowledge" and intervene for "greater justice, public accountability, democracy and quality in public services" (Fournier and Grey, 2000: 11). The resulting changes, welcomed by some, made the non-natural nature of administrative techniques newly visible. Beyond infamous influences of U.S. management practices, the authors argue that a further stage of management empowerment flowed from Japan, demonstrating new and sometimes contradictory fashions; indicating the "fragmented and unstable" field of management science; and providing clear targets for critical study. The evident changeability and lack of coherence and confidence in the future of management science "makes managers and management researchers if not receptive to critique then at least mindful of the deficiencies of their own knowledge base" (Fournier and Grey, 2000: 13).

CMS arose strongly in the U.K. based upon an apparently amenable critical and intellectual tradition lacking, for example, in the U.S., which according to the authors still exhibits the impact of positivism, McCarthyism, and the Cold War. In the U.S., many social science disciplines, as well as humanities disciplines, such as philosophy, continue to rally around positivist certainty with a concomitant disavowal of phenomenology and its suspect heritage (for a related discussion regarding U.S. philosophy's continental and analytical divide, see Maldonado-Torres, 2006). The U.K. apparently experienced a "fragmentation of the social sciences," revealing competing perspectives and an influential position for postmodernism and "a recognition of the socially constructed nature of social arrangements" (pp. 13–14). Such non-natural "social arrangements" clearly included instantiations of management and organization practices and principles.

Fournier and Grey (2000) argue that social scientists, whose departments and research opportunities were facing financial difficulties, appeared most ready to take advantage of the pragmatic and theoretical opportunities brought about by the advancement of U.K. university business schools. This category of migrants included many who became engaged with CMS. The authors do not mention that humanities departments also were experiencing fund cutting and departmental closings – and these displaced academics would have had similar impetus to find another university location for research and funding. Perhaps, at least initially, methodologies from these fields seemed less suited to research and publication based in business schools. However, some in humanities disciplines may have underestimated a compelling prospect given the number of social science and business-trained academics who have gone on to utilize philosophical thought and theory, if not methodologies, from humanities traditions to make sense of diverse contexts of management studies (See e.g., Czarniawska & Höpfl, 2002; Guillet de Monthoux, 1993; Jones, 2003; Karamali, 2007; Lim, 2007; O'Doherty, 2007; De Cock & Böhm, 2007; Rehn & Sköld, 2012; Sköld, 2010). Whether philosophers and literary theorists generally felt less at home or simply less attracted to business school environments is uncertain. Nevertheless, patterns of publication have shown the flow of a number of related theoretical and scholarly resources, including existential phenomenology, poststructural philosophy, and postcolonial studies, into business school disciplines.

Anti-performative research or perlocutionary performativity?

In their genealogy, Fournier and Grey (2000) consider what is meant by "critical," discerning "an anti-performative stance and a commitment to (some version of) denaturalization" (p. 8). They attend as well to the politics of CMS, which consists – in their rendering – of two positions, neo-Marxism and poststructuralism. It is worth noting that the discussion reflects a postmodern poststructuralism, which can be understood to have "an ideological framework against certain narratives" that goes beyond poststructural analysis per se (Gordon, 2006: 48). In short, the tools and insights available from poststructural analysis do not necessitate the attending postmodern ideologies, for example, regarding grand narratives. An analysis of this distinction in relation to CMS research could prove fruitful but will not be undertaken here. However, this rendering of the "politics" of CMS invokes ideologies that may obscure the decolonized potentials of the critical. For example, a decolonized "critical" may take issue with a commitment to an "anti-performative stance" (see interview with Gordon, this chapter).

Performative research is perceived as a key problem for CMS. "Performative research" indicates research that points out and develops implications that support performance of productive management. In their rendering, "performativity" marks efficiency with an economic motive that "subordinates knowledge and truth" (Fournier & Grey, 2000: 17). In other words, even if undertaken with concerns critical of mainstream business goals, performative research could be considered complicit with managerial intent, demonstrating the subordination of learning and research to other goals. In turn, the anti-performativity of the "critical" guides CMS observation, analysis and theorizing in what otherwise might be a field of unquestioning striving for, or achieving, aims unexamined by any but the most limited of economic sense.

Oddly, this is a rendering of the "performative" that lacks a poststructural lens: a brief discussion of this matter here will aid us in the following section on care. In line with a poststructural understanding, "performativity" describes manifestations of iterative gestures with the potential to produce diversities of identity, subjectivity and possibility (e.g., Borgerson, 2005; Butler, 1993). The kind of Austinian performative most readily adaptable to CMS research is *perlocutionary*. The perlocutionary performative "characterizes those utterances from which effects follow only when certain other kinds of conditions are in place" (Butler 2010: 147). In other words, "the perlocution implies risk, wager, and the possibility of having an effect, but without any strong notion of probability or any possible version of necessity" (p. 151). This mapping marks incompleteness and the potential for alteration, including shifts that contribute to processes unfolding without fixed, essential, or "natural" ends. Perhaps engaging with this version of the performative would alter the judgment the authors make regarding "performative research" in the sense that performativity marks not a matter of ways in which certain outcomes and insights can be operationalized but rather a further opportunity to engage the power relations embedded in declarations of the natural and essential that lead to management techniques and practices that further oppression and inequality. Perlocutionary performativity manifests disruption of essentializing, naturalizing and colonizing tendencies, marking failure in iterative gestures that opens possibilities for new emergences. A less compelling alternative would be for the CMS researcher to work with the *illocutionary* performative, speaking as a sovereign voice, constructing authoritative realities with utterances (Butler, 2010).

It has been argued that by raising questions and noting alternatives around various "imperatives," CMS has the potential to interrogate organizational reality, including illusions of the "naturalness" of relations and the way things just are, for example, around behaviors and attitudes often stereotypically associated with specific gender-demarcated groups (Maclaran, Miller, Parsons & Surman, 2009). Fournier and Grey (2000) write that the debates within CMS have

> led CMS writers to question the grounds for critique, their rights and ability to offer critique, and have alerted them to the paradoxical and even preposterous nature of their position as academic writers, condemned to provide critique that effaces or appropriates the voices of those in the name of whom they claim to speak.
>
> *(p. 21)*

It is disturbing to reflect upon the notion that CMS researchers would "claim to speak in the name" of their research subjects, even as they recognize their roles in "effacing or appropriating" processes. Nevertheless, the authors imagine an attempt to pursue research that does not harm and suggest a desire to decolonize the theory, the research practices and the positions and voices often drawn upon to fuel work in CMS (see also Alvesson, 2008). Surveying much of the CMS work published since 2000, however, suggests that this is far from a reality.

To summarize, then, Critical Management Studies attempts to "unmask power relations around which social and organizational life are woven" (Fournier & Grey, 2000: 19), raising tensions around outcomes of scholarly engagement or disengagement (pp. 22–26; Fournier, 2002). This includes attempts to draw upon emerging insights and principles to change the relations and situations of individuals enmeshed in them in less than flourishing ways. One of the most important insights around the potential of CMS is that those who study and pursue the course of management should understand that there are alternatives, diversities and points of cocreation that "mainstream management theory has treated as either irrelevant to the analysis of organizations or as a set of resources and constraints for the pursuit of performativity" (Fournier & Grey, 2000: 27). In other words, without the investigations and resulting understandings of CMS, much in the realm of management remains unaddressed and outside mainstream interest and consciousness, assumedly leaving the power relations and related oppressions and exploitations unexamined and in place. The turn to concerns for teaching and learning in management education (e.g., Beverungen, 2009; Grey, 2007; Willmott, 2006) – with notions of teachers and students communicating ideas and sharing the potential for insights – marks an opportunity to engage what has been characterized as an ethics of care in contrast to an ethics of criticism (Gabriel, 2009).

Is caring critical?

Human relations that emerge from an ethos of care may manifest qualities needed to offer new possibilities in a world of complex, often damaging interactions that support diverse aspects of social organization. Work in care ethics has highlighted the characteristics of subordinated groups, finding virtue in responses that support generous, nurturing or other-centered interactions and that also allay danger and retribution in oppressive relations. Related observations reveal semio-ontological links between marginalized identities and subject positions, such as blackness and femininity, and suggest a critical place for an ethos often reserved for the variously colonized (Borgerson, 2001). This is not to raise a call for adopting subordinated perspectives because there is something virtuous about doing so but rather to recognize the power in alternative versions and visions of the world even if we currently observe them functioning in less than optimal situations. For example, the humility perceived by Cornell that emerges in black philosophies of existence arises in part from lived realities of racism and struggle but at the same time proposes the necessity of positions of openness to the fully human and value-creating status of others – including those previously rendered invisible in the face of arrogant, colonizing fantasies of superiority.

Care ethics, favorably viewed, demonstrate attention to relationships and responsibility (Borgerson, 2007) and moreover a sense of acknowledging others' value in the world, in contrast to arrogance and defensiveness that block potential for intersubjectivity and generosity. Care ethics may engage an alternative to a narcissism that gauges everything in relation to oneself. The ethics of care were recently invoked as a balance against management studies' critical activities that arguably threaten to provoke a slide into academic cynicism, disciplinary irrelevance and irresponsible pedagogy (Gabriel, 2009).

Yiannis Gabriel opens a number of possible conversations regarding the future of CMS and critical reflective methods and moreover the meaning of, and distinction between, terms such as "criticism," "critique," and "critical reflection" (Gabriel, 2009: 381–382; Parker, 1995). The suggestion he puts forward might be analyzed in several directions: however, here the focus follows various potentials of Gabriel's call for the discipline and the disciples of critical management studies to engage with so-called care ethics, as well as his attempts to clarify and deepen notions involved in such an engagement. An analysis of "an ethic of criticism" rendered in terms of Gordon's work may suggest a "reconciliation" intrinsic to the possibility of education and hence pedagogy generally, thus implicating the future of management and organization at all levels.

The ethics of care also appear in an argument for "critical performativity" that contests the notion that CMS should remain disengaged and without performative intention (Spicer, Alvesson & Kärreman, 2009). Much of the potential for alteration discussed in Spicer, Alvesson and Kärreman's work would arise in conjunction with the notions of performativity previously put forward, that is, an understanding of the way in which iterative gestures continue to alter and shift over time, cocreating new possibilities and outcomes. This includes instances of iterations that, intentional or not, seemingly significant or not, slip continuously away from a sense of the natural or essential structure or way of doing things.

The authors offer several characteristics for their perspective on critical performativity, including an affirmative stance, optimistic focus on "micro emancipations," and a role for an ethic of care. According to the authors, an ethic of care involves "asking practical questions which care for participants' views at the same time as seeking to challenge the same participants" (Spicer, Alvesson & Kärreman, 2009: 547). In other words, CMS researchers assume an attitude of care that includes the need to "challenge" some aspect of the so-called participants' perception of the world.

Whereas the "challenging" aspect of the interaction might be supposed to enlighten the researchers, the tension between caring and challenging suggests that Critical Management Studies researchers know better than their participants, raising the problem, as they note, of "arrogance and elitism" in revealing instances of false consciousness – though this is not a term used in the article. The alternative, they argue, would be to "accept and legitimate" the social order, apparently represented by what emerges from the unchallenged research Other. The article presumes researchers who see truth and reality and whose thinking represents for them a global, universal vision (Dabashi, 2013). These researchers believe themselves to be in a position of responsibility to choose whether to attempt to interpret alternative perspectives for the participant – for example, the ignorant manager or the mainstream researcher. I do not intend to denigrate the difficulty of the quandary acknowledged here; nevertheless, decolonizing the "critical" may require an approach to this setup that is not considered here. Let us look a bit more closely.

Referring to the notion of "loving struggle" from philosopher of existence Karl Jaspers, the authors offer an image of a relationship that might allow a negotiation between researcher and participant that fosters CMS's potential for engagement, care and critical performativity:

> It involves recognizing the right of the other person to exist, and a simultaneous commitment to pushing, questioning and extending that other person in a way which encourages them to stretch their sense of who they are and might become.
>
> *(Fleming & Spicer, 2007, cited in Spicer, Alvesson & Kärreman, 2009)*

The Other person – here, the research participant – is conceived of as capable of altering and being altered in an exchange. Whereas recognizing "the right of the other person to exist" cuts somewhat below notions of the other as a source of value creation, the indeterminacy, openness and incompleteness that constitute being human is gestured to implicitly, and the theoretical implications of perlocutionary performativity are reasserted, again implicitly. The authors carry this forward by suggesting a "mystery-led approach," an "openness" to the unexpected, and an ability to connect with "local conditions" that may disrupt fondly held assumptions or the "theory-led protocol that dominates CMS" (p. 549). In sum, if CMS researchers are also willing to be "extended" and "stretched," then the contexts of being and knowing in which they are working, as well as the people with whom they engage, may disrupt broader CMS ideologies and universalizing tendencies brought into the field of investigation.

It is interesting to consider how close these statements of "caring" for the views of the other and "recognizing the right of the other person to exist" come to the notion of "humility" put forward by Cornell as crucial to the project of decolonizing the critical, and yet how extensive is the difference between these when brought into closer inquiry. In short, the caring relationship here becomes instrumental based upon the agentic perspective and sovereign desire of the CMS researcher, through which the notion of cocreation – or an ethical relation in a Levinasian sense of the absolute Otherness of the Other, unappropriated by the self-same – fades. Moreover, "openness" becomes an ideal methodological approach regarding research assumptions or theoretical frameworks, not an understanding of the irreplaceability of the participant or research subject.

Caring in CMS might need to become less of the so-called white man's burden to challenge the masses yet to come to consciousness, and more – attempted with an attitude of humility – a welcoming of the full humanity and realities of those with whom we share research interactions. A more carefully articulated and comprehended notion of care ethics – as well as reference to diverse related models of intersubjectivity and sociality – would help clarify and deepen the recommendations suggested by Spicer, Alvesson & Kärreman (2009). Moreover, a more thoughtful drawing out of the proposition might highlight the potential ontological implications that map onto colonizing backgrounds of critical theory.

It may be that a developed notion of care ethics in this context could intersect productively with the aspects of humility. Indeed, it was this impulse that led to the particular form of this chapter. Surely, CMS as a field must take responsibility for its own ignorance and arrogance, as well as for the reorientation and revisioning in hopes of broadening and animating ethical relationships. In short, postcolonial organization studies calls upon mainstream CMS to be reflective upon the implications of its own geography of reason, its illocutionary impulses, its parochialism, its ideologies and its racism.

Conclusion

In exploring the missions of Critical Management Studies and attending to claims of geographical grounding in a U.K. genealogy, this chapter has discussed scenarios around the devaluing and dehumanizing conditions of colonized relations to shed light on struggles to decolonize the "critical" in CMS. Can CMS researchers decolonize their research and theory and, in turn, address and reflect upon their own universalizing fantasies that deny epistemic limits in marking, idealizing or in other ways essentializing others? How might CMS participate with others, engage with others – as the colonized "find a way to meaningfully assert themselves as an epistemic limit to the imposition of white fantasy on who they can be in the world" (Cornell, 2008: 122)?

Hopes for decolonizing the critical in CMS reside in attending to the sociality of possible practices, guarding against anonymity and typicality with critical good faith, focusing on the potential of perlocutionary performativity and continually abdicating a delusional arrogated perspective in favor of humility that opens to the full humanity of others. One of Cornell's arguments is that by turning to the accounts of black philosophies of existence, we may grasp and act upon processes of "creolization" that sociologist Paget Henry defines as "a process of semio-semantic hybridization that can occur between arguments, vocabularies, phonologies, or grammars of discourses within a culture or across cultures" (Henry, 2000: 88, cited in Cornell, 2008: 132). Through creolization, critical management theorists and practitioners find themselves incomplete, decentered and, indeed, able to acknowledge their own human powers, and endure other', without flight into defensive attitudes, postures and positions. Multiplicities of being intertwine with the incompleteness of the human and defeat essentializing ontological and epistemic closures that impact upon the lived existence of colonized human beings, and others, in the world.

Despite performing situatedness and context in attempting to characterize CMS as born of U.K. conditions, including intellectual traditions, does some part of CMS desire, perhaps inadvertently, an idealization both in terms of genealogies and practices? In what way does challenging research participants to perceive their misunderstandings of the world in line with the theorizing, caring perspectives of CMS researchers make room for "the existence of the other"? As the traditions and resources of black existential philosophies, Southern Theory and other postcolonial thinking engage more explicitly with business school concerns, we see that new questions, critical positions and particular others address the arena of CMS. Indeed, approaching from alternative routes, we have reason to question that the relevant notion of *critical* necessarily emerges from European intellectual and academic traditions to the exclusion of those manifesting from elsewhere, including insights from colonial management and related racism that have been iterated and reflected upon in the experience and philosophy of the colonized.

And so we might ask, in what contexts CMS has had the opportunity to acknowledge, relate to and engage the Other? In the discipline of CMS, where might others typically appear in research, work life and global understanding? There are others as scholars and others as subjects of research whose life experiences and realities contest arrogated sensibilities and demand a rereading and revising regarding taken-for-granted universalized values, approaches and perspectives. In this sense, there are others whose potential as cocreative, intersubjective, epistemological and ontological limits require on the part of CMS a humility of perception and practice. Possibilities of inclusion emerge in this sense from attending to an already existing relation, debt and responsibility to these others from which some mainstream CMS academics over even the last decade have hidden.

It may be said that CMS has been more successful in addressing the inequalities of class than in confronting racism and the meaningful inequalities of global position and distribution – what has been called the global basic structure (Buchanan, 2004). A key move would be to engage the knowledge, expertise and conceptual sophistication of othered thinkers and practitioners: as authors – in many languages – whose work we read, draw upon and reference in our own publications; as scholars whom we invite to speak in our university seminar series and mentor our PhD students; and as colleagues whom we include in our edited books and with whom we write.

Perceiving agency, value and humanity in the world beyond CMS as usual is an initial step to decolonizing the critical and embodying a humility that offers understandings in the face of the broader world as we shift the geography of CMS reason. If situations of cocreation are understood to be not chosen, not "acceptable" perspectives, but rather the necessary conditions for being in the world, then CMS might begin to decolonize the critical in CMS by engaging the others that have participated in cocreating the identities and realities that CMS recognizes as its own. In other words, a self-satisfied Eurocentric perspective, including dogmatically universalized Marxist interpretations, refuses the cocreative contexts without which notions of Europe, Britain and CMS would not exist. If CMS is unwilling to decolonize the critical in CMS, none of this will change.

What Gordon says about disciplinary decadence offers positive analysis generally for CMS, in the sense that CMS attempts to recall its "birth" and by so doing allows contestation of founding myths, hypothesized roots and universalizing narratives. By maintaining an openness to alteration and shifting iterations and regenerations, as well as a questioning relationship to generalization and idealization, CMS may escape the "monstrous" existence that Gordon finds in human disciplinary creations that aspire to the eternal. An attitude of humility, then, in accepting the fact of coming into and going out of existence and the sociality of human processes – even those we would most like to claim as uniquely, autonomously conceived – may release CMS from the colonizing impulse toward a cocreative, coagentic understanding of critical management in an expanding and contracting world.

An interview with Lewis Gordon

JB: Cornell is gesturing to a Levinasian sense of "ethical" when she refers to your contribution concerning "humility" and attributing value and contribution to others in the world. Would you think of your approach to relationships and responsibility as intersecting with or being influenced by concerns similar to those of Levinas?

LG: I've been very critical of Levinas for many reasons. First, there is his Hellenizing of Judaism. The tendency to seek a Greek past is, as I see it, a legacy of Aryanism. The Germans liked the myth of Nordic tribes heading to the Mediterranean and inaugurating, through a mixture with Southern Mediterranean peoples, the Classical Age. (Ironic for an ideology of purity, no?) Second, there is the analytical structure of Levinas's argument. I wrote a long paper on deontic logic when I was a graduate student in which I raised the problem of the form of obligation versus the obligation of form. In effect, I was putting in logic terms what turns out to be Levinas's insight about ethics, where one could ask about the ethical implications of ontological commitments instead of the ontological status of ethics. I think he is right in that regard. Where I have a problem is the structure of how he sets up the question of the Other. It leads to so much inwardness that one ignores the social circumstances through which one could afford such ethical and moralistic luxury. An interesting comparison is Mulana Karenga. He, too, prioritizes the ethical. But for him, that leads to the obligation of engaging the social and historical world. The ignoring of black humanity was possible, e.g., through ignoring those realities. The Other, for Karenga, is not a demand that leaves one smitten and subordinated but instead *active*. This, too, is an insight I see from Frantz Fanon. If a colonized person looks at a colonizer as The Other to whom to *defer* and, echoing Derrida, *differ/defer*, then we are left simply with the maintenance of an unjust status quo. Philosophers of liberation and decolonial theorists such as Enrique Dussel, Nelson Maldonado-Torres, and others have posed such questions to Levinas (and also, in the context of critical theory, with communicative ethics) and to Habermas, and these extraordinary white men simply ignored them, while they reached out so much to their white counterparts in North America. It seems some others have a greater ethical demand than others. We see here the structure of the point raised by Fanon in *Black Skins, White Masks* and in *Les Damnés de la terre*: ethics ultimately requires equality instead of asymmetry. Political action is needed to rectify *that*. I think Drucilla Cornell shares this insight. She was a strong proponent of deconstructive approaches to the study of law and feminism, which led her to Levinas's thought. Her concerns as a labor organizer and jurist led her, however, to take seriously the convergence of class and gender in race and eventually into the question of thinking through justice in *political terms* and the demands of critical thought on race and Africana philosophy of existence in the *Ubuntu* work in South Africa and problems of culture raised by rethinking symbolic form or structure. Cornell has taken on the crucial question of the meaning of the human in the assertions of ethical, legal, and political life. This has led, in a word, to a saturated or thick conception of social reality and human agency. It makes Levinas insightful but woefully limited.

JB: Some argue that science should not become advocacy. This might mean not applying research insights and outcomes to advocate for particular applications or policies. Critical Management Studies has often tried to avoid contributing to research with managerial applications: they have said that CMS shouldn't result in better forms of oppression. Can a discipline maintain integrity, even when its insights are so closely related to dubious practical applications? Some have argued, sometimes in contrast, that in order to offer education for future management practitioners and academics, the outcomes and implications of CMS research *must* be articulated and moreover taught to students. Does philosophy have any similar concerns right now?

LG: Philosophy has similar concerns precisely because academic philosophy faces a similar problem. Analytical philosophy claims to be pursuing truth, but it does so in ways that are patently ethnocentric and preserving of the status quo – especially of elite institutions. One could argue, using Gramsci, that analytical philosophy is the organic philosophy of Anglo-liberalism and then neoliberalism. Although there are "left" analytical philosophers, the reality could be born out when methodological assumptions or presumptions are under critique: one finds a response not different from the Taliban. Continental philosophers collapse, often, into a form of Eurocentrism that makes them organic to the *cultural* maintenance of Euro-modernity. These two are not, however, the only alternatives, and in my book *Disciplinary Decadence*, I offer a critique of this false dilemma. In the end, I argue that both, in a failure of more rigorous metacritique, often fail to deal with reality. This is not an absolute claim, but my point is that those who are willing to go beyond their (ethnocentric) methodological dictates – i.e., going beyond analytical philosophy and continental philosophy – find themselves in a teleological suspension of disciplinarity for the sake of reality. There is incredible pressure in the study of management and business to be complicit with what is no less than market fundamentalism. The task is to achieve a proper level of self-critique. The other extreme, for instance – *anti*-management – fails to see that standards, rules, organization, and the variety of critical questions raised by management are *necessary*, especially where the institutions at work are large, complex, and modern. A decadent model turns away, however, from the multiple or diverse possibilities and resources from which to draw on ideas for the proper function of the institutions at hand. Here, then, the *critical* in Critical Management Studies must come to the fore.

References

Adler, P. (2002). Critical in the name of whom and what? *Organization, 9*(3): 387–395.

Alvesson, M. (2008). The future of critical management studies. In D. Barry & H. Hansen (Eds.), *The Sage handbook of new approaches in management and organization* (p. 13–26). London: Sage.

Alvesson, M., & Willmott, H. (Eds.), (2003). *Studying management critically.* London: Sage.

Beverungen, D. A. (2009). Whither Marx in the business school? PhD thesis, Leicester, UK, University of Leicester.

Bhaskar, R. (2011). *Reclaiming reality: A critical introduction to contemporary philosophy.* Oxford: Routledge.

Borgerson, J. L. (2001). Feminist ethical ontology: Contesting "the bare givenness of intersubjectivity." *Feminist Theory, 2*(2): 173–187.

Borgerson, J. L. (2005). Judith Butler: On organizing subjectivities. *Sociological Review, 53*: 63–79.

Borgerson, J. L. (2007). On the harmony of feminist ethics and business ethics. *Business and Society Review, 112*(4): 477–509.

Borgerson, J. L. (2008). Living proof: Reflections on irreplaceability. *The CLR James Journal, 14*(1): 269–283.

Borgerson, J. L. (2011). Bad faith and epistemic closure: Challenges in the marketing context. In M. Painter-Morland & R. ten Bos (Eds.), *Business ethics and continental philosophy*: 220–241. Cambridge: Cambridge University Press.

Borgerson, J. L., & Rehn, A. (2004). General economy and productive dualisms. *Gender, Work, and Organization, 11*(4): 455–474.

Borgerson, J. L., & Schroeder, J. E. (1997). The ethics of representation: Race and gender in images of Hawaii. *Cooley Law Review, 14*(3): 473–489.

Borgerson, J. L., & Schroeder, J. E. (2002). Ethical issues in global marketing: Avoiding bad faith in visual representation. *European Journal of Marketing, 36*(5/6): 570–594.

Borgerson, J. L., & Schroeder, J. E. (2008). Building an ethics of visual representation: Contesting epistemic closure in marketing communications. In M. Painter-Morland & P. Werhane (Eds.), *Cutting edge issues in business ethics*: 89–110. Springer.

Buchanan, A. (2004). *Justice, legitimacy, and self-determination: Moral foundations for international law.* Oxford: Oxford University Press.

Butler, J. (1993). *Bodies that matter: On the discursive limits of "sex."* New York: Routledge.

Butler, J. (2010). Performative agency. *Journal of Cultural Economy, 3*(2): 147–161.

Comaroff, J., & Comaroff, J. (2011). *Theory from the south: Or, how Euro-America is evolving toward Africa.* Boulder & London: Paradigm.

Connell, R. (2007). *Southern theory: Social science and the global dynamics of knowledge.* Cambridge: Polity.

Contu, A. & Willmott, H. (2005). You spin me round: the realist turn in organization and management studies. *Journal of Management Studies, 42*(8): 1645–1662.

Cornell, D. (2008). *Moral images of freedom: A future for critical theory.* Lanham, MD: Rowman & Littlefield.

Czarniawska, B., & Höpfl, H. (2002). *Casting the other: The production and maintenance of inequalities in work organizations.* London & New York: Routledge.

Dabashi, H. (2002). Dead certainties: The early Makhmalbaf. In R. Tapper (Ed.), *The new Iranian cinema: Politics, representation and identity*: 117–153. London: I. B. Tauris.

Dabashi, H. (2013). Can non-Europeans think? *Al Jazeera.* Retrieved on May 10, 2013 from www.aljazeera.com/indepth/opinion/2013/01/2013114142638797542.html.

De Cock, C., & Böhm, S. (2007). Liberalist fantasies: Žižek and the impossibility of the open society. *Organization, 14*(6): 815–836.

Disks, N. B. (2006). *The scandal of empire: India and the creation of Imperial Britain.* Cambridge, MA: Harvard University Press.

Fournier, V. (2002). Keeping the veil of otherness: Practicing disconnection. In B. Czarniawska & H. Höpfl (Eds.), *The production and maintenance of inequalities in work organizations*: xx. London: Routledge.

Fournier, V., & Grey, C. (2000). At the critical moment: Conditions and prospects for critical management studies. *Human Relations, 53*(1): 7–32.

Gabriel, Y. (2009). Reconciling an ethics of care with critical management pedagogy. *Management Learning, 40*(4): 379–385.

Gordon, L. R. (1995a). *Bad faith and antiblack racism*. Atlantic Highlands, NJ: Humanities Press.

Gordon, L. R. (1995b). *Fanon and the crisis of European man*. New York: Routledge.

Gordon, L. R. (1997). *Her majesty's other children: Sketches of racism from a neocolonial age*. Lanham, MD: Rowman & Littlefield.

Gordon, L. R. (2000). *Existentia Africana*. New York: Routledge.

Gordon, L. R. (2003). Irreplaceability: An existential phenomenological reflection. *Listening: A Journal of Religion and Culture*, 3(2): 190–202.

Gordon, L. R. (2006). African-American philosophy, race, and the geography of reason. In L. R. Gordon & J. A. Gordon (Eds.), *Not only the master's tools: African-American studies in theory and practice*: 3–50. Boulder & London: Paradigm.

Grey, C. (2007). Possibilities for critical management education and studies. *Scandinavian Journal of Management*, 23(4): 463–471.

Guillet de Monthoux, P. (1993). *The moral philosophy of management: From Quesnay to Keynes*. London: M. E. Sharpe.

Henry, P. (2000). *Caliban's reason: Introducing Afro-Caribbean philosophy*. New York: Routledge.

Henry, P. (2005). Africana phenomenology: Its philosophical implications. *CLR James Journal*, 11(1): 79.

Jack, G., and Westwood, R. (2006). Postcolonialism and the politics of qualitative research in international management. *Management International Review*, 46(4): 481–501.

Jack, G., Westwood, R., Srinivas, N., & Sardar, Z. (2011). Deepening, broadening and re-asserting a postcolonial interrogative space in organization studies. *Organization*, 18(3): 275–302.

Jones, C. (2003). Theory after the postmodern condition, *Organization*, 10(3): 503–525.

Karamali, E. (2007). Has the guest arrived yet? Emmanuel Levinas, a stranger in business ethics. *Business Ethics: A European Review*, 16(3): 313–321.

Lim, M. (2007). The ethics of alterity and the teaching of otherness. *Business Ethics: A European Review*, 16(3): 251–321.

Litvin, D. (2004). *Empires of profit: Commerce, conquest and corporate social responsibility*. Mason, OH: Thomson Publications.

Long, B. S., & Mills, A. (2008). Globalization, postcolonial theory, and organizational analysis: Lessons from the Rwanda genocide. *Critical Perspectives on International Business*, 4(4): 389–409

Maclaran, P., Miller, C., Parsons, E., & Surman, E. (2009). Praxis or performance: Does critical marketing have a gender blind-spot? *Journal of Marketing Management*, 25(7/8): 713–728.

Maldanado-Torres, N. (2006). Toward a critique of colonial reason: Africana studies and the decolonialization of imperial cartographies in the Americas. In L. R. Gordon & Gordon, J. A. (Eds.), *Not only the masters' tools: African-American studies in theory and practice*. Boulder & London, Paradigm.

McCumber, J. (2001). *Time in the ditch: American philosophy and the McCarthy era*. Evanston, IL: Northwestern University Press.

Mignolo, W. (2013). Yes, we can: Non-European thinkers and philosophers. *Al Jazeera*. Retrieved on May 10, 2013 from www.aljazeera.com/indepth/opinion/(2013)/02/(2013)2672747320891.html).

Mills, A. J., & Mills, J. H. (1999). From imperialism to globalization: Internationalization and the management text. In S. Clegg, E. Ibarra-Colado & L. Bueno-Rodriques (Eds.), *Global management: Universal theories and local realities*: 37–67. London & Thousand Oaks, CA: Sage.

Nechtman, T. (2010). *Nabobs: Empire and identity in 18th century Britain*. Cambridge: Cambridge University Press.

O'Doherty, D. (2007). Organization: Recovering philosophy. In C. Jones & R. ten Bos (Eds.), *Philosophy and organization*: London: Routledge.

Parker, M. (1995). Critique in the name of what? Postmodernism and critical approaches to organization. *Organization Studies*, 16(4): 553–564

Peruvemba, J. S. (2001). Do we really "know" and "profess"? Decolonizing management knowledge. *Organization*, 8(2): 227–233.

Prasad, A. (Ed.). 2012. *Against the grain: Advances in postcolonial organization studies*. Copenhagen: Copenhagen Business School Press.

Rao, H., Morrill, C., & Zald, M. (2000). Power plays: How social movements and collective action create new organizational forms. In B. Straw & R. Sutton (Eds.), *Research in organizational behavior*. New York: Elsevier.

Rehn, A., & Sköld, D. (2012). I love the dough: Rap lyrics as a minor economic literature. In C. Rhodes & S. Lilley (Eds.), *Organizations and popular culture information, representation and transformation*. London: Routledge.

Schroeder, J.E. & Borgerson, J. L. (2012). Packaging paradise: Organizing representations of Hawaii. In A. Prasad (Ed.), *Against the grain: Advances in postcolonial organization studies*: 32–53. Copenhagen: Copenhagen Business School Press.

Sen, S. (1998). *Empire of free trade: The East India Company and the making of the colonial marketplace*. Philadelphia: University of Pennsylvania Press.

Sköld, D. (2010). The other side of enjoyment: Short-circuiting marketing and creativity in the experience economy. *Organization, 17*(3): 363–378.

Smith, L. T. (2012). *Decolonizing methodologies: Research and indigenous peoples* (2nd Ed.). London & New York: Zed Books.

Spicer, A., Alvesson, M., & Kärreman, D. (2009). Critical performativity: The unfinished business of critical management studies. *Human Relations, 62*(4): 537–560.

Tapper, R. (Ed.). (2004). *The new Iranian cinema: Politics, representation and identity*, London: I. B. Tauris.

Varman, R., & Costa, J. A. (2013). Underdeveloped other in country-of-origin theory and practices. *Consumption Markets & Culture, 16*(3): 240–265.

Wild, A. (1999). *The East India Company*. London: HarperCollins.

Willmott, H. (2006). Pushing at an open door: Mystifying the CMS manifesto. *Management Learning, 37*(1): 33–37.

Zald, M. (2002). Spinning disciplines: Critical management studies in the context of the transformation of management education. *Organization, 9*(3): 365–385.

8

Sexualities and/in 'Critical' Management Studies

Jeff Hearn, Charlotte Holgersson and Marjut Jyrkinen

Introduction

This chapter explores the hidden but powerful aspects of management and organizations: sexualities and gender. In mainstream studies on management and organization, sex, sexuality and/or gender are still relatively seldom addressed or analyzed. For a long time, the issue of sexuality was neglected within organization and management studies, particularly within the mainstream research but also in critical approaches. This lack of focus on sexualities could be understood as resulting from several reasons. Firstly, there has been little focus on gender, bodies and embodiments in studies of organizations and management. In this sense, sexuality could be seen as one aspect of gender, albeit an aspect that was usually neglected relative to questions of work, authority and formal lateral and hierarchical organizational divisions (Hearn & Parkin, 1983). A second perspective on this neglect can be traced mainly due to the frequently cited, and indeed gendered, divide between private/public, defining sexuality as something belonging to the private life and thus not relevant for analysis and understanding of organizational life. A third approach to explanation is in terms of the assumed distinction of, on one hand, organizations as rational and, on the other, sexuality as part of the irrational, sometimes emotional and carnal that does not affect working life.

Sexuality takes many forms which impact directly on working life, labour processes, organizations, and management. Thus, one might imagine sexuality would be or could be a central feature of Critical Management Studies; yet this is far from so. Sexuality, or sexualities as it is more commonly named nowadays, refers to 'the social experience, social expression, or social relations of physical, bodily desires, by and for others or oneself. Others may be the same or different sex/gender or of in determinate sex/gender' (Hearn & Parkin, 1995: 57–58).

Moreover, in late modern societies, the borders and boundaries between the public and the private realms appear to be becoming more blurred for many people. This applies especially for those in many expert and management positions; new information and communication technologies (ICTs) enable flexibility but also even 24/7 availability; work has become more international and transnational, and travelling, including travel abroad, is an embedded part of work for many. Thus where the work starts and ends and what is so-called private time are under constant negotiation. Time used for work constitutes an increasing part of life for many, even with governmental directives in theory limiting work time in some parts of the world.

All these and indeed several other related avenues of analysis can be critiqued for artificial, human-made divisions and dichotomies that marginalize essential aspects of life and humanity. They (re)construct a disembodied ideal (male) worker and manager/leader and detach work from other aspects of life (Acker, 1990). Having said that, it is very important to place these questions of changing public and private relations in broader historical and cultural perspectives. Along with many black and postcolonial feminists, Patricia Hill Collins (1990) writing in a U.S. context, has analyzed how for many women and men of colour the strict separation of public and private domains has not been part of their historical experience. This is so most clearly when working within slave political economies, but it also operates in modified form when working as domestic servants or some other 'live-in' workers. Such historical and embodied arrangements of power have clear and direct implications for sexualities in work, workplaces and organizations. Indeed, drawing a line between work and non-work becomes very difficult, and as such drawing a line between sexuality and work is also hazardous.

Malestream approaches to work, public–private separations, organizations and management have been challenged by feminist and queer theory but also by poststructuralist, postcolonial and intersectionality theory that recognize that sexuality is a social power relation that exists and persists in intersection with other power relations such as gender, ethnicity, class, age, disability and race (Hearn, 2011). Depending on where the borders are drawn for the field of Critical Management Studies, there is either an almost complete lack of studies focusing on sexuality or an established body of literature on sexuality.

In the field of organization and management studies, it is mainly feminist and queer scholars who have approached the topic of sexuality, while scholars in what has become institutionalized as Critical Management Studies (with capital letters, as CMS) have to a far less extent been interested in exploring sexuality. The debate thus lies in what we are to include within the contested field of Critical Management Studies. Nevertheless, we will in this chapter adopt an inclusive approach. Thus we provide an overview of the critical study of the intersection between sexuality and management and identify some areas for future research.

Critical Management Studies and sexualities

Before proceeding with the particular aspects of CMS, sexualities and gender, it is perhaps helpful to consider how sexuality might be construed within the new 'mainstream' of Critical Management Studies. As has been lucidly explained, and at the same time constructed, by Alvesson & Deetz (1996, 2006), two main tendencies characterize Critical Management Studies: those drawing on or derived from Critical Theory in the Frankfurt School tradition and those drawing on or derived from postmodernism. In this latter case, postmodernism is used almost as an equivalent to poststructuralism. This is even though there are clear and perhaps as great divergences *within* postmodernism and poststructuralism (Seidman, 1995) as there are between them and Critical Theory. Thus resistance to postmodernism can be related with relative ease to Critical Theory and neo-Marxism (see Kincheloe & MacLaren, 1994), while anti-foundational ludic postmodernism much less so, if at all.

Having said that, the wellsprings of both the Critical Theory and postmodernist traditions have some clear connections with, as well as some disconnections from, matters of sexuality. First and perhaps foremost, there is the question of class, that is, economic class. In strictly economistic Marxism, sexuality has generally been seen as relatively unimportant and when considered at all seen as secondary to and derivative of class position and class relations. On the other hand, there is a strand even with Marx's own writing that sexuality, along with biology and the body, is to some extent socially produced, and even that division of labour is based in the (hetero)sexual act;

the latent slavery of women and children in the family is the first property and thus arguably the first oppression (Marx & Engels, 1976, 44, 46; see Hearn, 1991).

The use of class-type approaches, literally or metaphorically, has been taken up in many analyses of sexuality, which in turn have impacted on critical understandings of sexuality in and around organizations. Perhaps the most well known example of such a class metaphor is Catharine MacKinnon's various writings on sexuality, gender and the state (for example, MacKinnon, 1982). Other examples can be found in attempts to bring together Marxism and what used to be called, ambiguously, gay liberation (for example, Mieli, 1980). Either way, the notion of oppression can be transferred from the narrowly economic realm to the sexual realm, and thus with that the notion of sexual oppression may be seen as relevant in organizational and work contexts.

Perhaps unsurprisingly, this kind of argumentation and application is seen very differently by different researchers studying, for example, prostitution and the sex trade. This includes the debate on whether or not it is accurate to describe such activities through the lens of the concept of 'sex work', i.e. if and in which circumstances prostitution, pornography and other forms of the sex trade could be understood as ordinary work rather than as abuse and gendered violence. The sex trade – which can be defined as economic transactions where people's bodies and sexualities are offered for sale, and are sold, bought or delivered further and (ab)used in the name of clients' sexual wishes and desires (Jyrkinen, 2005) – has been and still is a topic which has divided the feminist movement, academic researchers, activism and non-governmental organization (NGO) work since the 1960s so-called sexual revolution (O'Connell Davidson, 2002; Jyrkinen, 2005). The anti-prostitution or (neo-)abolitionist position highlights the harmful effects of prostitution and places its roots and causes in patriarchal gender and class systems (for instance Coy, 2012). The pro-prostitution stand – supported by the sex industries, sex buyers and neo-liberal policy-makers – highlights the importance of the redefinition of prostitution as 'sex work' and thereby the need for it to be recognized like any other form of work (for example Bindman & Dozema, 1997). The latter position emphasizes the agency of women in prostitution and their right to 'choose' prostitution as their labour with legal(ized) rights. An anti-prostitution position highlights that the normalization of the sex trade mainly benefits the industries and the sex buyers and consumers, who are mainly men, instead of those who sell sex, mainly women and adolescent girls and boys (Jeffreys, 2012).

Although the sex trade forms a globally interlinked and effectively managed industry which offer high profits for the organizing levels and for the owners, the debates as regards the essence of such trade have raised surprisingly little interest in management and organization studies and CMS. For instance, the sex trade spills over to non-sex-trade-work contexts through questions of the consumption of pornography, the buying of sex during work trips or offering sex trade entertainment to business partners as part of meetings or recreation. These debates are, however, distinct from that on the concept of 'sexual work', which has been used in analyzing labour around and in relation to sexuality in organizations more generally (Bland, Brundson, Hobson & Winship, 1978; Hearn & Parkin, 1987/1995; also see Adkins, 1995, for a later discussion).

In addition, it should be noted that issues of sexuality have figured in a variety of other ways within broad Critical Theory traditions. This applies, for example, in Frankfurt School Critical Theory informed by psychoanalysis and cultural critique of mass media, New Left debates informed by sexual and other social movements, and developing post-Marxism informed by engagement with poststructuralist and related developments.

This brings us to the second main strand of CMS, that stemming from postmodernism, which in this context is often used synonymously with poststructuralism. Here, sexuality has had a different and in many ways greater significance. Poststructuralism is clearly in part a critique of structuralism and as such can be understood as a product of the undecidability of language.

This can be traced to many antecedents, from for example classical times, as with Heraclitus and the notion of perpetual flux, or, much later, Nietzschean presumptions, but the recent (in some sense modern) impacts are largely from the unsettlings of post–Second War facts and fictions (Silverman, 1992). In these poststructuralist debates, sexuality has loomed large here. There are complex intertwinings of sexuality politics and sexuality studies between the 'new sexual movements' of LGBTTIQ (lesbian, gay, bisexual, transsexual, transgender, intersex, and queer) and the poststructuralist revaluation of the power of sexuality. This is especially represented through the impacts of queer politics and queer theory, as well as the work of *inter alia* Michel Foucault (1976) and Judith Butler (1990).

Following and alongside groundbreaking work in ethnomethodology, symbolic interactionism, and gay and lesbian studies, Foucault set out a non-essentialized account of sexuality and its historical deployments. However, despite his massive impact on the discursive construction of sexuality and indeed the study of sexuality, he "says very little of sexual relations as they could be described or experienced, of even *women* and *men*, of gender relations" (Hearn & Parkin, 1995: 197). Butler (1990) also sees sexuality as inherently unstable and a regulatory fiction dominantly cast within what Rich (1980) named compulsory heterosexuality. Thus here sexuality is no 'add-on', as in some Marxisms and neo-Marxisms, but at the heart of the deconstructive project.

Interestingly, in both strands of CMS – the postmodernist and the Critical Theory strands – there has often, perhaps typically, been a lack of attention to gender and sexuality, along with an absence of sexuality, as part of an ignoring of feminism. Accordingly, CMS and sexuality have characteristically been difficult bedfellows. There are, of course, many other developments that are part of and impinge on CMS. These include postcolonialism and green politics and eco-political theory. In the first case, clear links to both these broad traditions are noted. Indeed, post-colonialism, like internationality theories, can be seen as a mediation between modernism and postmodernism. Postcolonialism has a significant place in problematizing not only the normative Western subject, but also the normative Western male (hetero)sexual subject, globally, generically and in studies of management and organizations.

Within green/eco-politics, questions of sexuality are addressed to much more variable extents and from varying positions, including at times naturalism and even conservative biologism. However, while the Critical Theory and postmodernist traditions can be said to be the two dominant strands, it is fair to say that CMS is now a very broad umbrella indeed, with many texts and examples from well beyond those perspectives. Finally, in this section it has to be pointed out that the critical "C" of CMS is sometimes overused, so that some contributions within CMS gatherings and conferences are little more than mainstream studies with, say, a qualitative angle. In such examples, social divisions, power, let alone gender and sexuality, may not figure, may not be thought of at all. Thus, Critical Management Studies scholarship might need a critical revision and self-reflections as well.

Focused literature on sexuality and organizations

The literature specifically addressing sexuality in work, organizations and management can be distinguished in terms of different strands. One strand of literature consists of theoretical and conceptual reviews of sexuality, as, for example, Hearn & Parkin (1987/1995), who made one of the first attempts to create a framework for understanding the linkages among organization, sexuality and gender. In their scheme it is useful to consider the concept of 'organization sexuality' (not organizational sexuality) in order to speak simultaneously of organization(s) and sexuality, rather than prioritizing one over the other or seeing one as determinant of the other. Other strands that will be presented focus on phenomena such as sexual harassment, the sexualization of work and 'the Other', heteronormative and heterosexist work cultures, ICTs and sexualities, as well as management change practices addressing sexuality.

Sexual harassment

A major strand of literature consists of the exploration of linkages between sexuality and managerial control and exploitation. Early examples are the revision of the Hawthorne study by Acker & Van Houten (1974) and the research by Cockburn (1983, 1991) that has highlighted how men, including managers, workers and researchers, mobilize sexuality to control women. An important body of literature within this strand of research concerns sexual harassment. Behaviours that could be perceived as sexual harassment are often presented on a continuum, from requests for dates, ogling and staring, offensive comments and gestures, to sexual propositions and physical assault. While there is no universal definition, most national statutes, according to McDonald (2012), contain similar elements, such as descriptions of the behaviour as unwanted and where the purpose or effect results in intimidation, hostility, degradation, humiliation or offensiveness. Statistics derived from national prevalence studies, cross-national meta-analyses and case studies show that, despite legislation, sexual harassment continues to be a problem mainly for women but also for some men (McDonald, 2012). Sexual harassment is, however, often under-reported due to a widespread defensive attitude towards sexual harassment. Studies show that individuals frequently downplay behaviours that could be labelled as sexual harassment. For example, a study by Collinson & Collinson (1996) found that women in male-dominated workplaces avoided defining their experiences as sexual harassment in order to be viewed as competent and as team players by colleagues and superiors. McDonald (2012) highlights that the extent to which sexual behaviour in the workplace is identified as sexual harassment is influenced by factors including political events, presence and implementation of organizational policies that name the issue and provide processes for complaints and the level of support by public institutions for anti-discrimination legislation.

The critical organizational literature offers a number of explanations for sexual harassment. Early explanations viewed sexual harassment as a result of sex role spillover. Men are commonly perceived as sexual agents and women as sexual objects, and in a male-dominated context, women's sex role becomes more highlighted than their work roles (Gutek & Morasch, 1982). Later approaches focus more on power perspectives, interpreting sexual harassment as an expression of men's dominance and women's subordination operating in different ways on individual, organizational and societal levels (for example Popovich & Warren, 2010). Sexual harassment against gay men and lesbian women is also discussed from a power perspective. For example, Epstein (1997) labels sexual harassment against gay men and lesbian women as heterosexist, drawing on Butler's concept of the heterosexual matrix. The heterosexual norm in workplaces is enforced by punishing those who deviate from heterosexual norms of masculinity and femininity, through homophobic anti-gay biases and gender hostility.

Empirical research into sexual harassment demonstrates that sexuality is used as a means of control and has challenged the dominant view of sexual harassment as an individual problem, where an isolated man occasionally harasses a woman victim, not a problem related to a workplace culture that tolerates ongoing harassment (Hearn & Parkin, 2001). Sexual harassment, as a part of exclusions from careers and as violations at work, is a serious problem nationally and globally. Framing the individualization as a "personal problem" disguises the gender and power relations at work. For instance, Acker (1991) writes about covert and overt control at work: covert control can be exercised, for example, through arguments about how 'women's emotionality', related to their bodies/sexuality, can disable their ability to accomplish demanding tasks in leadership and management. More overt control is actualized through sexual harassment or relegating women of childbearing age to non-managerial posts (Acker, 1991). Sexual harassment relates to career hurdles for many women, and, for example, Husu (2001) in her study on academic women has found that gender discrimination often takes place in very subtle and hidden forms, such as 'non-happenings' in the career. Often sexual harassment is disguised in fear of consequences to one's career and work organizations. Research on women managers by Jyrkinen & McKie (2012) has revealed the tendency to silence sexual harassment issues in organisations, as taking up issues on sexuality and violence might harm the organization, its managers/leaders and, in the process, in particular the victim. The silencing of organization violences has also been studied. Moreover, the idea that the victim is always a woman has been problematized. Lee (2000) has analyzed the experiences of male victims of workplace sexual harassment and how men who found verbal sexual allegations distressing were feminized. Other forms of sexual abuse and violence in organizations have also been explored, such as physical violence, initiation rites, rape and sexual assault within the military, as well as in residential and total institutions (for example Hearn & Parkin, 2001; Flam, Hearn & Parkin, 2010).

Sexualization of work and 'the Other'

The sexualization of some women's work is another topic of inquiry (Hearn & Parkin, 1987/1995). Adkins (1995) shows, for example, that women service workers are expected to engage in sexualized interactions with customers and colleagues (see Gutek & Morasch, 1982) and that this is so engrained in the workplace culture that it is almost impossible to resist. According to Folgero & Fjeldstad (1995), such cultures do not allow women to see themselves as victims of sexual harassment. In her analysis of the banking culture in the City of London, McDowell (1997) highlights the various ways in which women were sexualized and othered. She demonstrates how the use of sexualized language objectified and humiliated women, for example by referring to women in general or women colleagues as 'skirts', 'slags', 'brasses' and 'tarts' and referring to women colleagues as 'girls' in face-to-face interactions. The culture also included a range of 'practical jokes' involving sexy computer passwords, obscene messages, underwear and blow-up dolls. The women reported on how they were constantly reminded of their bodies and appearance through comments, sexualized jokes and gossip, as well as behaviour that could be interpreted as sexual harassment. This made these women visible in the organization and restricted to a narrow set of acceptable behaviours (McDowell, 1997). Furthermore, McDowell discusses how the sexualized jargon at the stock exchange also sexualizes men's labour. She observed a particular form of heterosexual machismo culture that othered alternative versions of masculinity. For example, the sexualized language and humour was centred around heterosexuality and the denigration of faithfulness, bisexuality and homosexuality. Gay men reported that they concealed their sexual preferences, and the only openly gay respondent revealed that he was subject of unwelcomed sexist jokes and behaviour.

Research on ethnicities, 'race' and gender in the context of imperialism and (neo)colonialism have revealed many racializations and sexualizations of 'the Other'. Gendered work and management and ownership relations are embedded with many forms of exoticizations and more direct subordinations of, in particular, black/non-white women in work and elsewhere (see McClintock, 1995). In the field of international relations, Enloe (1989) has explored how the international/transnational organizations and corporations, including war industries, have major impact on further gendering of work and othering of women, particularly 'foreign' women. Women as servants, helpers, wives, girlfriends and prostitutes become an integral part of organizing and enabling transnational work. However, women's work is often underpaid and even ignored as real work, which is the case of nannies, au pairs and maids who often play an important role in organizing care, for instance, in embassies and international and career-oriented relationships and families. The 'outsourcing' of care responsibilities to low-paid immigrant women has created neocolonial global care chains (Hochschild, 2000), which may enable work and careers for educated middle-class (white) women; interestingly, the question of the role of men in care is less seldom posed. However, the experiences of women of colour enhanced black feminists' critique on the universalism of liberal feminism and the neglect of race and class-based exploitation in activism and scholarly work (hooks, 1981; Crenshaw, 1991). The intersections of gender and class at work have been studied, for example, by Acker (1990), but many other aspects of intersections in management and organizations, such as sexualities and ethnicity, are still relatively rarely focused on. Intersectionality as a theory, as an approach and as a method has been developed during the last two decades in many fields, also including management and organization theory (Hearn, 2011). According to McCall (2005), intersectionality is the most important contribution of women's/feminist studies and other related fields thus far. Intersectional approaches are also important in management and organization studies, not least in CMS, and even more so as work and organizations are increasingly transnational and multicultural. We return to this question of intersectionality in the last part of the chapter.

Heteronormative and heterosexist work cultures

Uses and abuses of sexuality in managerial cultures that are still predominantly masculine and heterosexual (Hearn & Parkin, 1987/1995, 2001) has also been highlighted. Most organizations and managements embrace dominant heterosexual norms, ideologies, ethics and practices, for example, in constructions of men managers' reliance on wives in traditional marriage (Reis, 2004; Hearn, Jyrkinen, Piekkari & Oinonen, 2008; Holgersson, 2013) and the sexualized relationship between managers and secretaries, the office wife according to Kanter (1977). For example, Pringle (1989) discusses the manager relationship in terms of compulsory heterosexuality, master–slave and sadomasochism. Moreover, the heteronormativity of managerial cultures and the consequences for lesbian and gay managers have also been analyzed (for example, Lee, Learmonth & Harding, 2008; Pringle, 2008). Sexuality in the relationship between men has also been discussed. Scholars such as Roper (1996) and Holgersson (2013) have explored homosocial relations between male managers and in particular discussed the importance of homosocial desire between different generations of managers in situations of management recruitment and succession. This particular type of intimacy in formally heterosexual circumstances may appear non-sexual but nonetheless may construct and contain potentially erotic desire.

A significant, if often marginalized, strand of empirical research on sexuality, organizations and management that has developed from the 1970s and 1980s has been on lesbians' and gay men's experiences in workplaces. Weston and Rofel (1984) had already raised the issue of sexuality, class and conflict in a lesbian workplace in 1984. Many of the early studies were linked to campaigns or other political interventions against discrimination and violation. More recent studies have examined wider experiences of lesbians and gay men at work, including business (Woods & Lucas, 1993; Dunne, 1997), public sector (Humphrey, 2000; Rumens, 2008; Rumens & Kerfoot, 2009), police (Burke, 1993), military (Cammermeyer, 1995; Hall, 1995), and community (Oerton, 1996a, 1996b) organizations. As Creed (2006) notes, some of the recurring issues discussed are the career conditions for lesbians and gay men, conditions with different professions and the determinants and consequences of disclosure decisions within the workplace. More recently, there has been a growing body of research on transsexual, transgender and intersexual people at work and on what workers go through there when they change genders or are in non-binary, non-cisgender (that is, when the identity, body and gender assigned at birth do not match) categorizations and identifications (Lehtonen & Mustola, 2004; Namaste, 2000; Schilt, 2006; Schilt & Wiswall, 2008; Davis, 2009). For example, Schilt and Connell (2007) examine the process of transitioning from one gender to another when the process is openly discussed in the workplace, how the identities are crafted and how colleagues relate to the individuals post-transition.

Even so, the work conditions and work situations of lesbian, gay, bisexual, transgender, transsexual or queer people in management and indeed also in entrepreneurship continue to be a relatively neglected area of research. The so-called pink money, the business-related interests of lesbian, gay and (inter-)transsexual persons and consumers, is growing in many countries. This has been important in the increased attention in the media to lesbian and gay sexualities, but, at the same time, some kinds of media attention may strengthen the stereotypes and reproduce homophobia and dominant normative assumptions about sex and sexualities. The 2001 UK Gay and Lesbian Census conducted by ID Research found that 15% of lesbians and gay men who responded believe their sexuality has hindered their job prospects, even though 43% reported having managerial jobs. A 2005 UK survey of readers of the magazines *Diva* and *Gay Times* by Out Now Consulting (2005) found that half of the gay men and lesbian respondents reported they can be completely honest about their sexuality with work colleagues. The gay men respondents earned on average almost £9,400 more than the national average for men, the lesbian respondents about £6,000 more than the national average for women. Such figures from both these studies should, however, be treated with caution, as the data was from volunteers rather than random surveys. A more comprehensive U.S. analysis by Lee Badgett (2001) rejects the idea that lesbians and gay men are more affluent than heterosexuals. She considers the complex interplay of income and standard of living of gay men and lesbians with such factors as financial and family decisions, workplace discrimination and denial of health care benefits to partners and children.

Although much literature has highlighted how sexism, heterosexism, homophobia and heteronormativity in organizations perpetuate inequalities, scholars have raised concerns about focusing only on coercive aspects of sexuality and thus overlooking consensual sexual interactions in organizations and other more 'positive' interpretations of sexuality. Intimate relations such as sexual relations can indeed also be a source of pleasure, meaning and relief from boredom and resistance (Gherardi, 1995; Lerum, 2004). The meanings of sexual interactions in the workplace vary across both cultural and material contexts, and this consequently calls for further exploration into this approach both empirically and theoretically.

ICTs and sexualities

There is a broad range of technologically organized or related sexualized practices, which are pervasive in late modern times. Such techno-disembodied practices range from sex without embodied presence of another person to technological enhancements of one's (sexual) body (James & Carkeek, 1997). New information and communication technologies (ICTs) consist of a complex web of innovations that are constantly and rapidly changing and evolving. PCs, mobile phones, computer games, the Internet, email, Twitter and many other forms of social media and so forth are part of people's everyday life in many parts of the world, and ICTs are further blurring the division between public and private time and space. There is a huge global industry of and research and development on ICTs and their business adaptabilities, also in the areas of sex and sexualities. ICTs provide vast possibilities to organize sexualities, for meeting sexual partners and (re-)creating sexual identities and for experiencing new forms of sexualities. These include techno-sex, non-connection sex, virtual sex, Internet-based dating, cyber affairs and multimedia interactive sex and so forth (Hearn, 2006).

Technological innovations and the ICT industries are interlinked with and for the commercialization of bodies, sex and sexualities at least in three ways. First, new and older technologies are (ab)used for the sex trade through marketing of its products and services in printed and visual forms and through virtual encounters. Secondly, new technological innovations enable the creation of new modes of commercial sex, for instance interactive pornography through the Web and smartphones with 4G data capabilities. Thirdly, technologies as such profit from sex commerce through boosting the sex trade, which has been keen to develop new innovations for e-commerce and Web-based advertising methods. The sex traders are among the innovators and early adapters of the ICTs, as the business possibilities and profit making of the integrated and convergent technologies are extensive, and the existing legislative supervision and control mechanisms are nominal nationally and internationally. Within work organizations, the policies on ICTs and the use of and encounters with the sex trade products and services are often deficient or totally lacking (Jyrkinen, 2005, 2012).

As professional work is increasingly mobile, international and consisting often at least partly of distance work through ICTs, the non-interest in and deficiency of policies concerning the sex trade is rather surprising. Silences in organizations and management are often multidimensional and paradoxical and can indicate power and powerlessness; silences may have many purposes, meanings and representations that impact on internal organizational policies or non-policies. Silences on issues like the uses of commercial sexual services during work time and/or by the use of corporate ICTs and networks – for instance, for downloading and consuming pornography – may indicate that such activities are considered to be rare and nominal and thus not a problem. Or this may also indicate that the sex trade use within work contexts – be that during work trips or in contexts of entertaining business partners after meetings – are implicitly accepted or at least not against organizational ethical premises and possible codes of conduct.

Symbolic expressions of male sexuality, reflected often in organizational metaphors and language, can be used to increase the coherence and homosociality of male workers but can also be used as mechanisms for the control of women in organizations and even for control over (other and excluded) men at the workplace (Acker, 1990; Collinson & Hearn, 1994; Hearn & Parkin, 1995). Thus management's approval of sexist language or pornographic pictures in workplaces or the tolerance of (other) connections with the sex trade by the members of the organization in work-related contexts act as symbolic expressions of male dominance and significant control over women in work organizations. Women are thereby excluded from the informal male bonding through the embedded sexist 'body talk', as well as through homosociality constructed by the (ab)use of commercial sex services (Acker, 1990).

Management change practices addressing sexuality

Following the development of practices regarding diversity management, corporate social responsibility (CSR) and ethical leadership in many Western organizations, critical scholars have also studied if and in what way these practices address issues of sexuality. Sexual harassment is today an issue on the agenda of employers, and practices of handling complaints are in place, but, as McDonald (2012) notes, these efforts have been less than successful and there is still room for development. Another way sexuality is addressed in work for change is through diversity management. The discourse and practice of diversity have become a vehicle for voicing the experience of LGBT persons, for example, through affinity groups or networks (Githens & Aragon, 2009; Colgan & McKearney, 2012). However, as diversity management discourse seldom prioritizes issues of power, there is a risk that sexuality is incorporated as another area to be controlled and manipulated in service of a mainstream corporate agenda (Creed 2006). Nevertheless, scholars such as Holvino & Kamp (2009) argue that critical approaches to diversity management can indeed open more humanist discourses and practices. Colgan (2011), for example, analyzed the development of structures, policies and practices on sexual orientation diversity work in five organizations in the private sector in the U.K. In four of the studied organizations, sexual orientation equalities work began on social justice grounds before legislation was put in place. The managers interviewed did not perceive anti-discrimination legislation as a particularly important factor for their work for change. However, some managers found that the CSR agenda within their organization was an important trigger for the development of sexual orientation diversity policies and practices. Following Shen (2011), Colgan (2011) interprets CSR as a unifying term including social justice, legislative and business case rationales. Sexual orientation diversity work was used an example of a company's commitment to CSR. There were, nevertheless, challenges in implementing these policies and practices across a variety of national contexts.

Aspects of corporate social responsibility and of ethical leadership and managing are also relevant for both theory building and practice around sexuality. One area of interlinking theory and practice has been the development of ethical codes of practice. Ethical guidelines and codes of conducts of organizations have, however, seldom tackled issues related to sexuality and sexual exploitation. Research on tourism and the sexual abuse of children, prostitution and trafficking in human beings has emerged lately (for example, Glover, 2006; O'Connell-Davidson, 2004; Tepelus, 2008). Often initiatives to investigate and prevent sexual abuse in organizational contexts have a broader origin, for example from the work of international NGOs and international human rights conventions and their follow-up. However, important resolutions, such as United Nations Security Council Resolution 1325 to involve women in all aspects of the resolution of wars, do not necessarily reach the organizations at the grassroots level. Or, more precisely, they are not implemented by countries and their governments. Paradoxically, the interest and concern originates from NGOs, but countries and their politicians are still seldom in explicit focus when sex and sexualities are talked about.

As work has become more internationalized, the possibilities for the use and abuse of other people's intimacy and sexuality have also increased. The sex trade is a growing area of the (illegal/half-legal) industry. Although buying sex or related sexual abuses of the person have long taken place, for example under imperialism and colonialism, the intensity of some of these abusive sexual acts has in some respects increased through globalization. In business and other organizations, the hierarchies of the late class society are still often pronounced and perpetuate the use of this semi-legitimate power and the position of subordinates and people in the home country and abroad. Corporate social responsibility in relation to sexual abuses is thus an area where future research and activism need to be focused on.

A case example of these processes has been documented by Holgersson (2011). She has, for example, documented that although large Swedish multinational companies state that engaging in any form of sexual entertainment at work is against their ethical policies, such practices were seldom explicitly mentioned in the policies and training. Interestingly, following lobbying carried out by a network of NGOs and government officials, the Swedish government commissioned the Council for Development within Government Agencies (Krus, 2012) to develop tools that can support government agencies, work against commercial sex and the consumption of pornography. Moreover, the Swedish Women's Lobby carried out a campaign, (Corporate Compass – Policy on Sexual Exploitation) to urge business organizations to introduce codes of conduct against sex purchasing and other forms of sexual exploitation (Swedish Women's Lobby, 2013).

Future research: Sexuality, organizations and Critical Management Studies

Setting out a new agenda for CMS in relation to sexuality requires a critical look at what has been done thus far but, more importantly, what are the issues and perspectives that have been ignored or silenced. There is still a need for more research into sexuality in organizations in various contexts, particularly in the light of changing politics and practices across the world regarding gender and sexuality; the so-called third sector organizations, the NGOs or civil society organizations are becoming more prominent in taking care of many tasks that the official sector outsources, whether to business organizations or NGOs in the late modern societies. Such changing organizational contexts include private and public sector organizations, as well as organizations in civil society. Civil society organizations have received very little attention from critical management and organization scholars, and that may appear surprising considering that these organizations are one of the driving forces behind putting sexuality on the agenda. Although some of these activist organizations also challenge heteronormative cultures, as shown in, for example, Raeburn's (2004) study of lesbian and gay activism in U.S. corporations, there is still a lack of research into organizations that adopt this critical position towards heteronormativity. Here, the combination of empirical and conceptual findings from CMS and research on social movements and civil society holds much promise.

Other types of organizations that remain largely unexplored are the sexploitation organizations. Most empirical studies and theorizing are still carried out within what Hearn & Parkin (1987) have called 'subordinated sexual organizations', where the dominant ideology is that matters of sexuality are subordinated to the 'non-sexual' organizational task. Relatively little critical inquiry into management issues in sexploitation organizations – where sexuality is exploited for the benefit of managers and owners, either commercially or sexually, for example, the pornography industry – has been carried out. Moreover, few have studied the linkages between management in organizations where sexuality is overtly subordinated to the 'main aim' of the organization (for example where sexuality is banned [or not named] in corporate policies) and management in sexploitation organizations, where sexuality is indeed part of the main aim (for example when commercial sex is used in corporate entertainment).

The relation between sexuality and managerial discourse also needs to be re-examined. Calás and Smircich (1991) performed one of the first deconstructions of traditional leadership discourse by linking leadership to seduction, but further analysis of management and leadership discourses in relation to sexualities is needed, considering the continuous production of literature, both scholarly and popular, on management and leadership. For example, building on the work of Calás and Smircich and drawing on queer theory, Harding, Lee, Ford and Learmonth (2011) have added that seduction also informs managers' lay accounts of leadership and that these accounts are informed not only by heterosexual seduction but also by homoerotic seduction. Other scholars have highlighted the compulsory (hetero)sexuality embedded in the managerial discourse (for example Collinson & Hearn, 1994; Höök, 2001). By applying queer theory and recognizing the fluidity of our identities, scholars, such as Parker (2002), Bowring (2004) and Bendl, Fleischmann & Hofmann (2009), have sought to destabilize our understanding of management and challenged the many binary distinctions that characterize established management knowledge and practice.

The linkages between social media and organization sexuality are areas for further research. Research has already started to document sexual harassment on the Internet (for an overview, see Barak, 2005), also called 'cyber-sexual harassment', which includes displaying offensive and sexually explicit visual material on computers and mobile phones (McDonald, 2012). Sexualized hate on the Internet against feminists has taken place in many countries and can also be seen as a new form of sexualized harassment (Filipovic, 2007). Anonymity is a crucial part of new media discussions on sexualities and brings many aspects of empowerment to the fore, but, paradoxically, freedom of speech and anonymity can sometimes enable sexualized harassment and hate speech in new media. It has been noticed also that researchers on gender, ethnicity and immigration have met with sexualized harassment, hate speech and actual threats that limit their public presentations. Current legislation, policies and codes of conducts do not necessarily safeguard freedom from sexualized harassment that takes place through ICTs and in social media. Multidisciplinary research on virtual sexuality, legislation(s) and organizational policies is crucial for current and future management strategies and development.

As we have seen, much of the literature on sexuality within Critical Management Studies derives from gender, feminist and queer studies scholars. The relations to and intersections with other social divisions such as class, race, ethnicity, bodily ability and age continue to be taken into account in future studies. While there is an increasing amount of policy interest in age and ageing because of the demographic changes in most late modern societies, there is relatively little research on the intersections of gender and age in management and organizations. However, age and ageing can impact differently on women managers than their men colleagues, and women are often interpreted as 'ageing' earlier than men (Itzin & Phillipson, 1995; Ilmarinen, 2005). A survey study of the financial sector in the U.K. suggests that women experience more age discrimination than do men (Duncan & Loretto, 2004), and another U.K. study (Granleese & Sayer, 2005) found that women in higher education are discriminated against in ways that differ from those that men identify: women experience a triple jeopardy of discrimination because of age, gender and 'lookism'. Gendered ageism in organizations can be manifested through sexualized commenting on women managers' physical features and age, both by men and other women (Jyrkinen, 2014). Thus, age(ism), gender and sexualities in different managerial and organizational contexts would need more research and be an area of interest in CMS in the future. Intersections of age, gender and sexualities are highly relevant for CMS, for several reasons, including demographic change and reorganization of care through globalizing care chains.

In accordance with Pullen and Thanem (2009: 4), we argue that it is important to consider sexuality in relation to space, which would demand focus on 'the ways in which sexuality is performed, expressed and enacted in various spatial contexts of work and organizations, and the ways in which this may disrupt and enable various spaces and forms of work and organization'. They highlight the need to examine 'the ways in which queer sexualities are restricted and performed in various spaces and forms of work and organization' and highlight the centrality of the body in the organizing and managing of space(s).

Relatedly, as work for change on the societal and organizational levels continues, research needs to document and analyze how organizations accommodate changing categorizations of gender, for example, providing toilets without the traditional male and female markings, and how they work for more inclusive cultures. The jurisdictional woman/man sex/(cis-)gender bipolarity excludes transgender people, and research on other genders could enable development of inclusive organizational policies and practices. Issues of dress and appearance, with their frequent sexual and gender meanings and connotations, also need to be highlighted, not least in relation to questions of discrimination and legal employment law (Brower & Jones, 2013). CMS could offer a forum for all such further explorations.

A final area for future research concerns global and transnational developments. The globalization of gendered work, sexploitation in particular of women in and from developing countries, and the increase in power of transnational companies demand much further research and critical analysis. For example, in the area of sexual harassment, research conducted outside Western contexts has made important contributions by documenting the consequences of sexual harassment for female domestic workers and different perceptions of sexual harassment across cultural contexts (McDonald, 2012).

CMS has today developed into a very broad field of inquiry where at times what exactly is meant by its 'criticality' has become less apparent. There is, moreover, still a lack of attention to gender and sexuality within CMS. Reviewing the literature on sexuality in organizations, it is clear that that critical edge of CMS scholarship could be revitalized by learning from the literature reviewed – much of it from various disciplines outside what is usually described as CMS – that has focused on sexualities and organizations.

References

Acker, J. (1990). Hierarchies, jobs, bodies: A theory of gendered organizations. *Gender and Society, 4*(2): 139–158.

Acker, J. (1991). Thinking about wages. *Gender & Society, 5:* 390–407.

Acker, J., & Van Houten, D. (1974). Differential recruitment and control: The sex structuring of organizations. *Administrative Science Quarterly, 9*(2): 152–163.

Adkins, L. (1995). *Gendered work: Sexuality, family and the labour market.* Buckingham: Open University Press.

Alvesson, M., & Deetz, S. (1996). Critical theory and postmodernism approaches to organizational studies. In S. Clegg, C. Hardy, & W. R. Nord (Eds.), *Handbook of organization studies:* 191–217. London: Sage.

Alvesson, M., & Deetz, S. (2006). Critical theory and postmodernism approaches to organizational studies. In Clegg, S., Hardy, C., Lawrence, T. B., & Nord, W. R. (Eds.), *Handbook of organization studies:* 255–283. London: Sage.

Badgett, M. V. L. (2001). *Money, myths, and change: The economic lives of lesbians and gay men.* Chicago: University of Chicago Press.

Barak, A. (2005). Sexual harassment on the Internet. *Social Science Computer Review, 23*(1): 77–92.

Bendl, R., Fleischmann A., & Hofmann, R. (2009). Queer theory and diversity management: Reading codes of conduct from a queer perspective. *Journal of Management & Organization, 15*: 625–638.

Bindman, J., & Dozema, J. (1997). Redefining prostitution as sex work on the international agenda. Retrieved July 5, 2013 from http://www.walnet.org/csis/papers/redefining.html.

Bland, L., Brundson, C., Hobson, D., & Winship, J. (1978). Women 'inside' and 'outside' the relations of production. In Women's Studies Group, CCCS, University of Birmingham (Ed.), *Women Take Issue:* 35–78. London: Hutchinson.

Bowring, M. A. (2004). Resistance is not futile: Liberating Captain Janeway from the masculine-feminine dualism of leadership. *Gender, Work & Organization, 11*: 381–405.

Bowring, M. A., & Brewis, J. (2009). Truth and consequences: Managing lesbian and gay identity in the Canadian workplace, *Equal Opportunities International, 28*(5): 361–377.

Brower, T., & Jones, J. (Eds.) (2013). Dress and appearance codes in the workplace: Gender, sexuality, law and legal institutions, Special issue. *Equality, Diversity and Inclusion, 32*(5).

Burke, M. E. (1993). *Coming out of the blue: British police officers talk about their lives in 'the job' as lesbians, gays and bisexuals.* London & New York: Cassell.

Butler, J. (1990). *Gender Trouble: Feminism and the Subversion of Identity.* New York: Routledge.

Calás, M., & Smircich, L. (1991). Voicing seduction to silence leadership. *Organization Studies, 12*(4): 567–601.

Calás, M. B., & Smircich, L. (1996). From 'the woman's' point of view: Feminist approaches to organization studies. In S. Clegg, C. Hardy & W. Nord (Eds.), *Handbook of organization studies:* 218–257. London: Sage.

Calás, M. B., & Smircich, L. (2006). From the 'woman's point of view' ten years later: Towards a feminist organization studies. In S. Clegg, C. Hardy, W. Nord & T. Lawrence (Eds.), *Handbook of organization studies* (2nd Ed.): 284–346. London: Sage.

Cammermeyer, M. (1994). *Serving in silence.* Harmondsworth: Penguin.

Cockburn, C. (1983). *Brothers: Male dominance and technological change.* London: Pluto.

Cockburn, C. (1991). *In the way of women.* London: Macmillan.

Colgan, F. (2011). Equality, diversity and corporate responsibility: Sexual orientation and diversity management in the UK private sector. Equality, Diversity and Inclusion. *AN International Journal, 30*(8): 719–734.

Colgan, F., & McKearney, A. (2012). Visibility and voice in organisations: Lesbian, gay, bisexual and transgendered employee networks, *Equality, Diversity and Inclusion: An International Journal, 31*(4): 359–378.

Collins, P. H. (1990). *Black feminist thought: knowledge, consciousness, and the politics of empowerment*. Boston: Unwin Hyman.

Collinson, D. L., & Hearn, J. (1994). Naming men as men: Implications for work, organization and management. *Gender, Work & Organization*, 1(1): 2–22.

Collinson, M., & Collinson, D. L. (1996). 'It's only Dick': The sexual harassment of women managers in insurance sales. *Work, Employment & Society*, 10: 29–56.

Coy, M. (Ed.). (2012). *Prostitution, harm and gender inequality: Theory, research and policy*. Farnham, UK: Ashgate.

Creed, W. E. D. (2006). Seven conversations about the same thing: Homophobia and heterosexism in the workplace. In A. M. Konrad, P. Prasad & J. K. Pringle (Eds.), *Handbook of workplace diversity*: 371–400. London: Sage.

Crenshaw, K. W. (1991). Mapping the margins: Intersectionality, identity politics, and violence against women of colour. *Stanford Law Review*, 43(6): 1241–1299.

Davis, G. (2009). *Mobilization strategies and gender awareness: An analysis of intersex social movement organizations*. Unpublished manuscript, Department of Sociology, University of Illinois at Chicago.

Duncan, C., & Loretto, W. (2004). Never the right age? Gender and age-based discrimination in employment'. *Gender, Work and Organization*, 11(1): 95–115.

Dunne, G. (1997). *Lesbian lifestyles: Women's work and the politics of sexuality*. Basingstoke, UK: Macmillan.

Enloe, C. (1989). *Bananas, beaches and bases: Making feminist sense of international politics*. Berkeley: University of California Press.

Epstein, D. (1997). Keeping them in their place: Hetero/sexist harassment, gender and the enforcement of heterosexuality. In A. Thomas & C. Kitzinger (Eds.), *Sexual harassment: Contemporary feminist perspectives*. Buckingham: Open University Press.

Filipovic, J. (2007). Blogging while female: How Internet misogyny parallels real-world harassment. *Yale Journal of Law & Feminism*, 19: 295.

Flam, H., Hearn, J., & Parkin, W. (2010). Organisations, violations and their silencing. In A. Wettergren & B. Sieben (Eds.), *Emotionalizing organizations and organizing emotions*: 147–165, Houndmills: Palgrave Macmillan.

Folgero, I. S., & Fjeldstad, I. H. (1995). On duty-off guard: Cultural norms and sexual harassment in service organizations. *Organization Studies*, 16(2): 299–313.

Foucault, M. (1976). *The history of sexuality*. Vol. 1: *An introduction*. London: Allen Lane.

Gherardi, S. (1995). *Gender, symbolism and organizational cultures*. London: Sage.

Githens, R. P., & Aragon, S. R. (2009). LGBT employee groups: Goals and organizational structures, *Advances in Developing Human Resources*, 11: 121–135.

Glover, K. (2006). Human trafficking and the sex tourism industry, *Crime & Justice International*, 22(92): 4–10.

Granleese, J., & Sayer, G. (2005). Gendered ageism and "lookism": A triple jeopardy for female academics. *Women in Management Review*, 21(6): 500–517.

Gruber, J. E., & Morgan, P. (Eds.). (2005). *In the company of men: Male dominance and sexual harassment*. Boston: Northeastern University Press.

Gutek, B. A., & Morasch, B. (1982). Sex-ratios, sex-role spillover, and sexual harassment of women at work. *Journal of Social Issues*, 38: 55–74.

Hall, E. (1995). *We can't even march straight*. London: Vintage.

Harding, N., Lee, H., Ford, J., & Learmonth, M. (2011). Leadership and charisma: A desire that cannot speak its name? *Human Relations*, 64(7): 927–949.

Hearn, J. (1991). Gender: Biology, nature and capitalism. In T. Carver (Ed.), *The Cambridge companion to Marx*: 222–245. New York: Cambridge University Press

Hearn, J. (2006). The implications of information and communication technologies for sexualities and sexualised violences: Contradictions of sexual citizenship. *Political Geography*, 25(8): 944–963.

Hearn, J. (2011). Sexualities, work, organizations, and managements: Empirical, policy, and theoretical challenges. In E. L. Jeanes, D. Knights & P. Y. Martin (Eds.), *Handbook of gender, work, and organization*: 299–314. Chichester: Wiley.

Hearn, J., Jyrkinen, M., Piekkari, R., & Oinonen, E. (2008). "Women home and away": Transnational managerial work and gender relations. *Journal of Business Ethics*, 83(1): 41–54.

Hearn, J., & Parkin, W. (1983). Gender and organizations: A selective review and a critique of a neglected area. *Organization Studies*, 4(3): 219–242.

Hearn, J., & Parkin, W. (1987/1995). *'Sex' at 'work': The power and paradox of organisation sexuality* (1st/2nd ed.). New York: St. Martin's Press.

Hearn, J., & Parkin, W. (2001). *Gender, sexuality and violence in organizations: The unspoken forces of organization violations*. London: Sage.

Hochschild, A. R. (1983). *The managed heart: Commercialization of human feeling*. Berkeley: University of California Press.

Hochschild, A. R. (2000). Global care chains and emotional surplus value. In W. Hutton & A. Giddens (Eds.), *On the edge: Living with global capitalism*, London: Jonathan Cape.

Holgersson, C. (2011). "When in Rome . . ."?: On multinational corporations, codes of conduct and commercial sex. In A. Biricik & J. Hearn (Eds.), *Proceedings from GEXcel theme 9: Gendered sexualed trans-nationalisations, deconstructing the dominant: Transforming men, "centres" and knowledge/policy/practice, Spring 2011*: 105–115. Linköping & Örebro: Institute of Thematic Gender Studies, Linköping and Örebro Universities, GEXcel Work in Progress Series.

Holgersson, C. (2013). Recruiting managing directors: Doing homosociality. *Gender, Work and Organization*, *20*(4): 454–466.

Holvino, E., & Kamp, A. (2009). Diversity management. *Scandinavian Journal of Management, 25:* 395–403.

Höök, P. (2001). Management as uncontrollable sexuality. In Sjöstrand, S.-E., M. Tyrstrup & J. Sandberg (Eds.), *Invisible management: The social construction of leadership*. London: Thomson Learning.

hooks, b. (1981). *Ain't I a woman? Black women and feminism*. Boston: South End Press.

Humphrey, J. (2000). Organizing sexualities, organization inequalities: Lesbians and gay men in public service occupations. *Gender, Work and Organization*, *6*(3): 134–151.

Husu, L (2001). *Sexism, support and survival in academia: Academic women and hidden discrimination in Finland*. Helsinki: Department of Social Psychology, University of Helsinki.

Ilmarinen, J. (2005). *Towards a longer worklife! Ageing and the quality of worklife in the European Union*. Helsinki: Finnish Institute of Occupational Health and Ministry of Social Affairs and Health.

Itzin, C., & Phillipson, C. (1995). Gendered ageism: A double jeopardy for women in organisations. In C. Itzin & C. Phillipson (Eds.), *Gender, culture and organisational change. Putting theory into practice*: 84–94. London: Routledge.

James, P., & Carkeek, F. (1997). This abstract body: From embodied symbolism to techno-disembodiment. In D. Holmes (Ed.), *Virtual politics: Identity and community in cyberspace*: 107–124. London: Sage.

Jeffreys, S. (2012). Beyond 'agency' and 'choice in theorizing prostitution. In M. Coy (Ed.), *Prostitution, harm and gender inequality: Theory, research and policy*: 69–86. Farnham, UK: Ashgate.

Jyrkinen, M. (2005). *The organization of policy meets the commercialization of sex. Global linkages, policies, technologies*. Helsinki: Hanken School of Economics [http://hdl.handle.net/10227/118].

Jyrkinen, M. (2012). McSexualization of bodies, sex and sexualities: Mainstreaming the commodification of gendered inequalities. In M. Coy (Ed.), *Prostitution, harm and gender inequality: Theory, research and policy*: 13–32. Farnham, UK: Ashgate.

Jyrkinen, M. (2014). Women managers, careers and gendered ageism, *Scandinavian Journal of Management*, *30*(2): 175–185.

Jyrkinen, M., & McKie, L. (2012). Gender, age and ageism: Experiences of women managers in two EU countries. *Work, Employment and Society*, *26*(1): 61–77.

Kanter, R. M. (1977). *Men and women of the corporation*. New York: Basic Books.

Kincheloe, J. L., & McLaren, P. L. (1994). Rethinking critical theory and qualitative research. In N. K. Denzin & Y. S. Lincoln (Eds.), *Handbook of qualitative research*: 138–157. Thousand Oaks, CA: Sage.

Krus (2012). http://www.krus.nu/Verksamhetsomrade/Privat-pa-jobbet.

Lee, D. (2000). Hegemonic masculinity and male feminisation: The sexual harassment of men at work. *Journal of Gender Studies*, *9*(2): 141–155.

Lee, H., Learmonth, M., & Harding, N. (2008). Queer(y)ing public administration. *Public Administration*, *86*: 1–19.

Lehtonen, J., & Mustola, K. (Eds.). (2004). *"Straight people don't tell, do they . . . ?" Negotiating the boundaries of sexuality and gender at work*. Helsinki: Ministry of Labour. Retrieved from http://www.esr.fi.

Lerum, K. (2004). Sexuality, power, and camaraderie in service work. *Gender & Society, 18*: 756–776.

MacKinnon, C. A. (1982). Feminism, Marxism, method and the state: An agenda for theory. *Signs*, 7(3): 515–544.

Marx, K., & Engels, F. (1976). *The German ideology*. In *Collected works*, Vol. 5. New York: International Publishers.

McCall, L. (2005). The complexity of intersectionality. *Signs: Journal of Women in Culture and Society*, *30*(3) 1771–1800.

McClintock, A. (1995). *Imperial leather: Race, gender and sexuality in the colonial contest*. New York: Routledge.

McDonald, P. (2012). Workplace sexual harassment 30 years on: A review of the literature. *International Journal of Management Reviews, 14*: 1–17.

McDonald, P., Backstrom, S., & Dear, K. (2008). Reporting sexual harassment: Claims and remedies. *Asia Pacific Journal of Human Resources, 46*(2): 173–195.

McDowell, L. (1997). *Capital culture: Gender at work in the city.* Oxford: Blackwell.

Mieli, Mario (1980). Homosexuality and liberation: Elements of a gay critique. London: Gay Men's Press.

Namaste, V. (2000). *Invisible lives: The erasure of transsexual and transgendered people.* Chicago: University of Chicago Press.

O'Connell Davidson, J. (2002). The rights and wrongs of prostitution, *Hypatia, 17*(2): 84–98.

O'Connell Davidson, J. (2004). Child sex tourism: An anomalous form of movement? *Journal of Contemporary European Studies, 12*(1): 31–46.

Oerton, S. (1996a). *Beyond hierarchy: Gender, sexuality and the social economy.* London: Taylor & Francis.

Oerton, S. (1996b). Sexualizing the organization, lesbianizing the women: Gender, sexuality and flat organizations. *Gender, Work and Organization, 3*(1): 289–297.

Out Now Consulting Gay Times and Diva Readers Surveys. (2005). www.OutNowconsulting.com. Also see *Gay at home but not at work.* New study – UK gays unable to reveal sexuality at work. http://www.gaywork.com/page.cfm?Sectionid=5&typeofsite=storydetail&ID=269&storyset=yes.

Parker, M. (2002). Queering management and organization. *Gender, Work & Organization, 9*: 146–166.

Popovich, P., & Warren, M. (2010). The role of power in sexual harassment as a counterproductive behavior in organizations. *Human Resource Management Review, 20*: 45–53.

Pringle, J. K. (2008). Gender in management: Theorizing gender as heterogender. *British Journal of Management, 19*: 110–119.

Pringle, R. (1989). *Secretaries talk: Sexuality, power and work.* London: Verso.

Pullen, A., & Thanem, T. (2009). Editorial: Sexual spaces. *Gender, Work & Organization, 17*(1): 1–6.

Raeburn, N. C. (2004). *Changing corporate America from inside out: Lesbian and gay workplace rights.* Minneapolis: University of Minnesota Press.

Reis, C. (2004). *Men working as managers in a European multinational company.* Munich & Mering: Rainer Hampp Verlag.

Rich, A. (1980), Compulsory heterosexuality and lesbian existence. *Signs,* 5(4): 631–660.

Roper, M. (1996). 'Seduction' and 'succession': Circuits of homosocial desire in management. In D. L. Collinson & J. Hearn (Eds.), *Men as managers, managers as men: Critical perspectives on men, masculinities and management*: 210–226. London: Sage.

Rumens, N. (2008). Working at intimacy: Gay men's workplace friendships. *Gender, Work & Organization, 15*(1): 9–30.

Rumens, N., & Kerfoot, D. (2009). Gay men at work: (Re)constructing the self as professional. *Human Relations, 62*: 763–786.

Schilt, K. (2006). Just one of the guys?: How transmen make gender visible in the workplace. *Gender & Society, 20*(4): 465–490.

Schilt, K. & Connell, C. (2007). Do gender transitions make gender trouble? *Gender, Work, & Organization, 14*(6): 596–618.

Schilt, K., & Wiswall, M. (2008). Before and after: Gender transitions, human capital, and workplace experiences. *The B.E. Journal of Economic Analysis & Policy, 8*(1): Article 39. 26 pp. Retrieved from http://www.econ.nyu.edu/user/wiswall/research/schilt_wiswall_transsexual.pdf.

Seidman, S. (1995). *Social postmodernism.* Cambridge: Cambridge University Press.

Shen, J. (2011). Developing the concept of socially responsible international human resource management. *The International Journal of Human Resource Management, 22*(6): 1351–1363.

Silverman, K. (1992). *Male subjectivity at the margins.* New York: Routledge.

Swedish Women's Lobby. (2013). Corporate compass – Policy on sexual exploitation. Retrieved on June 26, 2013 from http://www.rattriktning.se/home.

Tepelus, C. M. (2008), Social responsibility and innovation on trafficking and child sex tourism: Morphing of practice into sustainable tourism policies? *Tourism and Hospitality Research, 8*(2): 98–115.

Weston, K. M., & Rofel, L. B. (1984). Sexuality, class, and conflict in a lesbian workplace. *Signs, 9*(4): 623–646.

Woods, J. D., & Lucas, J. H. (1993). *The corporate closet: The professional lives of gay men in America.* New York: Free Press.

9

Power failure
The short life and premature death of critical "diversity" research

Roy Jacques

Introduction

Critical signifiers have a short shelf life. French Impressionist paintings that once constituted a radical critique of perception are now sold as wallpaper. *Viva Guevara*: Che Guevara lives – as a T-shirt icon, $21.95 plus shipping. The complex contributions of a half-century of Continental critical theorizing are today being methodologically lobotomized into mere narrative analysis pretentiously rechristened "discourse analysis" (*cf.* Grant, Hardy, Oswick & Putnam, 2004; Fairclough, 1995). With Procrustean dependability, genuine radicals are systematically replaced by "tempered radicals" (Meyerson, 2001), upholding the status quo from their positions of privilege while providing just enough *faux* challenge to the powers that be to drive out any substantive one.

Where does diversity research stand in this regard? This is an important question to critical scholars. Can one resist the tyranny of the status quo by doing critical diversity scholarship, or is that term now an oxymoron? Has diversity scholarship become a tool for assuring that marginality remains marginal? Is a "tempered radical" merely a self-flattering term for a conservative?

In this chapter, rather than asking what diversity *does* or *should* mean in an abstract sense, I am asking what it *has* meant to date as a cultural production, primarily in the American case (i.e., in case of the United States). Using content analysis of the papers and symposia that have been presented in the conference programs of the Gender & Diversity Division of the Academy of Management of the United States, I have attempted to paint an empirical picture of the boundaries of diversity research.

Why the American case? The term 'diversity' originates from American research; American concerns have been central to shaping the meanings it has assumed. For better and for worse, Americans enthusiastically export diversity 'knowledge' worldwide through scholarly work, textbooks, popular writing and corporate products. American cultural values permeate American social thought, yet research rarely indicates awareness of this fact (Jacques, 1992). Just as Rabinow (1986: 241) encouraged us to "anthropologize the West" in order to make space for other social realities, an international understanding of diversity research must contextualize and critique the influence of American differences and American values on the production and shaping of this complex signifier.

The radical potential of diversity discourse

Jones (2004) refers to the two divergent potentials inherent in diversity discourse. On the one hand, she writes "To talk about diversity and difference is to talk about the constantly shifting power relationships between the margins and the centre" (p. 281). On the other hand, her title "Screwing Diversity out of the Workers" graphically suggests the negative potential of the diversity signifier to reinforce marginality. As American diversity research has become increasingly institutionalized, we would do well to heed Jones's phrase "constantly shifting power relationships". What has reinforced marginality is not sameness or difference per se but the *power* to determine how sameness or difference will become salient and which differences will be so.

At its point of emergence a generation ago, diversity discourse was inherently radical to a degree because it was destabilizing both to work organizations and to management theory in general. It is clear how the status quo was challenged by the movement of women and non-white people into positions of authority, but there is a second, less visible way in which diversity discourse has had radical potential. It challenges our understanding of the very object of organization and management theory – the universal individual. In the formative decades of what has become management discourse, the subject of knowledge was simply the human being – what applied to one presumably applied to all, subject to differences that could be specified as personal or situational 'variables'. We could be tall or short, educated or ignorant, skilled or unskilled, but presumably under these surface differences we are all alike.

From Walter Dill Scott (Scott & Clothier, 1923) to Rensis Likert (1967), organizational behavior was simply the behavior of 'people', who differed in their possession of psychological variables, such as personality, but who shared a universal framework in which the same variables had the same relationship to one another and to social reality. This generic subject facilitated the mass production of management knowledge about those who, in parallel fashion, mass-produced the goods of society. It was also, we should acknowledge, a relatively liberal response to earlier proto-managerialist writing grounded in social Darwinist and eugenic thought (e.g. Blackford & Newcomb, 1914). A detailed history of the generic employee as a subject of management knowledge may be found in Jacques (1992).

The assumption that we are all just people, the same as one another under the skin, was a progressive response to this "scientific racism" (Shipman, 2002). The generic subject of management research dominated for several decades, then began to erode. It became a white subject in the wake of the American Civil Rights movement. 'He' became a masculine subject as the gendered nature of management came under feminist scrutiny. Today, ethnicity, sexual orientation and a host of other identities mark the main subject of organizational research not as 'humanity' but as subgroups of our species who share identity group memberships. One could justifiably argue that the greatest insight of the last half-century regarding the subject in organizations has been the gradual discovery of the profound degree to which human 'nature' – social reality itself – is contingent upon the shaping forces of social identity.

This is the 'paradigm' problem that has been central to debates within the social constructionist, poststructuralist, postcolonial and other anti-essentialist perspectives which have emerged in critical social thought in the last few decades. People, it seems, do not simply differ in the *degree* to which they possess a group of universal variables; they also differ by social identity group in the *saliency* of these variables, in the *relationship* of these variables to each other and even in *which* variables structure perception, value, belief – and thus action – within that group.

This has been problematic for Empiricist social theory. The presumed homogeneity of human subjectivity was foundational to the still incomplete project of developing a cohesive set of testable propositions about human behaviour in organizations. The so-called Hawthorne effect was supposed to have been a discovery about 'people,' not the reactions of female, immigrant, young, poor people. Mintzberg's (1971) 'classic' study was about what 'managers' really do, not what white, male, Canadian managers of a certain age, status and relationship to Mintzberg *père* do. As a diversity literature has developed into a profusion of research clusters focusing on the uniqueness of one and then another identity group, the dream of producing "a general theory of action" (Parsons & Shils, 1967) has receded like a horizon. Receding along with it is the credibility of the management disciplines. At risk are jobs and extensive resources in the business schools and in work organizations; one should expect that this would create strong resistance to change. The signifier 'diversity', then, does not simply have the potential to challenge social privilege. It also threatens the still dominant (if quixotic) Empiricist project of creating a statistical academic discourse about the person in work organizations.

Method

This study is not – as some earlier reviewers have erroneously imagined – an example of hypothetico-deductive analysis done badly. No statistically testable hypothesis is intended in the design. This work may more appropriately be considered interpretive content analysis. Quantification is used to subjectively create a portrait of the terrain surveyed. The method employed in this study is similar to that of Mintzberg (1971). For further discussion on this topic, the reader is invited to refer to Prasad (2005) and Burrell and Morgan (1979).

Data for the present review consist of the titles and abstracts of all papers and symposia presented in the Gender and Diversity in Organizations programs at the 10 Academy of Management meetings 1998–2007. Since the division changed its domain from "women in management" to "gender & diversity" in 1998, the sample represents a comprehensive population of everything presented as symposia or research papers by this division in its first decade. Certainly, relevant work has also been done in other divisions of the Academy of Management and elsewhere worldwide. However, the sum total of presentations at so professionally central a conference can reasonably be supposed to constitute an excellent proxy for the scope, emphases, theoretical approaches and assumptions structuring American academic discourse on the topic. The data have not been updated for submissions 2008–present because this would change only the number of submissions, not the pattern of content.

Objective and subjective information about each submission was recorded in a database. Non-diversity-related contributions from other divisions were eliminated. To equate papers and symposia, a symposium was recorded as if it were a single, multiply authored paper. The final database consisted of $n = 949$ papers and symposia. Categories were developed inductively. Significance testing was not deemed relevant and was not conducted. Results are presented as tabulations and percentages designed to show descriptively where the effort of a decade of diversity research has been placed. Tabulation of key data may be found in Tables 9.1–9.3.

Table 9.1a An empirical definition of diversity, 1998–2007: Most popular themes.

	TOTAL		2007	2006	2005	2004	2003	2002	2001	2000	1999	1998
	%	Number	130	86	102	123	96	71	65	75	60	53
[Does not match total submissions due to multiple entries.]												
GENDER	**42.7**	*405*	**59**	**38**	**43**	**43**	**56**	**39**	**27**	**40**	**33**	**27**
Sex difference – Total	**38.7**	*367*	**56**	**36**	**38**	**40**	**50**	**31**	**25**	**38**	**30**	**23**
Male/female difference	26.1	*248*	35	17	29	28	39	26	18	24	18	14
Women	11.8	*112*	19	17	9	12	11	5	7	12	12	8
Men	0.7	*7*	2	2	0	0	0	0	0	2	0	1
Gendering of bodies	**4.0**	*38*	**3**	**2**	**5**	**3**	**6**	**8**	**2**	**2**	**3**	**4**
RACE/ETHNICITY	**13.8**	*131*	**21**	**14**	**21**	**17**	**12**	**10**	**12**	**11**	**8**	**5**
Race unspecified	6.1	*58*	11	7	8	5	7	4	4	6	3	3
Ethnicity unspecified	1.2	*11*	1	1	3	1	1	1	1	1	0	1
African-American, black	2.6	*25*	3	1	5	5	2	2	5	0	1	1
Hispanic American	1.4	*13*	4	0	2	1	1	1	1	2	1	0
Asian	0.4	*4*	1	1	1	0	0	0	0	0	1	0
people of color	0.2	*2*		0	0	0	0	1	0	0	1	0
minorities	0.6	*6*		0	0	0	1	1	1	2	1	0
ethnic (vs. non-ethnic)	0.1	*1*		0	0	1	0	0	0	0	0	0
native (vs. immigrant)	0.1	*1*		0	0	1	0	0	0	0	0	0
Indian (from India)	0.2	*2*		2	0	0	0	0	0	0	0	0
White	0.8	*8*	1	2	2	3	0	0	0	0	0	0

Table 9.1a (Continued)

	TOTAL		2007	2006	2005	2004	2003	2002	2001	2000	1999	1998
	%	Number										
CULTURE	**6.6**	**63**	**20**	**4**	**5**	**8**	**5**	**5**	**5**	**4**	**3**	**4**
Organizational culture	0.1	1				1						
National culture	0.0											
Unspecified, general	2.3	22	6	2	2	4	2	1	2	1	1	1
Australia	0.2	2	2									
Brazil	0.2	2	2									
U.S.	0.1	1										1
France	0.1	1	1									
Japan	0.1	1			1							
Mexico	0.1	1			1							
Korea	0.3	3	1			2						
China – PRC	0.8	8	1				1	2	1	1	1	1
China – Hong Kong	0.3	3	1								1	1
China – Taiwan	0.2	2	1							1		
India	0.2	2		1				1				
Ghana	0.1	1				1						
Turkey	0.1	1					1					
Norway	0.1	1						1				
Italy	0.1	1					1					
Europe	0.1	1							1			
Pakistan	0.2	2	2									
Sweden	0.2	2	2									
Holland	0.1	1							1			
New Zealand	0.1	1								1		
Religion – Unspecified	0.2	2	1	1								
Religion – Islam	0.1	1			1							
GENERIC DIFFERENCE – No identity specified	**29.0**	**275**	**43**	**30**	**33**	**55**	**23**	**17**	**21**	**20**	**16**	**17**

Table 9.1b An empirical definition of diversity, 1998–2007: Less common themes.

	TOTAL %	TOTAL Number	2007	2006	2005	2004	2003	2002	2001	2000	1999	1998
Hidden identities	**3.1**	**88**	**12**	**8**	**11**	**14**	**11**	**7**	**9**	**9**	**6**	**7**
LGBT specifically	2.7	29	3	2	5	3	3	2	3	3	5	0
Other (e.g. chronic illness, belief)	0.3	26	3	2	4	3	2	1	3	3	5	0
Disability	**2.0**	**19**	**1**	**2**	**0**	**4**	**4**	**2**	**4**	**1**	**1**	**0**
Physical	1.9	18	1	1	0	4	4	2	4	1	1	0
Mental	0.1	1	0	1	0	0	0	0	0	0	0	0
Appearance	**0.8**	**8**	**0**	**0**	**1**	**1**	**1**	**1**	**0**	**4**	**0**	**0**
Weight/obesity	0.4	4	0	0	1	1	1	1	0	0	0	0
Attractiveness	0.4	4	0	0	0	0	0	0	0	4	0	0
Age	**1.3**	**12**	**2**	**1**	**1**	**2**	**3**	**1**	**1**	**0**	**0**	**1**
Being a certain age	0.9	9	2	1	0	2	2	1	1	0	0	0
Caring for those of a certain age	0.2	2	0	0	0	0	1	0	0	0	0	1
Singles	0.1	1	0	0	1	0	0	0	0	0	0	0
Family type	0.4	4	0	2	1	1	0	0	0	0	0	0
Bullying	0.1	1	0	0	0	1	0	0	0	0	0	0
Social class	**1.6**	**15**	**6**	**1**	**3**	**2**	**0**	**1**	**1**	**1**	**0**	**0**
Class/caste	0.5	5	1	1	1	0	0	0	1	1	0	0
Privilege	0.2	2	0	0	1	1	0	0	0	0	0	0
Poverty	0.3	3	1	0	1	1	0	0	0	0	0	0
"Dirty work"	0.5	5	4	0	0	0	0	1	0	0	0	0

Table 9.2 Common perspectives and topics.

	%	n =	2007	2006	2005	2004	2003	2002	2001	2000	1999	1998
TOTAL SUBMISSIONS [some submissions uncategorizable]		952	123	119	95	133	108	80	83	80	73	58
Correcting perceptual bias	25%	235										
General		149	13	25	16	29	20	13	11	13	4	5
Personnel issues: Hiring, promotion, careers, etc.		77	10	6	8	6	8	5	4	9	11	10
Organizational justice. Justice – Perceptions		9	0	2	0	2	2	0	2	0	1	0
Relational Demography	33%	312										
General		142	6	30	14	24	24	14	8	11	8	3
Organizational justice – Empirical antecedents/consequences		3	0	1	2	0	0	0	0	0	0	0
Effect of diversity on organizational performance		119										
Positive		55	6	1	6	6	11	6	8	3	2	6
Negative		1	1	0	0	0	0	0	0	0	0	0
Situational (or relationship unclear from abstract)		63	14	1	4	14	4	1	4	10	11	0
Moderately constructionist: Social ID / Social Network Theory		48	6	11	8	5	4	2	6	3	2	1
"Identity-ist" and other antiessentialist	4%	42	8	5	0	3	2	8	4	2	6	4
Human Capital / Social Capital	1%	13	1	0	0	3	2	5	0	0	1	1
Work-life/work-family	10%	98	18	13	9	12	12	7	6	10	3	8
Personnel	8%	79	12	6	8	6	8	5	4	9	11	10
Violence/harassment	4%	38										
To women		22	0	0	4	2	4	2	4	3	2	1
To men, other identities		3	0	0	0	0	1	0	0	0	1	1
General unspecified		13	1	0	0	0	0	1	1	2	4	4
International comparisons	3%	32	2	4	3	11	1	3	5	1	1	1
EEO/affirmative action/glass ceiling	3%	32	4	4	5	1	0	2	11	1	2	2
Mentoring	2%	23	3	3	1	4	2	4	3	1	2	0
Decision making/rational action	4%	35	15	4	6	3	2	1	2	1	1	0
Privilege, creation/maintenance	1%	9	2	2	1	2	1	1	0	0	0	0
Backlash/resistance	0%	4	1	1	0	0	0	1	0	1	0	0

Table 9.3 Levels of analysis in GDO studies 1998–2007.

	TOTAL		2007	2006	2005	2004	2003	2002	2001	2000	1999	1998
	n =	%										
[Rows/columns may not total to 100% due to rounding.]												
Individual – total	506	61%	60%	70%	60%	62%	59%	56%	63%	66%	54%	60%
Individual – focus on marginal	308	37%	16%	45%	33%	37%	35%	41%	37%	46%	52%	53%
Individual – focus on dominant	77	9%	8%	17%	11%	12%	8%	6%	16%	8%	0%	2%
Individual – focus on both	121	15%	36%	8%	17%	13%	16%	9%	10%	12%	2%	4%
Group	100	12%	12%	8%	7%	9%	20%	17%	13%	12%	16%	9%
Organization	117	14%	15%	14%	18%	18%	15%	7%	6%	14%	16%	13%
Social/Structural	78	9%	10%	7%	10%	8%	4%	17%	15%	4%	11%	15%
Unable to categorize	25	3%	3%	2%	5%	4%	1%	3%	3%	4%	2%	4%
	826											

Reviewing the data

What identities are 'diverse'?

So, what has counted as diversity? As Figure 9.1 indicates, three groups constitute more than 85% of submissions reviewed. If one combines ethnicity and national culture, which have not systematically been distinguished as separate constructs in this literature, the proportion climbs to 92%. There are some interesting presences and absences in this data.

Gender

The 43% representation of gender studies is somewhat proportional to the fact that half of the world's population is female. What is more surprising is that most 'gender' research in this sample is not gender research at all. A well established distinction shared between mainstream and critical scholars has long been that 'gender' refers to socialized difference which is not inherently connected to the male or female body. Differences between male and female bodies are properly referred to as 'sex' differences. In the pool of *Women in Management* articles reviewed by Calás & Jacques (1988), this distinction had been rigorously observed. A generation later, apart from a few of the more traditional social psychology researchers who refer, properly, to sex difference or sex effects, it is commonplace to describe any article related to male/female difference as being about 'gender'. Of 405 submissions related to gender, only 38 in any way addressed the construction of masculinity/femininity. The remaining 90% simply studied differences between a male and a female pool of research subjects.

This practice constitutes an implicit return to social Darwinist trait theories, in which cognitive and behavioural attributes are attributed to subjects based upon 'physiognomy'. There is irony in this. Where sex difference has been studied, it has overwhelmingly been by researchers with progressive intent who sought to establish "no significant difference" between marginal and dominant populations in their ability to work effectively (Jacobson & Jacques, 1990). Socially, this has meant that there is no reason to presume women less effective than men. However, if researchers were not committed to maintaining male superiority, they showed total dedication to using the Empiricist tools of their training. Thus, decades after gender construction has been recognized, males and females continue to be used as proxies for gender, not because they are appropriate but because they are operationalizable.

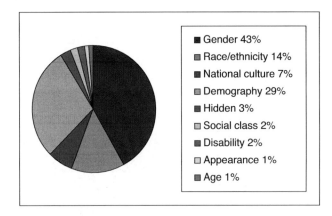

Figure 9.1   Topics researched

Among the 10% of these studies which did address gender construction, most were from Interpretive or anti-essentialist perspectives. Most represented the work of European contributors. This represents a backsliding in terms of the mainstream understanding of gender in the American academy. In the 1980s, there were even popular Empiricist models, such as the Bem Sex Role Inventory, which offered conceptual models for de-essentializing male/female difference. In the period covered by the present review, biological difference has been used unquestioningly as a proxy for male/female differences – within theory in which they are conceived to be social.

Race

Since the construct of race is not biologically meaningful, it is incumbent upon 'race' researchers to stipulate how this notion has been conceptualized in their research. For instance, to Benjamin Franklin, German immigrants to Pennsylvania c. 1800 were not white; to mainstream Americans of the late 1800s, Italian and Eastern European immigrants were not white (Jacques, 1992). Today, both are widely considered to be white in race research. What, then, constitutes whiteness?

These studies lack rigorous discussion of their central variable, relying instead on unexamined, populist, American notions of race. Of the "race/ethnicity" subcategories in Table 9.1a ($n = 131$), *all* refer to American racial difference. In the category "culture" ($n = 63$), a possible proxy for race, the majority compared a research sample in a 'diverse' (e.g. non-U.S.) country with 'the literature', which has of course been derived largely from American samples. This amounts to judging all other countries according to a U.S.-based deficit model. Table 9.3 identifies only 32 studies which were multinational comparisons; thus, a minimum of 84% of race studies were either studies of the U.S., or they compared the world to a U.S. template. There was no discussion of the difficulty of conceptualizing race or of the limits of generalizability.

Even among American studies of race, the tetralogy of white/black/Hispanic/Asian dominates the discussion. With every culture in the world represented in the American population, how has 'diversity' been narrowed to relations among these four (very heterogeneous) populations? The answer is inseparable from the specifics of American cultural history. What it means to be 'of color' in the U.S. is not automatically transportable to other countries. To be a 'black fella' in Australia or 'brown' in New Zealand is a meaningful signifier but one whose relationships of power and marginality in those countries are simultaneously similar to and different from race in America in complex ways irreducible to a 'variable'.

These studies constitute an a theoretical set of comparisons based on a random smattering of racial, ethnic and national categories. They underscore the need for theoretical frameworks to help us understand which differences count as 'diverse' (Konrad, Prasad & Pringle, 2006; Nkomo & Cox, 1996). Not only is our understanding constrained by simplistic and culturally specific American fault lines. At the other extreme, identifiable social groups worldwide can be 'diverse' for the purposes of research. How can one conceptualize cultural memberships in a way that both permits the expression of local voice and captures more generalizable aspects of the dynamics of marginalization?

Is national difference a proxy for race? In 59 studies, it is treated as such. One suspects that there is a great difference in the degree to which this category captures a coherent unit of analysis. At one extreme, to be Japanese is probably a highly salient category for (non-Ainu) Japanese. In contrast, between China and Indonesia, using nationality as a proxy for race is undermined both by the fact that China is multi-ethnic and by the presence of a significant Han Chinese ethnic minority in Indonesia. A 'race' comparison of Americans and Mexicans might sneak past a 'white' American reviewer, but what of a comparison of Americans to the Canadian 'race'? National difference is meaningful, but it is not reducible to ethnicity, and there has been an absence of discussion regarding how to theorize it.

One final thought on race is that this review does not contain a single paper discussing indigeneity. This may again result from the dominance of U.S. cultural history in shaping diversity discourse, since U.S. history with first peoples has been nearly genocidal. Contrast this to the experience of New Zealand, where first peoples (the Maori) still constitute about one-seventh of the population and have treaty rights with the British crown which (albeit incoherently) stipulate rights to some form of bicultural national co-governance. In this context, problems of marginality overlap with problems of indigeneity, but they are not entirely congruent.

Being 'brown' in New Zealand is a marker of marginality, but it is not historically associated with slavery. African-Americans do not claim to be indigenous Americans, but Maori do claim rights as the people of *Aotearoa*, the Maori land within which European New Zealand formed, marginalizing but not eliminating it. Maori share some issues such as health and housing with Sa'amoan, Tongan and other *Pasifika* New Zealanders, but only Maori have first-people rights, and each group has its distinct culture. This intersection of race and indigeneity has no complete parallel in American race discourse. In what ways can we extrapolate from American experiences and in what ways do these relationships have their own local shape and specificity? Worldwide, further examples are everywhere, yet the theoretical problem of Americanism shaping a diversity literature around American relationships constitutes a deafening silence in the literature.

Demographics

Incongruously, the second most popular category of diversity research does not even specify what is diverse about the subjects studied! Difference is specified only as 'demography' or 'identity', as though all differences are created equal. Examples of topics in this area would include the relationship between team diversity and team performance or the relationship between a company's diversity reputation and profitability. On the one hand, rising above the profusion of individual variables is theoretically laudable. As Tables 9.1a–9.1b show, the range of various differences is computationally intractable from a data processing perspective. Hypothetically, abstracting from individual identity differences to demography is a feasible way to make the problem tractable, but at what cost? When 'diversity' becomes 'demography', does what remains elucidate the relationships of diversity or remove them from analysis altogether? There are already entire fields dedicated to the study of all demographic difference among social groups. We call them sociology and anthropology. How, if at all, is diversity research not merely a pale reflection of these?

Absences

One notable absence in these articles is religion, the topic of a mere three studies. Although it is a formidable shaping force in the world today, religious identity has barely entered diversity discourse. Perhaps more surprising is the near absence ($n = 15$) of studies related to social class, caste or poverty, since exclusion from wealth is so tightly associated with marginality as to be almost definitional of it. While there is delicious irony in a field having removed the marginal from the diversity discourse, one might question how methodologically or socially appropriate this silencing is.

Topics addressed

The preceding section has considered *who* is considered diverse. This section will discuss *what* researchers have wanted to know about them. Again, a small number of categories account for the preponderance of work. Figure 9.2 summarises the results of this analysis.

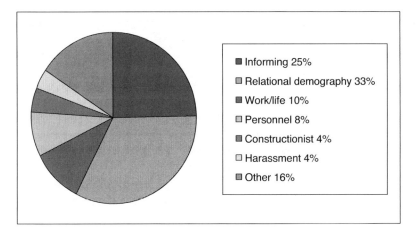

Figure 9.2 Topics addressed.

Relational demography

Fully a third of submissions utilized some form of social identity theory or social network theory to conceptualize diversity as a 'network imbalance'. Most often, this pool of submissions stipulated only that 'diversity' was the variable of interest, as though diversity itself is directly measurable without making operationalizing assumptions. Of this group, nearly half (45%) were attempts to describe the general network, abstracting people entirely out of the problematic. Of the remainder, the central topic of interest has been the effect of diversity on team performance, not on team members.

There has been one limited area of theoretical progress. A generation ago, it was widely accepted within this research that diversity improves team performance. This has given way to a more nuanced exploration of the conditions under which it does and does not. On the positive side of the ledger, promoting team performance has been one of the motivational wedges that diversity researchers have used to stimulate corporate interest in diversity. For this reason, the contribution of this stream of research should not be dismissed. At the same time, the prominence of this stream raises the threat that diversity might come to be understood only as an issue of profitability, to the exclusion of equity.

Informing people of misperceptions

Fully a quarter of all contributions (*n* = 235) have been implicitly informed by the Gospel of John (8:32), "You shall know the truth and the truth shall make you free". Marginality is conceptualized as an information deficit of the marginal, the dominant or both. No doubt, some marginalization is accomplished unknowingly by people who would act otherwise if they knew better, but how much? Probably not all and perhaps only a little. Ferguson (1984), in her analysis of patriarchy, suggests that the reason the privileged do not 'get it', despite ample, available evidence, is that privilege is pretty much the ability to *choose* to not get it. Provisionally, one might postulate three degrees of diversity issues, each with different dynamics in this regard:

1   Ignorance-based discrimination.
2   Accommodation.
3   Privilege maintenance.

All three of these may be simultaneously present, but the value of information differs among them. *Ignorance* may be well addressed by accurate information. When an expatriate manager has to work in a different culture or new immigrants enter a work group in which they are an unfamiliar minority, the challenge may be to generate and share information. However, with *accommodation*, challenges such as employment of workers with mobility restrictions or different religious holidays, the problems do not disappear when ignorance does. Workers *do* need special consideration; employers may face significant costs; co-workers may dislike accommodating. Addressing accommodation issues effectively requires some information but further requires dealing with workplace power issues. A commitment to social equity, as well as to knowledge, is demanded. The third type of issue, *privilege maintenance*, is well summed up by the old bumper sticker: 'I'm not deaf; I'm ignoring you'. Research directed merely at correcting ignorance does little to contribute to points 2 and 3 in the list. We would be well reminded that John (8:32) refers to personal revelation, not to social change.

Work/life balance

Fully a tenth of all studies have addressed issues of work and family roles. This is a potentially useful research stream, but is it diversity research at all? Every worker also has a life. There is nothing inherently 'diverse' about studying work and family roles. Historically, this body of research was produced as a gender issue due to women's well documented disadvantages relative to men in this area, but that is not necessarily what work/family research must – or does – study. When the research subject is gender-unspecified or when the study is about the problems of men, where is the diversity issue? A cross-cultural work/life comparison does not necessarily impinge on gender issues. If everyone has work and family problems and a general body of information is being developed about them, is this not a general societal issue?

Constructionism

The topics explored also suggest an important issue in terms of research assumptions. Fewer than 4% of these articles claim a social constructionist or anti-essentialist theoretical position. However, this entire body of work is implicitly constructionist because it assumes that the social reality studied can be changed. The submissions grounded in social identity theory and social network theory focus on the construction of identity. One of the largest categories explicitly focuses on cognition and perception. Topics such as group performance and mentoring are based on values, perceptions and beliefs which affect people's behavior towards each other. This is significant because it points to a red herring division among diversity researchers.

Certain dichotomous divisions from the so-called paradigm wars of the 1980s have become unproductively entrenched in our conventional wisdom. One of these is the opposition of "positivist to non-positivist" (Konrad, Prasad & Pringle, 2006). This need not be the case. For our research purposes, whether one believes in a constructed or an objective ultimate reality is unimportant. We have, *de facto*, defined the research problematic as one that is socially constructed through personal, interpersonal and institutional social forces.

One should not, however, suppose that objectivist methods are at all incompatible with researching a constructed problematic. Such methods can be useful for documenting empirically stable relationships, whether these are constructed or not. That they cannot deliver the Real is not a liability compared to other methods, since none can. Where there are differences of importance between researchers, they do not involve method, but epistemology, training and ideology. Taking the constructed nature of the problematic seriously would dramatically transform this body of research.

Levels of analysis

Nearly two-thirds (61%) of these studies focused on the individual and, of these, the preponderance focused on the marginal (Table 9.3). There is both positive and negative potential in this skewness. It is laudable to attempt to understand the marginal, but in these studies the marginal are not sources of voice but merely sources of data. As Miller (1976: xix) appropriately warned, "The close study of an oppressed group reveals that a dominant group inevitably describes a subordinate group falsely in terms derived from its own systems of thought". Focus on the individual sense-making of the marginal from the perspective of the dominant virtually guarantees a diversity literature that passively blames the victim by focusing on what the marginal can do about their marginality.

There are also aspects of marginalization, such as hiring and promotion decisions, which are not merely perceptions of the marginal. Were these issues not largely beyond the control of the marginal, they would not be diversity issues to begin with. A focus on the marginal draws research focus away from the relationships of power which create marginality.

Since diversity issues are primarily enacted at the group level, it is somewhat surprising that only an eighth of the studies focused on this level. Of these, the overwhelming majority focused only on the relationship between group composition and work performance. This is a legitimate topic but one marred by two significant problems. The first, discussed earlier, is a lack of theoretical coherence regarding what counts as group diversity. The second is the triteness of the problematic defined. Organizational reality is primarily a group reality, the place where the individual and the structural intersect. There is so much more to explore at this level than team performance.

The minority of studies (14%) which focused on the organizational level did not complement the group and individual level studies as much as they raised completely different topics. Of primary interest were personnel policy and the connection between diversity or 'diversity reputation' and performance. The small portion of studies which addressed the social/structural level of analysis (9%) included almost all of the submissions which identified themselves as poststructuralist, critical or postcolonial. Where other studies included this level, it was primarily about society as a supplier or a market – the effect of diversity on hiring or its effect on sales. This chapter's findings regarding levels of analysis are summarized in Figure 9.3.

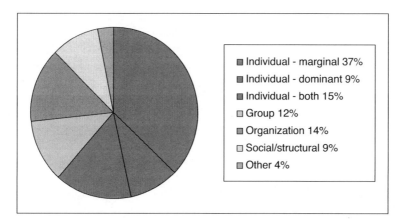

Figure 9.3 Levels of analysis.

Pervasively in this research, organizational reality is treated as something produced by individuals who behave as rational sense-makers. Since the group-, organizational- and social-structural levels are treated as more or less merely aggregations of individual efforts, all of society is treated as the product of such robotic individuals. This is a questionable view in general, but especially in the volatile area of diversity issues. In making the central research object the rational, individual mind, this research silences consideration of the role of either non-rational behavior or social-structural forces in maintaining privilege.

Funeral for a friend

Has 'diversity' become a dead signifier? The idea merits consideration. Terms such as oppression, marginalization, dominance, power, collusion, racism, sexism and privilege are rarely found in this literature. In 'diversity' discourse, everyone is well intentioned and self-determining; there is no battle for scarce resources; malicious intent and wilful ignorance barely exist. One of the central relations of power structuring 'diversity' discourse is the oxymoronic axiom that relations of power are unimportant. It is increasingly impossible within this discourse to say that somebody is getting screwed over.

Empirically, it seems that diversity discourse has settled into a narrow discursive space in which privilege and injustice are increasingly unrepresentable and the central diversity issue is its effect on corporate performance. Admittedly, this does not necessarily reflect the intentions of diversity researchers, many of whom do care about creating a more equitable workplace. Still, the largely unquestioned discursive boundaries of 'diversity' discourse make it a vehicle that does not go where most critical scholars would wish to take it.

One important contributor to this problem is a near universal failure to question what Burrell & Morgan (1979:105) refer to as "abstracted empiricism." As they explain:

> [A]bstracted empiricism represents a situation in which a highly nomothetic methodology is used to test a theory which is based upon an ontology, an epistemology and a theory of human nature of a more subjectivist kind.
>
> *(Burrell & Morgan, 1979: 105)*

Even the primarily Empiricist literature reviewed in this chapter has defined diversity as a constructed problematic, yet for 96% of the studies reviewed, social construction was a problem to transcend. The problem is recognized to be grounded in human perception; to have no objective basis apart from human consciousness; to be dynamic; to be influenced by the group, organizational and social context – but this in no way tempers the blind Empiricist belief that enough hypothesis testing will lead eventually to positive knowledge. Restricting the discourse to that which can be expressed as a statistically significant difference removes most of what matters from the phenomena studied. It also conveniently facilitates the kind of diversity discourse that an African-American colleague described to me several years ago when she referred to a particular diversity consultant as, "Making a quarter-million dollars a year telling white people what they want to hear."

Might a discourse of 'marginality' as an alternative discourse of difference better support progressive change? If a precondition of change is to state that some people are being treated unfairly, this seems increasingly necessary. The following questions and comments are offered as examples of topics which might interest a scholar of marginality but which have not been represented in the literature reviewed in this study. These are not tested propositions but plausible topics we might investigate more vigorously if we took the questioning of unfair privilege seriously:

- What general social relationships define marginality and diversity, regardless of the specific signifier through which they operate?
- How does affirming the identity of the marginal automatically undermine the entrenched self-interest of the dominant and produce resistance?
- What are the dynamics of the social pressures which push dominant identities together and marginal identities apart?
- Where are the voices of the Others in diversity research? The marginal cannot be fairly represented except in their own voices, and there are such voices in the literature – feminism, Afrocentric theory, postcolonial theory, *Ubuntu, kaupapa Maori*. Where are they in theory?
- It seems that, overall, marginal people are not uniformly better human beings, nor are the dominant merely evil, yet harm is done and privilege is experienced. What forces make this so?
- What are the overall and long-term consequences to the individual and to society of denying voice and dignity?
- How does privilege reproduce itself in a manner that is more or less transparent to the privileged?
- How do we understand the observable fact that those who possess marginal demographics do not necessarily act in solidarity with their demographic?
- How do the dynamics of 'getting ahead' reinforce the dynamics of dominance and marginality?
- How is marginality a source of blindness, as well as insight? How is the same true of dominance?
- To what extent is 'maturity' socialized behaviour? Cultures which appear 'childlike' to the observer may illustrate more about the observer's construction of maturity than about the deficiency of the Other. How can Western maturity be "anthropologized" as Rabinow (1986) suggests?
- What conflicts are associated with finding a meaningful place within the mainstream while simultaneously honouring a cultural heritage linked to marginality?
- What are the limits of pluralism (there is only one CEO, only one personnel policy . . .)?
- Given that the status quo is a production of dominant culture and that dominant culture values are embedded in 'excellent' management practice as well as in 'rigorous' research practice, how is equal access to the status quo is still not equitable to those of other backgrounds?
- How are the same stories told about the marginal (dirty, childlike, stupid, sexual and lazy) worldwide, regardless of the marker of marginality?
- Since marginality is everywhere linked to poverty, what is the place of social class membership in the study of diversity?
- What are the dynamics of ignorance? How does it operate to reproduce marginality? How does exclusion from the *savoir faire* required to move out of lower-status work (or unemployment) perpetuate privilege? How does ignorance result in unintentional collusion of the marginal with the dominant?

'Diversity' is an exhausted signifier

All these questions make up merely a sampler, but in them one can see that most of the terrain we could have explored in diversity research remains terra incognita. Mere acknowledgement of power relationships and inequity is impolite. This is analogous to petroleum scientists excluding the study of carbon. Myriad differences have been tabulated as markers of diversity, but mere difference is not inherently a diversity issue. Virtually all of the research reviewed measures one or more demographic differences without theorizing the relations of power that create privilege and marginality around that difference. As 'diversity' erodes into 'demographics', we are now all equally 'diverse'. The notion of inequity which motivated the old blacks-in-management and women-in-management research has been lost.

Whatever the axis of difference, just two things dependably determine which social differences will count as diverse – *membership* and *knowledge*. The dominant are members of the group with disproportionate power; the marginal are not, and they are labeled as such. Additionally, the dominant disproportionally learn to negotiate the relationships of power which lead to successfully turning dominant group membership into social privilege; the marginal not only do not have this opportunity but the 'common sense' within which they are raised is counterproductive in this regard. It follows that the antidote to privilege and marginality is *inclusion* and *education* – but not merely at the company level; both are general social issues relevant from cradle to grave. How do we develop a coherent body of theory around these two relationships, one which can inform progressive social action? To date, progress has been worse than disappointing in the organizational 'diversity' literature.

When the idea for this chapter first took shape several years ago, the working title was 'Toward a General Theory of Diversity'. The goal was to argue for a need to abstract from specific cases and analyze general fault lines of difference, to move from research fragmentation to more general theoretical models. One of the surprises of this research has been to find that such models are emerging, in social identity theory, in network analysis – some research even speaks specifically of "fault line analysis". Ironically, however, in such analysis, what gets lost is the fact that somebody is getting cheated and hurt, which was the motivating issue for this research area in the first place. No. What is needed is not merely abstracted general theory but general theory which remains connected to the pain and suffering of being short-changed in life.

Summing up, as diversity research has coalesced, three congenital and fatal flaws have become boundary conditions of this research. That is, they are not simply common; they are conditions of credibility:

1   *Lack of theory:* The field is moving away from, not closer to, coherent theories regarding the dynamics of privilege and marginality, despite a plethora of available models in the allied social sciences.
2   *Methodolatry:* The ability to speak of complex phenomena, values or emotions, which are all central to the dynamics of privilege and marginality, is fatally hampered by near universal acceptance among researchers of methods which involve statistical hypothesis testing, computation and therefore simplistic models and either/or findings. Refusal to accept the inadequacy of the generic employee has cost diversity research the ability to say very much of importance.
3   *Co-optation:* To be "within the true" (Foucault, 1970) of diversity discourse, one must treat organization members as people of good will. Racists, sexists, bigots, the self-interested and greedy do not exist. Further, one must design one's research to address diversity as a source of or barrier to competitive advantage rather than as an issue of ethics or justice.

This is not to say that all work using the signifier 'diversity' has exhibited these qualities. There are indeed examples of this research which recognize inequities and power relations and argue for change that goes beyond enhancing corporate profitability (see e.g. Prasad, Mills, Elmes & Prasad, 1997). The question this chapter poses is whether the signifier 'diversity' is a viable vehicle for achieving these goals or whether it is an exhausted signifier, the very use of which places research within the Procrustean grip of the status quo. The research reviewed in this chapter is a comprehensive population of all research presented for 10 years within the Gender & Diversity division of the Academy of Management. Given the centrality of this professional organization to management discourse within the American business school, it is a fair claim that these articles represent what can and cannot count as diversity research within that discourse. Further, since American management discourse colonizes business school discourse internationally (through textbooks, magazines, management celebrities, journals, the AACSB etc.; *cf.* Jacques, 1996), one must question whether there is any significant critical potential for a signifier that has been so thoroughly reduced to serving corporate profitability within that discourse.

For those who wish to decolonize corporatist American management discourse, resist the trivialization of 'identity' into 'demographics' and question inequity, two broad approaches are available. We can attempt to significantly change the discursive boundaries which inform diversity discourse, or we can work under a signifier or signifiers more congenial to our interests. No doubt, there will be some who would argue for the former strategy. They may be right; I doubt it. Only time will tell, but we already have a good deal of evidence suggesting that social change will not come from the 'tempered radicals' of the status quo – more bad-tempered radicals will be needed. After looking at the evidence, I lean in the direction of doing 'marginality' and leaving 'diversity' for the consultants.

References

Blackford, K.M.H., & Newcomb, H. (1914). *The job, the man, the boss.* Garden City, NY: Doubleday, Page & Co.

Burrell, G., & Morgan, G. (1979). *Sociological paradigms and organizational analysis.* Portsmouth, NH: Heinemann.

Calás, M. B., & Jacques, R. (1988). Diversity or conformity? Research by women on women in organizations. Paper presented at the Seventh Annual Conference on Women and Organizations, Long Beach.

Fairclough, N. (1995). *Critical discourse analysis.* Harlow, UK: Longman.

Ferguson, K. (1984). *The feminist case against bureaucracy.* Philadelphia: Temple University Press.

Foucault, M. (1970). Discourse on language. In *The archaeology of knowledge*: 215–238. London: Vintage.

Grant, D., Hardy, C., Oswick, C., & Putnam, L. (2004). *The Sage handbook of organizational discourse.* London: Sage.

Harrison, D. A., Price, K. H., & Bell, M. P. (1998). Beyond relational demography: Time and the effects of surface- and deep-level diversity on work group cohesion. *Academy of Management Journal, 41*(1): 96–107.

Jacobson, S. W., & Jacques, R. (1990). Of knowers, knowing and the known: A gender framework for revisioning organizational and management scholarship. Paper presented at the Academy of Management meetings, San Francisco, August.

Jacques, R. (1992). *Manufacturing the employee.* London: Sage.

Jones, D. (2004). Screwing diversity out of the workers? Reading diversity. *Journal of Organizational Change Management, 17*(3): 281–291.

Konrad, A., Prasad, P., & Pringle, J. K. (2006). *Handbook of workplace diversity.* London: Sage.

Likert, R. (1967). *The human organization: Its management and value.* New York: McGraw-Hill.

Meyerson, D. E. (2001). *Tempered radicals: How people use difference to inspire change at work.* Cambridge, MA: Harvard Business School Press.

Miller, J. B. (1976). *Toward a new psychology of women.* Boston: Beacon Press.

Mintzberg, H. (1971). Managerial work: Analysis from observation. *Management Science, 18*(2): B97–B110.

Nkomo, S., & Cox, T. (1996). Diverse identities in organizations. In S. Clegg, C. Hardy & W. Nord (Eds.), *The handbook of organizational studies*: 329–349. Thousand Oaks, CA: Sage.

Parsons, T., & Shils, E. (1967). *Toward a general theory of action* (2nd Ed.). Cambridge, MA: Harvard University Press.

Prasad, P. (2005). *Crafting qualitative research,* Armonk, NY: M. E. Sharpe.

Prasad, P., Mills, A., Elmes, M., & Prasad, A. (Eds.). (1997). *Managing the organizational melting pot.* Thousand Oaks, CA: Sage.

Rabinow, P. (1986). Representations are social facts: Modernity and post-modernity in anthropology. In J. Clifford and G. E. Marcus (Eds.), *Writing culture: The poetics and politics of ethnography*: 234–261. Berkeley & Los Angeles: University of California Press.

Scott, W. D., & Clothier, R. C. (1923). *Personnel management: Principles, practices, and point of view*. Chicago: A. W. Shaw.

Shipman, P. (2002). *The evolution of racism: Human differences and the use and abuse of science*. Cambridge, MA: Harvard University Press.

Part IV
Knowledge at the crossroads

10

Toward decolonizing modern Western structures of knowledge

A postcolonial interrogation of (Critical) Management Studies

Anshuman Prasad

At long last we seem to have recognized that neither is Descartes the last word on reason nor is Marx that on the critical spirit.

(Ashis Nandy, 1983)

In postcoloniality, every metropolitan definition is dislodged . . . all metropolitan accounts are set askew.

(Gayatri Chakravorty Spivak, 1993)

Observers of the current global scene generally seem to agree that we are living in a world which is going through far-reaching changes. Underscoring the significance of some of those changes, an editorial in the *Economist* (2010) argued a few years ago that ongoing transformations have literally created a new world in which existing global institutions have been rendered obsolete, and need major reform in order to remain relevant. Insisting on the urgency of such institutional overhaul, the editorial added: "The case for reform is overwhelming. America's unipolar moment has passed. [New] rules [are needed] . . . in a world where power is shifting" (*Economist*, 2010: 16).

The *Economist* editorial, needless to say, was mainly commenting in the context of large-scale shifts in the global economy, which have received extensive attention in academic, business and national policy-making circles (Goldman Sachs, 2003; Govindarajan & Gupta, 2000; National Intelligence Council, 2008, 2012; PricewaterhouseCoopers, 2011; Standard Chartered Bank, 2010; Wallerstein, 2000), and what the editorial specifically had in mind was the need for new rules of international governance involving, for instance, restructuring of the United Nations by expanding the Security Council to include major polities like Brazil, India, South Africa and others as permanent members. But might we, with due justification, further extend *The Economist*'s line of argument and propose that "the great shift of wealth and power to the . . . [non-West]" (Prestowitz, 2005), which seems to be occurring today, would likely necessitate changes not only in the rules and structures for international/geopolitical governance but also in the rules and structures that govern the production of *scholarly knowledge*?

It would appear that arguments that share certain aspects of such largely economy-based lines of thinking can easily be made by drawing upon the insights of world system analysis (see, e.g., Frank, 1998; Lee, 1996; Wallerstein, 2000, 2004a, 2004b). That, however, it is important to emphasize here, is *not* the principal line of reasoning proposed to be adopted . . . search for alternative knowledges. Rather, while recognizing the importance of the systemic shifts occurring today in areas like the world economy or geopolitical balance of power, this chapter seeks to locate the transformative impulse for radical revisions of current structures of knowledge in that *prior space of contestation* which gave rise long ago to impressive anticolonial liberation movements and sophisticated "theoretical practices of the freedom struggles" (Young, 2001: 159), and which, in more recent years, has witnessed the emergence of what has come to be called postcolonial theory (or postcolonialism). The objective of the present chapter, accordingly, is to develop a postcolonial theoretic critique of *modern Western approaches and structures of knowledge* (with particular focus on management studies and other social sciences) and to explore some of the ways in which postcolonial thinking might contribute to a radical reorientation of management knowledge and scholarship.

Before proceeding further, a word of caution might be in order. Anecdotal evidence seems to suggest that, at least in some circles of management scholarship, the rapid economic rise of the BRICS (Brazil, Russia, India, China and South Africa) and several other countries in Africa, Asia, and Latin America may have come to be viewed as a sign that the world has moved beyond the era of (neo-)colonialism. Such a position lacks merit and is not subscribed to in this chapter. Instead, while acknowledging the significance of ongoing systemic changes at the global level, the present chapter also seeks to provide a more nuanced reading of the current global conjuncture, a reading embedded in the traditions of postcolonial critique. Accordingly, while this chapter duly recognizes the force of various analyses anticipating and projecting a post-Western world order (see e.g., *Foreign Affairs*, 2010; Ikenberry, 2011; Kupchan, 2012; Layne, 2006), the chapter also takes serious note of a multiplicity of Western efforts designed to resist such a development[1] and of the persistence and/or renewal of (neo-)colonial practices in different parts of the world.

As a result, this chapter views the current historical situation neither as an era of renewed Western hegemony nor as a moment when the world has finally and decisively consigned (neo-)colonialism to the past, but rather as a period of large-scale systemic makeover of the kind that is commonly accompanied by *intense struggles* over disposition of geopolitical and geo-economic power, *as well as* over structures of knowledge. That being the case, one of the important motivations for this chapter is provided by the scholarly necessity of reflecting upon the variety of ways in which current structures of knowledge might come to be transformed in the course of those ongoing struggles. Indeed, in view of the continuing intensification of contemporary globalization, the increasing focus in management scholarship upon understanding the complexities of 'East–West' encounters[2] and the growing interest within management research in issues related to critical scholarship and postcolonialism, the present moment seems to provide a particularly opportune moment for engaging in those reflections.

The rest of this chapter is organized in four sections. The first section briefly outlines the scholarly contours of postcolonial theory. This section begins by reviewing the contributions of some of the key scholars of the genre – focusing, in particular, on those scholars' appraisals of modern Western knowledge – and thereafter discusses a number of important characteristics of postcolonialism as a vehicle for critique. The second section provides a historically contextualized understanding of the emergence of management as a professional/applied social science. The transformation of management into a social science is a somewhat recent development that can largely be traced back to the middle of the last century. However, the wider domain of Western social science has a considerably longer history. Hence, this section contextualizes the rise of modern management within the larger history of the growth of Western social science and highlights the significance of colonialism and neocolonialism for the construction of the social scientific approach to knowledge. In the third section, a variety of epistemological and ideological problems, limitations and dilemmas associated with modern Western social science and (critical) management studies are examined, and, following that, the fourth and final section of the chapter discusses some of the ways in which postcolonial theory might be helpful in addressing those difficulties and thereby radically reorienting social scientific and management scholarship.

As we proceed with this agenda outlined, it might be useful to add here that the expression 'modern Western approaches and structures of knowledge' (or 'modern Western structures of knowledge') is being employed here to refer to that prevailing combination of a specific epistemological worldview and a particular institutionalized organization of scholarly knowledge production, which is largely premised upon (1) a deep separation across the three realms of truth, ethics and aesthetics; (2) a binary epistemological divide between *nomothetic* natural sciences and *idiographic* humanities/arts; (3) the idea of nomothetic natural sciences as models for producing knowledge/truth; (4) the notion of social sciences as belonging to a domain of knowledge that inhabits a somewhat ambiguous space between the natural sciences and the humanities; (5) an institutional structure mostly based on the idea of 'disciplines' as generally reflected in today's university departments; and (6) a 'research industry' involving a hierarchically ordered system of academic journals, learned societies, scholarly conferences, doctoral programs and so on (Lee, 1996; Mignolo, 2000, 2002; Wallerstein, 2004a, 2004b). In addition, it seems important to emphasize also that this chapter primarily focuses upon Euro-American circuits of knowledge. Hence, the chapter might be of somewhat limited *direct* relevance for scholarly circles in the non-West, where the focus and content of management and social scientific knowledge, as well as the meanings and practices attached to institutions of knowledge and scholarship, are likely to be considerably different. Within those circles, however, the chapter might be helpful in raising new questions on issues of knowledge production.

Postcolonial theory and criticism: An overview

Briefly stated, postcolonialism may be understood as a theoretical and ethico-political response to the past and the continuing present of modern Western colonialism/imperialism and anticolonial resistance. Western colonialism is a phenomenon of considerable depth and density in geographical as well as historical terms. Not surprisingly, therefore, colonialism and anticolonial resistance have left a lasting imprint – economic, political, cultural, epistemological and the like – on the world. Moreover, even after the formal political end of Western colonialism, many of its dynamics have continued to live on through a variety of *neocolonial* forms of domination. Hence, adopting a scholarly vantage point which "identifies with the subject position of [the colonized and the] anticolonial activists" (Young, 2001: 19), postcolonialism endeavors to develop an in-depth critique of the complex dynamics of (neo-)colonialism and anticolonial resistance.

Postcolonial theory forms part of a very long tradition of oppositional criticism directed against modern colonialism. At the same time, postcolonialism also represents a somewhat new and unique approach for critiquing (neo-)colonialism on account of (1) its efforts to develop a more comprehensive critical understanding of colonialism and the colonial aftermath and (2) its creative mobilization of conceptual insights from a wide range of critical perspectives, including the "theoretical practices of the freedom struggles" alluded to earlier (Young, 2001: 159), Marxism/neo-Marxism, feminism, poststructuralism, deconstruction, psychoanalysis and others. Partly as a result of such theoretical eclecticism and syncretism, postcolonialism has developed into a considerably heterogeneous intellectual position with significant internal debates and contestations and should not be seen as representing a narrowly systematized and monolithic theory. Indeed, as Harding has pointed out, "such contestations are a productive process" (2009: 417) and need to be regarded as a major source of strength for the field of postcolonial inquiry.

The emergence of postcolonialism in the Western academic world is closely linked with the extraordinary success achieved by Edward Said's masterpiece, *Orientalism* (1978). Since then, postcolonialism has continued to deepen its influence and is beginning to be seen now as "one of the most important intellectual movements . . . if not *the* most important [intellectual movement]" in the Western academe during the past 50 years or so (Nichols, 2010: 111; italics in the original). Reflecting these developments, postcolonial theory has been extensively utilized in a range of scholarly disciplines including, for instance, anthropology, art and art history, cultural studies, geography, history, literary theory, media studies, philosophy, political science, sociology and many more (Lazarus, 2004; Loomba, Kaul, Bunzl, Burton & Esty, 2005a; Moranña, Dussel & Jáuregui, 2008; Williams & Chrisman, 1994).

Postcolonial theory is by no means a stranger to the scholarly field of management, and especially during recent years, there seems to have been growing recognition within the discipline regarding the value of postcolonialism as a powerful instrument for critique (Banerjee & Prasad, 2008; Jack & Westwood, 2009; Jack, Westwood, Srinivas & Sardar, 2011a; Prasad, 2003b, 2012b). As a result, the last several years have seen increasing numbers of management and organizational scholars drawing upon postcolonialism with a view to addressing a wide range of issues, including, for instance, workplace diversity and multiculturalism (Kalonaityte, 2010; Prasad, 1997b, 2006; Prasad & Prasad, 2002), international and cross-cultural management (Ailon, 2008; Fougère & Moulettes, 2007; Jack & Westwood, 2006, 2009; Kwek, 2003; Westwood, 2004; Westwood & Jack, 2007), globalization (Banerjee & Linstead, 2001; Gopal, Willis & Gopal, 2003; Mirchandani, 2004, 2005), bureaucratic management of Australian Aborigine affairs (Sullivan, 2008; Tedmanson, 2008), the lasting imprint of (neo-)colonialism on existing institutions (Harrison, 1997; P. Prasad, 2003), control and resistance in organizations (Mir, Mir & Upadhyaya, 2003; Pal & Dutta, 2008; Prasad & Prasad, 2003), organizational communication (Bradfoot & Munshi, 2007; Grimes & Parker, 2009), knowledge transfer across organizations and/or economies (Chio, 2008; Frenkel, 2008; Mir, Banerjee & Mir, 2008; Mir & Mir, 2009) and so on. Simultaneously, researchers have utilized postcolonialist ideas also for the purpose of critiquing different aspects of (production of) management knowledge (Frenkel & Shenhav, 2006; Ibarra-Colado, 2006; Jaya, 2001; Özkazanç-Pan, 2008; Westwood, 2004; Westwood & Jack, 2007).[3]

Before proceeding further, a brief word about the postcolonial theoretic terminology employed in this chapter might be in order. To begin with, following a common postcolonial practice, the words 'colonialism' and 'imperialism' will be used interchangeably in this chapter. Similarly, the chapter will mostly employ the expressions 'Europe' and 'the West' synonymously and also as "figure(s) of the imaginary" having "somewhat indeterminate geographical referents" (Chakrabarty, 1992: 1). In light of earlier debates regarding the appropriateness of the prefix 'post' (see e.g., Gandhi, 1998; Hall, 1996; Mishra & Hodge, 1991; Shohat, 1992), scholars often employ the term 'post-colonial' (i.e., with a hyphen) as a temporal expression that refers to the *period* that comes after the decolonization of the mid-20th century, whereas the term 'postcolonial' (note the absence of the hyphen) is used to indicate a *form of critical practice* with specific ways of thinking about (neo-)colonialism. The same terminological practice will be followed here as well. On a cautionary note, it might be worth emphasizing here that neither of these two terms ('post-colonial' or 'postcolonial') is intended to suggest that colonialism has decisively ended.

Furthermore, the word 'discourse,' as used in this chapter, will not be indicative of language alone but rather will refer to the "intersection of ideas and institutions, knowledge and power" (Loomba, 1998: 54). Consistent with this understanding of 'discourse,' the term 'colonial discourse' will be employed here to refer to "the body of knowledge, modes of representation, strategies [and institutions] of power, law, discipline, and so on, that are employed in the construction and domination of 'colonial subjects'" (Niranjana, 1992: 7). Any deviation in the chapter from these terminological usages will generally take place in relatively well-defined contexts where the different meaning of a given expression will be fairly obvious. With the preceding background, we may now turn toward taking stock of some of the contributions made by postcolonial theory, especially with respect to postcolonialism's engagement with modern Western knowledge.

Postcolonial theory and modern Western knowledge

As noted, postcolonialism has been employed by scholars to examine a whole host of important questions. However, amid the wide variety of topics addressed by postcolonial research, an issue that appears to have received careful and sustained attention across different disciplines involves the project for "a *radical rethinking of knowledge* . . . authored and authorized by colonialism and Western domination" (Prakash, 1994: 1475; italics added).[4] In this regard, we may usefully note that Edward Said's *Orientalism* (1978) itself offers an extended critique of modern Western knowledge. *Orientalism*, in brief, foregrounded the complicity of knowledge and power and proposed that colonialism involved not only military and economic control but also a discourse of domination that operated to secure specific representations of the Western colonizer and the non-Western colonized and thereby "consolidated certain ways of seeing and thinking which . . . [enabled the exercise of] colonial power" (Loomba, 1998: 43–44). For Said, in other words, colonialism invariably "involved epistemic as well as physical violence" (Young, 2001: 383), with each form of violence facilitating and reinforcing the other.

In the specific context of Orientalist knowledge, Said argued that while growing knowledge about the Orient provided the West with an overarching framework for viewing and dominating the Orient, in its own turn, increasing control over the Orient "itself spawned . . . [specific] ways of knowing, studying, believing and writing" (Loomba, 1998: 44). Hence, according to Said, Western colonial knowledge *about* the non-West invariably went hand in hand with Western colonial power *over* the non-West. In this regard, Said pointed to the crucial role played by Orientalist knowledge in producing an elaborate structure of hierarchical binaries (e.g., civilized/savage, modern/traditional, scientific/superstitious, the vanguard/the led, etc.) which relegated the Orient/non-West to a position of ontological *inferiority* and elevated the West into a position of ontological *superiority*, with the result that the West largely came to regard colonial rule not only as something *natural* but something that was even a Western *moral obligation* (Prasad, 1997b, 2006). Thus, Said's analysis underscored the profound and mutually reinforcing links between modern Western knowledge and the exercise of colonial power.

While *Orientalism* is undoubtedly the book Said is best known for, his subsequent writings have added further depth and refinement to many of the arguments introduced in that book. In that process, Said's scholarship has covered such themes as Western media's coverage of Islam, the Palestinian issue, the complex links between colonialism and culture, resistance to colonialism and so on (Said, 1979, 1981, 1993). Said's ideas have exerted a major influence on postcolonial theoretic research in management studies. For instance, his insights inform a large number of critical works dealing with workplace diversity and multiculturalism, otherness in organizations, cross-cultural management, issues of representation and so forth (Fougère & Moulettes, 2007; Kwek, 2003; Prasad, 1997b, 2006; Priyadharshini, 2003; Westwood, 2004).

If Edward Said mobilizes the notion of colonial discourse to interrogate modern/colonial Western knowledge, Ashis Nandy (1983, 1987, 1988, 2000) may be seen as drawing upon the psychology of colonialism and "the subversive radicality of . . . [Mahatma] Gandhi's counter-modernity" (Young, 2001: 340), with a view to raising highly troubling questions about colonial and neocolonial forms of knowledge. Following his interest in the psychology of colonialism, Nandy often focuses upon what he calls "second colonization" (i.e., the ideological colonization of mind and imagination that came after the 'first colonization' involving military conquest and occupation of colonial territory), and he offers the argument that it is this "second colonization" that has helped "generalize the concept of the modern West from a geographical and temporal entity to a psychological category" (1983: xi), with disastrous consequences for the *entire* world, Western as well as non-Western. For Nandy, in other words, the second colonization is something akin to "a universal malaise" that affects significant sections of the West as well as the non-West (Buell, 1994: 244).

One of Nandy's (2000) key concerns, hence, is with articulating a radical critique of certain pivotal ideas (e.g., modernity, the nation-state, science, instrumental rationality, Western secularism, development, etc.), which constitute the West as a psychological category and undergird modern structures of knowledge. Nandy frames his scholarship in terms of "defy[ing] the key categories of the Enlightenment" (2000: 85) and, for that purpose, seems to find his major inspiration *not* within the academic 'research industry' of the social sciences, but in the world of those intellectuals and activists (especially, perhaps, in the global 'South') who are relatively outside the circuits of social science and, therefore, can understand and work with nonmodern categories and structures of knowledge. In this process, Nandy also seeks to "provide a language where a dialogue can be established" between the modern social scientific 'expert'/academic and the nonmodern intellectual (2000: 33).

All in all, Nandy's defiant postcolonial vision for the future includes an epistemological approach which produces open-ended knowledge that refuses systematization, as well as a world of *plural* knowledges "in communication with each other in their own way, and sometimes not even in communication" (2000: 81). In addition to knowledge and epistemology, Nandy's writings have focused upon a variety of other issues, including religion and fundamentalism, popular culture, technology and development, the problematic nature of modern nationalism and so forth (1988, 1994, 1998, 2001). Within the scholarly discipline of management, Nandy's ideas have been utilized in studies dealing with a variety of issues, including knowledge and epistemology, and control and resistance in organizations (Prasad, 1997a; Prasad & Prasad, 2003).

While Nandy's theorization of second colonization serves as a vehicle for launching a radical critique of the consequences of modernity and modern Western knowledge, Homi Bhabha (1990, 1994) relies upon concepts like ambivalence, mimicry and hybridity to point toward certain intriguing weaknesses at the very core of modern/colonial discourse, which render such discourse into a somewhat unreliable instrument for establishing Western hegemony – in Antonio Gramsci's sense – in the colony. For instance, Bhabha (1994) highlights the ambivalence of colonial knowledge by pointing out that colonial knowledge simultaneously represents the non-West as desirable and undesirable, familiar and strange, weak/effeminate and yet full of menace, as an other "which is at once an object of desire and derision" (p. 67) and indeed as "a social reality which is at once an 'other' and yet entirely knowable and visible" (pp. 70–71). According to Bhabha, such ambivalence of colonial knowledge and discourse implies that, rather than being a cohesive and monolithic instrument for the exercise of hegemonic power, discourse comes to serve as a site where the colonizer's deepest anxieties are put on full display.

Similarly, moving away from earlier analyses of colonialism – which often adduced colonial mimicry (i.e., the imitation of the colonizer by the colonized) as evidence in support of their argument that the colonizer wielded hegemonic authority in the colonial situation – Bhabha contends that, far from consolidating hegemonic control, mimicry "simultaneously stabilizes and destabilizes" colonial power and knowledge (Young, 1990: 148). Bhabha points out that, rather than producing (among the colonized) figures who might be *exact* copies of the colonizer, mimicry produces only *partial* replicas who are *"almost the same but not quite . . . almost the same but not white"* (1994: 89; italics in the original). Mimicry, hence, needs to be seen also as an act of refusal on the part of the colonized "to obey the colonizers' narcissistic demand/command to be the 'same'" (Prasad, 2003a: 22). For Bhabha, therefore, mimicry represents "an ambivalent mixture of deference and disobedience" (Gandhi, 1998: 149) that persistently menaces colonial discourse and "[results in] paranoia on the part of the colonizer" (Young, 1990: 148).

Along parallel lines, Bhabha points to the process of hybridity to emphasize how, during the very course of exercise of colonial power itself, colonial discourse ends up being 'translated' by the colonized, who combine that discourse "with a range of differential knowledges . . . [and thereby] produce new forms of knowledge . . . new sites of power" which destabilize the colonizer's knowledge and power (1994: 120). Thus, through his theorization of ambivalence, mimicry, hybridity and related concepts, Bhabha highlights certain fundamental difficulties faced by colonial discourse in the process of the exercise of power. In so doing, Bhabha deals a serious blow to some earlier scholarly claims that interpreted colonial authority as largely being hegemonic and hence tended to occlude the resistant agency of the colonized. In management scholarship, Bhabha's insights have been employed to study a variety of issues, including the dynamics of knowledge transfer, representations of the 'other' in business journalism, the processes relating to the formation of canonized knowledge in management studies, workplace resistance, and so on (Frenkel, 2008; Frenkel & Shenhav, 2006; Prasad & Prasad, 2003; Priyadharshini, 2003).

In comparison with Bhabha, whose writings seem to exhibit a somewhat persistent preoccupation with the psychic economy/structures of colonial knowledge and discourse, the scholarship of Gayatri Chakravorty Spivak (1990, 1993, 1999) is recognizably much more "heterogeneous . . . and diverse" (Young, 1990: 157) and spans a considerably wider variety of interests. Nevertheless, interrogating Western knowledge has always been one of Spivak's important concerns, and this issue seems to have received renewed attention in some of her more recent works (e.g., Spivak, 2003, 2008, 2012).

Being deeply aware of the profound problems investing current (structures of) Western knowledge, Spivak is concerned with imagining new and different ways for transforming that knowledge. One of her suggestions, in this regard, calls for promoting extensive collaboration between the humanities and the social sciences. Spivak fully recognizes that there exist serious institutionalized hurdles working against transformative collaboration of the kind she has in mind. However, Spivak (2003) points out that, within today's social science, there already exist "strong tendencies [that] . . . (acknowledge) . . . the central role of the humanities" (p. 19), and she believes that those tendencies create a promising opening for genuine collaboration between these fields. In addition, Spivak proposes that Western knowledge needs to learn to recognize "the 'other' as producer of knowledge" (2003: 11). Spivak is critical of the blindness of Western knowledge to the presence of theoretical sophistication in the non-West and believes that attempts to transform Western knowledge need to learn to "infect" that knowledge with theories from the global 'South' (2003: 11).

Spivak may be said to be arguing, furthermore, that attempts to draw upon non-Western theories need to go beyond relatively elite corridors of knowledge in the 'South.' In particular, Spivak (2008) seems to insist that attempts to transform Western knowledge need to establish connections with non-Western *subaltern* groups – i.e., groups "removed from lines of social mobility" (p. 22) – and "learn to learn from below" (p. 43). In other words, Spivak (2008) may be seen as suggesting that a radical transformation of Western knowledge requires that scholars linked to various circuits of that knowledge "[give] up convictions of triumphalist superiority" (p. 43) and develop the necessary mindset and competencies that would allow them to "learn from people with no institutional education" (p. 5).

As noted earlier, Spivak's scholarship ranges over a wide variety of subject matters. Apart from critiquing modern Western knowledge and its structures, Spivak's writings have focused upon such themes as critical pedagogy, the problematic aspects of First World feminism, the value of 'strategic essentialism' in the service of progressive politics, globalization and the changing geopolitical/geo-economic order and so on (1987, 1990, 1993, 1999, 2012). Within the field of management, Spivak's ideas have been utilized in studies dealing with representational issues, pedagogical aspects of international and cross-cultural management, disciplinary critiques of management, and the like (see, e.g., Jack & Lorbiecki, 2003; Priyadharshini, 2003; Westwood & Jack, 2007).

The prominent place accorded to the idea of the 'subaltern' in Spivak's project for transforming Western knowledge attests to the importance of this concept in postcolonial thought. Although the notion of the 'subaltern' originates in Antonio Gramsci's *Prison Notebooks* of the 1920s and 1930s, this concept gained renewed emphasis within postcolonial circles as a result of the efforts of the Subaltern Studies Collective, a group of scholars devoted to investigating the condition of subalternity in the South Asian context. Inspired by the historian Ranajit Guha (1963, 1997), the Subaltern Studies project grew out of a feeling of intense dissatisfaction with the prevailing state of historiography relating to South Asia. Specifically, conceptualizing the 'subaltern' as a demographic category distinct from the elite, the Subaltern Studies Collective roundly criticized existing histories – whether colonialist, Marxist, or elite nationalist – for ignoring the *agency* of the subaltern.

Accordingly, many of the works of the collective have sought to revise South Asian history by providing a sophisticated understanding of subaltern agency. Moreover, the project for rewriting South Asian history has also grown into a critique of conventional Western historiography as such, including Western historiography's taken-for-granted "techniques and procedures" (Prakash, 1994: 1485), as well as into a critique of "Europe and the modes of knowledge . . . instituted [under Western auspices]" (Prakash, 1994: 1483). Following these developments, the subaltern has emerged within postcolonialism as an influential *epistemological position* for rethinking and reorienting current (structures of) Western knowledge (Chakrabarty, 1992, 2000). Moreover, although the subaltern perspective emerged with an initial focus on South Asia, it has since found global resonance and is being extensively utilized in studies dealing with many different areas of the world, non-Western as well as Western (Chaturvedi, 2000; Prakash, 1994; Mignolo, 2000; Prasad, 2003a).

As pointed out earlier, in addition to knowledge and epistemology, postcolonial scholarship has addressed a wide range of other important concerns. Apart from knowledge/epistemology, some of the questions taken up in postcolonial inquiry include, for instance, issues of otherness (Daunton & Halpern, 1999; Gidley, 1992; Sardar, Nandy & Davies, 1993), race/ethnicity and identity (Arias, 2008; Gilroy, 2000; Goldberg, 2002; Morales, 2008; Retamar, 1989), nation and nationalism (Bhabha, 1990; Butler & Spivak, 2007; Chatterjee, 1986, 1993; Chrisman, 2005; Mallon, 2005; Nandy, 1994), religion and secularism (Maldonado-Torres, 2008; Nandy, 1998; van der Veer, 2001), colonialism and sexuality (Stoler, 1995, 2002; Young, 1995), 'Third World' development (Escobar, 1995; Grosfoguel, 2008; Rahnema & Bawtree, 1997; Sachs, 1992), globalization (Appadurai, 1996; Behdad, 2005; Brennan, 2003, 2005; Cooppan, 2005), cultural aspects of colonialism (Dirks, 1992, 1998; Said, 1993), language, literature and rhetoric of empire (Brantlinger, 1988; Sharpe, 1993; Spurr, 1993; Suleri, 1992; Teltscher, 1995), the complex role of Western women in the colonial project (Chaudhuri & Strobel, 1992; Jayawardena, 1995), postcolonial feminisms (Alexander & Mohanty, 1997; Lewis & Mills, 2003; Mohanty, 2003; Mohanty, Torres & Russo, 1991) and many more.

The postcolonial project: Major characteristics

As the preceding review indicates, postcolonialism as a genre of critique has emerged from the intermingling of a variety of academic disciplines and approaches to scholarly inquiry, with the result that the field exhibits considerable heterogeneity. The heterogeneity of the field implies also that, as postcolonial theory has expanded impressively across various academic disciplines, scholars have tended to "move beyond narrow definitions of postcolonial [theory]" (Loomba, Kaul, Bunzl, Burton & Esty, 2005b: 3) and developed increasingly comprehensive conceptualizations of this area of research. Hence, a host of "research initiatives and political projects" that are committed to "a critique of Eurocentrism, racism, . . . colonial discourse" and related phenomena may now be viewed as forming part of the postcolonial oeuvre (Stam & Shohat, 2005: 293).

Accordingly, postcolonialism is now frequently seen to include not only those works that somewhat closely follow the broad research approaches suggested by the scholarship of Edward Said, Ashis Nandy, Homi Bhabha, Gayatri Spivak, Ranajit Guha and similar other figures but also various aspects of "other forms of adversarial knowledge" (Stam & Shohat, 2005: 293), such as critical race theory, border thinking, diaspora and migration studies, critical multiculturalism, world system analysis, transnational cultural critique, studies of indigenous knowledge systems and epistemologies, aborigine studies, whiteness studies, post-development critiques, and many more. Such a *comprehensive conceptualization* of postcolonial theory reflects a scholarly recognition that postcolonialism needs to be an intellectually broad-based approach with a view to serving as an effective instrument of critique. Moreover, such a comprehensive conceptualization implies also that postcolonialism has come to be seen now in a somewhat open-ended way, i.e., as a field with rather porous boundaries, which is "still discovering [itself, even as it] . . . is getting bigger" and is always on the move (Hulme, 2005: 42).

It is important to recognize here that the remarkable heterogeneity and dynamism of the field is accompanied, at the same time, by a number of intellectual and ethico-political commitments that are widely shared, in a variety of ways, by postcolonial researchers, and which may be said to lend an overall coherence to the postcolonial project. Among those, mention may be made of commitment toward:

1   Persistent critique of Eurocentrism (Blaut, 1993, 2000; Shohat & Stam, 1994; Prasad, 2012a);
2   Interrogating "the denial of coevalness," i.e., questioning that dubious but fairly common modern Western idea which locates inhabitants of different civilizations in a "chronological hierarchy" and views non-Western peoples as "removed from the present" (Mignolo, 2000: 283; citing Fabian, 1983);
3   Provincializing Europe, i.e., challenging Europe's appropriation of the universal (Chakrabarty, 1992, 2000; Prasad, 1997a);
4   Questioning the Western "subalternization of knowledge" which denies the status of 'genuine' knowledge to the heterogeneous knowledges of the conquered and the colonized and further extending such questioning by constructing "new loci of enunciation" from where alternative knowledges might be produced (Mignolo, 2000: 13);
5   Recognizing the mutual imbrications and inextricability of the processes of modernity and colonialism, such that each implies the other and is seen as contributing to "the making of the modern/colonial world" (Mignolo, 2000: 21),[5] with the result that the Western metropole and the non-Western colony come to be viewed as a "unitary field of analysis" (Cohn, 1996: 4);
6   Recuperating – and understanding the significance of – the long history of global linkages, interactions, and interdependencies generally ignored and/or underemphasized in modern/colonial Western historiography; and

7   Working against the grain of modern/colonial knowledge and discourse with a view to
     radically reorienting such knowledge/discourse (Bhabha, 1994; Mignolo, 2000, 2011; Prasad,
     2012a; Spivak, 1999, 2003, 2008).

The next section of the chapter situates Western social science within the broader dynamics
of colonialism and neocolonialism and offers a brief discussion of the emergence of modern
management as a professional/applied social science.

Western social science and the rise of modern management

Western social sciences are generally seen as making their first appearance on the European
scene during the 19th century (Wallerstein, 2004a). However, although the emergence of the
social sciences may indeed be viewed as a 19th-century event, this phenomenon is inextricably
linked with certain major developments taking place during the second half of the previous
century. The latter half of the 18th century seems to mark a somewhat pivotal period of
transition between the first and the second *phases* of European modernity and colonialism
(Mignolo, 2000, 2002). This period of transition is characterized by a range of far-reaching
developments, including a consolidation of the gradually occurring shift in the European
balance of geopolitical and economic power from the Iberian Peninsula toward northwestern
Europe, a switch from the epistemological framework of the European Renaissance to that of
the European Enlightenment, and rapidly gathering momentum in the European conquest
and colonization of foreign territory, especially in Asia (Darwin, 2008; Mignolo, 2000, 2002;
Panikkar, 1959). All these historical developments appear to have left crucial marks on Western
social science.

Modernity/colonialism and Western social science

The transitional interlude between the two phases of modernity/colonialism also served as the
historical moment when some European countries made significant advances toward *nation-state*
formation at 'home' and *colonial-state* formation in the conquered territories abroad (Cohn, 1996;
Dirks, 2006; Sen, 1998). In many ways, Britain – which began its colonial conquest of India
during the 1750s – is often seen as providing an early exemplar of the simultaneous unfolding of
the two, mutually reinforcing state-building processes.[6]

Taking the case of Britain as a first-mover that "set the tone" (Sen, 1998: 3) for future European endeavors in these areas, scholars have pointed out that state-formation activities of the
period were largely governed by two major ideas: (1) that any society was knowable by means
of a "series of facts" that were empirically observable and (2) that the power of a state depended
upon the "efficient use of these facts" (Cohn, 1996: 4). Moreover, it was believed also at the
time that the 'facts' necessary for effectively knowing and administering the state spanned a wide
domain covering the natural as well as the social worlds (Sen, 1998). As a result, state building in
the late 18th century – whether in Europe or in the colony overseas – relied upon gathering facts
pertaining to a broad assortment of social and natural fields. It is in this context of gathering of
wide-ranging facts that the colonies came to play a crucial role in shaping the emergence and
development of Western social science.

It is important to recognize here that whenever European colonizers invaded a distant territory overseas (e.g., when the British invaded India in the 1750s), they also came across a different
"epistemological space" with its own unique definitions and understandings of facts about the

(local) world, 'facts' that often dramatically diverged from the so-called facts of the colonizers (Cohn, 1996: 4). At the same time, however, in order to put their rule of the conquered colony on secure foundations, the European invaders needed to make the colony (with its own 'strange' universe of facts) less perplexing and frustrating and thereby more "familiar and governable" (Sen, 1998: 95). Hence, the *imperatives of colonial rule* (e.g., gaining control over local revenues and institutions of trade and exchange, supplanting the laws of the defeated regimes with new sets of laws, mapping of local terrain and roads and rivers of military significance, etc., for instance, in late 18th-century India) set the stage for the launching of a vast effort to collect, record, classify, document, catalog and archive a huge amount of facts about the territory and the world of the colonized. In this process, the colonial theater served as a crucial site where European understandings of a multitude of facts were repeatedly worked over, tested, and refined/consolidated (Dirks, 2006) and where a range of "investigative modalities" (Cohn, 1996: 5) were developed and/or perfected that enabled the gathering of those facts.

The term "investigative modality" has been formulated by Cohn to refer to "the definition of a body of information that is needed, the procedures by which appropriate knowledge is gathered, its ordering and classification, and then how it is transformed into usable forms such as published reports, statistical returns, histories, gazetteers, legal codes, and encyclopedias" (1996: 5). In the course of examining different aspects of the formation of a British colonial-state in India, Cohn (1996) offers insights into a number of investigative modalities, such as historiographical, observational, enumerative, museological and so forth. Considerations of space prevent us from providing a discussion of these investigative modalities, although the labels used by Cohn for different modalities do appear to be quite informative. What needs to be especially emphasized here, however, is that the elaboration of these investigative modalities in the colony, including the creation of specific "institutions and administrative sites with fixed routines" and methods for collecting facts, greatly influenced the subsequent development and transformation of many of these modalities into various 19th-century Western (social) sciences, such as economics, cartography, ethnology, tropical medicine and so forth (Cohn, 1996: 5).

In this context, furthermore, it deserves to be underscored also that the work involved in the elaboration of Western knowledge and investigative modalities in the colony necessarily required significant reliance upon local inhabitants (e.g., local groups of scholars, scribes, craftsmen, bankers, merchants, soldiers etc.), as well as upon a great variety of local knowledge and skills, including, for example, knowledge and skills in areas like accounting, administration, botany, medicine, terrestrial surveying and mapping and so forth (Harding, 2009; Raj, 2007; Washbrook, 1990). Thus, non-Western peoples and knowledge systems played a crucial role in the emergence of modern Western (structures of) knowledge.

Emerging out of the colonial and national state-building activities of the 18th century, a number of social scientific disciplines gradually became institutionalized during the course of the 19th century. The growth and institutionalization of social scientific disciplines (e.g., economics, history, political science, sociology, etc.) was significantly influenced also by the late 18th-century European "divorce between philosophy and science" (Wallerstein, 2004a: 2) leading to the eventual separation of the 'sciences' from the 'humanities' (or the 'arts'). Such intellectual parting of ways was accompanied by a number of other important developments, including a deep epistemological divide between *nomothetic* natural sciences (e.g., physics, chemistry, mathematics, etc.) and *idiographic* humanities (e.g., languages and literatures, philosophy, etc.), and a "radical separation . . . in the world of knowledge between the true, the good, and the beautiful" (Wallerstein, 2004a: 74). In the course of time, the various social sciences came to be divided between the two rival epistemological camps, with some of them (e.g., economics, political science or sociology) turning largely nomothetic during the 19th and 20th centuries, while disciplines like anthropology or history remained mostly idiographic.

During the course of the 19th and early 20th centuries, moreover, Western social sciences were gradually institutionalized as departments within the structure of the modern (Western) university – usually seen as emerging initially in Germany during the first half of the 19th century – and the *production* of new social scientific knowledge became increasingly concentrated in those specialized departments (Lucas, 1994; Oleson & Voss, 1979; Ross, 1979). Along with such growth of *university-based* research, most of the social sciences – with the exception of anthropology and Oriental studies – also began to principally focus on the Western world alone. Indeed, Wallerstein notes in this context that "at least 95 percent of all . . . [social scientific] scholarship from the period of 1850 to 1914, and probably even to 1945, originates in five countries [only]: France, Great Britain, the Germanies, the Italies, and the United States . . . [and] *most of the scholarship by most scholars is about their own country*" (Wallerstein, 1996: 3; emphasis added; quoted in Mignolo, 2000: 251). As a result, huge areas of the world came to be almost completely ignored by different social scientific disciplines.

Neocolonial imperatives and the new social science paradigm

If, as we've seen, European *colonial* imperatives had played a crucial role in the emergence and development of social science; this field of knowledge was significantly reoriented during the 1940s–1950s and subsequent years as a result of key *neocolonial* imperatives as well (Cohn, 1996; Lee, 1996; Wallerstein, 2004a). The dynamics of neocolonialism unfolded in a world characterized by at least three unique features: (1) it was a world populated by a large number of newly independent post-colonial states, (2) it was a world in which the United States of America had claimed the leadership of 'the West,' and (3) it was a world of intense rivalry between the United States and the Soviet Union primarily for control over non-Western areas of the world (Arrighi, 1994; McCormick, 1989; Pletsch, 1981). All these aspects of the mid-20th century global order significantly influenced the future development of Western social science.

We may begin by noting that, in the rapidly decolonizing world of the mid-20th century, the United States as the leader of the so-called 'First World' urgently needed to establish *neocolonial* control over the 'Third World' for a host of reasons, including (1) the necessity of ensuring continued access to important raw materials from territories that were no longer under European colonial control, (2) the need for finding/expanding overseas markets for American and/or Western products and securing safe investment outlets for American/Western capital, and (3) the requirement of setting up a worldwide network of military bases with a view to challenging the Soviet Union in the Cold War (Arrighi, 1994; Darwin, 2008; Escobar, 1995; Klare, 1974). However, the mid-20th century U.S. quest for neocolonial control faced a number of serious hurdles. For one, the U.S. government, as a close ally of virtually all major European colonial powers, was viewed with suspicion in large parts of the world. Similarly, the Euro-American capitalist model was suspect in many areas of the world because, among other things, it had precipitated the Great Depression that devastated the global economy and also because it was seen as an instrument of exploitative (colonialist) extraction. In addition, the United States suffered also from a serious deficit of cultural 'soft power' as large sections of 'Third World' elites viewed "America and Americans as uncouth and uncultured" (Guha, 2007: 164).

In contrast to the United States, the Soviet Union stood as an open supporter of decolonization, and, moreover, its message of Socialist egalitarianism held significant appeal in the 'Third World.' As a result, to the U.S. policy-makers, the middle of the 20th century appeared to be a period when "the free enterprise system [itself] was in peril" (Escobar, 1995: 71), and the neo-colonial imperatives just mentioned seamlessly metamorphosed into the Cold War program of action for defending the so-called 'free-world' of Euro-American capitalism. The Cold War program of action that ensued involved also a significant redesign of Western social science. As a result of that redesign, Western social science – which had been rooted thus far in the discourse of the 'civilizing mission' – was transformed and became grounded in the discourse of 'modernization and development' (Mignolo, 2000, 2002; Spivak, 1999). As will be discussed, such transformation significantly relied upon the tropes of 'useful knowledge' and 'precise knowledge' and involved not only major changes in the nature of social science but also a large-scale overhaul of the institutional structures of knowledge.

The opening move in the aforementioned transformation of Western social science seems to have been made around the time World War II ended, when significant sections (private and public) of policy-making circles in the U.S. began to argue that the task of conducting U.S. policy with respect to different countries and regions of the world was greatly hampered because of a serious lack of 'useful' knowledge (i.e., the kind of knowledge produced by social sciences like economics, political science or sociology) about the non-Western world. As noted earlier, such absence of knowledge was due to the fact that most Western social sciences had overwhelmingly focused on Western countries alone. The U.S. policy-makers, hence, demanded that the situation be rectified. Moreover, since the 1920s, major American universities had witnessed rapid growth of the "'scientific' social sciences . . . [involving] Parsonian sociology, Keynesian macroeconomics, systems analysis and operations research, demography, and statistics," and the U.S. policy-makers began expressing the need for "precise knowledge" about the 'Third World' derived on the basis of the *nomothetic* insights and increasingly *quantitative* procedures of the new *scientific* social sciences (Escobar, 1995: 37; see also Bottom, 2009). The U.S. response to all those stated needs was to result in a sweeping restructuring of Western social science and its institutional arrangements and, in the process, lead to a *further consolidation* of U.S./Western academia as a key site for making "pragmatic contributions to . . . [neo-]imperial rule" (Cohn, 1996: 12).

The U.S. response to the needs of the moment consisted of several elements, including (1) establishment of Area Studies programs at different universities, (2) consolidation of the discourse of modernization and economic development, and (3) reorganization of the field of business management on a 'scientific' basis (Bilgin & Morton, 2002; Carroll, 1959a; Escobar, 1995; Pletsch, 1981). The new Area Studies programs were intended to organize the production of knowledge about various world areas (e.g., East Asia, Latin America, South Asia, etc.) on the basis of application of different social sciences to each area (Bilgin & Morton, 2002; Wallerstein, 2004a). Area Studies programs were usually set up by the U.S. intelligence agencies working closely with a range of private foundations, and available internal documents suggest that "the intelligence function" of such programs was often fully recognized by the foundations (Cumings, 1997).[7] Gradually, Area Studies programs emerged in other Western countries as well.

The Area Studies programs fostered "the emergence of the three worlds schema" (Bilgin & Morton, 2002: 59) and shaped the growth of a new "social science paradigm" (Cohn, 1996: 14) that worked to *produce* the 'Third World.' This new paradigm for the social sciences was founded upon the progressivist narrative of modernization and development, which took the 'West'/'First World' as the norm and declared that the 'Third World' had no option other than to 'progress'/'modernize' and keep working to become an ever closer *replica* of the 'West.' Moreover, the new paradigm was committed also to the production of universalistic nomothetic knowledge by means of increasing reliance upon mathematics, statistics, quantitative techniques, electronic computing and reductive model building.

The social scientific transformation of Western management

The transformation of management/business administration into a new (professional, or applied) social scientific discipline may be seen as being linked to the growth of the new (i.e., nomothetic and quantitative) social science paradigm, as well as to the U.S./Western imperatives of neo-colonial control. University-based *business* education is generally regarded as a U.S. invention of the late 19th century. From those beginnings, business schools grew to become an important part of university structure in the United States, and, by the middle of the 20th century, degrees in business accounted for fully one-seventh of all university degrees being awarded across the country (Carroll, 1959b). Clearly, by the 1950s, business education in the U.S. had become a "numerical giant" and a big business (Carroll, 1959b: vi).

At that point in time, however, business education was mainly *vocational* in nature and pre-pared the student for a career in a specific business or industry. Moreover, business education at this time had relatively limited contact with the social sciences (economics being an excep-tion): business school courses were primarily designed to teach current business practices and were mostly taught by experienced (working and/or retired) business executives. Furthermore, business schools at that time, generally speaking, were not expected to *produce* new knowledge: business school faculty, for the most part, did not engage in scholarly research, and production of new business knowledge was seen as largely taking place *outside* the structures of the university (Carroll, 1961; Clinebell & Clinebell, 2008; Khurana, 2007).

The generally vocational character of business education in the United States during the 1950s, however, should not be taken to imply that business schools at that time were completely insulated either from the world of scholarship or from the domain of social science. For instance, as early as the 1920s, elite social science networks in the U.S. had expressed the need for redesign-ing business administration/management along social scientific lines, and starting in the 1920s, the Social Science Research Council (SSRC) and the Rockefeller Foundation had provided finan-cial support for scholarly research in business, including, for instance, the research by Adolf Berle and Gardiner Means on the separation of ownership and control in the large U.S. corporation and Elton Mayo's research that eventually established the Human Relations School of manage-ment (Bottom, 2009; O'Connor, 1999a, 1999b).[8] Similarly, Bottom (2009) has pointed out that the Ford Foundation's involvement with the project of transforming business management into an applied social science began during the 1940s itself. Notwithstanding such developments, however, it would appear that, for the most part, business schools in the U.S. during the middle of the 20th century continued to have a mainly vocational orientation in their overall makeup.

Thus, by the 1950s, business schools were an important part of the U.S. university system – indeed, going by student enrollment, they constituted a somewhat dominant presence within the university – but, at the same time, by generally electing not to engage in knowledge production, business schools presented a significant challenge for the scholarly ethos of the university, which increasingly saw the university as the preponderant site for producing new knowledge. Similarly, by frequently choosing to ignore most social sciences, business schools implicitly questioned the claim of the new social sciences that true knowledge about all aspects of the human/social world could be obtained only by relying upon those very social sciences themselves.

In a somewhat related fashion, business schools represented a problem for the new Area Stud-ies programs as well. Area Studies programs were part of a larger discursive apparatus that sought to entrench the ideology of modernization, and a specific model of 'Third World' economic development involving measures like free trade, private investment, minimal role for government in the economy and reliance upon the production of primary commodities (e.g., raw materials and cash crops) and relatively low-value manufacture. Such an ideology and its prescriptions for

'Third World' development were of considerable value for purposes of linking 'Third World' economies in a hierarchically subordinate relationship with the West and thereby furthering neocolonial control.[9] The said ideology's prescriptions for 'Third World' development, however, ran substantially counter to the actual *historical experience* of the economic development of Europe and the United States, which had extensively relied upon government intervention and support, protectionism and a concerted shift to high-value manufacture.[10]

By and large, therefore, the experience of business practitioners (who tended to provide the bulk of the professoriate at the U.S. business schools at that time) was a somewhat unreliable instrument and foundation for promoting the new (neocolonial) model of economic development being engineered by Area Studies and development economics. Moreover, practitioners tended to offer also a much more contingent, locally situated and particularistic knowledge about business and economics that stood in sharp contrast to the model of universalistic knowledge being promoted by Area Studies and the social sciences. Finally, as part of the larger project of exporting the model of free-enterprise capitalism, Area Studies specialists and U.S. policy-makers seem to have intended to make business education itself into an important export of the United States to the rest of the world (Bottom, 2009; Carroll, 1959a, 1961). However, business education in the U.S. around 1950 was too closely focused on the specificities of local businesses and industries to appear relevant outside the United States and, hence, was not readily exportable. Thus, for a variety of reasons, business education of the time came to be framed as a 'problem' in the United States and became a serious target for 'reform.'

Although, as already noted, some efforts to 'reform' business management along social scientific lines had been made as early as the 1920s (Bottom, 2009), things began moving rapidly on that front only in the 1950s when the Ford Foundation, the U.S. private philanthropy with the largest endowment at that time (Tadajewski, 2009), became seriously involved in promoting Area Studies, development economics and business education and research and, over different periods, invested close to $1.5 *billion* in support of those activities (Cumings, 1997; Escobar, 1995; Sheridan & Kushner, 2009). Financial support for these activities was provided by various other foundations as well.

The program for transforming business management into a 'scientific' discipline – as outlined in a major report commissioned by the Ford Foundation – called upon business schools in the U.S. to develop a *new* understanding of "the practice of business . . . [by] relating it to *what we have* in the way of *relevant* systematic bodies of knowledge" (Gordon & Howell, 1959: 127; italics added).[11] This implied, as the report's foreword (written by the Ford Foundation's vice president) pointed out, that business schools needed to move away from the prevailing vocational and locally situated approach for understanding the problems of management and build up an abstract and universalistic approach based upon "the application of the fundamental disciplines of the social and behavioral sciences . . . [and] of modern mathematical and statistical methods" (Carroll, 1959b: v).[12]

Toward those ends, the Ford Foundation and others sponsored a range of activities, including the training of business school faculty in (1) different social sciences, mathematics and statistics and (2) in the use of "electronic computing machines" with a view to promoting the application of quantitative methods in business research (Carroll, 1959a: 162). Simultaneously, the use of Parsonian functionalism was encouraged in management research (Parsons, 1956a, 1956b). In these and related ways, business management in the United States was sought to be transformed into a 'scientific' discipline designed to produce universalistic and nomothetic knowledge by means of relying upon existing knowledge in the other 'relevant' social sciences and an epistemological approach committed to functionalism, positivism and quantitative methods. The reward for such transformation, argued the advocates of change, would be "full academic status"

(Carroll, 1959b: v) and increased prestige for business schools. We turn now to the third section of the chapter, which will offer a critical evaluation of management as a social scientific approach to knowledge. Following that, in the chapter's concluding section, we will explore some of the ways in which postcolonial theoretic insights might be helpful in productively reorienting management and organization studies (MOS).[13]

(Critical) Management Studies as a social scientific enterprise: A postcolonial critique

In Eurocentric accounts, modern Western scientific/social scientific knowledge is frequently represented as the result of a relatively disinterested pursuit of 'pure' truth and/or as the outcome of certain processes that are considered to be largely *internal* to the geographical space of Europe/the West (Hellyet, 2003; Wallerstein, 2004a; Westfall, 1992). From this vantage point, modern Western knowledge is often viewed as one of the "gifts that Western imperial powers brought to their colonies" (Seth, 2009: 373). As we have seen, postcolonial theory offers a much less pristine view of modern Western knowledge.

From a postcolonial perspective, (1) modern Western knowledge – including knowledge in the field of management – has been decisively shaped by Western colonial/neocolonial "geopolitical presence" (Darwin, 2008: 161); (2) such knowledge has often aided and supported the (neo-)colonial project and, to use Headrick's (1981) terminology, served as one of the "tools of empire"; (3) the origins of modern Western knowledge can frequently be found in "the projects and practices of colonialism" and neocolonialism (Seth, 2009: 374); (4) modern Western knowledge has generally played a *"constitutive* role . . . for colonialism [and/or neocolonialism, i.e.,] . . . as a means of conceptualizing and bringing into being the colonial [or, neocolonial] project itself" (Seth, 2009: 375; italics in the original); and (5) non-Western knowledges, techniques, actors and sites have played significant roles – from the very early days and in a variety of ways – in the creation of modern Western knowledge and its structures (Cohn, 1996; Harding, 1998, 2008, 2009; Raj, 2007). Management and other social sciences, however, appear to be largely oblivious of these aspects of their own history and, moreover, as will be discussed, to suffer also from a variety of other problems and limitations.

Management studies as applied social science: Major limitations

The 19th- and 20th-century consolidation of Western social science was deeply informed by prevailing ideas of unity of knowledge, which posited science to be a unified field (Lee, 1996; Sardar, 2006). Hence, paralleling natural science, social science also came to be viewed, in the main, as being engaged in a Cartesian search for *certainty* on the basis of a quantitative approach and positivistic conceptions of "truth associated with observable facts and the laws governing their relations" (Lee, 1996: 179). This view of knowledge, however, is premised upon notions of Cartesian rationality that posits an ontological dualism between body and soul (matter and mind) and sees reason as an instrument for controlling the body and the material world (Apffel-Marglin, 1996). As a result, significant sections of MOS and several other social sciences seem to subscribe to a very narrow and ethically questionable paradigm of knowledge, a paradigm mostly defined in terms of *prediction and control* of human/organizational/social behavior and rooted in a somewhat dehumanized understanding of individuals as objects to be controlled and manipulated.

Postcolonial critics of modern Western knowledge (including knowledge in the MOS field) note that Cartesian rationality – which leads to a separation of truth from the good and the beautiful – is only one among many competing forms of rationality that continue to exist in different parts of the world. (Apffel-Marglin, 1996; Harding, 1998, 2008; Ibarra-Colado, 2006; Sardar, 2006). Conceptualizing cultures as "ways of knowing," or as "knowledge systems" (Marglin, 1990: 24), these scholars propose that modern Western knowledge merely represents a particular *culture-specific* knowledge system, one which is grounded in, and profoundly limited by, the perspectives of Cartesian instrumental rationality. Moreover, point out the critics, the modern Western knowledge system suffers also from an "imperialistic pretension to universality," which results in a "total inability to regard competing [knowledge] systems with anything but contempt, . . . [an] inability indeed even to contemplate the existence of competing systems" (Marglin, 1990: 25). As a result, MOS and other Western social sciences largely seem to *lack the capacity* to learn and benefit from the theoretical sophistication of non-Western knowledge systems.

The social scientific approach that has decisively shaped MOS over the last several decades suffers from several other problems as well. Western social science, as Bilgin and Morton point out, "was a creature of states," and not infrequently, it has become a tool at the service of the state (2002: 58). For instance, as this paper has already discussed at some length, social science has played a crucial role in the discursive production of the West/non-West dichotomy, as well as the three worlds schema and thereby facilitated the exercise of (neo-)colonial power. Relatedly, scholars in anthropology, economics, international relations, political science and other fields have long served as administrators and advisers for Western governments and greatly contributed toward furthering (neo-)colonial control.

Similarly, the social scientific approach informing MOS is considerably compromised also because of its close links with social evolutionism and modernization theory, as a result of which social sciences, generally speaking, are led to produce highly problematic and stereotyped knowledge about different societies and cultures by following the formula of placing societies/cultures in the familiar grid of West/non-West hierarchy (Blaut, 1993, 2000; Nederveen Pieterse, 2010). Modernization theory, we may note, was deeply influenced by Max Weber's "model of the difference between a modernizing and a traditional society" (Blaut, 2000: 27), a model linked to Weber's comparative studies of world religions that have drawn considerable criticism lately for their arbitrary hierarchization of different religions, Eurocentrism and 'cultural racism'[14] (Masuzawa, 2005; Steinmetz, 2006; Zimmerman, 2006). Weber's studies have provided some of the key ingredients for fleshing out the hierarchical dichotomy of 'modern versus traditional society' – constructed around notions of rationality, industrialization, urbanization, and so forth – which serves as an organizing principle for the comparative approach widely used in the social sciences for analyzing national societies. Within MOS, the troubling imprint of that dichotomy can be found in the research stream that builds upon Hofstede's comparative study of national cultures (for critiques of Hofstede, see, e.g., Ailon, 2008; Fougère & Moulettes, 2007; Kwek, 2003).

In many ways, therefore, MOS and other modern Western social sciences may be seen as representing "ethnocentric . . . [and] arrogant" (Lee, 1996: 192) attempts to claim exemplarity and universal validity for certain ideas, beliefs, representations and ways of thinking that happened to gain prominence in one particular corner of the world at a specific historical juncture. Western social sciences, in other words, are unremittingly Eurocentric. Not surprisingly, during past years, virtually all the social sciences including MOS have drawn criticism for their Eurocentrism (Amin, 1989; Blaut, 1993, 2000; Boyacigiller & Adler, 1991; Frank, 1998; Prasad, 2012a; Wallerstein, 1997).

The Eurocentrism of social science, moreover, is crucially linked to extremely disturbing Western beliefs about race which, as Young (1995) has emphasized, "[permeated] . . . the fabric of almost all areas of thinking" in the West (p. 64) and seem to have provided "*the* common principle of academic knowledge" during the 19th century (p. 93; italics in the original) and, indeed, *at least* up to the 1930s, if not even later (Nederveen Pieterse, 2010: 21). Racism, hence, has deeply informed the knowledge produced in virtually all the social scientific fields. Biological racism, however, seems to have been now largely rejected in social science. Nevertheless, 'cultural racism,' or 'neo-racism' (Balibar, 1999; cited in Zimmerman, 2006), continues to cast its deeply troubling shadows on a number of social sciences, including MOS. Cultural racism operates by defining culture largely as a *fixity*, with the result that "culture . . . [functions] like . . . nature and [locks] individuals and groups . . . into a determination that is immutable" (Zimmerman, 2006: 53; quoting Balibar, 1999). Neo-racism worked its way into social science largely via Max Weber's influential rendering of the world as "a differentiated space of immutable cultural areas" (Zimmerman, 2006: 68), with Europe apparently occupying the top rank in the hierarchy of global cultures. As a result, scholars see neo-racism to be "latent" in concepts like 'traditional society,' 'modern society,' and others that have seemingly "functioned neutrally" in MOS and other social sciences (Zimmerman, 2006: 74).

Parsonian functionalism and Western management scholarship

Not surprisingly, perhaps, the range of these identified problems is deeply ingrained in Parsonian functionalism (Parsons, 1937, 1951), the scholarly framework that rose to become one of the major reigning influences in social science and that was the "dominant perspective" (Burrell & Morgan, 1979: 163) – perhaps, even an "orthodoxy" (Reed, 2006: 20) – in MOS during the 1950s–1970s period. For Parsons, the modern West represented "the pinnacle of human achievement" (Burrell & Morgan, 1979: 55). Hence, in the Parsonian world, the task of "social science becomes that of identifying the structures or elements" of a social system which ensure the system's survival (Burrell & Morgan, 1979: 55).

Insofar as the field of MOS is concerned, the Parsonian framework influenced the growth of a number of theories and research programs – dealing, for instance, with formal organizational structure, systems approach, a variety of characteristics and features of organizations, relationship between organizations and their environments and the like (Burrell & Morgan, 1979; Casey, 2002; Scott, 1992) – which were generally driven by a concern for technical efficiency/effectiveness of Western management practices and organizations and were largely underpinned by the arbitrary assumption that *Western* forms of managing and organizing necessarily served as *universal* norms. This assumption is reflected, for example, in Homans' declaration that "the organization of the large formal enterprises . . . in modern [i.e., Western] society is modeled on, is a rationalization of, *tendencies that exist in all human groups*" (1950: 186–187; quoted in Scott, 1992: 7; italics added).[15]

Moreover, the Parsonian "utopianism of the present" (Zimmerman, 2006: 73) promoted an *idealized* image of the United States and the West, which led to status quo theorizing and marginalization of critique in management research. Consequently, MOS failed to pay adequate attention to issues of oppression surrounding, for instance, race, gender, class, managerialism and so forth.[16] Simultaneously, international management researchers became involved in producing knowledge that mostly tended to conclude that the "modes of leadership and governance . . . [and] management systems . . . [in 'Third World' countries were] patrimonial . . . authoritarian, . . . dysfunctional, irrational, inefficient, incompetent, unsophisticated, and so on" (Westwood, 2004: 61).

Thus, MOS became a part and parcel of the larger institutional apparatus engaged in the discursive production of the 'Third World' and became deeply complicit with the Western neo-colonial project. Structural functionalism today is no longer the force it once was. Nevertheless, as

Casey (2002: 14), for instance, points out, "many of its categories, methods, and imperatives . . . remain . . . generally operative . . . in organization studies" and continue to persist. Similarly, critics have noted that, in significant ways, current international management research routinely continues to essentialize, exoticize and denigrate the non-West (Jack & Westwood, 2010; Westwood & Jack, 2007).

The critical imagination in Western management scholarship

In addition to conventional functionalist research, MOS has a long history of critical and interpretive scholarship drawing upon a variety of theoretical and philosophical perspectives, such as, existentialism, phenomenology, ethnomethodology, hermeneutics, social constructivism, critical Weberianism, different forms of Marxism and neo-Marxism and so on (Burrell & Morgan, 1979; Morgan, 1983; Prasad, 2005). During recent decades, critical MOS research informed by feminism, postmodernism, poststructuralism, postcolonialism and so forth has appeared as well. Generally speaking, critique of management and organizations now constitutes an expanding area of research, and the area is rapidly being institutionalized (at the U.S. Academy of Management and elsewhere) under the contested label of 'Critical Management Studies' (CMS).[17] Needless to say, CMS scholarship has provided a useful alternative to the knowledge traditionally produced by functionalist management research in the West. Nevertheless, as will be discussed, *significant sections* of CMS continue to be marked by some of the limitations of Western social scientific knowledge identified earlier. Arguably, many of those limitations largely follow from certain problems that are deeply embedded in the very fabric of various theoretical/philosophical frameworks that inform CMS.

For instance, we noted earlier the questionable tendency in Western social science to refuse to accept non-Western knowledges as 'genuine' knowledge and, at the same time, to claim also that social science has the capability of producing universal truths. Those tendencies seem to be present in many of the philosophical frameworks that inform different sections of CMS. Indeed, Western thought has a long tradition of arguing that non-Western philosophies/knowledges are *not* 'genuine' philosophy/knowledge. An influential early 19th-century example of such belief can be found in Hegel's declaration that Chinese and Indian philosophy "must . . . be excluded from the History of Philosophy . . . [because] Philosophy proper commences in the West" (1955: 99).

It deserves to be emphasized here that such dismissal of non-Western knowledges/civilizations is, by no means, confined only to politically conservative Western philosophers like Hegel. For example, even a radical thinker like Karl Marx – arguably, one of *the* most important influences on the development of critical social science and CMS – fully subscribes to Hegel's philosophy of history (in terms of which Europe is seen as the teleological end point of universal history), as well as to the Hegelian history of philosophy (which dismisses non-Western philosophies as not being philosophical enough), with the result that Marx, the iconic Western philosopher of praxis and human emancipation, turns into a *defender* of brutal Western colonialism, which he comes to approvingly regard as "the unconscious tool of history" necessary for bringing the light of knowledge and civilization to the "semi-barbarian, semi-civilized" non-West (Marx, 1972: 581–582).[18]

Along with its general disregard for non-Western philosophies and knowledges, Western philosophy has long claimed also that it possesses the capacity to produce what Edmund Husserl calls, in his 'Vienna Lecture of 1935,' "absolute theoretical insights . . . through universal scientific reason" (Husserl quoted in Chakrabarty, 1992: 3). This belief leads to a further conviction that the West has at its command all the necessary *categories* that might be required for understanding the entire world. Or, as Jean-Paul Sartre puts it in his *Existentialism and Humanism* (1948), "Every project, even that of a Chinese, an Indian or a Negro, can be understood by a *European* . . . . There is always some way of understanding an idiot, a child, a primitive man or a foreigner if one has sufficient information" (Sartre quoted in Spivak, 1999: 171; italics added).

The belief in the West's exclusive access to Absolute Universal Reason animates a large galaxy of major Western philosophers and thinkers, such as Hegel, Heidegger, Husserl, Sartre, Merleau-Ponty, Karl Marx, Max Weber and others (Chakrabarty, 1992; Blaut, 2000; Halbfass, 1988), who have considerably influenced the development of CMS. The CMS field, by and large, has neither challenged such belief in any concerted fashion nor made meaningful attempts to encourage and facilitate the utilization of non-Western knowledges in management research.

Not surprisingly, perhaps, many of the philosophical perspectives informing various streams of CMS research tend to be deeply Eurocentric. Hence, for the most part, CMS also exhibits the problem of Eurocentrism identified earlier in the case of MOS and other Western social sciences in general. An important instance of the Eurocentrism of CMS may be found in its broad neglect of colonialism, a neglect that seems to have had significant scholarly implications. CMS, broadly speaking, appears to have unquestioningly accepted 'internalist' accounts of Western capitalism, which portray the development of Euro-American capitalism to be a product of certain dynamics that were largely internal to the West. As a result, to take merely one example out of many, CMS has largely failed to seriously examine the significance of colonialism for the emergence and development of the institutions of Western capitalism, including modern Western management practices and knowledge (Westwood & Jack, 2007). Hence, the Eurocentrism of large sections of CMS – as exhibited, in this instance, in their neglect of colonialism – may be said to have resulted in a highly partial and inadequate understanding of important management and organizational issues and phenomena.

As already noted, during recent decades, many CMS researchers have been drawing upon postmodernism and poststructuralism as well (Alvesson & Deetz, 2006). Despite their professed desire to give new directions to Western thought, however, it appears that postmodernism and poststructuralism remain deeply enmeshed in Eurocentric and universalistic ways of thinking. Postcolonial scholars, for instance, have critiqued postmodernism/poststructuralism for ignoring the dynamics of colonialism, for frequently treating the somewhat widely prevalent condition of European cultural angst as a global predicament, for seeking to consolidate a Eurocentric framework for viewing the cultural products of the non-Western world and for promoting a local cultural/epistemological attitude as a general movement having global relevance (Adams & Tiffin, 1990; Bhabha, 1994; Mignolo, 2000; Sardar, 1998; Spivak, 2008). Generally speaking, research in the CMS field does not seem to have made serious efforts to challenge these and related problematic tendencies exhibited by postmodernism/poststructuralism.

Critical Management Studies, as noted earlier, is a heterogeneous field comprising a variety of approaches to scholarly inquiry, and this chapter does not intend to offer close critiques of different streams of CMS research. Nevertheless, it might be useful here to take a quick look at one particular stream of CMS because of the long-standing commitment displayed by that stream to the project of institutionalizing CMS in a rather *narrow* fashion (for some examples of this stream, see Alvesson, Bridgman & Willmott, 2009; Alvesson & Willmott, 1992, 2003, 2011; Grey & Willmott, 2005a; etc.). Given space considerations, our examination of the said CMS stream – often referred to as the Manchester School of CMS (see Prasad, Prasad, Mills & Helms Mills, Chapter 2 in this volume) – must necessarily be somewhat brief.

We may begin by noting here that the Manchester School of CMS often makes rather extravagant claims about the special role played by researchers from Europe – or, perhaps even more narrowly, from Scandinavia and the U.K. – in the development of critical management scholarship[19] and seems to contend also that the growth of a sizeable body of critical literature in management was somehow *catalyzed* by the emergence of the "capitalized phrase *Critical Management Studies* . . . the title of the . . . collection [edited by Alvesson and Willmott] . . . that appeared in 1992" (Grey & Willmott, 2005b: 3; italics in original). Gestures like these attempt to draw somewhat arbitrary boundary lines through historical time and geographical and/or conceptual space and work to generate a considerably scaled-down and truncated map of the overall CMS terrain. Needless to say, such gestures, along with a deep-rooted commitment to Eurocentrism, serve also as important anchoring devices for this research stream's project to institutionalize a rather *narrow and provincial* version of CMS.

In this regard, furthermore, as a number of researchers have pointed out (see, e.g., Ashcraft, 2011; Ferdinand, Muzio & O'Mahoney, 2004, 2005; Prasad, 2008; see also Prasad, Prasad, Mills & Helms Mills, Chapter 1 in this volume), what seems also to distinguish the Manchester School of CMS research is a deep tension between, on the one hand (1) this school's routine espousal of the idea of CMS as a pluralistic intellectual domain characterized by considerable debates across widely divergent scholarly perspectives and, on the other hand (2) its determined attempts to consolidate a somewhat narrow and exclusivist intellectual map of the broader CMS terrain. With respect to intellectual perspectives, for instance, this school of CMS appears to ascribe a "rather narrow definition . . . to the notion of Critical Management Studies" (Ferdinand, Muzio & O'Mahoney, 2005: 1715), tending to view the conceptual landscape of CMS mostly in terms of neo-Marxist Critical Theory and certain aspects of postmodernism and/or poststructuralism alone. Similarly, in terms of object of inquiry, this school increasingly seems to investigate *micro- and/or meso-level* processes largely by means of focusing upon "very limited sections of the professional and managerial class" (Ackroyd, 2004: 167)[20] and, as a result, mostly overlooks wider dynamics involving *macro-level* concerns, such as race, ethnicity, subalternity, workplace diversity and multiculturalism, systemic corruption in different corporate sectors in the West, global economic structures/crises, neocolonialism, Eurocentrism and so on (Ashcraft, 2011; Prasad, 2008).

Such a narrowly defined research program is clearly problematic and would seem to be of rather limited value in a post-colonial and rapidly globalizing world. In some ways, however, what appears to be even more problematic is this school's insistent claim that, somehow, such a narrowly framed research oeuvre needs to be viewed as forming the core (or canon, or vanguard) of the *entire* CMS field (Ashcraft, 2011; Prasad, 2008). Such insistence on the part of a uniquely provincial and narrowly defined research stream within CMS – an insistence which, from a postcolonial perspective, may be regarded as a Eurocentric and modernist attempt to discipline knowledge, and to contain the force of the contestatory and liberationary impulses animating CMS – would hardly seem to promote the larger cause of radical critique in MOS.

Ashcraft (2011), for instance, has pointed out in this connection that the existence of the earlier identified tension in the writings of the Manchester School – namely, the tension between this school's copious declarations regarding the pluralistic nature of CMS, on the one hand, and its concerted efforts to institutionalize a highly restricted version of CMS, on the other – implies that this stream of research is constrained to resort to a variety of "repetitive, beguiling (discursive) sleights of hand" that seek to assign a marginal status to various other critical genres of scholarship and, in so doing, frequently do considerable disservice to the wider critical project in MOS (see also, Ashcraft's Chapter 6 in this volume). Parallel to this, Tatli (2011) has identified within this school a troubling absence of adequate self-reflexivity regarding its own dynamics of exclusion. Similarly, Prasad (2008) notes that this school appears reluctant to raise a number of critical questions including, for instance, "what might be . . . the ethico-political interests being promoted by . . . [that] variety of CMS" (p. 283). All in all, in other words, the Manchester School of CMS may be seen as providing a considerably limited form of critique within MOS/CMS research.

As the preceding discussion of critical as well as conventional management scholarship suggests, MOS may be seen as an approach to knowledge production which is defined by two analytically distinct – although "complementary and inseparable" – forms of *ethnocentrism*: epistemological and ideological (Mudimbe, 1988: 19).[21] Epistemological ethnocentrism connects MOS as social science to "an intellectual atmosphere which [lends the discipline] . . . status . . . significance . . . and credibility as . . . science in . . . [a specific] field of human experience" (Mudimbe, 1988: 19). Thus, elements like Cartesian rationality, positivism, universalism, and so on may be seen as manifestations of epistemological ethnocentrism. Ideological ethnocentrism, on the other hand, refers to "an intellectual and behavioral attitude [linked to] . . . the scholar's . . . consciousness, the scientific models of . . . [the] time, and the cultural and social norms of . . . society" (Mudimbe, 1988: 19). In MOS, ideological ethnocentrism mostly seems to express itself via notions like modernization, the hierarchical system of West/non-West dichotomies, and neo-racism. Generally speaking, the ideological ethnocentrism of MOS tends to result in a somewhat unthinking undervaluing of 'Third World' management practices and systems and a corresponding elevation/celebration of 'Western' ones (Westwood, 2004; Westwood & Jack, 2007).

As the final section of the chapter discusses, postcolonial theory offers several valuable ideas for (1) taking MOS beyond the intellectually debilitating confines of the previously identified twin forms of ethnocentrism and, in that process (2) for radically transforming the MOS field. In what follows, the chapter will first outline a number of important postcolonial considerations relevant to the project of reorienting MOS and then go on to discuss the significance of the need to rethink Western categories of knowledge. Thereafter, the chapter will offer some provisional suggestions for a critical postcolonial theoretic research agenda for the MOS field. Finally, the chapter will conclude with brief thoughts on the necessity of reimagining MOS as a multipolar domain of plural knowledges spread across different regions of the world. *Mutatis mutandis*, much of what follows may be seen as relevant for the CMS area as well.

The search for alternative knowledges: Toward a postcolonial reorientation of (Critical) Management Studies

Postcolonialism is a vehicle for critique and ethico-political transformation aimed at creating a more just and humane future. Hence, postcolonial theoretic insights have the potential to radically reorient MOS, effecting thereby far-reaching changes with respect to the field's theoretical foundations, disciplinary boundaries, institutional arrangements, and epistemological and methodological commitments. To begin with, postcolonial theory provides valuable suggestions for rethinking the foundational knowledge of MOS which, as we have seen, is significantly marked by Eurocentrism, Orientalism, neo-racism and the like. Specifically, critiques of modern Western knowledge offered by postcolonial scholars (e.g., Mignolo, 2000, 2002; Spivak, 2003) suggest that MOS researchers need to seriously look for theoretical inspiration *outside* the conventional boundaries of MOS. In this regard, moreover, MOS also needs to take into account the growing recognition in postcolonial and other critical circles that a belief in Western scholarship's traditional divide between the so-called two cultures – represented, respectively, by nomothetic and idiographic approaches to inquiry – has become a major hindrance to intellectual creativity (Mignolo, 2000; Spivak, 2008; Wallerstein, 2004a, 2004b). As a first step, therefore, MOS needs large-scale engagement with critical scholarship in other social sciences *and* humanities with a view to rejuvenating the field's theoretical foundations.

As we saw in an earlier section of the chapter, the social scientific transformation of business was based on the idea of management as an applied social science. In that process, however, the range of social sciences that were deemed 'relevant' for management was somewhat narrowly circumscribed and seems to have been largely limited to sections of economics, psychology and sociology. Moreover, in general, the humanities were considered 'irrelevant' for management. During recent years, researchers in the CMS and interpretive traditions have made praiseworthy attempts to draw upon other social sciences and the humanities, but much more extensive efforts in that direction might be necessary with a view to developing additional critical resources. It would seem that MOS researchers can gain substantially by engaging with critical scholarship in fields like anthropology, history, geography, international relations and the like in the social sciences and with cultural studies, feminist studies, race studies, religious studies and others in the humanities.

Postcolonial theory, of course, is not alone in emphasizing the need for interdisciplinarity, especially perhaps, when interdisciplinary engagement involves the crossing of disciplinary borders separating the humanities from the social sciences (see, e.g., Joshi, 1986; Wallerstein, 2004a, 2004b). Without getting into a discussion of different scholarly perspectives advocating collaboration between the humanities and social science, however, for a postcolonial theorist like Spivak (2003, 2008), a major benefit of such interdisciplinary exchange is to be found in the potential of the humanities to prepare the social sciences to offer *better* generalizations.

Spivak (2008) suggests that genuine collaboration between the humanities and a social science (e.g., MOS) requires that researchers do "not reject . . . [the social scientific] impulse toward generalization" (p. 46) and recognize that "the social sciences . . . can produce useful generalizations – *however limited*" (p. 228; italics added). For researchers in MOS and other social sciences, therefore, the project of engaging with the humanities offers an intellectual and ethico-political space for addressing many of the *limitations* of the social scientific imagination (identified earlier in the chapter) with a view to producing *improved* generalizations. In brief, following Spivak (2008), it is possible to suggest that a number of fields in the humanities (e.g., cultural studies, feminist studies, race studies, religious studies, etc.) seem to have the potential to provide MOS with that "exercise of the imagination" (p. 227) and "uncoercive rearrangement of desire" (p. 226) which, when combined with a "transnational [awareness of] . . . the dynamic [political and] geopolitical configurations of the globalizing world" (p. 226), might help develop within the MOS discipline a scholarly "habit of politically literate textured reading" (p. 229) that could, conceivably, lead to valuable generalizations about national and transnational processes involving businesses, organizations, industries, institutions, networks and so forth.

At the same time, in order to challenge Eurocentric habits of thought that seem to dominate the field, MOS researchers also need to develop a postcolonial historical sensibility built upon, among other things, the idea of "connected histories" (Subrahmanyam, 1997, 2005), "interactional history" (van der Veer, 2001: 8) or "horizontally integrative macrohistory" (Frank, 1998: 345). Such history draws attention to the rich record of global exchange and interactions in a variety of spheres (e.g., cultural, economic, intellectual, epistemological and the rest), and emphasizes not only that all cultures, whether Western or non-Western, bear significant imprints of influences emanating from other cultures but also that the *origins* of the various practices and institutions of Western modernity and Euro-American capitalism "cannot be neatly located . . . [within the 'West,' and] must be sought in the . . . [complexity] of [colonial] encounters" (van der Veer, 2001: 160).

Equally important, moreover, in tune with the suggestion made by Spivak (2008) and other postcolonial scholars, MOS researchers need to actively look *outside* the West and draw upon non-Western theoretical and philosophical resources also. In this regard, researchers need to keep in mind also that, in contrast to many Western countries where intellectual life has become largely dominated by "academic intellectuals," large sections of Africa, Asia and Latin America continue to have thriving worlds of public intellectuals who are *not* part of the "organized [research] industry" (Nandy, 2000: 33). Hence, in addition to drawing upon non-Western academic sources, MOS researchers also need to look beyond the academic world while engaging with the non-West.

Furthermore, in line with our earlier discussion of Spivak (2008), MOS researchers may also need to "learn to learn from below" (p. 43) and, toward that end, establish links with non-Western subaltern groups. Needless to say, the project of learning from the non-Western subaltern entails an unusually high level of difficulty, and space considerations here do not permit a detailed discussion of various issues relevant to this subject. In brief, however, Spivak's (2008) notion of 'learning to learn from the subaltern' revolves around a complex set of ideas which emerged as part of Spivak's attempts to develop a variety of pedagogical programs in collaboration with non-Western subaltern groups. Learning from the subaltern, as Spivak (2008: 38) cautions us, demands a "different way of epistemic access," one which rejects the idea of the subaltern as an "object of investigation for disciplinary information retrieval."

According to Spivak (2008), that different way of learning involves "a risky othering of the self" on the part of the 'researcher' (p. 267), as well as the 'researcher' adopting the role of an *apprentice* to the subaltern who is the "teacher" (p. 269). Such learning, moreover, is aimed at accessing/redefining, in a highly tentative fashion, the subaltern group's "older cultural habits" (p. 25), and/or "erased ethical scripts" (p. 38) which often appear considerably damaged because of the depredations of history but which still seem to offer the possibility of filling today's structures of capitalism "with . . . [a] more robust imperative to responsibility" (p. 24), an imperative which resists Western modernity's desire for "the extraction and appropriation of surplus . . . exploration and conquest of nature, and so on" (p. 24). While engaging with the subaltern, however, MOS researchers need to pay serious attention to Spivak's (2008) warning that 'learning from the subaltern' involves a process which is extremely slow and painstaking, and, furthermore, that it is also an undertaking that comes with no guarantees about the outcome.

As we proceed with our discussion of various other postcolonial theoretic ideas that might be helpful in facilitating critique of epistemological and/or ideological commitment to universalism, positivism, structural functionalism, Orientalism, the West/non-West hierarchy, racism/neo-racism and the like, it would be useful to recall that scholarly commitment to many of these highly troubling notions can be found even in the works of major Western philosophers/thinkers who have frequently provided inspiration to management research belonging to the interpretive and/or CMS genre. Hence, MOS researchers need to develop a much more critical and interrogative relationship with such intellectual sources. It is important to note here that postcolonialism does not require that MOS scholars completely reject those "Wise Men of Europe" (Spivak, 1999: 111). Rather, what postcolonial theory suggests is that, in the process of making use of those thinkers, MOS researchers also need to explicitly highlight and critique the *complicity* of such thinkers' ideas with the 'axiomatics of imperialism' (Spivak, 1999) and, in so doing, work to *decolonize* Western theory and philosophy (see, e.g., Spivak, 1999; Steinmetz, 2006; Zimmerman, 2006).

Needless to say, postcolonial theory suggests the need for a sustained program of critique directed at existing management knowledge and practices (including practices relating to the production of management knowledge in the academic 'research industry') and, in that process, developing a thoroughly revised and critical understanding of the same. The postcolonial critique of modern Western knowledge, moreover, extends into the methodological domain as well. In brief, postcolonialism seems to argue that the seriousness of the problems investing modern Western knowledge literally demands that we adopt an attitude of considerable skepticism toward the methods and procedures *responsible for producing* such flawed knowledge (Prakash, 1994). As regards methodology, therefore, postcolonial theory encourages significant exploration and inventiveness. For MOS researchers, this suggests the need for eclectic experimentation with various postpositivist approaches (Prasad, 2005) and with different critical and indigenous methodologies (Denzin, Lincoln & Smith, 2008).

In a related vein, postcolonial scholars emphasize the importance of quotidian practices and everyday experiences (Chakrabarty, 2000) – of "being more sensitive to our own lived experiences and those of others" (Behera, 2007: 359) – for knowledge production. In part, this methodological guideline may be seen as being linked to a desire not to fetishize 'data.' As Wallerstein (2004b) has noted, even idiographic social sciences like history and anthropology, while mostly rejecting the idea of universal generalization, continue to cling to "the scientific emphasis on empirical data" (p. 19). Hence, postcolonial scholars like Mignolo (2000), for instance, have sought to challenge the social scientific obsession with 'data' by such means as employing "casual conversations [*not* interviews] . . . as research method" and "anonymous rumor" as data (p. xi).

Along with the foregoing, postcolonial theory suggests that MOS researchers in the West need to learn new ways of studying non-Western management practices. To begin with, researchers need to learn not to automatically view *difference* as *deficiency* or *inferiority*. As we have seen, MOS researchers frequently regard non-Western management practices as 'inefficient' or 'flawed' simply because those practices happen to be different from the Western norm (Westwood, 2004). A postcolonial reorientation of MOS would require researchers to give up such intellectual laziness and learn the habit of viewing non-Western practices and institutions as situated responses to local contexts and requirements.

At the same time, however, researchers also need to learn not to regard non-Western practices that might appear 'similar' to Western practices to be exact replicas of practices that prevail in the West. As postcolonial scholars have pointed out, *difference* is frequently embedded in what might appear as the *same* (Bhabha, 1994; Nandy, 1983). Hence, as regards the study of non-Western management practices, MOS researchers need to develop a new habit of intellectual caution that (1) would allow them to recognize the embeddedness of those practices in local cultures, meanings and institutions and (2) would thereby enable them to understand the said practices only on the basis of such contextual embeddedness. The significance of contextual embeddedness for knowledge production, however, raises important questions about the *theoretical categories* that might appropriately be employed in MOS research dealing with the non-West.

Rethinking Western categories of knowledge

Postcolonial theory is rooted in the awareness that "the question of what we keep and what we discard from the heritage of [Western] modernity needs explicit and ongoing discussion" and negotiation (Inayatullah & Blaney, 2004; quoted in Behera, 2007: 359). Crucially, however, one of the major legacies of modernity/colonialism is the very constellation of categories that inform Western structures of knowledge. Hence, postcolonialism argues that, in the context of understanding non-Western societies and cultures, there is a need also for a critical reassessment of the theoretical categories that undergird Western social science (Bhambra, 2007; Escobar, 1995). Such a reconsideration of social scientific categories has important implications for MOS researchers.

In this regard, scholars have noted that the categories of Western social science are intimately linked to the idea that social life is characterized by its "separation . . . into [a number of relatively autonomous] functional spheres . . . [such as] the economy, the polity, society, culture, and the like" (Escobar, 1995: 60). Management and other social sciences generally regard these domains as "natural, presocial and universal" and as the "fundamental building blocks of all societies"

(Escobar, 1995: 61). What needs to be recognized, however, is that such a configuration of the social world is merely an aspect of Western modernity and simply does not obtain in large parts of Africa, Asia and Latin America.

Hence, a postcolonial theoretic overhaul of MOS would require that researchers interested in understanding non-Western management and organizational practices disavow the notion of the universality of the functional spheres that generally characterize the modern West. It follows, therefore, that MOS researchers need to discard the assumption of the existence of 'the economy' as a separate domain in all societies around the world. In other words, MOS researchers need to resist "the spontaneous impulse to look in every society for 'economic' institutions and relations separate from other social relations" (Godelier, 1986; quoted in Escobar, 1995: 61) and learn to rely upon *local categories* instead for purposes of understanding how social life might be structured in any particular society.

In a somewhat parallel fashion, postcolonial insights require MOS researchers to reevaluate their assumption regarding the universal usefulness of the category of 'the organization' as well. As Ibarra-Colado (2000) has pointed out, 'the organization' as a category is not particularly useful for understanding those *modes of organizing* that do not depend upon "instrumental rationality and the logic of the market" (p. 467). However, in large parts of Africa, Asia and Latin America, there exist alternative "modes of organizing," undergirded by "non-scientific" knowledges and associated "modes of rationality," which simply do not conform to market logic and the tenets of instrumental rationality (Ibarra-Colado, 2006: 474). Hence, those alternative modes of organizing and related rationalities can be understood only on the basis of a "historically and culturally" contextualized approach that relies upon *local categories* of knowledge (Ibarra-Colado, 2006: 474).

The said local categories of knowledge may be found (1) in local intellectual traditions of thought and speculation, as well as (2) in the form of "practical concepts . . . embedded in quotidian practices" (Chakrabarty, 2000: 6), including "rituals and beliefs, . . . [unique] forms of division of labor and . . . [other] activities, . . . rites and celebrations" and so on (Ibarra-Colado, 2006: 474). Hence, MOS researchers desirous of studying non-Western modes of organizing need to develop the necessary competencies that would enable them to acquire access to, and adroitness in the use of, such categories within the relevant non-Western country or region. Among other things, developing those competencies requires that researchers build up what may be called, following Spivak (2003), an 'idiomatic understanding' of the non-Western society in question, that is, an understanding based on extended, in-depth, non-Eurocentric and serious efforts to learn the society's history, culture, politics, language(s) and the like. Needless to say, such a postcolonial approach toward studying non-Western modes of organizing requires considerable prior intellectual preparation on the part of the researcher (Prasad, 2012a).

The complexities associated with the issue of adequately understanding non-Western modes of organizing raise troubling questions about the role of so-called Western management experts who take on paid and/or unpaid consulting and training projects in the non-West. While this chapter is not intended to provide a detailed critique of projects of that nature, a postcolonial theoretic reorientation of MOS does require that scholars develop a sceptical attitude toward such Western efforts supposedly directed at 'improving' non-Western practices of organizing. Generally speaking, it would seem that unless the Western 'experts' involved have made *substantial* prior investments toward developing an 'idiomatic understanding' (Spivak, 2003) of the non-Western region where the consulting/training project is to be carried out, the project is unlikely to offer much of value to the non-Western area concerned. Critical MOS scholars, therefore, need to view such 'experts' and their projects as 'case studies' in need of serious scrutiny and critique.

A postcolonial agenda for (Critical) Management Research

The preceding discussions have highlighted a range of valuable postcolonial theoretic insights for effecting a far-reaching – and, we might add, much needed – transformation of MOS as well as CMS. Drawing upon those insights, this part of the chapter seeks to offer brief outlines of a tentative postcolonial research agenda for the discipline. It is important to note, in this connection, that past postcolonial scholarship has pointed out that the task of fundamentally reorienting modern Western knowledge involves two interrelated and simultaneously unfolding projects: one of 'deconstruction' and the other of 'reconstruction' (Escobar, 1995; Mohanty, Russo & Torres, 1991; Nandy, 2000). The 'deconstructive'[22] project primarily focuses upon developing radical critiques of modern Western knowledge with a view to "dismantling" various problematic aspects of existing knowledges, practices and knowledge-producing institutions and structures (Escobar, 1995: 16). The 'reconstructive' project, on the other hand, is principally concerned with imaginatively "constructing new ways of seeing and acting" (Escobar, 1995: 16).

Accordingly, the provisional research agenda about to be suggested includes both (1) a scholarly program of 'deconstruction,' as well as (2) a scholarly program of 'reconstruction.' For the sake of convenience, moreover, each of these two scholarly programs, in its own turn, has been sketched out here in terms of its focus upon three somewhat distinct, though highly interrelated, aspects of MOS: (1) MOS knowledge, (2) organizational/managerial practices and structures and (3) practices and institutions of MOS research, including the constitutive dynamics of the MOS 'research industry.' All in all, therefore, the postcolonial agenda for MOS research proposed in this chapter spans the following six overlapping dimensions: (1) radical interrogation and deconstruction of existing MOS knowledge and theory; (2) critique of current managerial, organizational and institutional practices and structures; (3) critique of existing MOS epistemologies and/or methodologies, as well as the MOS 'research industry'; (4) imaginative reconstruction of new MOS knowledge; (5) creatively reimagining new and different modes of organizing involving 'other' work practices and structures; and (6) imaginatively envisioning new ways of doing research in the MOS field. These six dimensions are schematically laid out in Figure 10.1. Needless to say, our elaboration of the proposed research agenda under each of these dimensions is merely illustrative, rather than exhaustive.

As regards the first of these six dimensions (Cell-I, Figure 10.1), a postcolonial interrogation and deconstruction of existing MOS knowledge are intended to, among other things, deny the universalistic pretensions of MOS and to shed critical light on the many weaknesses/limitations of MOS knowledge stemming from, for instance, its complicitous links with the discourses of colonialism and/or neocolonialism. Accordingly, some possibilities for future research along this dimension might include (1) investigating the continued presence of colonialist/Orientalist binaries and/or (neo-)racist thought in extant theory and empirical research in a variety of areas

		FOCUS OF RESEARCH PROGRAM		
		MOS Knowledge	Current Practices	MOS Research Industry
AIM OF RESEARCH PROGRAM	'Deconstruction'	Cell-I	Cell-II	Cell-III
	'Reconstruction'	Cell-IV	Cell-V	Cell-VI

Figure 10.1 Postcolonial research agenda for management and organization studies (schematic).

including, for instance, management of workplace diversity, cross-cultural management, dynamics of gender and sexuality in organizations, tourism marketing and so on; (2) scrutinizing the role of Western MOS knowledge (e.g., in the field of international management) in furthering the interests of Western multinational enterprises (MNEs) and thereby facilitating the West's neocolonial domination of the 'Third World'; (3) bringing to light spectacular failures of Western theories of leadership, motivation, attribution, (Weberian) bureaucracy and so on in non-Western workplaces; (4) highlighting the provincial nature of Western MOS knowledge by bringing attention to the narrowness of MOS researchers' institutional affiliations, study samples and so forth; and (5) examining the economic, political and sociocultural consequences resulting from the adoption of Western MOS knowledge in 'Third World' work and employment sectors.

In a similar vein, a postcolonial critique and deconstruction of current management and organizational practices/structures (Cell-II) involves, among other things, developing a critical understanding of how contemporary managers, organizations and institutions might work to reproduce and further entrench the discourses of colonialism and/or neocolonialism. Hence, some possible avenues for future research under this dimension include (1) taking a critical look at the role played by corporate practices and structures of Western MNEs in designing a neocolonial international division of labor and the consequences of the latter for the economic, political and sociocultural well-being of 'Third World' peoples; (2) identifying the influence of Western private corporate interests on the formulation of (neo-)colonial and/or militaristic foreign policy agendas by governments of different Western countries; (3) investigating the significance of geopolitical considerations in the design and governance of global supply chains and international production networks; (4) studying the role of various policies, practices and structures of Western governmental foreign 'aid' agencies (e.g., United States Agency for International Aid) and/or international 'development' organizations (e.g., the International Monetary Fund or the World Bank), in perpetuating the discourses that ongoingly reproduce a neocolonial world order; and (5) understanding the psychological degradation and "cultural pathologies" (Nandy, 1983: 35) brought about within the 'West' itself as a result of various (neo-)colonial aspects of Western corporate practices and structures.

Parallel to what has been just stated, potential postcolonial critiques of current MOS epistemological/methodological commitments and dynamics of MOS 'research industry' (Cell-III) might focus upon in-depth examination of such issues, among others, as (1) consequences of the Eurocentrism/provincialism of major modern Western philosophers and thinkers whose ideas inform the foundational epistemologies/methodologies of MOS/CMS research; (2) factors that might perpetuate the reluctance of MOS/CMS researchers to employ non-Western epistemologies/methodologies for producing knowledge; and (3) the role of the institutional politics of publication and academia – involving, for instance, the deep ties binding together academic tenure and promotion decisions, faculty reward structures, enactment of various kinds of professional hierarchies, promotion within the discipline of a somewhat narrow set of so-called top-tier research journals, obsession with 'impact factors' and journal rankings and so on – in encouraging the continued production of epistemologically and/or ideologically ethnocentric MOS/CMS knowledge in the West.

Needless to say, moving from the scholarly program of deconstruction to one of reconstruction involves some important shifts in the suggested agenda for postcolonial theoretic MOS research. For instance, future research concerned with reconstructing MOS knowledge (Cell-IV) would likely involve focus upon at least two broad areas: (1) extensive rewriting of the history of the growth of MOS knowledge and different business/organizational practices, with a view to understanding the significance of the colonial and neocolonial encounters in shaping current knowledge and practice in fields like accounting, management, marketing and so on, and (2) utilizing new critical resources (from different social sciences and humanities, as well as from a variety of non-Western academic and nonacademic sources) in order to generate novel and nonconventional understandings of work and work-related practices.

Accordingly, possible directions for future research aimed at imaginatively constructing new MOS knowledge might include (1) historical studies that investigate the important role played by colonial and/or neocolonial dynamics in the emergence of different aspects of management knowledge and practice and, in so doing, provide new and revised understanding of those phenomena; (2) theoretical and/or empirical studies of non-Western philosophies and cultures which seek to identify local categories of knowledge with a view to producing non-Eurocentric understanding of non-Western practices of work and organizing; (3) non-Eurocentric comparative studies of organizational practices and structures (between organizations situated in the global 'North' and those in the global 'South') which firmly reject the West/non-West hierarchy and do not view 'difference' as 'deficiency'; (4) non-Eurocentric comparative studies of organizations (between organizations situated in different countries/ regions within the global 'South') which offer new insights into the extraordinary diversity and sophistication of work-related practices, arrangements and structures across various parts of the non-Western world; (5) empirical studies of cross-cultural 'translation' which provide in-depth understanding of inventive transformations of managerial and organizational practices in a global context; and (6) studies of creative resistance (in non-Western settings) directed against Western MOS discourse.

The fifth dimension of the proposed agenda – namely, creatively imagining new modes of organizing and work (Cell-V) – would seem to have especially close links with the fourth dimension just discussed, as well as with the second dimension of the agenda which focuses upon critiquing current management and organizational practices/structures. Accordingly, some suggestions for research along this dimension include (1) creatively drawing upon non-Western categories and practices of work for purposes of reimagining/redesigning Western approaches to management and organizing; (2) imaginative reconstructions of non-Western subaltern ways of relating to work and labor which might be helpful in giving a nonmodern and more responsible direction to modern Western organizational practices; and (3) carefully employing the insights provided by postcolonial critiques of Western management and organizations with a view to imagining new modes of organizing that might increasingly diverge from colonial and/or neo-colonial discourses.

Finally, as regards the sixth dimension – i.e., imagining new ways of doing MOS research (Cell-VI) – some future research possibilities include (1) developing new practices of non-Eurocentric inquiry that inventively combine different postpositivist and/or indigenous methodologies; (2) epistemological/methodological studies that draw upon non-Western philosophies and practices of knowledge creation with a view to reframing MOS research practices; (3) demonstrating the intellectual value of nonconventional conceptions of 'data'; (4) highlighting the irrelevance of traditional disciplinary boundaries for MOS research in a rapidly transforming world; and (5) developing creative ways of identifying non-Western categories of knowledge and thought.

Concluding thoughts: Toward a pluralistic world of multiple knowledges

The postcolonial theoretic emphasis on the necessity of embedding the production of management knowledge in local categories, histories, cultures and modes of organizing implies also that researchers need to seriously begin the process of reimagining MOS as a pluralistic world of *multiple varieties* of MOS spread across different areas of the globe. The reader may recall that this chapter's overview of postcolonial theory had drawn attention to postcolonialism's commitment to the project of plural knowledges. The project of plural knowledges, which has now gained considerable currency in different scholarly circles (Alatas, 2001; Behera, 2007; Ribeiro & Escobar, 2006; Visvanathan, 1997; Mignolo, 2011a, 2011b), is linked to the idea of cultures as knowledge systems and to the awareness that, throughout history, *all cultures have always produced knowledge*. As regards social science, the project of plural knowledges seeks to reinvent that approach to knowledge by means of imaginatively constructing a number of locally situated and non-Eurocentric social sciences in different parts of the world.

This chapter is not the place for a detailed discussion of the currently ongoing search for multiple social sciences. In brief, however, the project for multiple social sciences is neither anti–social science, nor nativist, nor relativist. Rather, that project seeks to create a variety of locally embedded social sciences in different regions of the world, all of which would (1) abandon goals of certainty and systematized knowledge aimed at totalized understanding and (2) produce instead open-ended knowledges informed by an awareness of their own limits. According to Mignolo (2002), the project for multiple social sciences represents a quest for the "decolonization of the social sciences" (p. 62), aimed at achieving what he calls "diversality," i.e., "diversity [of knowledge] as a universal project," committed to neither relativism, nor universal truth, but to "justice, equity, [and] human rights" (p. 90). A postcolonial theoretic reorientation of MOS may be seen as involving a somewhat similar decolonization of the MOS discipline as well.

It is important to emphasize here that the project of plural knowledges, multiple social sciences and different varieties of MOS holds great value not only for the 'non-West' but for the 'West' as well. During the last several decades, critics have drawn urgent attention to a range of crisis conditions confronting the world (see, e.g., Hopkins & Wallerstein, 1996; Sachs, 1992; Wallerstein, 2004a). Along with this, critics have also come to the realization that those crisis conditions – involving, for instance, the natural environment, growing polarization of income and wealth, the disappearing welfare state, increasing militarization, the decline of community and so on – seem to be linked to a much deeper crisis, namely, the crisis of modern/colonial Western knowledge, or what Harding (2009) has called "the epistemological crisis of the West" (p. 411).

Postcolonial scholars like Nandy (1983) maintain that the epistemological crisis may be seen as rooted in the "cultural and psychological pathologies produced by [colonialism and neo-colonialism]" *within the West itself* (p. 30), which caused considerable "long-term cultural damage" (p. 32) and set in place specific ways of seeing, thinking and acting that came to be regarded as 'normal' within Western modernity and Euro-American capitalism. Hence, the project for a plurality of knowledges and social sciences also represents a search for 'other' epistemologies and ethical systems that radically diverge from 'the normal' of modern Western knowledge and have a disruptive effect on the same. Or, to put it in other words, the said project represents a quest for different "mindsets that are *defective* for [Euro-American] capitalism" and Western modernity (Spivak, 2003: 33; italics added) – in the hope of "constructing new ways of seeing and acting" (Escobar, 1995: 16) that might provide a way out of the overwhelming situation of crisis in which all of humanity finds itself trapped today.

In that task of creatively constructing new ways of seeing, thinking, and acting, the cultures and epistemologies of Africa, Asia and Latin America – representing, in mutual solidarity, a "subversive 'non-aligned' force" (Escobar, 1995: 215), animated by "the spirit of Bandung" (Spivak, 2008: 237; see also Mignolo, 2011a, 2011b) – have a special role to play. By reimagining itself along the lines suggested by postcolonial theory, MOS/CMS has an opportunity to become an integral part of that radically transformative, intellectually exciting and ethically important project.

Notes

1 The wars being waged by the U.S.-led Western military alliance in places like Afghanistan, Iraq, Libya, Syria, etc. may be regarded as merely a few of the examples of such efforts.

2 For instance, for its 2011 annual meeting, the U.S. Academy of Management adopted the conference theme of "West Meets East: Enlightening, Balancing, Transcending".

3 For an excellent survey of the current terrain of postcolonial theoretic management research, see Jack, Westwood, Srinivas & Sardar (2011b).

4 Although the scholarly interests of postcolonial theory go considerably beyond issues of knowledge and epistemology, this overview – because of the specific focus of the present chapter – mainly highlights postcolonialism's engagement with matters related to knowledge/epistemology. Hence, the overview will offer merely a brief glimpse into those areas of postcolonial scholarship that might not be directly related to issues of knowledge/epistemology.

5 From this perspective, modernity and colonialism are seen as two faces of the same coin (Mignolo, 2000).

6 Basically, state building involved consolidating the control of various governmental bureaucracies over populations and territories.

7 See also Bilgin & Morton (2002) and Parmar (2012), among others, for discussions of the close links between Area Studies programs and the U.S. national security agencies.

8 To be precise, some of these research fundings came from the Laura Spelman Rockefeller Memorial (LSRM), a body that was eventually consolidated with the Rockefeller Foundation in 1929. For a brief history of LSRM, see, e.g., Rockefeller Archive Center (2011).

9 It needs to be noted that, notwithstanding its support for the idea of free-trade liberalism, the Postwar International Economic Order (PIEO) established under U.S. auspices also tended to diverge, in important ways, from the model of 'pure' economic liberalism. For one, even while promoting multilateral free trade, the PIEO also permitted intervention by governments to protect "a domestic producer . . . threatened with injury from import competition" (Ruggie, 1982: 397) and in pursuit of goals of domestic employment stability and social welfare (Nayar, 2005; Ruggie, 1982; Tang, 2006). These provisions – when coupled with the Cold War–related U.S. decisions to (1) strengthen the economies of Western Europe by opening American markets to Western European exports *without* insisting on a reciprocal opening of European markets and (2) to provide Western Europe with massive financial assistance by way of outright grants (*not* loans) under the Marshall Plan – allowed *Western European countries* the flexibility of adopting a variety of *Keynesian* social welfare and full employment measures at home (Nayar, 2005). At the same time, however, the PIEO operated quite differently insofar as the '*Third World*' was concerned. During the post–World War II years, for instance, in violation of the provisions relating to multilateral free trade and nondiscrimination – accepted under the General Agreement on Tariffs and Trade (GATT) of 1947 – the U.S. and other Western countries often "imposed quotas and non-tariff barriers" against exports from 'Third World' countries (Nayar, 2005: 69). As a result, the PIEO failed to facilitate large-scale liberalization of trade in those sectors (e.g., textiles and clothing) that were important to the 'Third World,' and the 'Third World' was denied many of the potential economic benefits of free trade. Moreover, the PIEO came to include two additional features: (1) a Western regime of 'foreign aid' for the 'Third World,' with specific policies aimed at "(creating) an open . . . world economy characterized by the dominance of market forces and . . . maximum freedom of private capital" (Wood, 1986: 21; quoted in Kaimowitz, 1992: 204–205) and (2) starting in 1948, a world of conditionalities devised by the International Monetary Fund (IMF), which generally required 'Third World' countries to adopt *anti-Keynesian* policies like "domestic austerity measures . . . [and] reduced public spending" (Ruggie, 1982: 407, n. 90). The fact that the IMF conditionalities – which came to be applied against the Third World with devastating effect during the 1980s and the 1990s – were written up as early as 1948, says volumes about the Western agenda motivating the PIEO. Along with this, Western pronouncements (on 'Third World' development) regularly promoted the ideology of orthodox liberalism and unfettered free trade.

10 Arrighi (1994: 293), for instance, has pointed out that, starting in 1883 and up to the interwar years, the United States alone adopted at least six rounds of major protectionist measures, the latest rounds coming during the 1920s and in 1930.

11 A somewhat similar report was brought out by the Carnegie Corporation as well (see Pierson, 1959).

12 Thomas H. Carroll, Ford Foundation's vice president, wrote a piece also in the second volume of the newly launched *Academy of Management Journal* (then called *Journal of the Academy of Management*) explaining the proposed reforms (see Carroll, 1959a). In general, the Ford Foundation (and many others who wrote on these issues at the time) tended to prefer the term 'behavioral sciences' over 'social sciences,' largely because

many members of the United States Congress seem to have interpreted the latter term as indicating an approach for introducing 'socialism' in the United States (Tadajewski, 2009).

13 The mid-20th-century social scientific transformation of business schools involved all fields of business management, including, e.g., accounting, finance, marketing, etc. However, our discussion in the next section unfolds within a context largely framed by the field of management and organization studies.

14 The concept of cultural racism is further elaborated on later in the chapter.

15 George Homans was a member, alongside Talcott Parsons and others, of the so-called Pareto Circle at Harvard University in the United States.

16 During the Cold War, such tendency toward marginalization of critique received further reinforcement from the prevailing ideological climate as well (Cooke, Mills & Kelley, 2005; Kelley, Mills & Cooke, 2006; Runté & Mills, 2006).

17 For a discussion of the contestation involving the CMS label, see Prasad, Prasad, Mills & Helms Mills (Chapter 1 in this volume). The following discussion mainly focuses upon the limitations of CMS as a critical perspective. However, much of this chapter's critique of CMS is generally applicable to MOS research that styles itself as 'interpretive' as well.

18 Marx's writings on colonialism first appeared in 1853. On the close links between Marx and Hegelian philosophy, see, e.g., Fetscher (1971).

19 For instance, a recent edited collection brought out by this CMS stream declares that two specific researchers, one each from Sweden and the U.K., "are two of the *founding fathers* of modern critical management studies" (see Alvesson & Willmott, 2011; italics added).

20 As Ashcraft (2011) notes, it is mostly the "white, Western, male, hetero, comparatively privileged knowledge workers who appear as the lead characters" in this stream of CMS. See also Ashcraft (Chapter 6 in this volume).

21 Mudimbe (1988) primarily focuses upon anthropology as a social scientific discipline. However, his insights, *mutatis mutandis*, appear relevant for all Western social sciences, including management studies.

22 We need to note that the notion of deconstruction evoked here (based on Escobar, 1995) is somewhat different from Derridean deconstruction.

References

Ackroyd, S. (2004). Less bourgeois than thou? *Ephemera, 4* (2): 165–170.
Adams, I., & Tiffin, H. (Eds.). (1990). *Past the last post: Theorizing postcolonialism and postmodernism.* Calgary: University of Calgary Press.
Ailon, G. (2008). Mirror, mirror on the wall. *Academy of Management Review, 33*: 885–904.
Alatas, S. F. (Ed.). (2001). *Reflections on alternative discourses from Southeast Asia.* Singapore: Pagesetters.
Alexander, M. J., & Mohanty, C. T. (Eds.). (1997). *Feminist genealogies, colonial legacies, democratic futures.* New York: Routledge.
Alvesson, M., Bridgman, T., & Willmott, H. (Eds.). (2009). *Oxford handbook of critical management studies.* Oxford: Oxford University Press.
Alvesson, M., & Deetz, S. (2006). Critical theory and postmodernism approaches to organizational studies. In S. Clegg, C. Hardy, T. Lawrence & W. Nord (Eds.), *The Sage handbook of organization studies* (2nd Ed.): 255–283. Thousand Oaks, CA: Sage.
Alvesson, M., & Willmott, H. (Eds.). (1992). *Critical management studies.* Newbury Park, CA: Sage.
Alvesson, M., & Willmott, H. (Eds.). (2003). *Studying management critically.* Thousand Oaks, CA: Sage.
Alvesson, M., & Willmott, H. (Eds.). (2011). *Critical management studies* (4 vols.). Los Angeles, CA: Sage.
Amin, S. (1989). *Eurocentrism.* New York: Monthly Review Press.
Apffel-Marglin, F. (1996). Rationality, the body, and the world. In F. Apffel-Marglin & S. Marglin (Eds.), *Decolonizing knowledge*: 142–181. Oxford: Oxford University Press.
Appadurai, A. (1996). *Modernity at large: Cultural dimensions of globalization.* Minneapolis: University of Minnesota Press.
Arias, A. (2008). The Maya movement. In M. Moranña, E. Dussel & C. Jáuregui (Eds.), *Coloniality at large: Latin America and the postcolonial debate*: 519–538. Durham, NC: Duke University Press.
Arrighi, G. 1994. *The long twentieth century.* London: Verso.
Ashcraft, K. L. (2011). Fringe benefits? Revising the fate of feminisms in CMS. Paper presented at the Academy of Management Annual Meeting, San Antonio, Texas, August.
Balibar, E. (1999). Is there a "neo-racism"? In E. Balibar & I. Wallerstein (Eds.), *Race, nation, class*: 17–28. London: Verso.

Banerjee, S., & Linstead, S. (2001). Globalization, multiculturalism and other fictions: Colonialism for the new millennium? *Organization, 8*: 683–722.

Banerjee, S., & Prasad, A. (Eds.). (2008). Special issue: Critical reflections on management and organizations: A postcolonial perspective. *Critical Perspectives on International Business, 4*(2/3).

Behdad, A. (2005). On globalization, again! In A. Loomba, S. Kaul, M. Bunzl, A. Burton & J. Esty (Eds.), *Postcolonial studies and beyond*: 62–79. Durham, NC: Duke University Press.

Behera, N. C. (2007). Re-imagining IR in India. *International Relations of the Asia-Pacific, 7*: 341–368.

Bhabha, H. K. (Ed.). (1990). *Nation and narration*. London: Routledge.

Bhabha, H. K. (1994). *The location of culture*. London: Routledge.

Bhambra, G. (2007). Sociology and postcolonialism. *Sociology, 41*: 871–884.

Bilgin, P., & Morton, A. D. (2002). Historicising representations of 'failed states': Beyond the cold-war annexation of the social sciences? *Third World Quarterly, 23*: 55–80.

Blaut, J. M. (1993). *The colonizer's model of the world*. New York: Guilford Press.

Blaut, J. M. (2000). *Eight Eurocentric historians*. New York: Guilford Press.

Bottom, W. P. (2009). Organizing intelligence: Development of behavioral science and the research based model of business education. *Journal of the History of the Behavioral Sciences, 45*, 253–283.

Boyacigiller, N., & Adler, N. (1991). The parochial dinosaur. *Academy of Management Review, 16*: 262–290.

Bradfoot, K., & Munshi, D. (2007). Diverse voices and alternative rationalities: Imagining forms of postcolonial organizational communication. *Management Communication Quarterly, 21*: 249–267.

Brantlinger, P. (1988). *Rule of darkness: British literature and imperialism, 1830–1914*. Ithaca, NY: Cornell University Press.

Brennan, T. (2003). From development to globalization. In N. Lazarus (Ed.), *The Cambridge companion to postcolonial studies*: 120–138. Cambridge: Cambridge University Press.

Brennan, T. (2005). The economic image function of the periphery. In A. Loomba, S. Kaul, M. Bunzl, A. Burton & J. Esty (Eds.), *Postcolonial studies and beyond*: 101–122. Durham, NC: Duke University Press.

Buell, F. (1994). *National culture and the new global system*. Baltimore, MD: Johns Hopkins University Press.

Burrell, G., & Morgan, G. (1979). *Sociological paradigms and organisational analysis*. Portsmouth, NH: Heinemann.

Butler, J., & Spivak, G. C. (2007). *Who sings the nation-state?* Kolkata (Calcutta), New York & Oxford: Seagull Press.

Carroll, T. H. (1959a). A foundation expresses its interest in higher education for business management. *Academy of Management Journal, 2*(3): 155–165.

Carroll, T. H. (1959b). Foreword. In R. A. Gordon & J. E. Howell, *Higher education for business*: v-vi. New York: Columbia University Press.

Carroll, T. H. (1961). Management education. *Academy of Management Proceedings*, 6–13.

Casey, C. (2002). *Critical analysis of organizations*. London: Sage.

Chakrabarty, D. (1992). Postcoloniality and the artifice of history. *Representations, 37*: 1–26.

Chakrabarty, D. (2000). *Provincializing Europe*. Princeton, NJ: Princeton University Press.

Chatterjee, P. (1986). *Nationalist thought and the colonial world*. London: Zed Books.

Chatterjee, P. (1993). *The nation and its fragments: Colonial and postcolonial histories*. Princeton, NJ: Princeton University Press.

Chaturvedi, V. (Ed.). (2000). *Mapping subaltern studies and the postcolonial*. London: Verso.

Chaudhuri, N., & Strobel, M. (Eds.). (1992). *Western women and imperialism*. Bloomington: Indiana University Press.

Chio, V. (2008). Transfers, training and inscriptions. *Critical Perspectives on International Business, 4*: 166–183.

Chrisman, L. (2005). Beyond black Atlantic and postcolonial studies. In A. Loomba, S. Kaul, M. Bunzl, A. Burton & J. Esty (Eds.), *Postcolonial studies and beyond*: 252–271. Durham, NC: Duke University Press.

Clinebell, S., & Clinebell, J. (2008). The tension in business education between academic rigor and real-world relevance. *Academy of Management Learning & Education, 7*: 99–107.

Cohn, B. (1996). *Colonialism and its forms of knowledge*. Princeton, NJ: Princeton University Press.

Cooke, B., Mills, A., & Kelley, E. (2005). Situating Maslow in Cold War America. *Group & Organization Management, 30*: 129–152.

Cooppan, V. (2005). The ruins of empire. In A. Loomba, S. Kaul, M. Bunzl, A. Burton & J. Esty (Eds.), *Postcolonial studies and beyond*: 80–100. Durham, NC: Duke University Press.

Cumings, B. (1997). Boundary displacement. *Bulletin of Concerned Asian Scholars, 29*(1). Retrieved on September 14, 2010 from http://www.mtholyoke.edu/acad/intrel/cumings2.htm.

Darwin, J. (2008). *After Tamerlane: The rise and fall of global empires, 1400–2000.* New York: Bloomsbury Press.

Daunton, M., & Halpern, R. (Eds.). (1999). *Empire and others.* Philadelphia: University of Pennsylvania Press.

Denzin, N., Lincoln, Y., & Smith, L. T. (Eds.). (2008). *Critical and indigenous methodologies.* Los Angeles: Sage.

Dirks, N. (Ed.). (1992). *Colonialism and culture.* Ann Arbor: University of Michigan Press.

Dirks, N. (Ed.). (1998). *In near ruins: Cultural theory at the end of the century.* Minneapolis: University of Minnesota Press.

Dirks, N. (2006). *The scandal of empire: India and the creation of imperial Britain.* Cambridge, MA: Harvard University Press.

Economist. (2010). Thinking the UNthinkable. November 13–19: 15–16.

Escobar, A. (1995). *Encountering development.* Princeton, NJ: Princeton University Press.

Fabian, J. (1983). *Time and the other.* New York: Columbia University Press.

Ferdinand, J., Muzio, D., & O'Mahoney J. (2004). Studying management critically (extended book review). *Organization Studies,* 25(8): 1455–1465.

Ferdinand, J., Muzio, D., & O'Mahoney J. (2005). Muddling with CMS: A reply. *Organization Studies,* 26(11): 1714–1716.

Fetscher, I. (1971). *Marx and Marxism.* New York: Herder & Herder.

Foreign Affairs. (2010). Special Issue: The world ahead. November–December, 89(6).

Fougère, M., and Moulettes, A. (2007). The construction of the modern West and the backward rest. *Journal of Multicultural Discourses,* 2: 1–19.

Frank, A. G. (1998). *Re-Orient: Global economy in the Asian age.* Berkeley: University of California Press.

Frenkel, M. (2008). The multinational corporation as a third space: Rethinking international management discourse on knowledge transfer through Homi Bhabha. *Academy of Management Review, 33*: 924–942.

Frenkel, M., & Shenhav, Y. (2006). From binarism back to hybridity: A postcolonial reading of management and organization studies. *Organization Studies, 27*: 855–876.

Gandhi, L. (1998). *Postcolonial theory.* New York: Columbia University Press.

Gidley, M. (Ed.). (1992). *Representing others.* Exeter, UK: University of Exeter Press.

Gilroy, P. (2000). *Against race.* Cambridge, MA: Harvard University Press.

Godelier, M. (1986). *The mental and the material.* London: Verso.

Goldberg, D. T. (2002). Racial rule. In D. T. Goldberg & A. Quayson (Eds.), *Relocating postcolonialism*: 82–102. Malden, MA: Blackwell.

Goldman Sachs. (2003). *Dreaming with BRICs.* New York: Goldman Sachs Group.

Gopal, A., Willis, R., & Gopal, Y. (2003). From the colonial enterprise to enterprise systems: Parallels between colonization and globalization. In A. Prasad (Ed.), *Postcolonial theory and organizational analysis:* 233–254. New York: Palgrave.

Gordon, R. A., & Howell, J. E. 1959. *Higher education for business.* New York: Columbia University Press.

Govindarajan, V., & A. Gupta. (2000). Analysis of the emerging global arena. *European Management Journal, 18*(3): 274–284.

Grey, C., & Willmott, H. (Eds.). (2005a). *Critical management studies: A reader.* Oxford: Oxford University Press.

Grey, C., & Willmott, H. (2005b). Introduction. In C. Grey & H. Willmott (Eds.), *Critical management studies: A reader* (1–15). Oxford: Oxford University Press.

Grimes, D., & Parker, P. (2009). Imagining organizational communication as a decolonizing project. *Management Communication Quarterly, 22*: 502–511.

Grosfoguel, R. (2008). Developmentalism, modernity, and dependency theory. In M. Moranña, E. Dussel & C. Jáuregui (Eds.), *Coloniality at large*: 307–331. Durham, NC: Duke University Press.

Guha, R. (Ramachandra). (2007). *India after Gandhi: The history of the world's largest democracy.* New York: HarperCollins.

Guha, R. (Ranajit). (1963). *A rule of property for Bengal.* Paris: Mouton.

Guha, R. (Ranajit, Ed.). (1997). *A subaltern studies reader.* Minneapolis: University of Minnesota Press.

Halbfass, W. (1988). *India and Europe.* Albany, NY: SUNY Press.

Hall, S. (1996). When was the 'post-colonial'? In I. Chambers & L. Curti (Eds.), *The post-colonial question*: 242–260. London: Routledge.

Harding, S. (1998). *Is science multicultural? Postcolonialisms, feminisms, and epistemologies.* Bloomington: Indiana University Press.

Harding, S. (2008). *Sciences from below: Feminisms, postcolonialities, and modernities.* Durham, NC: Duke University Press.

Harding, S. (2009). Postcolonial and feminist philosophies of science and technology. *Postcolonial Studies*, *12*(4), 401–421.

Harrison, J. (1997). Museums as agencies of neocolonialism in a postmodern world. *Culture and Organization*, *3*: 41–65.

Headrick, D. (1981). *The tools of empire*. New York: Oxford University Press.

Hegel, G. W. F. (1955). *Lectures on the history of philosophy* (3 vols.). London: Routledge.

Hellyet, M. (Ed.). (2003). *The scientific revolution*. Oxford: Blackwell.

Homans, G. (1950). *The human group*. New York: Harcourt.

Hopkins, T., & Wallerstein, I. (1996). The world-system: Is there a crisis? In T. Hopkins & I. Wallerstein (Eds.), *The age of transition*: 1–10. London: Zed.

Hulme, P. (2005). Beyond the straits. In A. Loomba, S. Kaul, M. Bunzl, A. Burton & J. Esty (Eds.), *Postcolonial studies and beyond*: 41–61. Durham, NC: Duke University Press.

Ibarra-Colado, E. (2006). Organization studies and epistemic coloniality in Latin America. *Organization*, *13*: 463–488.

Ikenberry, G. J. (2011). The future of the liberal world order: Internationalism after America. *Foreign Affairs*, *90*(3): 56–68.

Inayatullah, N., & Blaney, D. (2004). *International relations and the problem of difference*. New York: Routledge.

Jack, G., & Lorbiecki, A. (2003). Asserting possibilities of resistance in the cross-cultural teaching machine. In A. Prasad (Ed.), *Postcolonial theory and organizational analysis*: 213–231. New York: Palgrave Macmillan.

Jack, G., & Westwood, R. (2006). Postcolonialism and the politics of qualitative research in international business. *Management International Review, 46*: 481–501.

Jack, G., & Westwood, R. (2009). *International and cross-cultural management studies: A postcolonial reading*. New York: Palgrave Macmillan.

Jack, G., Westwood, R., Srinivas, N., & Sardar, Z. (Eds.). (2011a). Special Issue – Postcolonialism. *Organization*, *18*(3).

Jack, G., Westwood, R., Srinivas, N., & Sardar, Z. (2011b). Deepening, broadening and re-asserting a postcolonial interrogative space in organization studies. *Organization*, *18*(3): 275–302.

Jaya, P. S. (2001). Do we really "know" and "profess"? Decolonizing management knowledge. *Organization*, *8*: 227–233.

Jayawardena, K. (1995). *The white woman's other burden*. New York: Routledge.

Joshi, P. C. (1986). Founders of the Lucknow School and their legacy. *Economic and Political Weekly*, *XXI* (33), 1455–1469.

Kaimowitz, D. (1992). Aid and development in Latin America. *Latin American Research Review, 27*: 202–211.

Kalonaityte, V. (2010). The case of vanishing borders: Theorizing diversity management as internal border control. *Organization*, *17*: 31–52.

Kelley, E., Mills, A., & Cooke, B. (2006). Management as a Cold War phenomenon? *Human Relations, 59*: 603–610.

Khurana, R. (2007). *From higher aims to hired hands*. Princeton, NJ: Princeton University Press.

Klare, M. T. 1974. Indian Ocean and Japan in US grand strategy. *Social Scientist, 3*: 3–16.

Kupchan, C. 2012. *No one's world: The West, the rising rest, and the coming global turn*. New York: Oxford University Press.

Kwek, D. (2003). Decolonizing and re-presenting culture's consequences: A postcolonial critique of cross-cultural studies in management. In A. Prasad (Ed.), *Postcolonial theory and organizational analysis*: 121–146. New York: Palgrave Macmillan.

Layne, C. (2006). The unipolar illusion revisited. *International Security, 31*(2): 7–41.

Lazarus, N. (Ed.). (2004). *The Cambridge companion to postcolonial studies*. Cambridge: Cambridge University Press.

Lee, R. (1996). Structures of knowledge. In T. Hopkins & I. Wallerstein (Eds.), *The age of transition*: 178–206. London: Zed.

Lewis, R., & Mills, S. (Eds.). (2003). *Feminist postcolonial theory*. New York: Routledge.

Loomba, A. (1998). *Colonialism/postcolonialism*. London: Routledge.

Loomba, A., Kaul, S., Bunzl, M., Burton, A., & Esty, J. (Eds.), (2005a). *Postcolonial studies and beyond*. Durham, NC: Duke University Press.

Loomba, A., Kaul, S., Bunzl, M., Burton, A., & Esty, J. (2005b). Beyond what? In A. Loomba, S. Kaul, M. Bunzl, A. Burton & J. Esty (Eds.), *Postcolonial studies and beyond*: 1–38. Durham, NC: Duke University Press.

Lucas, C. J. (1994). *American higher education: A history*. New York: St. Martin's Press.

Maldonado-Torres, N. (2008). Secularism and religion in the modern/colonial world-system. In M. Moranña, E. Dussel & C. Jáuregui (Eds.), *Coloniality at large*: 360–384. Durham, NC: Duke University Press.

Mallon, F. (2005). Pathways to postcolonial nationhood. In A. Loomba, S. Kaul, M. Bunzl, A. Burton & J. Esty (Eds.), *Postcolonial studies and beyond*: 272–292. Durham, NC: Duke University Press.

Marglin, S. (1990). Towards the decolonization of the mind. In F. Apffel-Marglin & S. Marglin (Eds.), *Dominating knowledge*: 1–28. Oxford: Oxford University Press.

Marx, K. (1972). On imperialism in India. In R. C. Tucker (Ed.), *The Marx-Engels reader*: 577–588. New York: W. W. Norton.

Masuzawa, T. (2005). *The invention of world religions*. Chicago: University of Chicago Press.

McCormick, T. J. (1989). *America's half century*. Baltimore, MD: Johns Hopkins University Press.

Mignolo, W. (2000). *Local histories/global designs*. Princeton, NJ: Princeton University Press.

Mignolo, W. (2002). The geopolitics of knowledge and the colonial difference. *South Atlantic Quarterly*, *101*: 57–96.

Mignolo, W. (2011a). Geopolitics of sensing and knowing: On (de)coloniality, border thinking and epistemic disobedience. *Postcolonial Studies*, *14*: 273–283.

Mignolo, W. (2011b). *The darker side of western modernity*. Durham, NC: Duke University Press.

Mir, R., Banerjee, S., & Mir, A. (2008). Hegemony and its discontents: A critical analysis of organizational knowledge transfer. *Critical Perspectives on International Business*, *4*: 203–227.

Mir, R., & Mir, A. (2009). From the colony to the corporation: Studying knowledge transfer across international boundaries. *Group & Organization Management*, *34*: 90–113.

Mir, R., Mir, A., & Upadhyaya, P. (2003). Toward a postcolonial reading of organizational control. In A. Prasad (Ed.), *Postcolonial theory and organizational analysis*: 47–73. New York: Palgrave Macmillan.

Mirchandani, K. (2004). Practices of global capital: Gaps, cracks and ironies in transnational call centers in India. *Global Networks*, *4*: 355–374.

Mirchandani, K. (2005). Gender eclipsed? Racial hierarchies in transnational call center work. *Social Justice*, *32*: 105–119.

Mishra, V., & Hodge, B. (1991). What is post(-)colonialism? *Textual Practice*, *5*: 399–414.

Mohanty, C. T. (2003). *Feminism without borders: Decolonizing theory, practicing solidarity*. Durham, NC: Duke University Press.

Mohanty, C. T., Russo, A., & Torres, L. (Eds.). (1991). *Third World women and the politics of feminism*. Bloomington: Indiana University Press.

Morales, M. R. (2008). Peripheral modernity and differential *Mestizaje* in Latin America. In M. Moranña, E. Dussel & C. Jáuregui (Eds.), *Coloniality at large*: 479–505. Durham, NC: Duke University Press.

Moranña, M., Dussel, E., & Jáuregui, C. (Eds.). (2008). *Coloniality at large: Latin America and the postcolonial debate*. Durham, NC: Duke University Press.

Morgan, G. (Ed.). (1983). *Beyond method*. Beverly Hills, CA: Sage.

Mudimbe, V. Y. (1988). *The invention of Africa: Gnosis, philosophy, and the order of knowledge*. Bloomington: Indiana University Press.

Nandy, A. (1983). *The intimate enemy*. Delhi: Oxford University Press.

Nandy, A. (1987). *Traditions, tyranny and utopias*. Delhi: Oxford University Press.

Nandy, A. (Ed.). (1988). *Science, hegemony and violence*. Delhi: Oxford University Press.

Nandy, A. (1994). *The illegitimacy of nationalism*. Delhi: Oxford University Press.

Nandy, A. (1998). The twilight of certitude: Secularism, Hindu nationalism and other masks of deculturation. *Postcolonial Studies*, *1*(3), 283–298.

Nandy, A. (2000). The defiance of defiance and liberation for the victims of history. In V. Lal (Ed.), *Dissenting knowledges, open futures*: 3–93. Delhi: Oxford University Press.

Nandy, A. (2001). A report on the present state of health of the gods and goddesses in South Asia. *Postcolonial Studies*, *4*(2), 125–141.

National Intelligence Council. (2008). *Global trends 2025: A transformed world*. Washington, DC: National Intelligence Council.

National Intelligence Council. (2012). *Global trends 2030: Alternative worlds*. Washington, DC: National Intelligence Council.

Nayar, B. R. (2005). *The geopolitics of globalization*. Delhi: Oxford University Press.

Nederveen Pieterse, J. (2010). *Development theory* (2nd Ed.). Los Angeles, CA: Sage.

Nichols, R. (2010). Postcolonial studies and the discourse of Foucault. *Foucault Studies*, *9*: 111–144.

Niranjana, T. (1992). *Siting translation*. Berkeley: University of California Press.

O'Connor, E. (1999a). The politics of management thought: A case study of the Harvard Business School and the Human Relations School. *Academy of Management Review*, *24*: 117–131.

O'Connor, E. (1999b). Minding the workers: The meaning of 'human' and 'human relations' in Elton Mayo. *Organization, 6*: 223–246.

Oleson, A., & Voss, J. (1979). The organization of knowledge in modern America, 1860–1920. *Bulletin of the American Academy of Arts and Sciences, 32*: 10–31.

Özkazanç-Pan, B. (2008). International management research meets "the rest of the world." *Academy of Management Review, 33*: 964–974.

Pal, M., & Dutta, M. (2008). Theorizing resistance in a global context. In C. Beck (Ed.), *Communication Yearbook*: 41–87. New York: Routledge.

Panikkar, K. M. 1959. *Asia and Western dominance* (New Ed.). London: Allen & Unwin.

Parmar, I. (2012). *Foundations of the American century*. New York: Columbia University Press.

Parsons, T. (1937). *The structure of social action*. Glencoe, IL: Free Press.

Parsons, T. (1951). *The social system*. Glencoe, IL: Free Press.

Parsons, T. (1956a). Suggestions for a sociological approach to the theory of organizations—I. *Administrative Science Quarterly, 1*(1): 63–85.

Parsons, T. (1956b). Suggestions for a sociological approach to the theory of organizations—II. *Administrative Science Quarterly, 1*(2): 225–239.

Pierson, F. C. (1959). *The education of American businessmen*. New York: McGraw-Hill.

Pletsch, C. E. (1981). The three worlds, or the division of social scientific labor, circa 1950–1975. *Comparative Studies in Society and History, 23*: 565–590.

Prakash, G. (1994). Subaltern studies as postcolonial criticism. *American Historical Review, 99*: 1475–1490.

Prasad, Anshuman. (1997a). Provincializing Europe. *Culture and Organization, 3*: 91–117.

Prasad, Anshuman. (1997b). The colonizing consciousness and representations of the other. In P. Prasad, A. Mills, M. Elmes & Anshuman Prasad (Eds.), *Managing the organizational melting pot*: 285–311. Thousand Oaks, CA: Sage.

Prasad, Anshuman. (2003a). The gaze of the other. In Anshuman Prasad (Ed.), *Postcolonial theory and organizational analysis*: 3–43. New York: Palgrave Macmillan.

Prasad, Anshuman. (Ed.). (2003b). *Postcolonial theory and organizational analysis*. New York: Palgrave Macmillan.

Prasad, Anshuman. (2006). The jewel in the crown. In A. Konrad, P. Prasad & J. Pringle (Eds.), *Handbook of workplace diversity*: 121–144. Thousand Oaks, CA: Sage.

Prasad, Anshuman. (2008). Review of *Critical Management Studies: A reader*. *Academy of Management Review, 33*: 278–283.

Prasad, Anshuman. (2012a). Working against the grain. In Anshuman Prasad (Ed.), *Against the grain*: 13–31. Copenhagen & Malmo: Copenhagen Business School/Liber.

Prasad, Anshuman. (Ed.). (2012b). *Against the grain: Advances in postcolonial organization studies*. Copenhagen & Malmo: Copenhagen Business School/Liber.

Prasad, Anshuman, & Prasad, P. (2002). Otherness at large: Identity and difference in the new globalized organizational landscape. In I. Aaltio & A. Mills (Eds.), *Gender, identity and the culture of organizations*: 57–71. London: Routledge.

Prasad, Anshuman, & Prasad, P. (2003). The empire of organizations and the organization of empires: Postcolonial considerations on theorizing workplace resistance. In Anshuman Prasad (Ed.), *Postcolonial theory and organizational analysis*: 95–119. New York: Palgrave Macmillan.

Prasad, P. (2003). The return of the native: Organizational discourses and the legacy of the ethnographic imagination. In Anshuman Prasad (Ed.), *Postcolonial theory and organizational analysis*: 95–119. New York: Palgrave Macmillan.

Prasad, P. (2005). *Crafting qualitative research*. Armonk, NY: M. E. Sharpe.

Prestowitz, C. (2005). *Three billion new capitalists: The great shift of wealth and power to the East*. New York: Basic Books.

PricewaterhouseCoopers. (2011). *The world in 2050: The accelerating shift of global economic power: Challenges and opportunities*. London: PricewaterhouseCoopers LLP.

Priyadharshini, E. (2003). Reading the rhetoric of otherness in the discourse of business and economics. In Anshuman Prasad (Ed.), *Postcolonial theory and organizational analysis*: 171–192. New York: Palgrave Macmillan.

Rahnema, M., & Bawtree, V. (Eds.). (1997). *The post-development reader*. London: Zed Books.

Raj, K. (2007). *Relocating modern science*. New York: Palgrave Macmillan.

Reed, M. (2006). Organizational theorizing. In S. Clegg, C. Hardy, T. Lawrence & W. Nord (Eds.), *The Sage handbook of organization studies* (2nd Ed.): 19–54. London: Sage.

Retamar, R. F. (1989). *Caliban and other essays*. Minneapolis: University of Minnesota Press.

Ribeiro, G., & Escobar, A. (Eds.). (2006). *World anthropologies*. New York: Berg.

Rockefeller Archive Center. (2011). Rockefeller related organizations: Laura Spelman Rockefeller Memorial. Retrieved on May 11, 2011 from http://www.rockarch.org/collections/rockorgs/lsrmadd.php.

Ross, D. (1979). The development of the social sciences. In A. Oleson & J. Voss (Eds.), *The organization of knowledge in modern America, 1860–1920*: 107–138. Baltimore, MD: Johns Hopkins University Press.

Ruggie, J. G. 1982. International regimes, transactions, and change. *International Organization, 36*: 379–415.

Runté, M., & Mills, A. (2006). Cold War, chilly climate. *Human Relations, 59*: 695–720.

Sachs, W. (Ed.). (1992). *The development dictionary*. London: Zed.

Said, E. (1978). *Orientalism*. New York: Vintage Books.

Said, E. (1979). *The question of Palestine*. New York: Times Books.

Said, E. (1981). *Covering Islam*. London: Routledge.

Said, E. (1993). *Culture and imperialism*. New York: Alfred A. Knopf.

Sardar, Z. (1998). *Postmodernism and the other*. London: Pluto.

Sardar, Z. (2006). *How do you know?* London: Pluto.

Sardar, Z., Nandy, A., & Davies, M. (1993). *Barbaric others*. London: Pluto Press.

Scott, W. R. (1992). *Organizations* (3rd Ed.). Englewood Cliffs, NJ: Prentice Hall.

Sen, S. (1998). *Empire of free trade*. Philadelphia: University of Pennsylvania Press.

Seth, S. (2009). Putting knowledge in its place. *Postcolonial Studies, 12*(4): 373–388.

Sharpe, J. (1993). *Allegories of empire*. Minneapolis: University of Minnesota Press.

Sheridan, B., & Kushner, A. (2009). B–school backlash. *Newsweek*, August 17. Retrieved on May 20, 2010 from http://www.newsweek.com/id/209960.

Shohat, E. (1992). Notes on the "post-colonial." *Social Text, 31/32*: 99–113.

Shohat, E., & Stam, R. (1994). *Unthinking Eurocentrism*. New York: Routledge.

Spivak, G. C. (1987). *In other worlds*. New York: Methuen.

Spivak, G. C. (1990). *The postcolonial critic*. New York: Routledge.

Spivak, G. C. (1993). *Outside in the teaching machine*. New York: Routledge.

Spivak, G. C. (1999). *A critique of postcolonial reason*. Cambridge, MA: Harvard University Press.

Spivak, G. C. (2003). *Death of a discipline*. New York: Columbia University Press.

Spivak, G. C. (2008). *Other Asias*. Malden, MA: Blackwell.

Spivak, G. C. (2012). *An aesthetic education in the era of globalization*. Cambridge, MA: Harvard University Press.

Spurr, D. (1993). *The rhetoric of empire*. Durham, NC: Duke University Press.

Stam, R., & Shohat, E. (2005). Traveling multiculturalism. In A. Loomba, S. Kaul, M. Bunzl, A. Burton & J. Esty (Eds.), *Postcolonial studies and beyond*: 293–316. Durham, NC: Duke University Press.

Standard Chartered Bank. (2010). *The super-cycle report*. London: Standard Chartered Bank.

Steinmetz, G. (2006). Decolonizing German theory. *Postcolonial Studies, 9*(1), 3–13.

Stoler, A. L. (1995). *Race and the education of desire*. Durham, NC: Duke University Press.

Stoler, A. L. (2002). *Carnal knowledge and imperial power*. Berkeley: University of California Press.

Subrahmanyam, S. (1997). Connected histories: Notes towards a reconfiguration of early modern Eurasia. *Modern Asian Studies, 31*: 735–762.

Subrahmanyam, S. (2005). *Explorations in connected history* (2 vols.). Delhi: Oxford University Press.

Suleri, S. (1992). *The rhetoric of English India*. Chicago: University of Chicago Press.

Sullivan, P. (2008). Bureaucratic process as morris dance: An ethnographic approach to the culture of bureaucracy in Australian aboriginal affairs administration. *Critical Perspectives on International Business, 4*: 127–141.

Tadajewski, M. (2009). The politics of the behavioral revolution in organization studies. *Organization, 16*: 733–754.

Tang, A. T. F. (2006). Reconstructing embedded liberalism. *Journal of International Economic Law, 9*: 81–116.

Tatli, A. (2011). On the power and poverty of critical (self) reflection in Critical Management Studies: A comment on Ford, Harding and Learmonth. *British Journal of Management* [doi: 10.1111/j.1467–8551.2011.00746.x].

Tedmanson, D. (2008). Isle of exception: Sovereign power and Palm Island. *Critical Perspectives on International Business, 4*: 142–165.

Teltscher, K. (1995). *India inscribed: European and British writings on India, 1600–1800*. Delhi: Oxford University Press.

van der Veer, P. (2001). *Imperial encounters: Religion and modernity in India and Britain*. Princeton, NJ: Princeton University Press.

Van Maanen, J. (2011). Ethnography as work. *Journal of Management Studies, 48*: 218–234.

Visvanathan, S. (1997). *A carnival for science.* Delhi: Oxford University Press.

Wallerstein, I. (1996). Open the social sciences. *ITEMS* (Social Science Research Council), *50*: 1–7.

Wallerstein, I. (1997). Eurocentrism and its avatars: The dilemmas of social science. *New Left Review, 226*: 93–108.

Wallerstein, I. (2000). Globalization or the age of transition? *International Sociology, 15*: 251–267.

Wallerstein, I. (2004a). *World-systems analysis.* Durham, NC: Duke University Press.

Wallerstein, I. (2004b). *The uncertainties of knowledge.* Philadelphia: Temple University Press.

Washbrook, D. (1990). South Asia, the world system, and world capitalism. *The Journal of Asian Studies, 49*(3): 479–508.

Westfall, R. S. (1992). *The scientific revolution in the 17th century.* Oxford: Clarendon Press.

Westwood, R. (2004). Towards a postcolonial research paradigm in international business and comparative management. In R. Marschan-Piekkari & C. Welch (Eds.), *Handbook of qualitative research methods for international business*: 56–83. Cheltenham, UK: Edward Elgar.

Westwood, R., & Jack, G. (2007). Manifesto for a postcolonial international business and management studies. *Critical Perspectives on International Business, 3*(3): 246–265.

Williams, P., & Chrisman, L. (Eds.). (1994). *Colonial discourse and postcolonial theory.* New York: Columbia University Press.

Wood, R. E. (1986). *From Marshall Plan to debt crisis.* Berkeley: University of California Press.

Young, R. C. (2001). *Postcolonialism: An historical introduction.* Oxford: Blackwell Publishers.

Young, R. J.C. (1990). *White mythologies.* London: Routledge.

Young, R. J.C. (1995). *Colonial desire.* London: Routledge.

Zimmerman, A. (2006). Decolonizing Weber. *Postcolonial Studies, 9*(1): 53–79.

11

Debating Critical Management Studies and global management knowledge

Gavin Jack

Introduction

This chapter debates Critical Management Studies (CMS) within the context of existing critiques of the characteristics, structures and institutions of social scientific knowledge on a global scale. It engages with CMS as one particular area of so-called global management knowledge (GMK), defined by Tsui (2004) as the totality of scholarship undertaken about management and organizations by researchers across the globe. Tsui's use of the term 'global' spans geographical, demographic and epistemic issues. It questions just how diverse global management knowledge, as well as the academic workforce that creates it, actually is. Just who produces management knowledge and under what conditions? Where are they located, and what kind of knowledge do they produce? Under what conditions are theoretical insights and social experiences from the periphery of GMK and CMS possible?

The chapter pays attention, then, to CMS as one thread in a broader tapestry of academic knowledge, woven together by particular people in particular places using and producing differently valued theoretical and empirical knowledge under different conditions. I conceive of CMS as a sub-field of management studies constituted by a number of scholarly and institutional activities "for the expression of views critical of established management practices and the established social order" (group.aomonline.org/cms). The quotation indicates that this chapter is particularly geared towards discussion of activities and outputs associated with the Academy of Management's (AoM) CMS Division (of which I am co-chair at the time of writing) and the International Critical Management Studies Conferences and networks in the U.K. and Europe (at which I have organized streams and presented work).

As a forum for critical expression, CMS is no monolith and is intended to be diverse in terms of its disciplines, topics, perspectives and methods (Cunliffe, 2008). For me, such openness is best encapsulated in the notion of CMS as a scholarly entity which is in a permanent state of 'becoming' (as suggested by Roy Stager Jacques to students at an AoM doctoral colloquium, Chicago, 2009). As such, CMS scholarship is alive to (self-)critique and the need for (self-)reflexivity and ongoing transformation. For, as with any approach, some CMS voices, perspectives, places and activities seem in certain respects to matter more than others and thus carry the potential to exclude. This is despite the best of intentions and with all the willingness and openness to let it be/become otherwise.

Against this context, the chapter comprises a number of sections organized in accordance with two tasks. The initial three sections address the first task of 'provincializing' global management knowledge (encompassing CMS) and the wider social sciences. Drawing on previous literature, I note the metropole-periphery[1] system (Connell, 2007) in which scholars located in, as well as theories and ideas generated and exported from the Global North elsewhere, dominate the global production of social science knowledge. Presenting some evidence that is suggestive of similar structures of dependency within the institutions of CMS, I point to a certain Eurocentrism at the heart of CMS theory culture.

The next three sections engage with the task of reconstruction. If we accept that CMS can in certain respects be characterized as parochial and dependent upon Eurocentric structures of knowledge, how might interested scholars best respond to these limitations? Existing work by CMS scholars raises the spectre of multiple CMSs, that is, of decentring and decolonizing CMS with respect to peripheral and Indigenous knowledges. I critically discuss a world of many CMSs as a possible response to the epistemic limits of existing institutions. In doing so, I draw on insights from comparative literary theorist Aamir Mufti and sociologist Raewyn Connell to argue for a decentred, relational and mutually engaged multiplicity of CMSs.

The parochialism of GMK

There is no shortage of writing by mainstream and critical scholars alike on the narrow constituency and parochial nature of global management knowledge. These writings consistently identify demographic and epistemic diversity as two issues of concern in the production of knowledge about management and organization.

Beginning with demographic diversity, Boyacigiller and Adler (1991) discuss the quantitative (and qualitative – see below) parochialism of organization science. They note the measurably skewed demographic profile towards scholars institutionally located in the U.S., a finding largely since confirmed by a whole cottage industry of study dedicated to the historical analysis of the provenance of management research. This cottage industry typically proceeds through content analyses of one, or several, core management journals (either general or specialist) and profiles the scholarly output. Amongst other findings, these profiles typically confirm that authors located in a small number of countries situated in the Global North (predominantly countries in North America, Western Europe, and some others – the 'minority world') produce most of work; note that the majority world is significantly under-represented in the pages of our journals, unless as a site for data collection in multi-country studies designed by partners in the Global North; draw attention to English as the dominating language of management research; profile the Global Northern (and typically also white male) dominance of chief editorial roles and editorial board composition of leading journals (Jack & Westwood, 2009). The Academy of Management has sought to address some of these issues within its own sphere of influence, for instance through an explicit internationalization strategy (including the first AoM conference outside North America in 2013 in South Africa [AOM Africa Conference] – an interesting move worthy of debate) and explicit calls in the editorials of its key journals for more submissions by authors outside North America and Europe (see, for instance, Eden & Rynes, 2003).

Recent AoM membership data and its publication profile might show grounds for cautious optimism. Whilst domestic (by which the AoM means located within the U.S.) membership numbers have decreased, international (located outside the U.S.) numbers have increased. At July 1, 2014,[2] the AOM had 19,341 members: 10,196 domestic (U.S.); 9,145 (international). The gap between the numbers of domestic and international has closed since 2010, and indeed over that five-year period, there has been a 7.64% decline in domestic numbers compared to an 8.84%

increase in international numbers. Moving to Academy journals and taking the AMJ (*Academy of Management Journal*) as just one example, Kirkman and Law (2005) conducted an analysis of its scholarly output over the period 1970–2004. They identified an upward trend in the international content and orientation of the journal in the first five years of the 21st century, leading them to describe *AMJ* as a "truly international journal" (p. 383), with "many authors who are international scholars, . . . many samples collected outside North America, and/or . . . many topics related to international or cross-cultural management".

A more insidious problem, however, is that of 'qualitative parochialism' (Boyacigiller & Adler, 1991), since it is connected to the substantive characteristics of the knowledge and knowledge systems of GMK. Even though there might be grounds for (cautious and limited) optimism regarding the demographic diversification of the base of scholars producing management research, the existence of qualitative parochialism seriously undercuts claims to progress. Scholars have identified at least four interconnected features of qualitative parochialism.

First, the values underpinning many dominant theoretical frameworks for management research are U.S.-based (e.g. individualism, free will and low context communication preferences, as noted by Boyacigiller & Adler) and thus culture specific. Reflecting the ascendancy of the U.S. in the post-war social sciences, Boyacigiller and Adler (1991) suggest that an "implicit, and yet inappropriate universalism" (p. 262) accompanied the rise of U.S. management theory. In such an historical context, "it was easy for researchers – including non-U.S. researchers . . . to assume implicitly that American theories also dominated" (Boyacigiller & Adler, 1991: 265). Secondly, then, these parochial and ethnocentric models are often exported unquestioningly outside their cultural boundaries as if they are cross-nationally/cross-culturally valid and meaningful (Westwood, 2014). With regard to management scholarship in Latin America, for example, Ibarra-Colado (2008) describes how:

> [u]ntil now and dominantly, most of the Latin American researchers have been copying and pasting syllabus, theories, methodologies and other management fads and fashions manufactured in the Anglo-Saxon countries, *it doesn't matter if the appropriation is on mainstream theories or in those produced by critters or pomos* [critical management scholars or postmodernists].
>
> . . . [W]e can recognize some mechanisms that stimulate these copy-paste practices. For example, most of the Latin American scholars in the field do not recognize the colonial condition of the region and, consequently, they systematically deny the structural differences and asymmetries with the centre. The problem is seen as one of development and the solution is reduced to the appropriate application of those management and organizational knowledges produced in the most developed countries. This uncritical acceptance of Anglo-Saxon theories conditions the type of explanation of the problems of the region and the type of solutions to confront them, producing in this way a certain kind of *self-imposed coloniality*.
>
> (p. 933; italics added)

The export ("copying and pasting") of knowledge from Anglo-Saxon into Latin American countries fosters a "kind of self-imposed coloniality", according to Ibarra-Colado, where the framing of management problems and solutions of the former location becomes that of the latter. Such a process involves a disavowal of the colonial and neocolonial structures that make it possible in the first place, not to mention a marginalization of Indigenous perspectives on management and organization. Interestingly, Ibarra-Colado brackets both mainstream and critical, or postmodern, management research into this copy-and-paste exercise.

Inequality in the global division of academic labour is a third feature of the qualitative parochialism of GMK. Given the historical dominance of U.S./Global North theory, it is the case that most theoretical intellectual labour occurs in the minority world of GMK and is then exported (as noted) into other locations for testing or modification (typically within the purview of the functionalist paradigm and a hypothetico–deductive approach to knowledge generation), thus rendering scholars in the latter locations 'data collectors' for studies designed and controlled elsewhere. Prichard, Sayers and Bathurst (2007) describe this as the basis for a 'franchise model' that dominates global management research and makes it very difficult to develop distinctive, Indigenous perspectives on management and organization. Recent debates in Asian management research have tackled the issue of theory development in non-metropolitan locations, specifically of indigenous[3] theory development. Whilst offering important exemplars of how Asian management scholars might generate theory (sometimes indigenous to their contexts, sometimes not), the spectre of Global Northern meta-theory (and especially functionalist thinking) is still encoded in these progressive debates (Jack et al., 2013).

Finally, these forms of qualitative parochialism – especially the look to the center – are arguably being reproduced and perhaps intensified, thanks to "new neoliberal techniques of academic governance (league tables of universities, prestige rankings of journals, etc.) [that] tend to reinforce the dominance of the North-Atlantic metropole" (Connell, 2007: 289). Through national government assessments of 'research quality' (e.g. the ERA in Australia or the PBRF initiatives in New Zealand), for instance, researchers in these locations are measured on how much research they produce 'at world standard' (or equivalent terms). Of course, 'world standard' means publishing in journals associated with the centre, predictably the Academy journals and leading European ones. Prichard and colleagues (2007) argue that scholars located "closer to the NATO [North Atlantic Theories of Organization (Clegg, Linstead & Sewell 2000)] nexus" can "largely ignore" the resultant problem confronted by scholars located further away: "how to engage in research whose content, method, and format is at a distance and to varying degrees distinct from that produced by the particular location in which they find themselves" (pp. 27–28).

The parochialism of the global social sciences

This brief characterization of global management knowledge appears reflective of the situation within the social sciences more broadly. According to Connell (2007: vii), "Its [social science's] dominant genres picture the world as it is seen by men, by capitalists, by the educated and affluent. Most important, they picture the world as seen from the rich capital-exporting countries of Europe and North America – the global metropole". According to Connell, this status quo is part of an historical trajectory of the modern social sciences, which emerged at the height of European imperialism in the late 19th century. Her analysis shows how early social scientific interest, gleaned from the colonial encounter, in the knowledge systems of individuals and groups located in the periphery became expunged from emerging sociological knowledge.

As knowledges of 'the Other' were housed in the discipline of anthropology as studies of 'primitive societies', scholars in other social sciences became able to propagate "ethnocentric assumptions that amounted to a gigantic lie – that modernity created itself within the North Atlantic world, independent of the rest of humanity" (Connell, 2007: x). On this basis, Connell argues, key social science models, including functionalist sociology, modernization theory, neo-classical economics, were then exported to the rest of the world with the authority of the metropolitan centre. This export model continues today, part of a Western/Northern intellectual hegemony that mitigates against the successful widespread development of indigenous social scientific alternatives to the white, bourgeois, Eurocentric, androcentric biases of the center (Alatas, 2000; Harding, 1998; Keim, 2011; Loubser, 1988). Of course, alternative knowledge systems exist, especially Indigenous ones, but as in any hegemonic context, these are contained or discredited typically through various means, including, as Connell notes, intellectual discreditation or commercial exploitation by multinationals seeking IP rights.

Alatas (2003) characterizes the social sciences as a system of academic dependency fostered by the interconnected historical and contemporary forces of economic, political and importantly intellectual imperialism (Alatas, 2000). Academic dependency is "the condition in which the social sciences in certain countries are conditioned by the development and growth of the social sciences of other countries to which the former is subjected" (Alatas, 2003: 603). According to Alatas, the dimensions of such dependency relate to the realm of ideas, the media of ideas, the technology of education, aid for research, investment in education and demand in the West for Third World scientists (p. 604). Calls for a reversal of this situation have been thwarted by what Alatas sees as key structural and phenomenological barriers to change. The first is the inequitable global division of social science labour according to which First World scholars conduct both theoretical and empirical work, studies of their own and Third World societies and do more comparative work, whilst Third World scholars are typically confined to empirical work, studies of their own country and single-case studies. As Alatas (2000) incisively notes:

> You do not find Indian and Japanese scholars subcontracting data collection in Europe or in the United States, for research on culture, history, politics and social problems. You do not find Japanese and Indian scholars roaming all over the United States and Europe collecting data, publishing them at home, in their language, and then bombarding Europe and the United States with their published results on Europe and the United States.
>
> *(p. 30)*

The phenomenological barrier that Alatas has famously discussed in relation to the development of the social sciences in Asia (Alatas, 1974) is that of the 'captive mind' and the 'intellectual bondage' (Alatas, 2000) associated with it. The captive mind is "an uncritical and imitative mind dominated by an external source [Western categories and modes of thought], whose thinking is deflected from independent perspective" (Alatas, 1974: 692). It has the effect of deflecting attention from issues of local importance, of stifling intellectual creativity and cultivating docility (as per Ibarra-Colado's earlier note) and, in turn, of undermining the capacity for the development of a distinctive Indigenous tradition in social science.

So to/too CMS?

I now try to turn the critical lens onto CMS by considering some evidence for the existence within it of some of the problematic issues just raised with regard to GMK and the social sciences. In other words, is there evidence of quantitative and qualitative parochialism in the activities of CMS scholars and institutions? I have to acknowledge the trickiness of the following evidential base; first, it is difficult to paint a picture of a set of activities like CMS scholarship without falling into the trap of reification and perhaps even homogenization; second, it represents the particular choices I have made about how to portray CMS – others may choose different sources; third, it is hardly a portrayal of an objective reality that covers everyone's experience. That said, there are institutional statements and sources of information (e.g. CMS websites and domain statements, AoM membership data and meeting programs), as well as published and informal accounts of experiences of working and writing in CMS. The latter comprise some of the sources of my evidence, as well as my own position and experience as a self-identified CMS scholar and as former co-chair of the AoM CMS Division (2013–2014).

As noted in the provocative exchange between Tatli (2011) and Ford, Harding & Learmonth (2011), CMS scholarship includes plenty of calls for and examples of reflexivity, self-critique and 'external' critique. For instance, several of the *Speaking Out* pieces on the future of CMS (published in *Organization* (2008), *15*[6]) demonstrate a concern with the demographic and epistemic diversity of CMS. Bill Cooke (2008) (past chair of the CMS Division at the academy), for example, expresses "concerns I have about class, affluence, locality, masculinity and age, and the way these play out in CMS career paths and practices" (p. 912). Ann Cunliffe (2008) (past chair of the CMS Division at the academy) notes, "It's important to be more sensitive to issues of inclusion: intellectually, culturally and geographically. We have gotten better at moving beyond the image of CMS as male and Eurocentric, but not far enough" (p. 937). And within the AoM CMS Division, there have been professional development workshop presentations that express concern with the provincialism of CMS (A. Prasad, 2012; P. Prasad, 2012). How might we sketch out these concerns a little more?

If we turn first to the question of quantitative parochialism, the membership numbers and demographic profile of our main conferences and associations are interesting. The CMS division at the AoM is the most international of all the divisions and has a higher proportion of international vis-à-vis domestic members. As of July 1, 2014, there were 234 domestic (U.S.) members and 493 international members. Over the period 2010–2014, CMS Division membership numbers decreased, notably amongst domestic members. International numbers were also down but by a (significantly) smaller percentage. Declining membership is an academy-wide phenomenon, with a 13.56% decrease of domestic AoM members in the same period. In terms of conference attendance, the numbers of non-U.S. and non-U.K. participants are typically high, especially at the U.K. conferences, which now attract around 500 delegates. Unfortunately, I do not have the breakdown in numbers according to institutional affiliation. My sense in attending both U.S. and U.K. conferences and from my purview of co-chair elect, is that, whilst membership and conference attendance do attest to the high portion of non-U.S. and non-U.K. participants, the 'international' profile is skewed towards European nations and to a lesser extent Canada, Australia, New Zealand, and Brazil. Fewer members and delegates come from nations in Africa, Central America, the Middle East, South and South East Asia. Whilst there is evidence that CMS is certainly demographically diverse, certain parts of the world are still under-represented.

Moving to the question of qualitative parochialism, statements about the emergence of CMS are a useful starting point. Whilst scholarly outputs and activities that are oppositional to the mainstream of management studies existed before the informal/formal institutionalization of CMS, there is a creation narrative. As the editors of *Organization* write in their introduction to the *Speaking Out* pieces, "[T]he evident success of this area of scholarly endeavour [CMS], [is] now institutionalized in conferences in the U.K. and as a division of the Academy of Management in the U.S." (*Organization,* 2008: 911). In terms of the U.K., the 1st International Critical Management Studies Conference was held in Manchester in 1999 and has remained in the U.K. since (Lancaster, Cambridge, Warwick), apart from the 2011 meeting in Naples (and in 2015 back to the U.K. at the University of Leicester). As for the CMS Division at the AoM, it was initially instituted as an interest group (IG) in 1998 and awarded divisional status in 1998. Its chairs (as both an IG and a division from 2004 to 2012) have come from (in terms of institutional affiliation) New Zealand (2); the U.S. (5); Canada (1 – with two co-chairs); the U.K. (1); Brazil (1). A U.K.-centric narrative is also manifest in the following excerpt from the Critical Management website:[4]

> Having originated in business schools in the United Kingdom, CMS as a platform has audiences all over the world including Europe, Australia, Asia, Latin America, Canada and the United States.
>
> *(criticalmanagement.org)*

Interestingly in the preceding excerpt, non-U.K. locations are positioned as 'audiences' for CMS, suggesting that the CMS platform has a writerly centre in the U.K. and the English-speaking world (we would then have to exclude the writings from other European nations that have made substantive CMS contributions, including Sweden,[5] Denmark, the Netherlands, France, Germany, Italy, Poland and so on) and is transmitted/transmissible to all other receiving/peripheral locations. The nomination of Canada and the U.S. as separate nations (in which CMS has a following), as opposed to the other continents (minus Africa and Asia, unless this is included in Australasia) could be interpreted as a 'worlding of the world' that minimizes the importance of some parts of the globe (and the diversity and dynamism associated with them) whilst maximizing the importance of others. Of course, this sentence could also be interpreted as rhetorical flair or expedience on the part of the writer/s, with much less symbolic baggage than that attributed by my previous sentence. It is also appropriate to note that there are conferences and networks outside the Global North at which CMS work is presented, and where CMS scholars congregate, including APROS and ACSCOS in Asia-Pacific, the Iberoamerican Academy and LAEMOS in Latin America, and informal institutional seminars and personal connections.

Moving beyond numbers and historical narration, I do have concerns that the "theory culture" (Mufti, 2005) of CMS – that is to say, both the key theoretical frames and the embodiment and lived experiences of those frames amongst CMS scholars – exhibits parochialism. Some evidence for this includes the very critically reflective accounts of the diversity of CMS scholarship. For instance, Adler (2008) notes that:

> there is the risk that we become complacent about our internal heterogeneity. I see increasingly frequent references to "CMS theory" as if there were a single body of theory that characterized CMS. In reality, there is a buzzing confusion and profusion, running the gamut from poststructuralism to labour process theory, from Derrida to Marx, from radical postcolonial feminism to moderate social-democratic liberalism, from positivism to critical realism to social constructivism.
>
> *(pp. 925–926)*

And again from the Critical Management website (retrieved Sept. 2, 2014):

> As an umbrella research orientation CMS embraces various theoretical traditions including anarchism, critical theory, feminism, Marxism, post-Marxism, post-structuralism, post-modernism, postcolonialism and psychoanalysis, representing a pluralistic, multidisciplinary movement.

Whilst I do not doubt these expressions of theoretical pluralism, they do hide two things. First, most of these theoretical resources are Eurocentric; that is to say, they are connected with writers and traditions connected to particular linguistic and cultural contexts, typically in Europe (notably France, Germany, the U.K., Austria and Italy). A quick glance (as of September 2014) at the "theorists which can inform CMS research" page of the critical management portal also manifests this Eurocentrism, with a near exclusive listing of living and dead European or American writers (Spivak is an exception in this list). The references to the prefix 'post-' are also connected to Eurocentric periodizing categories – notably modernity/modern and postmodernity/postmodern – where 'Europe' is the centre of its own historicizing narrative and other places, variations on that history. CMS could thus be read as a critique of modernity, or at least a critical sociology of modernity. This is not to deny the existence within CMS of postcolonial and Indigenous perspectives that critique modernity as coloniality and attempt the difficult task of writing back from the periphery and of challenging the centre by learning from Indigenous knowledges and social experiences. However, I would certainly not want to overstate the extent to which Indigenous perspectives have found a place within CMS. Second, there exist relational differences and scholarly preferences between them. In my experience, there is comparatively less emphasis on anarchism, perhaps even feminism, than on some of the others.

In a presentation at the 2012 AoM meeting, Anshuman Prasad outlined a number of interconnected transformations in the world that raise serious questions about the "continued viability of *Eurocentric* approaches to knowledge" (emphasis in the original). Amongst others, these transformations are connected to the oft remarked geopolitical decline of the West, the economic crisis in the Eurozone, the rise of BRICS nations, environmental depletion and so on. These transformations undermine the power of the West and of its knowledge systems, to claim privilege and superiority in the organization of its and others economic and social affairs. However, Prasad argues that "most of CMS appears *blind* to this "epistemological crisis of the West" (Harding)" (emphasis in the original) is generated by these transformations and is so precisely because it is in large part a modern/colonial Western social science with accompanying epistemological and ideological limitations.

Reconstructing CMS as multiple CMSs?

If we accept that there are limitations and exclusions within CMS associated with its dominant institutional positioning and knowledge systems in/from the Global North, then how might it be otherwise? On what basis would non-metropolitan knowledges become knowable within our work? CMS scholars are addressing this complex issue, in part with the notion that we move from one CMS to multiple CMSs. The suggestion is to decentre CMS by creating a context in which a dominant Eurocentric epistemic space (connected to particular and dominant locations) becomes just one of several emergent epistemic possibilities connected to a more diverse set of geographical and cultural locations. Several CMS scholars have addressed this issue.

Anshuman Prasad (2012; see also his Chapter 10 in this volume) calls for no less than the decolonization of CMS, citing Arturo Escobar, Walter Mignolo, Chandra Mohanty and Ashis Nandy as some of the key theoretical sources for his suggested program of 'deconstruction', 'reconstruction' and 'diversality'. Inspired by Mignolo's notion of 'diversality', Prasad reimagines CMS as a "pluralistic world of *multiple varieties* of CMS spread across different areas of the world" (emphasis in the original). Recent critical work by Brazilian scholars also deploys Mignolo both to critique Northern/colonial social sciences (including CMS) and to inspire a different vision for the social sciences and other knowledge systems located in Brazil (and with implications for other Latin American contexts). For example, Faria, Wanderley, Reis and Celano (2013) call for a "decolonial-critical management studies" (D-CMS) and use a case study of a Brazilian organization to illustrate how D-CMS could be performatively accomplished through organizational practices of anthropophagy. In part, their paper is a response to their concern that "the performative turn within CMS could be used as a way of bringing "critical development" and "critical knowledge" to the "rest of the world" from a perspective of coloniality" (p. 208).

A recent special issue of *Organization* (2012, 19:2) on Southern voices in management and organizational studies, edited by Rafael Alcadipani, Farzad Rafi Khan, Ernesto Gantman and

Stella Nkomo, also represents an important contribution to decentring GMK. Whilst they do not explicitly focus on CMS, the issue is certainly relevant for it. In their editorial essay, they state their desire to "make [these] voices [beyond Northern academia] heard, without any particular commitments to Western theoretical framework or approaches" (p. 131) and to acknowledge the fact, so often overlooked by Northern perspectives, that "nations that comprise what today is the Global South have demonstrated the possession of relevant MOK [management and organizational knowledge] throughout history" (p. 133). They thus confront the stereotyping of Southern management practices as dysfunctional, affirm the importance of focusing on and learning from Indigenous perspectives and note the associated challenges of writing, listening to and understanding Indigenous knowledge. The special issue contains a number of papers that present Southern voices in their own terms and in interaction with Western categories and modes of thought. Readers might also wish to consult the *Organization* special issue on postcolonialism (2011) and the recent edited book by Westwood, Jack, Khan and Frenkel (2014).

Prichard, Sayers and Bathurst (2007) develop the concept of 'locale' as a foundation for responding to metropole–periphery relations in CMS and generating locally relevant and valuable CMS insights. Using examples from their joint research project on music, work and organization, they illustrate three different responses to the "predicament of management/social science researchers in New Zealand" (p. 26). That is, how to manage their peripheral location in the field of management research, whilst working in an institutional system that defines and rewards 'world class research' with regard to the institutional centre. These responses are:

- *Franchise model:* Sayers was involved in adapting and administering a questionnaire on styles of aesthetic labour in NZ as part of an existing, U.K.-led international comparative study. This involved using the theoretical framework, questionnaire instrument and key outlets (conferences and journals) of the centre in the NZ context. It is a form of imitation where "[w]ork *there* is repeated here in similar or refined forms: institutions and frameworks are imported, and efforts are made to reproduce the practices, processes and frameworks of the center in peripheral locations" (p. 30; italics in original).
- *Margin model:* Bathurst's work with Burundian refugees in New Zealand attempted to understand how these "musical refugees" would use their cultural capital in efforts to integrate socially. He found they do not use music to help them to become Kiwis but instead to express and preserve their Burundian cultural identity. Bathurst interprets this as a "marginal group choos[ing] to remain at the margin" (p. 32), a position with paradoxical challenges for cultural groups and researchers alike. For researchers, not complying with the centre may result in work being perceived indifferently, or worse.
- *Locale model:* Prichard's research on music calls for the integration of a sense of place into one's theoretical framework. Based on this notion, he argues for a third response that turns location into locale, a position that:

  does not ignore the centre's research problems or theoretical machineries, and nor does it react to these by tracing out the boundary positions. . . . it attempts to re-invent or re-imagine these as part of a response to the empirical and theoretical materials found or experienced in a particular location. This involves explicitly speaking back to the dominant theoretical and conceptual machines of the metropolitan centres.

  (p. 35)

The authors advocate this locale response as the "next step" for CMS researchers in peripheral locations. They make it clear that they are not suggesting that we ignore or dismiss NATO debates but "beg, borrow and steal from them in ways that turn location into a locale, a space from which to address both local issues and concerns and to speak back to the centre" (p. 39).

If we return to the humanities and social sciences disciplines, we can see similar and more concerted scholarly struggles with how to respond to institutionalized parochialism, especially in terms of disciplinary theory culture. In the final two sections of this chapter, I draw selectively on two authors whose perspectives can further animate debate in and about CMS and global management knowledge with regard to two issues of significance that emanate from the preceding concerns. First, how should we best confront the dominant Eurocentrism of our theory culture? Can it simply be ignored as we reach out for knowledge contained in non-Western, or Indigenous, languages, literatures and social experiences? Second, how might we conceive of a relational framework in which these multiple knowledges could sit together? Is a 'mosaic' of different and autonomous knowledge systems the right frame?

Mufti's global comparativism

Over the last 20 years in comparative literature, leading scholars (notably Said, 1978, 1993 and Spivak, 2003) and professional associations have recognized the Eurocentrism of their discipline's knowledge structures and debated ways to better address its global purview. The dominance of the languages and literatures of Europe (notably British, French and German) and North America as the principal axes of scholarly comparison represent the discipline's most pressing challenge. Literature(s) produced in languages of a non-Western origin have traditionally occupied the margins of this comparative literary world. The publication of the Bernheimer Report (commissioned by the American Comparative Literature Association) in 1993 made recommendations to address this scenario including, as noted by Mufti (2005), expanding the linguistic competences of scholars in order to ensure that literature is read in its original language of production, and incorporating so-called minority literatures into the curriculum as part of a "multicultural recontextualization of Anglo-American and European perspectives" (p. 478).

Since the publication of this report, Mufti argues that the inclusion of non-Western languages in the discipline remains minimal and that linguistic asymmetries continue (as also noted with reference to management and organization studies by Merilainen, Tienari, Thomas and Davies (2008). For instance, he describes how students who are working on "literatures in non-Western languages are expected to demonstrate a familiarity with at least the theoretical literature of one or more of the European languages" (p. 477). However, with regard to cultural literacy, no equivalent range is expected of students whose work is mainly conducted in the dominant European languages. Furthermore, he expresses the view that the inclusion of more so-called minority literatures (whether under the rubric of postcolonial literature, world literature or others) "most often represent[s] an accommodation with the status quo rather than an attempt to interrogate it rigorously" (p. 477).

According to Mufti, the reason for this scenario is that the reaching out to non-Western literature continues to rely on Eurocentric structures, for example through use of categories of Western literary history (romanticism, realism, postmodernism and so on) and through the naming and labelling of particular 'non-Western' genres, such as 'the Arab novel' or the 'Urdu short story'. To explain how the latter constitute examples of Eurocentrism, Mufti turns to Dipesh Chakrabarty's (2000) reflections on the 'informal developmentalism' that underpins much historical scholarship and rendered challenging his own writing about 'Indian' history. Informal developmentalism is the notion that ideas and history happen "first in the West and then elsewhere" (Chakrabarty, 2000: 6; in Mufti, 2005: 474). Europe acts as "the sovereign, theoretical subject" of all historical knowledge, so that histories that are supposedly 'Indian', 'Chinese' [or]

'Kenyan' . . . tend to become variations on a master narrative that could be called "the history of Europe" (Chakrabarty, 2000: 3; in Mufti, 2005: 474).

When literary theorists talk of genres like the 'Arabic novel' or the 'Urdu short story', the deployment of the adjectives presupposes but disavows the existence of an original 'European' novel or short story against which it requires a name. Thus they become knowable as an object of study (rather than as an active cultural media, as Mufti remarks with reference to Spivak), marked by difference within the discursive system of Orientalism. As Mufti incisively notes, under these epistemic conditions, we continue to be Eurocentric "even and perhaps especially when we attempt to tell the story of such non-European objects as Indian, Chinese, and Arabic literature" (p. 474).

The parallels to management research are most striking with respect to the recent growth of literature on 'African', 'Chinese' and 'Indian' management produced by mainstream academics and practitioners. Whilst seeming to offer a multicultural recontextualization of management theory and practice, the need to name them as 'African', 'Chinese' or 'Indian' suggests that they are knowable and intelligible only through the discourse of the centre. Alongside other problems with these genres (e.g. the essentialisms and problematic claims to authentic cultural knowledge in these texts or the commodification of Indigenous knowledge) (see Nkomo, 2011 in particular, for a critique), it is clear that turning to multiple versions or local forms of management knowledge could be problematic, especially if it is assumed that it solves the problematic of Eurocentrism by ignoring it. But what could we do instead? Can we simply rid ourselves of Eurocentrism in the effort to bring in other knowledges? What other kind of framework could we imagine?

On these questions, Mufti returns to his teacher Edward Said. Said's concept of contrapuntality outlined in *Culture and Imperialism* (1993) represents his response to the criticism that his pathbreaking work in *Orientalism* involved "bracketing off the cultural production and trajectories of non-Western societies or bringing to them modes of attention distinct from, and far less compelling than, those he has developed for a critical re-engagement with the Western tradition" (Mufti, 2005: 472).

Through contrapuntality, Said calls for a reconfiguration of the ways in which scholars read and relate to literatures and cultures on opposite sides of the colonial/imperial divide. For example, Mufti suggests that students could read Joseph Conrad's *The Heart of Darkness* together with Tayeb Salih's *Season of Migration to the North* or Jane Austen's *Mansfield Park* with C.L.R. James. To read these texts together is to come to understand how such societies "live deeply imbricated lives that cannot be understood without reference to each other" (Mufti, 2005: 478), not as discrete and autonomous entities to be read individually and separately (as would be the case with a more conventional comparative literature approach). Whilst each novel may draw out particular perspectives on the experience of colonization/imperialism for its key protagonists, a reading-together approach highlights the broader and shared historical context of the settings. From this perspective, Mufti (2005) argues that:

> The genuine alternative to this universalism of contemporary Eurocentric thought is not a retreat into the local, into so many localities, but rather a general account of the play of the particular in the universalizing processes of capitalist-imperialist Modernity.
>
> *(p. 485)*

This is the framework for Mufti's new global comparativism, and it involves a number of features inspired by Edward Said. First, a return to the past of the comparative literature discipline, one in which a transnational perspective was emphasized and which now needs to be renewed for current times. Second, a "double critical consciousness" (Laroui, 1967) is required, in particular regard to attempts "to reclaim traditions whose social basis is seen to have been destroyed by the processes of capitalist-colonial modernization" (p. 481). Mufti is reliant on Abdallah Laroui's essay on contemporary Arabic ideology in this regard. Laroui talks of the necessity of a double critical consciousness (toward both Arabic society and the Western Other) for understanding critically the postcolonial context of Arab societies. Mufti (2005) summarizes as follows:

> No self-described attempt to "return" to tradition, religious or secular, can sustain its claim to be autonomous of "the West", Laroui writes (p. 68), not even that of "the religious scholar" (cleric) whose claim to authenticity is based on a return to the purportedly uncontaminated doxa of religious tradition: "In contemporary Arab ideology, no form of consciousness is authentic . . .". . . . No attempt to explore one's own tradition can therefore bypass a histori-cal critique of the West and its emergence into the particular position of dominance. In this sense, the critique of the West is in fact a self-critique.
>
> *(p. 481)*

According to Mufti, then, we cannot, and should not, excise a critical engagement with Euro-centrism from the picture. Instead, Mufti calls for conscious movements between recognition and disavowal that engage critically with an awareness of "the already translated nature of the objects it seeks to approach":

> the emergence of a critical consciousness that is neither fully inside nor entirely outside metropolitan Western cultures, a critical consciousness that will undertake a radical critique of Western culture as a condition for exploring "contemporary alternatives to Orientalism".
>
> *(Said, 1978: 24; in Mufti, 2005)*

Finally, this new global comparativism requires a fundamental transformation of the train-ing, professional competences and expectations of literature scholars. Apart from a pedagogical rethinking of how core theoretical traditions should reappear in this framework, Mufti calls for students to be required to learn a non-European language, to broaden their cultural and intel-lectual knowledge, and to have a sound understanding of key terms like the Global North/the Global South that structure the field which they will reproduce.

Connell's work, to which I turn next, extends some of these themes at book length.

Raewyn Connell's *Southern Theory*

Raewyn Connell's (2007) *Southern Theory: The Global Dynamics of Knowledge in Social Science* is one of a recent number of texts that address the possibilities for a global sociology and global theoriz-ing about social relations (see also Keim, 2011; Hountondji, 2002; Rodriguez, Boatca & Costa, 2010). As a cognate discipline for CMS, Connell's sociological ideas are particularly pertinent, especially since they draw on postcolonial, decolonial and Indigenous perspectives that animate some of the recent critical work on CMS outlined earlier. The book is part revisionist disciplin-ary historiography – she describes the 'founding fathers' narrative surrounding Durkheim, Marx and Weber as one of sociology's foremost and unhistorical bad habits – and part rally cry and manifesto for "a new path for social theory that will help social science to served democratic purposes on a global scale" (2007: vii). Her ideas are numerous, but seem to be underpinned by three overarching themes.

First, Connell is committed to combating the persistent inequality in the global division of intellectual labour between 'theory' produced in the Global North and 'data' to be collected by locals in the Global South. In *Southern Theory*, she states that:

> colonised and peripheral societies produce social thought *about the modern world* which has as much intellectual power as metropolitan social thought, and more political relevance. Since the ground is different, the form of theorising is different too. Work needs to be done to develop the connections, as well as the contrasts, between these bodies of thought and those of the metropole.
>
> *(Connell, 2007: xii; italics in the original)*

As such, the choice of her title *Southern Theory* draws attention to the notion that social thought occurs in particular places and reminds us that scholars in the majority world do produce theory. Often, this theoretical work will take form in genres that are not consistent with the "professional disciplinarity of the metropole" (Connell, 2011: 289), thus requiring patience, cultural contextual understanding and a commitment to become educated in ways we are yet to know. To demonstrate the rich possibilities of Southern Theory, the lion's share of Connell's book is dedicated to discussion of selected texts on social theory by scholars from various locations where economic and/or cultural dependency (associated with varying kinds of imperialism or colonialism) have been challenged. These peripheral locations include:

- Postcolonial Africa, covering work by Akinsola Akiwowo, Moses Makinde, Olatunde Bayo Lawuyi, Olufemi Taiwo, John Mbiti, Kwane Gyekye and notably Paulin Hountondji, as well as debates about the African Renaissance Model;
- Modernizing Iran and the relationship between Islam and the West, covering work by Sayyid Jamal ad-Din (al-Afghani), Jalal Al-e-Ahmad, Ali Shariati;
- Latin America since World War II, especially in relation to ideas about dependency, autonomy and neoliberalism, with work by Raul Prebisch, Fernando Henrique Cardoso, Enzo Faletto, Marti Hopenhayn, Sonia Montecino, Nestor Garcia Canclini;
- India since the 1970s, including scholarly works by Ranajit Guha and Subaltern Studies, Indian feminism, Vandana Shiva, Veena Das, Ashis Nandy.

Connell demonstrates a particular 'readerly' disposition or attitude towards this scholarly endeavour. She reads and comments upon work by these scholars "as texts to learn from, not just about" (2007: viii), especially in terms of what they illuminate about the "project of theorising in the global periphery, its intellectual and practical problems, and its differing forms" (2007: viii).

She learns from these texts of the struggles and complexities of relations of dependency, including the conditions of possibility and constraints on asserting Indigenous knowledges as forms of intellectual resistance. She also highlights the double critical consciousness displayed by many of these authors in how they treat their topics of discussion.

Second, Connell is able to go further than Mufti in outlining specific characteristics and ideas for generating a "new science, prioritising the social experience and social thought of the majority world" (Connell, 2011: 288). I have summarized what I interpret to be the key characteristics and ideas presented in the whole book in Table 11.1. Her broad framework does share certain ideas with Mufti's (coincidentally). For one, she makes it clear that she does not support, or even think empirically possible, the idea that a collection of distinct knowledge systems would ameliorate, far less transform the status quo in the social sciences. She asserts this position on the following grounds:

Every significant development in the social sciences in the periphery makes *some* use of concepts or techniques from the metropole. It is therefore not realistic to imagine the future of world social science as a mosaic of knowledge systems – as a set of indigenous sociologies, indigenous economics, and so on, all functioning independently. . . . I will go so far as to say the only possible future for social science on a world scale involves a principle of unification.

(2007: 223)

For me, it is perhaps curious given her interest in relationality, as well as the various resistances and conscious silences of peripheral scholars/knowledge systems faced with the machinations of the centre, that she would suggest a "principle of unification" for the global social sciences. Admittedly it is a somewhat under-specified notion in Connell's text (one that would concern me), but it seems that what belies it is a concern that conversation rather than scholarly isolation of different traditions should underpin the future of the social sciences.

Like Mufti, Connell believes we need to begin from the notion that texts, ideas and even the institutional conditions in peripheral contexts are already hybridized and translated objects as a consequence of the colonial encounter. Our task is to recognize these relational conditions for knowledge, not place too circumscribed a focus on any one form of peripheral knowledge, and to explore formations of knowledge in relation to one another. In exploring these formations, Connell notes three potential strategies. First, by emulating the writerly strategies of some of the authors whose texts she discusses in the four locations previously listed (especially Shariati and Hopenhayn). She describes how adoption of a critical distance to metropolitan knowledge involves a willingness to challenge it and knowing when to leave it. Second, by generating greater connections between scholars and knowledges located in peripheral locations, encouraging those in rich semi-peripheral locations or elites in other locations in particular to deploy their resources to generate connections. Practices of connection could cover travel, patronage and sponsorship, publication and research network formation. Finally, and crucially, a reconfiguration of relations between the metropole and periphery requires greater dialogue and a collective learning process that will help to 'retool' scholars in the centre. In practical terms, for metropolitan scholars, this would mean reflecting on and looking for changes to the kinds of knowledges and affiliations we privilege in our research, the publication strategies and citation practices we adopt, the theory and readings we set in our teaching and the languages in which we read and write.

Table 11.1 Recommendations for social sciences on a world scale.

Name the pattern of inequality and register different situations of metropole/periphery (M/P) relations.

Undo the erasure of experience from the periphery (a constitutive mechanism of Northern Theory) to make a shared learning process possible.

Stop building models/social theory based on a privileged minority worldview.

Describe the characteristics/locations of the social scientific workforce, and evaluate the practices, contexts and institutions in which social science knowledge is produced.

Challenge and subvert any monologism in metropolitan perspectives based on a Southern Theory view (texts to learn from, not just about).

Avoid a future world of social sciences as a mosaic of distinct and independent knowledge systems.

Create the conditions and structures for a long-term educational process of retooling and reconfiguring social science based on respect and recognition of peripheral knowledge.

Expose, challenge and change the democratic deficits in the social sciences.

Source: Adapted from Connell (2007).

Table 11.2 Questions for debating a CMS in 'Becoming'.

Do we name colonialism and imperialism as the condition of possibility for the enterprise of CMS?

Are the viewpoints, perspectives and problems of metropolitan society/the Global North predominant in CMS?

Is CMS characterizable as an exporter of a set of Eurocentric theory, concepts and methods to peripheral locations? What happens to these exported perspectives in peripheral locations?

In what ways do the diverse and dynamic conditions of reception for CMS in peripheral locations play out in relation to local, Indigenous knowledges?

Where and how does Southern Theory circulate in CMS and with what effects? What distinctive perspectives, theoretical forms and empirical insights does it bring?

What are we to do with the existing fact of Eurocentrism? What are we to do with the phantasmic ideas of cultural autonomy, and how can we recognise and build upon the existing fact of cultural hybridity?

What are our structures for mutual learning and practices for connecting scholars in the metropole and the periphery?

Should all students of CMS be required to learn a second language, and especially a non-European/ non-English language as relevant to their research?

How do we address the need for greater linguistic and cultural literacy in CMS?

Should CMS share Connell's desire for a social science aimed at serving democratic purposes on a world scale? What is the epistemological basis for such a planetary knowledge? How can we avoid 'worlding the world'?

Do you agree that the mosaic of knowledges is an unrealistic and unhelpful way of conceiving of things? Do you think the future of CMS is/should be a multicentered one? Under what conditions?

What specific role should Indigenous knowledge play in this multicentered re-imagining? How can we learn from Indigenous struggles, knowledges and politics?

Source: Author

Conclusion

In this chapter, I set out to debate CMS in the context of existing critiques of both global management knowledge and the wider social sciences as Eurocentric and reproductive of inequalities between scholars and knowledge systems located in different parts of the world. The particular challenge for CMS at the Academy and in Europe that I see is the Eurocentrism of its dominant theory culture and the question of the conditions under which 'multiple CMSs' located across different geographical and epistemic spaces could become possible. By engaging with Mufti and Connell, I have outlined some of these conditions, emphasizing a focus on engaged and relational encounters between metropolitan and peripheral knowledge (not the development of autonomous systems), the need for a retooling of scholars in the centre with particular regard to linguistic competence and cultural literacy, and finally encouraging greater connections between scholars and knowledge systems (notably Indigenous knowledge and social experiences) in peripheral locations. I began by noting the notion of CMS in becoming, and I would like to end with it by drawing your attention to the questions I have posed in Table 11.2 as a basis (hardly exhaustive, of course!) for future debate about CMS.

Notes

1 I use the terms 'metropole-periphery' (from Connell, 2007) and 'core/center-periphery' interchangeably within the chapter.

2 The international membership numbers at July 1, 2014, are taken directly from official Academy of Management sources. Unfortunately the 'international' numbers available are not broken down by individual countries or continents. However, some indications (within limits – the costs of travel and accommodation for North America, for instance, are greatly prohibitive to conference attendance, especially for international members in countries and institutions with low levels of travel funding) of the location of international members might be extracted from the participant country numbers presented in the 2014 Academy of Management Annual Meeting Statistics (AOM Philadelphia 2014, Official Printed Program: 52). The number of international participants at the AOM conference in 2014 in Philadelphia by country were (countries with over 100 participants noted only): United Kingdom (694), Canada (484), Germany (426), Australia (321), Netherlands (313), France (255), Spain (211), Switzerland (197), Italy (178), Singapore (136), Taiwan (127), Denmark (124), Hong Kong (121), South Korea (105), Belgium (104), Finland (108). The United States had 4422 participants. There were participants from Africa (the highest number from South Africa – 15), India (91) and a number of other Asian and Latin American nations.

3 'Indigenous' can be a confusing, even misleading concept as deployed in some management research. An example is the concern amongst Asian management researchers to create theory relevant to local issues and experiences; at best, this might be signified by 'indigenous' with a small 'i'. This is not necessarily the same thing as talking about the histories and experiences of colonialism and imperialism, which created the very category of Indigenous peoples (with a capital 'I' for Indigenous). Perhaps a better adjective for researchers to use would be 'endogenous' when related to general forms of 'local' experience, and 'Indigenous' with more specific reference to groups subjected to colonial and imperialist histories.

4 The website (www.criticalmanagement.org) is a portal that, to quote from the site, aims to "gather information about CMS in one place as well as develop its own content (e.g. overviews on philosophers and CMS, overviews of themes researched within CMS, commentated bibliography etc.) through collaboration of the CMS community. The website works as a Wikipedia-type website, so everyone can contribute to its content" (retrieved September 2, 2014).

5 P. Prasad (2012) refers to the 'Anglo-Scandinavian' branding of CMS (so a slight amendment to a purely UK-centrist view of the genesis of CMS), with certain publications specifically pinpointing Alvesson and Willmott's (1992) *Critical Management Studies* as a foundational moment in the field. See also the present volume's introductory chapter by Prasad, Prasad, Mills and Helms Mills.

References

Adler, P. S. (2008). CMS: Resist the three complacencies! *Organization, 15*(6): 925–926.

Alatas, S. H. (1974). The captive mind and creative development. *International Social Science Journal, 26*(4): 691–700.

Alatas, S. F. (2000). Intellectual imperialism: Definition, traits, and problems. *Southeast Asian Journal of Social Science, 28*(1): 23–45.

Alatas, S. F. (2003). Academic dependency and the global division of labour in the social sciences. *Current Sociology, 51*(6): 599–613.

Alcadipani, R., Khan, F. R., Gantman, E., & Nkomo, S. (2012). Southern voices in management and organization knowledge. *Organization, 19*(2): 131–143.

Boyacigiller, N. A., & Adler, N. J. (1991). The parochial dinosaur: Organizational science in a global context. *Academy of Management Review, 16*(2): 262–90.

Chakrabarty, D. (2000). *Provincializing Europe.* Princeton, NJ: Princeton University Press.

Clegg, S., Linstead, S., & Sewell, G. (2000). Only penguins: A polemic on organisation theory from the edge of the world. *Organization Studies, 21*: 103–117.

Connell, R. (2007). *Southern Theory: The global dynamics of knowledge production in social science.* Cambridge: Polity Press.

Connell, R. (2011). Sociology for the whole world. *International Sociology, 26*(3): 288–291.

Cooke B. (2008). If critical management studies is your problem . . . . *Organization, 15*(6): 912–914.

Cunliffe, A. (2008). Will you still need me . . . When I'm 64? The future of CMS. *Organization, 15*(6): 936–938.

Eden, D., & Rynes, S. (2003). Publishing across borders: furthering the internationalization of AMJ. *Academy of Management Journal, 46*: 679–683.

Faria, A., Wanderley, S., Reis, Y., & Celano, A. (2013). Can the subaltern teach? Performativity otherwise through anthropophagy. In V. Malin, J. Murphy & M. Siltaoja (Eds.), *Getting things done: Dialogues in critical management studies*, Vol. 2: 205–224. Bingley, UK: Emerald Group Publishing.

Ford, J., Harding, N., & Learmonth, M. (2011). Who is it that would make business schools more critical? A response to Tatli. *British Journal of Management, 23*: 31–34.

Harding, S. (1998). *Is science multicultural: Postcolonialisms, feminisms and epistemologies.* Bloomington: Indiana University Press.

Hountondji, P. (2002). Knowledge appropriation in a post-colonial context. In CAO Hoppers (Ed.), *Indigenous knowledge and the integration of knowledge systems*: 23–28. Claremont, South Africa: New Africa Books.

Ibarra-Colado, E. (2006). Organisation studies and epistemic coloniality in Latin America: Thinking otherness from the margins. *Organization, 13*(4), 463–488.

Ibarra-Colado, E. (2008). Is there any future for critical management studies in Latin America? Moving from epistemic coloniality to 'trans-discipline'. *Organization, 15*(6): 932–935.

Jack, G., & Westwood, R. (2009). *International and cross-cultural management studies: A postcolonial reading.* Basingstoke, UK: Palgrave Macmillan.

Jack, G., Zhu, Y., Barney, J., Brannen, M-Y., Prichard, C., Singh, K., & Whetten, D. (2013). Refining, reinforcing and reimagining universal and indigenous theory development in international management. *Journal of Management Inquiry, 22*(2): 148–164.

Keim, W. (2011). Counterhegemonic currents and internationalization of sociology. Theoretical reflections and an empirical example. *International Sociology, 26*(1): 123–145.

Kirkman, B., and Law, K. (2005). International management research in AMJ: Our past, present, and future. *Academy of Management Journal, 48*(3): 377–386.

Laroui, A. (1967). *L'ideologie arabe contemporaine.* Paris: Essai Critique.

Loubser, J. J. (1988). The need for the indigenization of the social sciences. *International Sociology, 3*(2): 179–187.

Merilainen, S., Tienari, J., Thomas, R., & Davies, A. (2008). Hegemonic academic practices: Experiences of publishing from the periphery. *Organization, 15*(4): 584–597.

Mufti, A. (2005). Global comparativism. *Critical Inquiry, 31*(2): 472–489.

Prasad, A. (2012). Decolonizing critical management studies. Professional development workshop, Frontiers of Critique: Critical Management Studies in a Changing World, Academy of Management Meeting, Boston, August.

Prasad, P. (2012). Perils of provincialism in a globalizing world: Debating the Anglo-Scandinavian branding of CMS. Professional development workshop, CMS Unbound, Academy of Management Meeting, Boston, August.

Prichard, C., Sayers, J., & Bathurst, R. (2007). Franchise, margin and locale: Constructing a critical management studies locale in Aotearoa New Zealand. *New Zealand Sociology, 22*(1): 22–44.

Rodriguez, E. G., Boatca, M., & Costa, S. (Eds.). (2010). *Decolonizing European sociology: Transdisciplinary approaches.* Farnham, UK: Ashgate.

Said, E. (1978). *Orientalism: Western conceptions of the Orient.* London: Penguin.

Said, E. (1993). *Culture and imperialism.* New York: Vintage Books.

Spivak, G. C. (2003). *Death of a discipline.* New York: Columbia University Press.

Tatli, A. (2011). On the power and poverty of critical (self) reflection in critical management studies: A comment on Ford, Harding and Learmonth. *British Journal of Management, 23*: 22–30.

Tsui, A. S. (2004). Contributing to global management knowledge: A case for high quality indigenous research. *Asia Pacific Journal of Management, 21*: 491–513.

Tsui, A. S. (2007). From homogenization to pluralism: International management research in the Academy and beyond. *Academy of Management Journal, 50*(6): 1353–1364.

Westwood, R. (2014). De-centering management and organisation studies: On the eccentricity of US-based management and organisation theory and practice. In R. Westwood, G. Jack, F. R. Khan & M. Frenkel (Eds.), *Core-periphery relations and organization studies*: 53–78. Basingstoke, UK: Palgrave Macmillan.

Westwood, R., Jack, G., Khan, F. R., & Frenkel, M. (Eds.). (2014). *Core-periphery relations and organization studies.* Basingstoke, UK: Palgrave Macmillan.

12

Rethinking market-ing orientation

A critical perspective from an emerging economy

Alexandre Faria

Introduction

The concept of market orientation – a notion that may be seen as a condition as well as a consequence of neoliberal globalization – has become one of the most important in the field of marketing. Beginning in the early 1990s, influential marketing researchers argued that large business
firms that followed the concept of market orientation – i.e. firms that focused on either the needs
of consumers, the pattern of competition and intra-organizational coordination (Slater & Narver,
1990, 1998, 1999) or on the construction and use of market intelligence systems (Jaworski &
Kohli, 1993; Kohli & Jaworski, 1990) – achieved superior performance (measured in terms of
profitability). While the popularity of market orientation helped raise the status of the field
of marketing within large corporations and business schools, at the same time it also insulated
researchers (1) from criticisms about the relevance of the discipline and (2) from developments
in other scholarly fields concerning debates about different types of capitalism, the neoliberal
features of management knowledge and the changing geopolitical and geo-epistemic position of
emerging economies in the post–Cold War international context. Informed by a critical perspective that situates its locus of enunciation (Mignolo, 2000) in an emerging economy, this chapter
proposes that market orientation reproduces assumptions that are particularly problematic for
emerging economies, and, accordingly, that critique in marketing needs to be taken beyond the
'comfort level' of critical Anglo-American and/or European researchers.

Parallel to the territorial, material and ideological expansion of neoliberal globalization in
the post–Cold War years and its transformation into what has been called a neoliberal empire
(Harvey, 2003; Pieterse, 2004; Steger, 2009), market fundamentalism – i.e. an unquestioning
belief in the efficiency, effectiveness and moral legitimacy of market-based exchange in virtually all spheres of human life – invaded different areas of the world, including business research
and education. The marketization thesis – based on the argument that "non-market activity is a
vestige of a pre-capitalist past" (Williams, 2006) – became dominant in industrialized economies
and then was sought to be imposed on the rest of the world through the mobilization of both
hard and soft power mechanisms. Since 'non-markets' were seen by the Western literature as a
key feature of the rest of the world, the neoliberal representation of the market (i.e. the so-called
free market) and corresponding policies were aggressively promoted by the West in the rest of

the world. The project to promote the neoliberal market became something akin to a civilizing mission informed by the idea of "end of history" (Fukuyama, 1989), which aimed to eliminate all vestiges of 'non-market' on the earth. Through the mobilization of both hard and soft power mechanisms, the project of promoting the idea of the market appears to have achieved considerable success in the immediate aftermath of the Cold War.

Within the business research and education system, it seems that marketing academics and institutions were among the first to embrace and disseminate the idea that globalization equals 'free market'. Accordingly, wittingly or unwittingly, they also became participants in the project of *keeping invisible* the competing idea that globalization equals imperialism ruled by the only 'superpower', an idea advanced early in the 1990s by authors from Latin America (e.g. Santos, 1993) and elsewhere. Marketing literature, moreover, mostly ignored not only authors from the rest of the world but also Euro-American authors who portrayed globalization as a highly uneven process that "generates powerful sources of friction, conflict, and fragmentation . . . [with the result that] the interests of the few more often than not take precedence over the interests of the majority of humankind" (McGrew, 2008: 15), as well as those who highlighted the return of the militarization of markets after the September 2001 terrorist attacks on the U.S. as a reworking of the Cold War (Harvey, 2007) and the transformation of "market globalism" into 'imperial globalism' (Steger, 2009).

We may note that, at odds with the claims by Fukuyama (1989) and builders of what may be called the market-ing orientation project or design, the end of the Cold War was not framed as a discontinuity by a large part of the international relations community, including numerous practitioners as well as researchers. In his 25 April 2005 State of the Nation speech, for instance, President Vladimir Putin of Russia had declared that "the collapse of the Soviet Union was the greatest geopolitical catastrophe of the century . . . the epidemic of disintegration infected Russia itself" (Putin, 2005). The growing nuclear weaponization of different areas of the world and the launching of the global War on Terror by the U.S. President George W. Bush after the events of 9/11 have also been portrayed by the international relations literature as evidence that the Cold War is not over and that history and the world order remain in the making (Cox, 2008) and that market fundamentalism does not quite enjoy global hegemony.

Hence, one of the major priorities of the market-ing orientation design has been the delegitimation of ideas that could block the trajectory of expansion of the neoliberal order. The extraordinary rise of market-oriented management institutions in the post–Cold War era has been pushed by the corresponding grand strategy based on the diffusion on a global scale of the idea that the defeat of communism resulted in the 'natural' unlimited expansion of the market-oriented neoliberal order led by the United States.

However, the international relations literature has asserted since the early 1990s that such market-ing orientation is misleading as it assumes that countries and regions in general, and the lone 'superpower' in particular, would be voluntarily willing to dispense with the notion of state sovereignty. Accordingly, it is not surprising that, especially after the events of 9/11 and the rise of U.S. unilateralism, the market-ing orientation design in general and the Washington Consensus in particular were at the receiving end of numerous critiques voiced not only from the rest of the world but from within the U.S. itself (Philo & Miller, 2001; Harvey, 2003). For different reasons, those critical accounts from other fields of knowledge and/or regions of the world have been overlooked or kept invisible by both mainstream *and* critical marketing studies. This situation has enabled the successful trajectory of the concept of market orientation on a global scale in general, and in particular the 'invasion' of emerging economies by a neocolonial/neo-imperial perspective after the events of 9/11.

Accordingly, adopting the perspective of an emerging economy – in particular Brazil – I argue in this chapter that critical researchers need to embrace critiques of the market-ing orientation design being offered by Latin American authors (as well as authors from various other non-Western regions of the world), and by a range of other fields of knowledge, with a view to co-constructing an international critical perspective that goes beyond current Anglo-American and/or European contributions. In the second and third sections of the chapter, the successful trajectories of neoliberal market-ing orientation design and the concept of market orientation are critically analyzed. The fourth section focuses on the importance of rethinking market orientation from the perspective of an emerging economy located in Latin America. The final section provides suggestions for further critical developments in Brazil and other emerging economies.

On market-ing orientation

Market-ing orientation is a Euro-American design (with the U.S. playing the leading role in its construction) that was then transformed into a global design. It is based on the idea that U.S. capitalism defeated communism because of its intrinsic superiority and that neoliberal globalization represents the end of history and the corresponding triumph of Eurocentrism. In other words, market-ing orientation represents the final victory of the neoliberal design based on 'free market' and 'free enterprise' mantras. Correspondingly, marketing institutions and researchers, especially (but not only) in the U.S. share and disseminate on a global scale the idea that the marketization of the entire world is not just 'natural' and beneficial for all but also necessary. According to marketing authors and institutions, everything that is not part of the market has to (or will) become part of the market (Achrol & Kotker, 2000).

Market-ing orientation ignores not only history and authors from the rest of the world (in particular Latin America) who equate neoliberalism with neo-imperialism or neocolonialism (e.g. Santos, 1993), but also a vast Euro-American literature (of international relations, for instance) which challenges the argument that the post–Cold War period signifies a discontinuity and posits instead that the end of the Cold War actually represents the rise of a problematic world order with many powers, marked mainly by a "return to the shift of alliances and instabilities of the multipolar era that existed prior to World War II" (Goldgeir & McFaul, 1992: 467). Market-ing orientation, moreover, is linked to an understanding within certain international relations circles in the U.S. that although it is 'obvious' that Western civilization and its corresponding ideology constitute the pinnacle of human history, there are still fierce opponents of the Western liberal order who remain to be faced. It is therefore seen as legitimate for Western institutions to 'reform' those rivals according to the precepts of the Western model of civilization (Huntington, 1996).

Huntington's famous typology of civilizations which informs the market-ing orientation design is based on a neocolonial and racist dichotomy between Western and non-Western values: Western values supposedly represent liberalism, rationality, social equality and individual rights, whereas non-Western values are said to represent illiberalism, irrationality, social inequality and collective rights. Given such reasoning, the imposition of the market-ing orientation design on a global scale is regarded as a legitimate responsibility of the lone 'superpower'. As Huntington (1993) declares:

[T]he promotion of democracy, human rights, and markets are [sic] far more central to American policy than to the policy of any other country. . . . A world without US primacy will be a world with more violence and disorder and less democracy and economic growth than a world where the United States continues to have more influence than any other country in shaping global affairs.

(p. 83)

Correspondingly, the market-ing orientation design bestows on the West the responsibility of conquering the hearts and minds of opposing non-Western forces that allegedly represent 'backwardness' and 'threat'. Marketing academics and institutions, led by the U.S. and supported by Europe, have become completely enmeshed in the mission of transforming the market-ing orientation design into a global design. For them, even the notion of a different European capitalism (argued for by some) does not make sense in an era of global convergence. Although the concept of market orientation has been embraced and fostered by European researchers and institutions since the mid-1990s, there is no debate within this literature based on the theory of varieties of capitalism. Besides ignoring the *critical* marketing literature, researchers also ignore not only the disputes between Brussels and Washington regarding the making of markets and states in the European Union and Central and Eastern Europe (Bruszt, 2002) and between types of Western capitalisms (Morgan, Whitley & Moen, 2004), but also the strategic disputes between Oriental and Occidental globalizations (Pieterse, 2004) and between Western and non-Western capitalisms (Arrighi, 2007). Reinforcing in the post–Cold War era the subordination of the discipline to U.S. Cold War grand strategies (see Barksdale, Kelly & MacFarlane, 1978; Tadajewski, 2006), they fail to realize that the market-ing orientation design which informs the concept of market orientation has been fostered to a major extent by U.S. foreign policies and the neoliberal empire.

The many failures of the Washington Consensus and market fundamentalism which started in the mid-1990s (see, e.g. Stiglitz, 2003, 2008) created conditions for the recognition in the rest of the world that the market-ing orientation design aims not just to *eliminate* non-market forces in the rest of the world, but also to *keep invisible* Western non-market mechanisms which have informed the rise of neoliberal imperialism (Steger, 2009). Indeed, it also aims to preempt *alternatives* from the rest of the world in general and from emerging economies in particular. As pointed out by Pettigrew (1987), the higher-order strategic changes in a neoliberal world in which supposedly there is no alternative require the mobilization of power to both defeat and prevent competition "derived from the generation and manipulation of symbols, language, belief and ideology . . . through the possession, control, and tactical use of overt sources of power such as position, rewards or sanctions, or expertise" (p. 659). The legitimate mobilization of power to both defeat and prevent competitors has been reinforced by the unilateral diffusion, after the events of 9/11, of the idea that emerging economies represent a threat to the Western order (Jervis, 2003) and by the argument that the lone superpower should "eliminate them before they become legitimate challengers" (see Glosny, 2010: 104).

This dark side of the market-ing orientation design, which is crucially important from the perspective of emerging economies, has been addressed by critical authors from Latin America and in different fields of knowledge, such as international political economy, international relations, global sociology, geography and so on. Nevertheless, this literature has been ignored or successfully kept invisible by the marketing literature and corresponding institutions on a global scale. Interestingly and somewhat related to the reach and pervasive power of the market-ing orientation design, this literature has also been virtually overlooked by Anglo-American critical scholarship in both marketing and management studies.

How to explain this state of things? In the main, this chapter addresses three interrelated issues or ideas to explain this picture. In so doing, the chapter makes a scholarly contribution (from an emerging economy located in Latin America) which aims to go beyond the existing Anglo-American contributions in critical marketing and management studies. The first such issue or idea is that the market-ing orientation design has been overlooked in the Anglo-American world because the dispute between communism and capitalism has been replaced in the post–Cold War era by a neocolonial dispute, led by the U.S. and backed by Europe, between types of Western capitalism (Campbell & Pedersen, 2007; Morgan, Whitley & Moen, 2004), *at the expense of* alternatives and voices from the rest of the world (Arrighi, 2011). The management of ideas and meanings in this neoliberal world has been grounded on geopolitical processes "designed to create legitimacy for one's ideas, actions and demands, and to delegitimize the demands of one's opponents" (Pettigrew, 1987: 659).

The second issue is that academic institutions in management, led by the U.S. and seconded by Europe, have been playing a central role in constructing and spreading the market-ing orientation culture from the West towards the rest of the world (Clegg & Carter, 2007; Philo & Miller, 2001; Thrift, 2005). The extraordinary expansion of management knowledge and institutions over recent decades as a global design led by the U.S. and supported by Europe is related to the increasing importance of soft power – a term coined in the U.S. by Joseph Nye – within international relations circles, i.e. "the ability of a country to persuade others to do what it wants without force or coercion" (Nye, 1990). In other words, Western academic institutions of management embody the grand strategy of fostering a necessary but less costly U.S. post–Cold War hegemony.

Finally, the third issue being introduced here is that the big emerging economies – in particular Brazil, China, India, and Russia – have been portrayed by Euro-American institutions and authors as a threat, capable of not only challenging the U.S. hegemony but also constructing and disseminating *alternative capitalisms* or alternatives to the Western order on a global scale (Kagan, 2009; Trenin, 2006). In this regard, although many authors used to hold in past years that "bandwagoning" with the U.S. was the only option to these emerging economies (Van Ness, 2002), the subsequent crises of the neoliberal order and the consistent rise (or return) of emerging economies (Arrighi, 2011) have led large numbers of analysts to conclude that, although "the old winners are still winning . . . the terms on which they are winning cede more and more to emerging forces" (Pieterse, 2008: 707). Correspondingly, developments such as Russia's soft power strategies towards the Caucasus and Central Asia (Hill, 2006) or China's soft power programs in Africa and Latin America have become major issues within Euro-American international relations circles and help explain why emerging economies – especially Russia, India and China – have been portrayed as a threat to the West by the main builders of the market-ing orientation design.

These three interrelated issues help us understand the trajectory of the transformation of the market-ing orientation into a global design, as well as the successful trajectory of market orientation. Simultaneously, they also explain why researchers in Europe can freely point out that the mainstream fields of marketing and strategic management are non-neutral when it comes to U.S. interests (Knights & Morgan, 1991; Tadajewski, 2006), but those same researchers generally overlook the fact that *both* critical and mainstream versions of these fields remain *Euro-American* fields. European authors have been keen to point out that marketing and strategic management share a history of ethnocentrism and aversion to criticism and interdisciplinarity (Brownlie, Saren, Wensley & Whittington, 1999; Pettigrew, Thomas & Whittington, 2002), but the recognition of knowledges from the rest of the world and the corresponding provision of geo–epistemic conditions for the co-construction of a world in which many worlds and knowledges could coexist remain as gaps to be filled.

On the trajectory of market orientation

Given the geopolitical underpinnings and the successful trajectory of the market-ing orienta-tion design, it is not surprising that the successful trajectory of the concept of market orienta-tion within the marketing literature started as of the early 1990s. The first articles in the matter were published in the U.S. by two powerful institutional builders of the market-ing orientation design: the Marketing Science Institute and the *Journal of Marketing*. Those articles were based on statistical correlations and on the absence of market theorizing and showed that large business firms that followed the concept of market orientation achieved superior performance measured in terms of profitability (Jaworski & Kohli, 1993; Kohli & Jaworski, 1990; Slater & Narver, 1990).

Influenced and enabled by the market-ing orientation design in general and in particular by the imposition of hard power by the Washington Consensus, those studies reinforced the Euro-American mission of transforming that design into a global design and belief in a free market world order (Slater & Narver, 1998, 1999). More importantly, it helped in delegitimizing competing or alternative ideas and keeping invisible the dark geopolitical side of the market-ing orientation design. As such, market orientation may be correctly understood as a successful neoliberal reworking (in the post–Cold War era) of the mobilization of marketing as a resource of soft power.

During the Cold War period, the U.S. imposed free market and democracy on the Third World through the mobilization of hard power and also by imposing management institutions and market-ing disciplines. At that time, the main justification was that management and market-ing disciplines were necessary to deter the advance of communism. Due to the enduring sub-ordination of the discipline to U.S. grand strategies, the marketing literature has been silent on the extent to which this dark geopolitical side explains its successful trajectory in the Cold War period despite its low status within management academic institutions and large corporations. From the perspective of an emerging economy in Latin America, it is worth pointing out that the transformation of Chile into the first neoliberal experiment in the early 1970s, through the mobilization of free-market discourses, market-ing institutions, and military power by Euro-American great powers (Faria, Ibarra-Colado & Guedes, 2010; Harvey, 2007), has been kept invisible by the Euro-American marketing literature in particular and also by the management literature in general, in *both* mainstream and critical versions.

The concept of market orientation helped in establishing on global scale the idea of a new 'market-oriented world order' and also in keeping invisible the mechanisms mobilized by Euro-American great powers in the post–Cold War period. A few European authors dared to criticize the methodological assumptions and procedures followed by market oriented publications (e.g. Langerak, 2003; Henderson, 1998; Wensley, 1995), but, not surprisingly, they failed to recog-nize authors from the rest of the world who equated the market-ing orientation design with neo-imperialism or neocolonialism, as well as the embeddedness of those publications in the market-ing orientation design. In this respect what is even more interesting is that the concept of market orientation has been overlooked by critical marketing literature published in the Anglo-American world.

Spurred on by the dissemination of neoliberal discourses by the neoliberal empire, and by embracing the project of broadening the scope of marketing conveyed in the U.S. in the Cold War period (Kolter & Levy, 1969) to preempt the advance of communism, research in market orientation 'invaded' the realms of public as well as non-profit organizations. A large community of researchers from different countries, asymmetrically linked with U.S. researchers and institu-tions, applied the concept in Asia, Latin America and Eastern Europe (e.g. Hooley et al., 2000; Hooley, 2003), and both overlooked and helped in making invisible the dark geopolitical side of the market-ing orientation design.

Interestingly, this post–Cold War ambiguity involving neoliberals and neoconservatives which informs the rise of neoliberal empire was also a key issue in the Cold War. At that time U.S. liberals called on the U.S. "to stop supporting Third World dictators", and conservatives and neoconservatives in the U.S. warned "that the dictators would be replaced by pro-Soviet communists" (Kagan, 2008: 101).

Allegedly for economic reasons, emerging economies (more specifically Brazil, China, India and Russia) were subsequently taken as major target for the expansion of research in market orientation in recent years, particularly after the events of 9/11 (e.g. Felix & Hinck, 2005). U.S. marketing academics and institutions overlooked the sequential crises of the neoliberal order and the rise of the neoliberal empire (Pieterse, 2004) and claimed that researchers should recognize the "institutional failures" of emerging economies (Burgess & Steenkamp, 2006). This turn toward emerging economies from a neocolonial perspective was informed by the post-9/11 idea that the absence of market-oriented institutions in developing countries represented a global threat (see Faria & Wensley, 2011).

Critical research in marketing overlooked this geopolitical turn, a key post–Cold War reworking of the historical enmeshment of marketing discipline and institutions with U.S. foreign policies. This Cold War phenomenon (see Tadajewski, 2006) was strengthened in the early 1990s in accordance with the international relations literature, which disclaims the neoliberal idea that the end of the Cold War represents a historical discontinuity. The discipline was concerned just with critiques from top executives of business corporations and academics from strategic management (Mintzberg, Ahlstrand & Lampel, 1999; Whittington, 2001; Whittington & Whipp, 1992). As a result, market orientation was framed and embraced by the marketing community worldwide as the best way to raise the strategic status of marketing as a discipline in order to enable business organizations and societies to catch up with requirements established by the market-ing orientation design.

As critique in marketing is supposed to come from researchers and institutions involved with Critical Management Studies (e.g. Brownlie, Saren, Wensley & Whittington, 1999; Burton, 2005) and as the concept of market orientation was overlooked by them, researchers in emerging economies faced special difficulties to address the successful trajectory of market orientation from a critical perspective. From the perspective of an emerging economy located in Latin America, it is arguable that a major feature of Anglo-American critique in marketing in particular, and management studies in general, has been the virtual overlooking of the dark geopolitical side of both the market-ing orientation design and Western neoliberalism (see Faria, 2013). An example of this kind of Anglo-American critique in marketing studies, which became a sort of global design, in tandem with the successful trajectory of the market-ing orientation design, follows:

> In the world of business in the 1990s, the idea of marketing has central importance. . . . For Critical Theory, however, the myth of market freedom and with it the myth of marketing itself need to be unpacked. . . . Marketing is not a neutral way of looking at the world; it has distinctive power effects for organizations, managers, consumers and society as a whole. A critical approach to marketing will seek to reveal the conditions of possibility for marketing as a way of thinking about and doing particular social relations. In this way, it will link the critique of marketing to the critique of society.
>
> *(Morgan, 1992: 136)*

This type of Anglo-American critical approach aims to reveal the ideological feature of free market and marketing from a problematic perspective of universality. Correspondingly, researchers fail to address the geopolitical side of the market-ing orientation design and geo-epistemic and 'ideological' issues, which might help explain why 'universal' critique in marketing is invariably enunciated in the West, published in English, and informed by (almost only) European theories and theorists, all at the expense of criticalities and critical knowers and theorists from the rest of the world. It is arguable that this local design of critical marketing which emerged in the post–Cold War period in the Anglo-American world in the 1990s (e.g. Alvesson & Willmott, 1996; Morgan, 1992) and then became a global design represents a condition and outcome of the imposition of the market-ing orientation design on a global scale. In other words, from the perspective of the rest of the world, Anglo-American critical marketing can be also framed as an outcome and condition of the market-ing orientation design. Despite the intentions held by individual researcher and institutions, such critique is instrumental to the objective of 'preventing competition' from a perspective of geopolitics of knowledge.

It is not surprising that the publication of critical marketing literature in the United Kingdom, for instance, remains a privilege for a few academics and institutions (e.g. Saren, 2006; Saren et al., 2007; Tadajewski, 2010). Whereas it is correct to say that this critique has been ignored by the marketing literature in the U.S. and to a lesser extent in Europe, it is also correct to say that Euro-American critique has been instrumental for the reinforcement of the Western neoliberal order and corresponding subsuming of alternatives from the rest of the world.

In Brazil, where I live and work, the institutional and geopolitical conditions for the construction and legitimization of a critical perspective in marketing that addresses the geopolitical side of market-ing orientation design are not favorable, also for those reasons that have been overlooked by Anglo-American authors and institutions (there are important exceptions such as Cooke and Dar [2008]; Mills and Mills [2013]). It is not expected that academics and institutions from the rest of the world – when Brazil is portrayed as an 'emerging economy' rather than 'Third World' by Euro-American institutions, the notions of backwardness and threat assigned to the 'other' by Eurocentric ideas do not disappear – may question the 'dominant' literature (whether critical or mainstream). Such geo-epistemic obstacles have been reinforced in the post–Cold War period by the market-ing orientation design, and this helps explain the triumphant trajectory of market orientation in developing countries and the 'invasion' of emerging economies from a neocolonial perspective after the events of 9/11. Those selfsame geo-epistemic obstacles also explain why the trajectory of both the market-ing design and the concept of market orientation have been overlooked by Anglo-American critical marketing.

Arguably, Anglo-American critical management researchers are not just beneficiaries of such hegemonic design (Jack & Westwood, 2009) but also contributors for its diffusion as a global design that prevents alternatives from the rest of the world in general and in particular from emerging economies. Conversely, this picture supports the argument that critical perspectives from emerging economies which go *beyond* the Anglo-American contributions are necessary for the co-construction of a world in which many worlds and knowledges can coexist (see Faria, 2013; Cooke & Faria, 2013; Murphy & Zhu, 2012; Ibarra-Colado, 2008). Such international critical perspective might embrace the concept of geopolitics of knowledge. This concept has been uncovered and elaborated by academics from the rest of the world – in particular from Latin America – in the post–Cold War years as the colonial difference which started in the early 16th century with the 'discovery' of America by Eurocentric powers, a concept largely invisible to Euro-American researchers and institutions. In other words, it is correct to argue with Walter Mignolo that the geopolitics of knowledge "was not, and could hardly have been, a concern of Euro-American scholarships and thoughts" (2011: 119).

It has been argued in other fields of knowledge that the neo-liberal market-oriented project that was transformed into neo-liberal empire has been engendered through the asymmetric diffusion of market-ing oriented academic discourses – especially from the field of management. It has been clear for authors from those fields since the first moments of the post–Cold War years that the 'free market' was designed to benefit only a tiny minority, in detriment to a large majority (Câmara Neto & Vernengo, 2002; Chang, 2002; George, 1997). Their unheard claims suggest that the broad notion of 'critical marketing' is too important to be accepted by the rest of the world as a sort of niche to be mobilized and kept by a few Anglo-American researchers and institutions. Analogous critical arguments have been voiced by authors from different fields in Brazil since the early 1990s (e.g. De Paula, Ferraz, & Iooty, 2002; Oliveira, 1998; Paulani, 2005; Santos, 1993; Sola, 1993). but they remain virtually ignored by both mainstream and critical researchers not only in the Euro-American world but also in Brazil.

The darker geopolitical side of the market-ing orientation design helps explain why geopolitics of knowledge is so important and why it has been kept invisible. In the post–Cold War era, soft power has become as valuable as hard power to U.S. foreign-oriented policies and strategists. The U.S. post–Cold War hegemony in management knowledge in general and in marketing in particular can be explained in terms of the increasing deployment of soft power, especially after the events of 9/11 and the corresponding decay of the legitimacy of U.S. hegemony as a result of the launch of the global War on Terror.

Geopolitical management of knowledge has become even more important to the institutional builders of the market-ing orientation design after the Western neo-liberal crisis precipitated by Wall Street in 2008. A number of authors and institutions now share the idea that the victories of the neo-liberal order against non-Western opposing forces should not be framed as 'natural' or inevitable as proposed by the 'end of history' thesis. There is an understanding within international relations circles in the U.S. that the "reemergence of the great autocratic powers, along with the reactionary forces from Islamic radicalism, has weakened [the (neo-)liberal order] and threatens to weaken it further" (Kagan, 2008: 105). Neo-conservative strategists argue now that "the great fallacy of our era has been the belief that a liberal international order rests on the triumph of ideas and the natural unfolding of human progress. . . . What reason was there to believe that after 1989 humankind was suddenly on the cusp of a brand new order?" (Kagan, 2008: 102–104). Such reworking of the market-ing orientation design helps explain the 'market-oriented' invasion of emerging economies from a perspective of neocolonialism or neo-imperialism.

On emerging economies

After the events of 9/11, strategists of global corporations, large consultancy firms and management institutions raised the argument that a major challenge for business organizations in emerging economies is that their markets are still mired in problems/constraints that have long been mobilized by Western institutions to differentiate and hierarchize the West and the rest, civilization and barbarism, developed and underdeveloped, North and South. The marketing strategies of large Western corporations focusing on high-income consumers were taken by corporate strategists and strategic management researchers as the main target. They first asserted that products and strategies of large corporations aimed at the middle class in their home countries are not suitable for the huge base of low-income consumers in emerging economies, i.e. the so-called bottom of the economic pyramid (Brugmann & Prahalad, 2007).

This rather surprising concern with the mismatch between 'universal' knowledge from the Euro-American world and the institutional particularities of emerging economies in an era of convergence was led by strategic management authors and corresponding institutions. The marketing discipline responded promptly by admitting that large corporations bring to these markets not only their products, technologies and skills but also, implicitly, "the understanding of market structures from the context of developed countries" (Dawar & Chattopadhyay, 2002: 460). Both strategic management and marketing researchers kept untouched and invisible the market-ing orientation design and its dark geopolitical side.

Subsequently, strategic management authors and institutions asserted that strategic management concepts in general and 'global strategy' in particular were not working properly in emerging economies because of *institutional failures* in these contexts (Hoskisson, Eden, Lau & Wright, 2000; Khanna, Palepu & Sinha, 2005; Wright et al., 2005). They claimed that the "pre-capitalist" characteristics of emerging economies – in particular poverty, technological backwardness and corruption – largely explain the huge base of low-income consumers in those countries, and that these causes can and should be eliminated by the reinforcement and reworking of market-oriented institutions and corporate strategies. Influential scholars and institutions pointed out that although the concept of market orientation explains the performance of companies in emerging economies, researchers should recognize national specificities in "the world out there" in order to make the concept more effective (Despandhé & Farley, 2004; Liu, Luo & Shi, 2003). In order to rework market orientation, they also suggested that longitudinal research could provide a comprehensive understanding of how the concept actually works in those business organizations with superior performance in emerging economies (Kirca, Jayachandran & Bearden, 2005; Noble, Sinha & Kumar, 2002).

Strategic management researchers pointed out that, especially because of corruption, it is "impossible to do well in emerging economies without an understanding of how formal and informal institutions affect their firms and consumers" (Wright et al., 2005: 6). These researchers, however, have ignored and kept invisible the vast literature that points out that large corporations and market-oriented institutions explain a great deal of the problems observed not only in developing countries but also in developed economies (e.g. Block & Evans, 2005; Block, 2011). They also keep invisible the argument that corruption has achieved a *legal status* in the U.S. (Mahbubani, 2009) and that the neoliberal call to defend or impose the market-ing orientation design on others from a perspective of soft power and through the mobilization of neo-liberal imperial mechanisms has been a key issue in the U.S. foreign policy (Thomas, 2007). Corruption has been framed in the U.S. as a major feature of authoritative governments in emerging economies (especially China and Russia), which is supposedly encouraged by national institutions controlled by local elites. A major concern in the post-9/11 West is that the institutionalization of corruption in emerging economies could lead to the spread of global terrorism and disorder. This helps explain why authors and institutions in the U.S. claimed that the concept of market orientation had to be reviewed in order to become effective in emerging economies by transforming it into "emerging market-oriented strategies" (Dawar & Chattopadhyay, 2002: 472).

From the internal standpoint of the discipline, such a 'strategic' neocolonial approach on emerging economies was taken as necessary to build legitimacy of marketing within large corporations and management academic institutions. This invasion of emerging economies from a neocolonial perspective has been ignored by Anglo-American critique not only in the field of marketing but also in management studies. It is arguable that the virtual absence of dialogue between critical marketing and Critical Management Studies in the Anglo-American world is explained by the low status of marketing. An international critical perspective on management studies enunciated in an emerging economy in Latin America and through a perspective of pluriversality is necessary to challenge the pseudo-universality of Euro-American critique. Contemporary Euro-American literature points out that the hegemonic position of the U.S. in the field of management can largely be accounted for by political and ideological issues (Chiapello & Fairclough, 2002; Locke, 1996; Tadajewski, 2006). The neutrality of U.S. academia has been questioned by a growing number of researchers associated with Critical Management Studies (Clegg & Palmer, 1996; Cooke 2004; Frank, 2002; Mills & Hatfield, 1999; Prasad, 2003). However, Critical Management

Studies in general and critical marketing in particular have failed to address the dark side of geopolitics and recognize the pressing importance of creating conditions for the construction and legitimation of criticalities in management and marketing studies from the perspective of emerging economies.

Critical researchers in Brazil should not complain about this state of things. They/(we) should not wait for their/(our) colleagues from the Anglo-American world to address the dark side of the market-ing orientation design and recognize this invasion of emerging economies from a perspective of neocolonialism. Instead critical researchers in Brazil might take this as an opportunity and assume some further responsibility and propose the co-construction of an international critical perspective in marketing (and management studies) from a perspective of *pluriversality*. Emerging *economies* should be framed by us as 'emerging *powers*', as pointed out by some authors from the field of international relations. The main characteristic of emerging powers, from a theoretical perspective in international relations focused on transformation rather than on maintenance of the status quo (see Cox, 1981), is their capacity to challenge to some extent the hierarchy of the world system. From such a perspective, emerging economies can challenge the dominant position of the U.S. in the contemporary international context and also promote the revision of positions of countries which have been classified as developing countries. To quote MacFarlane (2002):

> Emerging powers are specific because their identity is dynamic; their position changes as their power grows and, at the same time, their capacity to shape results. They have some potential for systemic revisionism – a challenge for the hierarchy in the system in which they exist.
>
> *(p. 42)*

From a Brazilian standpoint, the extreme notion of revisionism attributed by some to emerging economies should be replaced by a perspective of pluriversality. From such a perspective, the international system should be challenged but not through the replacement of one 'universalism' by another 'universalism'. We should not reinforce Eurocentric universalism by presenting such international critical perspective (from an emerging economy located in Latin America) as a threat being mobilized by irresponsible 'barbarians' from the rest of the world. Rather, we are talking about a co-constructed international perspective which opens up possibilities for the co-construction of a world in which many worlds and critical knowledges can coexist.

While engaging with the dark side of geopolitics, we should be aware that institutional builders of the market-ing orientation design, such as the World Economic Forum and the Institute for International Economics, have claimed that emerging economies should not behave as 'free-riders'. The main idea here is that in an increasingly interdependent world the policies and strategies of emerging economies impact not only their own economies and those of neighboring countries but also the global economy (Boyer & Truman, 2005). From such a neocolonial or neoconservative perspective, emerging economies should behave as allies, not as U.S. competitors or opponents. This helps to explain why gurus in the field of marketing and strategic management claimed just after the events of 9/11 that large emerging economies are greatly important not only to the expansion of large corporations but also to ensure the security of the market; the reworking of market-oriented strategies and institutions are needed to eliminate not only corruption in emerging economies but also the threat of global terrorism (Prahalad & Hart, 2002).

An international critical perspective from Brazil should foster the engagement of colleagues from the Anglo-American world. Otherwise, as suggested by the notion of geopolitics of knowledge, such a critical perspective – even if it is enunciated in Brazil instead of China, India or

Russia – will inevitably be framed and classified by the market-ing orientation design as 'anti-market', 'anti-marketing', 'anti-U.S.' or 'anti-West' and then be eliminated or used as a justification for the mobilization of further soft power mechanisms by a neo-liberal empire paranoid about "whether non-Western countries such as China and India will seek to use their rising power to usher in a substantially different sort of international order" (Ikenberry, 2009: 83). As the 'benefits' provided by the Western neo-liberal order have become more problematic even for the Euro-American world, and the Critical Management Studies community has showed an increasing concern with neocolonialism, it is more likely that such international critical perspective is becoming feasible.

Building the legitimacy of such initiative should be considered a priority, as the lone 'super-power' is not expected to share its responsibilities with 'others' without reluctance and perhaps a bit of resentment. Conservative and neoconservative voices in the U.S. share an understanding, which is backed by an unbeatable amount of hard power mechanisms and resources, that there is no alternative to the market-ing orientation design (the so-called liberal order). There will always be a mission for the lonely 'superpower' in the post–Cold War era as the rest of the world in general and emerging economies in particular are framed as not being capable of taking major world-making responsibilities. As Kagan (2008) declares:

> [W]hether American [sic] power and expansiveness will continue to be the most pressing problem in the years to come, or whether it is the most pressing problem even today, is increasingly debatable. In a world heading today toward a more perfect liberal order, an old-fashioned superpower with a sense of global mission might seem a relic of the past and an obstacle to progress. But in a world poised precariously at the edge of a new time of turmoil, might not even a flawed democratic superpower have an important, even indispensable, role to play?
>
> (p. 86)

Final considerations

I have argued in this chapter that market-ing orientation is a powerful Euro-American design which has been transformed into a global design mainly by Western neoliberal forces and mechanisms. This design has been overlooked and kept invisible by *both* mainstream and critical marketing studies literatures and to some extent also by Critical Management Studies. The market-ing orientation design also explains the successful trajectory of the concept of market orientation, as well as the recent focus of market orientation on emerging economies from a neocolonial or neo-imperial perspective. From the perspective of an emerging economy located in Latin America (Brazil in particular), it has been argued that critical researchers in different parts of the world should embrace the vast critical literature on the market-ing orientation design put forward by different fields of knowledge and embrace the co-construction and legitimation of an international critical perspective in marketing and management studies that goes beyond the Anglo-American contributions.

The chapter is undergirded by three key interrelated issues. First, the dispute between communism and capitalism has been replaced in the post–Cold War period by a neocolonial dispute, led by the U.S. and seconded by Europe, between types of Western capitalism and orders, at the expense of alternatives and voices from the rest of the world. Second, academic institutions in management, led by the U.S. and seconded by Europe, have played a central role in the construction and diffusion of the market-ing orientation culture from the West towards the rest of the world from a perspective of soft power. Third, big emerging economies have been portrayed by Euro-American institutions and authors as a threat, capable of not only challenging the U.S. hegemony but also of constructing and disseminating alternative capitalisms or alternatives to Western capitalism and order on a global scale.

Given their increasing concern with the rise of Russia, India and China, institutional builders of the market-ing orientation design have framed and classified Brazil as "neither a military nor an economic hegemony capable of coercing its neighbors" (Armijo & Burgess, 2010: 36). According to these circles, the so-called Brazilian style is portrayed as "non-confrontational and consistent . . . [with] the viewpoint of the unipole and . . . status quo great powers, [and] greater inclusion of Brazil . . . [is regarded as] a congenial option" (Armijo & Burges, 2010: 36–37). Correspondingly, an international critical perspective enunciated in Brazil represents an important opportunity for a legitimate transformation of the market-ing orientation design and our engagement with the dark geopolitical side through the co-construction of a pluriversal perspective. By going beyond the Euro-American contributions, such an international critical perspective in marketing and management studies is aimed at further enhancing the conditions of possibility for the co-construction of a world in which many worlds and knowledges could coexist. I hope this chapter has showed that the field of marketing has become too important to be overlooked or marginalized by other fields of knowledge, including Critical Management Studies. Among other important outcomes, rethinking market orientation through such a perspective is an important step towards challenging the neocolonial logic that developing countries in general and emerging economies in particular represent 'backwardness' and a 'threat'.

References

Achrol, R., & Kotler, P. (2000). Marketing in the network economy. *Journal of Marketing, 63*(4): 146–163.

Alvesson, M., & Willmott, H. (1996). *Making sense of management.* London: Sage.

Armijo, L., & Burges, S. (2010). Brazil, the entrepreneurial and democratic BRIC. *Polity, 42*(1): 14–37.

Arrighi, G. (2007). *Adam Smith in Beijing.* London: Verso.

Barksdale, H., Kelly, W., & MacFarlane, I. (1978). The marketing concept in the U.S. and the USSR: An historical analysis. *Academy of Marketing Science, 6*(4): 258–277.

Biggadike, R. (1981). The contributions of marketing to strategic management. *Academy of Management Review, 6*: 621–632.

Block, F. (2011). Breaking with market fundamentalism. In J. Shepner & P. Férnandez-Kelly (Eds.), *Globalization and beyond.* University Park, PA: Penn State University Press.

Block, F., & Evans, P. (2005). The state and the economy. In N. Smelser & R. Swedberg (Eds.), *The handbook of economic sociology.* Princeton, NJ: Princeton University Press.

Boyer, J., & Truman, E. (2005). The United States and the large emerging-market economies: Competitors or partners? In C. Bergsten (Ed.), *The United States and the world economy: foreign economic policy for the next decade.* Washington, DC: Institute for International Economics.

Brownlie, D., Saren, M., Wensley, R. & Whittington, R. (Eds.). (1999). *Rethinking marketing: Towards critical marketing accountings.* London: Sage.

Brugmann, J., & Prahalad, C. (2007). New social compact. *Harvard Business Review, 85*(2): 80–90.

Bruszt, L. (2002). Making markets and eastern enlargement: Diverging convergence? *West European Politics, 25*(2): 121–140.

Burgess, S., & Steenkamp, J. (2006). Marketing renaissance: How research in emerging markets advances marketing science and practice. *International Journal of Research in Marketing, 23*(4): 337–356.

Burton, D. (2005). Marketing theory matters. *British Journal of Management, 16*: 5–18.

Câmara Neto, A., & Vernengo, M. (2002). Globalization, a dangerous obsession: Latin America in the post-Washington Consensus era. *International Journal of Political Economy, 32*(4): 4–21.

Campbell, J., & Pedersen, O. (2007). The varieties of capitalism and hybrid success: Denmark in the global economy. *Comparative Political Studies, 40*: 307–332.

Chang, H.-J. (2002). Rompendo o modelo: Uma economia política institucionalista alternativa à teoria neoliberal do mercado e do Estado. In G. Arbix, A. Comin, M. Zilbovicius & R. Abramovay (Org.). *Brasil, México, África do Sul, Índia e China: diálogo entre os que chegaram depois.* São Paulo: Unesp.

Chiapello, E., & Fairclough, N. (2002). Understanding the new managerial ideology: A transdisciplinary contribution from critical discourse analysis and new sociology of capitalism. *Discourse & Society, 13*(2): 185–208.

Clegg, S., & Carter, C. (2007). The sociology of global organizations. In G. Ritzer (Ed.), *The Blackwell companion to globalization*: Ch. 13, 272–290. Oxford: Blackwell.

Clegg, S., & Palmer, G. (1996). Introduction: Producing management knowledge, In S. Clegg & G. Palmer (Eds.). *The politics of management knowledge*. London: Sage.

Cooke, B. (2004). O gerenciamento do (Terceiro) Mundo. *Revista de Administração de Empresas, 44*(3): 62–75.

Cooke, B., & Dar, S. (2008). Introduction: The new development management.

Cooke, B., & Faria, A. (2013). Development, management and North Atlantic imperialism: For Eduardo Ibarra Colado. *Cadernos EBAPE. BR, 11*(2): I–XV.

Cox, M. (2008). From the Cold War to the War on Terror. In J. Baylis, S. Smith & P. Owens (Eds.), *The globalization of world politics* (4th Ed.): 66–82. Oxford: Oxford University.

Cox, R. (1981). Social forces, states and world orders: Beyond international relations theory. *Millennium – Journal of International Studies, 10*:126–155.

Dawar, N., & Chattopadhyay, A. (2002). Rethinking marketing programs for emerging markets. *Long Range Planning, 35*: 57–474.

De Paula, G., Ferraz, J., & Iooty, M. (2002). Economic liberalization and changes in corporate control in Latin America. *Developing Economies, 4*(2): 467–496.

Despandhé, R., & Farley, J. (2004). Organizational culture, market orientation, innovativeness, and firm performance: An international research odyssey. *International Journal of Research in Marketing, 22*(1): 3–22.

Faria, A. (2013). Border thinking in action: Should critical management studies get anything done? *Dialogues in Critical Management Studies, 2*: 277–300.

Faria, A., & Wensley, R. (2011). Rethinking authority and legitimacy in strategy: A perspective from an emerging economy. *Canadian Journal of Administrative Sciences/Revue Canadienne des Sciences de l'Administration, 28*(2): 188–201.

Faria, A., Ibarra-Colado, E., & Guedes, A. (2010). Internationalization of management, neoliberalism and the Latin America challenge. *Critical perspectives on international business, 6*(2/3): 97–115.

Felix, R., & Hinck, W. (2005). Executive insights: Market orientation of Mexican companies. *Journal of International Marketing, 13*(1): 111–127.

Fukuyama, F. (1989). The end of history. *The National Interest, 16:* 3–18.

George, S. (1997). How to win the war of ideas. *Dissent,* Summer: 47–53.

Glosny, M. (2010). China and the BRICs: A real (but limited) partnership in a unipolar world. *Polity, 42*(1): 100–129.

Goldgeier, J., & McFaul, M. (1992). A tale of two worlds: Core and periphery in the post–Cold War era. *International Organization, 46*(2): 467–491.

Harvey, D. (2003). *The new imperialism.* Oxford: Oxford University.

Harvey, D. (2007). *A brief history of neoliberalism.* Oxford: Oxford University.

Henderson, S. (1998). No such thing as market orientation: A call for no more papers. *Management Decision, 36*(9): 598–609.

Hill, F. (2006). Moscow discovers soft power. *Current History, 105*(693): 341–347.

Hooley, G. (2003). Market orientation of the service sector of the transition economies of Central Europe. *European Journal of Marketing, 37*(1/2): 86–106.

Hooley, G., Cox, T., Fahy, J., Shipley, D., Berac, J., Fonfara, K., & Snoj, B. (2000). Market orientation in the transition economies of Central Europe: Tests of the Narver and Slater market orientation scales. *Journal of Business Research, 50*: 273–285.

Hoskisson, R., Eden, L., Lau, C. M., & Wright, M. (2000). Strategy in emerging economies. *Academy of Management Journal, 43*(3): 249–267.

Huntington, S. (1993). Why international primacy matters. *International Security, 17*(4), 68–83.

Huntington, S. (1996). *The clash of civilizations and the remaking of world order.* New York: Simon & Schuster.

Ibarra-Colado, E. (2006). Organization studies and epistemic coloniality in Latin America: Thinking otherness from the margins. *Organization, 13*(4): 489–508.

Ibarra-Colado, E. (2008). Is there any future for critical management studies in Latin America? Moving from epistemic coloniality to trans-discipline. *Organization, 15*(6): 932–935.

Ikenberry G. (2009). Liberal internationalism 3.0: America and the dilemmas of liberal world order. *Perspectives on Politics, 7*(1): 71–87.

Jack, G., & Westwood, R. (2009). *International and cross-cultural management studies: A post colonial reading.* London: Palgrave Macmillan.

Jaworski, B., & Kohli, A. (1993). Market orientation: antecedents and consequences. *Journal of Marketing*, 57(3): 53–70.

Jervis, R. (2003). The compulsive empire. *Foreign Policy, 137* (July–August): 83–87.

Kagan, R. (2009). *The return of history and the end of dreams.* New York: Vintage Books.

Khanna, T., Palepu, K., & Sinha, J. (2005). Strategies that fit emerging markets. *Harvard Business Review, 83*(2): 63–76.

Kirca, A., Jayachandran, S., & Bearden, W. (2005). Market orientation: A meta-analytic review and assessment of its antecedents and impact on performance. *Journal of Marketing, 69*(2): 24–41.

Knights, D., & Morgan, G. (1991). Corporate strategy, organizations, and subjectivity: A critique. *Organization Studies, 12*(2): 251–273.

Kohli, A., & Jaworski, B. (1990). Market orientation: The construct, research propositions and managerial implications. *Journal of Marketing, 54*(2): 1–18.

Kotler, P. (2005). The role played by the broadening of marketing movement in the history of marketing thought. *Journal of Public Policy & Marketing, 24*(1): 114–116.

Kotler, P., & Levy, S. (1969). Broadening the concept of marketing. *Journal of Marketing, 33*: 10–15.

Langerak, F. (2003). An appraisal of the predictive power of market orientation. *European Management Journal, 21*(4): 447–464.

Liu, S., Luo, X., & Shi, Y. (2003). Market-oriented organizations in an emerging economy: A study of missing links. *Journal of Business Research, 6*: 481–491.

Locke, R. (1996). *The collapse of the American management mystique.* Oxford: Oxford University Press.

MacFarlane, S. (2006). The 'R' in BRICs: Is Russia an emerging power? *International Affairs, 82*(1): 41–57.

Mahbubani, K. (2009). Can America Fail? *The Wilson Quarterly (1976), 33*(2): 48–54.

McGrew, A. (2008). Globalization and global politics. In J. Baylis, S. Smith & P. Owens (Eds.), *The globalization of world politics* (4th E): 14–32. Oxford: Oxford University.

Mignolo, W. (2000). *Local histories/global designs.* Princeton, NJ: Princeton University Press.

Mignolo, W. (2011). *The darker side of western modernity: Global futures, decolonial options.* Durham, NC: Duke University Press.

Mills, A., & Hatfield, J. (1999). From imperialism to globalization: Internationalization and the management text. In S. Clegg, E. Ibarra-Colado & L. Bueno-Rodriguez (Ed.), *Global management: Universal theories and local realities.* London: Sage.

Mills, A., & Mills, J. (2013). CMS: A satirical critique of three narrative histories. *Organization, 20*(1): 117–129.

Mintzberg, H., Ahlstrand, B., & Lampel, J. (1992). *Sáfari de Estratégia.* Porto Alegre: Bookman.

Morgan, G. (1992). Marketing discourse and practice: Towards a critical analysis. In M. Alvesson & H. Willmott (Eds.), *Critical management studies.* London: Sage.

Morgan, G., Whitley, R., & Moen, E. (Eds.). (2004). *Changing capitalisms?* Oxford: Oxford University Press.

Murphy, J., & Zhu, J. (2012). Neo-colonialism in the academy? Anglo-American domination in management journals. *Organization, 19*(6): 915–927.

Nye, J., Jr. (1990). Soft power. *Foreign Policy*, 80: 153–171.

Oliveira, F. (Org.). (1998). *Globalização, regionalização e nacionalismo.* São Paulo: Unesp.

Paulani, L. (2005). *Modernidade e discurso econômico.* São Paulo: Boitempo Editorial.

Pettigrew, A. M. (1987). Context and action in the transformation of the firm. *Journal of Management Studies, 24*(6): 649–670.

Pettigrew, A., Thomas, H., & Whittington, R. (Eds.). (2002). *Handbook of strategy and management.* London: Sage.

Philo, G., & Miller, D. (2001). *Market killing: What the free market does and what social scientists can do about it.* Essex, UK: Pearson Education.

Pieterse, J. (2004). *Globalization or empire?* New York: Routledge.

Pieterse, J. (2008). Globalization, the next round: Sociological perspectives. *Futures, 40*: 707–720.

Prahalad, C., & Hart, S. (2002). The fortune at the bottom of the pyramid. *Strategy and Business, 26*: 2–14.

Prasad, A. (2003). *Postcolonial theory and organizational analysis: A critical engagement.* London: Palgrave Macmillan.

Putin, V. (2005) Annual address to the Federal Assembly of the Russian Federation, Retrieved on December 10, 2009, from http://www.kremlin.ru/eng/speeches/2005/04/25/2031_type70029type82912_87086.shtml

Santos, M. (1993). *Fim de século e globalização*. São Paulo: HUCITEC.

Saren, M. (2006). *Marketing graffiti: The view from the street*. London: Elsevier.

Saren, M., Maclaran, P., Goulding, C., Elliott, R., Shankar, A., & Catterall, M. (Eds). (2007). *Critical marketing: Defining the field*. London: Elsevier.

Slater, S., & Narver, J. (1990). The effects of a market orientation on business profitability. *Journal of Marketing*, 54(4): 20–35.

Slater, S., & Narver, J. (1998). Customer-led and market-driven: Let's not confuse the two. *Strategic Management Journal, 19*(10): 1001–1006.

Slater, S., & Narver, J. (1999). Market-oriented is more than being customer-led. *Strategic Management Journal, 20*(12): 1165–1168.

Sola, L. (Org.). (1993). *Estado, mercado e democracia. Política e economia comparadas*. São Paulo: Paz e Terra.

Steger, M. (2009). *Globalisms*. Lanham, MD: Rowman & Littlefield.

Stiglitz, J. (2003). *The Roaring Nineties. A new history of the world's most prosperous decade*. New York: Norton.

Stiglitz, J. (2008). The fall of Wall Street. *New Perspectives Quarterly, 25*(4): 46–49.

Tadajewski, M. (2006). The ordering of marketing theory: The influence of McCarthyism and the Cold War. *Marketing Theory, 6*(2): 163–199.

Tadajewski, M. (2010). Towards a history of critical marketing studies. *Journal of Marketing Management, 26*(9–10): 773–824.

Thomas, N. (2007). Global capitalism, the anti-globalisation movement and the Third World. *Capital & Class*, 92: 45–78.

Thrift, N. (2005). *Knowing capitalism*. London: Sage.

Trenin, D. (2006). Russia leaves the West. *Foreign Affairs, 87*: 85–93.

Van Ness, P. (2002). Hegemony, not anarchy: Why China and Japan are not balancing US unipolar power. *International Relations of the Asia-Pacific*, 2: 131–150.

Wensley, R. (1995). A critical review of research in marketing. *British Journal of Management, 6*: s36–s82.

Whittington, R. (2001). *O que é estratégia*. São Paulo: Pioneira.

Whittington, R., & Whipp, R. (1992). Professional ideology and marketing implementation. *European Journal of Marketing, 26*(1): 52–63.

Williams, C. (2006). Beyond marketization: Rethinking economic development trajectories in Central and Eastern Europe. *Journal of Contemporary European Studies, 14*(2): 241–254.

Wright, M., et al. (2005). Strategy research in emerging economies: Changing the conventional wisdom. *Journal of Management Studies, 42*(1): 1–33.

13

Social movements and organizations through a Critical Management Studies lens

Metaphor, mechanism, mobilization or more?

Maureen Scully

Introduction

This chapter examines social change efforts undertaken within corporations toward changing the corporation. These efforts are distinct from anticorporate activism or activism toward increased state regulation of corporations. Employee activists, particularly in North America where corporations play a dominant role in how regulation is implemented, leverage insider corporate knowledge to propel change. Social movement theories and organization theories have been brought together to shine a light on this phenomenon, which often renders the social movement aspect as a metaphor, mechanism or mobilization. Through a critical lens, I ask, "Are social movements in organizational settings meant to be 'more'?" Criteria for assessing whether a change effort is properly understood as a social movement could include critical explication of status quo problems that invite change, conflict, resistance of the powerful to change, redistribution, risk and envisioned alternatives. These criteria preserve the meaningfulness of "social movement." Globally conceived Critical Management Studies (CMS) sees also the limitations of incrementalism and the need for alliances within, across and outside corporations.

CMS scholars have many reasons to be interested in research on the phenomenon of social movements. CMS research often documents problems that would warrant or trigger social movement activism. By critically uncovering patterns in the status quo that systematically serve more powerful stakeholders, CMS scholars set the stage for when and why dissent is warranted; they often theorize how dissent is thwarted. These studies join a long tradition of revealing the "false promises" (Aronowitz, 1992) behind dominant discourses about democracy, meritocracy and markets. In the face of strong dominant ideologies proclaiming that the status quo is working well or at least in the best equilibrium attainable, CMS scholars take up the challenge of exposing what is not working. Instead of democracy, there is social exclusion; instead of meritocracy, there are biases that produce inequalities; and instead of effective free markets, there are captured markets that cluster capital with elites. Some CMS scholarship stops at the point of critique, but much work continues with the imperative to locate the forces that might halt the reproduction of the status quo and even generate fundamental changes. Thus, the study of social movements is relevant and even urgent. At the same time, organizational scholars who are rapidly adopting the social movement toolkit in management studies are tying it not necessarily to deep structural critiques or prospects for radical change but sometimes to a host of superficial change efforts. This essay takes up the project of bringing CMS principles into the lively and ongoing intersection of organization studies and social movement studies.

I argue that the particular way in which social movements theories have been brought into contact with organization theories has resulted in slippage away from a focus on radical resistance. Instead, nearly any organizational change effort becomes eligible for treatment as more or less of a "social movement." It is in the purview of CMS scholarship – that is, CMS scholarship revitalized and reenvisioned – to ensure that "social movement" remains deployed as a meaningful term, addressing the domains where conflict, power, resistance and discontinuous change are engaged. It will take larger-scaled change efforts to match the growing severity of the critiques that CMS scholars are offering.

In addressing social movements in this essay, a blurry line quickly emerges. Is the focus on the scholarship of social movements or on social movements per se? This essay retains what I think is some useful slipperiness along this borderline, where social movement scholarship and social movement activism touch one another. I argue that it matters what researchers choose to name as a social movement. We lose some of the force of both social movements as a concept and social movements as a form of meaningful social action when we classify too many kinds of change efforts under the category of social movement.

Researchers cocreate with activists a sense of what is possible when they study and write about social movements. In assessing social movements, we are called "to rethink the categories of success and failure as they relate to social movements and to social movement research" (Haiven & Khasnabish, 2014: 21). The writings of the "revolutionary intelligentsia" have historically operated at this boundary of scholarly exploration and concerned activism. Vaclav Havel – a philosopher, an activist mobilized by the Prague Spring social movement of 1968 and president of Czechoslovakia 1989–1991 – operated on this boundary: "[t]he intellectual should constantly disturb, should bear witness to the misery of the world, should be provocative by being independent, should rebel against all hidden and open pressure and manipulations . . ." (1991: 167). Social movement scholars can retain rigor and a measured tone while contributing to the toolkit of social activists, naming what is wrong that propels dissent and systematically identifying patterns of successful and unsuccessful social movement attempts. Moreover, scholars have the opportunity – and the imperative – to expand "the radical imagination" (Haiven & Khasnabish, 2014). Where I offer, in this chapter, a set of principles for what we should mean when we say "social movement," I am referring to the criteria that researchers should use when they locate, name and explain social movements. But occasionally I may veer over that necessarily blurry borderline, and I will sound as though I am trying to define what a fundamental social change effort should look like and seek to accomplish.

Setting a high bar for meaningful social change is challenging in this essay because I am looking at social movements as they are attempted via and within corporations. There is a necessary "tempering" (Meyerson & Scully, 1995) of social activism inside corporate walls. In my research, I have defended the local, tempered, finely gauged actions of insider social activists, noting where they are well suited to move the needle of change. At the same time, I have queried, perhaps in the spirit of "self subversion" (Hirschman, 1995), whether insider activism yields little more than distractions, small wins that remain small, or occasions to vent – all of which buffer elites and the status quo from more profound change. I do not think there is an answer to this question about whether modest change efforts are impactful or trivial. I think it is the question that is important.

The question prompts ongoing reflection, reappraisal and ultimately concern for meaningful change that remedies serious problems.

Now duly situated, this essay has three parts. First, I open by locating my domain of interest. I am looking at change efforts undertaken within corporations or workplaces. I distinguish these within-corporate efforts from the literature's increasing attention to "anticorporate" activism, which has grown since the 1990s both as a global phenomenon and as an area of study. The tools and concepts of social movements have been applied and advanced through the study of anti-corporate dissent, and indeed anticorporate dissent looks like what we would expect in evoking social movement with a critical edge. In contrast, the social movement arsenal of concepts has been borrowed into the domain of within-corporate change efforts with vigor, but also, rather curiously, with a bit of arms-length engagement where social movement remains more about analogy than activism.

Thus, the second part of this essay examines three ways in which the study of social movements has been taken up in management and organization scholarship: as a *metaphor* for organizational forms and processes, as a set of shared *mechanisms* across organizational and sociological studies of social action and with a focus on the processes of *mobilization* (sometimes more than the outcomes). Metaphors help us see phenomena in a fresh way (Morgan, 1980). Identifying fundamental mechanisms brings rigor to scholarship (Davis, 2006). Looking at the problem of mobilization connects to enduring puzzles about collective action in settings where complacency may be more rational (e.g., Olson, 1971). These formalisms in the uptake of social movement theory – metaphor, mechanism and mobilization – have created detours from studying the radical resistance that used to be at the heart of how we thought about social movements. It seems appropriate for CMS scholars to hold organization theory to account in using "social movement" in its radical sense.

Third, and toward this end, I lay out principles that should guide CMS researchers in identifying and even anointing change efforts as social movements. The principles are meant to reanimate a vigorous and aspirational view of social movements, both for scholars and for activists. The seven principles focus on (1) naming what is problematic in the status quo that might propel change, (2) surfacing conflicts and power dynamics, (3) locating visible and hidden blocking moves by elites and "institutional defenders" (Levy & Scully, 2007), (4) acknowledging the asymmetries of mobilization (center/margin, left/right), (5) highlighting serious risks – to body, livelihood, community, (6) envisioning alternatives, and (7) using some criteria for determining whether meaningful change has been accomplished.

In the closing section, I critically appraise some of my own research in the within-corporate domain, using these principles. I raise the question of whether the rise of scholarship on anticorporate activism has shown within-corporate efforts to be trivially incremental – or simply subject to different rules of engagement that need some renewed appraisal. I examine the potential for alliances across forms of activism – within, across and outside corporations.

Within-corporate and anticorporate activism

Activism that was aimed at changing corporations used to be achieved through actions aimed at the state, with the desire of making regulatory and legal changes that would then be applied to corporations. For example, to change organizational practices regarding discrimination on the basis of race and gender, activists in the U.S. lobbied for civil rights legislation. The creation of the EEOC (Equal Employment Opportunity Commission) located the need for change inside organizations and held organizations accountable through the courts. Researchers began to examine whether organizations' internal procedures for handling discrimination extended the spirit of civil rights legislation or "depoliticized" it into a set of local managerial dilemmas (Edelman, Erlanger & Lande, 1993).

The interest in within-corporate change efforts followed. Through a series of events and studies in the 1990s to the early 2000s, "the framework of social movements within organizations was an idea whose time seemed to have arrived" (Walker, 2012). For regulations to have an impact, it was important to look inside the organizational settings where they would be enacted, contested, negotiated and refined. Environmental regulations about pollution require new organizational routines and cultural embedding of new practices (Howard-Grenville, 2009). Regulatory protections for vulnerable groups, such as patients in hospitals with possibly overworked doctors, require new organizational practices regarding work flow and hours (Kellogg, 2011). The first generation of issues regarding workplace discrimination could be adjudicated in the courts, but remedies for "second generation" discrimination require looking inside organizations for embedded oversight of the opportunity structure (Sturm, 2001). Civil rights activists turned their lens on corporations and workplaces. Emerging civil rights quests, such as the Employment Non-Discrimination Act (ENDA) to protect GLBT (gay, lesbian, bisexual and transgendered) employees, linked societal and organizational change efforts from their inception (Armstrong, 2002; Creed, Scully & Austin, 2002).

Within-corporate settings appeared to be a promising place for change to occur. The workplace solved some problems of "resource mobilization" (McCarthy & Zald, 1977) because employees had ready access to email lists, conference rooms, photocopying codes and conference budgets. The foundational social movement problem of simply getting people to show up, for example in the school gym at night for some tenants' rights activism (Alinsky, 1971), was solved by the fact that employees were in the same place all day, all week. Social movement tactics could become quite strategic and well refined, as employees working in "micro-mobilization" (McAdam, 1988) settings had ready access to local levers for change. They could word just the right compelling framing of an issue and mobilize allies in nonthreatening ways through everyday encounters (Creed & Scully, 2000). They could read the political landscape and determine which elites might join cause with them and which would be blockers around whom they would have to maneuver (Kellogg, 2011). In their daily work routines, they could make technological trends like lean production in automobile assembly become a moment for making production more "green" (Rothenberg, Pil & Maxwell, 2001). Radical reform "the quiet way" (Meyerson, 2001) seemed not tame but clever.

The old problem that big societal promises tended to remain only loosely coupled to everyday organizational realities was reconsidered. Perhaps school reforms could move meaningfully into the classroom (Hallett, 2010). What might be platitudes about "diversity" could become the "umbrella" of protection that allowed insider activists to hold executives accountable, yielding unexpected changes like including secretaries in the bonus pool for high-technology teams (Scully & Segal, 2002). A rather hopeful tenor imbued studies of within-corporate change in this period. "Small wins" did not seem small or co-optive but rather like the cumulative means toward bigger ends that they were meant to be (Weick, 1984).

Much of this research on within-corporate activism focused on the U.S. It was more of a footnote to consider how corporate responses to regulatory changes in the U.S. might spread globally, as multinational corporations standardized their production processes and human resource management practices. In some cases, a more global lens exposed U.S.-centric shortcomings. For example, social movements met organization studies in tracking the diffusion of domestic partner benefits (DPBs) (Briscoe & Safford, 2008); DPBs extended employer health care benefits to partners of GLBT employees. However, GLBT employees in most nations need not worry about their employer's adoption of domestic partner benefits (DPBs) because health care is regarded as a right, not a commodity or employment benefit. Studies of DPB adoption are moot from a global vantage point, which globally oriented CMS scholars, digging for the root logics of issues like health care, would point out.

Cross-national comparative studies remained in the domain of social movement researchers per se, who sought broad patterns across time and place in the "dynamics of contention" (McAdam, Tarrow & Tilly, 2003). From these studies, ideas could be borrowed to understand within-corporate activism. For example, comparing the strategies of antinuclear activists in the 1970s and 1980s in France, Germany, the U.S. and Sweden allowed Campbell (2005) to offer a compelling elucidation of pivotal mechanisms of "political opportunity," extending them to become part of the available repertoire for organizational scholars. In France, activists encountered a state that was "closed, insulated, and centralized" (Campbell, 2005: 45) and thereby resorted to mass demonstrations and civil disobedience. In West Germany, the federalist and more decentralized state structures permitted the creation of a Green Party that accessed the courts to halt nuclear plant construction. In Sweden, policy-making gained legitimacy from public discussions, such that activists were able to push for a national referendum that resulted in phasing out commercial nuclear plans by 2010. In the United States, the two-party system, long a bulwark against third parties and structural change (Sombart, 1976), deflected social change. Antinuclear activism emerged instead through professional associations such as the Union of Concerned Scientists. The notion of "political opportunity structures" was imported from state to organizational settings (Campbell, 2005). A cross-national perspective enabled these insights. However, notwithstanding nods to the revolutions in Russia and China, these studies remained largely European focused until the 1990s.

In the 1990s, a more truly transnational lens on anticorporate activism disrupted and reawakened the study of activism, particularly at the boundary of sociology and organization studies. The "new social movements" (Laraña, Johnston & Gusfield, 1994) that had focused on identity and less on interests were updated to "even newer social movements" (Crossley, 2003). Anticorporatism "has been marked, at its most visible tip, by a series of high-profile protests directed against the new managerial elites of global capitalism: The World Trade Organization (WTO), the World Bank, the International Monetary Fund (IMF) and the parties to the Free Trade Agreement of the Americas (FTAA)" (Crossley, 2003: 287). Protests and scholarship, especially from the "global South," reradicalized both the analysis of grievances against corporations (e.g., Tauss, 2012) and the practices of radical social movement activism. From this kind of activism, there does not seem to be a clear, or even dotted, line into and through corporations and workplaces. The movement is against corporatism itself, and the issues are not just about workplace or production conditions but about community, life chances, and even food (Shurman & Munro, 2010).

Global financial crises and the rise of anticorporate activism require some serious reconsideration of within-corporate activism – its premises and its promises. The organic rise of the Zapatistas in Mexico in 1994 changed the nature and object of activism. Rather than remedying social problems such as discrimination and pollution via corporations, the corporation itself became the object of contestation. Instead of lobbying states to produce regulations that would rein in corporations, the whole premise of corporate power and its rapid and alarming consolidation came under fire. Even the nature of what the state is, as a player in the politics of global contestation, requires critical rethinking (Jammulamadaka, 2014: 1), from an arm's-length regulatory body to a notion of "the State as being made through ongoing public claim making by the citizens," where the state itself arises from "the specific histories and dynamics of nation making and the continuing colonial encounters and decolonization."

Metaphor, mechanism and mobilization

Invoking social movements in the study of organizations seems like a move that retains and advances some of these critical sensibilities, because "social movement" is such an evocative term. But what indeed does it evoke? It has historically meant examining conflicts of interests, dissent, pressure for change and reinvention of social systems. It invokes images of radical protests. Radical protests are not typically connected with mainstream organizational studies, where ideas about innovation and change remain tied to quests for productivity and competitiveness. The challenge, then, is to understand if potentially radical change can occur via organizations and whether the social movements lens sharpens what we see. Does this lens help us see if the resulting changes are shallow or profound? I argue that social movement concepts have been taken up largely in the categories of metaphor, mechanism and mobilization – and that the field needs "more."

Metaphor

Change processes in organizations can be better understood by looking at their analogues in the societal sphere, an insight by Zald and Berger (1978) that took some time to percolate into organization studies. They proposed that ousting top executives looks like a coup d'etat. Strategic rule breaking in the middle levels might be thought of as bureaucratic insurgency. Patterns of association on the shop floor that lead to dissent can be understood similarly as mass movements (Zald & Berger, 1978). The idea of overthrowing the CEO has gained new attention in corporate governance studies focused on boards' vigorous oversight, at the intersection of organizations and finance but not through a social movement lens (e.g., Ertugrul & Krishnan, 2011). The idea of bureaucratic insurgency, or "moves from the middle," has gained traction in organization studies, particularly through a rich vein of work on "issue selling" (e.g., Dutton, Ashford, O'Neill & Lawrence, 2001), which probes incremental, internal change and tactics such as bundling and timing. These studies are not anchored in social movement theories and are not designed to examine changes that might extend social movement issues and aims.

The "mass movements" metaphor is intriguing but has flourished in an entirely different strand of the literature. The idea of mass movements in and through organizations had its zenith in the 1970s, when labor process theory linked societal level concerns about workers' rights and unionization to shop floor activism at the point of production. The "associational density" in the workplace (Zald & Berger, 1978) was noted also by Edwards (1979) as a crucible for grievances and a locus for planned activism. But this vein of studies did not find its way into the "Venn diagram" linking organizations and social movements, even though it offers a direct treatment of radical social change via organizations. New social movement (NSM) studies steered away from the working class and the managerial elites as the main fault line of conflict, but Crossley (2003: 303) argues that these "older fracture lines" have not gone away but are simply joined and rejoined by new fracture lines.

A set of social movement metaphors encouraged researchers in organization studies to take a fresh look at the activism that might be roiling just under the surface in organization settings. While such activism may not involve marching around the building with placards, it could be seen as something bold, perhaps indeed like insurgency or a mass movement. This metaphor lent a kind of dignity and urgency to the efforts of organizational insiders to make changes that addressed urgent social problems, particularly ones where corporations are implicated. One workplace activist explained that, while her parents marched in the Civil Rights movement in the 1970s, her job was to expand civil rights inside the Fortune 500 in the 1990s (Scully & Segal, 2002).

Metaphors, however, are useful not only for what they illuminate but for where they break down and fail to translate across boundaries (Morgan, 1980, 1983). For example, social movements often seek to spread, to maximize their impact and to gain strength in numbers. Soon cases of diffusion of many types of programs were being likened to social movements, by dint of the common fact of diffusing. For example, the diffusion of total quality management (TQM) looks like a social movement in that it has passionate adherents who build allies to provoke discontinuous change. In posing this analogy, Hackman and Wageman (1995) were careful to show that the spread of TQM was *like* a social movement, not exactly a social movement per se.

This earlier carefulness in not slipping from the metaphor *of* social movements to characterization *as* social movements waned in the literature. Diffusion – itself a metaphor from chemistry and epidemiology – is not enough on its own to liken studies of organizational processes to social movements. Indeed, the social movement metaphor itself diffused widely. We may best understand a phenomenon at the edge of a metaphor's usefulness. Showing how certain kinds of change efforts are *not* in fact social movements – not quite bold, risky or linked to conflict against entrenched interests – is equally important. Clemens (2005: 351) ponders helpfully about whether organizations and social movements are really "two kinds of stuff," asking provocatively, "When tie-dyed activists and poor people's marches are central to the imagery of a theory, can that theory be transposed to corporate boardrooms and back offices without doing fundamental violence to our understanding of both phenomena?" As someone who has studied within-corporation activists, I tend to reply that corporate boardrooms may be the most practical setting in which to press for clean energy and living wages, particularly because the tie-dyed perimeter of the "Occupy" movement simply could not get traction to move from anger to reform. Brave employee activists inside corporations speak truth to power, even where their jobs and livelihoods are at stake. They make the boardroom contested terrain. But nonetheless, the burden of proof should fall to within-corporation studies to show that their topics and their analyses are not narrow, co-opted and depoliticized.

Mechanism

In digging appreciatively into a wide range of settings where activists attempt change, organizational scholars and social movement scholars have shared analytical tools. They have usefully informed one another, as each seeks to understand structural forms, political processes, collective identities and resource dependencies. The borrowings have moved in both directions. Organizational mechanisms explain how social movements find themselves assimilated or trending toward centrism (Michels, 1911). Identity dynamics are invoked to explain who joins social movements and finds allies (Polletta & Jasper, 2001) and, inside organizations, to illuminate the specific ways in which identities create or fracture alliances at work (e.g., Kellogg, 2011; Raeburn, 2004). The importance of available resources, compelling frames, political opportunities and mobilization channels are together taken as the essential toolkit at the organizations and social movements interface (McAdam, McCarthy & Zald, 1996).

The array of mechanisms has been helpfully characterized by Campbell (2005) as cognitive, relational and political, the latter including the kind of state dynamics previously discussed. Cognitive mechanisms have centered on the concept of "framing" social action (Gamson & Meyer, 1996). Processes of translation, from social movement slogans to locally adept organizational terminology (Creed, Scully & Austin, 2002), can push top leadership in organizations to adopt changes. Scanning the environment, activists find new organizational forms and building blocks to anchor their work. Relational dynamics include "networks [that] constitute the conduits through which new models, concepts, and practices diffuse and become part of an organization or movement's repertoire" (Campbell, 2005: 61). Working against the long history of employers' using identities to divide and conquer the workplace, workers sometimes mobilize across identities toward shared material interests (Kurtz, 2002), although all too often the identity emphasis crowds out materiality.

These mechanisms have opened up a rich understanding of how social movements happen, often in surprising ways and against the odds. At the same time, the focus on mechanisms has allowed a proliferation of studies with a diminished emphasis on the urgency of fundamental social change.

Mobilization

Collective engagement is a puzzle in its own right. Social movement theorists pioneered the concept of social movement organizations (SMOs) and showed how their rise, adaptation and spread permitted sustainable mobilization (e.g., Clemens, 1993; Minkoff, 1999; Zald & Ash, 1966). Mobilization happens via organizations, and organization theory lent fresh insight. New institutional theory, with its focus on the rise and diffusion of organizational forms and practices, was tapped, and, reciprocally, social movements became a new domain of inquiry for organization theorists using these institutional theory tools. Studies focused on the creation of new organizational forms as the outcome of mobilization processes, with detours from original social movement goals as itself a phenomenon of interest (e.g., Haveman, Rao & Paruchuri, 2007).

A focus on mobilization queries how people might do much with few resources, relying upon passion and commitment. This energy might be directed top-down by elites and might result in unlikely commitment to a corporate initiative, such as a quality program (Strang & Jung, 2005). The distinction between any kind of concerted activity and grassroots mobilization directed toward fundamentally disruptive change is important to retain. As McAdam (2007) writes, "The term 'collective action' is hopelessly broad. Taken at face value, it could plausibly refer to all forms of human social action involving two or more people. . . . But there is a far narrower subset of human action to which the term has been applied. . . . [C]ollective action refers to emergent and minimally coordinated action by two or more people that is motivated by a desire to change some aspect of social life or to resist changes proposed by others." The desire for change or resistance becomes foregrounded again, with the varied tactics, resources and structures of social movements as the supporting characters.

Overall, what is striking is a relative equanimity about the kind of change being discussed. The term "social movement" might seem to suggest changes that are radical, highly charged, sharply contested and consequential for the broader society, such as women's suffrage, civil rights, poor people's movements, or environmentalism. In contrast, the new domain of overlap in studying organizations and social movements (e.g., Rao, Monin & Durand [2003], as but one example) might consider anything from new professional practices (cuisines, accounting rules, nursing care) to new organizational forms (charter schools, microfinance) to newly salient identities (activist churchgoers). The changes studied are locally charged and may involve delegitimating old routines and inventing new ones, but they do not represent "crises of legitimation" in the broader societal sense. They are not about – nor toward – deep structural changes in power or resource distribution.

"More?"

The seven principles presented here are animated by the spirit of Critical Management Studies and the role it can play as a call to study action radically and to act radically. They can guide studies at the intersection of social movements and organizations.

1: Explicit recognition of what is problematic in the status quo that might propel change

The societal sphere is ripe with social crises that invite the attention of critical organizational scholarship. Inequality is widening, employment conditions grow meaner, corporations are better able to capture governments to receive favorable regulatory and taxation terms and activists raise voices in frustration but find fewer tactical avenues for dissent. Organizations are often implicated as the sources and perpetuators of these problems. Emile Zola, the French author, wrote passionately of the coal miners' strike in northern France in the 1860s, using sharp detail and sociological analysis, in his novel *Germinal* (1885/1974), to raise the profile of this social movement and provoke outrage about the terrible working conditions in the coalfields at that time. Important labor reforms followed the public reaction.

While social scientists chafe at being likened to novelists or journalists, vivid accounts of the presenting problems of social movements have their place in critically informed scholarship. Studies of social movements allow researchers to note in their own terms the severity of social conditions or to use the third person voice of activists who explain what has motivated their moral outrage. The "awakening of a sense of social injustice" (Deutsch & Steil, 1988) used to be considered the major trigger for social movement activism. Rich research on mechanisms and structural conditions has shown that more forces than outrage must align, but at the same time the sources of outrage should not fade from attention. Frames and opportunities will not be taken up without some sense that there is an urgent social problem requiring attention. It is possible to attend to the *why* of social movements as well as the *how*, as in the study of farm workers' mobilization and both the sense of injustice and the savvy tactics that made change possible (Ganz, 2009).

2: Attention to fundamentally conflictual interests and to the power dynamics that channel change efforts

Social movements are needed when there is a conflict of interests. Modest change efforts can occur through joint optimization or agreed-upon terms of change. Whether or not there is conflict might distinguish which kinds of change efforts belong under the purview of social movement studies. Many social theorists have investigated the fundamental puzzle of why the many seem to do the bidding of the few and how soft power remains cloaked (Dahl, 1961). Studies of how change agents lobby the powerful should question, beyond certain visible "moves" to address "top leadership" inside organizations, who the really powerful players are. In Japanese politics, there is a long held appreciation for the role of the kingmaker, or *kuromaku*, who pulls the strings behind the public façade of political party nomination fights but who remains carefully out of the press. The term derives from black-clad stage hands in Kabuki theater, who move props around on the stage in full view of the audience but who, by convention, remain invisible.

Equally shrouded in invisibility may be those whose lack of power puts them outside the scope of studies of within-corporate change. Invisible stakeholders may include factory workers in emerging economies, domestic caregivers for children or the elderly, homeless individuals and families or others. The precarious lives of invisible stakeholders are often inherent casualties of organizational operations in capitalist context. The concerns of the least well-off stakeholders may be overlooked if moves from the organizational middle dominate work at the intersection of social movements and organizations. While midlevel insiders can often best reach the levers for change, the wider implications of their agency, beyond their own interests and identities, come into view through a critical lens. For example, midlevel insiders in organizations can argue and organize effectively for fair forms of remuneration like domestic partner benefits (Creed, Scully & Austin 2002). However, "moves from the middle" are less likely to be effective in securing a living wage for low-paid front-line workers, better conditions for sweatshop workers or protections against union busting. The concerns of anticorporate activism set the concerns of within-corporate activism in sharper relief.

3: Understanding of when social movements are needed but do not happen because of blocking moves by "institutional defenders"

For all the focus on "institutional entrepreneurs," the subtle agency of "institutional defenders" in deflecting or resisting change should not be overlooked (Levy & Scully, 2007). Managers are sometimes puzzled when workers resist top-down changes (Prasad & Prasad, 2000). In a clever reframing, Bernard (1996) looked at "managers' resistance to change" when workers push for change.

Studies of social movements bias us toward instances where mobilization has occurred. But the absence of change is as important an area of study. Comparative historical sociology advanced the study of revolution by observing pairs of settings in which revolution might have occurred and either did or did *not* (Skocpol, 1979). The dynamics of social movements that did not occur or that did not prevail (Mansbridge, 1986) are just as vital to understand.

There is a selection bias emerging in the study of social movements that happen in and via organizations. Social movement efforts that are successfully blocked – by those who are invested in the status quo and can deploy ideologies that make change unthinkable and the status quo legitimate – are not salient and receive less attention. To read the current research on social movements and organizations, one could be forgiven for thinking that there has been a proliferation of successful agency. There are numerous accounts of framing of issues that actually worked, tactics that prevailed, political opportunities that were seized and allies that were converted. There is a striking disjunction between the hopefulness in these accounts and the continued rather dreary state of the workplace in many countries and corporations.

4: Acknowledgment of the asymmetries of mobilization (center/margin, right/left)

Social change efforts can be led by conservative as well as by radical forces (e.g., Teles, 2008). On the one hand, it may be that certain principles of social movements govern efforts from both the right and left – for example, the framing of critiques, the justification of tactics and the attempt to create an aspirational future that is widely appealing (Martin, Scully & Levitt, 1990). On the other hand, given the preceding principles, conservative change efforts work with – rather than against – the forces of power, legitimation and institutional preservation. They may be importantly distinct. Blocking moves from the conservative center of power often invoke different frames, or "rhetorics of reaction" (Hirschman, 1991), such as the perversity of attempted change.

5: Appreciation of the nature of risk – to body, livelihood, community – that distinguishes radical social movements

Social movements are serious endeavors. Activists – in organizational settings and outside – take significant risks precisely because there is likely to be push-back from the powerful. In the civic sphere, the risks may be bodily. In the workplace sphere, livelihood is at stake. There is renewed interest in organization studies in looking at how organizational life is inscribed on the body, which in the case of social movement activism involve the quite real physical risks of beating, pain, stress, food and housing insecurity and ostracism.

The nature of fear is an essential component for understanding social movements. Fear keeps people from protesting: fear of arrest, fear of loss of job, fear of marginalization, fear of police billy clubs. The fearfulness of protest in organizations based on insider knowledge is a brought to life in movies such as *Silkwood*, *Matewan*, *Norma Rae*, *Insider* and *North Country*. Karen Silkwood raises concerns about workers' radiation exposure and dies in a car accident of dubious nature. Miners protest brutal conditions in Matewan and face brutal suppression. The main character in *Norma Rae* joins the outsider union organizer to embolden coworkers to take collective action, risking the only jobs around. A cigarette company insider makes public some damaging company documents on the dangers of smoking and risks injury to both himself and, more frighteningly, to his family. A sexually harassed miner advocates for women's rights and finds herself an intimidated lone voice. Vivid storytelling reminds us of how scary real social movement activism can be. These films are the *Germinal* of our age.

6: Willingness to see envisioned alternatives

This section opened with the idea that a view of social movements informed by CMS should start with clarity about what is desperately wrong with the status quo. If that is so, then an envisioned alternative is warranted. Moreover, it is important to keep in mind this bigger picture of needed change as a way to appraise incremental change.

The necessity of a strategy of "small wins" (Weick, 1984) has gained traction at the intersection of social movements and organizations. What is sometimes lost is the risk of the classic problem of "goal displacement" (Selznick, 1949), whereby these small wins are means that become ends. The small wins need to be appraised in terms of whether and how they create momentum or steps toward the needed bigger wins that would remedy fundamental inequities and problems. It is difficult to find appropriate criteria by which to gauge whether small wins are steps on a ladder toward the ultimately desired and more profound change. In Weick's (1984) example that "ending world hunger" will cause activists to be overwhelmed and to stall while holding a canned food drive is imaginable and feasible, the idea was not to supplant world hunger as a concern. Adding "radical imagination" to strategy and tactics is the next frontier for social movements (Haiven & Khasnabish, 2014).

7: Appraisal of organizational social movements using some criteria for whether they effectively created substantial and meaningful change

What are the criteria by which a change effort is a small step, a detour or distraction or a meaningful change? A "yardstick of change" (Scully & Segal, 2002) requires appreciating what is meaningful change for those on the ground while keeping some analytical distance in looking at the remaining changes needed. For example, a group of insider activists working to enhance civil rights in the workplace was blasé about the selection of the first African-American to join the corporate board, claiming that particular "win" was distant from the everyday micro inequities they experienced at work. But they were quite excited that people were wearing a diversity T-shirt that they had designed with the company logo because this software company had a T-shirt culture with new shirts for product launches, company softball teams and the like. When they saw people wearing the diversity T-shirt to work, the internal activists felt they had made a profound incursion into the company culture. The challenge is to keep in mind the local meaningfulness of small wins that may seem trivial but are rather poetically profound in their home setting, while not losing sight of the big picture. Keeping in mind that the broader set of discrimination issues anchors small wins as milestones en route to more major changes.

A more critical appraisal of the outcomes of these change efforts is needed, including analyses across efforts, particularly in a literature that studies small wins one at a time. This appraisal must include limited successes, retrenchment of powerful interests, lessons from failures and movements not even attempted. Where small wins and micro mobilization processes are invoked, we need more critical appraisals of whether and how they eventually accrue to significant wins and macro implications. Redistribution of power and resources is a good benchmark for whether fundamental change has occurred; defining and measuring these are future directions for a meaningful study of social movements within corporations in a world of anticorporation protests.

Critical reassessment

In closing, I briefly reconsider a study of employee activist groups addressing diversity issues in the workplace (Scully & Segal, 2002) using the preceding principles. While this study was designed explicitly to draw upon the radical edge of social movement theory, that premise merits questioning. Does this study examine an instance of within-corporation activism that belongs properly in the category of social movement? Does the insider activism itself achieve meaningful changes that accord with a strong notion of what is a social movement? Looking at this study takes me back to that borderland between social movement research and social movements per se, discussed at the opening of this essay.

The study examined newly forming "employee resource groups" formed along social identity dimensions in the 1990s, including race, gender, and sexual orientation. The research tapped the radical aspirations of the change effort through the words of the activists themselves. As researchers, we were surprised at how these activists, who wore their corporate masks most of the time, could give voice to their radical motivations to be involved in a change effort to address diversity. Their framings made explicit linkages to the Civil Rights movement and questioned the rise of the term "diversity" and the disappearance of direct mention of "race." In this sense, the within-corporation activism was a vehicle for more radically envisioned societal change.

However, we did not report on the stories of incredible frustration about how little changed, what a strong hold the dominant, corporate "presentation of self" had in the workplace and how frequently the activists just had venting sessions. It seemed so startling that they had made any inroads at all that we focused there, acknowledging their brave and clever agency. To the extent we considered organizational elites, it was where a few of them offered "air cover" for the work of activists, hence the quirky metaphor, given to us by an activist, which forms the paper's title: "Passion with an Umbrella" (Scully & Segal, 2002).

Moreover, we lost the context of the state because the state's reach had seemingly hit a limit regarding enforcement of civil rights legislation. However, Jammulamadaka (2014) demonstrates how the state's regulations very specifically affect the options and outcomes of activism, sometimes providing legitimacy for activists' claims and sometimes providing loopholes for more powerful players. The state is the ultimate "umbrella" under which internal activists can push for policy enforcement – and toward which they should direct energies for better policies.

Activists lobbying the state, activists staging anticorporate protests and activists working inside corporations are different fronts for social movements. While activists may spar over whose approach is better, the approaches can be synergistic. Some of the employees we interviewed also engaged in community activism outside work, and they brought that sensibility back into the organization. Taking these types of activism together and recognizing the porousness and shared goals among them might provide social movement researchers with a promising place to train their lens – and activists a promising way to engage their joint energies.

In conclusion

Concepts from social movements have made important contributions to organization studies, revealing metaphors, mechanisms and mobilization methods. But a truly critical approach will do "more": Examine how radical change efforts attempt to address societal problems and alter patterns of legitimacy and distribution, particularly on behalf of the least well-off.

It is possible that the recent trends in engaging and studying anticorporate activism have rendered within-corporate activism obsolete. The field of within-corporate activism keeps moving sideways – to find new kinds of change efforts in many kinds of organizations. Instead, the field may need to look vertically – how to embed within-organization change efforts within anticorporate efforts and rapidly shifting global contexts. How does mobilization of the homeless, who often are not able to find work, link to mobilization of those who are working? How does the mobilization to expand schooling options link to the mobilization to make front-line jobs more sustainable?

Change movements can sometimes be big tents, where more mainstream actions and their "left flank" all have a place. That works only if there is reciprocal awareness. It may be too easy for scholars and activists in the within-corporate domain to lose awareness of actions in the anticorporate domain. And the latter domain should not underestimate how shareholders and boards of directors can redirect corporate actions in behind-the-scenes ways. When change agents struggle over who is "merely reformist" or who is "grandly radical," solidarity is fractured. Micro mobilization reattached to macro mobilization is the direction for future work. If it is possible to create alliances within, across and beyond organizational settings, social movements may find multiple levers for making change in complex environments. Social movements should be neither too "melancholic" about failure in the face of big challenges nor too "triumphalist" in the face of small wins (Haiven & Khasnabish, 2014: 137); instead, "research politics" and "scholar activism" might find a new path.

References

Alinsky, S. (1971). *Rules for radicals: A pragmatic primer for realistic radicals.* New York: Vintage.
Armstrong, E. A. (2002). *Forging gay identities: Organizing sexuality in San Francisco.* Chicago: University of Chicago Press.
Aronowitz, S. (1992). *False promises: The shaping of American working class consciousness.* Durham, NC: Duke University Press.
Bernard, E. (1996). Management resistance to change: A case of computer information systems. In C. Bina, L. Clements & C. Davis (Eds.), *Beyond survival: Wage labor in the twentieth century.* Armonk, NY: M. E. Sharpe.
Briscoe, F., & Safford, S. (2008). The Nixon–in–China effect: Activism, imitation, and the institutionalization of contentious practices. *Administrative Science Quarterly, 53*(3): 460–491.
Campbell, J. L. (2005). Where do we stand? Common mechanisms in organizations and social movements research. In G. F. Davis, D. McAdam, W. R. Scott & M. N. Zald (Eds.), *Social movements and organization theory*: 41–68. Cambridge: Cambridge University Press.
Clemens, E. S. (1993). Organizational repertoires and institutional change: Women's groups and the transformation of U.S. politics, 1890–1920. *American Journal of Sociology, 98*(4): 755–798.
Clemens, E. S. (2005). Two kinds of stuff: The current encounter of social movements and organizations. In G. F. Davis, D. McAdam, W. R. Scott & M. N. Zald (Eds.), *Social movements and organization theory*: 351–366. Cambridge: Cambridge University Press.

Creed, W. D., & Scully, M. A. (2000). Songs of ourselves: Employees' deployment of social identity. *Journal of Management Inquiry*, *9*, 391–412.

Creed, W.E.D., Scully, M. A., & Austin, J. R. (2002). Clothes make the person? The tailoring of legitimating accounts and the social construction of identity. *Organization Science*, *13*(5): 475–496.

Crossley, N. (2003). Even newer social movements: Anti-corporate protests, capitalist crises and the remoralization of society. *Organization*, *10*(2): 287–305.

Dahl, R. (1961). *Who governs? Power and democracy in an American city*. New Haven, CT: Yale University Press.

Davis, G. F. (2006). Mechanisms and the theory of organizations. *Journal of Management Inquiry*, *15*(2): 114–118.

Deutsch, M., & Steil, J. M. (1988). Awakening the sense of injustice. *Social Justice Research*, *2*(1): 3–23.

Dutton, J. E., Ashford, S. J., O'Neill, R. M., & Lawrence, K. A. (2001). Moves that matter: Issue selling and organizational change. *Academy of Management Journal*, *44*(4): 716–736.

Edelman, L. B., Erlanger, H. S., & Lande, J. (1993). Internal dispute resolution: The transformation of civil rights in the workplace. *Law and Society Review*, *27*(3): 497–534.

Edwards, Richard C. (1979). *Contested terrain: The transformation of the workplace in the twentieth century*. New York: Basic Books.

Ertugrul, M., & Krishnan, K. (2011). Can CEO dismissals be proactive? *Journal of Corporate Finance*, *17*(1): 134–151.

Gamson, W. A., & Meyer, D. S. (1996). Framing political opportunity. In D. McAdam, J. D. McCarthy & M. N. Zald (Eds.), *Comparative perspectives on social movements*: 275–290. Cambridge: Cambridge University Press.

Ganz, M. (2009). *Why David sometimes wins: Leadership, organization, and strategy in the California farm worker movement*. New York: Oxford University Press.

Hackman, J. F., & Wageman, R. (1995). Total quality management: Empirical, conceptual, and practical issues. *Administrative Science Quarterly*, *40*(2): 309–342.

Haiven, M., & Khasnabish, A. (2014). *The radical imagination*. London: Zed Books.

Hallett, T. (2010). The myth incarnate recoupling processes, turmoil, and inhabited institutions in an urban elementary school. *American Sociological Review*, *75*(1): 52–74.

Havel, V. (1991). *Disturbing the peace*. New York: Vintage.

Haveman, H. A., Rao, H., & Paruchuri, S. (2007). The winds of change: The progressive movement and the bureaucratization of thrift. *American Sociological Review*, *72*(1): 117–142.

Hirschman, A. O. (1991). *The rhetoric of reaction: Perversity, futility, jeopardy*. Cambridge, MA: Harvard University Press.

Hirschman, A. O. (1995). *A propensity to self-subversion*. Boston: Harvard University Press.

Howard-Grenville, J. (2009). *Corporate culture and environmental practice: Making change at a high technology manufacturer*. Cheltenham, UK: Edward Elgar.

Jammulamadaka, N. (2014). Theorising the state (or its absence?) in anti-corporate protest: Insights from India. Paper presented at the Academy of Management Annual Conference, Philadelphia, August.

Kellogg, K. C. (2011). *Challenging operations: Medical reform and resistance in surgery*. Chicago: University of Chicago Press.

Kurtz, S. (2002). *Workplace justice: Organizing multi-identity movements*. Minneapolis: University of Minnesota Press.

Laraña, E., Johnston, H., & Gusfield, J. R. (Eds.). (1994). *New social movements: From ideology to identity*. Philadelphia: Temple University Press.

Levy, D., & Scully, M. (2007). The institutional entrepreneur as modern prince: The strategic face of power in contested fields. *Organization Studies*, *28*(7): 971–991.

Mansbridge, J. (1986). *Why we lost the ERA*. Chicago: University of Chicago Press.

Martin, J., Scully, M., & Levitt. B. (1990). Damning the past, justifying the present, and neglecting the future. *Journal of personality and social psychology*, *59*(2): 281–290.

McAdam, D. (1988). Micromobilization contexts and recruitment to activism. *International Social Movement Research*, *1*(1): 125–154.

McAdam, D. (2007). Collective action. *Blackwell encyclopedia of sociology*. Malden, MA: Blackwell.

McAdam, D., McCarthy, J. D., & Zald, M. N. (Eds.). (1996). *Comparative perspectives on social movements: Political opportunities, mobilizing structures, and cultural framings*. Cambridge: Cambridge University Press.

McAdam, D., Tarrow, S., & Tilly, C. (2003). Dynamics of contention. *Social Movement Studies*, *2*(1): 99–102.

McCarthy, J. D., & Zald, M. N. (1977). Resource mobilization and social movements: A partial theory. *American Journal of Sociology*, *82*(6): 1212–1241.

Meyerson, D., & Scully, M. (1995). Tempered radicalism and the politics of ambivalence and change. *Organization Science*: 6: 585–600.

Meyerson, D. E. (2001). Radical change, the quiet way. *Harvard Business Review, 79*(9): 92–104.

Michels, R. (1911). *Political parties: A sociological study of the oligarchical tendencies of modern democracy.* Whitefish, MT: Kessinger Publishing.

Minkoff, D. C. (1999). Bending with the wind: Strategic change and adaptation by women's and racial minority organizations. *American Journal of Sociology, 104*(6): 1666–1703.

Morgan, G. (1980). Paradigms, metaphors, and puzzle solving in organization theory. *Administrative Science Quarterly, 25*(4): 605–622.

Morgan, G. (1983). More on metaphor: Why we cannot control tropes in administrative science. *Administrative Science Quarterly, 28*(4): 601–607

Olson, M. (1971). *The logic of collective action: Public goods and the theory of groups.* Cambridge, MA: Harvard University Press.

Polletta, F., & Jasper, J. (2001). Collective identity and social movements. *Annual Review of Sociology, 27*: 283–305.

Prasad, P., & Prasad, A. (2000). Stretching the iron cage: The constitution and implications of routine workplace resistance. *Organization Science, 11*(4): 387–403.

Raeburn, N. C. 2004. *Changing corporate America from inside out: Lesbian and gay workplace rights.* Minneapolis: University of Minnesota Press.

Rao, H., Monin, P., & Durand, R. (2003). Institutional change in Toque Ville: Nouvelle cuisine as an identity movement in French gastronomy. *American Journal of Sociology, 108*(4): 795–783.

Rothenberg, S., Pil, F. K., & Maxwell, J. (2001). Lean, green, and the quest for superior environmental performance. *Production and Operations Management, 10*(3): 228–243.

Scully, M., & Segal, A. (2002). Passion with an umbrella: Grassroots activists in the workplace. *Research in the Sociology of Organizations, 19*: 125–168.

Selznick, P. (1949). *TVA and the grassroots: A study in the sociology of formal organization.* Berkeley: University of California Press.

Shurman, R., & Munro, W. A. (2010). *Fighting for the future of food: Activists versus agribusiness in the struggle over biotechnology.* Minneapolis: University of Minnesota Press.

Skocpol, T. (1979). *States and social revolutions: A comparative analysis of France, Russia and China.* Cambridge: Cambridge University Press.

Sombart, W. (1976). *Why is there no socialism in the United States?* Armonk, NY: M. E. Sharpe.

Strang, D., & Jung, D. (2005). Organizational change as an orchestrated social movement: recruitment to a corporate quality initiative. In G. F. Davis, D. McAdam, W. R. Scott & M. N. Zald (Eds.). (2005). *Social movements and organization theory*: 280–309. Cambridge: Cambridge University Press.

Sturm, S. (2001). Second-generation employment discrimination: A structural approach. *Columbia Law Review, 101*(3): 458–568.

Tauss, A. (2012). Contextualizing the current crisis: Post-Fordism, neoliberal restructuring, and financialization. *Colombia Internacional, 76*: 51–79.

Teles, S. M. (2008). *The rise of the conservative legal movement: The battle for control of the law.* Princeton, NJ: Princeton University Press.

Walker, E. T. (2012). Social movements, organizations, and fields: A decade of theoretical integration. *Contemporary Sociology, 41*(5): 576–587.

Weick, K. (1984). Small wins: Redefining the scale of social problems. *American Psychologist, 39*(1): 40–49.

Zald, M. N., & Ash, R. (1966). Social movement organizations: Growth, decay, and change. *Social Forces, 44*(3): 327–341.

Zald, M. N., & Berger, M. A. (1978). Social movements in organizations: Coup d'etat, insurgency, and mass movements. *American Journal of Sociology, 83*(4): 823–861.

Zola, E. (1885/1974). *Germinal* (trans. C. Smethurst). London: Edward Arnold.

14

The usual suspects? Putting plagiarism 2.0 in its place[1]

J. Michael Cavanaugh

> There is nothing which so generally strikes the imagination, and engages the affections of mankind, as the right of property.
>
> William Blackstone (Underkuffler, 1990: 127)

This essay constitutes an attempt to loosen the grip of the largely judgmental discourse framing student plagiarism by auditioning a self-checking discussion about the landscape of plagiary and, not least, our connection to it.[2] Behind this effort lies a concern that in the rush to finger the 'usual' student suspects, academic faculty members risk undertheorizing student plagiarism *as a social practice*, alienating students in the process. In effect, emphatic and unreflexive efforts to shore up ratified notions of intellectual property (IP) may produce as much irony[3] as desired results because we, faculty, may not fully appreciate what we are up against. Mindful of the reputational and example-setting implications of tight-lipped countermeasures and locating students as one link in a chain of contingent events, I hope to award faculty with a richer appreciation of the social and institutional coordinates of e-student plagiarism within the academic workplace.

Introduction: It's complicated

> Rather, copyright is an ongoing social negotiation, tenuously forged, endlessly revised, and imperfect in its every incarnation.
>
> *(Lethem, 2007: 63)*

> On YouTube, 'you can get a whole story in six minutes,' he [a 17-year-old high school student] explains. 'A book takes so long. I prefer the immediate gratification.'
>
> *(Richtel, 2010a)*

In his challenging August 9, 2010, *New York Times* blog post, 'Plagiarism Is Not a Big Moral Deal,' Stanley Fish (2010a) argues that it is better to view plagiarism as a professional transgression rather than a universal, moral one. He writes:

And if you're a student, plagiarism will seem to be an annoying guild imposition *without a persuasive rationale* [my italics] . . . knowledge of what is and is not plagiarism in this or that professional practice is not something that will be of very much use to you unless you end up becoming a member of the profession yourself. It follows that students who never quite get the concept right are by and large not committing a crime; they are just failing to become acclimated to the conventions of the little insular world they have, often through no choice of their own, wandered into. It's no big moral deal; which doesn't mean, I hasten to add, that plagiarism shouldn't be punished – if you're in our house, you've got to play by our rules – just that what you're punishing is a breach of disciplinary decorum, not a breach of the moral universe.

In the space of time it takes to text message 'crime and punishment,' Fish's words triggered 635 email posts, the vast majority deeply offended by his churlish breach of faith. Plagiary, Fish was archly instructed, was theft, a character defect, a punishable crime, no middle ground, end of story. Surprised by this crescendo of indignity, Fish issued a defense appearing a week later (2010b), more soberly entitled, 'The Ontology of Plagiarism: Part Two.' In 'Part Two,' Fish patiently explains again that his intention was not to school students to cut corners, moral or otherwise. University students, like it or not, must play by house rules. But, Fish repeated, we live in many literary houses, each operating with its own, though not necessarily exclusive, rule set. What counts as original work depends on consensus anchored in particular times and places. Plagiary, therefore, may result in an expulsion in the academy or launch a lawsuit in Hollywood. It may just as easily serve as a sign of deference in some non-Western cultures (Valentine, 2006) or be shrugged off as mere copying in oral religious sermonizing (Swearingen, 1987; Miller, 1991).

To a scholar with the constructionist bona fides of Stanley Fish, intellectual property is an in-the-moment, 'tenuously forged' constellation of social relationships, a manifestly *human*, consequently debatable, endeavor to the core. Wiser all around, he feels, to approach the topic of plagiarism from the possibility latent in an epistemological perspective than a rock-bottom ontological one (Ashworth, Bannister & Thorne, 1997). Indeed, Fish avers, *whereas we faculty may venerate originality and property as sacraments doesn't mean that our students – the vast majority just passing through the 'little insular world' of the academy – necessarily do.* Taking a lesson from Dr. Fish, perhaps it's time to ask whether the moralizing remedy of choice deployed in universities across the land is up to corraling the broadband (cultural/institutional) changes in composition and literacy purportedly well underway (Woodmansee, 1994; Lessig, 2001; Vaidhyanathan, 2001; Posner, 2002). Are we inadvertently grounding plagiary policies in a sectarian misrepresentation of our own making, straining student–faculty ties and our own credibility to boot? After all, the movie and book-retailing industries resorted to punishing underage consumers until peremptorily relegated to the dinosaur wing. Borrowing (stealing?) a page from Professor Fish's contrarian thesis, I think his plucky swim against the tide merits a second, more tempered look. What follows constitutes an attempt to pick up where he leaves off.

The state of the art

[A]ll my best ideas were stolen by the ancients.

Ralph Waldo Emerson (McLemee, 2004)

A cursory computer search of *The Chronicle of Higher Education* and *The New York Times* quickly reveals that plagiarism is no stranger to the Academy. In 2006, *The China Daily* found that nearly two-thirds of the 160 Chinese academics it surveyed admitted to lifting parts of their publications

(Pocha, 2006). More recently, the Faculty Senate at Simon Fraser University adopted a stigmatizing grade 'worse than an F' for magpie-like impiety – 'FD,' or 'failed for academic dishonesty', perhaps in an attempt to shame, Hester Prynne-like, the perpetrators (*The Chronicle of Higher Education*, 2009). Following a lengthy investigation, 39 graduates of Ohio University's School of Mechanical Engineering were summarily ordered to rewrite their master's theses (some dating back 20 years) – or else (Bartlett, 2006). And by now we all know by heart the story of Kaavya Viswanathan, the precocious Harvard freshman who 'internalized' her favorite authors and then 'unintentionally' (albeit liberally) purloined their words. After an anonymous caller tipped *The New York Times*, her publisher, Little, Brown, took less than a Manhattan heartbeat to cancel her six-digit book advance (Rich, 2006).

The academic rap sheet scrolls on. But these instances of skullduggery duly noted, apparently what rattles some academicians inner-*pares res* is the threat posed by 'the digital challenge' (Leeds & Lohr, 2005), that is, that legions of file-swapping students are mercenary masters of the cut-and-paste. Indeed, dating back to the 1960s, the perennial literature surveying undergraduate and graduate student cheating appears to confirm worst-case fears – that cheating of one form or another is near endemic with business and economic majors, with honors students, no less, headlining the way (Ashworth, Bannister, & Thorne, 1997; McCabe, Butterfield, & Trevino, 2006). Throw in the viral contaminatory power of the Web, and it only follows that before things completely unspool, the onus falls on faculty to raise the ante for digital natives who fail to accept academic proprietary manners on our terms (Coombe, 2006).

Nevertheless, would not a more measured reading of reported cases of plagiary suggest that a one-dimensional construct hardly fits all (McLemee, 2004)? Punishments, it appears, vary with the social rank of the accused and academic discipline (Demirjian, 2006). And akin to the floating concepts of privacy and traffic yield signs, plagiarism and intellectual property are variously defined, that is, housebroken, as Professor Fish might put it. Besides, the P2P (person-to-person) phenomenon – downloading, mixing, cutting and pasting – long predates the Power-Book and the Net. And, after nearly 50 years of data crunching, can we confidently assume that cheating surveys yield actionable data? If nothing else, fixes placing responsibility squarely on students alone come at a premium (Hoover, 2002). It is sufficient justification, I suggest, to inquire if the reigning crime and punishment (C&P, or 'gotcha') metaphor is epistemologically adequate for the analytic and corrective tasks at hand. Not least, stiff penalties notwithstanding, what are the odds that the multitasking Facebook demographic will bother to hew the C&P line (Richtel, 2010a)?

Point of order

[T]he way we diagnose our students' condition will determine the kind of remedy we offer.
Parker J. Palmer (1998: 41)

Which is to propose that the *Judge Judy*[4] – or juridical predilection of the academy's quick-draw, lay-down-the-law – reaction to the 'rising tide' of student plagiarism be revisited (Cohen, 2005). Of course, the hyperaggressive, 'red meat' construct to whack the P-beast should come as no surprise given plagiarism's alleged power to upend the academy's 'stable rhetorical universe,' not to mention its tribal governing authority and identity (Bizzell, 1982; Kolich, 1983). On the other hand, putting students in their place appears at odds with academia's hallowed humanistic ideals and self-sustaining institutional goal of conscripting star students into academic discourse communities (Gordon & Palmon, 2010). Nor, come to think of it, does it reflect very kindly on who we think our students are and are about, or our sense of identity with them. Perhaps – just perhaps – an absolutist remedy may be called for on qualified occasion, but professional prudence and some sobering hindsight caution that we not fall into the habit of morphing students into litigants vis-à-vis the media industry.

Besides, I suspect that such raw exertions of social control as embodied every afternoon in the unctuous Judge Judy's courtroom or instances of student 'perps'[5] summoned before university review boards not only beg critical contextual factors but, in the rush for closure, understate the self-defeating pitfalls that tough loving is likely to engender. Arguably, the stark, vestigial "bad apples versus good" moral narrative is polemically cathartic and restorative of a sense of nominal control. A reassuring rhetorical device wherein faculty remain the unquestioned 'schoolmasters' and the root of the crisis is ascribed to an 'easily problematized' target population, that is, shifting the burden of proof to the rogue, low-hanging caricature of the malingering student (Campbell, 1999). But default hermeneutics of this sort, Terry Eagleton (1983) cautions, tend to set in motion a moony consolation that events can be dialed back to an unproblematic, sepia-toned, 'before.' In sentimental thrall of a preferred social reality, he adds, we effectively defuse hermeneutic forms of 'suspicion' *keen to think through* how social and individual agency are mutually produced.

So, pause to (re)consider. If seeing flashing red results in consigning heuristic academic conventions of analytic ambivalence to the sidelines, we risk transposing the problems of social structures onto the very people (here a student demographic of unprecedented diversity [Perfetto, 2010]) who embody them. Policies of containment are predicated on the commonplace denominator that a generation of preschool-admission-tested, 'teach-to-the-test,' 'early admission,' 'patch-writing' (Howard, Rodrigue & Serviss, 2010), grade-obsessed American students, armed with petabyte-sized laptops, BlackBerrys and Ritalin[6] prescriptions, preordains plagiary (Hafner, 2001). *No need to look further.* Oriented by this 'necessary abstraction' (McGrath, 2011), the disciplinary remedy is localized and privatized to upgrading individual behavior *without changing anything else.* Note, however, the reductive price tag for what amounts to taking sides. Specifically, the dueling either/or (virtue/vice) construction of convenient targets entails the wholesale erasure of the extenuating life contexts and institutional positioning arguably organizing plagiarism. In effect, the deflective rhetorical leap of naming and blaming brackets the issue so as to *insulate ourselves* from both the problem and our students.

Also keep in mind that ethical binaries[7] ask us to endorse a credulous baseline cultural homogeneity. The overwhelming prosecutorial slant of the Judge Judy brand of plagiarism discourse, that is, presupposes that students and faculty work from the same enduring characterizations of authorship and ownership. And that this dubious body of 'lived understandings' embodies and originates in an inevitable and universalized system of intellectual property enshrined by none other than the Founders in Article I, Section 8 of the United States Constitution (Schultz, 1993). That same Delphic, 27-word Copyright Clause, by the way, launched a down-to-the-present game of Prisoner's Dilemma over the nature of a robust intellectual commons. Anyone willing to bet the house that most of today's students find this vision compelling?

Conventional wisdom holds that the Academy in the ideal constitutes a knowledge arena prizing the strategic, eyes-wide-open notion of the examined life (*auctoritas*)—domain where unimpeachable absolutes are by definition dismissed as 'epistemologically provincial' (i.e., intellectually complacent). Where might we turn, then, if, upon careful examination, the C&P school of plagiary is found to operate with too many absences showing? Found too simple, paradoxically resembling its nemesis by spreading credit too thin? Is there more to student plagiarism than meets the normalizing eye? If so, a squinty-eyed, 'make my day' fixation on propping up ratified notions of academic intellectual property (along with our own credibility to exercise authority), arguably binds us to a counterproductive underestimation of student plagiarism as a *social* phenomenon and *our role* in this ongoing construction.

Second thoughts

> I began to have second thoughts. The truth was that, although I said I'd been robbed, I didn't feel that way.
>
> *(Gladwell, 2004: 41)*

For the record, while I have issues with recent extensions of copyright authority (Darnton, 2009),[8] I don't harbor a soft spot for source amnesia, whether crass, unintended, self-plagiaristic, kleptomanic or otherwise. And I don't teach in a monastery, my institutional affiliation notwithstanding. From firsthand experience, I readily acknowledge that some students appear determined to do whatever it takes. Many probably succeed, but, of course, not everyone. Each year, at my institution anyway, a handful of miscreants are caught red-handed, if not always abashedly red-faced, and disciplined to varying degree as each faculty member and school handles run-ins with plagiarism in their own *ad hoc* way. This informal situation may soon go the way of big city newspapers (Rodriquez, 2009), as faculty grow more adept at deploying antiplagiarism software and adjudication and as punishments are applied more evenhandedly, that is, formalized across the university. Meanwhile, until that day dawns, the likelihood of apprehending and disciplining offenders remains more the exception than the rule.

Before we wedge ourselves into a tighter epistemic corner, therefore, might we better use the 'crisis' as a ripe heuristic moment to pilot the self-checking question: are we, indeed, asking the appropriate questions? In straightforward Geertzian terms (Geertz, 1973), is the vice and disqualification discourse thick enough? Is C&P, in brief, *up to the explanatory task, or has it lost its spell?* For example, rather than take the crime metaphor at its un-nuanced face, might it also prove beneficial to reframe the 'crisis' as reflecting not only instances of narcissistic trespass (MEism. com) but as a possible indicator and portent, if you will, *of a larger cultural struggle over who governs the definition, production and certification of legitimate knowledge* – a (passing in the night) storytelling contest of divergent orders of knowing in which students, as incongruous as that may sound, actually play an oversized role?[9] Assigning students a less passive role in defining IP *in our house*, no less, holds promise to reward members of the academy with a complementary understanding (one closer to our own professed breadth and depth ideals) of the defining issues/authority at hand (Graff, 1995; Bizzell, 1998). At the same time, this inclusive step injects a sensitivity of the effects that varying responses on our part are likely to produce *and to teach* regarding the scope of faculty–student connection.

As a probationary departure, why not embark on easing the tight-fisted hold of the us/fallen angels binary validating the C&P prism by recasting plagiary as 'plagiary,' as a *community*-achieved 'speech-event' (Smith, 1998; Musson, Cohen & Tietze, 2007)? And then use this reversal of perspective as rationale for mirroring our own working assumptions? This exit strategy may well free up retrospective space to begin transforming the plagiary cat-and-mouse into a real-time mutual teaching moment for students *and* faculty alike to fashion a *collective* understanding of ourselves. Making it thinkable, where it wasn't before, to view the academy's prosecutor's mode with the same curiosity as the purported problem to be rectified. The research site for the construction of plagiary is effectively scaled up to include not just isolated cases of student (mis-)behavior but the academic *cultural* landscape writ large.

Coming to terms

> Unlike academic knowledge, . . . new media literacy is structured by the day-to-day practices of youth participation and status in diverse networked publics. This diversity of youth

values means that kids will not fall in line behind a single set of literacy standards that we might come up with, even if those standards are based on the observations of their own practices.

(Ito et al., 2010: 344)

From a constructivist optic, Paul de Man (1919–1983) pretty much says it all:

Far from there being nothing outside of the text, everything was out there, waiting to be called back into reality by the power of words.

(Kernan, 1990: 187)

This was de Man's succinct warrant, as I read it, to cut the Stockholm syndrome of orthodox (timeless, irreversible, closed-book) belief systems down to (human) size. The reenvisioning of established truth as a language form (Cunliffe, 2001; Boje, Oswick & Ford, 2004) – half full, contingent, all too human achievement – opened the door to demystifying scrutiny, including what a particular truth says about the world, how it goes about saying it and whose values it expresses (Bazerman, 1989; Coombe, 1989). No longer beyond question, gospel demoted to human artifact invited testing, debate, heresy and innovation. Unveiled as perishable, historical constructions, hardcore truths – whether of the political, social, economic or scientific variety – all yield to T. Kuhn's (1977) provisional prevailing wisdom thesis. In common with the transitory nature of retreating glaciers, the 'natural' rate of unemployment, accounting standards, straightforward meanings, papal primacy, home ownership and even house rules, sacred cows' days are likewise numbered. To paraphrase Kuhn, an axiomatic mentality arrives to red carpet fanfare, eventually overstays its welcome (i.e., lame duck status – reaches a tipping point where questions outnumber and outweigh answers placing the 'common sense' itself in question) and, over the course of time, falls out of fashion (loses its grip, its incontrovertible status). With the regularity of semesters, definitive narrative bell curves come and go.

This portrayal of entropic decay, mind you, seldom occurs overnight or without intense struggle (Durkheim, 1965; Hannah & Freeman, 1984). But even stone tablets, market fundamentals (Frank, 2000), handwriting, and the book (Bell, 2005) are, in theory, not exempt.[10] Cases in point: due to broad cultural/technological transformations, the self-evident plausibility consecrating modernist conceptions of the self-sufficient author, the sanctity of intellectual property, and received notions of plagiary (Jones, 1991) are similarly under review, i.e., topical – in question and jeopardy (showing their age) (Sebberson, 1993; Rorty, 1998; Posner, 2002; Lethem, 2007; Heffernan, 2009; Lessig, 2010). The extended reach of property over the last three decades has split legal scholars over the seesawing balance between intellectual property rights and the public domain (Boyle, 1997; Lessig, 2002; Rose, 2005; Goodman, 2009). Academics in Literary and Composition Studies whittle away at rusty 18th-century Romantic notions of authorship and originality propping up copyright extension (S. Miller, 1990; C. R. Miller, 1996; Woodmansee, 1994; Coombe, 2006). Likewise, historians and sociologists of knowledge sift through the genealogical pedigrees of contemporary definitions of intellectual property (Belknap, 1982; Buranen & Roys, 1999). Adding another chorus to this (de-)composing process, champions of open sourceware and 'sharing economies' vociferously declaim that dated notions of property in use today actually impede finding solutions to the intermeshed ecology of 21st-century challenges (Lessig, 2001; Vaidhyanathan, 2001; Baca, 2006, Schmidt, 2007).

And while we sleep, the Internet nation, our students, likely more than less oblivious of the *Sturm und Drang*, collectively test our patience, our envelopes, and possibly even our relevance (Fitzpatrick, 2002), right before our very eyes. Is giving due credit only 'academic' to many students (Heffernan, 2008; N. Cohen, 2009; P. Cohen, 2009; Lewin, 2009)?[11] As much as some may wish otherwise, in the case of IP, no one-truth, compositional ground zero apparently exists today, if it ever did (Schultz, 1993; Coomb, 1998). Everything considered, perhaps we all might be better off redirecting the relentlessly tactical energy expended building better mousetraps to mapping richer and more negotiable models of the cultural topography of plagiarism.

In house

> I think the gulf between academic and student culture can be closed only by starting respect-fully from where students already are.
>
> *(Graff, 1995: 276–277)*

We faculty face a host of lingering questions. Take enforcement, for example. Can it be safely assumed that colleagues carry a secret wish to be law enforcement constabulary (Porter & DeVoss, 2006)? Or would most prefer to avoid head-butting, student/parent versus instructor melo-dramas? Moreover, as of this writing no statistical consensus yet exists regarding the scope of (or even definition of) plagiarism (Foucault, 1987; Buranen & Roys, 1999). If we looked hard enough, would we find that some curricular designs proffer perverse incentive to plagiarize?[12] Is punishment meted out evenly across disciplines and schools? Plus, the common sense regard-ing plagiarism's ubiquity is based nearly exclusively on student self-reporting polls which must, statistically speaking, always be taken with a confirmationally biased grain of salt (Bakalar, 2010). At this point, the 'evidence' collected to date appears circumstantial at best, while normalizing the adversarial trope. What *is* certain is that the *anti*plagiarism *business* is a growth industry. Specifi-cally, a mushrooming paper mill sector (bad) and its purported foil, plagiarism-detecting software systems (good), hint at a symbiotic market for both services (Bartlett, 2009; Dante, 2010; Truong, 2010). While hard 'evidence' of turpitude may be anecdotally soft, that has not prevented the construction of plagiarism into a crisis of epic proportion and a scalable, entrepreneurial market for deception and detection (Altheide, 2002).

Which brings us to the two proverbial elephants in our house (Bell & King, 2010): (1) how much longer will the canonical *MLA Handbook* own the privilege of the last word? Suppose for a moment that a meaningful fraction of our computer-literate students – our protégés, no less – are, in fact, not on the same (timeless) page. Are not, in fact, apprentices to our master model of slow, sustained, focused literacy (Kapitzke, 2011), but, as it were, distractedly troop-ing (and streaming) through (Connelly, 2011; Parker-Pope, 2010; Richtel, 2010b). And that perhaps, unwittingly, but nonetheless quite literally, students in general are busy writing their own pragmatic digital style guide beneath our out-of-joint noses. For argument's sake, might the plagiarism 'crisis' extend canonically beyond interpersonal misunderstanding or indiscre-tions or outright villainy? Is it conceivable that the point-and-click generation blithely oper-ates from an alternative literacy (Leu, Kinzer, Coiro & Cammack, 2004, Gee, 2006; Valentine, 2006, Carr 2010) regarding the baroque fine print interpretations of intellectual property, originality and/or authorship? That, in short, the academy's organizing centrality and vision of solidarity and continuity may not be shared, *nor even comprehended*, by more students than we might care to consider? Making it thinkable, even feasible, then, that students, disconcert-ing though it may sound, are well along on a *de facto* 'restatement' of the rules of composition (Berlinski, 2008). If that registers, then waging jihad on student piracy may potentiate as much Whack-a-Mole (Sisario, 2010) as law and order, particularly in light of the avowed borderless zeitgeist of cyberspace. In the very least this twist also puts the efficacy of stopgap 'mechanisms of discipline' (Campbell, 1999) from off-the-rack honor codes, preemptive doses of education, obligatory readings of style guides, to the castor oil of example-setting punishments (failing grades, suspensions, expulsions) in interpretive play.

Given our investment in the algorithm of proprietary grievance, dare we entertain the thought that our firewall of declaratory inoculations – warnings, prophylactic seminars and, most recently, oath taking (Arnold, 2010) – fail to scarecrow? That is, carry little street cred with 'generation download'? We, in effect, declare a grudge match on student plagiary, but only the home team shows. Taking threat assessments at their word or possibly worried that our bluff might be called, many academic authorities are scrambling to erect a foolproof infrastructure of integrity relying heavily on electronic spyware (or, more politely, verification software) to amass proof beyond a reasonable doubt. In this capacity the personal computer functions as a paradoxical, interactive medium, one capable of giving as well as profiling. Regarding the latter, in light of its inherent panoptic potential to expose (Foucault, 1979; Ryan, 1987; Boyle, 1997; Kovacs, 2001) – spyware's unparalleled normative sweep, if you will; literally hiding in plain sight, why would anyone dare indulge in stolen pleasures? Factor in Foucault's program to unearth the genesis of hearts and minds, *self*-policing subjectivity, and *why even contemplate* cheating? Quote:

> [H]e who is subjected to a field of visibility, *and who knows it*, assumes responsibility for the constraints of power; he makes them play spontaneously upon himself; he inscribes in himself the power relation in which he simultaneously plays both roles; *he becomes the principle of his own subjection.*
>
> *(Foucault, 1979; in Hall & duGay, 1996; my italics).*

Under the naked circumstances (Purdy, 2005) – ever fearful of leaving a digital trail, 'subjects' instinctively conform, i.e., work from the same dog-eared MLA page. No more lame alibis. No more plea bargaining. No more get-out-of-jail-free cards.

Yet, it's a little early for end zone dancing. As with ethical binaries, the 'internalization of control' (Foucault, 1993) comes with a catch, i.e., it fails to satisfy Geertz's litmus test of thickness. The backdrop mosaic of social factors, not to mention the 'governing mentalities' embedded in such push-button technology and those it targets, are once again shunted to the sidelines. And while these tools of 'the gaze' make it easier to uncover, if not situate, incidents of rule breaking, including those of delinquent scholars (Carlson, 2005), *we still lack the analytical wherewithal to explain why anyone in this totally transparent landscape would – as apparently countless digital Millennials swimmingly do 24/7 – stake their reputations against such casino-like house odds in the first place?*

A predicament, unless, *unless* the panoptic inmates turn out *not* to be the undeviating, self-interested Benthamite actors that the internalization edifice revolves around. What does this portend for self-disciplining if students live worlds apart, conscience-free in another cultural literacy (Hall & duGay, 1996)? Don't appreciate our house rules about paying down intellectual debts? Punch in primarily to make the grades necessary to win a fast-track ticket to the mother of all shows – the marketplace? If the student 'body' escapes 'docility' (cut their puppet strings), are we, bluff called, out of moral ammo?

Then there's the companion elephant: what, precisely, does the disciplinary option *teach* students, i.e., the take-away life lessons? Are they ones we have closely examined, ratified and want students to emulate? After all, from Maslow's fusty Hierarchy of Needs (Maslow, 1943) to more contemporary versions of Expectancy Theory, I know of no work in the vast terrain of Motivational Theory that sanctions low-trust leadership models (Steel & Konig, 2007). After the dust has settled, how do we calibrate the *disconnective* cost of catechetic suspicion to the fabled 'conversation' and 'hospitality' underwriting the fecundity of university life (Sen, 2006; Haughey, 2009)? Over and over again Lawrence Lessig pleads that the vital diversity and creative health of democracy hinges upon how we decide 'how far free access should reach' (2001, 2002, 2010). Might the same be said of the large spirited heterogeneity of the academic house? Hence, the need to pay special attention to what the endorsement of exclusion may mean for the culture of intellectual ferment that is the university *and* the legitimacy of academic authority.

Taken together, these inward-looking questions are of vital importance for the cultural ecology of the university, particularly if the forensic metaphor represents a sputtering narrative form low on expressive power. Narrative theorists stress that we live in and out of 'storied' cultural spaces woven together with language (Bizzell, 1987; Miller, 1989; Law, 1991; Golinski, 1993; Fish, 1998; Rodden, 2008; Herman & Vervaeck, 2009). Is it really going out on a limb to propose that the socio-political constraints that configure the manufacture of knowledge apply equally to plagiarism? By acknowledging the contingency of the subject – devising more flexible ways to think about plagiarism *and its layered backstory complexity*, we, alongside other constituencies in this ongoing interpretive process, are better positioned to hash out property and plagiary narratives that a listening (connected), dialogic consensus can live with (Gergen, 1999; Coombe & Herman, 2001). Smooth sailing? Unlikely. For if the hissy response to Stanley Fish's bedeviling foray is any indication, finding some sort of middle ground may be asking too much for those steeped in the venerable (and now vulnerable?) Gutenberg organizing principle of immersion (Kapitzke, 2001). Nevertheless, the fate of the deep reading agenda, I believe, ultimately hinges on our self-overcoming readiness to hot potato the C&P filibuster to better size up the impact of the meandering, 'task-saturated' literacy(-ies) of the plugged-in on student engagement (Carr, 2010, Kinzer, 2010).

Afterword: It takes a village[13]

> As social practices, all literacies – including information literacy – are situated responses to specific political economies of educational contexts and classrooms (453).
>
> *(Cushla Kapitzke, 2001)*

Bear in mind first that, like IP, or constructionism, or the 'intent' of the framers of national constitutions, or mathematics, universities are open-ended works-in-progress, something we all habitually do together. And, second, my hunch is that university students absorb as much outside of the classroom ('extracurricular' learning – life lessoning) as inside the classroom (exposure to official curriculum).[14] Where might these suppositions lead? For one, school is never out. Learning goes on around the clock, in *and* out of class, whether we direct it or not. (Perhaps extracurricular learning derives its power from the underappreciated cultural fact that we are always and everywhere 'in class.') It also follows that every member (and event, object) of the university inclusive of faculty, students, administrators, the board of directors, the night-shift of janitors, anguished decisions to thin the ranks of the university's support services, choice of commencement speakers, grading rubrics, campus racial realities, the content and configuration (specialisms) of the core curriculum, sports programs, where we invest (vote) our endowment dollars, overwhelmingly female secretarial staff, antiplagiarism campaigns – you name it – is, willy-nilly, a teacher in her or his (or its) own right. And what each of us teaches the other through word and deed permeates the quotidian social fabric of the university, ultimately affecting our communal ability to connect and act creatively. Why walk the plank of self-examination? Simply because it is an honored academic tradition, one accommodating a devout curmudgeon and an offbeat perspective or two. Moreover, if self-engagement is not enfranchised at the university, then where?

It is perhaps difficult for many of us to acknowledge this tacit agenda given our investment in the classroom and the off-radar nature of extracurricular learning. But *this* off-screen education,

I'll venture, is what constitutes the university's deep core curriculum: the university's unquestioned common sense. It is not a curriculum casually forgotten at the close of each term. It's so ingrained that we embody it, are disciplined to *feel* it. Indeed, the deep curriculum derives its staying power because we are up to our necks in it. It's the radioactive (osmotic) house we make together. Yet, since it is customary to situate industrial-strength learning in the classroom, we tend not to give the informal curriculum its due.

If we are concerned with the content and quality of the university's teaching mission, as I am convinced we are, it follows that house rules must be regularly engaged. And, when warranted, we must be open to the reworking of the life lessons contained therein. *We in the university are not in the business of leaving well enough alone.* Our relevance, remember, rests on our ability to extend the theoretical base along with student horizons, by composing more adequate portraits of how we go about everyday living – together. Doing our level best, that is, to navigate the divide between formal classroom (the talk) and campus life lessons (the walk) (Grabtree & Sapp, 2003). After all, it's complicated. Meaning that how we deal with plagiary – as a lack of morality or a pedagogic moment, say – is both telling and representative – a finger on the pulse of student/faculty relations, but also a vehicle by which to better gauge what students and faculty are teaching one another. And, as such, it is a double-check opportunity for building the kinds of university learning we want to happen and be known for (Biggs, 2001).

Notes

1 For Pat and Dan.
2 This essay draws upon my U.S.-based experiences and may have special resonance for academics who are familiar with the idiosyncracies of the 'American' (i.e., U.S.) system and culture. It is my hope, however, that the ideas being discussed in this chapter might trigger useful debates on intellectual property rights (IPR) in other academic circles as well.
3 Irony by way of unwanted consequences: digital push-back and potential lawsuits. When file swapping, officially authorized or otherwise, appears to have evolved into a rite of digital passage, don't expect members of the *Wired* generation to simply roll over. Many are returning fire in court and/or busy configuring adroit, one-step-ahead-of-the-law file-sharing software without end (Pareles, 2005). I suspect that if the Academy blindly emulates the take-no-prisoners model of the Recording Industry Association of America, it chances mutating answers into problems.
4 A popular commercial television show in the United States.
5 'Perps' is a term commonly used by police departments in the United States to refer to 'perpetrators' of crimes.
6 A drug for attention-deficit hyperactivity disorder (ADHD), prescribed to extremely large numbers of students in the United States.
7 Binaries paradoxically depend on codependent association. Per Binde reminds us that 'separation and unification, and contrast and similarity, are not modes of conceptually organising the world that exclude each other, but rather that *imply* (the original) each other . . . [T]he distinction between them can be maintained only by constant monitoring, discussion, negotiation, and affirmation of their relationships, since each of the domains is defined in relation to the others' (p. 25).
8 When first drafted in 1790, the first copyright act set the length of copyrights and patents for 'limited times' (i.e., 28 years). Reflecting different motivations, the Sonny Bono Copyright Term Extension Act of 1998 extended copyright authority to the lifetime of the author plus 70 years.
9 Cushla Kapitzke (2001) details what academic literacy is up against: 'The nonlinearity of hypertext sequencing is fast obliterating the conventional categories of knowledge and its hierarchical organization in, for example, the DDC. Furthermore, the ephemeral and hybrid nature of digital environments tends to elide differences between the real and virtual worlds, and therefore between factual and fictional ones. Information literacy derives from a print-based culture, and its logic as it currently stands maintains distinctions between, for instance, fiction and nonfiction, and between reading for pleasure and reading for information. These distinctions and their associated practices, such as the reading of novels in time reserved for silent, sustained reading (SSR), are becoming increasingly obsolete and discriminatory. For many youth today,

particularly in advanced capitalist countries, reading is no longer performed alone with a book, but is a shared activity undertaken with and around a computer screen while engaged in conversation with others who are in the room, in cyberspace, or in both.' See Kapitzke (2001: 452–453). See also Alison Gopnik's (2010) review of Stanislas Dehaene's *Reading in the Brian: The Science and Evolution of a Human Invention* (Viking, 2010), *New York Times*, January 3, 2010.

10 Before going out of business in March 2015, Rapid-Share, a leading file-hosting company based in Switzerland, reputedly used to offer a rich buffet of pirated music and e-books free to subscribers. When a reporter once prodded a company spokesperson about the content stored on Rapid-Share's servers, her (fore?)telling response was 'for us, everything is just a file, no matter what' (Stross, 2009).

11 The average student is largely socialized (pixilated?) in language use via television and the computer, so it's plausible that they function with little, if any, appreciation of the antecedent foundation of academic intellectual discourse. The makings for a cultural divide? See Bizzell (1978).

12 Consider, for example, the potential moral squeeze points built into the last, crunch time, projects-fall-due week closing every semester for, say, honors students, or lackluster students, for that matter. Different, but perhaps only by a matter of degrees from the ethics-testing pressure points scientists and business practitioners are often compelled to negotiate in the gray space of professional life.

13 Adapted from the Executive Summary for the November 22, 2005, Workshop on Shareholder Engagement and Jesuit University Endowment Management prepared by J. Michael Cavanaugh.

14 Time for some Math 101. Full-time students at my place of employ are required to take a minimum of 15 hours of class a week. That leaves 153 hours or 91% of each academic week, give or take, free for extracurricular 'class time.'

References

Altheide, D. L. (2002). *Creating fear: News and the construction of crisis*. New York: Aldine de Gruyter.

Arnold, C. (2010). Graduate students sign MBA oath. *Fairfield University Currents: Campus Edition, 36*(10): 1.

Ashworth, P., Bannister, P., & Thorne, P. (1997, June). Guilty in whose eyes? University students' perceptions of cheating and plagiarism in academic work and assessment. *Studies in Higher Education, 22*(2): 187–203.

Baca, M. R. (2006). Barriers to innovation: Intellectual property transaction costs in scientific collaboration. *Duke Law and Technological Review, 4*. Retrieved from LexisNexis Academic.

Bakalar, Nicholas. (2010). With baby on board, lying about a smoking habit. *The New York Times.* Retrieved from http://www.nytimes.com.

Bartlett, T. (2006, March 10). Ohio U. investigates plagiarism charges. *The Chronicle of Higher Education.* Retrieved from http://chronicle.com.

Bartlett, T. (2009, March 20). Cheating goes global as essay mills multiply. *The Chronicle of Higher Education.* Retrieved from http://chronicle.com.

Bazerman, C. (1989, Winter). Introduction: Rhetoricians on the rhetoric of science. *Science, Technology, & Human Values, 14*(1): 3–6.

Belknap, R. L. (1982). Review of Michael Holquist & Caryl Emerson, *The Dialogic Imagination: Four Essays* by M. M. Bakhtin. *Slavic Review, 41*(3): 580–581.

Bell, D. (2005, May 2). The bookless future: What the Internet is doing to scholarship. *The New Republic.* Retrieved from http://tnr.com.

Bell, E., & King, D. (2010, September). The elephant in the room: Critical management studies conferences as a site of body pedagogics. *Management Learning, 41*(4): 429–442.

Berlinski, D. (2008, April). The evidence of things not seen. *Harper's*, 17–21. Retrieved from http://www.harpers.org.

Berrett, D. (2011, April). Skimming the surface. *Inside Higher Ed.* Retrieved on April 19, 2011 from http://www.insidehighered.com.

Biggs, J. (2001). The reflective institution: Assuring and enhancing the quality of teaching and learning. *Higher Education, 41*: 221–238.

Bijker, W. E. (1995) *Of bicycles, Bakelites, and bulbs: Toward a theory of technological change*. Cambridge, MA: MIT Press.

Binde, P. (2001). Nature in Roman Catholic tradition. *Anthropological Quarterly, 74*(1): 15–27.

Bizzell, P. (1978). The ethos of academic discourse. *College Composition and Communication, 29*(4): 351–355.

Bizzell, P. (1982). College composition: Initiation into the academic discourse community. *Curriculum Inquiry, 12*(2): 191–207.

Bizzell, P. (1987). Review of *Invention as a Social Act* by Karen Burke LeFevre. *College Composition and Communication*, *38*(4): 485–486.

Bizzell, P. (1998). Beyond antifoundationalism to rhetorical authority: Problems defining "cultural literacy." In M. Bernard-Donals & R. R. Glejzer (Eds.), *Rhetoric in an antifoundational world: Language, culture, and pedagogy*: 33–64. New Haven, CT: Yale University Press.

Blackstone, W. (1990). Commentaries "2" in Laura S. Underkuffler. "On Property: An Essay." *The Yale Law Journal*, *100*(1): 127–148.

Boje, D. M., Oswick, C., & Ford, J. D. ((2004). Language and organization: The doing of discourse. *The Academy of Management Review*, *29*(4): 571–577.

Boyle, J. (1997). A politics of intellectual property: Environmentalism for the net? *Duke Law Journal*, *47*(1): 87–116.

Buranen, L., & Roys, A. M. (1999). *Perspectives on plagiarism and intellectual property in a postmodern world.* Albany, NY: SUNY Press.

Campbell, N. D. (1999). Regulating 'maternal instinct': Governing mentalities of late twentieth-century U.S. illicit drug policy. *Signs*, *24*(4): 895–923.

Carlson, S. (2005, June 10). Journal publishers turn to software to root out plagiary by scholars. *The Chronicle of Higher Education*. Retrieved from http://chronicle.com.

Carr, N. (2010). *The shallows: What the Internet is doing to our brains.* New York: W. W. Norton & Co.

Cavanaugh, J. Michael. Executive Summary. Proceedings of Workshop on Shareholder Engagement and Jesuit University Endowment Management, Fairfield University, Fairfield, CT, November 22, 2005.

Chace, William M. The decline of the English department. *The American Scholar* (September 1, 2009). Retrieved on March 10, 2015 from https://theamericanscholar.org/the-decline-of-the-english-department/#.VP7hlI4lmxw.

Cohen, A. (2005, October 9). Want social condemnation with your justice? Tune in Judge Judy. *The New York Times*. Retrieved from http://www.nytimes.com.

Cohen, N. (2009, February 2). Some fear Google's power in digital books. *The New York Times*. Retrieved from http://www.nytimes.com.

Cohen, P. (2009, February 25). In tough times humanities must justify their worth. *The New York Times*. Retrieved from http://www.nytimes.com.

Connelly, M. (2011, February 28). More Americans sense a downside to an always plugged-in existence. *The New York Times*. Retrieved from http://www.nytimes.com.

Coombe, R. J. (1989, Winter). Room for maneuver: Toward a theory of practice in critical legal studies. *Law & Social Inquiry*, *14*(1): 69–121.

Coombe, R. J. (1998). *The cultural life of intellectual properties: Authorship, appropriation, and the law.* Durham, NC: Duke University Press.

Coombe, R. J. (2006). Authorial cartographies: Mapping proprietary borders in a less-than-brave world. *Stanford Law Review*, *48*(5): 1357–366.

Coombe, R. J., & Herman, A. (2001). Cultural wars on the net: Intellectual property and corporate propriety in digital environments. *The South Atlantic Quarterly*, *100*(4): 919–947.

Cunliffe, A. L. (2001). Managers as practical authors: Reconstructing our understanding of management practice. *Journal of Management Studies*, *38*: 351–371.

Dante, E. (2010, November 12). The shadow scholar: The man who writes your students' papers tells his story. *The Chronicle of Higher Education*. Retrieved from http://chronicle.com.

Darnton, R. (2009, February 12). Google and the future of books. *The New York Review of Books*. Retrieved from http://nybooks.com.

Demirjian, K. (2006, May 11). What is the price of plagiarism? When someone steals another's words, the penalties can vary widely. *The Christian Science Monitor*. Retrieved from http://www.csmonitor.com.

Durkheim, E. (1965). *The elementary forms of the religious life.* New York: Free Press.

Eagleton, T. (1983). *Literary theory: An introduction.* Minneapolis: University of Minnesota Press.

Fish, S. (1998). Rhetoric. In M. Bernard-Donals & R. R. Glejzer (Eds.), *Rhetoric in an antifoundational world: Language, culture, and pedagogy*: 33–64. New Haven, CT: Yale University Press.

Fish, S. (2010a, August 9). Plagiarism is not a big moral deal. *The New York Times*. Retrieved from http://www.nytimes.com.

Fish, S. (2010b, August 16). The ontology of plagiarism: Part two. *The New York Times*. Retrieved from http://www.nytimes.com.

Fitzpatrick, K. (2002). The exhaustion of literature: Novels, computers, and the threat of obsolescence. *Contemporary Literature*, *43*(3): 518–559.

Foucault, M. (1979). *Discipline and Punish*. New York: Vintage Books.

Foucault, M. (1987). What is an author? In V. Lambropoulos & D. N. Miller (Eds.), *Twentieth-century literary theory*: 124–142. Albany, NY: SUNY Press.

Foucault, M. (1993). About the beginnings of the hermeneutics of the self: Two lectures at Dartmouth. *Political Theory, 21*(2): 198–227.

Frank, Thomas. (2000). *One market under God: Extreme capitalism, market populism, and the end of economic democracy*. New York: Doubleday.

Gee, J. P. (2001). Reading as a situated language: A sociocognitive perspective. *Journal of Adolescent & Adult Literacy, 44*(8): 714–725.

Gee, J. P. (2006). Oral discourse in a world of literacy. *Research in Teaching English, 41*(2): 153–159.

Geertz, C. (1973). Thick description: Toward an interpretative theory of culture. In C. Geertz, *The Interpretation of Culture*: 3–30. New York: Basic Books.

Gergen, K. J. (1999). *An invitation to social constructionism*. London: Sage.

Gjoen, H., & Hard, Mikael. (2002, Spring). Cultural politics in action: Developing user scripts in relation to the electric vehicle. *Science, Technology, & Human Values, 27*(2): 262–281.

Gladwell, M. (2004, November). Something borrowed: Should a charge of plagiary ruin your life? *The New Yorker*. Retrieved from http://www.newyorker.com.

Goleman, D. (2009). *Ecological intelligence: How knowing the hidden impacts of what we buy can change everything*. New York: Broadway Books.

Golinski, J. (1993). Review: The rhetorical maelstrom. *Isus, 84*(4): 746–749.

Goodman, E. (2009, April 3). Putting the care back in health care. *The Daily Hampshire Gazette*. Retrieved from http://www.gazettenet.com.

Gopnik, A. (2010, January 3). Mind reading. *The New York Times*. Retrieved from http://www.nytimes.com.

Gordon, M. E., & Palmon, O. (2010). Spare the rigor, spoil the learning. *Academe, 96*(4): 25–27.

Grabtree, R., & Sapp, D. (2003, Fall). Theoretical, political, and pedagogical challenges in the feminist classroom: Our struggles to walk the walk. *College Teaching, 51*(4): 131–140.

Graff, G. (1995, May). Conflict pedagogy and student experience. *College Composition and Communication, 46*(2): 276–279.

Hafner, K. (2001, June 28). Lessons in internet plagiarism. *The New York Times*. Retrieved from http://www.nytimes.com.

Hall, S., & DuGay, P. (1996). *Questions of cultural identity*. London: Sage.

Hannah, M. T., & Freeman, J. (1984, July). Structural inertia and organizational change. *American Sociological Review, 49*(2): 149–164.

Haughey, J. C. (2009, July). *Where is knowing going: The horizons of the knowing subject*. Washington, DC: Georgetown University Press.

Heffernan, Virginia. (2008). Content and its discontent: Why new forms of media must evolve along with new technology. *The New York Times Magazine*, December 7, 16–18.

Heffernan, V. (2009, June 9). Image in a haystack. *The New York Times*, 14.

Herman, L., & Vervaeck, B. (2009, January). Narrative interest as cultural negotiation. *Narrative, 17*(1): 111–129.

Hoover, E. (2002, May). Honor for honor's sake? *Chronicle of Higher Education*. Retrieved from http://chronicle.com.

Howard, R. M., Rodrigue, T. K., & Serviss, T. C. (2010, Fall). Writing from sources, writing from sentences. *Writing and Pedagogy, 2*(2): 177–192.

Ito, M., et al. (2010). *Hanging out, messing around, and geeking out: Kids living and learning with new media* (John D. and Catherine T. MacArthur Foundation Series on Digital Media and Learning). Cambridge, MA: MIT Press.

Jones, D .B. (1991, Summer). Book review of Alvin Kernan's *The Death of Literature. Modern Language Studies, 21*(3): 107–109.

Kapitzke, C. (2001). Information literacy: The changing library. *Journal of Adolescent & Adult Literacy, 44*(5): 450–463.

Kernan, A. (1990). *The death of literature*. New Haven, CT: Yale University Press.

Kinzer, C. K. (2010, September). Considering literacy and policy in the context of digital environments. *Language Arts, 88*(1): 51–61.

Kolich, A. M. (1983, February). Plagiarism: the worm of reason. *College English, 45*(2): 141–148.

Kovacs, A. (2001). Quieting the virtual prison riot: Why the internet's spirit of 'sharing' must be broken. *Duke Law Journal, 51*(2): 769–785.

Kuhn, T. S. (1977). *The historical structure of scientific discovery: The essential tension.* Chicago: University of Chicago.

Law, John. (1991, April). Theory and narrative in the history of technology: Response. *Technology and Culture, 32*(2), Part 1: 377–384.

Leeds, J., & Lohr, S. (2005, June 28). No pot of gold in court ruling for studios. *The New York Times.* Retrieved from http://www.nytimes.com.

Lessig, L. (2001). *The future of ideas: The fate of the commons in a connected world.* New York: Random House.

Lessig, L. (2002). The architecture of innovation. *Duke Law Journal, 51*(6): 1783–1801.

Lessig, L. (2010, January 26). For the love of culture: Google, copyright, and our future. *The New Republic.* Retrieved from http://www.tnr.com.

Lethem, J. (2007, February). The ecstasy of influence: A plagiarism. *Harper's Magazine, 314*(1881): 59–71.

Leu, D. J., Kinzer, C. K., Coiro, J. L., & Cammack, D. W. (2004). Toward a theory of new literacies emerging from the Internet and other communication technologies. In R. E. Rudder & N. J. Unrau (Eds.), *Theoretical models and processes of reading*: 1570–1613. Newark, DE: International Reading Organization.

Lewin, T. (2009, August 9). In a digital future, textbooks are history. *The New York Times.* Retrieved from http://www.nytimes.com.

Mahler, J. (2009, August 2). The soul of the city. *The New York Times Book Review.* Retrieved from http://www.nytimes.com.

Maslow, A. H. (1943). A theory of human motivation. *Psychological Review, 50*(4): 370–396.

McCabe, D., Butterfield, K. D., & Trevino, L. K. (2006). Academic dishonesty in graduate business programs: Prevalence, causes, and proposed action. *Academy of Management Learning & Education, 5*(3): 294–305.

McGrath, B. (2011, January 31). Does football have a future? The N.F.L. and the concussion crisis. *The New Yorker*, 41–51.

McLemee, S. (2004, December 17). What is plagiarism? A special report on plagiarism. *The Chronicle of Higher Education.* Retrieved from http://chronicle.com.

Miller, K. D. (1991). Voice of deliverance: The language of Martin Luther King, Jr. and its sources. *The Journal of American History, 78*(1): 120–123.

Miller, C. R. (1996, May). This is not an essay. *College Composition and Communication, 47*(2): 284–288.

Miller, S. (1989). *Rescuing the subject: A critical introduction to rhetoric and the writer.* Carbondale & Edwardsville: Southern Illinois University Press.

Miller, S. (1990, February). Cross-cultural underlife: A collaborative report on ways with academic words. *College Composition and Communication, 41*(1): 11–36.

Musson, G., Cohen, L., & Tietze, S. (2007, February). Pedagogy and the 'linguistic turn': Developing understanding through semiotics. *Management Learning, 38*(1): 45–60.

Palmer, P. J. (1998). *The courage to teach: Exploring the inner landscape of a teacher's life.* San Francisco: Jossey-Bass.

Pareles, J. (2005, June 29). The court has ruled so enter the geeks. *The New York Times.* Retrieved from http://www.nytimes.com.

Parker-Pope, T. (2010, June 6). An ugly toll of technology: Impatience and forgetfulness. *The New York Times.* Retrieved from http://www.nytimes.com.

Perfetto, G. (2010). The end of higher ed enrollment as we know it: What colleges and universities need to understand before it's too late. White Paper #1. Retrieved from www.admissionslab.com.

Pfaffenberger, B. (1992). Technological dramas. *Science, Technology, & Human Values, 17*: 282–312.

Pocha, J. S. (2006, April 9). Internet exposes plagiarism in China. *Boston Globe*, A7.

Porter, J. E., & DeVoss, D. N. (2006). Rethinking plagiarism in the digital age: Remixing as a means for economic development. WIDE Research Center Conference. Retrieved from http://www.wide.msu.edu/widepapers/devossplagiarism.

Posner, Richard A. (2002, April). On plagiarism: In the wake of recent scandals some distinctions are in order. *The Atlantic Monthly, 289*(4): 23–25.

Purdy, J. P. (2005). Calling off the hounds: Technology and the visibility of plagiarism. *Pedagogy, 5*(2): 275–296.

Rich, M. (2006, May 3). 'Opal Mehta' won't get a life after all. *The New York Times.* Retrieved from http://www.nytimes.com.

Richtel, M. (2010a, November 21). Growing up digital, wired for distraction. *The New York Times.* Retrieved from http://www.nytimes.com.

Richtel, M. (2010b, February 28). Outdoors and out of reach: Studying the brain. *The New York Times.* Retrieved from http://www.nytimes.com.

261

Rodden, J. (2008, Winter) How do stories convince us? Notes toward a rhetoric of narrative. *College Literature, 35*(1): 148–175.

Rodriquez, R. (2009, November). Final edition: Twilight of the American newspaper. *Harper's, 319*(1914): 30–38.

Rorty, R. (1998). The contingency of language. In M. Bernard-Donals & R. R. Glejzer (Eds.), *Rhetoric in an anti-foundational world: Language, culture, and pedagogy:* 65–85. New Haven, CT: Yale University Press.

Rose, C. M. (2005, September). *Privatization: The road to democracy.* Discussion Paper No. 06-11, University of Arizona Legal Studies. Retrieved from http://ssrn.comabstract=881877.

Ryan, A., (Ed.). (1987). *John Stuart Mill and Jeremy Bentham: Utilitarianism and other essays.* London: Penguin.

Schmidt, S. (2007). Review: J. Demer. Steal the music: How intellectual property law affects musical creativity. *Enterprise and Society 8*(1): 217–219.

Schultz, D. (1993). Political theory and legal history: Conflicting depictions of property in the American political founding. *The American Journal of Legal History, 37*(4): 464–495.

Sebberson, D. (1993). Reviewed works: *Textual dynamics of the professions: Historical and contemporary studies in writing in professional communities.* C. Bazerman & J. Paradis. *Rhetoric Society Quarterly, 3*(2): 50–54.

Sen, A. (2006). *Identity and violence: The illusion of destiny.* New York: W. W. Norton.

Sisario, B. (2010, November 27). U.S. shuts down web sites in piracy crackdown. *The New York Times.* Retrieved from http://www.nytimes.com.

Smith, R. E., III. (1998). Hymes, Rorty, and the social-rhetorical construction of meaning. In M. Bernard-Donals & R. R. Glejzer (Eds.), *Rhetoric in an antifoundational world: Language, culture, and pedagogy:* 227–253. New Haven, CT: Yale University Press.

Steel, P., & Konig, C. J. (2007). Integrating theories of motivation. *Academy of Management Review, 31:* 889–913.

Stross, R. (2009, October 4). Will books be Napsterized? *The New York Times.* Retrieved from http://www.nytimes.com.

Swearingen, C. J. (1987, April). A comment on 'Martin Luther King borrows a revolution.' *College English, 49*(4): 476–478.

Truong, K. (2010, June 24). A new tool to catch plagiarism in admissions essays. *The Chronicle of Higher Education.* Retrieved from http://chronicle.com.

Underkuffler, L. (1990). On property. *The Yale Law Journal, 100:* 127–148.

Vaidhyanathan, S. (2001). *Copyrights and copywrongs: The rise of intellectual property and how it threatens creativity.* New York: New York University Press.

Valentine, K. (2006, September). Plagiarism as literacy practice: Recognizing and rethinking ethical boundaries. *College Composition and Communication, 58*(1): 89–109.

Woodmansee, M. (1994). *The author, art, and the market.* New York: Columbia University Press.

Worse than an F: Canadian university pioneers new grade for failure. (2009, June 24) *The Chronicle of Higher Education.* Retrieved from http://chronicle.com.

15

Teaching management critically
Classroom practices under rival paradigms

Gabriela Coronado[1]

Since the inclusion of management education (ME) in universities, there have been many debates around what it should be and whose interests it should reflect. Different perspectives on its value for business and/or society have divided the academic and professional communities. There is, however, agreement that universities need to provide knowledge and intellectual skills to prepare graduates to play a role in organizations where they will be employed. But what are the skills and knowledge needed, and whose interests define them? Should business schools respond to or challenge business interests?

Business schools[2] have an important role in determining what and how they teach, but they are exposed to multiple economic, academic and ideological demands. It is widely acknowledged that "coinciding with the period of neoliberalism, there has been a shift from considering education as a public good to education as a private consumer good" (Joseph, 2012: 240). In this process, the mission of universities as a service to society has shifted to become creators of products to be bought by students, to acquire skills that potential employers from business organizations demand. As a commodity, a degree stamped by a particular university becomes part of what Pfeiffer & Fong (2002) refer to as the pedigree syndrome. What matters is not the knowledge but what the degree symbolizes in measurable outcomes: university ranking, certification, grades.

Under these pressures, academics like myself, teaching in management programs, have to respond to procedures designed by universities to deliver education in a commoditized way, which claims to respond to student market demands and business expectations. In this context, curriculum development and the design of specific knowledge products (subjects and degree programs) respond to multiple pressures from universities and their business and academic stakeholders. As such, management education cannot be dissociated from the existing management paradigms and the legitimation of their knowledge, that is, the discursive regimes (Fairclough & Wodak, 1997) that have shaped the evolution of academic thinking, practice and pedagogy in universities. In this chapter I address the differences in the two existing paradigms in management, one represented by *mainstream management* and its hegemonic discursive regime of neo-liberalism and managerialism, the other *Critical Management Studies* (CMS), which questions the legitimacy of dominant hegemonic business ideologies.

With a focus on Critical Management Education (CME), I will discuss the implications of the coexistence of these different paradigms and how both shape forms of knowledge and pedagogical practices employed in universities to teach business students. In my argument, I use critical readings of documents from management discursive communities (see Hardy & Thomas, 2012), including the business community and mainstream management discipline and the textbook industry that serves them.

Drawing on an autoethnographic approach, understood as personal self-reflexivity directed to my experience of educational practice (Coronado 2009b), I reflect on the challenges of making management students critical, referring to my own practice as a critical management educator teaching in an undergraduate management degree in an Australian university. I relate those experiences to CME and share some strategies I have developed. In particular, I will refer to students' engagement with, or resistance to, CMS and emphasize the importance of assignments as a driving force for promoting critical thinking and indirect forms of opposition to the hegemonic paradigm.

Implications of the paradigm divide in management education

Historically, different academic disciplines have played a role in defining dominant forms of knowledge. As discursive regimes, they have limited the scope of inquiry and excluded alternative ways of thinking. According to Foucault (1971), a discursive regime defines what is legitimate knowledge (accepted as 'truth' or 'sense' for the specific community), constraining who can say what to whom and how it can be said (Coronado 2012). What prevails are hegemonic forms of knowledge, which constitute and reproduce academic disciplines as paradigms, i.e., a "constellation of concepts, values, perceptions and practices shared by a community which forms a particular vision of reality that is the way the community organizes itself" (Clarke & Clegg, 1998:9).

In the management discipline, the hegemonic discourse is held by two interconnected sectors: the mainstream management academics and the business community, whose interests and demands are at the center of the first group. Both share the dominant ideology in contemporary society, neoliberalism (Munck, 2005). Neoliberalism, like all ideologies, is complex and has been defined in many ways at different times (see Thorsen's 2009 review). For my argument. I use the term in Harvey's (2005) sense:

> Neoliberalism is in the first instance a theory of political economic practices that proposes that human well-being can best be advanced by liberating individual entrepreneurial freedoms and skills within an institutional framework characterized by strong private property rights, free markets and free trade. The role of the state is to create and preserve an institutional framework appropriate to such practices.
>
> *(p. 2)*

Neoliberalism's assumptions have been naturalized and globally spread, defining free market state policies. At a micro level, neoliberalism is represented as managerialism, an ideology that assumes that independently of different values, aims, industries or countries, all organizations are basically similar and can be managed in the same way, through generic business technics and skills mostly defined by the American model of business management (Hodge, Coronado, Duarte & Teal, 2010). Neoliberalism and managerialism as constitutive of the management discursive regime are the hallmarks of the hegemonic management paradigm.

University teachers are under pressure to conform to these managerial models, which define how we perform our educational practices and what knowledge and skills we teach to business students. Through different discourses and practices, the hegemonic management paradigm shapes the work academics do in business schools, impacting their capacity to teach management critically. Among these pressures, we can refer to managerial forms of "quality" control, the role of business as university stakeholders, and the influence of the textbook industry. These are not the only ones, but they represent some of the main *obstacles* for critical educators.

Universities increasingly respond to the pressures of neoliberal policies that use funding systems to define education and research. Instruments of "quality" control have been imposed in the form of policies and regulations for standardization and consistency in the "product" to produce the graduate attributes demanded by the workplace. These regulatory instruments respond to external pressures. At the national level, constraints from the funding models and curriculum audits are used to ensure international consistency in the quality of higher education, so that universities can compete successfully in the global education markets (de Meyer, 2012; Vaara & Faÿ, 2012).

One relevant Australian instance is the creation of national bodies such as the Tertiary Education Quality and Standards Agency (TEQSA), a regulatory and quality agency for higher education. In their own words: "TEQSA's primary aim is to ensure that students receive a high quality education at any Australian higher education provider" (http://www.teqsa.gov.au/). Other influences defining ME include the role of business advisers in assessing management degrees and the demands for certification from professional associations. The expectation is to achieve homogeneous business programs that respond to business needs. In the words of the Business Council of Australia, "The challenges involved in adapting to new and changing workplaces. . . require effective generic skills. Generic skills including communication, teamwork, problem solving, critical thinking, technology and organizational skills have become increasingly important in the workplace" (BCA, 2011: 8). That is to say, with minor differences, demands on management education include the development of intellectual skills similar to other disciplines, such as liberal arts and social sciences (Khorn, 2012).

Management degrees offer similar programs, with subjects with almost identical titles, using textbooks that represent minor variations of the same content. In this standardization process, the textbook plays a crucial function as an instrument to reproduce the dominance of mainstream management. Textbooks define content and teaching approaches that carry ideologies and values reflecting business interests to be transmitted in business schools (Coronado, 2012). In common pedagogic practice, every subject design must include one textbook, and the content and structure of the teaching program follows its structure. In this way the omnipresent textbook industry defines what forms of knowledge are acceptable, limiting the possibility of introducing *counter-hegemonic* alternatives. Decisions on what is published are based on what sells in the massive management degrees offered by neoliberal universities.

Even so, in practice there are still opportunities to circumvent this dominance. I have always struggled with the use of textbooks and resisted their use. As I explained to a colleague:

> If you don't use the textbook, students say the course is "unstructured", but if you use it you have to spend so much time criticizing it. What else can you do? The problem is that students still believe that if it's in the textbook it must be true. They always expect you to tell them what is right or wrong, and of course this means according to the textbook.
>
> *(May 20, 2012)*

I tried compiling customized readers, with different perspectives from CMS and other disciplines (sociology, political science, complexity theory). This practice is not uncommon in other disciplines, but in management my students rejected it every semester. I also tried customized textbooks, which allowed me to provide readings in a glossier format. Even though students had to pay a higher price, they found this more acceptable, and despite some limitations it did provide critical perspectives from other disciplines (e.g., Coronado, 2009a). This kind of resistance to the ideologies of the hegemonic paradigm is limited, and still dominant discursive instruments control the dissemination of knowledge. Critique is allowed but under their terms, i.e., as long as they are aligned with their assumptions, values and ideologies.

It would be simplistic to suppose that hegemonic and counter-hegemonic paradigms do not include competing perspectives. They do. Without ignoring such complexity, however, it is still possible to identify basic points that divide the two paradigms. The divide is evident in the critique of ME appearing in Adler, Forbes and Willmott (2007):

> For many, work is premised on relations of subordination, exploitation, and intimidation. What we tend to find in textbooks and curricula in place of these topics, is a series of 'code words'. Sweatshop exploitation, the vast inequalities of the global value chains, endemic economic disenfranchisement and the palpable alienation of the many are addressed (as if to protect ourselves from the mess that such issues provoke) by way of phrases like 'strategic choices', 'corporate social responsibility' and 'diversity', while alienation, disenfranchisement and subordination seem to be expressed in term of the problematics of 'trust' and 'commitment' and 'loyalty'. . . what is taught is not meant to reflect current realities and 'disturbances' but to provide a sketch of ideal relations and circumstances that managers ought to try and create.
>
> *(p. 133)*

In agreement with this view my intention is to stress key differences that characterize the tension between the two perspectives interacting within business schools. In Figure 15.1, I represent the two paradigms, highlighting key qualities that typify paradigm distinctions as transmitted in ME.[3]

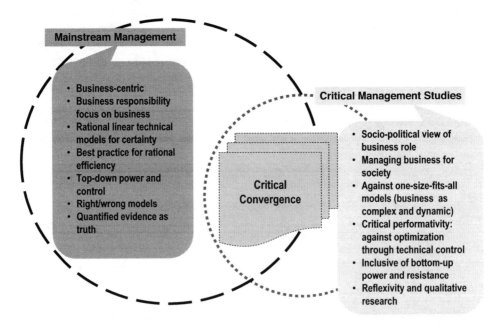

Figure 15.1 Contrasting mainstream and critical management paradigms.

As shown in the figure, the two paradigms are characterized by opposite emphases on some aspects of business practice and the significance or otherwise of the social impacts of those practices. Mainstream management gives priority to the ideologies, needs and processes involved in improving the efficiency of business for being profitable at any cost. As such, its objectives can be defined as business-centric and the consideration of impacts of business practices as restricted to business performance and interests. Any negative impact outside business is seen as collateral. To fulfill those priorities, emphasis in ME is put on the importance of management models that rationally, and using measurable facts, ensure certainty. In this way, the models defined as right promote the expectation that it is possible to identify and apply best practices to achieve business efficiency independently of contextual conditions. Business performance is guaranteed by the application of one-size-fits-all procedures. Under these rational models, top-down forms of power and control are legitimized in the hands of top executives, acting on behalf of corporate interests.

In contrast, the Critical Management Studies paradigm emphasizes the responsibility of business in society and highlights the existence of ideological forms of hegemonic power embedded in business practices. Through critical analysis of business performance its *de facto* status is denaturalized, exposing how management's existing models have ideological and ethical implication, perpetuating historical, economic, political and social forms of domination. Consequently, CMS scholarship incorporates debates on socio-political analysis of business organizations embedded in complex and dynamic power relations, in which potential resistance from all levels of the organization and society emerge. Based on those objectives, critical thinking and reflexivity are promoted in management education for students to uncover false assumptions regarding business performativity.

It needs to be noted that the diversity inherent in any paradigm demands recognition of existing self-critical perspectives that might converge with other paradigms. Academic management communities produce an exchange of perspectives that are more or less critical of hegemonic ideologies, generating an overlap. This is especially important when referring to CME, where academics not regarded as CMS also engage critically. In that respect, it is crucial to recognize that management as taught in ME includes many ways in which knowledge is represented, questioned, contradicted and transformed. Critical pedagogies have often been used in mainstream management, and when it comes to defining the mission, curriculum and pedagogies of business schools, discursive convergence and coexistence of different paradigms become evident. Paradigm concurrence constitutes one of the challenges CMS academics face when trying to teach management critically, since each paradigm carries ideologies that serve opposing interests.

CMS as a counter-discourse has been generated by dissenting academics with different disciplinary backgrounds (e.g., anthropology, sociology, psychology, etc.) employed by business schools. It is interdisciplinary and heterogeneous but unified around debates that emerge from critical views of the role of business and management in society. CMS academics and their allies focus their research precisely on the critique of hegemonic management theories and practices. Even if CMS can be considered as an "active and subversive intervention into managerial discourses and practices" (Spicer, Alvesson & Karreman, 2009: 538), its overlaps with some mainstream critical perspectives have opened up the possibility of its acceptance as part of the academic management landscape.[4]

Many CMS scholars are well-known and have published extensively in top journals and highly respected editorial houses (see, for example, Alvesson, Bridgman & Willmott, 2011; Jack & Westwood, 2009; Prasad, 2003, 2012; Willmott, Kenny & Whittle, 2011). Although some of their publications can be useful resources for teaching business students, with few exceptions (e.g., Clegg, Khornbergger & Pitsis, 2005; Knights & Willmott, 2007), those are oriented toward higher research degrees or master's courses (including MBAs), rather than large undergraduate courses where students are just beginning to acquire basic academic skills. Consequently, CMS perspectives are still underrepresented in educational resources used in undergraduate ME.

Challenges for critical approaches to management education

Having worked in the management program of a business school, I assume the presence almost everywhere of a diversity of academics, holding both critical and noncritical perspectives. I have also found, however, some agreement around the importance of critical thinking as a key graduate attribute. Therefore, the expectation that management students will acquire critical thinking can be seen as a discursive convergence between opposed paradigms. Such convergence is not uncommon within discursive regimes and can be explained in terms of what Hodge and Kress (1988) call the ideological complex. By understanding discourse as an ideological complex, we can recognize how contradictions can be incorporated within a hegemonic ideology to neutralize counter-discourses.

Appropriation of a critique in rhetorical terms can get around resistance without always transforming its effects of dominance. A clear example of the ideological complex in management education is the way business ethics and corporate social responsibility have become part of the managerial perspective in textbooks (e.g., Arnold, Beauchamp & Bowie, 2012; Steiner & Steiner 2011). Another example is how management programs are incorporating the United Nations' Principles for Responsible Management Education (PRME) initiative by simply adding the word "responsibility" without any other change (Solitander, Fougère, Sobczak & Herlin, 2012).

The discursive convergence around critical thinking may offer a potential opening to teach CMS in management. But the question arises: is critical thinking in CME critical of the managerial paradigm or merely a tool to increase the latter's dominance? The ideological differences of the two paradigms create problems for critical teaching in business schools, where students are exposed to both, but these are usually presented as if the difference does not exist. Given that the two management approaches are divided by ideology, it is likely that uses of the term "critical thinking" will have different aims, depending on the respective paradigm.

The challenge for CMS, then, is to respond to a demand defined by mainstream management, which according to Datar, Garvin and Cullen (2011) must:

> reassess the facts, frameworks, and theories that they teach (the "knowing" component), while at the same time rebalancing their curricula so that more attention is paid to developing the skills, capabilities, and techniques that lie at the heart of the practice of Management (the "doing" component) and *the values, attitudes, and beliefs that form managers' world views and professional identities* (the "being" component) [my emphasis].
>
> (p. 456)

CMS academics have to acknowledge those demands, understood by their schools as legitimate, and at the same time denaturalize the assumptions of those who share "the managers' world views."

Although CMS academics are still a minority, some hold senior positions based on their research strengths, which are valued by university funding systems (see Contu, 2009). They also have allies who may not be entirely convinced of various aspects of the heterogeneous CMS agenda (e.g., radically questioning business or Eurocentrism) but who share the belief that critical views of management and critical pedagogies are important. The contrasting assumptions of the two paradigms interact in business schools' attempts to define ME, with implications for teaching CMS and CME approaches in business schools.

Critical thinking in management education

Since both academic groups are immersed in the management ideological complex, it is not surprising to encounter some convergence around what is quality education. I find it difficult to imagine, for instance, any opposition to what the Business Council of Australia expects from universities: "to produce graduates who have . . . 'The ability to think independently, critically analyse issues and problems, and to adapt thinking and analytical skills to different contexts and new problems'" (BCA 2011; report in Hall, Agarwal & Green, 2012: 21).

Despite such convergence, these skills are interpreted *differently* under the two paradigms. There is no doubt that CMS academics agree that graduates should be critical thinkers, but it is expected that their understanding of the term "critical" is different:

> The CMS use of the term critical signifies more than an endorsement of the standard norms of scientific skepticism or the general value of "critical thinking." It also signifies more than a focus on issues that are pivotal rather than marginal. Critical here signifies radical critique. By radical is signaled an attentiveness to the socially divisive and ecologically destructive broader patterns and structures – such as capitalism, patriarchy, imperialism, and so forth – that condition local action and conventional wisdom. By critique, we mean that beyond criticism of specific, problematic beliefs and practices (e.g., about teamwork), CMS aims to show how such beliefs and practices are nurtured by, and serve to sustain, divisive and destructive patterns and structures; and also how their reproduction is contingent and changeable, neither necessary nor unavoidable.
>
> *(Adler, Forbes & Willmott, 2007, p. 137)*

An examination of how critical thinking is understood in ME makes clear that the term "critical" is used mainly in the BCA sense, bounded by the ideological values of the hegemonic paradigm that CMS questions. This can be illustrated with how textbooks describe critical thinking:

> The ability to think critically and analytically is a **conceptual skill**. It involves the ability to break down problems into smaller parts, to see the relation between parts, and to recognize the implications of any one problem for others. As we assume ever-higher responsibilities in organizations, we are called upon to deal with more ambiguous problems that have many complications and longer term consequences.
>
> *(Schermerhorn, Campling, Poole & Wiesner, 2011: 22; bold in the original)*

This implies a skill that can be applied irrespective of what is the problem, who is affected and who is responsible. It indicates that thinking critically is a form of clear reasoning, useful for analysis independently of the subject matter (see also Datar, Garvin & Cullen, 2011). The assumption that practices are neutral appears in many other aspects of management textbooks. They presume a rationalistic management approach with clearly defined models that are taught to students without recognizing the inherent complexities of the contexts of application or the power dimensions.

One common criticism of ME is its detachment from reality: "it is clear that many people's experience of organizations is one that differs substantially from the presentation of work organizations found in conventional classrooms and textbooks" (Prichard, 2009: 53). Such lack of connection between models proposed in management teaching and the real organizations they are applied to is also criticized by university business stakeholders. As in the case of the term "critical," convergence between business and critical academics on this issue too can be rather superficial. Businesses demand that management models are taught for more efficient control over workplace practice, so that managers reproduce businesses interests. From a critical perspective, the aim is for students to recognize that what they learn in mainstream management textbooks hides the reality of power underlying business practice and managers' workplace behavior. From this perspective, the link with reality does not consist of merely learning models for business to be successful but learning the internal dynamics of such success and its impacts at the societal level.

Since the two distinct paradigms cohabit in business schools with some overlaps around how "critical" is understood, critical pedagogies can be applied to both forms of ME. Both may produce critical responses to business practices, but they do so in unpredictable ways. CME does not operate in a vacuum but includes a diverse range of experiences, values and ideologies carried by teachers and students. Thus, even if we hold a CMS perspective, our intent to transform students into critical thinkers does not necessarily mean they will become critical of business values and ideologies. Students are responsible for their own learning and subsequent practices.

Consistent with the principles of a critical education, we need to recognize students' right to hold their own views, even if they reject our critique. Not to allow disagreement with critical perspectives on business would legitimize anti-CME claims that students are at risk of becoming confused: "[t]o engage such students in modes of critique that attack their dominant positions without enabling them to construct alternate subject positions is to risk their cultural displacement, alienation and disillusionment" (Fenwick, 2005: 34). Even if I agree with the importance of "enabling" alternative positions, the assumption that students share the dominant position seems to ignore the diversity currently existing in business schools.

In my experience, students are capable of integrating critical perspectives into a complex framework for when they are or will be participating in the workforce. When criticizing business practices in classes, I have encountered more resistance than disillusionment. But the resistance is not simply a rejection of the critique. Students may accept the validity of the criticism but challenge it because of the reality of the workplace, where questioning business power can be the difference between being employed or not.

Applying critical pedagogies demands recognition of students' different backgrounds. I teach in a non-elite Australian university attended by students from diverse cultural backgrounds. This case is different from that in many other universities, where "the typical students of the critical management educator are not those at the margins of society, but at the centre" (Perriton & Reynolds, 2004: 71). Many of my students speak English as a second language and are the first generation in their family to enroll in tertiary education. Even if they are exposed to mainstream management in other courses, critical perspectives can tap into their underlying empathy with CMS views. After the first moment of surprise (as they will have mostly encountered noncritical perspectives), students can quickly recognize that in exploitative business practices they will be the ones exploited, as their parents were.

In this context I will discuss some CME approaches and the implications for CMS academics teaching in business schools. I describe some tactics I have explored to teach management critically in my classroom practice and how students have reacted.

Teaching management with critical pedagogies

It is possible to identify a number of different critical pedagogies in the Critical Management Education literature (see Grey, 2007). In many cases, these accounts focus on the application of one or another approach, emphasizing how it improves the learning experience, i.e., how to better learn what is on offer. Often these critical approaches do not explicitly question the hegemonic management discourse. Even more invisible is the role of educational resources in teaching practice.

The use of specific materials, for example case studies, is not uniform, and even if claims can be made for their value in learning, there are enormous differences in how to use them and what questions to ask. The case studies included in mainstream textbooks are generally used to reinforce the content presented in the chapter and to ensure that specific knowledge is attained, while implicit ideologies are internalized (see Nicolai, 2004). But using case studies detached from their original aims offers scope to critically question the accepted management models. Audiovisual materials present similar patterns, especially as packaged by business education providers. The use of such resources as critical pedagogies to promote critical thinking or problem solving might improve learning but not always the critical questioning advocated by CMS, unless the case studies used are provided by CMS academics themselves (Rostis & Mills, 2010).

The use of films and TV documentaries not controlled by the business education industries can offer more to support multiple modes of learning and provide broader scope for CME (see Panayiotou, 2011). However, what lecturers do with any of those resources is not well known, except occasionally when academics reveal how they use them (e.g. Mathews, Fornaciari & Rubens, 2012; Mallinger & Rossy, 2003). Outside these published accounts, we can only rely on our own experiences and those of colleagues that we overhear in meetings, corridors or the lunch room. Hence my account of attempts to teach management critically as presented here comes from everyday experience in my university, school and program.

An autoethnography of my undergraduate classroom

Coming from anthropology to teach management, I found the CMS agenda invaluable and consistent with my previous interest in Freire's (1972) Liberation Education as a pedagogic framework. In ME, some have questioned the application of Freire's emancipatory pedagogy, arguing that it applies only to the "oppressed," the main target of Freire's literacy programs. Perriton and Reynolds (2004: 73) propose an alternative pedagogy, "pedagogy of refusal," to teach "the privileged business student," based on refusing to follow the dominant ideology of managerialism. Without discounting the potential of this form of critical pedagogy for CMS, attempts to limit Freire's usefulness and value for CME – on the unfounded assumption that business students are all privileged – appear to be flawed. Moreover, Freire's critique of power relations inherent in the hegemonic system of education – what he refers to as the "banking" system of education, where students are passive recipients of information "deposits" from lecturers – is highly pertinent for management education because it questions not only (1) the university model of commoditized education under which we have to teach but also (2) the resources provided by the hegemonic discourse, namely, textbooks and other educational techniques, which reproduce student passivity and a relatively uncritical embrace of hegemonic ideologies by students.

Another key point in Freire's approach, which underlies the CMS paradigm, is the development of critical social consciousness, i.e., making students aware of how domination operates so that they are able to understand the conditions of power and oppression, independently of how "oppressed" they are personally. When we teach management uncritically, we reproduce the conditions to perpetuate *intellectually* "oppressed citizens," indoctrinating them into the hegemonic business discourse. CMS and liberation education are conceptually deeply intertwined, and I try consistently to follow this critical pedagogy.

Although I draw on other critical pedagogies as well (see Coronado, 2011), Freire's philosophical principles are the foundation of my CMS approach, always undergirding the "social contract" I use to construct relationships in class. From the beginning, an explicit agreement is established between me and the students emphasizing the dialogic character of the learning process. I also use his ideas in analytical practices required for classroom activities and in the design of assignments in which students are guided to discover "untested feasibilities," i.e., what is possible but hidden by taken-for-granted assumptions (Freire, 1972: 85). By challenging those assumptions, students might find possible solutions not seen before.

I applied these principles in the first subject I designed in the management degree in 2002, namely, Business Society and Policy. In my first week, I questioned the banking system of education and outlined the dialogic expectations of the class, emphasizing the students' right (even obligation) to question my perspective. I systematically worked on developing trust, so that students could believe that, irrespective of my position of power in the student–teacher relationship, I would not give them a failing grade for disagreeing with me. Every semester, I share the following real story from the early days of my teaching:

> Once, one student worked very hard to defy my views on capitalism. He demonstrated an excellent understanding of the readings and used counter-arguments to sustain his perspective. He got a high distinction.

Also, I challenged the assumption of there being only one right answer when dealing with dilemmas involving ideological positions. In a Socratic approach, I generated group discussions where all points of view were invited for debate, including my having to play devil's advocate when everyone agreed with me (see Fallon, 2006, on uses of Socratic method in teaching business ethics).

In the second week, I introduced the study of capitalism based on a reading from the *Communist Manifesto* (Marx & Engels, 1970). I now recognize my naivety about business students, who were not expecting to find Marx as a main reading. After a bit of shock, my approach still generated critical thinking and some acceptance of criticism of capitalism. It is clear to me now that students generally tend to be conservative when it comes to innovations in ways of teaching. Any change from past precedents provokes a measure of rejection. Word of mouth to other students seemed to ease acceptance of my new approaches in later years.

In developing this subject, I realized that explicitly reading and discussing Freire and Marx was counterproductive. Without changing the principles and the themes, I subsequently introduced these ideas in a more understated way. The ideas were received with less resistance but still with transformative outcomes: better informed students who were convinced by the critical arguments and students who intelligently challenged my views.

Other less socially oriented subjects pose a different challenge: How to teach management critically and still respond to students' needs to learn relevant skills to work within the mainstream paradigm? This question kept me awake when designing Global Strategy and Management and Managing Professionals. Although in general my approach was the same, I explored different ways to promote critical thinking adapted to the specificity of each subject, scaffolding content, learning outcomes, tutorial activities and assignments (Biggs, 2004). Reflecting on my 10 years' experience teaching management. it is clear that when dealing with two paradigms in the same program, as in my case, it is advantageous to introduce critical views of the hegemonic discourse in a less confrontational way. My main strategy to subvert the boundaries imposed by hegemonic discourse and practices has become to promote critical thinking through different assignments.

Assignments in my view constitute the best opportunity for developing critical perspectives in the context of predominant managerialism. Consistent with the discourse of neoliberal education, assignments are measurable outcomes linked to the final destination. Thus, they are the focus of students and represent one of the few spaces left in which academics have a dutiful audience. Besides, assignment design provides a level of flexibility that can defeat bureaucratic forms of control. Common assessment modes such as essays, research reports, case studies, film analysis, presentations and even exams can be designed in multiple forms for different goals. Assuming that each assignment has its corresponding process of learning in tutorial activities, I expect that individual values and ideologies (mine and students') will be the undercurrents in the learning process, to be discovered, reflected on, debated and their implications taken responsibility for.

In three subjects I designed from scratch, my assessments included reflection on experiential learning (Cunliffe, 2004), use of sociological imagination (Mills, 1979; Duarte, 2009), ideological analysis (Chiapello & Fairclough, 2002), case analysis, Web-based research (Coronado, 2011) and introduction of complexity thinking (Levy, 2002) for students to respond to uncertainty by analysis of multiple scenarios. In all cases I included the search for unseen possibilities, the ultimate outcome for Freire's transformative education. All assignments were connected to concepts subtly aligned with CMS perspectives (sometimes included in the readings, always in lecture notes or lecture presentations). In all cases I required students to conclude by proposing alternative ways to deal with the issues at stake and identify ethical dilemmas.

Similar types of assignments were uniquely developed and adapted to challenges posed by subject content. All were aligned with tutorial activities for developing analytical skills, through reflections on how theory applies (or does not apply) to practice and continuous discussion of values and ideological implications of management practices. I emphasized the rejection of decontextualized, simplistic interpretations when found in conventional management interpretations. (See Figure 15.2 for how assignments were adapted at different moments of development in different subjects.)

Each assignment required students to question theoretical assumptions, discover real organizational challenges and reflect continuously on ideological assumptions and values. In my experience, constantly applying critical thinking (in the CMS sense) indirectly in assignments fulfilled the aims stated in managerial discourse (promoting critical thinking, problem-solving skills, applicability of theory to practice) and also exposed students to counter-discourses, giving them the opportunity to decide what kind of citizen/managers they wanted to become.

Subjects / Assignments	1. Business, Society and Policy (2nd year)	2. Global Strategy and Management (3rd year)	3. Managing Professionals (1st year Financial Advising)
Reflective Journals	a. Based on 3 key learning from each week reading using sociological imagination to link macro and micro business practices b. To document the process of research including suggestions to "solve" the problems and reflecting on ethical dilemmas.	Based on weekly questions around aspects of complexity and students' reflections on attempts to oncover unseen possibilities.	Evaluation of theories in practice, link between issues discussed in class and previous knowledge, or future professional management practice. Included *Description* (e.g., How did we work as a team?) *Critical explanation or analysis* (of specific situation that triggered attention; connects past experience with current thoughts) and *Reflection* (rethinking experience during the "learning situation" for future professional practice.
Case Analysis	Group analysis of 1 case including *3 individual reports* on one perspective each, and *1 group report* jointly produced comparing the 3 perspectives, highlighting ethical dilemmas and proposing alternative ways of managing the conflicts.	*Case analysis:* Company to be researched using weekly themes (for research).	*In tutorial activities:* For teams to evaluate theoretical perspectives applied cases studied from real organizational researched stories. Case problems for virtual team discussion and in exam (see below).
Research	*Individual research project* based on selection of research question on different social impacts of business practice (e.g., child labor, discrimination, health impacts and marketing, fair trade)	*Report/portfolio:* Identify variation under the recognition of complex environments. Highlight uncertainty and question rationality. Concluding with evaluation, pointing out problems and ethical dilemmas and suggesting recommendations.	*Team:* Professional research report to develop independent and collaborative forms of inquiry, drawing on Web-based research on professional firms and associations and informal face-to-face interviews. Analytical tools designed by teams in class to classify and compare data collected.
Presentations	*Team: Video analysis* from TV documentaries, highlighting conflicts from the interaction between business and society, ideological positions represented and ethical dilemmas, if any. To finish proposing a question for class discussion.	*Team: Complexity & Global Management* Application of Readings under a comparative frame of different multinationals researched by individuals	
Online discussion (part of Reflective Journals)	Using sociological imagination and ethical reasoning to explain: Why capitalism is considered an unjust system?		Contribution and reflections from the virtual team work around a designated problem solving activity.
Exam (when policy make it compulsory)	3 questions to be selected out of 6 given in advance. Students to write 3 short discussion essays explaining and discussing their perspectives.	3 Questions on complexity concepts to be answered through short discussion essays substantiating own perspectives in response to the questions.	Based on 2 problem-solving questions considering the perspective of the manager and of a professional. students discuss the problem, evaluate options and propose a solution according to each role.

Figure 15.1 Critical assignment designs in different subjects.

274

Conclusion

The challenges that CMS academics face in teaching management critically are complex and require dealing with multiple interests represented by various stakeholders involved in reproducing the hegemonic management paradigm. Given the university context and its identification with the hegemonic paradigm, CMS academics need to find alternative strategies to fulfill their critical objectives in teaching management degrees. First, we must survive as employees in a managerialist university, and second, we have to overcome the limitations imposed by the dominance of the managerial discursive regime and its instruments of control over management education.

Teaching management critically under these paradigms requires a continuous struggle to counteract the constraints on management degrees imposed by university management systems, as they try to make education a "commodity" – mass-produced, consistent and with quality controls that conform to the international competitive environment. As a minority position, CMS-rooted critical approaches to ME need to be strategically presented, providing critical intellectual skills commonly accepted as legitimate in conventional ME, while disseminating critical perspectives on business and management. In terms of my own experience, these strategies should not be confrontational so that they might circumvent resistance from students used to mainstream approaches, while also passing unnoticed by hegemonic forms of managerial control.

Although my account is anecdotal, I do not suppose my situation is unique. Like many other academics, my quotidian practice is just a constant quest to fulfill my educational aims, trying to contest a hegemonic ideology in my teaching and my praxis. By identifying discursive practices that influence the way in which ME has developed under the hegemonic discourses, I have uncovered some challenges that the CMS field faces in introducing a counter-hegemonic version of business education. Reflecting on my own classroom experiences and student responses, I have also shared in this chapter some positive strategies to help overcome the obstacles to teaching CMS under these difficult conditions.

Notes

1 I want to thank my colleagues in Organisational Studies, School of Business in UWS for sharing reflections on their teaching experience. Thanks in particular to Dr. Wayne Fallon for his constant experimentation in teaching management from a CMS perspective and for his feedback on a previous version of this text.
2 I refer to business schools in generic terms, but my focus is only on the discipline of management.
3 For this comparison, I draw on CMS publications (such as Adler, Forbes & Willmott, 2007; Alvesson & Willmott, 2011, 2012; Alvesson & Spicer, 2012; Fournier & Grey, 2000), together with the analysis of textbooks I have evaluated for my undergraduate teaching (e.g., Hill, 2010; Steiner & Steiner, 2008).
4 It is now possible to find CMS sessions in mainstream academic conferences (e.g., Critical Management Studies Division of the Academy of Management in the United States [http://group.aomonline.org/cms/Index.htm] or ANZAM, the Australian New Zealand Academy of Management). Critical views have a significant presence in organizational studies conferences and journals (APROS and *Organization*), and CMS has another Biannual International Conference as well.

References

Adler, P. S., Forbes, L. C., & Willmott, H. (2007). Critical Management Studies. *The Academy of Management Annals*, *1*(1): 119–179.

Alvesson, M., & Spicer, A. (2012). Critical leadership studies: The case for critical performativity. *Human Relations*, *65*(3): 367–390.

Alvesson, M., Bridgman T., & Willmott H. (Eds.). (2011), *The Oxford handbook of critical management studies*. Oxford: Oxford University Press.

Alvesson, M., & Willmott, H. (2012). *Making sense of management: A critical introduction* (2nd Ed.). London: Sage.

Arnold, D. G., Beauchamp, T. L., & Bowie, N. L (2012). *Ethical theory and business* (9th Ed.). Old Tappan, NJ: Pearson Higher Education.

BCA. (2011). *Lifting the quality of teaching and learning in higher education.* Melbourne: Business Council of Australia.

Biggs, J. (2004). *Teaching for quality learning at university: What the student does.* Berkshire, UK: Open University Press.

Chiapello, E., & Fairclough, N. (2002). Understanding the new management ideology: A transdisciplinary contribution from critical discourse analysis and new sociology of capitalism. *Discourse & Society, 13*(2): 185–208.

Clarke, T., & Clegg, S. (1998). *Changing paradigms: the transformation of management knowledge for the 21st century.* London: HarperCollins Business.

Clegg, S., Khornbergger, M., & Pitsis, T. (2005). *Managing and organizations: An introduction to theory and practice.* London: Sage.

Contu, A. (2009). Critical Management Education. In M. Alvesson, T. Bridgman & H. Willmott (Eds.), *The Oxford handbook of critical management studies*: 536–550, Oxford: Oxford University Press.

Coronado, G. (Comp.) (2009a). *Business, society and policy 200158, Customized Book of Readings.* Sydney: Pearson Education.

Coronado, G. (2009b). From autoethnography to the quotidian ethnographer: Analysing organizations as hypertexts. *Journal of Qualitative Research, 9*(1): 3–17.

Coronado, G. (2011). Web-based research as critical pedagogy: A reflection on its application to undergraduate management education. *Journal of University Teaching & Learning Practice, 8*(2), Article 6. Retrieved from http://ro.uow.edu.au/jutlp/vol8/iss2/6.

Coronado, G. (2012). Constructing the 'neocolonial' manager. Orientalising Latin America in the textbooks. In A. Prasad (Ed.), *Against the grain: Advances in postcolonial organization studies*: 155–177. Copenhagen: Copenhagen Business School Press.

Cunliffe, A. L. 2004. On becoming a critically reflexive practitioner. *Journal of Management Education, 28*(4): 407–426.

Datar, S. M., Garvin, D. A., & Cullen, P. G. (2011). Rethinking the MBA: Business education at a crossroads. *Journal of Management Development, 30*(5): 451–462.

de Meyer, A. (2012). Reflections on the globalization of management education. *Journal of Management Development, 31*(4): 336–345.

Duarte, F. (2009). Rekindling the sociological imagination as a pedagogical "package" in management education. *Journal of Management Education, 33*(1): 59–76.

Fallon, W. (2006). Rethinking 'business is business': A criticalist perspective on teaching business ethics. *Australian Journal of Professional and Applied Ethics, 8*(2): 78–92.

Fairclough, N., & Wodak, R. (1997). Critical discourse analysis. In T. A. van Dijk (Ed.), *Discourse as social interaction*: 258–284. London: Sage.

Fenwick, T. (2005). Ethical dilemmas of critical management education. Within classrooms and beyond. *Management Learning, 36*(1): 31–48.

Foucault, M. (1971). Orders of discourse. *Social Science Information, 10*(2): 7–30.

Fournier V., & Grey, C. (2000). At the critical moment: Conditions and prospects for critical management studies. *Human Relations, 53*(1): 7–32.

Freire, P. (1972). *Pedagogy of the oppressed,* Harmondsworth, UK: Penguin.

Grey, C. (2007). Possibilities for critical management education and studies. *Scandinavian Journal of Management, 23*: 463–471.

Hall, R., Agarwal, R., & Green, R. (2012). The future of management education. Scoping paper, Australian Business Deans Council, March. Retrieved on April 23, 2012 from http://www.abdc.edu.au/events.html.

Hardy, C., & Thomas, R. (2012). Strategy, discourse and practice: The intensification of power. *Journal of Management Studies* [doi: 10.1111/joms.12005, Consulted February 13, 2013].

Harvey, D. (2005). *A brief history of neoliberalism.* Oxford: Oxford University Press.

Hill, C.W.L. (2010). *Global business today.* Sydney: McGraw-Hill.

Hodge, B., Coronado, G., Duarte F., & Teal, G. (2010). *Chaos theory and the Larrikin Principle. Working with organisations in a neo-Liberal world.* Copenhagen: Copenhagen Business School Press.

Hodge, B., & Kress, G. (1988). *Social semiotics.* Oxford: Polity Press.

Jack, G., & Westwood, R. (2009). *International and cross-cultural management studies: A postcolonial reading.* New York: Palgrave Macmillan.

Joseph, C. (2012). Internationalizing the curriculum: Pedagogy for social justice. *Current Sociology*, *60*(2): 239–257.

Khorn, M. (2012). Wealth or waste? Rethinking the value of a business major. *The Wall Street Journal*, April 5, 2012. Retrieved on June 13, 2012 from http://csi.sagepub.com/content/59/4#content-block.

Knights, D., & Willmott, H. (2007). *Introducing organizational behaviour and management*, London: Thompson.

Levy, D. (2002). Applications and limitations of complexity theory in organization theory and strategy. In J. Robin, G. J. Miller & B. Hildrot (Eds.), *Handbook of strategic management*: 67–87. New York: Marcel Dekker.

Mallinger, M., & Rossy, G. (2003). Film as a lens for teaching culture: Balancing concepts, ambiguity, and paradox. *Journal of Management Education*, *27*(5): 608–624.

Marx, K., & Engels, F. (1970). Communist manifesto. In *Karl Marx and Frederick Engels Selected Works*: 35–47. London: Lawrence & Wishart.

Mathews, C. S., Fornaciari, C. J., & Rubens, A. J. (2012). Understanding the use of feature films to maximize student learning. *American Journal of Business Education*, *5*(5): 563–574.

Mills. C. W. (1979 [1959]). *The sociological imagination*. New York: Oxford University Press.

Munck, R. (2005). Neoliberalism and politics, and the politics of neoliberalism. In A. Saad-Filho & D. Johnston, *Neoliberalism: A critical reader*: 60–69. London: Pluto Press.

Nicolai, A. (2004). The bridge to the "real world": Applied science or a schizophrenic tour de force? *Journal of Management Studies*, *41*(6): 951–976.

Panayiotou, A. (2011). Deconstructing the manager: discourses of power and resistance in popular cinema. *Equality, Diversity and Inclusion: An International Journal*, *31*(1): 10–26.

Perriton, L., & Reynolds, M. (2004). Critical Management Education: From pedagogy of possibility to pedagogy of refusal? *Management Learning*, *35*: 6–7.

Pfeiffer, J., & Fong, C. T. (2002). The end of business schools? Less success than meets the eye. *Academy of Management Learning and Education*, *1*(1): 78–95.

Prasad, Anshuman. (Ed.). (2003). *Postcolonial theory and organizational analysis*. New York: Palgrave Macmillan.

Prasad, Anshuman. (Ed.). (2012). *Against the grain: Advances in postcolonial organization studies*. Copenhagen: Copenhagen Business School Press.

Prichard, C. (2009). Three moves for engaging students in Critical Management Studies. *Management Learning*, *40*: 5–68.

Rostis, A., & Mills, J. H. (2010). A pedagogy of the repressed? Critical management education and the teaching case study. *International Journal of Management Concepts and Philosophy*, *4*(2): 212–223.

Schermerhorn, J. R., Jr., Campling, J., Poole, D., & Wiesner, R. (2011). *Management: An Asia-Pacific perspective*. Milton, Queensland: Wiley.

Solitander, N., Fougère, M., Sobczak, A., & Herlin, H. (2012). We are the champions: Organizational learning and change for responsible management education. *Journal of Management Education*, *36*: 337–363.

Spicer, A., Alvesson, M., & Karreman, D. (2009). Critical performativity: The unfinished business of critical management studies. *Human Relations*, *62*(4): 537–560.

Steiner, G., & Steiner, J. (2011). *Business, government and society: A managerial perspective*. Sydney: Irwin McGraw-Hill.

Thorsen, D. E. (2009). The neoliberal challenge. What is neoliberalism? Working paper, Department of Political Science, University of Oslo, October 10. Retrieved on June 13, 2012 from http://folk.uio.no/daget/neoliberalism2.pdf 26/05/2012.

Vaara, E., & Faÿ, E. (2012). Reproduction and change on the global scale: A Bourdieusian perspective on management education. *Journal of Management Studies*, *49*(6): 1023–1051.

Willmott, H., Kenny, K., & Whittle A. (2011). *Studying identity and organizations*, London: Sage.

Part V
History and discourse

16
History of-in-and Critical Management Studies

Terrance G. Weatherbee

Introduction

This chapter is a theoretical exploration of the scholarly activities associated with the 'historic turn' (Clark & Rowlinson, 2004) as currently unfolding in both Management and Organization Studies (MOS) and Critical Management Studies (CMS). It is a synthesis of work which has taken place in organization studies over the last two decades constructed through my own effort(s) at investigating the processes of knowledge production occurring at the sites where History and MOS/CMS intersect and interact.[1] The focus of this enquiry was to understand the potentials of the turn to history for MOS/CMS when history is viewed as a process rather than as a product or outcome and to identify the implications this has for advancing our collective and future efforts at historiographical understanding (Weatherbee, Durepos, Mills & Helms Mills, 2012) in MOS/CMS. Though sections of this chapter deal with events antecedent to the present, and while this work is both historically and historiographically informed, the chapter itself is *not* intended to be read as a *history*.[2]

Prior to engaging with the contemporary activities within the historic turn, it is considered apropos to briefly illustrate the conditions within which contemporary MOS/CMS developed for two reasons. First, it fills a lacuna as the interactions between historical context and the development of these fields remain largely underexplored and unacknowledged (Stager Jacques, 2006). Second, because each area has traditionally maintained a different orientation towards the importance of history and historiography in research, entering the turn through a historiographic space in this way will highlight specific aspects of the conditions which saw the emergence and crystallization of the call for a historic turn. It will also situate the potential for history-work and its interrelation with the pursuit of historiographical understanding within MOS/CMS.

The loss of history and the emergence of the historic turn[3]

The following section summarizes the conditions and processes leading to the marginalization of historical consideration from MOS thought and research activities – whether those were conceptual, theoretical or substantive – a circumstance which was both concomitant with and constitutive of the entry and development of MOS as a separate field within the academy (Khurana,

2007; Weatherbee, 2012). It also provides the context for understanding how the dominant form of historical thinking in organization studies has come to be as it is.

Throughout the 20th century, management and business researchers slowly replaced 'rules of thumb' and 'anecdote' with increasingly scientific approaches (Khurana, 2007).[4] In doing so, they set organizational and business studies on an ahistorical trajectory.[5] This trajectory was further buttressed as the emergent MOS borrowed its foundation from the Policy/Administrative Science branch of Sociology (see, for example Parsons, 1956a, 1956b). A disciplinary domain where method and theory development had already largely moved to one based upon experimental and quantitative paradigms. In its marriage to the Social Sciences, MOS increasingly distanced itself from the Humanities (Zald, 1993) as it embraced a positivistic and functionalist approach to research (Burrell & Morgan, 1979; Weatherbee, 2012). This orientation would firmly sediment as MOS found its home within business school practices (Clark & Rowlinson, 2004). The marginalization or exclusion of history from introductory and pedagogical business texts (Stager Jacques, 2006) would follow despite protests from scholars who saw history as an important subject for the education of business practitioners and researchers alike (see, for example Bedeian, 1998; Cummings & Bridgman, 2011; Van Fleet & Wren, 2005; Wren, 1987; Wren & Van Fleet, 1983).

As history and historiographic considerations in MOS were quantized, marginalized and finally almost excised from business research and curricula, the ahistorical condition reached an equilibrium which would perpetuate itself.[6] In large measure, the only interaction with historical considerations that remained in MOS would be abandoned to only those with a special interest in history[7] or relegated and confined to the sub-specialties of Strategy and Business History (Khurana, 2007; Weatherbee, 2012). This slow evisceration would continue for almost a century before the absence of active historical consideration would become viewed as problematic by a broader group of scholars and researchers in both MOS and CMS (Booth & Rowlinson, 2006; Clark & Rowlinson, 2004; Kieser, 1994). The return to history was also a gradual process. It commenced in the early 1990s and evolved over the next two decades, somewhat more vigorously in the second half.[8]

In a review of the activities which could be categorized as taking place within the historic turn, Mills, Weatherbee and Durepos (2013) identified several distinct yet overlapping shifts present in the renewed trajectory of historiographic research in MOS/CMS during this time. These included approaches to historical and historiographic issues described as Factual (e.g. Chandler, 1994) , Contextual (e.g. Kieser, 1994), Methodological (e.g. Booth & Rowlinson, 2006) and Epistemic (e.g. Weatherbee, Durepos, Mills & Helms Mills, 2012). These shifts did not displace one another – as in an evolutionary series – but rather the later approaches tended to be added to the overall changes in the stratagems for historical consideration in research. What the analysis revealed was a return to historical consideration which was ongoing, shifting and variable with regard to how the past was/is being conceptualized. As will be argued in the following sections, this condition still holds, and it has several critical implications for understanding the process of ordering knowledge of the past in both MOS/CMS.[9]

The Factual and Contextual efforts of the turn first viewed the lack of historical consideration in organizational theory in general (Kieser, 1994) and the distancing of MOS from the humanities in particular (Zald, 1993, 1996) as two concerns. These centered on the absence of historical consideration of the contexts in which organizational theory was developed and in the exclusion of active consideration of the socio-contextual aspects of management research. In the case of the former, it was believed that history could more fully inform those engaged with theory development in MOS. In the case of the latter, it was believed that the relevance of MOS research to the practices of management required re-engagement from a more humanistic and less scientistic orientation.

Concurrent with and sympathetic to the expression of concern focused on the ahistorical and overly scientific nature of MOS research was a growing movement in research which was founded in alternatives to the mainstream approaches of knowledge production in MOS. Many of these alternatives were critical of MOS thought and incorporated historical perspectives as levers of critique. These various positions converged in their reaction to what was perceived as the increasingly hegemonic presence and spread of managerialist ideology, both within the academy and in the sphere of business practice outside. Broadly speaking, these researchers and their efforts have been described as critical studies of management (Mills & Helms Mills, 2012). These emerging and alternative approaches stemmed from various positions including critical sociology-, Marxian-, feminist-, critical theory-, postmodern- and poststructuralist-based critiques (Adler, Forbes & Willmott, 2007). Somewhat later, the appellation 'Critical Management Studies' would become a signifier for these critiques of managerialism, critiques which interrogated both the practice of management and its academic research arm – MOS (Fournier & Grey, 2000).[10] While historical consideration was often the basis for these alternative approaches, it would be some time later before a more contemporary 'CMS critical edge' would be brought to the historic turn (Durepos, 2014, forthcoming). This process would take another decade to more fully develop, and when it did, it would raise additional methodological and epistemic issues for consideration.[11]

From these critical and alternative-to-the-mainstream perspectives, the canonical history of MOS was largely read as a unitary re-presentation supported by a system of beliefs founded upon a simplistic historiography unproblematically assumed as a linear chain of chronological progress – a version of the past which had been so thoroughly naturalized throughout Western society and MOS that it went largely unquestioned by business researchers. It was a system with a history which not only valorized the benefits of managerialism and management theory – presenting both as progressive, scientific, timeless and universal (Booth & Rowlinson, 2006) – but which simultaneously concealed the hegemonic nature of its particularistic socio-political worldview (Weatherbee & Durepos, 2010). A dominance perpetuated by a historiography in which non-ideologically sanctioned and less than savory historical influences on/in/of management had effectively been written out (Cooke, 1999, 2003).[12]

A short time after the institutionalization of CMS within the Academy of Management, the call for the historic turn would become somewhat more formally recognized, heralded by the arrival of a critically oriented journal founded in 2006. The journal, *Management & Organizational History*, was intended to be a forum for critical and alternative approaches to history and historiography. It was designed to be an outlet that could recapture and renew historically informed research and theorizing in MOS from a critical perspective. It was to be a space for those forms/methods of historiographic research that were not being addressed elsewhere in the mainstream of organization studies, e.g. in publications such as the *Journal of Management History*.[13]

Many of the first and early scholars turned their attention to the potentials existing at the intersection of history and MOS and focused on exploring the terrain and on mapping potentials. These efforts sketched out theoretical challenges and identified the empirical potentials to be found in a renewed historicized approach (Booth & Rowlinson, 2006; see, for example, the terms of engagement as laid out by Stager Jacques, 2006, and for a more detailed description of the 'mapping' of the 'terrain', readers are referred to Weatherbee, Durepos, Mills & Helms Mills, 2012). These early scholars also encouraged engagement with additional methodological and epistemic issues for future research.

Methodological formulated work drew upon contemporary debates in History in order to explore the different ways in which history-work in MOS/CMS could be married with theory of History. For example, in employing a Munslowian framework (Munslow, 1997, 2000, 2010)

Rowlinson, Stager Jacques and Booth (2009) show how much mainstream history-work was still bound by modernist tenets, sensibilities and practices of historians. They explicated the differentials of historical treatment and interpretation in MOS along modernist reconstructionist and constructionist variants and advocated for moving beyond these. They argued for expanding the range of historiographic methods used and for adopting a more postmodern and deconstructionist orientation towards history-work in MOS.

The epistemic thematic has witnessed other work to interrogate disciplinary notions of the past and their relationship with history. Efforts have been made to deconstruct the dominant notions of the relationship between the past and history, theory and method, as found in both modernist and postmodernist historiography (Mills, Weatherbee & Durepos, 2013). One of the outcomes of this research was an increasing interest in doing history-work that moved beyond simply the address of (or lack thereof) history *in* MOS to include a focus on historiography *and* MOS (Weatherbee, 2013; Weatherbee & Durepos, 2010). This latest Epistemic orientation has been one which draws upon Mannheim's conceptualization of the Sociology of Knowledge (1985) as informed by amodernist notions of Latourian Actor-Network Theory (Latour, 1993, 2005a, 2005b). From this position, Durepos and Mills are using Anti-History to advance history work beyond the modernist reconstructivist/constructivist notions of a past–history relationship *while* avoiding the dangers of relativist history that modernists ascribe to poststructural deconstructionist approaches. They propose that the way forward is through an amodernist and relational view of history-work (Durepos & Mills, 2011; Durepos & Mills, 2012) and to move the engagement with history beyond the modern-postmodern contours which have consumed much of the debate in the discipline of History for the last two decades (Durepos, 2014, forthcoming).

Finally and most recently, various efforts are underway to build upon the Anti-History approach to investigate how historiographic processes influence knowledge production and theory development by identifying those historiographic and social processes which have structured the fields of both MOS (J. Foster, Mills & Weatherbee, 2014) and of CMS (Mills & Helms Mills, 2012). Particular attention is being given to the investigation of how the social nature of historiography results in the exclusion or inclusion of various aspects of the past. The intent is to identify the manner in which broader socially generated processes and mechanisms, both inside and outside MOS/CMS, lead to the writing-out (Cooke, 1999) or writing-in (Weatherbee, 2014) of events or persons of the past on a ideological or socio-political basis. These efforts represent a new focus in the historic turn and are signal of a potential sociological shift to the treatment of history and historiography (Foster, Mills & Weatherbee, 2014; Mills, Weatherbee & Durepos, 2013) with focus on the historical and social constraints upon disciplinary knowledge production (Weatherbee, 2014, under review).

In addition to the factual-, contextual-, methodological-, epistemic- and emerging sociological-focused thematic, there has been a wealth of other approaches or styles of address to the issue of history in MOS/CMS. These include counterfactual, virtual or counter-narrative histories (MacKay, 2007; Maielli & Booth, 2008; Mordhorst, 2013) and a broadening of interest in using history to more fully inform management education (Cummings & Bridgman, 2008; Topping, Duhon & Bushardt, 2006). Finally, there are efforts to more fully inform those who wish to engage with historical consideration in their research with methodological articles and texts published specifically for this purpose (see, for example, Bell & Taylor, 2013; Musacchio & Mutch, 2013).

A great deal of work has been expended over the decade since the latest call for a 'Historic Turn' went out. The return to historical consideration is now engendering increased attention in both the mainstream (see the works by Greenwood & Bernardi, 2014; Rowlinson, Hassard &

Decker (2013), in *Organization* and the *Academy of Management Review*, respectively) and critical strands (Weatherbee, Durepos, Mills & Helms Mills, 2012) of MOS. Explicit historical thought is starting to return to theory development (W. Foster, Suddaby, Minkus, & Wiebe, 2011; Rowlinson & Hassard, 2013; Rowlinson, Hassard & Decker, 2013), and historiographic study is being used to expand disciplinary knowledge which was previously missing, lost or unresearched (Le Texier, 2013). The naturalized version of the past development of MOS is being interrogated further (Hassard, 2012; Mills, Weatherbee & Durepos, 2013) and in this respect may be somewhat less hegemonic in stature as research problematizes the common sense notions of history underpinning MOS (Mills, Weatherbee & Durepos, 2013).

In sum, it is fair to say that there has been a small explosion of historically oriented work covering a wide gamut of subjects, approaches and areas. The results have seen positive growth in a wide range of methodological, conceptual, theoretical and empirical concerns that have been collectively raised both in MOS and CMS. However, while the scale and scope of research with a historical orientation are accumulating, almost all of this work retains MOS as its central subject and focus of inquiry. Few efforts have been made to turn a gaze upon critical studies of management or the institutionalized variant Critical Management Studies, employing a historical rather than a theoretical or methodological lens.[14] In fact, despite a comprehensive search of the literature, only one such effort could be located, an article by Mills and Helms Mills in *Organization* (2012). The use of their work is a reflexive and potentially fruitful way to explore the interrelations of the tenets of historical consideration with the narrated pasts of CMS. This is the main focus of the next section.

Deconstructing history(-ies) of CMS

In a reversal of the traditional directionality found in most CMS critiques, the work of Mills and Helms Mills turns a historiographically informed gaze towards critical studies of management/CMS. Their interest in doing so appears to have stemmed from two impulses. The first arose from the historiographical investigation focused on exploring the origins of CMS. Relatedly, the second was founded in their efforts at understanding how scholars of critical management studies/CMS; at least those who have produced accounts of the origin(s) of CMS, construct, narrate and re-present the CMS past. Mills and Helms Mills' objective was, in part, to surface and problematize the underlying notions associated with the past–history relationship as presented in historical descriptions of CMS found in the literature.

Their analysis used several journal articles and one book chapter. Each was chosen on the basis that it was either explicitly authored or presented as a history of CMS or because the text heavily imbricated their focal subject from a historical perspective on critical studies/CMS.[15] Their analysis determined that each had differentially assumed, interpreted, and employed particular past–history logics in their versioning of a CMS past. Though each text could be read as having "contribute[d] to a sense of the history of the field [CMS]" (2012: 118), when apprehended together, i.e. the narrative-sum of each text read against the other, the unfolding, variable and relational nature of contemporary versus 'historicized' CMS identity was foregrounded. For Mills and Helms Mills, this meant that even after decades of critical studies of management and the institutionalization of CMS within the Academy of Management, that CMS still remains a "contested actant" (2012: 126).[16]

The turning of a reflexive and historic gaze upon these versions of the past of CMS is particularly revealing in several respects. First, it highlights the ways in which common sense and un-problematized notions of the past-as-history are dominant circulations in the network. Second, by shifting a historic gaze from a perspective which problematizes looking from CMS outwards – to one that problematizes inwards – they reveal how historiographic processes interact with political, theoretical and geographical interests within the network. Third, its reveals how these re-presentations of CMS origins may delimit or bound the activities within CMS and influence what is seen as legitimate CMS scholarship.[17] Finally, it highlights the central role that the CMS collective-identity-problematic[18] has had on notions of the CMS past, on the historical representations of CMS offered to the network, and on the topology of knowledge production over the 'life' of the CMS institutional project.[19]

It is difficult to gainsay the conclusions reached by Mills and Helms Mills regarding the CMS past(s) and the extant histories which re-present them. In fact, the common starting point between their efforts and this one may best be described as beginning with a case of violent agreement. However, their work also presents us with an interpretive paradox viz. discussion of a CMS past and how such a discourse of the past is constructed. In the final sentence of their article, they employ a quotation from Ibarra-Colado: "[i]n short, 'the future of CMS must be imagined as a set of multiple dialogues and conversations … across different regions and cultures'" (Mills & Helms Mills, 2013: 934). This quotation is taken from a relatively short but historically based article, and the work describes the colonization of the Latin American Academy by the Western one (Ibarra-Colado, 2008: 127). In this brief but powerful polemic, Ibarra-Colado recounts some of the major historical elements that have led to a colonization which, he argues, resulted from the adoption of the academic norms of research and writing as found in the Western Academy (in this case both MOS and CMS) by the Latin American one.

On the one hand, Ibarra-Colado's observations concerning the scholarly and hegemonic domination of 'the rest by the West' appears to arise from an assumption that the present of CMS has been absent of a multiplicity of dialogue. This is a perspective which sees the CMS past as having led to a condition that he argues is somehow singular, perhaps unitary in and of itself or, at the very least, CMS as part of a unitary and hegemonic Western project.[20] However, on the other hand, we have a multiplicity of origin histories available within CMS which, arguably, reflect an ongoing conversation about the CMS past. Even if these non-consensual views of a CMS past reflect to a certain extent the theoretical and political divides found within the contemporary CMS tent (Adler, 2002), this circumstance begs several questions. What is the relationship between the contested nature of CMS and the way(s) its past has been/is being constituted as 'history'? Is it the case that the predominant norm of the past–history relationship – the way we think about history in the modernist, Enlightenment tradition of Western European thought[21] – is the very condition which contributes to Mills and Helms Mills' fifth observation "that the various histories tend to reinforce the idea of csm/CMS as an Anglo-American project" (2012: 127)? Finally, if CMS has been historically constituted as a 'contested actant' is it because the conceptualization of the past–history relationship remains largely unquestioned and taken for granted?[22]

An appropriate starting point to attempt to answer these questions, or at least for exploring their resonance with the present condition of origin histories in CMS, is to envision the objects of Mills and Helms Mills' analysis otherwise! Instead of viewing these works as outcomes of historiographic research undertaken by specific *individuals*, we could instead reposition them within a *collective* process of doing history-work. While analytical movement away from the deconstruction of histories *of* CMS to a process-oriented investigation of history-work *in* CMS is possible, to do so requires four moments of reframing. The first is to acknowledge the ontological difference between the past and history. The second is grounded in an understanding that the purposes of doing history-work within a collective context are attempts to find meaning within the past. The third moment comes in recognizing that any collective *discourse of the past* is multi-purposeful and multi-constructed. The final moment is recognizing that disciplinary History and the conventions and practices within it constitute just one mode of thinking and one way of doing history-work. Each of these is discussed in more detail in the sections to follow.

The past–history relationship and epistemic fallacy[23]

With few scholars in MOS/CMS trained in the methods (Bedeian, 1998; Greenwood & Bernardi, 2014) or exposed to the theoretical debates (Weatherbee, 2013) in History, the orthodoxy of the past–history relationship is generated by our experience as scholars and persons. First, in the Kuhnian sense of new scholar entry, we are expected to learn the discipline's stock of past knowledge, our canon. Once it is mastered, we may then seek to contribute to the literature ourselves as guided by disciplinary boundaries and conventions previously established. In this process, we learn to both interpret and contribute to the discipline's past – to do history-work by engaging with the knowledge we inherit.[24] The second source, also imbricated with the first, is a Western and culturally derived formulation of the past–history relationship. There are two aspects to this second formulation. The first is the 'common sense' orientation we believe exists between the past and history, and the second is the role that we see Historians assuming in the production of it (Mills, Weatherbee & Durepos, 2013; Rowlinson et al., 2013; Rusen, 2005a).[25] Together, these serve to establish the legitimacy of history-work – a history taken as an accurate reflection/reconstruction/representation of the past world – based upon a presumed correspondence between the empirical fact(s) from the past and the history(ies) produced from them. This approach has been coined "history of a particular kind" (Munslow, 2000: 18) and can be problematic if the reality of the past world becomes equated/conflated with the representations we produce of it (Jenkins, 2003; Munslow, 2010).

Contrary to the evidence given to us by our disciplinary and our common sense notions of the past, the actuality of the past world is no longer accessible to us. All that is available are the remnants of material trace, both natural and constructed. These traces are the 'facts' which historians seek, collect and use in the construction of their histories. Therefore, there is an ontological distinction which needs to be made between the past-as-it-was and any history that is a representation of it (Munslow, 2010). As a past–history relationship cannot be based upon theories of correspondence, from this it follows that the past world has no pre-given ordering to it. Hence the articulation of the past–history relationship is itself the basis for our ordering of trace(s) to produce knowledge of the past (Foucault, 1973). However, possession of ordered knowledge of the past is an insufficient condition for generating historical understanding of the past, as knowledge of the past, in and of itself, is just a collection of traces or 'facts'—whether these facts are found in an individual's memory, an organization's archive, or a disciplinary canon. In order to have a *meaningful sense* of the past, what Lukacs terms a remembered past (1968), first requires that historical knowledge be given purposive meaning (Carr, 1961). The way in which a culture inheres meaning to knowledge of the past is through how history-work collectively establishes a past–history relationship and orients the collective to the past, the present and the future. This temporal orientation and the mechanisms whereby it is achieved, its purposes and how it is maintained through time have been conceptualized as Historical Consciousness (Rusen, 2007c).

Historical Consciousness: How we order the past-present-future

As temporality of experience is part of the human condition, all individuals and collectives maintain an orientation to the past. However, even though collective Historical Consciousness is a universal phenomenon (Rusen, 2005b), *how* knowledge of the past is produced and used is a culturally specific, collectively determined and learned practice (Rusen, 2007b). Variation in how cultures and collectives produce such historical knowledge, indeed even how they determine what *is* historical knowledge, flows from culturally and/or collectively determined meta-historical assumptions (Megill, 1994; White, 1973) or modes of historical thinking (Rusen, 2005a). Modes of historical thinking are a constellation, or set, of organizing assumptions, concepts and practices which "educate us on how to know, deal and think about the past" (Liakos, 2010). These modes are the ways and means in how a collective makes sense of the changes in the world through varying acts of interpretation, translation and the purposes to which we put knowledge of the past to use (Minear, 1940).

Taken together, Historical Consciousness and modes of historical thinking represent the totality of *how* a collectivity gathers, categorizes, organizes, expresses and uses knowledge of the past to achieve historical understanding in the present. Therefore, cultural discourses of the past are collective processes which arise from and are constituted by the various mechanisms employed to produce historical representations *and* the purpose(s) to which these representations are put (A. Assmann, 2008a; Rusen, 2007a). So it is the sum of all such history-work, whether disciplinary or not, which comprises "the human effort to understand the present and expect the future by understanding and interpreting the past." (Rusen, 2007b: 4). Or, to restate and extend Ermarth (2007), it is necessarily both "historical conventions" and *history-work* which serve as our "basic tools of thought" (p. 51).

While in the case of the Western experience, the academic field of History has traditionally been given the societal responsibility for constructing history (Iggers, 2002) history-work is conducted by persons, groups and institutions outside the discipline as well. But it is the outcomes of both forms of history-work which inform the historical understanding of the collective in which they operate. And the collective's past-present-future orientation influences the history-work ongoing both outside and inside the discipline (Rusen, 2004). Recognition of the mutual constitution of the past from both within and without History invokes the revisiting of the relationship between History and Memory Studies[26] since now "memory has a history" and "history is itself a form of memory" (A. Assmann, 2008b: 62). If a collectively held sense of the past is founded upon the totality of the collective's meaningful knowledge of the past – whether it is text-based history, a film, a museum display or even an academic article – and the work which produces such knowledge – be it disciplinary or not – this is a signal of the potential for the theoretical and analytical collapse between History and Memory Studies as both are *ways* in which a collective orients itself to the past though both may have different *means*. This is a position that is increasingly being explored and argued for as History and Memory Studies co-evolve (see, for example Confino, 2011; Olick & Robbins, 1998; Rasmussen, 2009; Tamm, 2013). It is also a position I am sympathetic to and one which directly bears upon the issue at hand: the role that CMS 'histories' play in the construction of a CMS discourse of the past.

From memory to history and back again: A discourse of the past?

While a full discussion of the effects that History and Memory Studies are having upon one another is beyond the remit of this chapter,[27] there have been several theoretical developments which make a repositioning possible of CMS 'histories' in the liminal space between these two areas of study. As distinctions, both epistemological and ontological, which previously existed between History and Memory Studies are made porous, perhaps even arbitrary, one of the more significant lines of theorization has focused on the interrelationships between the collective processes of memory making and collective remembering and the processes of transformation of collective memory into history (A. Assmann, 2008a, 2008b; J. Assmann, 2008). Table 16.1

Table 16.1 Relationships between collective memory and history.

	Conceptualizations of Collective/Cultural Memory and Disciplinary History			
	Halbwachs	A. Assmann	J. Assman	Rusen
Individual level	–	Neuronal	Autobiographical memory	Autobiographical memory
Social level	Collective Memory	Social memory	Communicative memory (Intergenerational)	Historical consciousness and modes of historical thinking and disciplinary history-work
		Archived memory (unused but potentially meaningful)	Cultural Memory (incorporates disciplinary and non-disciplinary history-work)	
Relationship to disciplinary history	Dead memory	Functional memory (meaningful and used)		

presents a brief overview of some of the relationships now theorized between collective memory and history in this respect.[28]

This suggests that a collective discourse of the past is comprised of all the ongoing processes involved in the production, consumption and exchange of both 'memory' and 'history'. Returning to our own CMS 'histories', the objects of Mills and Helms Mills' analysis may now be viewed as elements *within* a process and not just outcomes *of* a process. In other words, they need to be seen as contributing to a sense of the CMS past rather than as reflections or reconstructions of either 'a' or 'the' CMS past – read as being part of the ongoing construction of a sense of a CMS past rather than as a determinant of it.

CMS and the historic turn: Potentials

If we were to abandon the dominant correspondence theory of the past–history relationship and view our notions of the past as an open process of becoming rather than as one foreclosed by an outcome orientation of history-work, our CMS histories could now be considered as antenarratives (Boje, 2011). Repositioning them as *antehistories* within a collective discourse of a CMS past would have several desirable outcomes. First, it abandons the notion of a fixed past as produced by a collective focus on history-work-as-outcome. Second, it would bring into sharper relief the multiple processes involved in history-work and our collective efforts in constructing and reproducing a discourse of the past. Third, it would reconcile the oft contradictory nature of re-presentations and interpretations of the past within the discourse itself. Rather than focusing on issues of what actually happened, it permits a greater focus on how and why such interpretations come to be and what purpose(s) they serve. Fourth, it avoids epistemic foreclosure of interpretations of the past by opening up the discourse to the multiplicity of ontologies involved in doing history-work. Finally, as "[n]o one owns the past, and no one has a monopoly on how to study it, or, for that matter, how to study the relation between the past and present" (White, 2007: 25), it creates a space between history *and* CMS which would allow CMS and the historic turn to proceed otherwise.

For both MOS and CMS, being more reflexive about history-work, whether from a meta-theoretical, meta-historical, or empirical level, means we must acknowledge that our history-work is polysemous. This is a critical observation, despite the similarity of the epistemic and ontological concerns raised in the 'history-culture wars' (Munslow, 1997) to those of our own 'paradigm wars' (Pfeffer, 1993; Willmott, 1993), as the subject of history has remained (and remains) only a silent participant. As much of the ongoing disciplinary conversations – the discussions, debates and exchanges in MOS and CMS – have centered on the inter-paradigmatic differences in meta-theoretic assumptions, this has meant that, unlike the history-culture wars, meta-historical assumptions and the subject of history, are generally *not part of* these conversations (Durepos, 2014, forthcoming). Even with the influence of the 'posts' (including postcolonialism, which, along with feminist history and others remains absent from our analysis) and a reinvigorated renewal of meta-theoretic debates, the past-history relationship has remained largely untouched.

Given the historically derived nature of paradigms themselves (Burrell & Morgan, 1979) and the perspective of hindsight, this seems a somewhat paradoxical and surprising circumstance. However, and more importantly, the absence of meta-historical discussions has meant that their consonance, or dissonance, with MOS/CMS's own meta-theoretical assumptions has also rarely been fully explored. These are the ontological and epistemological leaps needed to surface the historically contingent nature of our taken-for-granted knowledge and the ways in which we collectively relate the past to the present and the future. This is critical as what we perceive, interpret and constitute as the past-as-history holds the potential to change attitudes and move collectives to action (Carpenter, 1995; Durepos, 2014, forthcoming).

Through surfacing and interrogating our meta-historical assumptions, we can begin to see how our fields of study (both MOS and CMS) are constituted as much by the discourse of the past we collectively construct as they are by any scientific discourse or imperative of managerialism. An understanding of how a sense of the past is produced and consumed would further inform us as to how disciplinary boundaries and knowledge have come to be (Mills, Weatherbee & Durepos, 2013). Perhaps this is a route whereby Ibarra-Colado's (2008) concern could be addressed? By avoiding history-work of a particular kind, one in which the pursuit of what actually happened simply reifies the past into the form of the content we give it, it becomes possible that CMS could be reimagined as something other than "a creature of the global north" (Parker, 2013: 173).

Notes

1 To differentiate between the discipline of history and the outcome of history-work – a history of something – the term 'History', with a capitalized 'H', will be used to indicate the discipline (conventions, etc.); 'history-work' will be used as an umbrella term for all forms of research or production of representations of the past, and 'history' will refer to a product or outcome.

2 It is taken as a given that the terms 'past' and 'history' are perspectival and based upon various epistemological and ontological positions. The problematics of extant notions and understandings of these terms will be addressed later in the chapter. Given that scholarly understanding is subject to the unfolding and temporal nature of lived experience – in both the collective and academic senses, as well as the individual and personal senses – the chapter is a spatio-temporally bounded construction and work-in-progress. While I have employed the concepts and terminologies associated with historiography when speaking to past events, the reader should consider this work an act of storying (Czarniawska, 1997; Gabriel, 2000) of the past. A narrative reflecting the meaning(s) I have given to my own experiences of/with CMS over the last decade and my own participation in being shaped by (and perhaps in a small way in shaping?) CMS and the historic turn within it. Thus, the textual presentation, by necessity, imbricates my personal with my scholarly understandings as they relate to CMS. So while grounded in 'verifiable' traces of the past and while employing a historiographic method, the narrative is devoid of any intent to re-present a fixed or stable version of what has happened. In other words, while the traces have been framed in a particular way – it is not the only possible way! It should be read as a *living story* (Boje, 2001).

3 The intent here is to demonstrate how 'history', as formally promulgated in disciplinary literature, may sediment over time into the background to become taken for granted and remaining unquestioned (see, for example, Czarniawska, 1998).

4 The reliance on rule-of-thumb approaches on the part of business was a position which was heavily critiqued by Wallace B. Donham, the second dean of the Business School at Harvard (Donham, 1922b). Paradoxically enough, one of the first formalized approaches in the development of an early theory of business within the university was itself heavily historical. Donham believed that by emulating natural science methodology, i.e. the collection of empirical data from records of business decisions and subsequent analysis, a scientifically based theory of business was achievable. This was the genesis of the renowned Harvard Business Case approach (Donham, 1922a). However, despite a great deal of effort put into this project by Harvard, it would ultimately be supplanted by economic and statistical approaches (Weatherbee, 2012).

5 While the term 'ahistorical' is employed to describe contemporary organization studies, it is not to imply that MOS or CMS is unhistorical. There is much of History and 'history' in MOS and CMS. It is just that both are employed largely unreflexively and without consideration for the epistemological and ontological implications of their use (for a more detailed exploration of this, see Durepos, 2015).

6 Ultimately, MOS would so fervently embrace a scientific and quantitative orientation that some two decades later it would be assessed as having become overly scientific and analytically oriented as to make the research being conducted within so abstract as to be irrelevant to practitioners (Porter & McKibbin, 1988). The debate which coalesced around the issues of academic rigor versus practical relevance spawned a critique of MOS and its relationship with the business school model which remains ongoing and unresolved (Pfeffer & Fong, 2002; Trank & Rynes, 2003; Tushman, O'Reilly, Fenollosa, Kleinbaum & McGrath, 2007).

7 Within the Academy of Management structure, the Management History Division is one of the originals at the formation of AoM. The division is also been consistently one of the smallest (Stiles et al., 2010). There has also been a long-running and active set of scholars interested in the history of business and businesses outside of the AoM. For example, the Business History Conference association (http://www.thebhc.org/) has been in place since 1954. In other areas, there has been significant intersection between history and business strategy, e.g. stemming from the important works of Alfred Chandler (Chandler, 1962, 1980, 1990, 1994). However, the work in these areas has had relatively little impact or influence upon other sub-fields within MOS or business education overall (Stager Jacques, 2006).

8 It is understood that the selection of a beginning for any historical narrative is the decision of the author (White, 1987) and that there are few 'natural' beginnings in the social realm. This time frame was chosen as it is the canonical one portrayed in the literature (see, for example Clark & Rowlinson, 2004; Rowlinson, Stager Jacques & Booth, 2009). It is also understood that the enactment of the 'turn' is still ongoing and underway. Indeed, this contribution may be considered part of this process. Therefore, it is likely that the activities of the address of history in MOS and CMS will evolve into the future. So it is also likely that any future description may undoubtedly portray it differently than is the case here.

9 The common sense everyday approach to the past, one which reflects our everyday experience, tends to be based upon the idea that there is a past reality somewhere out there waiting to be found or uncovered through the discovery and accumulation of 'facts'. Therefore, there are various forms of knowledge within the discipline (facts, theories, etc.) which become taken for granted, not because they are valid but because they have a strongly narrated 'history' underscoring their validity. The pig iron work calculation and Maslow's Theory of Motivation are two such taken-for-granted elements in MOS historiography. Similar examples can be found in terms of other orthodoxies of context, methods and epistemological considerations.

10 It is understood that the ongoing construction of CMS, whether considered as a community, brand, label, social movement or scholarly field, is a socially heterogeneous, highly fluid and contested process in both contemporary and historical terms. This will become apparent as the discussion in this work unfolds. Because the collective identity of CMS remains contested, so too are its origins and its 'history' (see, for example, Mills & Helms Mills, 2012). As the intent of this project is, in effect, to apply the tenets of the historic turn to CMS the constitutive relationship between the past, identity and 'history' will be addressed separately in later sections.

11 Arguably, while critical of the lack of history in MOS, Keiser's positioning is not synonymous with the 'critical' of either critical theory or the critical nature of a postmodern/poststructural 'critique' of History. Neither is Zald's positioning on history, although the call to see more a more humanistic MOS is.

12 It should be emphasized that even with the advent of postmodern/poststructural and postcolonial thought, the notion of History (as a discipline and as the outcomes produced by Historians) is still dominated by Western notions of what History is and how histories are to be produced (Iggers, 2002).

13 This is not to say that other journals did not previously accept critical articles which were historically based (Dye, Mills & Weatherbee, 2005) or those which used alternative approaches to do history work, e.g. Foucauldian archeao-genealogical methods (Burrell, 1988). However, *M&OH* was the first journal specifically dedicated to critical and alternative historiographic approaches in MOS.

14 While both critical studies of management and CMS have been the focus of much critique – some reflexive, some not – these critiques have been made from personal, political or theoretical sensibilities (Clegg, Kornberger, Carter & Rhodes, 2006; Cooke, 2008; Cunliffe, 2008; Marens, 2013; Thompson, 2004) and more recently from a postcolonial and epistemological standpoint (Faria, 2013; Faria, Wanderley, Reis & Celano, 2013; Ibarra-Colado, 2006, 2008) While many of these address the past of CMS – and as such are historically oriented – they do not take a historiographical perspective, nor do they problematize notions of the past or the representations of CMS history.

15 While the article by Burrell, Reed and Calas (1994) predates the formalization of CMS in institutional terms, it positions critical studies of management as breaking away from the mainstream 'past' of organization studies, and in this sense it is a prospective account of the potential for the emergence of CMS. The remaining publications, an article by Adler, Forbes and Willmott (2007) and one by Hassard, Hogan and Rowlinson (2001), are both accounts of the origins of CMS from a 'common sense' and retrospective notion of the past–history relationship. A few other sources speak to some elements of the past of critical studies of management (Grey & Willmott, 2005) or to the origins of CMS (The Origins of Critical Management Studies, 2013). Other sources, while not specifically written as historiographies, do contain fragmentary commentary on the past of both (see, for example, Fournier & Grey, 2000). Finally, it should be noted, that the article by Mills and Helms Mills, while an interrogation of canonical versions of the past, must also now be included amongst them. In this regard, it should be positioned as an example of a relational historiography (Durepos, 2014, forthcoming).

16 While the contested nature of CMS is not especially revelatory – the variety of answers to the question 'What is CMS?' is an open secret – the novelty of their historiographic approach and the identification of several articulated pasts of CMS within the literature are!

17 As noted by Mills and Helms Mills, all of the authors of these histories were involved in the activities or promotion of critical studies of management/CMS. Therefore, the authors are also informed by their own personal scholarly 'histories' and experiences as they too had part in the activities they render historically in their writing.

18 As our professional activities in academe – what we study, research and teach – all contribute to how we see ourselves and our sense of self (Alvesson, 2001; Jawitz, 2009); our work as scholars may be considered "an experience of identity" (Wenger, 1998: 215). This plays an especially significant and central role for those who associate themselves with CMS (Clegg, Kornberger, Carter & Rhodes, 2006) as our "collective visions of self" tend to "become not so much the 'main show' as important resources in the formation of personal notions of self." (Alvesson, Ashcraft & Thomas, 2008: 16). As "CMS distinguishes a kind of discourse and/ or type of academic (in the main) that, in varied ways, problematizes established canonical forms of doing and representing 'management!" (Willmott, 2006: 36), the collective identity of the 'we' in CMS remains a highly diverse collection of personalized meanings (Alvesson et al., 2008) as CMS is a "catch-all term used to describe a pluralistic and diverse field of work or intellectual movement" in order to "maintain its identity" (Willmott, 2013: 151). The diversity of approaches to MOS and the varied theoretical positions used has meant that it is difficult to use normative terminology to identify what the institutionalized CMS is at a collective level. This is perhaps why CMS has been described variously, and alternatively, as a school or branch of MOS (Kettunen, 2013), a sub-field of MOS (Malin, Murphy & Siltaoja, 2013) and even as an insurgency or social movement rather than a coherent collective whose glue was "a distinctive domain of knowledge" (Willmott, 2013: 126). I personally see CMS as a scholarly outlet that allows me to participate in a project to improve the way in which we think about the world of organizing and organizations. I am not overly fussed about how it is categorized, though I recognize that identities are constructed through the activities of both insiders and outsiders and, in the collective sense, may be seen to be the outcome of processes of social construction (Berger & Luckmann, 1967) over which I may have little to no influence.

19 This observation also reflects some of my own experiences and concerns viz. the issue of domain-bounded legitimacy. For example, I have always wondered why there is more than some discomfort and disagreement evident between the feminist and critical management elements with the structural organization of the AoM. I once attended a symposium entitled "The Uneasy Marriage Between Feminism and CMS," (Benschop et al., 2006) where much of the discussion centered on scholarly exclusionary practices of the this-does-not-belong-here form. I have had papers which use a critical historiographic lens to critique MOS which were panned by critical management reviewers as being more suitable for history sessions and

history track reviewers, suggesting that the work is really a critical orientation on an element of MOS, e.g. organizational behavior, and that the paper should be submitted to another "more appropriate sub-field" track. While certainly not a new observation, for me personally this reinforces notions that the way we organize and structure disciplines has as much effect on what and how we theorize as the results of any scholarly enquiry. To resituate this observation in historical terms, the way in which we interpret and present the past within the CMS network also serves to delimit what questions are considered worth answering in scholarly terms. I see this as a very un-reflexive problematic and contrary to much of what we speak about on an ongoing or day-to-day basis within csm/CMS.

20 In many ways, Ibarra-Colado's critique centers on CMS as part of a larger project – the Academy and Western views of 'doing' academics – a view which collapses CMS into MOS on grounds of epistemological colonization. While his point of critique is valid and I am in sympathy with it, it will only be touched upon briefly in this work. And then it remains an oblique touch in that it is only to highlight how patterns of historical consciousness vary across cultures.

21 Western Historiography is still dominated by realist history in the modern tradition (Iggers, 1997), and, despite the linguistic and cultural turns, the discipline of History still remains dominated with Rankeian tenets of doctrinal realism- and correspondence-based methods of reconstructing the truth about past events (Wilder, 2012).

22 Even the most cursory review of the CMS literature shows patterns which reveal how un-reflexively we engage with notions of 'history' and the 'past'. A search in several top critical journals on the terms 'history', 'historiography' and the phrase 'in the past' reveals how often we refer to the past and its representations without specific reference to the ways we think about the past and history. Searches of *Organization*, *Culture and Organization* and *Human Relations* show that the use of 'history' and 'in the past' is extremely common. They are almost ubiquitously used within the full text of articles. Yet these same terms are almost non-existent in the Title, Abstract or Keywords fields of these works. Using *Organization* as an example, the term 'history' is found within the full text of 537 articles for all work published in the period 1994–2014. In this same period, only 11 articles have 'history' in the title field, 37 in the abstract, and 11 in the keyword fields. Search on the term 'the past' resulted in 2 article titles, 18 incidents in abstracts, 280 times in full text and once in keyword. 'Historiography' is even more limited and is found in only 2 article titles, 4 abstracts, 24 times in the full text and once in any of the other searchable fields. Despite the contention that CMS work tends to be more historically informed than that of MOS (Rowlinson, 2004), the CMS literature appears to be no different in its embedded assumptions than is the MOS literature. For example, in the *Academy of Management Journal*, the term 'history' is found in 1114 articles with only 7 instances in the Title field, 47 in the Abstract field, and 18 in the Keyword field. Similar patterns are also observed in the *Academy of Management Review*. The term 'historiography' may be found only on two occasions in *AMJ* and four times in *AMR*. While these results cannot be considered comprehensive or complete, they certainly may be read as linguistic signs which signal how naturalized reference to the past has become and how under-problematized the past–history relationship remains in the patterns which inhere in the language we use to describe and communicate our research and theorizing.

23 Following Bhaskar (1997), the phrase 'epistemic fallacy' is used to refer to the condition where our epistemological beliefs have been collapsed into our ontological beliefs concerning the past. This is a hyper-realist notion of the past and a circumstance which, despite the debates of the 'history wars', still remains the default for both disciplinary (Iggers, 1997, 2002) and non-academic or popular history (Munslow, 2010). While the past world did happen and while we can be assured that the past was comprised of persons, places and 'things' (even postmodern historians will agree to this; see Jenkins, 2003) the ontology of the prior (our past world) and the ontology of our representations (our histories) are categorically of two different orders (Munslow, 2010).

24 As has been argued elsewhere (Durepos, 2014, forthcoming; Weatherbee, 2013; Weatherbee & Durepos, 2010) we are both the producers and consumers of our own histories – even while we are naïve concerning the methods and theories appropriate to understanding the complex nature of the past–history relationship of our knowledge and its construction.

25 It is recognized that this is a Western and Eurocentric view of History and of history.

26 The concept of Cultural/Collective/Social Memory and the related emergence of a field tentatively labeled Memory Studies remain a somewhat ambiguous and loose conceptualization in the literature(s). Part of the reason for this is that its antecedents include the natural sciences, social sciences and humanities (disciplines including psychology, history, sociology and literary studies), as well as the intersections of media and cultural history, history and sociology, neuroscience and social psychology, and cognitive psychology and history (Erll, 2008).

27 Memory Studies finds its antecedent largely in the work of Halbwachs, who saw collective memory and history as distinct from one another; collective memory was living memory in the present, while history was dead memory from the past (Halbwachs, 1992). Unfortunately, Halbwachs never addressed the relationship between these two (Olick & Robbins, 1998), and a great deal of effort has been taken since to theorize the interrelationship between collective memory, cultural practices of remembrance, History and historiography. As history has been variously viewed as "a method of research ('inquiry'), a place ('the past'), a process (temporality), a practice (memorialization, celebration, remembrance), a literary or, more precisely, rhetorical genre (history writing), and even a manifestation of an ontological category (humanity)" (White, 2002: 10), there has been a great deal of scope for enquiry. Efforts at exploring the linkages were accelerated by the 'memory boom' occurring at the end of the last century which increased the empirical pressure on both historians and cultural theorists to reconsider the notions of both collective memory and the practices of disciplinary history (Tamm, 2013). Readers are referred to the debates and discussions in Assmann (2008b), Kansteiner (2002), Klein (2000) and Tamm (2013) for a more detailed and comprehensive perspective on this issue.

28 The relationship between collective memory and history is very resonant with the triadic system of story forms proposed by Boje (2011). Boje's Living Story and Fixed Narrative forms conceptually resemble the notions associated with intergenerational storytelling (living memory) and history as a fixed object belonging to Cultural Memory, respectively. It is also possible, from a process perspective, to see the extant CMS Histories as forms of antehistory, analogous to Bojeian antenarratives.

References

Adler, P. (2002). Critical in the name of whom and what? *Organization, 9*(3): 387–395.

Adler, P., Forbes, L., & Willmott, H. (2007). Critical Management Studies: Premises, practices, problems and prospects. *The Academy of Management Annals, 1*(3): 119–179.

Alvesson, M. (2001). Knowledge work: Ambiguity, image and identity. *Human Relations, 54*(7): 863.

Alvesson, M., Ashcraft, K., & Thomas, R. (2008). Identity matters: Reflections on the construction of identity scholarship in organization studies. *Organization, 15*(1): 5–28.

Assmann, A. (2008a). Canon and archive. In A. Erll & A. Nunning (Eds.), *Cultural memory studies: An international and interdisciplinary handbook*: 97–107. New York: Walter de Gruyter.

Assmann, A. (2008b). Transformations between history and memory. *Social Research, 75*(1): 49–72.

Assmann, J. (2008). Communicative and culture memory. In A. Erll & A. Nunning (Eds.), *Cultural memory studies: An international and interdisciplinary handbook*: 109–118. New York: Walter de Gruyter.

Bedeian, A. (1998). Exploring the past. *Journal of Management History, 4*(1): 4–15.

Bell, E., & Taylor, S. (2013). Writing history into management research. *Management & Organizational History, 8*(2): 127–136.

Benschop, Y., Calas, M., Fletcher, J., Forray, J., Helms Mills, J., Stager Jacques, R., . . . Tienari, J. (2006). *Symposium: The uneasy marriage between feminism and CMS*. Paper presented at the Critical Management Studies Group of the Academy of Management Annual Conference, Atlanta, August 15.

Berger, P. L., & Luckmann, T. (1967). *The social construction of reality*. Middlesex, UK: Penguin.

Bhaskar, R. (1997). *A realist theory of science* (2nd Ed.). London: Verso.

Boje, D. (2001). *Narrative methods for organizational and communication research*. Thousand Oaks, CA: Sage.

Boje, D. (Ed.). (2011). *The Future of Storytelling and Organizations: An antenarrative handbook*. New York: Routledge.

Booth, C., & Rowlinson, M. (2006). Management and organizational history: Prospects. *Management and Organizational History, 1*(1): 5–30.

Burrell, G. (1988). Modernism, post modernism and organizational analysis 2: The contribution of Michel Foucault. *Organization Studies, 9*(2): 221–235.

Burrell, G., & Morgan, G. (1979). *Sociological paradigms and organizational analysis: Elements of the sociology of corporate life*. London: Heinemann.

Burrell, G., Reed, M., & Calas, M. (1994). Why organization? Why now? *Organization, 1*(1): 5–17.

Carpenter, R. (1995). *History as rhetoric: Style, narrative, and persuasion*. Columbia: University of South Carolina Press.

Carr, E. H. (1961). *What is history? The George Macaulay Trevelyan Lectures delivered in the University of Cambridge*. London: Macmillan.

Chandler, A. (1962). *Strategy and structure*. Cambridge, MA: MIT Press.

Chandler, A. (1980). *The visible hand: The managerial revolution in American business*. Cambridge, MA: MIT Press.

Chandler, A. (1990). The enduring logic of industrial success. *Harvard Business Review*, March–April: 130–114.

Chandler, A. (1994). *Scale and scope: The dynamics of industrial capitalism*. Cambridge, MA: MIT Press.

Clark, P., & Rowlinson, M. (2004). The treatment of history in organization studies: Towards an 'historic turn'? *Business History*, *46*: 331–352.

Clegg, S., Kornberger, M., Carter, C., & Rhodes, C. (2006). For management? *Management Learning*, *37*(1): 7–27.

Confino, A. (2011). History and memory. In A. Schneider & D. Woolf (Eds.), *The Oxford history of historical writing*, Vol. 5: *Historical writing since 1945*: 36–51. Oxford: Oxford University Press.

Cooke, B. (1999). Writing the left out of management theory: The historiography of the management of change. *Organization*, *6*(1): 81–105.

Cooke, B. (2003). The denial of slavery in management studies. *Journal of Management Studies*, *40*: 1895–1918.

Cooke, B. (2008). If Critical Management Studies is your problem. *Organization*, *15*(6): 912–914.

Cummings, S., & Bridgman, T. (2008). Strawman: The reconfiguration of Max Weber in management textbooks and why it matters. Best Paper Proceedings of the Academy of Management Annual Meeting, Anaheim, California.

Cummings, S., & Bridgman, T. (2011). The relevant past: Why the history of management should be critical for our future. *Academy of Management Learning & Education*, *10*(1): 77–93.

Cunliffe, A. (2008). Will you still need me . . . When I'm 64: The future of CMS. *Organization*, *15*(6): 936–938.

Czarniawska, B. (1997). *Narrating the organization: Dramas of institutional identity*. Chicago: University of Chicago Press.

Czarniawska, B. (1998). *A narrative approach to organization studies*. Thousand Oaks, CA: Sage.

Donham, W. (1922a). Business teaching by the case system. *The American Economic Review*, *12*(1): 53–65.

Donham, W. (1922b). Essential groundwork for a broad executive theory. *Harvard Business Review*, *1*(1): 1–10.

Durepos, G. (2015). ANTi-history: Toward amodern histories. In P. Genoe McLaren, A. J. Mills & T. G. Weatherbee (Eds.), *The Routledge companion to management and organizational history*. London: Routledge.

Durepos, G., & Mills, A. (2012). *ANTi-history: Theorizing the past, history, and historiography in management and organizational studies*. Charlotte, NC: Information Age Publishing.

Durepos, G., & Mills, A. J. (2011). Actor-network theory, anti-history and critical organizational historiography. *Organization*, *19*(6): 703–7221.

Dye, K., Mills, A. J., & Weatherbee, T. G. (2005). Maslow: Man interrupted: Reading management theory in context. *Management Decision*, *43*(10): 1375–1395.

Erll, A. (2008). Cultural memory studies. In A. Erll & A. Nunning (Eds.), *Cultural memory studies: An international and interdisciplinary handbook*: 1–15. New York: Walter de Gruyter.

Ermarth, E. (2007). The closed space of choice: A manifesto on the future of history. In K. Jenkins, S. Morgan & A. Munslow (Eds.), *Manifestos for history*: 50–66. New York: Routledge.

Faria, A. (2013). Border thinking in action: Should critical management studies get anything done? In V. Malin, J. Murphy & M. Siltaoja (Eds.), *Dialogues in critical management studies*: 277–300. Bingley, UK: Emerald.

Faria, A., Wanderley, S., Reis, Y., & Celano, A. (2013). Can the subaltern teach? Performativity otherwise through anthrophagy. In V. Malin, J. Murphy & M. Siltaoja (Eds.), *Dialogues in critical management studies*: 205–224. Bingley, UK: Emerald.

Foster, J., Mills, A., & Weatherbee, T. G. (2014). History, field definition and management studies: The case of the New Deal. *Journal of Management History*, *20*(2): 225–243.

Foster, W., Suddaby, R., Minkus, A., & Wiebe, E. (2011). History as social memory assets: The example of Tim Hortons. *Management & Organizational History*, *6*(1): 101–120.

Foucault, M. (1973). *The order of things; An archaeology of the human sciences*. New York: Vintage Books.

Fournier, V., & Grey, C. (2000). At the critical moment: Conditions and prospects for critical management studies. *Human Relations*, *53*(1): 7–32.

Gabriel, Y. (2000). *Storytelling in organizations: Facts, fictions, and fantasies*. New York: Oxford University Press.

Greenwood, A., & Bernardi, A. (2014). Understanding the rift, the (still) uneasy bedfellows of history and organization studies. *Organization*, *21*(8): 907–932.

Grey, C., & Willmott, H. (2005). *Critical management studies: A reader*, Vol. 9. Oxford: Oxford University Press.

Halbwachs, M. (1992). *On collective memory* (L. Coser, Ed.). Chicago: University of Chicago Press.

Hassard, J. (2012). Rethinking the Hawthorne Studies: The Western Electric research in its social, political and historical context. *Human Relations*, *65*(11): 1431–1461.

Hassard, J., Hogan, J., & Rowlinson, M. (2001). From labor process theory to critical management studies. *Administrative Theory & Praxis*, *23*(3): 339–362.

Ibarra-Colado, E. (2006). Organization studies and epistemic coloniality in Latin America: Thinking otherness from the margins. *Organization, 13*(4): 489–508.

Ibarra-Colado, E. (2008). Is there any future for critical management studies in Latin America? Moving from epistemic coloniality to 'trans–discipline'. *Organization, 15*(6): 932–935.

Iggers, G. (1997). *Historiography in the twentieth century: From scientific objectivity to the postmodern challenge.* Hanover, NH: Wesleyan University Press.

Iggers, G. (2002). The professionalization of historical studies and the guiding assumptions of modern historical thought. In L. Kramer & S. Maza (Eds.), *A companion to Western historical thought*: 225–242. Oxford: Blackwell.

Jawitz, J. (2009). Academic identities and communities of practice in a professional discipline. *Teaching in Higher Education, 14*(3): 241–251.

Jenkins, K. (2003). *Refiguring history. New thoughts on an old discipline.* London: Routledge.

Kansteiner, W. (2002). Finding meaning in memory: A methodological critique of collective memory studies. *History and Theory, 41*(2): 179–197.

Kettunen, P. (2013). CMS – A solution or an extra problem for management research? In V. Malin, J. Murphy & M. Siltaoja (Eds.), *Dialogues in critical management studies*: 53–60. Bingley, UK: Emerald.

Khurana, R. (2007). *From higher aims to hired hands: The social transformation of American business schools and the unfulfilled promise of management as a profession.* Princeton, NJ: Princeton University Press.

Kieser, A. (1994). Crossroads: Why organization theory needs historical analyses – And how this should be performed. *Organization Science, 5*(4): 608–620.

Klein, K. L. (2000). Special issue: On the emergence of memory in historical discourse. *Representations, 69*: 127–150.

Latour, B. (1993). *We have never been modern.* Cambridge, MA: Harvard University Press.

Latour, B. (2005a). On recalling ANT. In J. Law & J. Hassard (Eds.), *Actor-network-theory*: 15–25. Oxford: Oxford University Press.

Latour, B. (2005b). *Reassembling the social: An introduction to actor-network-theory.* Oxford: Blackwell.

Le Texier, T. (2013). The first systemized uses of the term 'management' in the eighteenth and nineteenth centuries. *Journal of Management History, 19*(2): 277–285.

Liakos, A. (2010). What is historical critique about? *Historein, 10*: 144–152.

Lukacs, J. (1968). *Historical consciousness: Or the remembered past.* New York: Harper & Row.

MacKay, R. (2007). 'What if?': Synthesizing debates and advancing propsects of using virtual history in management and organization theory. *Management & Organizational History, 2*(4): 295–314.

Maielli, G., & Booth, C. (2008). Counterfactual history, management and organizations: Reflections and new directions. *Management & Organizational History, 3*(1): 49–61.

Malin, V., Murphy, J., & Siltaoja, M. (2013). Beyond critique: Towards transformative practice in critical management studies. Editor's Introduction. In V. Malin, J. Murphy & M. Siltaoja (Eds.), *Dialogues in critical management studies*: xiii–xxxi. Bingley, UK: Emerald.

Mannheim, K. (1985). *Ideology and utopia: An introduction to the sociology of knowledge.* New York: Harcourt Brace.

Marens, R. (2013). What exactly did you expect from CMS? American business schools as an expression of futile relations. In V. Malin, J. Murphy & M. Siltaoja (Eds.), *Dialogues in critical management studies*: 3–22. Bingley, UK: Emerald.

Megill, A. (1994). Jorn Rusen's theory of historiography bewtween modernism and rhetoric of inquiry. *History and Theory, 33*(1): 39–60.

Mills, A., & Helms Mills, J. (2012). CMS: A satirical critique of three narrative histories. *Organization, 20*(1): 117–129.

Mills, A., Weatherbee, T., & Durepos, G. (2013). Reassembling Weber to reveal the-past-as-history in management and organization studies. *Organization, 21*(2): 223–241.

Minear, P. (1940). Historical consciousness vs. historical knowledge. *Journal of Bible and Religion, 8*(2): 72–76.

Mordhorst, M. (2013). From counterfactual history to counternarrative history. *Management & Organizational History, 3*(1): 5–26.

Munslow, A. (1997). *Deconstructing history.* London: Routledge.

Munslow, A. (2000). *The Routledge companion to historical studies.* London: Routledge.

Munslow, A. (2010). *The future of history.* London: Palgrave Macmillan.

Musacchio, A., & Mutch, A. (2013). In search of historical methods. *Management & Organizational History, 8*(2): 105–110.

Olick, J., & Robbins, J. (1998). Social memory studies: From "collective memory" to the historical sociology of mnemonic practices. *Annual Review of Sociology, 24*: 105–140.

The Origins of Critical Management Studies. (2013).

Parker, M. (2013). 'What is to be done?' CMS as a political party. In V. Malin, J. Murphy & M. Siltaoja (Eds.), *Dialogues in critical management studies*: 165–181. Bingley, UK: Emerald.

Parsons, T. (1956a). Suggestions for a sociological approach to the theory of organizations – I. *Administrative Science Quarterly*, *1*(1): 63–85.

Parsons, T. (1956b). Suggestions for a sociological approach to the theory of organizations – II. *Administrative Science Quarterly*, *1*(2): 225–239.

Pfeffer, J. (1993). Barriers to the advance of organizational science: Paradigm development as a dependent variable. *The Academy of Management Review*, *18*(4): 599–620.

Pfeffer, J., & Fong, C. (2002). The end of business schools? Less success than meets the eye [discussion]. *Academy of Management Learning and Education*, *1*(1): 78–96.

Porter, L., & McKibbin, L. (1988). *Management education and development: Drift or thrust into the 21st century?* New York: McGraw-Hill.

Rasmussen, S. (2009). Mythico-history, social memory, and praxis: Anthropological approaches and directions. *History Compass*, *7*(3): 566–582.

Rowlinson, M. (2004). Historical perspectives in organization studies: Factual, narrative, and archeo-genealogical. In D. E. Hodgson & C. Carter (Eds.), *Management knowledge and the new employee*: 8–20. Burlington, VT: Ashgate.

Rowlinson, M., & Hassard, J. (2013). Historical neo-instituionalism or neo-institutionalist history? Historical research in management and organization studies. *Management & Organizational History*, *8*(2): 111–126.

Rowlinson, M., Hassard, J., & Decker, S. (2013). Strategies for organizational history: A dialogue between historical theory and organization theory. *Academy of Management Review*, *39*(3): 250–274.

Rowlinson, M., Stager Jacques, R., & Booth, C. (2009). Critical management and organizational history. In M. Alvesson, T. Bridgman & H. Wilmott (2011) (Eds.), *The Oxford handbook of critical management studies*: 286–303. New York: Oxford University Press.

Rusen, J. (2004). Historical consciousness: Narrative structure, moral function, and ontogenetic development. In P. Sexias (Ed.), *Theorizing historical consciousness*: 63–85. Toronto: University of Toronto Press.

Rusen, J. (2005a). *History: Narration, interpretation, orientation.* New York: Berghahn Books.

Rusen, J. (2005b). How to compare cultures? The case of historical thinking. *Koers-Bulletin for Christian Scholarship*, *70*(2): 265–289.

Rusen, J. (2007a). How to make sense of the past – Salient issues of metahistory. *The Journal of Transdisciplinary Research in South Africa*, *3*(1): 169–221.

Rusen, J. (2007b). Introduction. In J. Rusen (Ed.), *Time and history: The variety of cultures*: 1–4. New York: Berghahn Books.

Rusen, J. (2007c). Making sense of time: Toward a universal typology of conceptual foundations of historical consciousness. In J. Rusen (Ed.), *Time and history: The variety of cultures*: 7–18. New York: Berghahn Books.

Stager Jacques, R. (2006). History, historiography and organization studies: The challenge and the potential. *Management and Organizational History*, *1*(1): 31–49.

Stiles, C., Lamond, D., Spell, C., Murphy, P., Janney, J., Humphreys, J., Govenkar, M., Gibson, J. (2010). *Management History Division Five Year Review Report.* Briarcliff Manor, NY: Academy of Management.

Tamm, M. (2013). Beyond history and memory: New perspectives in memory studies. *History Compass*, *11*(6): 458–473.

Thompson, P. (2004). Brands, boundaries and bandwagons: A critical reflection on critical management studies. In S. Fleetwood & S. Ackroyd (Eds.), *Critical realism in action in organisation and management studies*: 54–70. London: Routledge.

Topping, S., Duhon, D., & Bushardt, S. (2006). Oral history as a classroom tool: Learning management theory from the evolution of an organization. *Journal of Management History*, *12*(2): 154–166.

Trank, C. Q., & Rynes, S. L. (2003). Who moved our cheese? Reclaiming professionalism in business education. *Academy of Management Learning and Education*, *2*(2): 189–205.

Tushman, M., O'Reilly, C., Fenollosa, A., Kleinbaum, A., & McGrath, D. (2007). Relevance and rigour: Executive education as a lever in shaping practice and research. *Academy of Management Learning & Education*, *6*(3): 345–362.

Van Fleet, D., & Wren, D. (2005). Teaching history in business schools. *Academy of Management Learning and Education*, *4*(1): 44–56.

Weatherbee, T. (2012). Caution! This historiography makes wide turns: Historic turns and breaks in management and organization studies. *Management and Organizational History*, *7*(3): 203–218.

Weatherbee, T. (2013). *The historic turn in MOS: Getting beyond false consciousness in our history-work.* Paper presented at the Academy of Management Annual Conference, Orlando, Florida.

Weatherbee, T. (2014). *Historiographic processes: The writing-in and writing-out of MacKenzie King from MOS history.* Paper presented at the Academy of Management Annual Conference, Philadelphia, Pennsylvania.

Weatherbee, T., & Durepos, G. (2010). *Dar'wren'ian evolution in Management: Implications of the ethics of epistemology for the scholar.* Paper presented at the Academy of Management, Montreal, Quebec, August 8–9.

Weatherbee, T., Durepos, G., Mills, A. J., & Helms Mills, J. (2012). Theorizing the past: Critical engagements. *Management & Organizational History,* 7(3): 193–202.

Wenger, E. (1998). *Communities of practice: Learning, meaning and identity.* New York: Cambridge University Press.

White, H. (1973). *Metahistory: The historical imagination in nineteenth-century europe.* London: Johns Hopkins University Press.

White, H. (1987). *The content of the form: Narrative discourse and historical representation.* London: Johns Hopkins University Press.

White, H. (2002). Foreword (T. Presner, Trans.). In R. Koselleck (Ed.), *The practice of conceptual history: Timing history, spacing concepts.* Stanford, CA: Stanford University Press.

White, H. (2007). Afterward: Manifesto time. In K. Jenkins, S. Morgan & A. Munslow (Eds.), *Manifestos for history*: 220–231. New York: Routledge.

Wilder, G. (2012). From optic to topic: The foreclosure effect of historiographic turns. *American Historical Review,* 117(3): 723–745.

Willmott, H. (1993). Breaking the paradigm mentatity. *Organization Studies,* 14(5): 681–719.

Willmott, H. (2006). Pushing at an open door: Mystifying the CMS manifesto. *Management Learning,* 37(1): 33–37.

Willmott, H. (2013). Changing institutions: Critical management studies as a social movement. In V. Malin, J. Murphy & M. Siltaoja (Eds.), *Dialogues in critical management studies*: 123–163. Bingley, UK: Emerald.

Wren, D. (1987). Management history: Issues and ideas for teaching and research. *Journal of Management,* 13(2): 339–350.

Wren, D., & Van Fleet, D. (1983). History in schools of business. Retrieved on January 7, 2013 from http://www.thebhc.org/publications/BEHprint/toc121983.html.

Zald, M. (1993). Organization studies as a scientific and humanistic enterprise: Toward a reconceptualization of the foundations of the field. *Organization Science,* 4(4): 513–528.

Zald, M. (1996). More fragmentation? Unfinished business in linking the social sciences and the humanities. *Administrative Science Quarterly,* 41(2).

17

Let them eat ethics

Hiding behind corporate social responsibility in the age of financialization

Richard Marens

On July 13, 2011, a blog entry on the website of Adbusters, a Vancouver-based antiglobalization group known primarily for its satirical mock advertisements, put out a call for demonstrations on Wall Street that would echo those of Egypt that drove Mubarak out of power. Although the movement would soon become associated with the maldistribution of wealth and income under the unifying slogan "We are the 99%," the original call for action actually touched on a broader range of issues:

> [I]nstead of being caught helpless by the current power structure, we the people start getting what we want whether it be the dismantling of half the 1,000 military bases America has around the world to the reinstatement of the Glass-Steagall Act or a three strikes and you're out law for corporate criminals. Beginning from one simple demand – a presidential commission to separate money from politics – we start setting the agenda for a new America.
>
> *(Adbusters, 2011)*

Thus, the manifesto that would end up triggering the Occupy movement went far beyond complaints about distribution to include a critique of the military-industrial complex, the quashing of regulation, the ubiquity of financial fraud, and the corruption of politics through money. For the participants in the eventual movement, this was not so much a list of distinct grievances as a catalogue of symptoms, the end result of rule by a plutocracy that was quite willing to resort to violence in order to direct economic gains to top corporate management and their financial world allies to the exclusion of nearly everyone else. Yet this cluster of abuses that so many rallied against coalesced in an era in which major firms, as well as many smaller ones, professed to practice an elevated level of corporate social responsibility (CSR), a stance promoted for over a generation by the denizens of the new academic field of business ethics, who had educated many of these managers in the nuances of CSR. Yet, despite these claims on the part of corporate leaders that they were embracing an elevated level of social responsibility, thousands of people were willing to express their skepticism by joining street demonstrations, sleep in cold parks and risk beatings and arrest, often traveling long distances for the honor of doing so. Greedy bankers or ruthless executives have been denounced throughout most of the history of the United States, leaving the question as to why would an era of globalized business provoke such a reaction, especially at a time during which top executives were actively claiming to "do better" and were even endowing business school chairs and conferences in order to imbue their successors with an appreciation of social responsibilities.

Before even beginning to answer this question, it needs to be understood that CSR is not actually a new idea but has actually existed as at least an informal construct since the early days of widespread incorporation. But it becomes especially prominent during times and in places in which the power of corporate leaders to exploit communities and their own employees, as well as that of financiers to embezzle (legally or not), faced the fewest institutional checks, especially the countervailing power of government. This is not to say that corporate social responsibility is occasionally trotted out as a cover story to divert attention away from rapacious behavior by telling a "big lie" or that it is simply an advertising slogan for suckering those consumers who naively hoped to find "good" corporations that they could feel fine about patronizing. Certainly, there is some truth in both presumptions, but not all professions of CSR are insincere and there are certainly examples of such programs producing a degree of good, at least at the local level. Understanding the role of CSR within globalization requires more than merely dismissing it as cynical and largely dishonest public relations.

Hanlon and Fleming (2009) argue that the intended purpose of contemporary CSR is to legitimize the power of corporate decision making during our neo-liberal era of global reach subjected to relatively few institutional or governmental constraints. What executives and their academic allies project by promoting CSR is not only a distraction away from reprehensible behavior but something more fundamental, a rationale for the very freedom of action that grants corporate managers the autonomy to choose to behave reprehensibly or responsibly. In effect, CSR is a justification for enlightened despotism. Corporate figures and their academic allies embrace CSR because of the need for such a justification in an age of neo-liberalism, in which corporate decision making has become relatively unfettered by regulation and when government has become increasingly less viable as alternative provider of employment or economic security. Promoting CSR not only attempts to reassure the world that corporate executives are worthy of the autonomy to wield great power over so many people's lives, it also generates a set of expectations that pressures the recalcitrant among this stratum to fall in line at least rhetorically, so as not to blow a good thing for everyone else.

What Hanlon and Fleming claim for the contemporary role of CSR can be generalized to cover the entire history of CSR, not surprisingly since the legitimation of unequal economic power has a history that extends back centuries before the Industrial Revolution. As Weber (1978) astutely observed, the Catholic Church promoted *caritas* throughout the Middle Ages as a means of ameliorating class conflict, as typified in the celebration of the alms-giving of Duke Wenceslaus of Christmas carol fame, who shortly after his death was simultaneously canonized by the Church and posthumously promoted to the title of "King" by the Holy Roman Emperor. What interests us here, however, is the more restricted history of *corporate* social responsibility, which is largely an American story or at least has been until these last two decades (Kinderman, 2010). Matten and Moon (2008) have tried to extend the construct by distinguishing "explicit" CSR from a more implicit version that they associate with Japan and the European continent, in which CSR is actualized piecemeal by firms acceding to the corporatist pressures exerted by regulators, unions and trade associations. Kinderman (2010), however, correctly dismisses the labeling of accommodating behavior as "social responsible," not only because it stretches the definition of the term so that simply refusing to break the law becomes "socially responsible" but because European business leaders themselves do not view such behavior as practicing CSR.

CSR begins as an American story because that is where, during the early decades of the 20th century, the large publicly traded corporation achieved its zenith in terms of national pervasiveness, global significance, and, perhaps most significantly, political and legal autonomy. As the economic importance and social and political influence of large corporations increased, various segments of the American public reacted with alarm, not only blue-collar labor leaders and professional liberal reformers, but also socially conservative figures worried about the erosion of such presumed American values as self-reliance and individual entrepreneurship. In response to these reactions, CSR became the legitimizing principle of the corporate push-back through the use of economic, political and, quite often, physical force. Managerially defined CSR eventually faded into the background as depression, war and the informal and uneasy pluralism that characterized American corporate political economy through the first postwar generation reduced the autonomy of corporate leaders to a degree, while "the great compression" of postwar American incomes demobilized any serious threat from the politics of class conflict, a demobilization hastened by the Red Scare of the era. With the rise of neo-liberalism in the 1980s, however, an environment emerged, not only in the United States this time but to some degree throughout the rest of the industrialized world, that was not too dissimilar to what existed in the first third of the century in the U.S.: an environment characterized by weak unions and light levels of regulation. This time, there was not only an American revival of the need for legitimizing CSR; the need spread abroad with the advent of globalization.

In this latest dissemination, the corporate leadership would find a new ally. If CSR is an inherently voluntary choice on the part of the top managers of a particular corporation, it is also a moral choice, and a new academic discipline would emerge within business schools that would arise to offer to both assist managers in making these choices and to train their successors. Academics had engaged with the social responsibilities of corporations before 1980 but only sparingly and typically in books and articles intended for the general public. Moreover, from the famous exchange between Dodd (1932) and Berle and Means (1932), to the literature that emerged from informal quasi-field of "business and society" during the course of the postwar generation, the discussion was often skeptical of managerial intentions, even occasionally critical, and would not have pleased many corporate executives. What developed after 1980 was the new discipline of business ethics, far more accepting of executive power and autonomy as the starting point of discussion than was previous academic discourse and, as a result, far more successful in institutionalizing themselves within American business schools.

Yankee origins

It was in the United States where a literature first emerged that attempted to define the specific social responsibilities that ought to attach to corporations. Certainly, discussions of the morality of various forms of business behaviors hardly had to wait for the great American merger movement at the end of the 19th century to commence. In the Western world, Catholicism had long advised and instructed craftspeople, merchants and bankers as to the acceptable limits of commercial conduct (Marens, 2005), and the Protestant moral philosopher Adam Smith (1776) was hardly shy about condemning the irresponsibility of the East India Company or the tendency of master craftsmen to engage in restraint of trade. When the Industrial Revolution did arrive, both the Catholic Bishop Ketteler of Mainz and the pious Anglican Lord Shaftesbury assumed leadership roles as advocates of 19th-century reform. When the new corporate giants emerged at the end of the 19th century, however, the specific question as to the social responsibilities that ought to attach to this new organizational form was first and foremost an American preoccupation.

There are a number of reasons why this question was especially relevant in the U.S. First, the uniquely American transcontinental railroads owned by private interests not only produced technological, financial and organizational innovations that allowed for large-scale enterprise but also generated an extensive internal market, while stimulating that same market through the railroads' own demands for fuel, rails, equipment even capital (Roy, 1995; Standiford, 2005). This multifaceted impact stimulated the growth of a population of large industrial and retail corporations that far exceeded that in the rest of the industrializing world. Other nations, most notably Britain and Germany, possessed their own giant firms but not as many and not so spread across as many industries (Schmitz, 1995). Moreover, large businesses were historically constrained in older nations by their corporatist interplay with other institutions: guilds, parliaments, courts, estates, church and the like, along with the networks of patronage that traditionally mediated relationships among these institutions (Gerstenberger, 2005). Britain possessed the weakest corporatist[1] traditions, but the firms behind that nation's industrialization were typically much smaller than equivalent American firms, and while Britain actually pioneered railroad construction, these were hardly of the same size and power of their American counterparts.

Britain, along with Germany, also possessed something missing in the United States, a parliamentary system in which labor-based parties could push back against the growing power of larger businesses (Holt, 1977). By contrast, the United States was governed through a federal system in which the central government was slow to intervene economically, and the various state governments were often outflanked or overwhelmed by national corporations. Worse, a continuum of perpetrators of state violence, ranging from federal troops to state national guards to local police to deputized Pinkerton guards, waged the most violent war against organized labor anywhere in the industrial world (Goldstein, 1978; Norwood, 2002; Taft & Ross, 1969). While unions hung on in smaller shops and construction, they made virtually no inroads into the new corporate giants before the Depression beyond a very few niches for skilled workers within the growing swarms of industrial workers. Moreover, the craft-based American Federation of Labor could not even manage to organize the few corporate opportunities that occasionally presented themselves (Marens, 2012). As unions failed to make headway within the new corporate world, the development of a generalized employment-at-will doctrine around the turn of the 20th century left individual employees, including those in the new white-collar occupations, virtually without enforceable rights (Feinman, 1976).

The result by the end of World War I was a large population of giant corporations facing few legal or institutional restraints, especially with regard to the treatment of employees. A degree of regulation was imposed by state and federal governments, but outside of the railroad regulation, these tended to be mild and sometimes, as in the case of meat inspection or workers compensation, even supported to some degree by larger firms hoping to either reassure consumers, to reduce lawsuits or even to impose higher unit costs on smaller competitors (Barkan, 1985; Weinstein, 1981). This managerial autonomy was further bolstered by the self-confidence and resources generated by tremendous commercial success. At the time of the American Civil War, the nation was largely an exporter of minerals and agricultural commodities. By 1900, it was exporting as many manufactured goods as Great Britain, while simultaneously supplying a much larger and wealthier domestic market. Moreover, much of the U.S. growth in production and export belonged to the dynamic "high-tech" sectors of the time: locomotives, industrial machinery, electrical equipment, typewriters and farm machinery (Kirkland, 1961). European commentators warned of the growing American "menace" using the kind of terms that American pundits fearfully employed in the 1980s with regard to Japanese Toyotas and consumer electronics (Flint, 1901). There was at least one important difference, however, with later American fears regarding Japan. The wealth accumulated by this industrial success combined with the devastation of World War I led to the emergence of New York as the new financial capital of the world, a status Tokyo has never obtained, and that allowed continued American dominance of the world economy even after its relative industrial decline in the later years of the 20th century (Pollin, 2003). The new American corporate order had collectively accumulated vast economic power along with the legal autonomy to use as it saw fit.

Worries over these developments was not restricted to the American political left, or to liberal reformers, or even to alliances of the two factions, as in the efforts of Florence Kelley (1899) to unite consumers and workers, or to the Worker's Health Bureau's largely quixotic attempts to interest organized labor (predominantly craft-based at the time) to focus more on improving general working conditions (Rosner & Markowitz, 1989). While it may not be obvious today, the large corporation was hardly a "conservative" institution but in many ways a radical break with tradition and ideologically a threat to the myth of the individual proprietor that had pervaded American history, offering instead an unmanly dependence on the white-collar bureaucracies of these monopolist corporations (Davis, 2000). Judge Grosscup (1905), for example, who had displayed no sympathy to those Pullman strikers he had once sentenced to jail, warned in print about a decade after that strike that the new large corporations were posing a threat to the very entrepreneurship that Americans so cherished. Even as undeniable a product of big business as the second John Rockefeller (1916) worried, after the shock of the Ludlow Massacre, that the new steam and electrical technology that powered modern business had "by necessity erected large-scale barriers between employers and men, thus making it more difficult to understand each other" (p. 113). As America's leading "serious" newspaper columnist expressed it on the eve of World War I:

> In the last thirty years or so American business has been passing through a reorganization so radical that we are just beginning to grasp its meaning. At any rate for those of us who are young to-day the business world of our grandfathers is a piece of history that we can reconstruct only with the greatest difficulty. We know that the huge corporation, the integrated industry, production for a world market, the network of combinations, pools and agreements have played havoc with the older political economy. The scope of human endeavor is enormously larger, and with it has come, as Graham Wallas says, a general change of social scale.
>
> *(Lippman, 1914: 35–36)*

Creating CSR

The beginnings of CSR were an ideological response to all of these various concerns raised by a diverse set of critics regarding the impact of these large and autonomous corporations on American life. One can find precedents within corporate America dating back at least to Carnegie's professions of *noblesse oblige* in his *Gospel of Wealth*, published in 1889, when corporate consolidation was only beginning. By the beginning of the 20th century, a sizable minority of corporations had already experimented with a variety of employee uplift and welfare programs (Tolman, 1909; Tone, 1997). As long as control of the workplace was contested by employees, organized into unions or not, these various initiatives never really coalesced into any single of coherent view of the social responsibilities that should attach to the new business organizations. Carnegie himself was no longer credible as a spokesperson for enlightened capitalism after suffering the embarrassment of the shooting war at his Homestead works (Standiford, 2005).

It was labor peace that brought a more fully developed CSR into being, but it was the peace of conquest with CSR serving as a program of pacification. Having crushed organized labor's efforts to gain or solidify entry in the new corporate world shortly after the end of World War I, while increasingly bureaucratizing white-collar employment and neutralizing most regulatory tendencies that might have survived the short-lived Progressive Era, the leaders of American corporations felt compelled to define for a wary public how they intended to use their economic power and legal autonomy. To defend and consolidate these gains, corporate leaders needed to convince the American public that the rise of corporate domination was indeed a general boon for society, especially for employees, whom the firms still ultimately depended upon and, because of changes in immigration law, could no longer be replenished through waves of new arrivals (Slichter, 1929). William Leiserson (1929), an early academic expert on labor and employment relations, warned that even if large-scale labor unrest had become a thing of the past, business still needed to attend to a myriad of smaller-scale problems in dealing with employees, not only for good public relations but for the more pedestrian reasons of preventing turnover and improving efficiency. Avoidable industrial accidents, wage cuts, speedups, arbitrary treatment at the hands of supervisors and foremen and a general failure on the part of many companies to adequately share the prosperity they enjoyed hardly brought confidence in the ability of the new corporate order. These publicized failings ran counter to the rather explicit promise that the commercial promoters and their political allies had made during the course of the of the 19th century that a series of incremental extensions of the rights of corporations and incorporators (granting full limited liability, allowing holding companies, broadening corporate purpose) would bring economic prosperity to the entire society (Dodd, 1954; Roy, 1995). Moreover, the shock of the Russian Revolution made much of the American elite, from trust-busting Woodrow Wilson (1919) to the son of the builder of the greatest of all the trusts (Rockefeller, 1916), quite aware that the reaction to irresponsibility could even prove deadly. As even conservative economist Arthur Hadley (1896), who, while president of Yale actually encouraged his students to work as scabs (Norwood, 2002), warned, "Those who fear the effects of increased governmental powers must prove by their acceptance of ethical duties to the public that they . . . are preparing to accept the heavy burdens and obligations which the industrial present carries with it" (quoted by Heald, 1970: 29).

Business leaders responded with a mixture of advocating enlightened self-interest and calls for civic virtue. As early as 1896, the antiunion Hadley had actually argued that slightly higher wages than necessary for bringing in workers provided a competitive advantage over less generous employers, a sentiment echoed by the president of Studebaker a generation later, asserting that "[i]t is the duty of capital and management to compensate labor liberally, paying at least the current wage and probably a little bit more, and give workers healthful surroundings and treat them with the utmost consideration" (Forbes, 1924: 113). An editorial in *Forbes Magazine* (1917) had already turned this virtue into a patriotic duty, claiming that "[g]iven their [employees'] power to help or hinder a firm, the employer who does not do everything in his power to satisfy his men is not only short-sighted from his point of view but is an enemy of national peace and harmony" (p. 112). And a decade later, the publisher of that same magazine complained under his own byline that this sage advice was too often ignored, with too many workplaces still tending "to breed socialists, communists, and other unwholesome agitators" (Heald, 1970: 107).

Some workplaces did try to satisfy and motivate their workers with a variety of representation plans, corporate welfare programs, various benefit packages and sometimes higher-than-market wages. As might be imagined, the seriousness of these efforts varied enormously, from Gerard Swope, president of General Electric, a one-time tutor at Hull House and an acquaintance of Florence Kelley, offering to allow union representation for his employees if the unions could agree on a single union to serve as the counterparty (they couldn't agree), to the sham works councils of International Harvester used to cover up rapacious personnel policies (Ozanne, 1967). Even when sincerely implemented, however, these programs often proved to be valued considerably less by employees than their would-be benevolent managers anticipated. Works councils at Ludlow and an employee subsidized stock plan offered by U.S. Steel may have indeed been appreciated to some degree, but neither prevented strikes at either company over working hours and pay (Selekman & Van Kleeck, 1924; Tarbell, 1925). Even where pay was significantly more generous than necessary to simply bring workers into the plant, most famously at Ford Motor Company, the quid pro quo was often an intensified working pace (Toller, 1930).

Still all of this effort, or professed effort, at better employment relations did pay off in public relations. Looking back on the eve of the Depression, Owen Young (1929), chair of General Electric, argued that after a generation of trial and error, large firms had not only mended their ways but had actually become far more considerate of employee welfare than smaller firms. National Cash Register, a usually enthusiastic promoter of corporate welfare, was largely forgiven its monopolistic practices on that account (Sealander, 1988). Nor was blue-collar labor the only target of supposed managerial beneficence. Corporate white-collar job ladders, denounced by critics as deadening bureaucracies, were now framed, not without some truth, as opportunities for ambitious men who would otherwise lack the capital to compete as entrepreneurs (Davis, 2000). Heinz and Hershey, among other food and clothing manufacturers, even tied enlightened personnel policies to the wholesomeness of their products (Tone, 1997).

From this use of supposedly progressive personnel policies as a societal boon, it was a fairly short step for the more thoughtful business leaders to argue for a new way to look at the large corporation. Young (1927) told one Harvard audience:

> We think of managers as no longer partisan attorneys of either group [capital or labor] against the other. Rather we have come to see them as trustees of the whole undertaking, whose responsibilities are to see to it on the one side that the invested capital is safe and that its return is adequate and continuous, and on the other side that competent and conscientious men are found to do the work and that their job is safe and their earnings are adequate and continuous.
>
> *(p. 392)*

Other executives expressed similar views. Not surprisingly, these included his subordinate, Gerard Swope, who argued that both the public and employees should be considered ahead of stockholders. Robert Wood Johnson, of Johnson & Johnson, echoed these sentiments, declaring:

> It is to the enlightened self-interest of modern industry to realize that its service to its customers comes first, its service to its employees and management second, and its service to its stockholders last. It is to the enlightened self-interest of industry to accept and fulfill its share of social responsibility
>
> *(Quoted by Foster, 1999: 224).*

Swope, Young, and Johnson were unusually liberal for corporate executives and, to varying degrees, supporters of the New Deal, but even Liberty Leaguer Alfred Sloan (1941), a harsh critic of Roosevelt, acknowledged in his memoirs that "industrial management must expand its horizon of responsibility. . . . It must consider the impact of its operations on the economy as a whole in relation to the social and economic welfare of the entire community" (p. 145). Other celebrity executives of the time echoed these sentiments. Eastman argued that anything for the betterment of humanity is good business, while Heinz saw his food company as being responsible to grocers, employees and customers as well as to stockholders (Heald, 1970). Gary, hardly a bleeding heart, saw himself as "occupying a position of balance among . . . investors, employees, customers, competitors, and all others who may be interested in, or affected by, the actions or attitudes of the managers" (Tarbell, 1925: 100).

While little remembered today, the so-called Roaring Twenties was a period in which corporate managers were sufficiently autonomous from pressures from government, investment bankers, and labor unions to develop their own definition of their responsibilities. While Berle and Dodd conducted their academic debate as to whether this was a good or bad thing, one issue that they agreed upon was that corporations owed their employees some degree of security and shared prosperity (Marens, 2010). Ironically, when managerially driven CSR was revived in both the business and academic worlds a half-century from the beginning of the Depression, this would be the element that would not be resuscitated.

Pluralist interlude

With the coming of the Depression, the New Deal, industrial unionism, hot and cold wars and fiscal demand management, the social, political and economic environment changed for the American corporation and, with it, the autonomy of corporate managers to decide for themselves exactly where their responsibilities lay. Instead, for the duration of that first postwar generation, corporate social responsibilities were defined in the context of pluralism, that informal and ultimately transitory Americanized version of European-style corporatism, in which various organized interest groups – churches, universities, agriculture, trade associations, along with corporations and labor unions – would alternately compete and cooperate, refereed by a mildly regulatory state that would energize the process when necessary with moderate Keynesian demand management. While this may have been a simplified and idealized view of reality, there was some truth to it (Schattschneider, 1960), and, realistic or not, it was at least a broadly accepted ideal (Bell, 1960).

In such a setting, it was unsurprising that the focus of discussions of the responsibilities of corporations would shift from what enlightened corporate executives would decree to what the society itself would demand or expect from the managers of these enterprises. With the expansion of postwar higher education, especially business schools vying for a legitimate place in the university, academics would increasingly involve themselves in this discussion, but it actually began outside of it, in such places as *Human Relations in Modern Business* (Biggers, 1949), a booklet produced by a consortium of business, labor and clergy organized by Robert Johnson, organized around the guiding principle of "Co-operation, not conflict" (p. v). The publication was excerpted in *Harvard Business Review*, which published a similarly themed piece two years later, ostensibly authored by Frank Abrams (1951), CEO of Esso (now Exxon), and the first of several CSR pieces the journal published during the 1950s, although many of the others would be written by academics.

The scholars who turned to the topic during the 1950s were typically specialists in industrial relations or macroeconomics with some background in government, labor union or foundation work that endowed them with some knowledge of how businesses actually interacted with other institutions. Contributors to this discourse included Howard Bowen, Neil Chamberlain, J. M. Clark, Ernst Dale, Peter Drucker, John Kenneth Galbraith, James Kuhn, Karl Kaysen, Sumner Slichter and even the generation-older Ben Selekman, who had conducted studies with working-conditions reformer Mary Van Kleeck in the early 1920s (Selekman & Van Kleeck, 1924). A very few academic philosophers also contributed (Brown, 1983), but considerations of the morality of business practices were largely the province of industrial relations and economics specialists. *A Moral Philosophy for Management*, for example, which ran through five editions between 1959 and 1963, was written by Selekman (1959), a pioneering industrial relations scholar.

For the postwar generation of scholars, discussing corporate social responsibilities was a side-line to their "serious" scholarship and was often targeted to students or a general audience in either the *Harvard Business Review* or through books, often published by that Taylorist reformer and early human resources educator Ordway Tead, working at Harper & Brothers. A handful of younger academics, however, attempted to establish instead a new academic discipline within business schools during the 1960s and 1970s with the aim of studying both the normative and empirical aspects of the impact of business upon society. "Business and Society," as the field was generally known (sometimes expanded to "Business, Government, and Society"), attempted to institutionalize itself with specialized courses, PhD programs, conferences and founding both an academic (*Business & Society*)and a practitioner-oriented (*Business and Society Review*) journal, but with only limited and isolated success in establishing itself as a full-blown discipline. Its novelty and institutional uncertainty generally failed to attract better scholars away from established disciplines or law schools, especially since there was a reasonable degree of uncertainty as to the degree of intellectual freedom that a new scholar could expect within a business school environment (Marens, 2010).

The 1950s cadre of CSR scholars did not agree on every point, but they were typically quite skeptical about the propriety or ability of corporate executives to define their own social responsibilities. Howard Bowen (1953), in writing what has been regarded on the founding text of the study of CSR asserted, "The businessman's viewpoint is that management should function as a trustee mediating among the several interest groups, but that the power of decision-making should rest exclusively with management . . . is . . . just another application of the familiar but discredited doctrine of benevolent use of power" (p. 42). Economist Karl Kaysen (1957), who would serve in the Kennedy Administration, echoed Bowen's opinion in even harsher terms:

> But what management takes into account is what management decides to take into account, and however responsible management policy is, it is responsible only in terms of the goals, values, and knowledge of management. No direct responsibility, made effective by formal functioning machinery of control, exists. No matter how responsible managers strive to be, they remain in the fundamental sense irresponsible oligarchs in the context of the modern corporate system.
>
> *(p. 316)*

While others may not have used such blunt language, business leaders and the business school administrators who catered to them were unsurprisingly suspicious of intellectuals accusing them of discredited doctrines or even irresponsible oligarchy. Bowen himself was briefly the victim of the Red Scare when he was pressured to abandon the deanship of the University of Illinois School of Business after charges of "radicalism" (Solberg & Tomilson, 1997). While the era of explicit McCarthyism ended by the late 1950s, the rise of the social movements of the 1960s provoked a new reaction a decade later, exemplified in the infamous future Supreme Court Justice Lewis Powell's (1971) letter to the United States Chamber of Commerce, in which he accused reform-ers and liberals of posing a far more serious threat to the business establishment than "upfront" socialists and communists. As the seventies preceded, and as business leaders felt increasingly har-ried by Naderites and environmentalists as well as becoming more overtly hostile to unions and Keynesian stimulation (both of which they blamed, not entirely unfairly, for inflation and lack of competitiveness on world markets), the business establishment was hardly tolerant of suggestions that it required further constraints to ensure responsible behavior (Marens, 2010). Typical of the era were both the transformation of the once mildly Keynesian think tank, the Committee for Economic Development, toward an antiregulatory stance due to pressure from its corporate patrons (Clark, 1976; Collins, 1982) and an article written by the CEO of a defense contractor "Corporate Support of Education: Some Strings Attached" (Malott, 1978), advocating, without any apparent irony, the teaching of more laissez-faire economics in American universities.

In reality, the corporate leadership had little to fear from the first group of full-time business and society scholars who had begun to make their way into business schools during the 1960s. Whether it was because they lacked the experience or sophistication of their "part-time" 1950s predecessors or because they engaged in self-censorship to survive in business school settings, the result was a body of work that was generally unthreatening. They did, however, make the decision to broaden their own ranks by recruiting moral philosophers into their world, and some of these newcomers proved more feckless, at least initially. Often inspired to analyze the ethics of business by the enormous success of Rawls's *Theory of Justice*, a defense of egalitarian and democratic economic systems, these philosophers came to the subject with the presumption that "ethics had implicit in it standards that were independent of the wishes of corporations." According to one of these business ethics pioneers:

> Those in business ethics did not see ethics as coming after economics and law but as restraints on economic activity and as a source for justifying law and for proposing additional legal restraints on business when appropriate. As a result business ethics and business ethicists were not warmly received by the business community, who often perceived them as a threat – something they could not manage, preaching by the uninformed who never had to face a payroll.
>
> *(DeGeorge, 2005, p. 22)*

The second wave of academic philosophers who followed these business ethics pioneers would learn the lesson of this rejection well.

Non-consequentialism with a vengeance

By the early 1980s, top management at many major American corporations were actually facing a far more objectively deadly threat to their own careers than that posed by pesky reformers or demanding labor leaders. Attacks from shareholder activists, corporate raiders and their allies in the finance professoriate were taking their toll with a new, well funded argument. For these attackers from what might be considered the political "right" (Clawson, Neustadtl & Weller; 1998; Pollin, 2003), the problem was not that corporate executives were failing to fulfill their broad set responsibilities but that they were ignoring their single, supposedly inviolable obligation to stockholders to do whatever they legally could to raise the price of shares. Whether through coincidence or shrewd observation, a small group of moral philosophers saw their opportunity to offer to help rescue these besieged executives by offering to legitimize their power and autonomy, provided that they agree to wield these in an ethical manner through the heuristics that these ethicists would provide. By acknowledging executives' right to guide their companies largely free of interference from impatient stockholders, greedy unions or meddlesome regulators, these ethicists intended to guide corporate managers toward ethical leadership and thus use their managerial autonomy to benefit both corporations and the larger society in ways that regulators or union officials could not hope to match and that the more short-term-focused investors and investment managers were unconcerned with matching.

These philosophically trained ethics "entrepreneurs" actually had very little experience with business or even with government or labor unions, in sharp contrast with the postwar generation of business and society academics. But they seemed to understand, at least implicitly, how patronage had worked down the ages for moral philosophers, whether it be Aristotle serving Philip and Alexander, Locke residing in the household of one of England's largest landowners, or even Kant writing hagiography to Frederick in the hope, ultimately vain as it turned out, of an invitation to Berlin (Kuehn, 2001; Marens, 2011). This new cadre of ethicists emulated these icons and broke with practices established by the first wave of business and society scholars by making corporate executives subjects, not objects, of ethical analysis, assuming the point of view of the top executives of American corporations. They would do for these executives what Young, Swope, Abrams, Johnson, Heinz, Eastman, Johnson and even Rockefeller Jr. had done for themselves, or at least allowing their names to appear in the byline.

They departed from this earlier group, however, in one crucial aspect. Even though corporate America had by the 1920s successfully defeated organizing labor, employees' legal challenges and the great bulk of workplace regulation, it still required the cooperation of its employees, and so there was a great deal of attention paid to the need to offer, or at least claim to provide, secure, well compensated, humanized employment. While these goals were often honored in the breach, there was some degree of specificity with regard to discussions of pay, job security, welfare programs, benefits and the like, subjects that were also strongly emphasized by the postwar business and society academics. Concerns for the welfare of employees, however, were reduced to vague generalities by the post-1980 generation of business ethics (and what remained of business and society) scholarship because the need to mollify employees was no longer viewed by top managers as crucial to their own success, and the new cohort of business ethicist possessed neither the necessary knowledge nor the integrity to advocate for employees. The rise of globalization, the political defeats of organized labor, the increased practicality of moving both manufacturing and white-collar work abroad and a sense that American labor was earning more than it deserved – all meant that employee buy-in was regarded as less important than it had been in the past. What mattered was the perception of a company's "value" – that is, "stock price" – and a firm viewed as overly generous, such as Costco, faced skepticism in the financial markets with regard to its future (Holmes & Zellner, 2004). Moreover, given the increasing malleability of accounting numbers, there were more certain ways of attracting investment and enhancing "value" than putting one's hopes in the vagaries of a high-road sharing of prosperity with employees (Partnoy, 2003). Whether by chance or design, the new generation of business ethicists benefited from failing to broach such a touchy subject with their patrons.

Ethicists focused instead on promoting abstract prescriptions as to how to manage both effectively and ethically by applying virtue ethics (Solomon, 1992), social contract theory (Donaldson, 1982) and Kantian deontology (Freeman, 1984). In this, they followed historical precedent. Aristotle was quite explicit that only men of leisure would have the opportunity to cultivate virtues (Wood, 2008), while Locke (1697), who despised the poor, restricted his argument for political rights, up through the right to overthrow a king, to those who owned property (Becker, 1992). Even Kant rarely missed a chance to flatter his king, arguing that he was wiser than any Parliament, and what Kant (1967) praised as Frederick's tolerance of argumentation and disagreement, provided it was followed by strict obedience, could serve as the template for the modern workplace "empowerment" programs that ethicists praise (e.g., Goodstein & Wicks, 2007; Rehbein, Waddock & Graves, 2004).

Much as business and society scholars of the 1950s published nonacademic books to promote their pluralistic view of CSR, two nonacademics books by philosophers, one by Donaldson (1982), the other, later but more widely read, by Freeman (1984), began this process of offering advice to managers, implicitly accepting as legitimate their power and autonomy to make major moral choices. Reflecting this thrust, the Society of Business Ethics, originally founded in 1980 as part of the American Philosophical Association, switched its meeting time and location in 1989 to coincide with the Academy of Management meetings. What the new business ethics asked of executives was never made concrete: executives would honor the interests of "stakeholders" and somehow referee whenever interests of different stakeholders came into conflict. Exactly how stakeholders would come together and present their agenda was largely left unexamined, although Freeman, writing with Evan (a sociologist), did endorse the idea of board representation, although he has neither pursued the idea nor explained its mechanics over the ensuing generation (Freeman & Evan, 1990).

Alternatively, executives were urged to comply with implicit social contracts that the executives themselves would deduce or define (Donaldson & Dunfee, 1995), or possibly fulfill a set of Aristotelian virtues that were as banal as they were venerable (Solomon, 1992). Like William Frederick (1998), possibly the leading figure of the second generation of business and society academics who emerged during the 1960s, these business ethicists, whom he had at one time encouraged to become involved with business studies, "continued devotion to the noncontextualist abstractions found in the lore of conventional philosophy," requiring a "nearly studied ignorance of what has actually taken place within the American business world" (p. 44).

This ignorance proved useful in fulfilling the prophecy of Richard DeGeorge (1991), a philosopher at the University of Kansas and host in 1974 of what might have been the very first business ethics conferences: "[i]f Business Ethics is tailored to the wishes of established business, then it will become the inculcation of established norms, a handmaid of business's vested interests, and it will cease to have the objectivity and critical function that justifies it as an academic field" (p. 49). Kahn's (1990) study of the *then* new field of business ethics, presumably researched a couple of years before its publication date, reported a professed interest among business ethicists in applying social science to their scholarship and making it truly interdisciplinary. With the exception of a smattering of social psychology, however, business ethicists continued to studiously avoid the relevant empirical social science generated outside of business schools. Hiding behind the nonconsequentialist rule-based approach to ethics, ethicists avoided the sources of "accumulation by dispossession" that has run rampant between the 1960s to 1990s. One would search in vain for informed discussion within this literature regarding any number of topics that would presumably raise all kinds of ethical issues: union avoidance or elimination, reductions in benefits coverage, upper redistribution of income, the politics of deregulation, the operation of the military (or prison) industrial complex, the constant downward pressure on taxes, the forcing of employees to train their outsourced replacements in return for severance pay or the extortion of state and local governments for relocation or even "stay put" subsidies (Armour, 2004; Brofenbrenner, 1994; Clawson, Neustadtl & Weller, 1998; Leroy, 2005; Logan, 2002; Melman, 1987; Mishel, Bernstein & Shierholz, 2009; Partnoy, 2003). Ethicists and the remaining social science–oriented business and society academics prefer to focus on such banalities as bribery (bad) or philanthropy (good). While existing laws and regulations are mentioned from time to time, virtually no business ethicist has been so rude as to bring up the political undermining of proposed regulation or the flouting of extant ones.

Ethical progress in such law-driven areas as discrimination, product safety and pollution is ballyhooed, but the logical conclusion that further laws or additional regulations may generate even more gains is simply never drawn (Marens, 2011). For all the teeth-gnashing over the short-term pressures that Wall Street supposedly puts on corporate management to turn them away from ethical management, no ethicist is so radical as to endorse Nobel laureate James Tobin's transaction tax, meant, in part, to make ownership of stock a more permanent decision. This aversion was on full display when the Ethics Institute of the Business Roundtable – an institute run by academics on behalf of an organization for CEOs that was initially formed to block legislation to make it easier to organize unions (Mills, 1979) – issued its study on "short-termism," which made no mention of such a tax (Krehmeyer, Orsagh & Schact, 2006).

Moreover, in a supposedly globalized marketplace, used to justify the increasingly rapacious treatment of American workers, other nations are rarely mentioned except as the objects of American-based management. One would be hard put to find a suggestion that the United States, as a society, might learn something from CSR practices initiated elsewhere. For American business ethics, there is simply no conceivable alternative to the American version of contemporary capitalism. Even its Canadian neighbor's single-payer health insurance, which has attracted some businesses because it relieves them of a major uncertainty (Krugman, 2005), would never be broached because it would eliminate a source of profits for the insurance industry, while empowering workers to exit and government to further tax and regulate. Germany's works councils, which might well have contributed to the nation's far stronger ability to hold onto high-wage manufacturing and which is generally regarded positively by German executives (Wever, 2008), are apparently an unknown entity to stakeholder enthusiasts, even though one might think they would embrace a stakeholder institution within a highly successful economy. Yet at a Society of Business Ethics meeting a few years back, among the few items left in the publishers' display room at the tail end of the conference closing giveaway were several copies of a special issue on works councils by the *British Journal of Industrial Relations*. One can only assume that business ethicists either do not know what works councils are, or they are well aware that they would be viewed negatively by corporate executives as an unwanted government interference that forces management to share power in certain spheres with their employees.

What little discussion of the real world that occurs in the literature is essentially framed as a Manichean struggle. There are occasionally discussions of "bad" firms: the tobacco companies, Enron, WorldCom and other scofflaws, along with perhaps a few others, such as Walmart, which are singled out as rapacious. On the other side is the firm whose leadership promotes an ethics program or claims some kind of fidelity to stakeholder relationships, essentially relabeling paternalism as stakeholder management. Evidence that might expose these claims to skepticism is simply ignored. Hence we read about Johnson & Johnson's handling of the Tylenol crisis a generation ago, Starbucks' partnership with its employees, Royal Dutch Shell's environmental sensitivity, the late Robert Galvin operating Motorola as a paragon of stakeholder management, or even praising Citibank for instituting an ethics program a few years before the collapse of financial markets (e.g., Goodstein & Wicks, 2007; Lawrence, 2002; Post, Preston & Sachs, 2002). On the other hand, the literature has literally nothing to say about the recent Johnson & Johnson factory scandals (Thomas & Abelson, 2012), or the reasons Starbucks has been convicted in three states of retaliating against union organizers (Allison, 2009), or how Galvin kept dossiers on Americans who opposed military spending, fought unionization and allowed Motorola to become the first major corporation to impose a drug test on its employees (Marens, 2006). As for lionizing Citibank's alleged turn to the ethical side of the force in the early 21st century, this should hardly require further comment (Enrich & Mollencamp, 2007; Partnoy, 2003).

Theoretically, business ethics need not have gone down the sycophantic road, at least not so far down. Within the 2500-year tradition of Western ethical writings, alternative models might certainly have been pursued. Smith and Mill are honored by every single business ethics textbook, and it would be impossible to paint either as "antibusiness." Yet Smith's skepticism of restraint of trade and corporate boards (and a degree of sympathy for workers' weak bargaining position vis-à-vis "combinations of masters"), and Mill's sympathy for workers' struggles, the need for all groups to self-protect and not simply depend on the benevolence of their social superiors (although he was hypocritical on this point when it came to India) and his willingness to try to weigh the evidence in ambiguous situations – would put them beyond the pale for "serious" business ethics. One might think that, given contemporary controversies that culminated in the Occupy movement, John Rawls's (1971) central concerns regarding a fair distribution of income and the erosion of democracy by wealth would be constantly cited, especially since he is easily the most cited contemporary philosopher in the business ethics literature. In actuality, very few ethicists apply Rawls this way; Harris (2006) and Hsieh (2009) provide rare exceptions. The overwhelming majority of citations to Rawls either are a passing mention or invoke "the veil of ignorance," his heuristic for establishing social rules. In fact, when ethicists do occasionally invoke his "difference principle" regarding fair distribution, it has been applied to a variety of subjects – bribery, immigration, access to health care, rulemaking and so on – but almost never to the distribution of income.

But as a practical matter, if the field had conducted closer scrutiny on the actual record of the aggregated decisions of corporate executives, it might have faced extinction, at least within business schools. In the era of financial hypertrophy, in which governments are expected to subsidize but rarely tax and almost never compel, a posture that offered "constructive criticism," let alone "loyal opposition," would never have gained traction. Tenure in business schools, ethical consulting gigs, endowed chairs and places at the Business Roundtable's Institute for Ethics were not intended for skeptics, let alone critics. Howard Bowen (1978), hardly a radical but a supporter of unions, Keynesian fiscal policies, and some degree of government regulation, gave up on corporate social responsibility as early as 1978, even before American wage stagnation was clearly underway. It became clear that business and financial leaders, along with most of the politicians they support, encouraged policies that would allow them to pocket the gains that businesses accrued, sometimes by paying their own employees or contractees less, sometimes by exploiting government procurement, research, or even direct subsidies and sometimes by simply cooking the books and exploiting the gullibility of the managers of institutional investments, many of whom are responsible for handling the retirement capital of workers. Even these pension funds themselves have been routinely looted in a more direct manner to the benefit of top management (Schultz, 2011). In a lucky-you-have-a-job world, irrelevant philosophical babble was all that ever had a chance of selling.

Note

1   "Corporatist" is used here in the political sense of the word, not as a reference to business corporations.

References

Abrams, F. W. (1951). Management's Responsibilities in a Complex World. *Harvard Business Review*. 29–34.
Adbusters (2011). Occupy Wall Street, July 13. Retrieved on November 8, 2012 from: http://www.adbusters.org/blogs/adbusters-blog/occupywallstreet.html.
Allison, M. (2009). Starbucks faces more union woes: Third union case for coffee giant. *Seattle Times*, January 6: A6.
Armour, S. (2004). Workers asked to train foreign replacements. *USA Today*, April 6: 1B.
Barkan, I. D. (1985). Industry invites regulation: The passage of the Pure Food and Drug Act of 1906. *American Journal of Public Health*, 75: 18–26.
Becker, R. (1992). Ideological commitment of Locke: Freemen and servants in the two treatises of government. *History of Political Thought*, 8: 632–656.
Bell, D. (1960). *End of ideology: On the exhaustion of political ideas*. New York: Free Press.
Berle, A. A., & Means, G. C. (1932). *Modern corporation and private property*. New York: Macmillan.
Biggers, J. D. (1949). *Human relations in modern business*. New York: Prentice Hall.
Bowen, H. R. (1953). *Social responsibilities of the businessman*. New York: Harper & Row.
Bowen, H. R. (1978). Social responsibilities of the businessman: Twenty years later. In E. Epstein and E. D. Votaw (Eds.), *Rationality, legitimacy, responsibility: Search for new directions in business and society*: 116–130. Santa Monica, CA: Goodyear.

Brofenbrenner, K. (1994). Employer behavior in certification elections and first contracts: Implications for labor law reform. In S. Friedman, R. W. Hurd & R. A. Oswald (Eds.), *Restoring the promise of American labor law*. 75–88. Ithaca, NY: ILR Press.

Brown, C. C. (1983). *The dean meant business*. New York: Columbia University Graduate School of Business.

Clark, L. H. (1976). Rehabilitation project: Once-mighty CED panel of executives seeks a revival, offers advice to Carter. *The Wall Street Journal*, December 17: A38.

Clawson, D., Neustadtl, A., & Weller, M. (1998). *Dollars and votes: How business campaign contributions subvert democracy*. Philadelphia: Temple University Press.

Collins, R. (1982). *Business response to Keynes*. New York: Columbia University Press.

Cooper, J. M. (1980) *The Army and civil disorder*. Westport, CT: Greenwood Press.

Davis, C. (2000). *Company men: White collar life and corporate cultures in Los Angeles*. Baltimore, MD: Johns Hopkins University Press.

DeGeorge, R. T. (1991). Will success spoil business ethics? In R. E. Freeman (Ed.), *Business ethics: The state of the art*: 42–55. New York: Oxford University Press.

De George, R. T. (2005). Keynote speech given at Markkula Center's Third Biannual Business Ethics Conference. Retrieved September 16, 2012 from: http://www.scu.edu/ethics/practicing/focusareas/business/conference/presentations/.

Dodd, E. M. (1932). For whom are corporate managers trustees? *Harvard Law Review*, *45*: 1145–1163.

Dodd, E. M. (1954). *American business corporations until 1860*. Cambridge, MA: Harvard University Press.

Donaldson, T. (1982). *Corporations and morality*. Englewood Cliffs, NJ: Prentice Hall.

Donaldson, T., & Dunfee, T. W. (1995). Integrated social contracts theory: a communitarian conception of economic ethics. *Economics and Philosophy*, *11*: 85–112.

Enrich, D., & Mollenkamp, C. (2007). Citigroup likely to propose cuts of 15,000 jobs. *The Wall Street Journal*, March 26: A1.

Feinman, J. M. (1976). Development of employment-at-will rule. *American Journal of Legal History*, *20*: 118–135.

Flint, C. R. (1901). Business situation in the United States and the prospects for the future. *North American Review*, *172*: 381–393.

Forbes, B. C. (1924). Our men build their souls into Studebaker cars. *Forbes Magazine*, April 26, 95–97, 108, 113, 132.

Forbes Magazine (1917). Fact and comment, October 13: 111–114.

Foster, L. G. (1999). *Robert Wood Johnson: The gentleman rebel*. State College, PA: Lillian Press.

Frederick, W. C. (1998). Moving to CSR4: What to pack for the trip. *Business and Society*, 37: 40–59.

Freeman, R. E. (1984). *Strategic management: A stakeholder approach*. Boston: Pitman.

Freeman, R. E., and Evan, W. (1990). Corporate governance: A stakeholder interpretation. *Journal of Behavioral Economics*, *19*: 337–359.

Gerstenberger, H. (2005). *Impersonal power: History and theory of the bourgeois state*. Chicago: Haymarket Books.

Goldstein, R. J. (1978). *Political repression in modern America*. Boston: G. K. Hall.

Goodstein, J. D., & Wicks, A. C. (2007). Corporations and stakeholder responsibility: Making business ethics a two-way conversation. *Business Ethics Quarterly*, 17: 375–398.

Grosscup, P. S. (1905). How to save the corporation, *McClure's Magazine*, February, 443–448.

Hadley, A. T. (1896). *Economics*. New York: Putnam's Sons.

Hanlon, G., and Fleming, P. (2009). Updating the critical perspective on corporate social responsibility. *Sociology Compass*, 3: 937–948.

Harris, J. (2006) How much is too much? A theoretical analysis of executive compensation from the standpoint of distributive justice. In R. Kolb (Ed.), *The Ethics of executive compensation*: 67–86. Malden, MA: Blackwell.

Heald, M. (1970). *The social responsibilities of business: Company and community, 1900–1960*. Cleveland, OH: Case Western Reserve University Press.

Holmes, S., & Zellner, W. (2004). The Costco way: Higher wages mean higher profits, but try telling Wall Street. *Business Week*, April 12, 76.

Holt, J. (1977). Trade unionism in the British and U.S. steel industries, 1880–1914. *Labor History*, 18: 5–35.

Hsieh, N. (2009). Corporate social responsibility and the priority of shareholders. *Journal of Business Ethics*, 88 (Supplement): 553–600.

Kahn, W. (1990). Toward an agenda for business ethics research. *Academy of Management Review*, 15: 311–328.

Kant, I. (1967). The nature of enlightenment. In R. Wines (Ed.), *Enlightened despotism, reform or reaction?*: 14–17. Boston: Heath Co.

Kaysen, C. (1957). Social significance of the modern corporation. *American Economic Review*, 47: 311–319.

Kelley, F. (1899). Aims and principles of the National Consumers League. *Journal of Sociology*, 5: 289–304.

Kinderman, D. (2010). Free us up so we can be responsible: The co-evolution of corporate social responsibility and neo-liberalism in the UK, 1977–2010. *Socio-Economic Review*, 10: 29–57.

Kirkland, E. C. (1961). *Industry comes of age: Business, labor, and public policy*. New York: Holt, Rinehart, & Winston.

Krehmeyer, D., Orsagh, M., & Schact, K. N. (2006). Breaking the short-term cycle. Business Roundtable Institute for Corporate Ethics: 1–24. Retrieved on June 18, 2014 from http://www.darden.virginia.edu/corporate-ethics/pdf/Short-termism_Report.pdf.

Krugman, P. (2005). Why jobs head north. *The New York Times*, July 25, A19.

Kuehn, M. (2001). *Immanuel Kant: A biography*. New York: Cambridge University Press.

Lawrence, A. T. (2002). Drivers of stakeholder engagement: Reflections on the case of Royal Dutch/Shell. In Sandra Waddock (Ed.), *Unfolding stakeholder thinking*: 185–200. Sheffield, UK: Greenleaf Publishing

Leiserson, W. M. (1929). Contributions of personnel management to improved labor relations. In *Wertheim lectures on industrial relations: 1928*. Cambridge, MA: Harvard University Press.

Lippmann, W. (1914). *Drift and mastery: An attempt to diagnose the current unrest*. New York: M. Kennerly.

Locke, J. (1697) Proposed Poor Law reform. Reprinted in H.R.F. Bourne (Ed.) (1969). *Life of John Locke*: 379–390. London: Scientia Verlag Aalen.

Logan, J. (2002). Consultants, lawyers, and the 'union free' movement in the USA since the 1970s. *Industrial Relations Journal*, 33: 197–214.

Malott, R. H. (1978). Corporate support of education: Some strings attached. *Harvard Business Review*, July–August: 133–138.

Marens, R. (2005). Timing is everything: Historical contingency as a factor in the impact of Catholic social teaching upon managerial practices. *Journal of Business Ethics*, 57: 285–301.

Marens, R. (2006). What is to be done? Theory, research, and reforming American capitalism in the twenty-first century. *Business Ethics Quarterly*, 16: 599–617.

Marens, R. (2010). Destroying the village to save it: Corporate social responsibility, labour relations, and the rise and fall of American hegemony. *Organization*, 17: 743–766.

Marens, R. (2011). Speaking platitudes to power: Observing business ethics in an age of Institutional Turbulence. *Journal of Business Ethics*, 94: 239–253.

Matten, D., & Moon, J. (2008). "Implicit" and "Explicit" CSR: A conceptual framework for a comparative understanding of corporate social responsibility. *Academy of Management Review*, 33: 404–424.

Melman, S. (1987). *Profits without production*. Philadelphia: University of Pennsylvania Press.

Mills, D. Q. (1979). Flawed victory in labor law reform. *Harvard Business Review*, May–June: 92–99.

Mishel, L., Bernstein, J., & Shierholz, H. (2009). *State of working America*. Ithaca, NY: Cornell ILR Press.

Norwood, S. H. (2002). *Strikebreaking and intimidation: Mercenaries and masculinity in twentieth century America*. Chapel Hill: University of North Carolina Press.

Ozanne, R. (1967). *A century of labor-management relations at McCormick and International Harvester*. Madison: University of Wisconsin Press.

Partnoy, F. (2003). *Infectious greed: How deceit and risk corrupted the financial markets*. New York: Holt.

Pollin, R. (2003). *Contours of descent: U.S. economic fractures and the landscape of global austerity*. New York: Verso Press.

Post, J. E., Preston, L. E., & Sachs, S. (2002). *Redefining the corporation: Stakeholder management and organizational wealth*. Stanford, CA: Stanford University Press.

Powell, L. F. (1971). Attack on the American free enterprise system. *Memorandum to the National Chamber of Commerce*. Retrieved on June 21, 2009 from http://www.mediatransparency.org/story.php?storyID=22.

Rawls, J. (1971). *A theory of justice*. Cambridge, MA: Belknap Press.

Rehbein, K., Waddock, S., & Graves, S. B. (2004). Understanding shareholder activism: Which corporations are targeted? *Business & Society*, 43: 239–267.

Rockefeller, J. D. (1916). Labor and capital – partners. *Atlantic Monthly*, January 10, 12–21.

Rosner, D., and Markowitz, G. (1989). Safety and health as a class issue: The Workers' Health Bureau of America during the 1920s. In D. Rosner and G. Markowitz (Eds.), *Dying for work: Workers' safety and health in twentieth-century America*: 53–64. Bloomington: Indiana University Press.

Roy, W. G. (1995). *Socializing capital: The rise of the large industrial corporation in America*. Princeton, NJ: Princeton University Press.

Schattschneider, E. E. (1960). *The semi-sovereign people.* New York: Holt, Reinhart, & Winston.

Schmitz, C. (1995). *Growth of big business in the U.S. and Western Europe.* Oxford: Oxford University Press.

Schultz, E. (2011). *Retirement heist.* New York: Penguin.

Sealander, J. (1988). *Grand plans: Business progressivism and social change in Ohio's Miami Valley, 1890–1920.* Lexington: University Press of Kentucky.

Selekman, B. M. (1959). *A moral philosophy for management.* New York: McGraw-Hill.

Selekman, B. M., & Van Kleeck, M. (1924). *Employees' representation in the coal mines.* New York: Russell Sage Foundation.

Smith, A. (1776/1902). *Wealth of nations.* London: Methuen & Co.

Slichter, S. (1929). Current labor policies of American industry. *Quarterly Journal of Economics, 32*: 393–435.

Sloan, A. P. (1941). *Adventures of a white collar man.* New York: Doubleday, Doran & Company.

Solberg, W. U., & Tomilson, R. W. (1997). Academic McCarthyism and Keynesian economics: The Bowen controversy at University of Illinois. *History of Political Economy, 2*: 55–81.

Solomon, R. C. (1992). Corporate roles, personal virtues: An Aristotelian approach to business ethics. *Business Ethics Quarterly, 2*: 317–340.

Standiford, L. (2005). *Meet you in hell: Carnegie, Frick and the bitter partnership that transformed America.* New York: Crown Publishers.

Taft, P., & Ross, P. (1969). American labor violence. In H. D. Graham & T. R. Gurr (Eds.), *Violence in America: Historical and comparative perspectives*: 221–301. Washington, DC: National Commission on the Causes and Prevention of Violence.

Tarbell, I. M. (1925). *The life of Elbert H. Gary.* New York: D. Appleton & Co.

Thomas, K., & Abelson, R (2012). J & J chief to resign one role, *The New York Times,* February 21, B1.

Toller, E. (1930). Ford through German eyes. *Living Age,* May 1, 299–302.

Tolman, W. H. (1909). *Social engineering.* New York: McGraw Publishing Co.

Tone, A. (1997). *Business of benevolence: Industrial paternalism in progressive America.* Ithaca, NY: Cornell University Press.

Weber, M. (1978). *Economy and society,* Vol. II. Berkeley, CA: University of California Press.

Weinstein, J. (1981). *Corporate ideal in the liberal state.* New York: Greenwood Press.

Wever, K. S. (2008). Learning from works councils: Five unspectacular cases from Germany. *Industrial Relations, 33*: 467–481.

Wilson, W. 1919, *State of the Union Address to Congress.* Retrieved October 12, 2011 from http://www.infoplease.com/t/hist/state-of-the-union/131.html.

Wood, E. M. (2008). *Citizens to lords: A social history of Western political thought from antiquity to the middle ages.* New York: Verso.

Young, O. D. (1927). Dedication address. *Harvard Business Review,* 5 (July): 385–394.

Young, O. D. (1929). Business sermon. *Nation's Business,* April, 161–163.

18

Towards a genealogy of humanitarianism

Revealing (neo-)colonialism in organizational practice

Adam Rostis

Introduction

In this chapter, I take a critical approach to the humanitarian organization as a central but undertheorized element of the organization of work. As a contribution to critical organizational scholarship, I will show how Foucault's genealogy can be used as a method for Critical Management Studies. In brief, genealogy will be used to defamiliarize humanitarianism through an examination of a specific organization and a particular historical intersection that has given rise to humanitarianism in its present form: the Nigerian Civil War of 1967–1972 and the involvement of an instantly recognizable humanitarian organization – the Red Cross. My main interest is to explore the question of how humanitarianism has become a *taken-for-granted* social construction aimed at alleviating suffering. In so doing, I seek to understand the effects on people and organizations when humanitarianism is wielded as a weapon of common sense. These effects are ironic and hidden because war and disaster have a sense of urgency that compels individuals to accept radical change at the same time as they silence resistance to change. However, the result is the opposite of change: it is the preservation and reinforcement of existing power relations under the guise of neutral humanitarianism.

I believe the trajectory taken by humanitarianism is coincident with that of colonialism and decolonization. Using postcolonialism as a theoretical framework, I will argue that resistance to humanitarianism has yet to be realized. The history of the Red Cross intersects with colonial and post-colonial periods in a way that provides a useful analytical framework. This intersection provides an opportunity to understand how historical representations and contemporary experiences of organization have been shaped by colonialism. Through this examination, I will show how humanitarianism is woven into our thinking about organizations and society. I will describe how humanitarianism requires us to believe that a set of extraordinary circumstances exist requiring immediate attention and justifies what Nietzsche has called "an excess of history" (Nietzsche, 1985). This excess hides contingencies, contexts and alternative explanations with the result that they are forgotten as inconvenient extras thus staunching any debate over the validity of a claim or idea; in this case, the claim is the naturalness or taken-for-granted nature of humanitarianism. I will problematize humanitarianism by arguing that the continued existence of humanitarian organizations is dependent upon the historical construction of humanitarianism such that it appears to be a static principle that has always existed and is based upon universally accepted values, principles and beliefs.

Beyond a contribution to Critical Management Studies, my motivation for this work is twofold. First is the need to understand the paradoxical behavior of humanitarian organizations: although humanitarianism appeals to the supposedly universal principle that we are all human and therefore all equally deserving of help, humanitarian aid is very selective of the type of suffering that will receive attention (MacFarlane & Weiss, 2000; Marten, 2004). My second motivation is that the humanitarian organization is an understudied aspect of organizations. This is surprising given the extent to which these organizations are involved in people's lives and the amount of trust and legitimacy they are given and with which they are imbued. Beck (1999: 44) argues that NGOs have a "blank cheque for an almost unlimited store of trust" because of their pure public image. Fiering (1976: 196) notes that "of all the great themes of eighteenth-century social thought, humanitarianism has received the least study in intellectual history." Lambert & Lester (2004: 324) argue that a "critical, postcolonial reappraisal" of those "who constituted the nexus of globalized philanthropy in the early nineteenth century is long overdue." Bankoff (2001: 19) suggests that "[i]nadequate attention . . . has been directed to considering the historical roots of the discursive framework within which hazard is generally presented" and that this framework is told within a story of "them and us, where the 'us' is the West . . . and the 'them' is everywhere else."

I will show that humanitarianism is a historical construction and that it has been and always will be subject to change. This implies there is room for resistance to humanitarianism in its current form. Foucault's genealogy instructs us to look for this change in historical points of intersection that give rise to new historical trajectories. I believe the Biafran War of 1967–1970 is just such an intersection that enables us to see the contingent and constructed nature of humanitarianism. It represents the height of the decolonization period in Africa, and it witnessed a fracture and disruption in the taken-for-granted status of the Red Cross as the *de facto* representative of global humanitarianism. Biafra is particularly important because during the war, a new form of humanitarianism emerged through the acts of individuals resisting the existing humanitarian order in a hybridization process well known to postcolonial scholars. These individuals included both recipients of humanitarian aid and those involved in implementing humanitarian action. The key aspect of postcolonial theory for this chapter is that organizations are blind to existing practices that have their origin in colonialism because of the pervasiveness of the colonial period: it influenced all aspects of the lives of both colonizer and colonized. As a method, genealogy decenters common sense, and so, combined with postcolonial theory, I believe it is well suited to reread the practices of the Red Cross to show the extent to which it is a postcolonial organization.

Theoretical framework: Postcolonialism

By the start of World War I, a few European nations held huge amounts of foreign land as colonies. Global power on a scale never before seen was concentrated in the hands of a few European nations, including Britain, France, Belgium, Portugal, Spain and Germany. European societies were organized, in part, to administer and extract surplus value from vast tracts of foreign geography and their subjugated distant populations. However, there was more to colonialism than the profit and power bestowed on Europe: postcolonial scholars claim that imperialism and colonization have more interesting and analytically useful properties beneath their surface and that these are relevant and applicable even today (Prasad, 2005). When combined with the observation that colonialism left virtually no aspect of social and economic life untouched, it is further claimed that colonialism's retreat in the independence struggles following World War II have left a residue of markers of colonial practices in social and political life (Said, 1994).

I believe there are three justifications for a postcolonial analysis of humanitarianism. The encounter between humanitarians and the populations they intend to serve is one that is between the West and the rest (De Waal, 1997). It largely reflects an established Western epistemology and politico-economic order and the drive to establish this primacy globally in so-called underdeveloped countries of the South through development. Humanitarian practice ranges over populations that were once ruled by distant European powers in a period and process known as modern Western colonialism (Banerjee & Prasad, 2008). Colonialism was extensive and long-lasting: it ranged over most of the planet's geography at its height and has a history of about 500 years (Banerjee & Prasad, 2008). Colonialism "involved the subjugation of one people by another" (Young, 2001: 15), and it was extraordinarily diverse in its approach to subjugation and methods of administration depending upon the colonizing country and the intention of the colonizer (Young, 2001). And so this coincidence of humanitarian practice and colonial practice in targeting the same specific populations and geographies is the first reason that I believe there is justification in somehow linking humanitarianism with colonialism. This should happen within a framework of theory that seeks to describe the ongoing and pervasive effects of colonization. This theoretical framework is known as postcolonial theory.

On the surface, domination appears to be the central practice of colonialism. However, domination is not peculiar to the colonial period, so what is it about this particular form of domination that made it so successful? Furthermore, how was consent gained among both colonizer and colonized to maintain distant rule? Perhaps part of the answer to these questions lies in colonialism being sold to both colonizer and colonized as being done "for a good reason," that is, to improve the lives of the colonized. In this sense, colonialism affected not only the colonized but the colonizers: a sense of duty was evident in European society that this domination was in fact a civilizing mission enabled by viewing the colonized as inferior or subordinate (Said, 1994) but redeemable through a process of civilizing or development.

The key phrase in my description of colonialism relevant to the study of humanitarianism is that colonialism is ongoing and pervasive. Colonialism was not just another form of domination: it was so extensive and has such a long history that Young (2001) and Banerjee & Prasad (2008: 91) argue that it "is an episode of particular significance in human history." Postcolonial theory reflects upon this significant phenomenon and is a framework for interpreting and analyzing the condition of former colonies and colonizers. While there is no longer an overt process of holding land and directly ruling populations, there remain "elements of political, economic and cultural control" (Banerjee & Prasad, 2008: 91). This ongoing form of colonialism is referred to as neocolonialism. However, one practice that extended from the colonial to the neocolonial is the concept of "duty to care": this is the belief that the colonizing power has an obligation to civilize and improve the colonized. In the post-colonial, these become neocolonial practices under one or the other banners of development, democratizing or rescuing (from war or disaster).

This conception of the colonized as being at the receiving end of the West's duty to improve may also have allowed the West the space to imagine itself. In other words, colonialism enabled the West to understand itself in relation to what it was not, to judge itself in relation to what it does not do, and to see possibilities in relation to what others do not have (Said, 1994). However, resistance to colonial rule, authority and the conceptualization of the colonized as being inert and objectified was also a defining feature of colonialism (Said, 1994). What is apparent from all of these practices is that the border between colonizer and colonized, between domination and resistance is an artificial one. Colonialism was not something that was done to the Other without effect on the colonizing society, and resistance did not suddenly appear at an appointed time in history. It is also suggested by postcolonial scholars (Prasad, 2005; Said, 1994) that the border between the colonial era and today is also artificial: if sought after, the residual markers of colonialism can be found today in the routines of organizations. I contend that they are notably present in the practices of humanitarian organizations engaged in contact with crisis.

I must acknowledge that there is considerable room for confusion here due to terminology: is there really such a difference between postcolonial, post-colonial, and neocolonial, together with their various 'isms'? I follow the convention adopted by Prasad (2003) and use the term "post-colonial" to refer to the period following the end of colonization, although it is problematic in itself to suggest that colonialism has in fact ended. Therefore, I understand the "post-" period to refer to the end of major European colonization in Africa and Asia at the end of World War II and later up to the present. I will use "postcolonialism" to describe the study of the effects of colonialism on countries, individuals, and organizations in the post-colonial period.

Decentering common sense: Genealogy as method

Central to this chapter is the development of a genealogy of humanitarianism. Through archival research of primary and secondary source documents, this genealogy will reveal the effects of constructing humanitarianism as a unique, extraordinary, and urgent event. Two major features of genealogy make it a unique method and distinguish it from traditional histories. First, genealogy is concerned with a history of the present (Castel, 1994; Meadmore, Hatcher & McWilliam, 2000). In other words, a genealogy does not portray the present manifestation of something as the inevitable outcome of a series of past events. It relies on a second feature, problematization, to understand how present problems have become defined and understood in their current form. It does not view the present as solidified. The result of a genealogy is that the present loses its inevitable and natural feeling, and in its place is a sense of the many trajectories from which the present has been derived (Meadmore, Hatcher & McWilliam, 2000). The accomplishment of these two features is achieved through an examination of the descent and emergence of various historical trajectories, a trajectory here being a path, albeit an unintended or undirected one, taken through the historical record.

Genealogy as method

One has to rely on secondary interpretations of Foucault's genealogical work (Castel, 1994; Kendall & Wickham, 1999; May, 1993), as well as examples of it in practice (Jacques, 1992; Jacques, 1995), to understand the method of genealogy. His method, it has often been said, is to write a history of the present (Foucault, 2002; Gutting, 2005; May, 1993). The reason for beginning with the present is that many things in the present are "intolerable" (Gutting, 2005). The intolerability of things is found in institutions or practices that are lodged in a seemingly permanent fashion in the present as oppressive features of society. A history of the present embarks on a reexamination of these features to demonstrate their contingent and impermanent nature. For example, when looking at Foucault's genealogy of discipline, the intolerability of prisons and the lack of prison reform are given as one motivation for embarking on the work (Gutting, 2006; Mills, 2003). But how do we know that the current state of prisons is in fact intolerable beyond the knowledge given by his opinion? It is certainly common sense to me, given my experience as a member of my culture at this point in human history, that capital punishment as a sentence for prisoners is intolerable. The answer might be to consider as intolerable any practice, institution or concept that presents itself as being as natural, taken-for-granted or permanent.

For example, Gutting (2006: 10) shows the outline of developing such questions in areas such as madness. How could we do anything except set up asylums to treat the mentally ill? How to deal humanely with criminals except by imprisoning them? In the case of my present work on humanitarianism, one could conceive as intolerable the various humanitarian impera-tives. How could we not consider the survivors of a disaster as vulnerable? How could we not but help the starving except by feeding them? This seems to be a much better and productive guide to identifying questions that are amenable to genealogy. But how is genealogy actually done in practice?

A considerable amount of historical work is required in conducting a genealogy, and this work provides the justification for any claims made in a genealogy (Gutting, 2006). This includes detecting the uninevitability of current institutional forms or concepts through iden-tifying accidents, contingencies and random occurrences and in examining the broader scale of historical development that can be found in existing histories (Gutting, 2006). Genealogies are not intended to be a complete history but are selective in mining the archive with the goal of uncovering artifacts that help us understand the present (Flynn, 2006). Foucault uses the term "archive" to refer to the way in which statements are formed within a society at a point in time (Prasad, 2005). It works with the details of history to discover how a discourse emerges and persists (May, 1993). However, genealogy is also archival in its method in the more com-mon sense of the word: it is "gray, meticulous, and patiently documentary" (Foucault, 1984: 76), and it involves working within physical archives and with primary and secondary source texts (Mills & Helms Mills, 2011).

The archival nature of genealogy implies that existing methods for accessing archival research can be used (see, for example, Hill, 1993). Materials are collected, kept and then depos-ited into archives in an unsystematic manner and create multiple layers of documentation with various incomplete sections (Hill, 1993). Thus, while the use of archives by genealogy brings with it the strength of existing archival methodology, it also presents a weakness: the limited completeness of the archival record. Genealogy confronts this with another strength: it uses existing histories both as a supplement to missing primary sources and as a counterpoint to its own genealogical project (Prado, 2000). It does not dismiss existing histories; on the contrary, these can provide bridges between long periods where there are no primary sources. The reuse of history helps point to a continuous and unfolding historical picture that is useful for geneal-ogy in that they serve to contrast the accidents and contingencies displayed in a genealogical approach. These written histories are themselves useful guides to dominant accounts of reality at different points in time.

If the question posed by history is "What is our past?" then genealogy asks "What is our present?" The response to this question involves a departure from traditional histories in two sig-nificant ways. First, genealogy does not portray the present as the inevitable outcome of a select series of past events. Second, it relies on establishing a relevant problematization to understand how the present has come to be defined and understood in its current form. For the genealogist, the present emerged and descended from a series of discontinuities that could have, under differ-ent circumstances and in a different context, produced something quite different. The result of a genealogy is that the present loses its inevitable and natural feeling, and in its place is a sense of the many trajectories from which the present has been derived (Meadmore, Hatcher & McWil-liam, 2000). The accomplishment of these two features is achieved through an examination of the descent and emergence of various historical trajectories.

Descent, emergence and problematization

Descent deconstructs the taken-for-granted nature of the present, enabling the genealogist to identify the precontexts of the taken-for-granted. It involves investigating and understanding the various pieces of an event or concept to demonstrate that contingencies, accidents and mistakes were encountered along the road to its emergence as a given or inevitable fragment of knowledge (Hook, 2005; Meadmore, Hatcher & McWilliam, 2000). The appearance of unity is seen instead as a myriad of singular events spread across multiple domains (May, 1993). While descent disturbs the given, emergence points out the interaction of the details of descent that have resulted in their appearance as a given (Hook, 2005; Meadmore, Hatcher & McWilliam, 2000). Put another way, emergence views history as a struggle of multiple forces, with no clear goal or evidence of progress, struggling for dominance (May, 1993).

The problematization of the present is at the core of genealogy. Castel (1994) explains that institutions, propositions of a philosophical, scientific, or moral nature, regulations on behavior or conduct or indeed anything that is produced by discourse are key to understanding what Foucault meant by problematization. Problematization does not create an object or explain something that already exists. Rather, it enables institutions, propositions or regulations to be seen for what they are: the sites of claims to truth and the ways of governing the behavior of others. Problematization thus reframes the conduct of historical analysis to understand how it has transpired that the present has come to be accepted as inevitable or natural. Therefore, one can look at the conditions by which a concept has come into being or rather the history surrounding a concept in order to understand it (Patton, 1978). As well, a concept exists because of the rules or grammar that must be followed or used in order for it to be understood (Patton, 1978). One should examine the text to determine what is not said – in other words, to identify the absences (Assiter, 1984).

However, while there are other interpretations of events, problematization is not a license to rewrite history (Castel, 1994). It must make a contribution beyond that made by other disciplines to the same topic (Castel, 1994). Furthermore, recasting a problem in terms of the history of how it has become seen at the present time has its own issues, as discussed by Castel (1994). First, one should be wary of projecting today's concerns onto the past as today's problems and concerns will be different in the future. Second, using a genealogy as a justification for searching back to the beginning of recorded history is fruitless: problematizations emerge at a specific point in time. A feature of the genealogical approach is that the researcher cannot claim to have examined the entire archive (Poster, 1987). Third, problematizations do not repeat themselves but occur as background noise in a continuity of other events and emergences. Fourth, in a particular span of history, a problematization may appear to be insignificant against the backdrop of other events or emergences that carry greater weight at the time. Fifth, as a problematization spans large historical periods, the method of studying a problematization must rely on primary and secondary sources by rereading historical documents as well as secondary sources from historians.

In sum, Foucault's genealogy rejects a linearity of explanation and uncovers the silences, accidents and intersections that have resulted in a taken-for-granted approach to knowledge; it acts as a counterweight to a process of forgetting created by an excess of history. These other ways of knowing are part of the silenced voices of the victims of crises; seeking out these silences should be part of the empirical work of a genealogy. The method of genealogy relies heavily on archival research, and, for practical reasons, this chapter will situate the exploration of humanitarianism within the archives of a specific organization: the Red Cross. It is important to note that "the archive" for Foucault is a decentralized construct. It is not only a physical container embodied in libraries and national "archives," but it is the belief that discourse is scattered everywhere and traces of its development can be found in multiple locations. This would include existing literature, histories, documents and practices of organizations.

Foucault's archive and the physical archive

My research strategy for choosing archival material was to look at material from the Red Cross archives in Geneva from the Biafran Civil War, as I believed that it indicated a point of rupture in humanitarianism. Both the IFRC and the ICRC are headquartered in Geneva, and both have physical archives with policies related to public access. The IFRC has a 30-year moratorium on accessing material, while the ICRC's is 40 years. Since my research was conducted in 2009, this meant that I could have access to certain material dealing with events occurring before 1979 for the IFRC and before 1969 for the ICRC. In practical terms, this meant that although I could access material on Biafra within the IFRC archive, I was not permitted access to Biafra-era materials from the ICRC. There was, however, a considerable amount of material from the ICRC contained within the IFRC archive. Therefore, despite not having direct access to the Biafra material in the ICRC archives, I was able to fill in the gaps through the archival material in the IFRC, together with third-party reports. In total, I examined 2670 pages of documentation from these two archive sites.

Results of the study: The Red Cross in Biafra

The Red Cross is an organization that is instantly recognizable for its humanitarian pedigree. In 1864, it was agreed to establish national societies dedicated to caring for battlefield casualties and to enshrine the principles and conventions of these societies in international law (Moorehead, 1999). The emblem used to identify the neutral volunteers on the battlefield was a red cross on a white background, the reverse colors of the Swiss flag; eventually the organization came to be uniquely known by this symbol, and the committee eventually became today's International Committee of the Red Cross (ICRC) (Moorehead, 1999). The power of the agreement among states gave the Red Cross leave to intervene in conflict, obliged armed forces to respect the neutrality of Red Cross volunteers and compelled nations to accept the establishment of Red Cross national societies (Forsythe, 2005). Since its creation in 1864, the Red Cross has diversified outside of armed conflict, and this causes some degree of confusion for outsiders to the organization as the Red Cross is actually three different organizational forms: the International Committee of the Red Cross (ICRC) and the International Federation of Red Cross and Red Crescent Societies (IFRC) are both based in Geneva, and the National Societies are based in each of the 186 member countries (ICRC, 2005). The two "international" organizations are often referred to as the International Red Cross, and the other organizations as the National Societies. By agreement among the International Red Cross, the IFRC focuses its attention on natural disasters and recovery from conflict, while the ICRC has the guardianship of international humanitarian law and concerns itself almost exclusively with conflict and issues surrounding conflict (Forsythe, 2005). The International Red Cross refers often to its network of national societies and a legion of volunteers in disaster relief and recovery.

The Red Cross was created with the consent of, and existed alongside, colonial states using state power and sanction to achieve humanitarian goals (Moorehead, 1999). Indeed, the International Committee of the Red Cross (ICRC) today holds pseudo–state power through its guardianship of international humanitarian law (Forsythe, 2005). Its organizational development was shaped through decades of European conflict, most notably World Wars I and II. But what is conspicuously absent from the Red Cross formation stories is that it was formed by colonial European powers in a Europe that was actively colonizing. The Nigerian Civil War (also known as the Biafran War) of 1968–1971 was a post-colonial war in that it followed after the decolonization of most African states and was at the end of most African independence struggles. The expectation by the Red Cross was that the parties in that conflict would behave rationally according to principles tested in over 100 years of European wars. However, the Biafran War was fought in the media as well as on the battlefield, and in effect both sides utilized civilians to convince the world of the rightness of their cause. In Biafra, the template for provision of assistance did not fit with contemporary reality.

Nigeria: Independence and conflict

Nigerian independence from Britain in 1960 resulted in a nominally democratic, civilian government ruled in this post-colonial period (Meredith, 2005). Existing histories of Nigeria seem to agree that the country, like others in colonial Africa, had pre-independence borders that served colonial interests, did not reflect the cultural divisions that existed within countries and in fact set the stage for future conflict (Meredith, 2005; Post, 1968). One of these conflicts was a coup in 1966 that put in place a military government (Diamond, 2007) that was at odds with an oil-rich region of Nigeria known as Biafra. Biafra possessed oil resources and was peopled by the Igbo, a minority ethnic group (Post, 1968). The specific events of the beginning of the Biafran War have been detailed numerous times (see, for example, Kirk-Greene & Wrigley,1970; Meredith, 2005; Gribbin, 1973). In summary, though, a declaration of independence in 1967 by Biafra was opposed by the federal government of Nigeria. The overwhelming military power of federal Nigeria meant that the Biafrans were effectively surrounded. However, the conflict persisted because of a proxy Cold War that was fought throughout Africa (de Montclos, 2009). Additional matériel and resources supplied to the Biafrans enabled them to extend their resistance. The eventual military success of Nigeria was through attrition: after 30 months of blockade, the population within Biafra was faced with shortages of food, currency and commodities (Falola, 2008). Before the Biafran rebellion collapsed, humanitarian organizations and humanitarian individuals maintained a sustained effort to prevent starvation and render aid to soldiers and the civilian population.

Biafra and humanitarianism

De Waal (1997: 73) contends that "an entire generation of NGO relief workers was molded by Biafra." Biafra was "the first humanitarian effort dominated by NGOs" (De Waal, 1997: 73) and while the ICRC receives the credit for the organization of the relief effort, the combined efforts of church groups in providing aid must not be forgotten. In fact, the Joint Church Aid (JCA) delivered an amount of aid that was "surpassed only by the Berlin airlift" (De Waal, 1997: 73). The war itself was of no great interest initially to the press or to people outside of Nigeria (De Waal, 1997). However, the key to its eventual impact on the world was the simplification of the complexity of the conflict through images of starving children that were reminiscent of Nazi concentration camps (De Waal, 1997). Not only did this provide the motivation for people to do something for the distant, suffering stranger, but it enabled the Biafran rebel combatants to seize upon something with which they could promote their cause (De Waal, 1997).

At one extreme, the humanitarian intervention influenced the conflict by prolonging it through the provision of food, medicine and foreign currency to the Biafrans who were, by all accounts, surrounded by the military forces of federal Nigeria and effectively blockaded. The success of the humanitarian response, as evidenced through the volume of financial resources contributed, can be attributed to the claim that the Biafran War was a personal war: people witnessed images and appeals through direct media such as television and advertisements in newspapers that utilized the image of starving children to motivate action on the part of those outside the war (Perham, 1970). The largest and most scrutinized of these organizations was the ICRC.

In Biafra, the archives of the Red Cross revealed several themes. First, there was a struggle for control between the ICRC and the Nigerian government and also with other parts of the Red Cross organization. This struggle was for control of the meaning of the war, as well as for the control of the humanitarian operation. Second, the war in Biafra was an exceptional event that justified the lack of success that the Red Cross had in convincing the Nigerian government and the Biafran rebels to respect the Geneva Conventions, and the Red Cross authority. Third, colonial attitudes regarding Africa surfaced in the organizational practices of the Red Cross.

A struggle for control

Biafra was a war fought not only between soldiers "on the ground" but also between competing interests of the ICRC, the Nigerian Red Cross, the Nigerian and the Biafran governments. The struggle was not just over land, but it also included a struggle over the meaning of the war and over control of the massive relief operation. As the literature continually emphasizes (Forsythe, 2005, 2007; de Montclos, 2009; Moorehead, 1999), this was a highly televised and public conflict, with highly emotive imagery influencing public perceptions of the war. As a result. there were huge opportunities for the Biafran and Nigerian governments, as well as for the Red Cross, to control the public's perception of the war. Biafra, through its use of a public relations firm, took out advertisements in major newspapers and on television to convince people that genocide was taking place and to argue for the correctness of their independence cause (Forsythe, 2005; Gribbin, 1973; Moorehead, 1999; Perham, 1970). Archival material from the Red Cross also reveals a struggle between the Nigerian Red Cross and the ICRC for control of the meaning of the relief operation as well as the physical operation.

The Nigerian Red Cross

In its final review of the relief operation, the Nigerian Red Cross (NRC) stated that the "relief operation did not start with the declaration of war, it started as far back as 1963 during the flood disaster at Abeokuta" (RCRCC, 1968: 2) and that it was the NRC that made the request for "experts to come and ascertain the type of assistance needed" (RCRCC, 1968: 2). This seems to be an effort at renarrating the story from one where outside experts make decisions to one where the NRC called for outside expertise and where the war and relief operation existed under circumstances different from what those outside Nigeria might think. In effect, the Nigerian Red Cross tried to influence the narrative such that it becomes viewed as a stable organization in the midst of crisis.

The ICRC

For its part, the ICRC attempted to exert control through its access to donors, resources and responsibility under International Humanitarian Law (the Geneva Conventions). It was "thanks to large scale technical assistance which had been provided for several years by Scandinavian Red Cross Societies [that] the Nigerian Red Cross was able to work throughout the whole territory" (ICRC, 1970: 2). The ICRC "sent in delegations . . . to ensure that supplies and financial assistance, as are provided are put to the best use possible, and in accordance with the wishes of donor Societies" (RCRCC, 1968:6). The International Red Cross also exerted its financial control and authority through visits of the LRCS's financial controller, who "paid a visit to Nigeria during which he had the opportunity to have a look into the financial situation and also to advise the [NRC] in the procedure of financial control" (LRCS, 1970: 4). Therefore, the International Red Cross acted as a gatekeeper of resources: "the ultimate authority for planning, finance and administration . . . was exercised by the ICRC Headquarters in Geneva" (NRC, n.d.: 5). It was also up to the International Red Cross to decide who gets aid as "the Red Cross must see that only the needy receive relief in proportion to their degree of need based on medical intervention" (LRCS, 1970: 1). Agreements in place at the international level prevented the NRC from directly appealing to donor societies. In response to a letter sent by the NRC to all Red Cross national societies, the secretary-general of the LRCS responded regretfully that "[y]ou know our sympathy for the cause of Nigeria and how much we want to be helpful" but "[t]here is . . . an agreement in force between the ICRC and the League, and you know that the ICRC have insisted that owing to the specific circumstances in Nigeria . . . the matter of relief to victims . . . should be handled by the International Committee" (Beer, 1968). It was also the ICRC that influenced the human resources used in the operation as "the rule followed in the ICRC's close cooperation with the Nigerian Red Cross was not to place a non-African in a post until after it had been ascertained that it could not be filled by an African" (ICRC, 1969a: 5). Many archival documents show the ICRC's attempt to exert control through the Geneva Conventions. For example, the ICRC "draws attention to the principles . . . embodied in the 1949 Geneva Conventions which today are universal . . . the ICRC expects instructions to be given . . . that these rules shall be strictly applied in all circumstances" (ICRC, 1969b). In the "relief operation which the ICRC is conducting," it "expects governments and responsible authorities to enable it to continue" the operation (ICRC, 1969b). There was also an expectation that victims should behave in a certain fashion, and the struggle for control extended to placing them at fault for not behaving correctly. For example, August Lindt, the ICRC's chief delegate for the operation, noted that "[it] must be avoided . . . creating a refugee mentality among the beneficiaries of relief, i.e. that they become accustomed to receiving supplies without working for their subsistence. Otherwise they would end up by enjoying this situation" (ICRC, 1969a: 2). Finally, the International Red Cross and the non-Nigerian donors decided when the emergency was over: "Mr. Sverre Kilde of the Norwegian Red Cross . . . maintained that as the emergency phase was over Red Cross action should be considered as concluded" (NRC, n.d.: 5).

For the ICRC, the exceptional nature of the conflict was used to explain why the Geneva Conventions were not followed and why there was so much suffering despite the intervention of the organization. The relief coordinator for the ICRC argued that "resettlement and rehabilitation is [sic] not normally considered one of the Red Cross activities. However, it has been done in some countries where all normal administration and authorities have broken down, and no other agencies were able to carry out plans for resettlement" (Kilde, 1966: 1). To be clear, the war was exceptional for the ICRC because the organization was involved in rehabilitation work that it normally did not undertake; this included mass feeding of civilians. It was also exceptional in that a party to the conflict was not a recognized state and that neither the recognized Nigerian government nor the unrecognized Biafran government consistently extended protections to citizens affected by the conflict; in other words, civilians were neglected deliberately. It seems that the conditions of the war caused humanitarianism to break down, not that humanitarianism (through the Geneva Conventions) didn't work for a particular set of circumstances. This is more clearly stated by the LRCS when it observed that "[t]he structure of the 'Biafran' forces, with their military, para-military militia and civil defence units . . . made a 'regular warfare', abiding to the Geneva Conventions, nearly impossible" (LRCS, 1968: 17).

Essentialization

The archival material does show an essentialization of Africa. This included broad generalizations about the nature of Nigeria and Nigerians. For example, the ICRC believed that in Africa "it was easier than in Europe for displaced persons to resettle and speedily become self-supporting, owing to the free land available and the quick harvests" (ICRC, 1969a: 2). This reflected the *terra nullius* (Fitzmaurice, 2007; Marten, 2004) conceptualization of Africa that, because the land on the continent was not under anyone's direct control or ownership (according to European notions of ownership), the land was therefore free from political or social claims and available to be settled. The Red Cross observed that the "scope for health services is unlimited in a developing country" (LRCS, 1968: 12), but "tribal antagonism made Red Cross work impossible in some places" (LRCS, 1968: 8). That the ICRC believed it had a duty to care is evident in the archival material. First, the organization had taken on the burden of costs that was "particularly difficult and heavy owing to [the ICRC's] character" (ICRC, 1969a: 6). It had "a responsibility to so many governments" and "appealed to the parties involved in the conflict to see to it that its impartial work of charity meets no further hindrance" (ICRC, 1969c).

Government of Nigeria and the victims of the conflict

The archival material reveals resistance on the part of the government and citizens of Nigeria. The resistance is found in the whole operation to remove the ICRC from controlling the relief operation, but it can also be found in the general population. Sverre Kilde, an LRCS delegate, noted that displaced persons had "formed their own association with a committee in each of the Provinces and they are working in close connection with the provincial officials. This association may turn out to be an advantage in the way it may be easier to collaborate. But on the other hand this association can be a heavy pressure group" (Kilde, 1966: 2). Even the Geneva Conventions were resisted and adapted to the Nigerian context. The Nigerian Armed Forces adopted a Code of Conduct for the Armed Forces that was based on the Geneva Conventions but held out certain specific exceptions such as mercenaries who "will not be spared: they are the worst of enemies" or youths and school children who "must not be attacked unless they are engaged in open hostility" (Federal Republic of Nigeria, n.d.).

(Neo-)Colonialism in humanitarian organizations

The post-colonial world has witnessed a weakening of the ability of the state to look after citizens (Agamben, 2005; Ophir, 2003; Redfield, 2005). Examples of this can be found in sub-Saharan Africa where nations have widely varying abilities to provide services to citizens. This weakening is broadly referred to as the failure of states (Hendrie, 1991; Ophir, 2003) but may more properly be attributed to the precarious ability of many nations to manage the multiple pressures of economic decline, conflict and disasters under conditions of a limited economic base. This state of permanent emergency has challenged the established disaster discourse and makes space for novel approaches to humanitarianism (Alexander, 2006; Bello, 2006). These approaches often include the privatization of aid and relief, and, despite appearances, they are not inherently beneficial to the population affected and may serve corporate or other interests (Banerjee, 2008). Underlying all these approaches is a discourse that depicts disasters as sudden shocks that temporarily divert a society from a deterministic movement forward (Alexander, 2006; Stefanovic, 2003). Evidence for this view can be found in the flourishing business in *sans-frontières* organizations ranging from Reporters- to Veterinarians- to Engineers-*sans-Frontières*.

Meinecke (1970) and MacIntyre (2007) develop arguments that there is now a borderless imperialism because local practices and knowledge have been replaced with those of the stranger. This does not result in greater inclusion of the local but rather conquest of the local by strangers. Laws that are valid for all of humanity (such as International Humanitarian Law and the Geneva Conventions) mean that there can be no laws peculiar to the local situation, and so there is no check against outside ambition. This creates "an imperial administration of the stranger" (Ossewaarde, 2007), resulting in the inability of the locals to set their own goals. Even though humanity is globalized, the individual human must live somewhere local. Hanging on to this locality through resistance to strangers and becoming strange is seen in forms such as "nostalgia, protest, terror and hope" (Ossewaarde, 2007). What do borders mean in a borderless world? What role is there for resistance to humanitarianism that relies on this borderless movement?

Resistance, stakeholders and borders

A specific contribution of postcolonial theory to Critical Management Studies is to reveal the historical context of management practices that have their genesis in colonialism (Özkazanç-Pan, 2008; Prasad, 2003). The genealogy of humanitarianism that I have outlined has revealed the extent to which these organizations perpetuate colonialism by hanging on to colonial practices unawares (Kwek, 2003; Prasad, 2003). The perceived colonial duty to look after the less advanced (Said, 1994) is evident from the texts studied as they reveal that the Red Cross views disaster-affected individuals as vulnerable people, forming vulnerable populations not capable of protecting themselves or even of having the ability to decide whether to accept the care being offered.

By extension, the state is also judged on its vulnerability and capacity to administer to its population, as evidenced from the Red Cross duty to intervene in conflict as afforded to it by international law. This behavior is consistent with Narayan's (1995: 136) argument that the relative capacity or vulnerability of individuals is "contested terrain" and is liable to variation depending upon who defines these terms. In this case, the definitions are made within the organizations that are in turn products of former colonizing nations. This echoes the observation of Lambert and Lester (2004) that colonial philanthropists did not argue against imperialism and an empire; rather, they sought to curb the excesses of imperialism.

This sentiment and approach still exist in the practices of the Red Cross as far as conflict and disaster are concerned. They take conflict and disaster as givens and seek to curb the excesses of violence and risk, respectively. Following on from this perspective, the clients of humanitarian organizations are viewed as vulnerable, and these same organizations are granted authority to intervene through international law. It is therefore argued that the current practices of the Red Cross are an extension of a colonial past.

Postcolonial theory argues that colonialism and resistance were dependent upon each other for their very existence as meaningful constructs. It also implies that colonization contained within it the seeds of change and eventual replacement with another set of power relations through a process of resistance. Given the argument that humanitarian organizations are part of a discourse that has a common colonial past, one would expect to see some accounting of resistance within these organizations. However, there is no place in the policies of the Red Cross for states or individuals to resist humanitarianism. This is in contrast to empirical evidence presented in documented cases of resistance to aid; these can be found, for example, in Ethiopia during the famines of the 1980s as explained by Hendrie (1991). In this case, resistance by the vulnerable was met with shocked incredulity by the humanitarian organization, together with claims of malfeasance lodged against the resisters. The obvious reason for this position of the humanitarian organization and for omission of resistance in the humanitarian discourse is that resistance seems illogical and counter to the goal established by the organizations to help those populations considered vulnerable. Just as the colonized subject was the receiver of a duty to care or to civilize, so the construction of the idea of vulnerability and vulnerable persons has no room for the subjects to participate in the definition or their inclusion in these categories (see, for example, Furedi 2007a, 2007b).

Since humanitarianism, vulnerability and aid are now "common sense," how can an individual or state choose to refuse aid or define the terms with which aid is accepted? Unmasking common sense can be achieved by noticing what is not said and by observing that the silences within discourse contain the possibility for change (Foucault, 2002; Marcuse, 2002; May, 1993). These silences do exist around resistance and the refusal of humanitarianism in, for example, the Biafran War. Thus, a space can be opened in the humanitarian discourse to include resistance. This space can be used to reimagine the individual recipient of humanitarianism from that of a passive subject of a distant duty to care into an active participant in the discourse.

Perhaps a first insight into this problem can be obtained by recalling that management theory compartmentalizes its ontology by drawing a boundary line at the organization (Burrell & Morgan, 1985; Johnson & Duberley, 2000; Weatherbee, Dye & Mills, 2008). Just as it is often necessary to hold some variable constant to solve an equation, the constant of the organizational equation is the individual external to the organization. This ontology has excluded relevant social actors, in particular those without voice yet still negatively affected by organizations. As an example, individuals living in communities impacted by the social and environmental decisions of industry have sought to influence decision making so that profit yields to local interests and conditions. Thus, exclusion from decision making results in resistance by external groups that seek to have a legitimate voice in internal decision making that affects the world outside of the firm.

In response, organizations engage in legitimizing processes that reduce resistance by including these external groups as partners or stakeholders. But clearly organizations do not admit all to the decision making process. In the case of disaster survivors and humanitarian organizations, aid recipients have enormous legitimacy as they provide to the vulnerable population so central to the existence of the humanitarian organization. Therefore, it becomes possible to admit the recipients of aid to the humanitarian discourse. I am suggesting that resistance to the humanitarian organization is an act of decolonization in a post-decolonization period. The task now becomes one of suggesting how this resistance might emerge within the humanitarian discourse. What can be learned from resistance and decolonization to guide this process?

Learning from decolonization

Resistance as a political movement resulted in decolonization through independence from the colonizing power (Fanon, 2004; Said, 1994). However, the state that replaced the colonizer often reproduced the colonial structures of power, albeit under the guise of trying to change existing conditions, liberating the population or seeking economic freedom. Pointing to examples from Chile and Cuba, Mignolo (1991) argues that decolonization projects were set to fail from the outset because the initial conditions were the same; that is, they used a logic that came from within modernity – socialism, in the cases of the two preceding examples. Therefore, resistance was futile because it is governed by the same epistemology and ontology that resulted in oppression. In the case of resistance to humanitarianism, the parallel would be the establishment of local humanitarian organizations. Interestingly, the Red Cross has already taken this approach through its global network of national societies. How, then, can resistance be conceptualized so that it avoids reproducing the existing discourse, albeit in a local disguise?

Mignolo (1991) argues for a solution that originates outside of modernity, and in the case of this chapter, the solution would be separate from the logic that created and perpetuates humanitarianism. However, according to Mignolo (1991), caution should be exercised so that the result of such a delinking does not result in furthering the essentialism overseen by the colonial project. In decolonizing from humanitarianism, one may attempt to attribute different ways of knowing about helping to the group that is delinking. This can result in an epistemology that is appropriate only to the decolonized and that stands in contrast to Western knowledge of humanitarianism, which views the survivors of conflict or disaster as receivers of a duty to care and improve as part of a continuing colonial discourse. In other words, a new essentialism regarding humanitarianism may emerge. Mignolo rejects the development of an equal but opposite essentialism in favor of the acceptance of more than one approach to knowledge: a hybridity of knowledge. Hybridity is part of the postcolonial perspective that sees the interaction of the colonizer and colonized as being implicitly interdependent (Bhabha, 1994; Prasad, 2005). The role of essentialism is challenged by hybridity: one cannot speak of the fundamental characteristics of the Other when these are increasingly shared with the colonizer. Mignolo (2007) uses the argument of delinking and shared cultural space to introduce the concept of border thinking or border epistemology. This notion contrasts quite sharply with the colonial ideal of the frontier.

Borders identify a geographical space and divide it into countries, defined by politics and often ordered as a result of colonial power sharing rather than respect for the cultural or linguistic heritage of those on either side. But a border implies the existence of people on either side and the possibility of exchange and movement between the sides. This is in contrast to the concept of the frontier, which conjures images of pushing into the unknown and the new (Mignolo & Tlostanova, 2006). Border thinking is achieved by accepting the idea of multiple perspectives. In terms of epistemologies, the frontier is characteristic of the modernist view, while the border adopts the view that multiple ways of knowing are possible. The frontier represents "the hubris of the zero point" (Mignolo & Tlostanova, 2006: 214). In other words, through colonialism, modernity's legacy has been the belief that it occupied new spaces and thus was able to gain an understanding of itself through a comparison to what it is not; the zero point or point of comparison is this "empty" colonized space. I suggest that disasters are a new uncharted territory seized upon by the West to rule ideologically over former colonial states: disasters most often play out on the same physical territory that was once colonized by Europe. Disasters present humanitarian organizations with a ready stock of souls to be discovered and rescued, be they tsunami survivors or the victims of financial disaster. I have shown how postcolonial theory can interrogate and expand Critical Management Studies through the defamiliarization of the humanitarian organization.

References

Agamben, G. (2005). *State of exception*. Chicago: University of Chicago Press.

Alexander, D. (2006). Globalization of disaster: Trends, problems, and dilemmas. *Journal of International Affairs*, 59(2): 1–22.

Assiter, A. (1984). Althusser and structuralism. *British Journal of Sociology*, 35(2): 272–296

Banerjee, B. (2008). Necrocapitalism. *Organization Studies*, 29(12): 1541–1563.

Bello, W. (2006). The globalization of disaster: The rise of the relief-and-reconstruction complex. *Journal of International Affairs*, 59(2): 281–296.

Bhabha, H. (1994). *The location of culture*. London & New York: Routledge.

Burrell, G., & Morgan, G. (1985). *Sociological paradigms and organisational analysis: Elements of the sociology of corporate life*. Farnham, UK: Ashgate.

Castel, R. (1994). "Problematization" as a mode of reading history. In J. Goldstein (Ed.), *Foucault and the writing of history*: 237–252. Oxford, UK: Blackwell.

Fanon, F. (2004). *The wretched of the earth.* New York: Grove Press.

Flynn, T. (2006). Foucault's mapping of history. In G. Gutting (Ed.), *The Cambridge companion to Foucault* (2nd Ed.). New York: Cambridge University Press.

Forsythe, D. (2005). *The humanitarians: The International Committee of the Red Cross.* New York: Cambridge University Press.

Foucault, M. (1984). Nietzsche, genealogy, history. In P. Rabinow (Ed.), *The Foucault reader:* 76–100. New York: Pantheon.

Foucault, M. (2002). *Archaeology of knowledge.* New York: Routledge.

Furedi, F. (2007a). Coping with adversity: The turn to the rhetoric of vulnerability. *Security Journal, 20*(3): 171–184.

Furedi, F. (2007b). From the narrative of the blitz to the rhetoric of vulnerability. *Cultural Sociology, 1*(2): 235.

Gutting, G. (2005). *Foucault: A very short introduction.* Oxford University Press.

Gutting, G. (2006). Introduction – Michel Foucault: A user's manual. In G. Gutting (Ed.), *The Cambridge companion to Foucault.* New York: Cambridge University Press.

Hendrie, B. (1991). The politics of repatriation: The Tigrayan refugee repatriation 1985–1987. *Journal of Refugee Studies, 4*(2): 200–218. Retrieved from http://jrs.oxfordjournals.org/cgi/content/abstract/4/2/200.

Hill, M. (1993). *Archival strategies and techniques.* Thousand Oaks, CA: Sage.

Hook, D. (2005). Genealogy, discourse, "effective history": Foucault and the work of critique. *Qualitative Research in Psychology, 2*(1): 3–31.

ICRC. (2005). Discover the ICRC. Retrieved from https://www.icrc.org/eng/resources/documents/publication/p0790.htm.

Jacques, R. (1992). Re-presenting the knowledge worker: A poststructuralist analysis of the new employed professional. Amherst, MA, University of Massachusetts.

Jacques, R. (1995). *Manufacturing the employee: Management knowledge in a postmodern world.* Newbury Park, CA: Sage.

Johnson, P., & Duberley, J. (2000). *Understanding management research: An introduction to epistemology.* Newbury Park, CA: Sage.

Kendall, G., & Wickham, G. (1999). *Using Foucault's methods.* Thousand Oaks, CA: Sage.

Kwek, D. (2003). Decolonizing and re-presenting culture's consequences: A postcolonial critique of cross-cultural studies in management. In A. Prasad (Ed.), *Postcolonial theory and organizational analysis: A critical engagement*: 121–148. New York: Palgrave Macmillan.

Lambert, D., & Lester, A. (2004). Geographies of colonial philanthropy. *Progress in Human Geography, 28*(3): 320–341.

MacIntyre, A. (2007). *After virtue: A study in moral theory* (3rd Ed.). Notre Dame, IN: University of Notre Dame Press.

Marcuse, H. (2002). *One-dimensional man: Studies in the ideology of advanced industrial society.* London: Routledge.

May, T. (1993). *Between genealogy and epistemology: Psychology, politics, and knowledge in the thought of Michel Foucault.* University Park: Pennsylvania State University Press.

Meadmore, D., Hatcher, C., & McWilliam, E. (2000). Getting tense about genealogy. *International Journal of Qualitative Studies in Education, 13*(5): 463–476.

Meinecke, F. (1970). *Cosmopolitanism and the national state.* Princeton, NJ: Princeton University Press.

Mignolo, W. D. (2007). *The idea of Latin America.* London: Blackwell.

Mignolo, W. D., & Tlostanova, M. V. (2006). Theorizing from the borders: Shifting to geo- and body-politics of knowledge. *European Journal of Social Theory, 9*(2): 205.

Mills, A., & Helms Mills, J. (2011). Digging archeology: Postpositivist theory and archival research in case study development. In R. Piekkari & C. Welch (Eds.), *Rethinking the case study in international business research.* Northampton, MA: Edward Elgar.

Mills, S. (2003). *Michel Foucault.* New York: Routledge.

Moorehead, C. (1999). *Dunant's dream: War, Switzerland, and the history of the Red Cross.* New York: Carroll & Graf.

Narayan, U. (1995). Colonialism and its others: Considerations on rights and care discourses. *Hypatia, 10*(2): 133–140.

Ophir, A. (2003). The contribution of global humanitarianism to the transformation of sovereignty. Paper presented at the International Workshop on Catastrophes in the Age of Globalization, Neve Ilan, Israel.

Ossewaarde, M. (2007). Cosmopolitanism and the society of strangers. *Current Sociology, 55*(3): 367.

Özkazanç-Pan, B. (2008). International management research meets "The rest of the world." *The Academy of Management Review, 33*(4): 964–974.

Patton, P. (1978). Althusser's epistemology: The limits of the theory of theoretical practice. *Radical Philosophy*: 8–18.

Prado, C. (2000). *Starting with Foucault: An introduction to genealogy* (2nd Ed.). Boulder, CO: Westview Press.

Prasad, A. (2003). The gaze of the other: Postcolonial theory and organizational analysis. In A. Prasad (Ed.), *Postcolonial theory and organizational analysis: A critical engagement* (1st Ed.): 4–43. New York: Palgrave Macmillan.

Prasad, P. (2005). *Crafting qualitative research: Working in the postpositivist traditions.* Armonk, NY: M. E. Sharpe.

Redfield, P. (2005). Doctors, borders, and life in crisis. *Cultural Anthropology, 20*(3): 328–361.

Said, E. W. (1994). *Culture and imperialism.* New York: Vintage.

Stefanovic, I. L. (2003). The contribution of philosophy to hazards assessment and decision making. *Natural Hazards, 28*(2): 229–247.

Weatherbee, T., Dye, K., & Mills, A. J. (2008). There's nothing as good as a practical theory: The paradox of management education. *Management & Organizational History, 3*(2): 147–160.

19

Deconstructive criticism and Critical Management Studies

Steve McKenna and Amanda Peticca-Harris

The Anglo-American poet W. H. Auden wrote that poetry makes nothing happen. In some sense, substituting Critical Management Studies (CMS) for poetry, this statement might be relevant to the work of critical scholars or at least be posed as a question – does CMS make anything happen? This, of course, is a difficult if not impossible question to answer. Perhaps all we can do as critical scholars is challenge and deconstruct the world as it is, not always with an alternative in mind but guided by the possibility that there are alternatives: alternative societies, alternative ways of organizing, alternative ways of managing, alternative ways of working. Perhaps critical research, working at many levels in many areas, with the lived experiences of people (and in other ways), might at least find some way of influencing the structures, ideas and thoughts of society, organizations and people in ways where alternatives might be considered and where a difference can be made. This is the hope of this chapter: that deconstructive criticism might enable an appreciation of what is excluded from consideration in the world(s) and begin to identify other possibilities and forms of resistance to the 'normal' that enable alternative conversations with those engaged in those world(s).

Any attempt to discuss 'deconstruction' is instantly implicated in a conversation with Jacques Derrida (1976, 1978). While acknowledging a debt to Derrida, this chapter does not attempt another discussion of 'who' or 'what' is Derrida, or indeed, 'what' is 'deconstruction'. However, what is important for our way of thinking about *deconstructive criticism* (Culler, 1982) is Derrida's thought that deconstruction "is not a discursive or theoretical matter, but rather a practico-political one, and one that always occurs in what are called in rather hasty and summary fashion, institutional structures" (Derrida, quoted in Hill: 26). Within the space of Critical Management Studies, this particular idea of deconstruction seems to us to be important. How can deconstructive criticism have a practical and political agenda? What can it say about the heterogeneity of the social and organizational world? What can it say about marginalized voices, not only of the oppressed, but hidden voices as they appear in many places and particularly in the organizational world? How can we use an understanding of these voices within the broader project that seeks alternatives to conventional managerialism? In the following, we hope to answer some of these questions, but first, how do we intend to use deconstructive criticism?

Deconstructive criticism, as we intend to use it, is informed by the ideas of Derrida (1976, 1978), particularly logocentrism, problematization, the idea of the Other and close reading, as far as we understand them and can experiment with them. Primarily in this chapter, however, we consider and apply the ideas of the Russian philosopher and literary theorist Mikhail Bakhtin (1981, 1984a, 1984b, 1986, 1995) in order to illuminate how deconstructive criticism can contribute to a practico-political agenda by investigating the voices of managers and managerialism in the 21st century. We illustrate this through a deconstruction and interrogation of aspects of three narratives written by managers. Aspects of these narratives have previously been analyzed (McKenna, 2010), but we use them again here to highlight how hidden voices in managerial narratives represent alternatives to the dominant discourse of contemporary management and also, perhaps, to the actual practice of management.

Bakhtin's dialogical approach

We assume a dialogical approach to be a form of deconstruction. While there has been some work in management and organizational studies which has engaged Bakhtin, the more radical aspect of his ideas have largely been ignored and marginalized in favor of his ideas relating to polyphony or multi-voicedness per se (Belova, King & Sliwa, 2008; Sullivan & McCarthy, 2008). In applying Bakhtin, we focus particularly on the differentiation between two functions of a narrative: the *representational function*, the simple story an author is telling, and the *interactional functioning*, how the narrative is positioned in the wider material world and the other voices in that world. So, when writing a narrative, not only does a manager describe and represent the world, but the words position the author, position others in the narrative and position the events reported in a wider material and discursive context. A text therefore does not exist as a stand-alone but fits inside of, reacts to and potentially disrupts a larger discursive context of which it is a part. Equally important, however, is that it says something about material reality, about life and lived experience and action.

The way a manager positions him-/herself interactionally in a narrative is related to what is available to the manager to describe and represent his/her experiences. In other words, how does a manager think about the experiences in the context in which he/she has to think and which largely shapes how he/she can think? Bakhtin (1981, 1984a, 1984b, 1986, 1995) explains this by noting that to understand an 'utterance' it "is necessary to understand the meaning of the utterance, the content of the act, and its historical reality" (Bakhtin & Medvedev, 1995: 149). In our examples, a manager is connecting diverse experiences together through a dialogue within the narrative. In analyzing such texts, we can investigate and deconstruct how managers position themselves in specific ways relative to others, society and history (Wortham, 2001).

In order to investigate the interactional positioning and identification a manager might take in a narrative, it is necessary to know something of the time and place within which the text was constructed (Holquist, 2004). A narrative is written within a specific location at a particular time within a prevailing regime of truth (Foucault, 1995). This regime of truth, perhaps also an ideology, shapes how a manager should 'think' and 'be' at that time in that place (Sarup, 1996). Deconstructing a written narrative dialogically requires some assessment of the relationship between text and context. For a critical scholar, this means infusing the interpretation of a managerial narrative with an explicitly political agenda. At the most simplistic level, it means asking, as we read managerial narratives, what else is going on in this narrative besides what might appear obvious? For example, a manager might write or say, "During the change, it was necessary to downsize the business by 300 staff". A monologic interpretation (Holquist, 2004) of this statement would accept the content as is, assuming that it was 'necessary' to fire 300 staff without any consideration of the implications of such an act or whether there was an alternative. Such an interpretation simply *represents* the narrator's position without relation to the broader context or about the broader context. The statement – "During the change, it was necessary to downsize the business by 300 staff" – is treated as if it is separate from the world beyond the narrative/text itself. A dialogical approach would deconstruct and disrupt this statement in various ways by posing questions that position the author of the text in a broader context in order to open up space for alternative voices to be heard. For example, how is the text written? Does the author imply that 'downsizing' is natural, normal, acceptable? Does the author position him-/herself against others who oppose downsizing, such as trade unions, communities?

When writing or speaking about events in his/her life, a manager immediately opens a space or a dialogue within which the manager is an active participant. In this sense, "nothing is ever one, it is always at least two" (Hill, 2007: 25). In writing or speaking about events, managers shape and position themselves practically. They portray their identities, the identities of others and a view of the social, economic and organizational world. They engage with wider discourses and place themselves within these discourses and the material world beyond. This is all specific to a particular time and place. When a manager says or writes something, there is always a trace and a glimpse of something else, the 'other', within the narrative constructed by the narrator and outside it. A narrator is always constructing something with a sideward glance at the world outside the words/text. This world and the manager's view of it are the basis for a manager's action within it.

Managers write or talk about events in their organizational and professional lives within an existing grand discourse and social, political and economic context (Alvesson & Kärreman, 2000). These contexts and discourses shape the way managers (re)present their organizational and professional world and where and how they position themselves within it. In a very practical sense, their stories contribute to, perpetuate, perhaps sometimes challenge the dominant discourse and material reality of the world in which they exist. A challenge for deconstructive criticism is to work out how we might unpick the way managers' position themselves in the world, how they position others and how they ignore or reject the possibility of alternatives to a particular dominant way of thinking. Furthermore, how can we, as critical scholars, influence the way managers think about managing in a way that raises the possibility of alternatives?

Bakhtinian tools for analysis

To "make linkages between history, structures, and individual lives in the service of an intellectual and political purpose" as a researcher (Mir & Mir, 2002: 121), it is important to enter the lived world and experiences of managers. Critical unpicking of the language and lives of managers requires appropriate politically informed tools of interpretation. Wortham (2001) developed such tools and concepts from his use of Bakhtin's ideas: *mediation, voicing* and *ventriloquation*. These concepts/tools lend themselves to application from a critical perspective.

The concept of *mediation* indicates how a text and its context should be construed. This construal is related to how we as researcher/readers and the narrator are addressed by the world itself. Critically motivated researchers would see the world in a political and ideological way and look to construe a narrative in a particular way and to search for alternatives within the lives of managers themselves as they represent them. Initially, however, we are looking for the elements of a narrative that indicate how managers see the organizational and managerial world in which they operate.

Bakhtin (1995), in his consideration of the novel, argued that novels contain a multiplicity of *voices* and socio-ideological belief systems that are voiced by the narrator. A manager will embody, in their narrative, points of view about themselves and the world, but these points of view are shaped within the ways managers are 'supposed' to think in the socio-ideological belief systems which prevail. They inhabit what they speak and write about, and it will have practical outcomes in their thoughts and actions (Daskalaki, 2012). For Althusser (2001: 115), "*all ideology hails or interpellates concrete individuals as concrete subjects* by the functioning of the category of the subject" (original italics). The manager is called, or hailed, to be a particular kind of subject, to be a particular kind of managerial person who is relevant to the needs of capitalism in a specific time and place. The managerial 'being' is subjectively fixed and normalized (Clegg, 1998; Foucault, 1995). Managerial narratives represent how managers are 'hailed', but they also contain the threat or the promise of something else (Derrida, 1982): other voices that they marginalize and peripheralize. The manager is in a dialogue with the other voices reflected in other characters, institutions and interests which are recognizable in the narrative. They often reflect what is different, what is an alternative, but which is ignored. For example, managers might privilege the idea and the identity of managers as being 'for change', being 'flexible', 'enterprising', 'taking responsibility' and might marginalize the idea that management is about building loyalty, community and a respect for the past.

A concept related to voicing is *ventriloquation*. Managers not only articulate their own voice(s) in their narratives, they also articulate alternative voices for themselves, give voices to other characters and to organizations and society. In this sense, managers may articulate many identities or 'ways of being' for themselves, for example as a moral self, conforming self or rebellious self (Collinson, 2003; Tappan, 1999). However, they will also organize and ventriloquate the voice(s) of other characters, and by characters we mean more than simply an individual character in the narrative. Characters can be, for example, society, an organization, a political and/or ideological position.

Bakhtin's (1981, 1984a, 1984b, 1986, 1995) ideas and concepts offer one way for the critical deconstruction of narratives. In the following sections, we apply these ideas and concepts to written managerial narratives. We suggest that using these ideas we can deconstruct narratives to show central features of ideological, societal, organizational and managerial discourses that dominate the way managers think and act. If managers are hailed in a particular way, they will practice management in that way. This practice, as identifiable in their stories, reflects a political and ideological position that hides and also reveals alternatives within the narratives themselves. In a small way, the content of the alternatives might act as a way of engaging managers with the many voices of organizational life and indeed enable them to reflect on their own voice.

Managerial text 1: Maureen

Maureen's narrative is set in a small health care clinic in New Zealand, in which she is the clinic manager, in a broad context of changing management in the public sector related to the idea of new public management (NPM) (i.e., the infiltration of corporate style management into the public sector). The clinic was established by a group of women doctors who were frustrated by having to work in male-dominated organizations. In particular, they were frustrated by the lack of power to change the dominant culture and structures of these organizations. They were motivated to create an alternative organization based on a greater balance among work, family and other activities and commitments in their lives in order to lead a more fulfilling life. In describing the establishment of the clinic, Maureen gives voice to the doctors and the wider context in which their initiative takes place. She has not yet entered the narrative with her own voice. She describes a group of 'feminist' doctors who are of the view that health care is male dominated with a certain culture and structures. This male-dominated world excludes women from power and involvement and the opportunity to change the way this world operates. Maureen does not indicate that she accepts this view of the world in health care; she is simply ventriloquating/ speaking for the doctors.

Maureen writes herself into her narrative when she becomes practice manager at the clinic. She notes how the clinic "changed the order of things" in the medical community in Smalltown.[1] It was a feminist organization seeking to establish an alternative idea of a clinic. The vision of the clinic was reflected in its *Ground Rules,* a set of guidelines specifying how conflict would be resolved, decisions would be made and how the organization would be managed. Its overall emphasis was on collective decision-making. The *Ground Rules* represented a statement of principles. As the practice manager, Maureen positions herself relative to the *Ground Rules.*

> The *Ground Rules* still exist in their original format six years after the opening of the business, and have not yet been revisited. Nor has the Mission Statement. No change has been made to the original business plan which was put together to apply for funding. All of these were put together to guide a young business still coming to terms with its environment. Now that they are established, they need to look at these things and assess whether they are still relevant.

What is of interest here is how Maureen accepts and perpetuates a discourse of change. The *Ground Rules,* a statement of the clinic's fundamental purpose, is negotiable for Maureen. It cannot be a constant organizing principle in a changing environment. Principles should be disposable if circumstances change. A commitment to operating a business as a collectivity should be jettisoned if the business environment requires something different of a business.

Maureen's self and interactional position in the narrative

As Maureen's narrative progresses, her own voice becomes increasingly prominent and also juxtaposed with other voices in the narrative. This is a development of her earlier voicing of the organization as 'feminist' and being outmoded. She begins to associate the feminist aspect of the organization to ineffectiveness and positions her 'self' in this setting.

> The practice needed to recruit an accountant. . . . [I]t was a long drawn out affair in which the better qualified male was overlooked in favor of a less able female because of the strong promotion by the lesbian partner. I believe that at this point we must stop using the term 'team' in conjunction with the organization. From my perception of what happened, a division occurred because those who had not been able to promote their chosen candidate felt manipulated, and power politics began to take over as the dominant frame of the organization. However, the perpetuation of the myth of the 'feminist' organization was tacitly acknowledged as more important. Because the feminist culture implied that 'women working together should be able to resolve these differences', the issue became a taboo subject and the feminist culture started to become a prison.

At a monological level, this is simply a story of a manager seeking to implement organizational change. However, when read dialogically, Maureen is positioning herself against alternative forms of organizing. For example, the 'feminist culture' became a 'prison'; it was becoming a site of manipulation, power and politics; it was unable to make effective change. In all of these ways, Maureen promotes what she feels is a rational, meritocratic approach to organizational management and rejects the possibility of alternatives. Her self and interactional positioning is further emphasized in the following passage describing the effects of change initiatives taken by Maureen.

> I was not deliberately initiating change to change the balance of power, I felt genuinely unable to operate in such an unstructured way, when the processes required were very structured. . . . I think I was imposing a mechanistic order on a politicized situation. . . . The order and structure was needed because the dominant culture had changed from being one of synergy, excitement and teamwork, to being one of power and domination within the organization. Their desire to see themselves as a feminist organization had become more important than the need to recognize that they were no longer working as a team. They were trapped in a prison perpetuating the myth of a feminist organization. They and the organization had become rigid and inflexible.

We are not here concerned with the veracity of Maureen's monological account but with her dialogical positioning of voices. Maureen's voice is that of the professional manager, adopting one particular view of the organizational world. She believes that structure, order, logic and rationality are necessary in the clinic, thus invoking "positions and ideologies from the larger social world" (Wortham, 2001: 40). This view is juxtaposed with that of the 'feminist' alternative, which is inflexible and rigid and dominated by individuals whose primary concern is power and domination.

The simple 'story' (monology) of Maureen's narrative is of a practice manager in a clinic attempting to effect change. However, when we search for other voices in the narrative through a dialogical approach, we can see the dialogue of voices. Maureen represents one way of managing and organizing, which she pursues in practice against recognizable other ways.

Managerial text 2: Colin

Colin is a manager in a small engineering firm. At the beginning of his narrative, he describes the changing environment within which his company, Engco,[2] operates and which is characterized by increasing global competition in a deregulated market for steel products. The senior management of the company, the level above Colin, had restructured in the face of new competition; however, Colin suggests that this has had no impact. He goes on to voice senior management as ineffective.

> I felt that senior management, many of whom had been at Engco for many years, had little idea as to how to change the business in any real way. They played with structures but were afraid to take any of the hard and necessary decisions that were required. They could not get past the kind of view of the business as a family club. Senior management treated staff as their children, many had worked at Engco for years, but this was not good for performance. Workers were sheltered from the realities of the marketplace by senior management who wanted to play 'happy families'.

Colin voices his view of what is required to change Engco against the current situation, which he voices as paternalistic and family orientated. He implies that such an approach to managing Engco is unlikely to help it succeed in a new competitive environment. It is outdated and shelters workers from 'realities'. Colin is narratively situating his position against that of an alternative mode of organizing, which he rejects.

Like Maureen, as Colin's story progresses, he places himself in it more centrally, and, also like Maureen, he voices himself as something of a savior, full of modern, more relevant ideas about how to manage.

> I was approached by the Managing Director and asked if I would like to take a more active role by becoming production manager. Instead I insisted that I become General Manager of the whole division under the condition that some long serving staff must leave, as they didn't fit into my plans for the new Engco Sheet metal Division.

Colin voices himself as the 'can-do', heroic, enterprising figure. His view of the organizational world has no place for loyalty and paternalism. Some workers who have spent much of their working lives at Engco are disposable and need to leave the business. The business, he argues, needs "rapid transformation"; it "had a problem with too much loyalty and commitment". The business "needed new and flexible ways because the old ways don't work, and they needed new and flexible people". Moreover, rigid "outdated thinking is holding the company back. Senior management had traditional thinking". Colin's narrative clearly voices alternative approaches to organizing and managing: rigidity (in Colin's view) against flexibility; loyalty and commitment against a more transactional, efficiency-oriented approach to relationships; paternalism against individualism. Colin represents two opposing belief systems in his narrative: the new, more enterprising way or the old, more family-oriented way.

Sennett (2007) has identified how there is a social deficit of institutional loyalty in the world today: "loyalty is dead, and each vigorous employee ought to behave like an entrepreneur" (Sennett, 2007: 65). Colin is such an enterprising self (du Gay, 1994, 2004). He articulates this 'type' precisely; he is it, and in being so, the alternative is voiced as archaic. Yet it is dialogically present in Colin's narrative, and as such he gives voice to its existence.

Managerial text 3: Cameron

> City management is under pressure. Fiefdoms prevail, protecting inefficiency and duplication. There is pressure from government to save money and to do more things with less. Change is inevitable and my role was to be a champion of change.

And so starts Cameron's narrative. He already identifies himself as a champion of change against the other voices he introduces – those protecting fiefdoms and therefore inefficiency. Cameron positions himself in his narrative very early and in a more self-interested way. He serves his own interest and in doing so is serving the interests of city management and government. In particular he rails against those who have developed 'cults' within city management and who work only to maintain their power.

> I was at war with losers and clueless technocrats. The battle with these people was to be in the ascendancy in your department and in the organization. I would fight them in a different fashion. The environment would not have seen the battle fought that way before and therefore had no strategy to combat my tactics. Those who would resist would be put to the sword. It was a case of the past or the future.

As with Maureen and Colin, Cameron voices a battle between modern and non-modern ways of organizing. Indeed, even his language of 'cults' and 'fiefdoms' reflects this juxtaposition. In the lengthy passage which follows we get a clear sense of Cameron's interactional positioning in his narrative and how he voices the context within which he is operating.

> My first day my new manager, T, had a uniform ready for me to wear. I politely refused and we reviewed the reasons I was appointed. It was obvious that the decision to establish the role was not one that T wanted. Indeed the role she had in mind was one of operations management. To my horror I found myself thrust into managing parking operations for the city. Psychological contracts my arse! This was a pathological manager ensuring immediate dominance over me and distancing herself from the chaos I was about to find. That chaos had a name. It was parking. This was the leper of the organization. No one likes a parking officer.
>
> But I befriended parking officers. I was one of them, an untouchable to members of the public. With the management team I used facts, refused to listen to emotion, delivered on time and under budget. I actioned the requests of my staff quicker than God.
>
> Six months into my role at parking things changed. I discovered my boss, T, was sleeping with my Head of Department. They were lovers. She was divorced and he married. It was the unspoken scandal. I finally had a way to win. T was promoted into obscurity, but just when I thought I had won I found out I had lost. I became her replacement. Then four months later the organization decided to restructure.

Cameron goes on to narrate the roles he was performing at this point: parking operations manager; acting parking services divisional manager; manager of business development; human resources manager, traffic and parking services; acting group manager, traffic and roading services. He was in so many management meetings across the organization that he was hearing the same message given a completely different spin depending on which management group was meeting: "I was so busy at no stage did it ever occur to me neither to ask for help nor to seek any. None was ever offered. Finally it was Christmas".

In this segment of the narrative, Cameron is indicating the complexity and pressure of his role(s) in a volatile and political context. However, beyond this, he is placing himself interactionally with respect to others. He is also positioning himself in a politically charged context giving a flavor of a different 'reality' of organizational life. Increasingly, Cameron moves from the 'heroic figure' he portrays himself at the beginning of his narrative to a person who is increasingly sucked into a chaotic, irrational and dysfunctional situation. He arranges the voices in different ways such that we see beneath the surface of city government by means of Cameron's interpretation of it. In particular, his own voice changes as the narrative progresses; initially he voiced himself in a hero's narrative, ready to fight whatever battles needed to be fought in order to win. Later he becomes a disillusioned and stressed manager, beaten down by the weight of the organization he sought to confront. Finally, he physically and mentally collapses.

> On December 26 whilst sitting in the sun on our lawn I felt sharp pains from within my gut. Within three days I had been rushed to hospital suffering from severe dehydration and loss of blood. My immune system had stopped functioning and I was seriously ill. Within the week my body weight had dropped from 98 kgs. to 85. The only relief was morphine for the pain. I realized that the nonsense was crazy. I wanted to be the last man standing, but in the end realized that this was a lonely and worthless place to be.

Discussion

In this chapter we have offered one way of undertaking *deconstructive criticism* using ideas from the Russia literary theorist and philosopher Mikhail Bakhtin (1981, 1984a, 1984b, 1986, 1995). In our discussion section, we attempt to connect this approach to some important features of Derridean deconstruction as a way of indicating the 'diversity' of this idea. Hill (2007: 117) has noted that:

> If it (deconstruction) could be characterized or defined at all, it was not as a single, repeatable, applicable method or methodology. Some programmatic strategy dominated by a final goal already visible on the horizon. Deconstruction more closely resembled a style, a way of reading and writing texts, addressing them with finesse, nuance, and all available sophistication, and with a different pen held, so to speak, in either hand.

In addition, we want to say some more about the practico-political aspects of this type of deconstructive criticism – of what use is it in challenging dominant thinking about management?

To deconstruct texts in this way is to recognize the importance of the process of construction as well as the idea that they can be deconstructed. What is in the narratives of Maureen, Colin and Cameron is important because of what is included and how they include it. It is also a reflection of the way perhaps that they are shaped to think about their professional lives and management in particular: what is available to them as a discourse to explain their managerial lives? In deconstruction, however, we are also interested in what might be concealed or excluded, not as the 'real truth' that is discovered underneath the surface, but as a way of opening space for further exploration, to push another agenda, to raise alternatives. It is in this sense that Bakhtin's ideas connect to key Derridean ideas, four of which seem to us of particular importance in appreciating the value of deconstructive criticism in general and in a practico-political sense: logocentrism, problematization, the Other and close reading of the text.

The notion of logocentrism, as we understand it, is to center things as a coherent whole (Derrida, 1976). All concepts in this way of thinking have a kind of self-evident aspect to them – e.g. 'truth', 'value', 'ethics' – as well as to concepts such as 'management' or 'change'. In conventional management and organization studies, many concepts operate logocentrically therefore marginalizing alternatives. In the texts produced in the managerial narratives of Maureen, Colin and Cameron, what it means to be a manager and how the manager should act or not act are part of managerial and organizational logocentrism, as is the perception that managers should be 'enterprising', 'for change', competitive and so on. As a way of thinking, logocentrism offers a sense of stability and order at any given time; the world can be divided between the 'right' and 'wrong', between the 'way' and the 'other way(s)'. In the case of our three narratives, there are signs that they accept a 'way' something is or should be, both as a process and as a 'presence' (Derrida, 1976). In undertaking a *deconstructive criticism* of the texts, the purpose is not to offer another 'center' but to open the space to problematizing the text and its content and also therefore the nature of the managerial world.

In some ways, all texts are 'obvious'. To use Bakhtin's (1995) terms, there is a monologic element to all narratives. However, to deconstruct texts is not to find 'solutions' to the meaning of the text; it is to disrupt its apparent obviousness, and this is done by raising contradictions that may exist within the text, partly through placing it in a 'bigger' context. In this sense, all texts are carnivalesque; they are a pageant of color, activity and playfulness. There are within them complexity, ambiguity and discontinuity that should be surfaced in order that they might be problematized in all sorts of ways, including discursively and ideologically. Our texts have much that is not 'obvious'. A Bakhtinian dialogical approach helps to bring out that which is not obvious for further deconstruction, not closure, as we have attempted to do in this chapter. By deconstructing managerial narratives, we can not only problematize them but highlight their ideological and multi-voiced nature. Managerial narratives contain within them the submerged alternative discourses of the organizational and managerial world. There is in them the possibility of alternatives even though our managerial narrators may reject them: the feminist organization based on principles of a better whole-life balance; the family-oriented organization based on loyalty and commitment to employees; the manager who ultimately dis-identifies with the 'rat race'.

Related to logocentrism and problematization of the text is the Derridean idea of the Other who appears in many voices in texts. Polyphony, the notion of multivoicedness, is a central element of Bakhtinian (Bakhtin, 1995) thought, whereby 'other' voices are marginalized, trivialized or silenced. It seems to us that, for Derrida, silencing 'otherness' is an attempt to prevent opposition or contradiction and alternatives (Derrida, 1976). It is important to be committed to raising all of these contradictions in texts, to find other suppressed voices, alternatives and things silenced. In the written narratives of Maureen, Colin and Cameron, it seems to us that that a dialogical reading can surface other voices and give space to and for them. Part of this deconstructive process is recognizing that any concept contains both itself and its opposite. To recognize the existence of others, it is important to 'look' for what a text excludes as well as includes. The dialogical approach of Bakhtin (Holquist, 2004) facilitates this process of looking. It enables a way of seeing beyond logocentrism and beyond the obvious and the center, which is what a monologic approach implies. To do this disrupts the text and surfaces alternative possibilities about the text in its relationship with context. It also raises the possibility of material and discursive alternatives. For example, in all of the narratives reported in this chapter, there are ideas and notions that present the possibility of other ways of doing things, of managing, of organizing, which might be practically and politically more socially responsible. While narrators themselves may denigrate alternatives, they give presence to their existence.

Close reading involves a very specific and detailed consideration of a text. There is much to be 'found' in very short pieces of text through close reading. Close reading can be undertaken of anything that can be considered a text; for example a sound or an image could be a text that is subject to close reading. In a close reading, a text is dissected thoroughly in terms of its narrative, metaphors, structure, syntax and other critical aspects of literary analysis. For Derrida (1978), to deconstruct is to first show a deep commitment to the original work. The texts constructed by our three managers are powerful because they are *their* stories, *their* recollections. To show respect for the way they describe and interpret aspects of their professional lives is a precursor to draw out complexities, discontinuities and doubts. Identifying the otherness of a text requires a recognition of what is in the original and why it is there. In this chapter, our reading of Maureen, Colin and Cameron has not been 'close enough', but what we have attempted to do in using Bakhtin's (1981, 1984a, 1984b, 1986, 1995) ideas is to show that texts hide themselves within texts and to draw out the dialogical enables us to see that all is not obvious. In a Derridean sense, we have tried to open a text rather than simply interpret it in another way. In practical terms, can we use this *opening* to enhance a critical agenda? Can it, to repeat our opening question, make anything happen?

There is no easy answer to this question, but perhaps an early move might be related to the teaching of management in business schools. Does the teaching of management and managing in business schools currently reflect the many possible ways of managing, or are they themselves the one-dimensional perpetrators of a dominant managerial discourse and 'reality'? And to what extent are we, critical scholars, complicit in this situation? Similarly, with alternative forms of organizing, are these reflected in business school programs? Wouldn't it be helpful to consider what a 'feminist organization' or 'feminist organizing' looks like? How can loyalty and commitment be taught in a socially responsible and politically subversive way rather than as throwaway words used by mealymouthed managers to manipulate the workforce? What if organizations were thought of as communities of people rather than profit-motivated mechanisms, how might this impact modes of management? In the business school context, it is likely that critical scholars can offer only small resistance to the tidal wave of managerialism through their teaching. Whether this can make things happen or not is another matter, but at least we can say we tried – hard.

Notes

1   A pseudonym.
2   A pseudonym.

References

Althusser, L. 2001. *Lenin and philosophy and other essays.* New York: New York University Press.
Alvesson, M., & Karreman, D. (2000). Varieties of discourse: on the study of organizations through discourse analysis. *Human Relations, 53*(9): 1125–1149.
Bakhtin, M. (1981). *The dialogic imagination.* Austin: University of Texas Press.
Bakhtin, M. (1984a). *Problems of Dostoevsky's poetics.* Minneapolis: University of Minnesota Press.
Bakhtin, M. (1984b). *Rabelais and his world.* Bloomington: Indiana University Press.
Bakhtin, M. (1986a). *The problem of speech genres.* Austin: University of Texas Press.
Bakhtin, M. (1995). Heteroglossia in the novel. In S. Dentith (Ed.), *Bakhtinian thought*: 195–224. London: Routledge.
Bakhtin, M., & Medvedev, P. N. (1995). Material and device as components of the poetic construction. In S. Dentith (Ed.), *Bakhtinian thought*: 144–156. London: Routledge.
Belova, O., King, I., & Sliwa, M. (2008). Introduction: Polyphony and organization studies: Mikhail Bakhtin and beyond. *Organization Studies, 29*(4): 493–500.
Clegg, S. (1998). Foucault, power and organizations. In A. McKinlay & K. Starkey (Eds.), *Foucault, management and organization theory*: 29–48. London: Sage.
Collinson, D., L. (2003). Identities and insecurities: Selves at work. *Organization, 10*(3): 527–547.
Culler, J. (1982). *On deconstruction: Theory and criticism after structuralism.* Ithaca, NY: Cornell University Press.
Daskalaki, M. (2012). Personal narratives and cosmopolitan identities: An autobiographical approach. *Journal of Management Inquiry, 22*(4), 394–413.
Derrida, J. (1976). *Of grammatology.* Baltimore, MD: Johns Hopkins University Press.
Derrida, J. (1978). *Writing and difference.* Chicago: University of Chicago Press.
Derrida, J. (1982). *Margins of philosophy.* Chicago: University of Chicago Press.
du Gay, P. (1994). Making up managers: Bureaucracy, enterprise and the liberal art of separation, *British Journal of Sociology, 45*(4): 655–674.
du Gay, P. (2004). Against 'enterprise' (but not against 'enterprise', for that would make no sense). *Organization, 11*(1): 37–57.
Foucault, M. (1995). *Discipline and punish.* New York: Vintage Books.
Hill, L. 2007. *The Cambridge introduction to Jacques Derrida.* Cambridge: Cambridge University Press.
Holquist, M. (2004). *Dialogism.* London: Routledge.
McKenna, S. 2010. Managerial narratives: A critical dialogical approach to managerial identity, *Qualitative Research in Organizations and Management, 5*(1): 5–17.
Mir, R., & Mir, A. (2002). The organizational imagination: From paradigm wars to praxis. *Organizational Research Methods, 5*(1): 105–125.
Sarup, M. (1996). *Identity, culture and the postmodern world.* Athens: University of Georgia Press.
Sennett, R. (2007). *The culture of the new capitalism.* New Haven, CT: Yale University Press.
Sullivan, P., & McCarthy, J. (2008). Managing the polyphonic sounds of organizational truth. *Organization Studies, 29*(4): 525–542.
Tappan, M. A. (1999). Authoring a moral self: A dialogical perspective. *Journal of Constructivist Psychology, 12*: 117–131.
Wortham, S. (2001). *Narratives in action.* New York: Teachers College Press.

Part VI
Global predicaments

20

The 'iron' in the iron cage

Retheorizing the multinational corporation as a colonial space

Raza Mir and Ali Mir

The economic power of multinational corporations (MNCs) has continued to grow over the last few decades. For example, the inflows of foreign direct investment, a key marker of MNC investment, crossed $1.6 trillion in 2012, with over $500 billion reported as mergers and acquisitions (UNCTAD, 2012), leading to a more concentrated global economy. The top 500 MNCs of the world showed revenue growths in excess of 10% and profit growths in excess of 15% in 2012, despite the global economic downturn (*Fortune*, 2013), and their revenues routinely exceeded the GDP of most nations; if firms and nations were listed together (annual revenues alongside national GDP), each of the top five corporations in the world (Royal Dutch Shell, Walmart, Exxon Mobil, Sinopec and China National Petroleum) would be ranked as a top 30 nation.[1] This concentration of economic power within a few private entities has led to a great sense of unease among other economic actors, in light of troubling signs that MNCs have intensified the deployment of their size and scope to operate in zones that exist beyond the reach of institutional governance. For example, corporations have been known to leverage their spatial breadth to avoid paying taxes to nation-states (Schwartz & Duhigg, 2013). They have been accused of large-scale violations of labor laws (Bajaj, 2013), and their activities have led to profound environmental degradation (Krauss, 2013). MNC responses to the problems they create have been characterized by obfuscation and impunity. For example, the global firms indirectly implicated in the April 2013 collapse of the Rana Plaza in Dhaka that led to the death of over 1000 Bangladeshi workers have refused to accept any legal or moral ownership for the labor conditions in Bangladesh. Likewise, BP has been accused of a highly legalistic and evasive approach to its obligations in the aftermath of the 2010 oil spill in the Gulf of Mexico. These actions and several others like them indicate that MNCs increasingly operate in a climate of impunity, with the imprimatur of law and theory. Critical management scholars have a duty to analyze their actions and develop alternative theories that will act as counterweights to the largely acquiescent praise that passes for international business research in mainstream academia. In this chapter, we attempt to address one facet of such an alternative theory, by exploring the theoretical linkages between an organization and a colony.[2] We base our theory on an empirical project, the analysis of capability transfer across national boundaries within an MNC. Many theorists have regarded capability transfer as the single most important source of advantage of an MNC and in fact theorized it as the *raison d'être* of the diversified and spatially distributed firm. For example, Kogut and Zander (1996: 503) suggest that the spatially diversified firm "be understood as a social community specializing in the speed and efficiency in the creation and transfer" of capabilities. In other words, capability transfer is an existentially defining characteristic of the family of firms of which an MNC is part. These theorists use the ideas of the sociologist Emile Durkheim, who had suggested that "since the division of labor becomes the chief source of social solidarity, it becomes, at the same time, the foundation of the moral order" (Durkheim, 1893; quoted in Kogut & Zander, 1996: 505), to theorize that capability transfer legitimizes firms such as MNCs. Given the salience accorded to capability transfer by mainstream theorists of the MNC, we contend that an analysis of capability transfer will lead to generalizable conclusions about the MNC itself.

The rest of this chapter comprises four sections. First, we examine theories of the MNC and subject them to critical reappraisal. We then discuss capability transfer across international boundaries, both at the theoretical level and through empirical findings based on ethnographic research. We then discuss our rationale for viewing MNC capability transfer practices as colonial practices. Finally, we conclude with a discussion that makes a case for a new approach to theorizing the MNC.

Theories of the MNC: A reappraisal

One of the earliest theories of the MNC was the internalization hypothesis (Hymer, 1960). It theorized the MNC through a special case of the transaction cost thesis. The emergence and success of MNCs were linked to their ability to internalize operations across national boundaries, which in turn allowed them to reduce risk, enhance economies of scale and scope, manage externalities and reap the arbitrage advantages of international heterogeneities (Buckley & Casson, 1976; see Collinson & Morgan, 2009, for a succinct review). Several other theories of the MNC have come to the fore, such as the eclectic paradigm (Dunning, 1977), financial theories (Choi & Levich, 1990), knowledge-based approaches (Kogut & Zander, 1993) and institutional examinations of isomorphic and divergent trends within MNCs (Morgan & Kristensen, 2006).

In this chapter, however, we are interested in highlighting the public policy elements that provide the essential conditions of existence of the MNC. The basic argument being made here is that the MNC is not legitimized on the basis of economic logic alone but that a variety of coercive institutional mechanisms support its perpetuation and growth. Our contention here is that, in their current state, MNCs have become agents of *imperialistic exploitation* (Mir & Sharpe, 2009).

Exploitation, as used in the Marxian sense (Bottomore, 1983: 157–158), is defined as the ability of a capitalist institution or apparatus to appropriate the surplus value generated by labor. The power of the capitalist to exploit labor is predicated upon three conditions. First, the ownership of productive assets has to be rendered limited; only a minority of stakeholders in society is granted access to ownership rights. Second, workers are not afforded the option to appropriate their own surplus value; exploitation works when their only possible means of livelihood is to enter the labor force as wage employees. Finally, exploitation is kept in place by a variety of institutions and state apparatuses.

While these three conditions can be found in some measure in all corporate institutions, they are especially visible in the conduct and the governance of MNCs. First, the access to MNC ownership is much more restricted than access to other forms of capital. Koechlin (2006: 378) has argued that, despite the default assumptions of the mobility of global capital, "the process of capital accumulation is much less global than we tend to presume." Differential access to global stock markets, currency convertibility and credit supply arrangements function as effective barriers to ownership of MNC stock by large sections of global society. The role of private equity firms in restricting ownership access to individuals despite capital availability has been well documented (Briody, 2004). While such an assertion runs contrary to the rhetoric of global fund markets and mobile finance capital, empirical studies have shown that a large portion of U.S. MNCs provide their own capital in lucrative investments abroad (UNCTAD, 2012). In effect, MNCs are far more closely held than local firms.

Second, MNCs are increasingly associated with actions that Marx termed "primitive accumulation," the act of dispossessing peasants across the world of their lands, thereby moving them from precapitalist modes of accumulation into a situation where they have little to trade except their labor. In the words of Harvey (2005: 159), "the main substantive achievement of neoliberalization has been . . . the commodification and privatization of land and the forceful expulsion of peasant populations (and) the conversion of various forms of property rights (common, collective, state, etc.) into exclusive private property rights." While the term "primitive" suggests a temporal antecedent to the practice of capitalist accumulation, the process continues even in present times. Sometimes in an exquisite irony, primitive accumulation is often carried out on behalf of the MNC by the state itself. The Chinese government regularly dispossesses peasants of their multicropped lands to enable the setting up of so-called Special Economic Zones for MNCs (Holmstrom & Smith, 2000). Likewise, land has been forcibly acquired from farmers by the state in Liberia (Ibrahim, 2004) and Russia (McCauley, 2001). The government of India's controversial 2006 acquisition of multicropped fields for the South Korean MNC POSCO provides a recent example of this phenomenon. Reports quoted Jeong Tae Hyun, the CEO of the giant steel corporation, stating that "we came to India for the iron ore and will go forward with the plan only if we are given a captive mine."[3]

Of course, the concept of exploitation has undergone a transformation in the past several decades. The spread of governmental technologies ensures that the state plays a role in reversing the more egregious effects of exploitation by capital (Chatterjee, 2007). Likewise, the rapid erosion of regimes of feudalism, the spread of education and political consciousness among the dispossessed and the patterns of urban migration seen in countries like India and China ensure that exploitation becomes a much more nuanced phenomenon than earlier conceptualizations would have described it (Sanyal, 2007). However, we argue that at the heart of this complicated enterprise, the fundamental nature of exploitation remains the same, especially for the poor in the Third World.

As we argue in this chapter, conditions in the past two decades (especially since the emergence of neoliberal regimes in many Third World nations) have led to a resurgence of the older patterns of imperialism (Gatade, 1997). MNCs, through their promise of global investment (and periodic threats to withdraw it), have been able to influence nation-states as well as local capitalists substantially, leading to the reemergence of extractive regimes (the extraction refers here not only to materials such as minerals and crops but also to surplus value through regimes of outsourcing and offshoring). They have been abetted by an entire secondary network of institutions that have aggressively pursued the goal of capital mobility, elimination of sovereign protection for local industries, currency convertibility and immunity for corporations from local laws (Baker, Epstein & Pollin, 1998). Consider, for example, that much of debt provision to the poorer nations by the International Monetary Fund and the World Bank has been linked to tariff reductions, corporate tax reductions, removal of barriers to MNC entry in specific industrial sectors, reduction of barriers to foreign exchange repatriation, currency convertibility, reduction of administrative tasks by foreign investors and, in specific cases, immunity from local laws relating to labor and environmental protection.

While our analysis is located primarily in the present age, we contend that actions by states and political actors on behalf of international capital are not new; in fact, they present a continuum from earlier actions, which we have now come to recognize as being inherently imperialistic in character. For example, in the 18th century, the British Army underwrote the physical and military security of the East India Company. Headrick (1988: 379) points to the fact that "trade did not follow the flag as come wrapped in it." Likewise, the rule of Central American colonies by the Spanish from 1520 to 1820 was administered by private enterprise, and once influence moved to the United States vide the Monroe Doctrine of 1823, U.S. troops were sent 36 times to this region between 1822 and 1964 to support the interests of U.S. corporations (Faber, 1993). Imperialist adventures form the basis of many actions that are now accepted MNC practices. The first joint stock company was formed by Genoese merchants to run plantations (Verlinden, 1970). The first instance of a joint venture between a government and a private entrepreneur was between Queen Elizabeth I and a slave trader (Rodney, 1974: 83). The East India Company, which was active in a number of nations in the 18th century, was organized into national subsidiaries reminiscent of a geographically specialized MNC. Essentially, many organizational forms as we know them were experimented upon in the regimes of colonialism (Mir, Mir & Upadhyay, 2003).

In conclusion, we would like to summarize our theoretical argument thus: the economic logic that supports the existence of MNCs elides the political reality that it was supported by a variety of coercive, exploitative and imperialistic practices. The MNC would hardly be as hegemonic in the world as it currently is without the support of these social and political institutions that allow it to dictate terms to its terrain in the long run. Bringing these factors back into the theories of the MNC will doubtless complicate our theorizing, but we ignore these realities at the peril of being marginalized, or worse, acting as abettors of the exploitative practices that MNCs wage on poorer people all over the world.

Capability transfer across international boundaries

Organizational theorists have dwelt at length about capability flows within corporations (see Argyres, Felin, Foss & Zenger, 2012 for a review). They talk about capability *creation* (Nonaka, 1998), its *codification* (Zander & Kogut, 1995) and its *transfer* (Chen, 2004). However, most researchers of organizational capability do not deal adequately with the historical experiences of power differences and economic imbalances that undergird the international encounter. In this chapter, we use our research in an MNC to uncover the tensions between an organization and other subsidiary organizations it encounters internationally, which are enveloped in relationships that are characterized by a significant power differential. Here, the directionality of capability transfer is opposite to the one mainly theorized in our field. In this case, the source of the capability turns out to be a contractor of the MNC, and the headquarters of the corporation becomes the recipient of the capability.

The construct of organizational capability has been dealt with extensively in the field of organizational theory (Ali, Peters & Lettice, 2012). Most research on organizational capabilities is devoted to the study of three interrelated processes. First, there is the issue of *capability creation* (Nonaka, 1994), primarily through routines of organizational socialization and teamwork. The challenge of the organization is to "create" capability and to facilitate systems whereby individual capability turns into social capability. The discussion of capability creation is often framed in terms of "value," or its ability to deliver rent for the organization (Rodan & Galunic, 2004). Second, capability can provide value only if it is communicable across the organization. Researchers speak of *capability codification* (Kankanhalli, Tanudidjaja, Sutanto & Tan, 2003), or the act of rendering it context independent. The communicability of capability across geographic boundaries is predicated upon its codifiability and its routinization, or at least an understanding of which elements of it can be codified and routinized and which of them cannot (Zander &

Kogut, 1995). Finally, there is the issue of actual *capability transfer* (Bierly & Chakrabarti, 1996), one of the most heavily studied empirical areas in the last decade, which has also been used to reach a number of profound theoretical conclusions. For instance, capability has been depicted as a construct that epitomizes the boundaries of the firm (Conner & Prahalad, 1996). It confers organizational identity upon workers and is the basis for an organizational culture and tradition. It has been argued that firms exist primarily because they are able to transfer capability within their boundaries (Kogut & Zander, 2003). Capability transfer has thus become the basis of a critique of the transaction cost theory (Ghoshal & Moran, 1996), which offers a view of the firm based on relatively negative attributes such as bounded rationality and opportunism.

This deployment of capability in the new theory of the firm is especially important to our formulation, for it uses capability to elevate firms from the ground of efficiency into the moral terrain. Thus, "firms exist because they provide a social community of voluntaristic actions that are structured by organizational principles that are not reducible to individuals" (Kogut & Zander, 1992: 384). These firms derive their superiority over markets consequent to their ability to offer "higher order organizational principles" to their constituents. These higher order principles comprise "shared coding schemes," "values" and a "shared language" (Kogut & Zander, 1992: 389).

Overall, one can observe from an analysis of the literature that capability is now considered the most strategic resource of organizations (Zack, 1999). In other words, its importance is predicated upon its ability to deliver value to an organization. Most theorists agree that while capability resides in various parts of organizations, it originates primarily in the minds of individuals (Davenport & Prusak, 1998). The challenge for organizations is to turn individual capability into social (organizational) capability (Nonaka, 1998). Firms are perceived to be the most efficient entities to coordinate such tasks (Hedlund, 1994). However, the availability of capability stocks within a firm is characterized by a lot of heterogeneity. Capability tends to be "sticky," and therefore best practices do not spread easily within organizations. In order to help this spreading, more attention should be paid to social ties in intraorganizational as well as interorganizational capability transfer (Szulanski, 2003).

Capabilities are usually embodied in organizational routines (Nelson & Winter, 1982). In order to transfer it, firms need to codify capability. However, the challenge here is that the more codifiable the capability, the easier it is to imitate (Zander & Kogut, 1995). The absorptive capacity of the recipient unit in organizations is believed to be a key contingency variable in capability transfer (Cohen, 1998). Motivational and dispositional issues at the level of the source unit can affect capability transfer (Gupta & Govindarajan 2000: Szulanski, 1995). Finally, one needs to better understand the relationship between data, information and capability either as a hierarchical ordering or as mutually constitutive entities in order to better understand the value effects of capability and take advantage of them.

Empirical analysis

To illuminate our theoretical position, we briefly report on an empirical study that emerged out of a comprehensive ethnography of a U.S.-based MNC and its Indian subsidiary (see Mir & Mir, 2009 for an elaboration on the research methodology). The organization being described in this chapter is code-named Reagent and is one of the leading manufacturers of consumer products in the world, with annual revenues in excess of $25 billion. It is based in the U.S. but operates in over 100 countries, and we were granted access to its Indian subsidiary, which has been operational for over 50 years. Reagent had first begun operations in India as an exporting house and had eventually developed its own manufacturing plants around three decades ago. Reagent-India had been incorporated as an Indian corporation, and its shares had initially been quoted on the Indian stock exchange. However, since the mid-1990s, they were no longer traded because Reagent-India was now fully owned by its parent company. Reagent-India was designated a "fully integrated operating subsidiary," which meant that it manufactured most of the products needed for the domestic market in-house. It owned three manufacturing facilities and also used around 20 third-party manufacturing locations in India. Outsourcing was a recent aspect of Reagent-India's business, because it was only since 1992 that MNCs had been allowed under Indian company law to use contract manufacturing facilities.

Capability transfer and the case of Satish Enterprises

When the R&D people of Reagent came up to me and showed me their plans, they acted as if they were dealing with very big secrets. They gave me these big multicolored binders and said, "you should be very careful – this material should not be photocopied. You should just look at it and tell us whether you can do it or not." At first I got a little excited, thinking that I would see some very new information. But after I studied it for 2–3 days, I called them up and asked them to take it back. I told them, "Thank you very much. But really your process is not going to work at all because it is far too expensive. You are asking me to buy completely all new kinds of equipment just to manufacture a simple product, one that I already manufacture far more efficiently. There are many companies with similar products as yours, who give me their manufacturing contracts, and they are all happy with my way. Why do you want your process to be three times as expensive when the product itself is quite the same?

(Sreekanth Reddy, owner of Satish Enterprises, a Reagent contractor)

Located on the outskirts of the southern Indian city of Hyderabad in an industrial complex known for the manufacture of generic pharmaceutical products, Satish Enterprises was a site where we observed and documented a relatively untheorized occurrence, one where a contractor from the Third World became the source in a capability transfer transaction.

As mentioned, outsourcing had been a recent aspect of Reagent-India's business. This explained their apprehension while dealing with a third-party manufacturer. The manufacturing operation being discussed here related to a product named Soledone, a global cash cow for Reagent. While Soledone generated substantial international revenues for Reagent, they had not yet introduced the product into India. Imitations of Soledone had already been introduced into the Indian market by a variety of competitors, and it was evident to Reagent that, were they to succeed in India with the brand, they would have to match the competitors' price. Thus, cost of manufacture was a major priority for them. However, the corporate headquarters continued to be wary of using subcontractors for those of their products that had significant international market share. As Scott Burbank, the vice president of Reagent's International Marketing Division, explained to us, "Contract manufacturers across the world present a tremendous saving in expenditure as well as mindspace. However, we do work with global brands here. And we cannot risk a problem at India jeopardizing the market for our products all over the world."

Reagent had long expressed a preference for importing its new products into India rather than having to produce them in-house. The only reason their in-house manufacturing operations had been hitherto so diversified (and consequently, scale-inefficient) was that the import substitution–oriented macroeconomic policies of the Indian state had forced their hand thus. Of late, following a broader trend of neoliberal economic reform, the import policy of the government had been relaxed to the extent that several small-volume, high-value products were allowed to be imported. However, there was another problem. The weak Indian rupee made it unfeasible to import high-volume products. Also, Reagent-India had made a policy decision to limit in-house manufacture wherever possible, so that it could reap the benefits of cost reduction through downsizing. Thus, when they decided to launch Soledone, they were forced to explore the outsourcing option. Satish Enterprises was one of the plants being considered.

A visit to the Satish plant confirmed that it operated on a philosophy that was radically different from that of the Reagent-India plant. For example, while Reagent-India required all workers in the plant to wear shoes and cover them with disposable plastic outers, the Satish plant required its workers to take off all their footwear before they entered the plant. Barefoot, they then walked into the plant through a 20-feet-long shallow pool of disinfectant. At the other end, they were given rubber *chappals* (Indian slippers). As Mr. Reddy explained, "This policy is ideal for Indian conditions. First of all, the kind of workers we employ are not used to wearing shoes. If they do not wear any shoes outside the factory, we feel that there is no point in asking them to wear shoes at work. Their feet are dirty anyway, and shoes will actually bring in more bacteria than my method." A variety of similar indigenous innovations marked Satish's operations, from recruitment policies that relied on caste affiliations, to the provision for worker substitution for those in the workforce who had agricultural responsibilities (many workers continued to have some agrarian linkages and also tilled their crops during the rainy season; they were allowed to nominate replacements within reasonable limits), down to the spicy lunches that offered an interesting counterpoint to Reagent's bland fare.

However, we do not wish to romanticize the operations of Satish Enterprises. Unlike the unionized workers of Reagent-India, the workers at Satish worked longer hours, they earned lower salaries and had fewer benefits, and their workplace did not have many of the amenities that the Reagent-India workers took for granted, such as air-conditioned cafeterias or rest areas. Their work routines appeared to be more "Taylorized" than in Reagent-India. The hum of activity at Satish was far less inflected with the sounds of conversation than at Reagent-India. Indeed, these were the main reasons why their manufacturing costs were lower than those of Reagent-India. Mr. Reddy was proud of his factory, "I really think that we are as efficient as any factory in Reagent. Also, our cost is lower because we don't waste any money on false prestige."

Reagent had developed five possible manufacturing processes for Soledone. All of them involved the utilization of capital equipment that no pharmaceutical contractor in India possessed. If the equipment dictated by Reagent's production manual were to be purchased, Soledone would have emerged with a substantial cost disadvantage with respect to its local competition. The marketing department had conducted research that suggested that Indian consumers were quite happy with Soledone's competitors and were unlikely to pay a premium price based solely on its status as an international brand.

At the heart of the problem was the procedure by which the final product would be purified against bacterial contamination. All of Reagent's prescribed production techniques used pasteurization, a process by which the product was rapidly heated and cooled for bactericidal effect. However, the temperature control required in this process would have to be very sophisticated, for Soledone was also a flavored oral product, and its flavor could be altered for the worse if the temperature went beyond a narrow range for too long. The computerized heating and cooling apparatus that would be needed by the process was formidable in its cost. The problem kept being debated in the corporation until Mr. Reddy of Satish Enterprises aggressively promoted his indigenous solution to Reagent. His description of the process is worth repeating verbatim, for it also suggests his technological prowess, a competence that had accrued to him through sustained experience of contract manufacture with several organizations, including Reagent-India's direct competitors-to-be:

They (Reagent corporate) said they did not like chlorination because of two things – one is that it is carcinogenic. Any residue of chlorine that was more than 2 ppm. (parts per million) is bad for human beings in the long run. I told them that in my process, the residual chlorine is brought down to 1 ppm. or less without any problem. Nobody believed me when I said that, but I have achieved it batch after batch. The second thing they said was that you have to use ozonization in the process in order to achieve some kind of bactericidal quality. I said there's no need to ozonize, because one can use chloron with hydrogen peroxide and 0.4% chloroform and that will do the exact same job by itself.

They did not believe me at first. So I said that, you know, chlorination will help you also not to use preservatives. And the less preservatives you use, the more your manufacturing efficiency. And they asked, how can that be done? So I said you add bromidium to the process. And that will take care of it. Then they asked how I would get rid of the bromidium catalyst. I said I have a good recovery system and I have been using it for many of the products that I manufacture. When they found I was giving technically feasible answers to all their questions, they had no choice. So they said OK, you can try.

And I used aluminum chloride, which I made by adding some hydrochloric acid to aluminum scrap. And did the reaction with sodium carbonate – actually through the bicarbonate route. And I was able to get about 80% efficiencies. Once I made a full batch, they subjected it to a number of really comprehensive tests for taste, flavor, color, and carcinogenics. And they found that it was as good as any of their other products in other plants.

As the quote shows, the technical mastery of Satish over the manufacture of Soledone was far greater than that of Reagent itself. Much of this mastery, of course, was also achieved through diffusion: Satish had been working as a subcontractor in Soledone's product range for several years. But still it represented a major innovative effort. As Scott Burbank remarked to the lead researcher, "[T]his guy [Reddy] is an amazing engineer. He is like your Indian filmmaker Satyajit Ray, who made all those great movies with primitive equipment and low raw film stock. He is a master at improvising under constraints." Apart from their technological proficiency, it appeared as if organizations like Satish were engaged in an inadvertent act of "cross-pollination" of ideas, where capability about a complicated manufacturing process that had been distilled across experiences with several corporations was being offered to Reagent.

Eventually, after much deliberation, the managers at Reagent were persuaded to take a chance with Satish's process. The finished product of Soledone matched the U.S. product in all lab tests, and after several trial runs, the process was adopted as the official Soledone manufacturing protocol by Reagent India. It cost substantially less than it would have, had the earlier production processes been used. Based on the cost advantages, Reagent-India was eventually able to manufacture Soledone competitively in the Indian market and establish it as a successful product for Reagent-India's product range.

One would have imagined that Satish's process would be valued by Reagent as an example of the good that comes out of a partnership between two professional organizations. However, we found that while the process was indeed valued by the organization, it was done in an unexpected fashion.

While searching for data on the R&D function at Reagent, we came across their annual R&D report, prepared by Sudesh Bhonsle, the VP of Reagent-India's R&D division. Among one of the annual achievements of his department for the year, Mr. Bhonsle mentioned, "[T]his year, we have, under the guidance of corporate, developed a new way of manufacturing Soledone that uses chlorination instead of pasteurization. This process, which uses a chlorination technique, has led to an over-50% reduction in the production cost of Soledone. The process has been thoroughly documented for ISO 9000 certification (annexure enclosed), and is under consideration for manufacture at other Reagent locations." It appeared that not only had Reagent appropriated Satish's systems as proprietary, but also they were being presented as local innovations by Reagent-India! Even the headquarters team was not averse to taking some credit for it! There was no mention of Satish Enterprises in the entire report.

The next time we met Mr. Bhonsle, we asked him about this report. His reaction was defensive. "Of course the process is ours. Satish had some ideas, but most of them came from studying the plans supplied to them by Tarrytown (Reagent's headquarters city). And my team worked constantly with them to fine-tune their process. It is not as if they came up with it on their own. And once we stabilized the process, we documented it as a matter of routine. It is part of our corporate policy. Anyway, before we began manufacture, Reddy had signed an agreement that all patents derived from this process would belong to us."

On our next trip to Satish, we asked Mr. Reddy for an explanation. After all, his account of the hard sell he had needed to get his process approved by the corporate visitors seemed to be at odds with Bhonsle's account, which suggested that the main ideas had come from Tarrytown, New York. He smiled wryly and appeared disinclined to elaborate. All he mentioned initially was that the company had asked him to sign "many papers" before the operation commenced and made it very clear that his "cooperation" on the issue of subsequent patents was an important factor for getting Reagent's business. Upon probing regarding who in his opinion was the actual "owner" of the innovative process of Soledone manufacture, this was the explanation he offered, laced with a number of requests that we do not share this information with Reagent personnel.

> After the first 12 batches had passed QA [quality assurance] inspections, Mr. Bhonsle came to me with Mr. O'Neill of Reagent corporate. He asked me whether I could give them all the minute details of my process. They had a number of forms, which they asked for my assistance in filling out. They collected batch-sheet information, and even observed the manufacture of one entire batch. I knew that this would be part of their local reports. I knew that in a way, they were stealing my information, but that is not a big thing for me. They are not going to manufacture it in India. And if they do it in other places, or if someone gets promoted for this reason, what is my problem? So I allowed them to note it down. They wrote down all the protocols and they have sent it to Tarrytown. My main worry is that they may eventually replace me with another contractor who will use my process, but that is a risk I had to take to get Reagent's business.

As a footnote, it must be mentioned that Reddy was a prominent absentee at a subsequent gala organized by Bhonsle and his team to launch an extension of Soledone in Reddy's hometown. When asked for a reason for his absence, he said, "[T]hey mentioned that this would be a celebration for the entire 'Reagent family.' Why should the family servant be part of the family celebration?"

The presence of the colony

> Global change does not require so much a transfer of capability from one part of the globe to the other as it does the investment in different types of global dialogues that can create new capability contextualized in multiple sites. This requires investments in dialogues that can initiate localized creativity and imagination and foster newer meanings and texts.
>
> *(Bouwen & Steyaert, 1999:304–305)*

Perhaps the ultimate example of the "presence of the colonial" in this case comes from the direction of capability flow, in which the arrow points from the subsidiary to the headquarters, rather than vice versa. If organizational theories are not set up to understand these dynamics, then one must conclude that they exhibit an ideological character. Also, as philosophers like Bakhtin (1981) as well as organizational theorists like Nonaka (1994) have stressed, capability that resides in individuals or isolated bodies can be integrated into a larger framework only through a spirit of social sharing, conversation and dialogue, which remained absent in the preceding vignette. Somewhere in a server housing the electronic archives of Reagent's production processes, there is a stored document about the manufacture of Soledone using the technique of chlorination. A patent may also have been filed about the process. As this incident shows, this document is the ultimate artifact of reverse capability transfer. Not only has capability been transferred across locations and internalized by an organization, it has moved from public to private ownership. In effect, capability has been transformed into property.

It is important to note that we do not believe that Reddy or Satish is the owner of the capability that was transferred. This particular capability emerged through a diffusionary process in which Reagent's competitors, Reddy and Satish, Reagent itself, and a number of other actors beyond the view of our empirical inquiry participated socially and produced a complex set of routines that led to a cheap form of manufacture and value creation. But in the eyes of the law, Reagent emerged as the ultimate owner of the capability. This was not done by methods that would be considered illegal; the paperwork was completed, "permissions" were sought and given and all patent laws were followed, including newer laws that had recently been enacted by the Indian government to ensure that organizations like Reagent were comfortable operating in the country. Interestingly, in response to a World Trade Organization directive, the Indian government enacted a policy effective January 1, 2005 that would protect manufacturing processes (Indian patent law hitherto protected only products).[4] Under this new law, Reagent would be able to charge Satish for the subsequent use of the chlorination process and restrict the firm from using the process as a contractor for other firms. Reddy and Bhonsle, the conduits through which capability "flowed" into Reagent's corporate stock, were appropriately compensated for their actions, Reddy monetarily so and Bhonsle through corporate recognition. But the end result is an act of privatization of capability acquired from a social and public realm, with perpetual property rights accruing to one group. Various work routines (Reagent's documenting system), socialization mechanisms (that attune Bhonsle toward recording and Reddy toward acquiescence) and infrastructures (Reagent's reporting system) are deployed in this process of capability transfer in an unexpected direction.

Perhaps counterintuitively, we contend that it was Reagent rather than Satish that behaved unwisely in this transaction. Satish's ceding of its property rights to Reagent is more an act of compulsion than oversight. Satish Enterprises is a flexible and agile organization, which is quite in touch with India's new status as a cog in the wheel of an emergent corporate globalization. For example, its ability to innovate in the manufacture of Soledone is also reflected in other spheres, such as the indigenous work practices it uses, as well as Reddy's ability to communicate effectively with Reagent's highly qualified technical managers. However, it remains a small-scale operation and will need to operate under the shadow of organizations like Reagent to survive in industrial India. Its very survival depends on its ability to provide capability and other benefits to the likes of Reagent. It thus assumes the role of the "local enabling class," the local elite who choose the passive role of the *accomplice* over the far more fraught one of the *opponent*. Capability transfer of the kind mentioned in this example merely cements that role further.

Reagent, of course, emerges the putative "victor" in this transaction. But moral judgment apart, the capability accrued to it inadvertently sows the seeds of its eventual delegitimization in the international arena, a risk factor that in our opinion outweighs the gains of the appropriation of capability stock. The observation by Scott Burbank comparing Reddy with the Indian filmmaker Satyajit Ray, who produced works of art under considerable constraints, demonstrates clearly how capability is context dependent. Working under severe resource constraints is not Tarrytown's competence, so in that sphere it appears that Satish has a capability advantage. However, rather than develop Satish as a complementary partner to its competencies, Reagent chooses a mercantilist approach to capability, treating the process as a zero-sum game and moving in to amass its capability stock at Satish's expense.

The uncontested appropriation of local capability by Reagent again points toward the absence of the dialogic element in the capability transfer process. Its stock of intellectual property has increased, but such coercive practices present mere short-term fixes. Had Reagent been more sensitive, it might have attempted more dialogic and equitable relations with Satish Enterprises and might have gained much more in a win-win long term.

Discussion

In this chapter, we have used our research on capability transfer to derive some relatively under-theorized conclusions about the MNC. We contend that an MNC that has a more egalitarian (less colonial) approach to capability is more sensitive of dialogic issues despite the existence of power differential favorable to itself. When it achieves its ends through coercive means, it ends up a loser despite potential short-term gains.

This is not to say that such coercion remains unresisted but rather that the modes of resistance are often left untheorized in the mainstream. Satish's responses to Reagent's regimes of expropriation must necessarily take highly subtle forms. In an atmosphere where the political, normative and even the theoretical decks are stacked against it, Satish's resistance to Reagent's domination is not clearly visible, unless one examines its interactions with Reagent closely for actions that take on a more passive, "routine" dimension (Scott, 1985). For instance, instead of more confrontational practices such as lawsuits, there is a subtle disengaging. Reddy refuses to confront the powers of Reagent directly but does refer to their appropriation as "stealing." He mocks their "multicolored binders" and their inability to adapt their operations to Indian conditions. Moreover, his refusal to extend Satish's relationship with Reagent beyond the economic into the normative realm (as evidenced in his refusal to become a part of the Reagent "family") shows us how in the power-inflected interaction, resistance functions by reducing open confrontations, replacing them with "subtle subversions," by acts of "disengagement" and by "ambiguous accommodations" (Prasad & Prasad, 1998).

In his prescient analysis of the emerging phenomenon of the "bureaucracy," Max Weber had worried that citizens who were new to bureaucracy would be subject to an "iron cage" of mystifying rules and control systems that would be opaque but implacable (Ritzer, 2004: 55). In this chapter, we have argued that the continued installation of systems of bureaucratic control in poorer nations by MNCs recalls in many ways the emergence of the Weberian bureaucracy in the West. Our image also focuses on the term "iron," which implies that the subjection of entrepreneurs like Satish Enterprises and other workers from poorer nations to the logic and control of MNCs will be characterized by harsh and coercive mechanisms, and people who resist the rapid ingress of MNCs into their lives on its own terms may not necessarily be equipped with the theoretical wherewithal to oppose on its own terms. Not only is iron a symbol of power, coercion and incarceration, it is also an extractable commodity, which reflects our contention that despite a variety of subtleties that have entered the discourse and practice of MNC presence in poorer nations, their extractive character has continued to be an important aspect of their presence.

At the risk of being repetitive, we would caution against seeing this case merely as an example of malfeasance on the part of Reagent. While that aspect is obvious, an exclusive focus on individual criminality prevents us from seeing this form of appropriation as a part of the discourse of colonialism. Colonial practices have fundamentally involved the appropriation of indigenous knowledge by colonists, often using emerging regimes of intellectual property rights to deprive the natives of this knowledge, many of whom had been conditioned to see such knowledge as public. MNCs have been the primary beneficiaries of many of these property rights and often have attempted to dispossess citizens of the poor nations of the world of the most indigenous of products, as exemplified by the application by WR Grace and Company to patent local medicinal herbs like *neem*[5] or the attempts by RiceTec to patent indigenous strains of rice like *basmati*.[6] MNCs are constantly attempting to deploy intellectual property rights as a means of earning monopoly rents from public goods, and it was perhaps in anticipation of this global era that Karl Marx had remarked that, once the windmill was invented, the emperor, the nobles and the priests began to fight over who owned the wind (Marx, 1866, 1977: 496). Of course, all this occurs under the seemingly benign framework of rules and science; as Sandra Harding has argued, regimes of science and law under capitalist frameworks are fundamentally Eurocentric and serve to provide intellectual legitimacy to imperialist enterprise (Harding, 2008).

In the hierarchized global economy, Reagent had power and legitimacy, backed not only by their economic advantage over Satish and the Indian economy but also by the weight of certain traditions in organizational theory that presented its perspective as appropriate. Eschewing a dialogic relationship, they utilized their power to appropriate local knowledge and legitimized their actions through a legal framework. However, that legitimacy existed only at their end and was predicated upon elaborate definitions of knowledge and property they crafted without any discussion with their subaltern counterparts. To that extent, their actions could be considered colonial. It would be safe to say that had Reagent exhibited a less than colonial approach to capability appropriation, they might have emerged from this transaction much better equipped to negotiate the minefield of intercultural relations in the international arena and not have to resort to various coercions and loss of relatedness in India.

Despite eventually adding to the capability stock of an organization as rich in resources as Reagent, Satish Enterprises remained a site of an authoritarian discourse, where the dialogic mode of communication remained suspended. Our challenge as organizational theorists is to develop an understanding of capability transfer, and, by extension, a theory of the MNC that is more sensitive to these issues, and to develop theories that allow for a more equitable sharing of capability and a more effective design for the accumulation and distribution of social products.

Resistance to this form of MNC control continues to be manifested (Banerjee, 2006; Wu, 2005), but in the terrain characterized by academia and theory, such resistive acts often get represented as irrational responses to inevitable change. Our chapter will hopefully tilt in the other direction and offer an empirical analysis of why we think the MNC is the new avatar of the colonialists of the 19th and early 20th centuries. In effect, our chapter may be viewed as an attempt to theorize the real as well as theoretical "bars" of the exploitative iron cage of MNCs.

Notes

1 Data developed by comparing corporate statistics from http://money.cnn.com/magazines/fortune/global500/2013/full_list/ and national data from http://data.worldbank.org/indicator/NY.GDP.MKTP.CD. (All websites in this chapter were last accessed on October 20, 2013.)

2 Our analysis is based on previous work, including Mir & Mir (2009), Mir, Banerjee & Mir (2008) and Mir & Mir (2011).

3 http://steelmillsoftheworld.com/news/newsdisplay_cntry.asp?slno=5315.

4 http://www.lorandoslaw.com/Publications/Changes-in-Indias-Patent-Law.shtml.

5 http://www.twnside.org.sg/title/pir-ch.htm.

6 http://www.alt.no-patents-on-seeds.org/index.php?option=com_content&task=view&id=74&Itemid=42.

References

Argyres, N., Felin, T., Foss, N., & Zenger, T. (2012). Organizational economics of capability and heterogeneity. *Organization Science*, *23*(5): 1213–1226.

Ali, S., Peters, L., & Lettice, F. (2012). An organisational learning perspective on conceptualising dynamic and substantive capabilities. *Journal of Strategic Marketing*, *20*(7): 589–607.

Bajaj, V (2013). Doing business in Bangladesh. *The New York Times*, September 14. Retrieved from http://www.nytimes.com/2013/09/15/opinion/sunday/doing-business-in-bangladesh.html.

Baker, D., Epstein, G., & Pollin, R. (1998), *Globalization and progressive economic policy*. Cambridge: Cambridge University Press.

Bakhtin, M. (1981). *The dialogic imagination: Four essays by M. M. Bakhtin* (Michael E. Holquist, Ed. Caryl Emerson & Michael Holquist, Trans.). Austin: University of Texas Press.

Banerjee, B. (2006). Land acquisition and peasant resistance at Singur. *Economic and Political Weekly*, *41*: 4718–4720.

Bierly, P., & Chakrabarti, A. (1996). Generic knowledge strategies in the U.S. pharmaceutical industry. *Strategic Management Journal*, Winter Special Issue. *17*: 123–135.

Bottomore, T. (1983). *A Dictionary of Marxist thought*. Cambridge, MA: Harvard University Press.

Bouwen, R., & Steyaert, C. (1999). From dominant voice toward multivoiced cooperation. Mediating metaphors for global change. In D. Cooperrider & J. Dutton (Eds.), *Organizational dimensions of global change. No limits to cooperation*: 291–319. Thousand Oaks, CA: Sage.

Briody, D. (2004). *The iron triangle: Inside the secret world of the Carlyle Group*. New York: Wiley.

Buckley, P., & Casson, M. (1976). *The future of the multinational enterprise*. London: Homes & Meier.

Chatterjee, P. (2007). Democracy and economic transformation in India. Unpublished manuscript, Center for the Advanced Study of India.

Chen, C.-J. (2004). The effect of knowledge attribute, alliance characteristics, and absorptive capacity on knowledge transfer performance. *R & D Management*, *34*(3): 311–321.

Choi, F., & Levich, R. (1990). *The capital market effects of international accounting diversity*. Chicago: Dow-Jones Irwin.

Cohen, D. (1998). Toward a knowledge context: Report on the first annual U.C. Berkeley forum on knowledge and the firm. *California Management Review*, *40*(3): 22–39.

Collinson, S., & Morgan, G. (2009). *Images of the multinational corporation*: 247–266. London: Blackwell.

Conner, K., & Prahalad, C. K. (1996). A resource-based theory of the firm: Knowledge versus opportunism. *Organization Science*, *7*(5): 477–501.

Davenport, T., & Prusak, L. (1998). *Working knowledge: How organizations manage what they know*. Boston: Harvard Business School Press.

Dunning, J. (1977). Trade, location of economic activity and the MNE: A search for an eclectic approach. In B. Ohlin, P. Hesselborn & P. M. Wijkman (Eds.) *The international allocation of economic activity: Proceedings of a Nobel symposium*: 395–418. Macmillan & London.

Faber, D. (1993). *Environment under fire: Imperialism and the ecological crisis in Central America*. New York: Monthly Review Press Books.

Fortune (2013). The Fortune 500. May 20. Retrieved from http://money.cnn.com/magazines/fortune/fortune_archive/2013/05/20/toc.html.

Gatade, S. (1997). *Globalisation of capital: An outline of recent changes in the modus operandi of imperialism*. New Delhi: Lok Dasta Press.

Ghoshal, S., & Moran, P. (1996). Bad for practice: A critique of the transaction cost theory. *Academy of Management Review*, *21*(1): 13–47.

Gupta, A., & Govindarajan, V. (2000). Knowledge flows within multinational corporations. *Strategic Management Journal*, *21*(4): 47–490.

Harding, S. (2008). *Sciences from below: Feminisms, postcolonialities and modernities*. Durham, NC: Duke University Press.

Harvey, D. (2005). *A brief history of neoliberalism*. Oxford: Oxford University Press.

Headrick, D. (1988). *The tentacles of progress: Technology transfer in the age of imperialism*. New York: Oxford University Press.

Hedlund, G. (1994). A model of knowledge management and the N-form corporation. *Strategic Management Journal*, Summer Special Issue, *15*: 73–90.

Holmstrom, N., & Smith, R. (2000). The necessity of gangster capitalism: Primitive accumulation in Russia and China, *Monthly Review*, *51*(2): 1–21.

Hymer, S. (1960), *The international operations of national firms: A study of direct foreign investment*. Cambridge, MA: MIT Press.

Ibrahim, J. (2004). *Democratic transition in Anglophone West Africa.* East Lansing: Michigan University Press.

Kankanhalli, A., Tanudidjaja, F., Sutanto, J., & Tan, C. (2003). The role of IT in successful knowledge management initiatives. *Communications of the Association for Computing Machinery.* 46(9): 69–80.

Koechlin, T. (2006). US multinational corporations and the mobility of productive capital: A skeptical view. *Review of Radical Political Economics, 38*(3): 374–380.

Kogut, B., & Zander, U. (1992). Knowledge of the firm, combinative capabilities, and the replication of technology. *Organization Science, 3:* 383–397.

Kogut, B., & Zander, U. (1993). Knowledge of the firm and the evolutionary theory of the multinational corporation. *Journal of International Business Studies, 24:* 625–645.

Kogut, B., & Zander, U. (1996). What firms do? Coordination, identity, and learning. *Organization Science,* 7(5): 502–518.

Kogut, B., & Zander, U. (2003). A memoir and reflection: Knowledge of the firm and the evolutionary theory of the multinational corporation 10 years later. *Journal of International Business Studies, 34*(6): 505–516.

Krausse, C. (2013). Halliburton pleads guilty to destroying evidence after gulf spill. *The New York Times,* July 25, 2013. Retrieved from http://www.nytimes.com/2013/07/26/business/halliburton-pleads-guilty-to-destroying-evidence-after-gulf-spill.html.

Marx, K. (1977/1868). *Capital,* Vol. 1. New York: Vintage.

McCauley, M. (2001). *Bandits, gangsters and the Mafia: Russia, the Baltic States and the CIS since 1991.* New York: Pearson Education.

Mir, R., & Sharpe, D. (2009). The multinational firm as a system of exploitation and domination. In Glenn Morgan and Simon Collinson (Eds.), *Images of the multinational corporation:* 247–266. London: Blackwell.

Mir, R., & Mir, A. (2009). From the corporation to the colony: Studying knowledge transfer across international boundaries, *Group and Organization Management, 34*(1): 90–113.

Mir, R., & Mir, A. (2011). Organizational change as imperialism. In David Boje, Bernard Burnes & John Hassard (Eds.), *Routledge companion to organizational change:* 425–439. London: Routledge.

Mir, R., Banerjee, B., & Mir, A. (2008). Hegemony and its discontents: A critical analysis of organizational knowledge transfer, *Critical Perspectives on International Business, 4*(2/3): 203–227.

Mir, R., Mir, A., & Upadhyay, P. (2003). Toward a postcolonial reading of organizational control. In Anshuman Prasad (Ed.), *The gaze of the other: Postcolonial theory and organizational analysis:* 47–75. New York: Palgrave Macmillan.

Morgan, G., & Kristensen, P. (2006). The contested space of multinationals: Varieties of institutionalism, varieties of capitalism. *Human Relations, 59*(11): 1467–1490.

Nonaka, I. (1994). A dynamic theory of organizational knowledge creation. *Organization Science, 5*(1): 14–37.

Nonaka, I. (1998). The concept of "Ba": Building a foundation for knowledge creation. *California Management Review, 40*(3) Spring: 40–54.

Prasad, A., & Prasad, P. (1998). Everyday struggles at the workplace: The nature and implications of routine resistance in contemporary organizations. *Research in the Sociology of Organizations, 15:* 225–257.

Rodan, S., & Galunic, C. (2004). More than network structure: How knowledge heterogeneity influences managerial performance and innovativeness. *Strategic Management Journal, 25*(6): 541–551.

Rodney, W. (1974). *How Europe underdeveloped Africa.* Washington, DC: Howard University Press.

Sanyal, K. (2007). *Rethinking capitalist development: Primitive accumulation, governmentality and post-colonial capitalism.* New Delhi: Routledge.

Schwartz, N., & Duhigg, C. (2013). Apple's web of tax shelters saved it billions, panel finds. *The New York Times,* May 20. Retrieved from http://www.nytimes.com/2013/05/21/business/apple-avoided-billions-in-taxes-congressional-panel-says.html.

Scott, J. C. (1985). *Weapons of the weak: Everyday forms of peasant resistance.* New Haven, CT: Yale University Press.

Szulanski, G. (1995). Unpacking stickiness: An empirical investigation of the barriers to transfer best practices inside the firm. INSEAD Working Paper, November.

UNCTAD (2012). *World Investment Report 2012.* Retrieved from http://www.unctad-docs.org/files/UNCTAD-WIR2012-Full-en.pdf.

Verlinden, C. (1970). *The Beginnings of modern colonisation* (Yvonne Freccero, Trans.). Ithaca, NY: Cornell University Press.

Wu, Y. (2005). Rethinking 'capitalist restoration' in China. *Monthly Review, 57*(6): 50–61.

Zack, M. H. (1999). Managing codified knowledge. *Sloan Management Review, 40*(4): 45–58.

Zander, U., & Kogut, B. (1995). Knowledge and the speed of the transfer and imitation of organizational capabilities. *Organization Science, 6*(1): 76–92.

21

"We're not talking to people, we're talking to a nation"

Crossing borders in transnational customer service work

Kiran Mirchandani

Introduction

The field of Critical Management Studies (CMS) is often said to have emerged out of the engagement of management scholars with the rich history of European critical theory. The Frankfurt School and its protégées represent, however, just one of the many genealogies of CMS. Scholars of antiracism, feminism, diaspora, postcolonialism and globalization have fundamentally shaped and given meaning to the notion of the "critical" within the CMS tradition. More than an interest in the exercise of elite power and the construction of organizational labor processes, these scholars have focused on the experience of organizational life from the perspective of those who are marginalized. The centering of those on the margin has provoked questions about border creations and crossings as well as the practices through which inclusion and exclusion is exercised within organizations. Rather than starting with the traditional pillars of management (such as organizational behavior, marketing, operations and finance), CMS involves documenting the processes through which organizations conceal and yet operate upon assumptions of an ideal worker and the mechanisms through which workers who deviate from this norm are penalized. CMS scholars have also questioned mainstream approaches to diversity and inclusion in management studies, especially given that managers are often the primary benefactors of class inequities supported by neoliberalism and capitalism.

This chapter highlights this approach to Critical Management Studies through the analysis of the experiences of transnational call center workers employed in India to provide telephone-based service to customers in the West. As a setting, call centers have historically provided Critical Management Studies scholars a rich site within which issues of power, language, control and resistance can be examined. Theorists have noted that although call center work is often promoted as "professional" work through the use of job labels such as "Customer Service Executive" and as an outcome of the clean, office-like environment of work (which resemble professional white-collar jobs), the jobs themselves are highly routinized, scripted and monitored. The use of automated dialing technologies facilitates the intensification of workflow in conjunction with the continual monitoring of work in relation to performance targets. There now exists over a decade of insightful research on how control is exerted in call centers through forms of electronic surveillance (Fernie et al., 1998), work intensification (Taylor, Mulvey, Hyman & Bain, 2002) and competitive performance management systems (Knights and McCabe, 2003; Flemming, 2009). Others have documented the ways in which workers resist these forms of control, either through collective action or more frequently through individual strategies aimed at reducing call flow and gaining control over scripts (Bain & Taylor, 2000; Barnes 2004; Mulholland, 2004). Central to these analyses have been attempts to document worker experiences within call centers. In the process of providing information, workers are required to engage in substantial amounts of emotional labor – which involves doing one's work in ways which make customers feel a particular way. Emotional labor takes skill and practice as it requires the management of self-feeling as well as learning strategies to recognize customer needs, appease angry customers and mirror the organizational brand.

Feminist and antiracist scholars have added to these analyses by highlighting the complex ways in which worker–customer interactions in call centers are embedded within social contexts that are stratified. In their detailed ethnography of hospitality work, for example, Dyer, McDowell, & Batnitzky (2010) show how particular workers occupy a privileged position in clients' perceptions of ideal service workers. This privilege is closely tied to workers' gender, ethnicity and migration histories. In U.K. hotels, for example, white migrants who are perceived as "cosmopolitan" are given front office jobs in hotels, while African or Caribbean migrant workers who have few labor market alternatives are seen as most suitable for doing repetitive and unpleasant cleaning work. Workers from certain countries are constructed as hardworking and passive, while others are less suitable because they are perceived to have a propensity to make demands. As Dyer and colleagues (2010) summarize, "[A]ttributes based on supposed national characteristics construct workers as more or less eligible for different types of work" (p. 653). In a similar manner, call center work is structured not only by local social hierarchies but, increasingly with the offshoring of this work, by transnational racialization. In the past decade, there has been a dramatic shift in the nature of customer service work as global processes have facilitated the exchange of services across national boundaries. With the growth of telecommunications technology, the service economy no longer requires the colocation of customer and worker, and call centers serving clients across geographical spaces and national boundaries have emerged. This has led to the emergence of new geographies of stratification and resistance, as well as new insights for the field of Critical Management Studies.

Building on these analyses of the social organization of call center work, this chapter focuses on how, in their daily work, transnational call center workers cross borders and make sense of relationships that constitute and are constitutive of globalization. Conceptualizing call center work in terms of its border crossings rather in terms of tasks required pinpoints the relational nature of this work. Given the location of call center workers as intermediaries between organizations and their customers, much of workers' jobs involves interpreting the needs and expectations of clients and managers and performing their jobs in line with these expectations. In transnational call center work, these expectations are influenced by national histories and global inequalities. With the offshoring of customer service work, workers living in countries with colonial histories have emerged as top contenders for these jobs. Out of these countries, India has appeared first on the list of most desirable future locations for offshore service work (Aggarwal, Aspray, Berry, Lenway & Taylor, 2004: 10) largely because of its two million college graduates each year, 80% of whom are English speakers.

As in many call centers around the world, customer service work in India involves working in highly monitored, routinized, performance-oriented jobs. Workers are employed in full-time, relatively well paid jobs but report high levels of stress, frequent abuse on calls and exhaustion due to the fact that they often work in night shifts when call volumes from customers in the West are high. While analyses of these work processes sheds light on their work experience, interviews with workers reveal a subterraneous mountain of invisible activity that involves interpreting and crossing boundaries. Drawing on analysis conducted for a study on the work experiences of customer service agents in India who serve clients in the West (Mirchandani, 2012), in this chapter I explore three boundaries that Indian workers traverse as an integral part of their work in call centers: boundaries of class, of nation and of production.

Borders and their crossings

Class borders

Russell (2008) notes that "call centre work is the information economy's equivalent of semi-skilled labor, meaning that employment entails greater skill than the blue-collar operator positions of the factory era, but cannot be meaningfully considered knowledge work" (p. 199). At the same time, employment in Indian call centers "is very much identified with the creation of a new middle class and the prosperity that accompanies it" (Thite & Russell, 2009: 255). Research by Van den Broek (2004) similarly reveals that transnational call center workers identify themselves as part of an elite class of professionals (p. 61). Call center workers therefore occupy shifting and often ambiguous class borders. Their work is constructed as "professional," and yet the work processes involved are highly routinized. In addition, the work requires servitude and deference and allows for little worker discretion. One young man interviewed for this project characterizes his work environment as a "a very professional environment. People respect the work you do and if you do a very nice job then there's always a package waiting." This enactment of the notion of professionalism sets up two sets of relations that structure customer service jobs: first, a total commitment to the organization, which requires workers to be independent, entrepreneurial self-managers who maximize their performance, and second, a total subservience to customers.

Organizational commitment and the limits to job autonomy

Noronha and D'Cruz (2009) characterize professionalism in call centers as a form of "socio-ideological control" (p. xi). This is because the implicit association of professional work with responsibility, control, mental challenge and creativity is purposefully produced in call centers, even though the labor process in place results in highly monitored and routinized jobs. Indeed, customer service agents talk about themselves as engaged in professional, elite work. Workers are not only producers but also occupy an important social position as India's new consumers. As Fernandes (2006) argues, Indian's new middle class is epitomized in those involved in transnational jobs not only in terms of their access to wealth but also in terms of the lifestyle of consumption. Krishnamurthy (2004) notes that the growth of call centers in India has increased the disposable income of middle class youth, who are simultaneously the producers as well as an important force behind the proliferation of consumerism (p. 11). At the same time, they are allowed – indeed required – to engage in consumption activities associated with middle- and upper-middle-class lifestyles in India. One worker explains:

> We have parties. Friday parties. Sometimes they take us to parties to five star hotels. I would have never been myself. But because the company is sponsoring we used to go there. The booze is on the house. You can eat and drink and have fun and meet so many people . . . it

helps us to build team spirit and come back and get fresh and start working afresh. When we come back, that time is the time to work at our best. So we know, that OK, the managers can do so much for us. So we should also do good for the managers. So we kind of work really hard. So it helps both of us. The managers as well as us.

(Krishnamurthy, 2004: 43)

Despite the access to middle-class lifestyles, as Poster (2007a) summarizes, call center workers occupy contradictory class locations. Like knowledge and managerial workers in transnational corporations, they have access to the global economy through their telephone conversations with customers. Yet they earn considerably less than knowledge and managerial workers and share job features, such as the lack of autonomy of tasks and time, that are typical of lower-level service jobs (p. 65). One worker describes his job in the following terms:

You are bonded. You don't have the choice. When they want to go for lunch [you go] . . . you cannot tell, I want this shift. Even if I want to leave, I have to ask.

Williams and Connell's (2010) study of retail workers sheds light on the ways in which organizations make use of such contradictory class orientations among workers. Workers in expensive, high-end retail stores often receive poor wages, and they are incented to accept these because of "perks" such as employee discounts. The opportunity to be associated with a brand is itself presented as a work-related benefit, and workers are constructed primarily as consumers interested in making well priced purchases rather than workers who need to work to sustain their livelihoods through enriched, well paid jobs. In a similar way, one worker notes:

We have had competitions ranging from gift vouchers, to having TVs, handycams, and home theatres and all that. It's really good. I mean you won't have actually bought this for the family. So it's like me giving a gift for the family. It feels good.

Although call center workers clearly appreciate the possible access to luxury goods, they also express significant job challenges due to their night work, long hours and stringent performance evaluations. Rather than addressing these challenges, companies use luxury goods as "perks" to motivate workers to perform. These perks do not result in any shift in the labor process, as noted by some respondents. One man with four years of experience in call centers notes that managers often encourage workers to emulate lifestyles depicted in Western popular media, such as excessive drinking, smoking and sharing personal challenges, because it helps workers to deal with on-the-job stress. He prefaces the following quote by talking about his own life and how he thoroughly enjoys music, drinking in moderation and going out. He notes, however, that young workers in call centers:

[f]eel that by doing these things they are, you know, mirroring these Westernized guys. The most important thing that hurts me personally is that these people, when we have process parties, these managers bribe teams. They tell that if your team is among the first three I'll give you money [for parties]. [At parties] these youngsters, they like to cry and scrap the family as not a united family. . . . [They] drink so much [they] start vomiting. Which is what upsets me. So nobody is there to tell them what is good, what is bad. And they are young. And believe me, commercially, unfortunately, the Managers and the Team Leaders are exploiting this kind of thing. They know that tomorrow they'll have to work for twelve hours. . . . These are gestures. Indirect bribes.

Negotiating customer–worker class positions

Class borders are also transnationally occupied in daily worker–customer encounters. Customers frequently exercise their positional power over workers, responding to poor service or their objections to offshoring by treating workers with aggression. One worker reports:

> At times they used to get hostile. They used to say, no, I would like to speak to someone who speaks English. I am speaking English! How is it that I am not speaking English? Sometimes we used to get . . . weird calls. There were times when people used to be kind of cranky and crazy. They just want to speak to someone who speaks English and also knows the product process very well. We know the process but still they are not comfortable speaking to an Indian.

At the same time, unlike in the West where call centers often offer poorly paid, part-time, or temporary precarious jobs, Indian workers have salaries that are higher than those offered in local industries for full-time jobs and even some benefits such as van or health services. Indian call center workers also highlight their higher educational qualifications and class positions vis-à-vis their Western customers, not all of whom are as highly educated. Workers often cast their customers as less educated and technologically adept. One woman working for a loans process reports:

> We need a lot of patience because means, sometimes they are, means the borrowers are so dumb, they can't understand [both laugh]. They can't understand, Means like, if you're co-browsing with the borrowers, or if you're giving simple answers also, they don't understand, means like, often we have to repeat one answer, we have to repeat it many times.

In these ways, careful attention to the experiences of customer service workers shed light on the lived and experiential nature of class relations. Acker (1999) argues that conceptualizing class as a social relation allows for a shift away from a notion that certain criteria define one's class within a pre-given structure of hierarchies (p. 57). Rather, as Reay (1998) notes, "what it means to be middle or working class, black or white, female or male shifts and changes, not only from one historical era to another, but for individuals over time as they negotiate the social world" (p. 266). Class negotiation is a central part of the work that customer service agents engage in as part of their jobs.

National borders

Aneesh (2006) characterizes transnational service work as "virtual migration" with a very different relationship to the nation compared to more conventional forms of labor migration. He notes that under the system of virtual migration, "labor bypasses the state borders while the immigrants' body stays within national temporal spaces" (p. 65). Workers therefore migrate and remain simultaneously and, in this, perform "border work" in relation both to the nation to which they migrate and to the nation within which they stay. Workers receive training on the histories and cultures of countries in the West where their customers reside. Much of this training occurs either through an engagement with popular culture (watching movies and television shows) or reading lists of Hofstede-inspired stereotypes of people in the West. One woman describes that she was successful at her job because she understood Western culture. She gained this familiarity through movies: "I used to see a lot of movies . . . during my school time, college time. I used to go for a lot of English movies. Even I had cable in my house. I used to see movies every day."

A training manual contains sections entitled "Appreciating Western Culture," which contains a summary of Americans and Britishers in bullet form:

> People from the United Kingdom are generally: conservative and class conscious, reserved, law abiding and principled, ethnocentrically arrogant, conscious about time.
>
> *(NIIT, 2003: 5.5)*

> The following are some of the basic traits of Americans and the rules governing their social and family relationship: appreciate equal opportunity, forthright, informal, independent, materialistic, value time, sensitive to gender and diversity issues.
>
> *(NIIT, 2003: 3.6)*

Based on films, trait characterizations during training and most importantly their own experiences of annoyed and aggressive customers on the telephone, workers make sense of their customers and reach a wide variety of conclusions on what Americans, Britishers or Australians are like. Many of their characterizations serve to justify the frequently abusive customer service interactions that are part of their daily work experience. One worker reports, "American client, he'll say, 'what the hell are you doing?'. . . For us, it's a very big thing, what this person has said, we really take it to heart. But out there, it's just a common thing. It's that way." Another recounts, "Brits, they are so sarcastic that you know, they'll eat you psychologically, slowly, slowly and God forbid. If anybody tries to be over smart and uses a jargon, he is gone because English is their language."

Based on interviews with British citizens engaged in conversations about belonging and community, Skey (2011) observes that rather just than a geographical entity, the nation is also constructed on a daily basis via common sense nationalism that serves to construct the subject positions of insiders and outsiders. Customers in the West often express anger during customer service interactions; they may be frustrated by the long wait times or may desire solutions tailored to their individual needs. Often workers make sense of customer anger by relating it to the nation to which they belong, employing ethnic stereotypes in order to differentiate themselves from people who routinize aggression as "just a common thing." Workers respond to the need to define violent customers as routine and normal by identifying the superiority of Indian work norms. One man working in a bank process describes a customer who was angry about being charged a fee for a bounced check:

> One cheque bounces and they get $30 overdraft fee. So they are like, why did you charge me? And they say, because you are an Indian you are charging me. If it was an American they would have given me a waiver . . .

This man goes on to say that this caller's perspective is misguided as in his experience:

> Americans have an attitude. Saying, this is not my job. I will not do this. But in India it's like, even if it's not my job I will try to do it. That's the difference between Indian and American communities.

Commonsense nationalism, therefore, occurs not only among those in power but is also exercised by those not in power in order to maintain self-worth in light of aggression. In their daily interactions, workers continually construct and cross the borders of nations – their own and their customers'. One man notes that customers in the West are threatened by India:

After 15–20 years this world will be ruled by India and China. Because there are over one million [Indian] people in London. There are many Chinese. In fact there is a Chinatown in US. All hotels in the US are run by Sardarjis. And Hinglish is a word that has been added in the dictionary last year. . . . This is acknowledgement by Oxford people sitting in Oxford. So these are small differences that you know, we know, that Indians and Chinese are now taking up the entire world. There is nowhere you won't find these people, especially Europe and US. So fifteen years down the line, not literally with guns and swords, but psychologically, India and China will be ruling for sure.

Another worker notes that she wishes she could respond differently on calls by sharing her experience with customer aggression:

They literally say, at times, that "you bloody Indians don't know how to speak English. Can I speak to someone who can speak English"? We transfer the call but they should not say that. . . . "Sir, I can speak many languages. Can you? Think about that. You don't have to humiliate anyone".

Poster (2007b) argues that working in Indian call centers also necessitates a host of activities broadly characterized as "national identity management" (p. 271). This includes adopting an American accent, using a Western alias and becoming familiar with American popular culture. Workers are required simultaneously to take personal responsibility for their work and pretend to be someone else. One woman explains:

When I'm doing the job I have to be myself. Even if I don't want to be I have to be because the person is calling over a number. . . . He is calling from such a far distance to get some resolution. I cannot just mimic or just act like anybody else. I have to be myself and resolve the issue. . . . People might not pronounce your name properly. Because here in India they have certain mythological names like Ishwar and all that I mean UK or US people won't pronounce it properly. They won't understand it properly. The communication would be, you know, indirect. So they want a name which suits them.

A key part of "national identity management" includes workers' responsibility to "represent India" to the world in a way that protects and enhances offshoring. This representation evokes a rhetoric of traitors and ambassadors that is sprinkled through training programs, media reports and workplace discourses. A high-profile diplomat, Shashi Tharoor (2007), refers to India's call center industry in the following way:

The call centre has become the symbol of India's newly globalised workforce: while traditional India sleeps, a dynamic young cohort of highly skilled, articulate professionals works through the night, functioning on US time under made-up American aliases, pretending familiarity with a culture and climate they've never actually experienced, earning salaries that were undreamt of by their elders (but a fraction of what an American would make) and enjoying a lifestyle that's a cocktail of premature affluence and ersatz westernization transplanted to an Indian setting.

Thrift (2002) notes that contemporary capitalism has "increased the demand for workers to act as . . . 'branded bodies', literally embodying the look and feel of their employers' corporate identity" (p. 206). On one hand, state branding practices have to be enacted over the phone by workers who are seen as the frontline ambassadors of Brand India.

> Many a times I got a customer where I wasn't speaking in an American accent. I was tired so I forgot to speak in an American accent. And I started speaking like how I do right now. . . . The quality people came and told me I was doing wrong. He told me that the customer said that can you give the phone to somebody who knows English because he wasn't understanding your neutral English. This is what the quality people do. It was very important to get to know all these things. It was very important for my colleagues to know all these things because we get to know what America is all about. Because we are not talking to people. We are talking to a nation.

Production borders

Indian call center workers continually straddle the borders between production and social reproduction. Weeks (2007) summarizes this duality in service work: "processes of production today increasingly integrate the labors of the hand, brain, and heart as more jobs require workers to use their knowledge, capacities for cooperation and communicative skills to create not only material but increasingly immaterial products" (p. 238; see also Adkins & Jokinen, 2008). These connections between production and reproduction fundamentally structure transnational service workers' daily lives. Van den Broek (2004) notes that "workers literally embody the service they provide. So rather than producing tangible products like cars or clothing, interactive service workers and call center workers particularly, trade in aesthetics and emotions – that is, workers sell attitude, personality and voice" (p. 60). Patel (2006) similarly argues:

> Unlike silicon [sic] chip *production* in Taiwan, maquiladoras [sic] in Mexico, or McDonald's in France, transnational customer service employment represents a shift from exporting the production of material goods or culture to a full scale *reproduction* of identity and culture. In contrast to McDonald's selling french fries in Paris, but not requiring an American accent from its French employees, call centre operations are based on the availability of workers trained to embody an American identity and cultural cues.
>
> *(p. 21)*

As part of their jobs, workers perform a host of emotional labor for which they draw on their socialization, childhood and educational experience. One woman working for a lost baggage claim process in which she frequently confronts angry customers notes:

> We cannot shout on passengers. We have to be cool. Most of the time, calm and patient. We cannot lose our patience. Because they are customers and we have to deal nicely with them. Talking patiently and nicely, you don't have to learn anywhere. It comes directly from your family.

Emotional labor involves managing self-feeling in order to effectively perform a job. Workers not only have to speak on the phone in ways that show empathy and caring, but they also have to hide their own negative reactions. A young woman with a convent education notes that she thought call center work would be easy given her English language skills and her personality:

> I just keep on talking and talking. My energy is still there. Even if I speak for eight hours, I'm interested in speaking [giggles]. So I had thought that the BPO (Business Process Outsourcing)

would be a great job for me. But then later on what I experienced is that speaking eight hours continuously with the same procedure, with the same accent, with the same verbiages, you get pissed off. . . . Even if you are angry, you have to keep your angriness with you only. You can't show. You have to always keep a smile on your face.

Feminist scholars have long highlighted the embodied nature of service work, however; as Bryson (2007) notes, much of the analysis of emotional labor is based on the analysis of the body while customer service agents interact with their voices rather than with their bodies (p. 36). Workers' bodies are carried through their voices, and, in this context, workers are trained to speak and sound in particular ways to their customers. Despite frequent customer abuse, workers in India are encouraged to develop empathy and care for customers. A manager shared the following experience with a caller asking for a large loan:

> [The customer] said, "I met with an accident. I have nobody to care for me". She was just going on as if there was nobody with who she can talk. She's pouring everything into me. I said, OK, let me listen. She was so glad that at the end of the call she said, "Why don't you come and have Christmas dinner with me?" So I said, "I'm sorry, but you're calling India." She said, "Whenever you come here you just come to my place" and she gave me her address. That gives me satisfaction. OK, I spoke to a lady who was very elderly, of my mother's age and I build a relationship with her. Every year, I call her at Christmas time. She wanted me to call her Granny. She didn't feel she is calling a call center. She feels she calls somebody she knows.

The manager goes on to note that this relationship-building benefits the company because she may tell her friends about her positive service experience. Only because of his managerial status, however, is he able to go "off script" with the customer. For most workers, such an exchange would translate into a poor performance evaluation, not only because the exchange does not follow the organizationally sanctioned script but also because the call exceeds the time allocated for calls. Workers are encouraged to invest emotionally in order to come across as sincere and interested, without undermining the high-paced, time-bound nature of interactions.

Call center work also depends on a complex infrastructure through which workers' family and home responsibilities can be met. Mukherjee's (2008) study of IT professionals reveals that professional women depend on parents and in-laws as well as on domestic help for child care and housework (p. 33). The normalization of night work and the lack of state and organizational responsibility for workers' temporal dislocation have resulted in a gendered incorporation of low-paid service workers who provide the invisible support for the industry. Sassen (2008) argues that "professional households need to function like clockwork . . . these households should be reconceptualized as part of [the infrastructure of global cities] and the low-wage domestics as strategic infrastructure maintenance workers" (p. 464). Indeed, many workers note that given their night shifts, they often spend much of the daytime attempting to catch up on their sleep. Workers rely on domestic workers and parents for domestic work. Workers with household responsibilities have to do considerable work to engage in their paid jobs while also attempting to sleep during the day when their families are awake.

Border crossings and authenticity work

Conceptualizing work in terms of border crossings highlights the relational nature of social life. It shows that organizational members make sense of and perform their work in relation to social norms, national histories and processes of stratification. Call center work has received substantial coverage in the CMS literature in the past decade. Studies include analyses of labor market trends, trade agreements, corporate decision-making processes, surveillance, performance mechanisms, national and international policies. While these studies provide a perspective on call center work, this chapter has a fundamentally different starting point: knowledge is gleaned from workers' interpretive work on the social context within which the globalization of service work exists. Transnational service work depends on the continual interpretation and management of borders of class, nation and production.

In order to be effective in their jobs, customer service workers in India have to understand customer expectations of ideal workers and try to emulate this ideal. This labor, termed "authenticity work," involves a process of proclaiming legitimacy (Mirchandani, 2012). For Indian customer service agents, it involves simultaneously constructing themselves as foreign workers who do not threaten Western jobs, as legitimate colonial subjects who revere the West, as real Indians who form an offshore model workforce and provide the cheap immobile labor needed in the West, as flexible workers who are trainable and global, as workers who are far away yet familiar enough to provide good service. Authenticity work is fundamentally relational in nature; it is the work of reading the preferences of those in power and attempting to adjust or meet those expectations. Transnational call center workers provide a vivid illustration of this labor, which pervades many jobs in the contemporary service-based economy.

References

Acker, J. (1999). Rewriting class, race, and gender: Problems in feminist rethinking. In M. M. Ferree, J. Lorber & B. B. Hess (Eds.), *Revisioning Gender*. 44–69. Thousand Oaks, CA: Sage.

Aggarwal, A., Aspray, W., Berry, O., Lenway, S. A., & Taylor, V. (2004). Off shoring: The big picture (Chapter 1). Retrieved from ACM (Association for Computing Machinery) website: http://www.acm.org/globalizationreport/chapter1.pdf.

Aneesh, A. (2006). *Virtual migration: The programming of globalization*. Durham, NC: Duke University Press.

Bain, P., & Taylor, P. (2000). Entrapped by the 'electronic panopticon'?: Worker resistance in the call centre, *New Technology, Work and Employment, 15*(1): 2–18.

Barnes, A. (2004). Diaries, dunnies and discipline: Resistance and accommodation to monitoring in call centers, *Labour and Industry, 14*(3): 127–137.

Bryson, J. R. (2007). The 'second' global shift: The off shoring or global sourcing of corporate services and the rise of distanciated emotional labor. Geografiska Annaler – Series B. *Human Geography, 89*(s1), 31–43 [doi:10.1111/j.1468–0467.2007.00258.x].

Dyer, S., McDowell, L., & Batnitzky, A. (2010). The impact of migration on the gendering of service work: The case of a west London hotel. *Gender, Work and Organization, 17*(6) 635–657.

Fernandes, L. (2006). *India's new middle class: Democratic politics in an era of economic reform*. Minneapolis: University of Minnesota Press.

Fleming, P. (2009). *Authenticity and the cultural politics of work: New forms of informal control*. Oxford: Oxford University Press.

Frenkel, S., Korczynski, M., Shire, K., & Tam, M. (1998). Beyond bureaucracy? Work organisation in call centers, *International Journal of Human Resource Management, 9*(6): 957–979.

Knights, D., & McCabe, D. (2003). Governing through teamwork: Reconstituting subjectivity in a call and processing centre. *Journal of Management Studies, 40*(7): 1587–1619.

Krishnamurthy, M. (2004). Resources and rebels: A study of identity management in Indian call centers. *Anthropology of Work Review, 25*(3–4): 9–18 [doi:10.1525/awr.2004.25.3–4.9].

Mirchandani, K. (2012) *Phone clones: Authenticity work in the transnational service economy*. Ithaca, NY: Cornell University Press.

Mukherjee, S. (2008). Producing the IT miracle: The neoliberalizing states and changing gender and class regimes in India. Doctoral dissertation. ProQuest Dissertations and Theses Database (UMI No. 3345013).

Mulholland, K. (2004). Workplace resistance in an Irish call centre: slammin', scammin', smokin' an' leavin'. *Work, Employment and Society, 18*(4): 709–724.

NIIT (2003). *Certificate in customer service: Student guide-I.* New Delhi: Sona Printers.

Noronha, E., & D'Cruz, P. (2009) *Employee identity in Indian call centres: The notion of professionalism.* New Delhi: Response.

Palm, M. (2006). Outsourcing, self-service and the telemobility of work. *Anthropology of Work Review, 27*(2): 1–9 [doi:10.1525/awr.2006.27.2].

Patel, R. (2006). Working the night shift: Gender and the global economy. *ACME: An International E-Journal for Critical Geographies, 5*(1), 9–27. Retrieved from http://www.acme-journal.org/index.html.

Poster, W. R. (2007a). Saying 'good morning' in the night: The reversal of work time in global ICT service work. *Research in the Sociology of Work, 17*: 55–112 [doi:10.1016/S0277–2833(07)17003–5].

Poster, W. R. (2007b). Who's on the line? Indian call center agents pose as Americans for U.S.-outsourced firms. *Industrial Relations, 46*(2): 271–304 [doi:10.1111/j.1468–232X.2007.00468.x].

Reay, D. (1998). Rethinking social class: Qualitative perspectives on class and gender. *Sociology, 32*(2): 259–275 [doi:10.1177/0038038598032002003].

Russell, B. (2008). Call centers: A decade of research. *International Journal of Management Reviews, 10*(3): 195–219 [doi:10.1111/j.1468–2370.2008.00241.x].

Sassen, S. (2008a). Two stops in today's new global geographies: Shaping novel labor supplies and employment regimes. *American Behavioral Scientist, 52*(3): 457–496 [doi:10.1177/0002764208325312].

Sassen, S. (2008b). Unsettling master categories: Notes on studying the global in C. W. Mills' footsteps. *International Journal of Politics, Culture, and Society, 20*(1–4): 69–83 [doi:10.1007/s10767–008–9030-z].

Skey, M. (2011). *National belonging and everyday life: The significance of nationhood in an uncertain world.* Hampshire, UK: Palgrave Macmillan

Taylor, P., & Bain, P. (2006). Work organisation and employee relations in Indian call centers. In J. Burgess & J. Connell (Eds.), *Developments in the call center industry: Analysis, changes and challenges*: 36–57. London: Routledge.

Taylor, P., Mulvey, G., Hyman, J., & Bain, P. (2002). Work organisation, control and the experience of work in call centres. *Work, Employment and Society, 16*(1):133–150.

Tharoor, S. (2007) The coolies are scheduling the trains. *Times of India*, April 15, 2007. Retrieved on September 1, 2010 from http://timesofindia.indiatimes.com/home/opinion/shashi-tharoor/shashi-on-sunday/The-coolies-are-scheduling-the-trains/articleshow/1927078.cms.

Thite, M., & Russell, B. (2009). Managing work and employment in Australian and Indian call centers. In M. Thite & B. Russell (Eds.), *The next available operator: Managing human resources in Indian business process outsourcing industry*: 253–278. New Delhi: Response Books.

Thrift, N. 2002. Performing cultures in the new economy. In P. du Gay & M. Pryke (Eds.), *Cultural economy: Cultural analysis and commercial life*: 201–234. London: Sage.

Van Den Broek, D. (2004). Globalising call center capital: Gender, culture and work identity. *Labor & Industry, 14*(3): 59–75.

Weeks, K. (2007). Life within and against work: Affective labor, feminist critique, and post-Fordist politics. *Ephemera – Theory & Politics in Organization, 7*(1): 233–249. Retrieved from http://www.ephemeraweb.org/journal/index.htm.

Williams, C., & Connell, C. (2010). Looking good and sounding right: Aesthetic labor and social inequality in the retail industry, *Work and Occupations, 37*(3): 349–377.

22

Microfinance

A neoliberal instrument or a site of the 'other's' resistance and contestation?

Nimruji Jammulamadaka[1]

I share with you a deep enthusiasm for what this remarkable tool [microcredit] can be in the future of poverty eradication.

> (James Gustave Speth, administrator, United Nations Development Programme,
> October 2, 1995)

Microcredit programs have brought the vibrancy of the market economy to the poorest villages and people of the world.

> (James D. Wolfensohn, president, World Bank, July 11, 1996)

[M]icrocredit makes life at the bottom of the pyramid worse. Contrary to the hype about micro-credit, the best way to eradicate poverty is to create jobs.

> (Karnani, 2007)

Why Microfinance Doesn't Work: The Destructive Rise of Local Neoliberalism

> (Bateman, 2010)

"The Tools of Empire? Micro-Finance, Neo-Liberalism, and the Vietnamese State"

> (Delaney, 2010)

Bangladeshi rural women's honor and shame are instrumentally appropriated by micro-credit NGOs in the furtherance of their capitalist interests.

> (Karim, 2008)

As these quotes eloquently convey, microfinance/microcredit[2] is an 'instrument'. For champions[3] like the World Bank, United Nations Development Programme (UNDP), United States Agency for International Development (USAID), the Bill & Melinda Gates Foundation or the Ford Foundation, microfinance is the magic bullet that breaks the vicious cycle of poverty leading to empowerment and growth. Dissenting voices have called it a blunt instrument which may improve incomes for some but fails to target the very poor (Buss, 1999; Hulme & Mosley, 1996, 1997; Karnani, 2007; Rahman, 1999). For critics, microfinance is a tool that furthers neoliberal interests: its "primary function . . . is to link the *unification movement at the supranational level*[4] with local social policy. Consequently, the *rules and norms of the global unification movement* are extended to the level of individuals within local communities"[5] (Weber, 2001: 5; emphasis added). Given that a detailed review of these literatures and positions is not possible here,[6] this summation at the risk of oversimplifying the nuances in the positions mentioned above moves ahead.

Of those positions, some are closer to each other than they appear at first sight, and some are polar opposites. In spite of the conceptual distance between these positions, what ties them together is their view of the *Other*. These positions cast the *Rest of the world*, the places where microfinance is actually being practised, as passive. To the extent that entities like Grameen Bank or Self Employed Women's Association (SEWA) Bank (India) are mentioned,[7] it is only that – a mere mention. These places and organizations are cast as experiments, as pilots, which worked/ did not work and therefore can now be used/not used by the West. For instance, the Declaration of the Microcredit Summit (Washington, D.C., 1997), ostensibly made by 3000 participants from 137 countries, states, "There now exist both a substantial *track record of accomplishments* . . . poor people are a *good credit risk* . . . bad loan ratios are comparable to or below those of *conventional banking*. . . . *Industrialised nations are developing models* for organizational sustainability that will further accelerate . . ." (p. 9; emphasis added). The language and its articulation evident in these excerpts make it apparent as to who is *speaking*. The World Bank's Consultative Group to Assist the Poor (CGAP) organized and paid for this summit. The 'experiments' have worked, and *They* (Summit Campaign,[8] RESULTS[9] and CGAP) can now drive the program to put '100 million poor people out of poverty'. The speech and impetus are shifted silently to the Western agencies.

The critics of this 'neoliberal tool', on the other hand, have seen the *Rest* as passively falling in line as they do not have the choice, the capacity or the power to resist. "[T]here is a virtual absence of the state in the rural economy . . . They [Grameen Bank and others] constitute a modern land-lord with a global vision" (Karim, 2008: 12), so the poor and their countries have no choice, and even though the poor do exploit the NGOs, "the balance of power is with these NGOs [Grameen Bank]" (Karim, 2008: 9). The analysis of Weber (2001) on the complicity of microfinance to the Washington Consensus also alludes to this 'choicelessness' of the Rest. "The way in which the Post-Washington Consensus policy framework is consolidated means that it actually aims at dele-gitimating the politics. . . . This is tantamount to an attempt at 'social closure'. Genuine political struggle – political contestation – of development is undermined" (Weber, 2001: 26).

This chapter takes objection to such a view of the Rest. It argues that the Rest is anything but passive. By engaging with the Indian experience and its enmeshing with global microfinance, the chapter argues that microfinance is not merely an instrument that can be *deployed on* the Rest but is a site of *active politics* – of appropriations by the West, of imaginative wresting of spaces, of the deployment of possibilities by the various actors on all sides and an unperturbed resistant ground-level practice. By drawing on several published materials like reports, review papers, and case studies of practitioners, government and global agencies, this chapter (through critical discourse analysis) constructs an account of microfinance as it has emerged in Indian community space, its engagement with the Indian state, its encounter with the West and its continuing aftermath. The analysis looks at the implications of this experience for the reading of global microfinance as a harmonizing and hegemonic practice of the West.

Emergence of microfinance in India (late 1970s and the 1980s)

The 1970s marked a period of great turbulence in Indian public space. The young nation's enthu-siasm for and expectations of its sovereign government were being replaced by considerable disil-lusionment. The public was beginning to realize that the government was ineffective in coping with famines and providing for the security and development of its people, and that at this time, voluntary and civil effort was required not to free the nation from British domination but to free it from the clutches of poverty and deprivation. As a result, the voluntary action, which was very popular during India's freedom struggle but which had slowed down after independence, saw a revival.[10] The development stalwarts of today (e.g., SEWA, SWRC (Social Work and Research Center), BCT (Barefoot College Tilonia), PRADAN (Professional Assistance for Development Action),[11] Seva Mandir, etc.) all had their genesis during that period. These were formed by people seeking to build the nation.

By the late 1970s, several such NGOs[12] in India were grappling with the issue of mobilizing people. They were exploring mechanisms for social intermediation that could mobilize the latent social capital among the poor and use it for improving their material conditions. They were also dabbling in forming groups based on various criteria. These NGOs realized that they had more positive experiences working with groups of women even for issues other than women's empowerment and that women, unlike men, were keen on lifting their families out of poverty. Building on these experiences, the NGOs encouraged the women to save tiny amounts of cash or kind in their groups to help tide them over tough times and avoid expensive borrowing. Such micro savings were used to support a needy member by lending to her in times of crisis. The following montage conveys these efforts and origins without going into a detailed cataloguing of the origins of microfinance in India:[13]

- BCT, an NGO from Andhra Pradesh in South India, encouraged women to save 10 paise per week in the late 1970s.[14] Some of the women saved this money by putting away a fist-ful of rice from every meal they were cooking. The savings by the women's group reached Rs.3000 within a matter of a year for a single village. This process continued, and the women's groups deposited over Rs.50,000 in a bank in the second year and used it to finance their consumption and production needs through lending amongst themselves (*The Week*, 1988).
- SEWA bank, a *"confluence of three movements – the labour, cooperative and women's movements"* (Shetty, 2012:207) was founded when the 4000 members of the Self Employed Women's Association, a women's trade union formed in 1972, contributed Rs.10 each to start a cooperative bank in 1974 in Gujarat, Western India, to meet their needs for savings and credit products.
- Myrada, an NGO working with Tibetan refugees in Karnataka, South India, was forming credit management groups of the community in 1984–1985 to mobilize capital and help the refugees manage their own lives and needs. Myrada named these groups as self-help groups (SHGs) in 1987 (Tankha, 2012).

Thus, across various parts of India, NGOs, working with communities, were experimenting with multiple approaches to mobilize and create people's institutions. These SHGs were the innovations of the local people, mechanisms that they stumbled upon and created through trial and error to cope with the challenges of their lives in order to build solidarity amongst themselves and to tackle their consumption or production needs while freeing themselves from usurious informal credit. These were not donor-induced interventions, nor were they blindly mimicking the Grameen Bank's[15] microcredit model of borrowing based on joint liability. It is important to note here that the Grameen Bank model is only one among many different models of microfinance practised around the world.

Around the same period, the government of India too was actively looking for mechanisms to improve access to rural credit. The All India Debt and Investment Survey 1981 showed that the informal sector provided 38% of total rural household debt. The poor were particularly dependent on the informal sources, and bank financing (both credit and savings) had very high transaction costs for banks and rural poor alike (Siebel & Dave, 2002). All the previous governmental efforts, such as cooperative credit societies, bank nationalization (done in the 1960s) and subsidies through commercial and rural banks (done in the 1980s) had failed. There were massive defaults, and the target population was being excluded from the formal financial system. The government realized that it could not provide the much needed credit to the rural poor in a cheap and cost-effective manner and was actively scouting for mechanisms to enable this. It formed NABARD (National Bank for Agriculture and Rural Development), an apex bank, in 1983 for this purpose. NABARD saw productive possibilities in the SHGs being formed and facilitated by NGOs and entered into a dialogue with them.

The government of India was among the first to lay claim to and appropriate the 'SHG innovation' of NGOs and the community. In 1982, it launched the Development of Women and Children in Rural Areas (DWCRA) program for forming women's groups and routing subsidized credit to them (Bishnoi & Singh, 2007). It was felt that, through this process, at least some of the money would be in the hands of the women who could use it to improve the condition of their families. The voluntary organizations played along, and in most cases facilitated this large-scale program.

On the international scene, Germany was implementing its own domestic version of informal financial intermediation. Observing the developments in Asia, namely Indian, Bangladeshi and Indonesian experiences, GTZ (one of the German donors) turned to Asia and participated in the APRACA (Asia-Pacific Rural and Agricultural Credit Association)[16] (Siebel, 2005). In 1986, GTZ shared their bank-linkage idea with the APRACA at Nanjing Workshop, and in Kathmandu in December 1986 the linkage approach was adopted by the APRACA (Tankha, 2012). Some Indian organizations, including NABARD, were members of APRACA. Back in India, informed by its exchanges with NGOs and the APRACA, NABARD supported an action research project of Myrada in 1987 by providing a grant of $21,978 (Rs.1 million) for onward lending to credit management groups of women in Myrada's intervention areas. The lessons learnt in this project paved the way for microfinance in India (Rao, 2008).

These early steps in microfinance were being taken at a momentous time for India. In 1991, India had sought help from the International Monetary Fund (IMF) to tide over its macroeconomic crisis. Liberalization and privatization ensued bit by bit. Initially, these developments had not touched microfinance, but in the later years, they became a key driver for its acceleration. The following account of developments in this area covering a period of roughly 20 years has been divided into four quinquennia for the sake of convenience.

1990–1995: Hesitant and modest moves

In July 1991, NABARD started a pilot project to lend to 500 SHGs promoted by NGOs. The guidelines specified that the groups should have been in existence for six months and have demonstrated a capacity to manage themselves as well as their savings. The credit ratio was fixed in the range of 1:1 to 1:4 (savings to credit) per group, but ideally that ratio was not expected to be more than 1:2 (Tankha, 2012). During these early years, 1991–1995, a total of 2122 SHGs were linked and Rs.0.02 billion was lent to them (NABARD data cited in Tankha, 2012). NABARD was funding this scheme by refinancing the commercial banks who were actually lending to the SHGs. Other national and international agencies, like Friends of Women's World Banking (FWWB) (India) and International Fund for Agriculture Development (IFAD), were also funding some of these NGOs and SHGs. The size of the groups varied from 15 to 25 and then settled on 20 members.

The SHGs promoted by the NGOs in the late 1970s and 1980s had emerged as quite mature and competent groups. These voluntary organizations were actively co-creating federations of SHGs as community-based and -owned membership organizations to manage both their savings and credit and other developmental activities. Sri Padmavathi Mahila Sangham (in Andhra Pradesh) was the first SHG federation to be registered in the country. SHG promotion was still a non-mainstream activity; not many NGOs were engaged in this. The vocabulary in use during this period was 'SHGs', 'capacity building', 'revolving loan fund' and 'thrift'. The terms 'microfinance' and 'microcredit' were conspicuous by their absence; so too were the emphases on scaling up, and operational and financial self-sufficiency. The most prevalent model at the time was the NGO-promoted SHG-federation model. Federations were primarily mechanisms to ensure that decision-making remained in the hands of the community (and thus built their competence), not simply a method of achieving economies of scale or disbursing credit.

1996–2000: Crisis and campaign

In 1996, both the Reserve Bank of India and NABARD had specified that lending to SHGs was to be treated as part of regular operations of banks and should be incorporated into their plans. Bankers were encouraged to promote SHGs. Training for both promotion and assessment of SHGs for bank financing was provided to bankers through NABARD. Later, NABARD explicitly prohibited retention of SHG's savings as explicit or implicit collateral by banks. Slowly, lending to SHGs was gathering momentum. In 1996–1997 alone, close to 4000 SHGs received funds for onward lending. For the first time, the Grameen Bank model was being mentioned in some places in India and being practised by a few like SHARE of Andhra Pradesh.

These positive experiences were occurring in the midst of an unfolding crisis in agriculture and rural India. The structural adjustment policies mandated by the IMF led to neglect of infrastructure building in agriculture along with rising input costs and subsidies. (Chand, n.d.). Post–World Trade Organization (WTO), the impact on agriculture was even more severe. "GDP in agriculture rose at the rate of 3.16 percent during 1990–91 to 1995–96 [i.e. before WTO reforms] and at the rate of 1.75 percent during 1996–97 to 2001–02 [i.e. post WTO reform period]" (Chand, n.d.). The steady decline in agriculture led to a vast loss of livelihoods in the rural areas (Gupta, 2005), posing a great challenge to the liberalization agenda of the government of India. Elections in some of the key states showed that the voters rejected *liberalization* and IMF-sponsored policies.

But all was not well with the IMF and the World Bank either. A United Nations Conference on Trade and Development (UNCTAD) study showed widening disparities: the rich 20% had 83% of the world's income by 1990 (Bello, Bullard, Chomthongdi, Adams & Shalmali, 2000). The failure of structural adjustment in Africa and Latin America was only too obvious. The rise in absolute poverty and the intense hardships faced by the people posed a severe threat to the legitimacy of the Washington Consensus. Amidst all this, at a meeting of the Donor Working Group in Paris in June 1994, CGAP[17] was launched for concerted and coordinated funding of poverty alleviation. With a $30 million initial grant and office space from the World Bank, CGAP began addressing poverty so that 'adjustment had a human face' (World Bank, 2004). The World Bank's Sustainable Banking with the Poor project started studying some of the models from the global inventory of 1000 microfinance practitioners it put together in 1995–1996 (Ledgerwood, 1999). Grameen Bank featured prominently in these studies as a replicable, scalable, sustainable and cost-effective model (Khandker, 1996), marking out Muhammad Yunus/ Grameen Bank as the brand ambassador of microfinance.

Poverty and women's empowerment emerged as key themes against a backdrop of structural adjustment policies from conferences held under the UN auspices (e.g., World Summit on Social

Development[18] and the Beijing Conference on Women[19]). These record-setting events effectively demonstrated that the Rest cannot be taken for granted. It was during this time that John Hatch (FINCA[20] founder), along with Sam Daley-Harris (RESULTS Foundation president), realized that programs need to be scaled up to tackle the poverty problem. Grameen's model of joint liability groups was scalable, and Muhammad Yunus was supporting their proposal. Together, they embarked upon the "100 million poor by a decade" goal for microcredit, i.e., the Microcredit Summit Campaign (Davis & Khosla, n.d.). CGAP saw this development as an opportunity to quickly deliver credit for microenterprise to the poor and thereby alleviate poverty and enhance women's empowerment. The Summit Campaign showed a way for the Washington Consensus to redeem itself as a poverty alleviator. In February 1997, with the sponsorship of CGAP and the UN, the Microcredit Summit Campaign to reach 100 million poor with microcredit within a decade was launched at a global conference of 3000 delegates (including heads of state, microfinance practitioners and civil society members).

The campaign mobilized a 'scale' frame for microfinance by focusing attention on the vastness of poverty and therefore the need to pursue models that could be 'scaled up to large numbers quickly'. The scale frame laid emphasis on "building sustainable, scalable financial institutions." (Davis & Khosla, n.d.: 19). The campaign played multiple roles: "goal-setter, progress counter, convener and conference organizer, political mobilizer and advocate, commissioner of new research and writing on core themes, packager of tools, information disseminator and best practice trainer" (Davis & Khosla, n.d.: 5). As Davis and Khosla suggest, the campaign worked on "mobilizing structures (by strengthening the networks of organizations and individuals in the field), political opportunities (by generating unprecedented international exposure) and framing processes (by giving the field a goal to rally around)" (p. 22).

The United Nations, various donor agencies through CGAP and the World Bank all actively promoted microfinance in almost all of their activities. When their microfinance approaches were criticized for prioritizing financial sustainability and *not* meeting the needs of the poor, the campaign advocated that financial sustainability would enable meeting the needs of the poor. Thus dissent was systematically seen as myth which needed to be shattered, and the campaign worked hard at it "by deliberately calling into question some of the field's dominant ideologies and (re-framing) them as opportunities to 'do better'. The campaign didn't ignore the field's myths, but rather incorporated them into their plan of action and strategy" (p. 20).

RESULTS became the agency which tracked the performance of microfinance organizations throughout the world. That, officially, RESULTS was an NGO helped the Washington Consensus remain in the background, but it should come as no surprise that CGAP (or rather the World Bank because, even after eight years, the World Bank provided the bulk of the funding for CGAP[21]) is the biggest sponsor for the summit/campaign. The campaign, through capacity-building programs, popularized poverty assessment tools and credit management tools like financial ratios to assess financial self-sufficiency. It did not explicitly push for the Grameen model but gently prodded practitioners in that direction by celebrating those organizations which achieved such sufficiency and scale (Davis & Khosla, n.d.). CGAP, on the other hand, was explicit. While its first phase (1995–1998) was aimed at consensus building and the development of common vocabulary in the field by supporting practitioners (67% of its Phase I budget went to grants to practitioners around the world), its second phase (1998–2003) explicitly focused on commercialization of microfinance and capacity building. It positioned itself as a "knowledge generator" of best practices: this expenditure increased from 5% to 47% in Phase II (World Bank, 2004: viii).

Thus *people's innovation* of self-help was *appropriated* as microfinance by the West. The campaign and CGAP positioned themselves as the "knowledge generators" through the promotion of performance metrics and best practices when in fact the innovations were being made by common people. The Summit Declaration stated that "it is difficult to incorporate a successful microcredit program into an institution that has relief or social-service approach to helping the poor," thus strategically privileging the credit supply–focused, scalable Grameen Bank model. In other models like SHGs that focused on group processes in saving-lending decisions so as to develop member competencies, credit supply started after six to twelve months of group formation. But since all performance measures and rhetoric of success revolved around recovery rates and financial sustainability, these path-dependent SHG models fared adversely on financial parameters as break-even was delayed; they were also difficult to scale as replicating group processes in large numbers is difficult.

By selectively appropriating a 'successful' credit supply technique and the empowering effects of other models, the campaign generated the myth of empowerment through scalable microfinance. Empowerment was assumed away in the measurement and was explicit only in public speeches, where it served to depict microfinance as a mechanism of women's empowerment instead of an exploitative tool. A cursory perusal of the various capacity-building tools promoted by these agencies and widely available on the Internet reveals this. The West conveniently *usurped* an idea that did not belong to it, transmogrified that idea in a fashion that benefitted its own purposes, turned it into the standard of excellence (delinked from the local experience) and then promoted itself as the benevolent 'knowledge generator' and evaluator of the practice of these ideas in local communities. This appropriation was probably necessary to redeem the loss of faith in Western-sponsored institutions.

Back in India, the Indian government, challenged by its own people on poverty alleviation, also jumped onto this microfinance bandwagon. The hesitant steps of the early years gave way to a massive policy focus on SHG and microfinance promotion. Interestingly, the words 'microfinance' and 'SHGs' started to be used synonymously. A special microfinance fund was created to provide money for SHGs. The government's subsidy schemes were also refashioned to the SGSY scheme to make them more like the SHGs.

In the civil society space, the October 1998 conference of the Women's World Banking (WWB)[22] in India, while alluding to the global refrain on microcredit, also stressed the vision of "building strong, sustainable institutions committed to serving poor women, with poor women leading the way" (Barry, 1998). The Consensus Report (1998) of the conference on "Building India's leadership in Microfinance" explicitly recognized the vision of "Microfinance . . . through investments in institutions and people . . ." (p. 2). It acknowledged that, "in a country as large and diverse as India, different approaches, methodologies . . . are needed . . . and should be encouraged" (p. 3). The strategy involved "building a strong . . . community-based development financial institutions (CFIs) with the help of NGOs and others" (p. 3). It positively stressed that "[E]xperience in India demonstrates the success of people's structures . . . groups. . . . in which people have a stake in the ownership and governance of the organizations. . . . They create the permanent organizing structures at the local levels . . . more emphasis needs to be placed on building upon indigenous organizations . . ." (p. 6). There was a clear recognition of the benefits of intermediation provided by the NGOs, and therefore it advocated the creation of distinct organizational arrangements for managing microfinance in/by the NGOs, as well as greater policy support through appropriate legal apparatus and necessary funding. Though Washington's performance standards were acknowledged by the self-regulatory body Sa-Dhan,[23] it is interesting to note that out of the 11 founding members, all but one were community-based self-help promoters and earliest innovators of this idea in India. One can make an educated guess about the bent of the discussions on standard setting in this body.

Thus the second quinquennium, which was marked by a crisis of the state and the neoliberal regime, represented the full-scale appropriation of the idea and practice of microfinance both by the Indian government and the World Bank.[24] An extensive rhetoric and set of practices emerged and consolidated around scale and financial sustainability, and even though the Indian practice also used some of this rhetoric, it explicitly deviated by clearly acknowledging the SHG practice in India and the need for its furtherance. Thus, the Indian practitioners *resisted* falling in line with the global practice and chose to suitably modify it to meet their needs. It is a case of shrewd politics that features an overt surface acceptance of the Western rhetoric and then its overhaul to suit local needs.

2001–2005: Accelerated microfinance

Riding on the heavy inflow of funding, advocacy and promotional activity, both by the Indian government and World Bank, Indian SHGs and microfinance grew phenomenally. Several models, including the Grameen model, individual banking and commercial finance companies, were in operation now. By 2005–2006, over 2 million SHGs had been provided bank linkage (Tankha, 2012). While the largest number of new clients was added by the Grameen replicators, "federations seemed to be *a fait accompli*" with the existence of over 60,000 SHG federations in the country by 2005 (Ghate, 2007). The SHG promoters far outnumbered the Grameen microfinance institutions (MFIs). Grameen replicators, however, gathered all the attention in the media for their meteoric growth, adding thousands of clients per month. These replicators found great favor (for scale and financial sustainability) in the West, with SKS Microfinance's founder Vikram Akula meriting a book with Harvard Business Publishing.

The regulation and capacity building of Indian microfinance were still within the control of the earliest SHG innovators (Sa-Dhan), who, while consistently favoring the SHG model, kept the space and debate open for Grameen replicators. The SHG people acknowledged that their operating costs were higher but pointed out also that SHGs were more sustainable and actually led to empowerment. SHG promoters also warned of an imminent implosion in the Grameen model, noting that the over 90% recovery rates of the Grameen model would plummet once the seven or eight loan ascendency cycles were complete (refer to note 15) because the Grameen model did not focus on enhancing and facilitating the capacity and capability of the client. The 2002 edited book by India's leading microfinance experts, *Beyond Microcredit: Putting Development Back into Microfinance*, proclaimed this.

That the government of India encouraged the rhetoric of empowerment helped. So did NABARD's comfort with and faith in the SHG model. The dual organizational model of the SHG promoting NGOs/community-owned microcredit MFIs[25] was explicitly promoted as against the Grameen replicators. Several such NGO/MFIs (federations) were formed during this period. Sanghamitra is one such MFI promoted by Myrada. In this Myrada/Sanghamitra model, the size and purpose of loans are controlled by the community group, and so are the savings. Sanghamitra explicitly contracts with federations and NGOs for capacity building of the community groups. While financially sustainable and managed by conventional finance personnel, Sanghamitra has an explicit corporate policy of not pursuing scale blindly and managing a limited portfolio of Rs.30–35 crores. It intends to spread the impact by enabling the formation of other Sanghamitras in other places (Fernandez, 2005).

This quinquennium was thus a prolific time: huge growth in outreach, multiple models, vibrant innovations and live debates. Microfinance in India was far from homogenization or harmonization by the West. The community and the NGOs continued to thrive and strongly controlled the trajectory without creating polar oppositions. In fact, much of the growth by the NGO/MFIs was achieved by tapping into the funds made available by the West's new focus on microfinance and by using the terms and ideology of microfinance as an umbrella that was opened when the NGOs needed it and closed when it became a hindrance.

2006 to 2010 and after: An implosion and reassertion

The sector's growth continued during this period. CGAP was bringing out documents on issues that NGOs need to consider while transforming into MFIs (Lauer, 2008). In 2010, Vikram Akula's SKS had successfully launched an initial public offering that was oversubscribed, opening the doors to private equity instead of grant or soft loan funding for microfinance. The top five MFIs in India were Grameen replicators who reached out to 14.6 million clients. Yet, the people-based SHG models were more popular. In 2010, while SHG membership was at 59.6 million, MFI clients stood at 26.7 million, but the MFI average loan size was higher at Rs.6870 as against Rs.4572 for SHGs. There were over 166,700 federations (Puhazendhi, 2012). Regulation was still marked by interim, ad hoc pronouncements by the Reserve Bank of India and the government, both of which were trying to straddle the twin objects of empowerment and fiduciary control (Jammulamadaka, 2011). The debate was still wide open.

Grameen replicators started showing early signs of crisis in 2009 with intermittently falling recoveries in some pockets in South India. The loan ascendency cycles were almost complete for several old clients. And then in late 2010, the crisis was full-blown, with suicides by the loanees (some were SKS clients) to avoid harassment. It was called India's 'subprime crisis'. There were also concerns that the promoters were building personal wealth using public funds (Sriram, 2010). In the race to scale up, these MFIs were competing with one another, lending to the same individuals and/or in volumes way above the repayment capacity of the borrowers (e.g. a loan of Rs.150,000 for a weekly income of Rs.600) (*The Hindu*, 2012). The state government of Andhra Pradesh reacted sharply by bringing in a very strict regulation that curtailed MFI operations. The challenges and problems of the highly scalable credit-only approach were manifest, and fiduciary regulation became strong, putting brakes on the Grameen juggernaut.

Through all this turmoil, organizations like Myrada/Sanghamitra continued to perform as per their mandate. Sanghamitra had reached only 8000 SHGs by March 2008 with an average loan of Rs.60,000/SHG even after 13 years of existence (paltry by Grameen standards). Yet they were also financially self-sufficient and even managed to achieve an A credit rating by M-Cril, the microfinance credit rating agency (M-Cril, 2008). Another NGO/SHG microfinance practitioner, SKDRDP, demonstrated that SHG-based operations did not imply 'small is beautiful' and that growth in outreach was possible by reaching out to 0.11 million SHGs. Though a late entrant into microfinance, SKDRDP is the sixth largest MFI in India and the largest NGO/MFI anywhere in the world. They continue to remain an NGO and provide a range of interventions and capacity building for managing SHGs, livelihoods, health and a host of other services. SKDRDP aims at an annual growth of 50%.

The implosion in credit disbursal and defaults in South India livened the debate among the various models. Government now saw most MFIs as the villains destroying rural well-being against whom the public needed to be protected. Capital supply for microfinance was affected, with bank lending becoming cautionary. This adversely affected even the NGO/SHG practice, and greater attention was brought onto the differential risks and benefits associated with the different models. ACCESS's annual report on the state of sector in 2012 read, "It is not necessarily because all the microfinance institutions (MFIs) were irresponsible or were not conscious of their responsibility to customers and society obligations; but like in any other industry, in microfinance industry too there were a few erring institutions that were not mindful of the hardship caused to their clients through their methods." A common code of conduct was now practiced by all, including the Grameen replicators. Myrada's founder, Aloysius Fernandez, in an interview explicitly stated, "SHGs were never intended to be financial (intermediation) institutions only . . . they were empowering institutions which included building self-confidence, social values . . . the habit of savings gave the members a degree of independence from large farmers (who are the money lenders) which got strengthened by Bank [sic] loans . . . It was the management of savings and credit which was empowering, not provision of credit per se" (Puhazendhi,2012: 35).

Community-based federations became strong institutional options for institutional sustainability of microfinance. This zeitgeist was reflected in the Microfinance India summit awards of 2010. SKDRDP was awarded the Microfinance India Institution of the Year (the previous year's winner had been a Grameen replicator). In the same ceremony, Aloysius Fernandez, the founder of Myrada/Sanghamitra, received the Individual Who Made Significant Contribution to the Sector award, and Ela Bhatt of SEWA received the Special Jury award. In 2011, Sanghamitra received the MFI of the Year award in the small and medium category alongside Ujjivan, a Grameen replicator in the large MFI category. Things had come full circle. There was now pressure on NABARD to examine ways of providing policy support to NGOs for developing and strengthening the capabilities of such federations and other community-based SHGs, especially given the renewed focus of NABARD on SHGs in its SHG-2 program (Srinivasan, 2012).

This period of the last quinquennium and after has thus seen the microcredit bubble burst. There was a crisis of survival and everybody suffered. The Summit Campaign too had some fretful moments brought on by this crisis. But the sector has shown signs of recovery. There has been a reassertion of the SHG and its empowering effects, as well as its rediscovery by the mainstream microfinance community in the country. The Summit Campaign may not have paid much attention to these shifts in meaning and practices on the ground in India, but it all still remains part of *microcredit*!

Conclusion

From the vantage point of 'hegemony' or 'ideology critique' (Mumby, 2004), it is difficult to accommodate any notion of resistance since domination is complete and the agency of the Other is limited to futile attempts at localized interpretations of 'fixed meanings' and 'ideologies'. Thus resistance itself gets narrowly framed and is seen as operating within the interstices of hegemonic domination. This appears to be the view shared by the *critics* of microfinance, and therefore their understanding of 'the Other in microfinance' is reduced to one of passivity. But the Indian tale of microfinance is far removed from such a hegemonic view of global microfinance that limits the agency of the Rest. This tale of Indian microfinance is a tale of resistance through 'informed and knowledgeable action' by the NGOs/SHGs with insights into the 'discursive and political conditions' of the discourse of microfinance, or what Mumby (2004) calls dialectics of power and resistance.

As our discussion shows, the NGO/SHGs were engaged in an ongoing effort with the government, fellow Grameen replicators and Summit representatives and others to fix and refix meanings and practices of microfinance. The NGO/SHGs were thus both participants in and creators of the discourse of microfinance in India. While NGO/SHGs let the West or even the Indian state appropriate a practice that was theirs without much noise, the NGO/SHGs retained control on those aspects that mattered most to their world, namely, the way microfinance was understood and practiced in India. The West did seek and continues to seek to 'discipline' this field through the discourse of performance management, but the Indian practice remains resistant by building in structural defenses and enablers in Indian policy. The account here has amply demonstrated that Indian SHG pioneers are anything but naïve. The manner in which Sa-Dhan (i.e., the SHG/NGOs) in coordination with the government-enabled plurality of practice, even though several key members of Sa-Dhan differed radically with the other Grameen replicator models, is a profound statement on voice and representation. They did point out the dangers of alternate models but never sought to homogenize or harmonize the field. Instead, they kept an animated debate alive, demonstrating how democratic politics can be practised.

One could argue that this resistance does not mean much, because, as things stand, the deep structure of domination is still in favor of privileging the West and that the West continues to seek to discipline and 'civilize' the Rest. Given that no domination can ever be total, these ground-level resistances are only to be expected, and this just provides further evidence of oppressive structures because these resistances remain only in the margin, on the periphery, and are not permitted to be the voice of the Centre. That Myrada/Sanghamitra[26] has been a persistent and perennial practice in India does not alter the fact that the Summit Campaign continues to frame and exemplify microfinance globally – that the 'Centre' remains forever the 'Subject'.

But this argument misses a point. This Centre is a Subject in a frame where it has appointed itself as the Centre/Subject. In a similar fashion, Myrada/Sanghamitra is a Subject in a frame which matters (more) to Myrada/Sanghamitra's life-world, namely, Indian microfinance. There is no reason or purpose for Myrada/Sanghamitra or for any of the other NGOs/SHGs of India to eschew this Subjecthood for being a Subject in the Centre created by the West, for this would then imply a simple trading of the Centre and periphery where the periphery is the new Centre. The domination continues; only the tyrant is now different. The very fact that Myrada/Sanghamitra has resisted this reversal underlines the transformative character of the politics being played: it is a displacement of the Centre-periphery in favor of multiple centres-peripheries, a recognition and acknowledgement of the fact that life-worlds in Africa, Latin America or elsewhere in Asia could throw up different possibilities and that *they* – the NGO/MFIs of India – do not have a legitimate right/locus to intervene. That the West is unable to see *this* as transformative politics and instead views this as naïve localism is because of its implication in Eurocentrism and the resulting inability to imagine multiple subject positions.

Notes

1 The author wishes to acknowledge the feedback received from Jessica Heinemann-Piper and Pragyan Rath and the comments received from anonymous reviewers in improving this essay.
2 The term 'microfinance' refers to the provision of a range of financial services to the poor, including savings, credit and insurance services. Microcredit, on the other hand, is distinguished by an exclusive focus on provision of credit to the poor. The terms 'microfinance' and 'microcredit' have been used interchangeably in this chapter unless otherwise specified in the text.
3 A cursory look at the websites of all multilateral, bilateral, private donor agencies and international NGOs reveals this posture.
4 'Supranational unification movement' refers to the convergence in global institutional and legal frameworks, policies and practices of the global trade regime and global development architecture. It draws upon private international trade law.
5 See Weber (2001) and Karim (2008) for the critical views.
6 See the working paper by Murdoch and Haley for a good summary of the various studies on microfinance: http://www.microfinancegateway.org/gm/document-1.9.29382/analysis%20of%20the%20effects.pdf
7 Refer to the Microcredit Summit Declaration of 1997: http://www.microcreditsummit.org/declaration.htm. Accessed 1 March 2013.
8 The Summit Campaign is a registered nonprofit based in the United States. The campaign was launched at a conference organized in 1997 by the RESULTS Foundation with the explicit aim of promoting microfinance for poverty alleviation and reaching 100 million poor. See http://www.microcreditsummit.org/about-the-summits2.html.
9 RESULTS is a political advocacy organization based in the United States. Headed by Sam Daley-Harris, it spearheaded the campaign and continues its monitoring to date.

10 See Jammulamadaka (2009) for an overview of NGOs and their development in India.

11 All of these are grassroots NGOs in India.

12 'NGOs' ('nongovernmental organizations') is the common nomenclature today to identify organizations like these. However, all such organizations were called voluntary organizations to acknowledge their altruistic nature. The term 'voluntary organizations' draws attention to the fact that these organizations and their workers are part of the community in multiple ways, and the distinction between the community and the organization as an external agent is extremely difficult and probably superfluous.

13 Refer to Tankh (2012), Shetty (2012) and others for an overview of the origins of microfinance in India.

14 It is difficult to even pinpoint the exact date because it emerged through a series of casual conversations amongst the NGO members and the community.

15 Grameen Bank model uses groups of five members who receive loans within weeks of group formation. Members repaying loans automatically qualify for larger loans, leading to a series of seven or eight progressively larger loans or loan ascendency cycles and thus providing an incentive for loan repayment. The savings credit and member management is done by the bank staff.

16 APRACA, formed in 1977, is a Food and Agriculture Organization–supported association of central banks and rural banks to promote rural finance.

17 The ten members who founded CGAP in 1995 are the World Bank, UNDP, African Development Bank, Asian Development Bank, UNCDF, U.S., Canada and the Netherlands. Initially known as Consultative Group to Assist the Poorest, it was later rechristened as Consultative Group to Assist the Poor.

18 March 1995, Copenhagen, Denmark.

19 Held in 1995, this conference highlighted the vulnerability of women and their ability to manage money (credit and enterprise).

20 FINCA provides financial services to the world's lowest-income entrepreneurs. It is an anti-poverty organization whose work is aimed at creating employment and reducing poverty worldwide. It is headquartered in Washington, D.C. (www.finca.org). Both FINCA's and RESULTS' websites reveal that they are very closely connected with USAID and the World Bank and thus part of the key ideation group in microfinance. FINCA's founder was a USAID staff member, and he was actively involved in poverty alleviation projects in Latin America. The RESULTS' board includes key U.S. policy-makers.

21 See the Consultative Group to Assist the Poor, the World Bank Operations Evaluation Department.

22 WWB's affiliates from 60 countries, along with practitioners and government representatives from across India, participated in this conference.

23 Sa-Dhan was informally launched in August 1998 and formally in 1999 as a standards-setting body for microfinance practitioners in India in the wake of global and national policy developments on microfinance. SHARE is the only Grameen replicator out of the 11 founding members, which included PRADAN, Myrada, RGVN and FWWB.

24 'The World Bank' is being used here to refer to the West broadly.

25 The NGO and the MFI federation worked in close co-operation with each other. This organizational model served to situate decision making within the hands of the community and enabled capacity building support by the NGO even while pursuing fiduciary and legal compliance.

26 'Myrada/Sanghamitra' is used as a general term for NGO/SHG practitioners.

References

Barry, N. (1998). Inauguration speech at the Women's World Banking Global Meeting, Ahmedabad, October 30.

Bello, W., Bullard, N., Chomthongdi, J-C., Adams, C. & G. Shalmali (Eds.), *Prague 2000: Why we need to decommission the World Bank and IMF*. Bangkok: Focus on the Global South.

Bishnoi, I., & Singh, V. (2007). Awareness of DWCRA programme among rural women. *International Journal of Rural Studies, 14*(1). Retrieved on March 5, 2013 from http://www.vri-online.org.uk/ijrs/April2007/Awareness%20of%20DWCRA%20programme%20among%20rural%20women%20in%20India.pdf.

Buss, Terry. (1999). Microenterprise in international perspective: An overview of the issues. *Journal of Economic Development, 1*(1). Retrieved from www.spaef.com/sample.html.

Chand, Ramesh. (n.d.). *Impact of trade liberalization and related reforms on India's agricultural sector, rural food security, income and poverty*. Retrieved on March 5, 2013 from http://depot1.gdnet.org/hind/pdf2/gdn_library/annual_conferences/fifth_annual_conference/chand_paper.pdf.

Consensus Report. (1998). The workshop of leading microfinance practitioners on building India's leadership in microfinance, New Delhi, August 1–2.

Davis, S., & Khosla, V. (n.d.). Taking stock of the Microcredit Summit Campaign: What worked and what didn't work 1997–2006? What is needed 2007–2015?. Retrieved on March 5, 2013 from www.microcreditsummit.org/papers/Assocsession/DavisKhosla.pdf.

Delaney, J. (2010). The tools of empire? Micro-finance, neo-liberalism, and the Vietnamese State. *Canadian Journal of Development Studies, 29*: 3–4.

Fernandez, A. (2005). "Why Sanghamitra is different?" Retrieved on March 5, 2013 from http://www.microfinancegateway.org/gm/document-1.9.24232/89.pdf.

Fisher, T., & Sriram, M. S. (2002). *Beyond microcredit: Putting development back into micro-finance.* New Delhi: Vistaar.

Ghate, P. (2007). *Microfinance in India: A state of the sector report, 2007.* New Delhi: Sage.

Gupta. (2005). Imperialism, liberalisation regime and the devastation of Indian agriculture. *People's March, 6*(4). Retrieved on March 5, 2013 from http://www.bannedthought.net/India/PeoplesMarch/PM1999–2006/archives/2005/april2k5/Agriculture.htm.

Harper, M., Iyer, L. & Rosser, J. (2012). *Whose sustainability counts?* New Delhi: Sage-Vistaar.

Hulme, D., & Mosley, P. (1996). *Finance against poverty. Vol. 2: Country case studies.* New York: Routledge.

Hulme, D., & Mosley, P. (1997). Finance for the poor or poorest? Financial innovation, poverty and vulnerability. In G. D. Wood & I. Sharif (Eds.), *Who needs credit? Poverty and finance in Bangladesh.* Dhaka: University Press.

Jammulamadaka, N. (2009). Do NGOs differ? How, with what consequences? *Vikalpa*, December.

Jammulamadaka, N. (2011). Microfinance in India: Promotional policy of fragmented ad hoc reactions. 3rd International CIRIEC Research Conference on the Social Economy, Valladolid, Spain, April 6–8 [ISBN. No. 978–84–95003–85–0].

Karim, L. (2008). Demystifying micro-credit: The Grameen Bank, NGOs, and neoliberalism in Bangladesh. *Cultural Dynamics, 20*(5): 5–29.

Karnani, A. (2007). Microfinance misses its mark. *Stanford Social Innovation Review*, Summer. Retrieved on March 5, 2013 from http://www.ssireview.org/articles/entry/microfinance_misses_its_mark

Khandker, S. R. (1996). Grameen Bank: Impact, costs and program sustainability. *Asian Development Review, 14*(1): 65–85. Retrieved on March 5, 2013 from http://www.microfinancegateway.org/gm/document-1.9.28425/1835.pdf.

Lauer, K. (2008). Transforming NGO MFIs: Critical ownership issues to consider. Occasional Paper 13. Washington, DC: CGAP.

Ledgerwood, J. (1999). *Microfinance handbook: Sustainable banking with the poor.* Washington, DC: World Bank Publications. Retrieved on March 5, 2013 from https://openknowledge.worldbank.org/bitstream/handle/10986/12383/18771.pdf?sequence=1.

M-Cril. (2008). Rating of Sanghamitra rural financial services. Retrieved on March 5, 2013 from http://www.m-cril.com/Sanghamitra.pdf.

Microcredit Summit. (n.d.). Declaration and plan of action. Retrieved on March 5, 2013 from http://www.microcreditsummit.org/declaration.htm and http://www.microfinanceindia.org/content/68/previous-awards.php.

Mumby, D. (2004). Discourse, power and ideology: Unpacking the critical approach. In D. Grant, C. Hardy, C. Oswick & L. L. Putnam (Eds.), *The Sage handbook of organizational discourse.* Thousand Oaks, CA: Sage.

Puhazhendi, V. (2012). *Microfinance India: State of the Sector Report 2012.* New Delhi: Sage.

Rahman, Aminur. 1999. Micro-credit initiatives for equitable and sustainable development: Who pays? *World Development. 27*(1): 67–82.

Rao, Muralidhara K. (2008). MFIs in India: An overview. In K. G. Karmakar (Ed.), *Microfinance in India* (pp. 57–66). New Delhi: Sage.

Seibel, H. (2005). *SHG banking in India: The evolution of a rural financial innovation and the contribution of GTZ.* Mumbai & New Delhi: NABARD.

Shetty, S. L. (2012). *Microfinance in India: Issues, problems and prospects: A critical review of literature.* New Delhi: Academic Foundation.

Siebel, H., & R. H. Dave. (2002). Commercial aspects of SHG-banking in India. Paper presented at the seminar on SHG-bank Linkage Programme, New Delhi, November 25 –26.

Srinivasan, G. (2012). *Microfinance India: The social performance report 2012,* New Delhi: Sage.

Sriram, M. S. (2010). Commercialisation of microfinance in India: Discussion of the emperor's apparel. *Economic and Political Weekly, XLV*(24), June 12: 65–73.

Summary of Consensus Report on Building India's Leadership in microfinance. (1998). Women's World Banking Global Meeting, Ahmedabad, November 6.

Tankha, A. (2012). *Banking on self help groups: Twenty years on.* New Delhi: Sage.

The Week. (1988). Man of the Year: Dr. Parameswara Rao. December 27–January 2.

Weber, H. (2001). The imposition of a global development architecture: The example of microcredit. Working Paper 77/01. Coventry: CSGR.

The World Bank. (2004). The Consultative Group to Assist the Poor: Addressing challenges of globalization: An independent evaluation of the World Bank's approach to global programs. Retrieved on March 5, 2013 from http://lnweb90.worldbank.org/oed/oeddoclib.nsf/DocUNIDViewForJavaSearch/C29F384 F74E0EC5785256F240050D440/$file/gppp_cgap_wp.pdf.

23

Exceptional opportunities

Hierarchies of race and nation in the United States Peace Corps recruitment materials

Jenna N. Hanchey

A few years ago, I was contacted by the U.S. Peace Corps recruiter at a large public university in the United States, who asked if I would be part of a panel of returned volunteers at a recruitment event. She then said she would love to meet me and that I was welcome to stop by her office anytime to reminisce about Peace Corps experiences. I took her up on her offer and dropped by one day to chat. When I entered the office, a small room on the fourth floor of the student center, she was in the midst of a conversation with someone else. Sitting down to wait, I noticed a colorful display on my right. A rack of pamphlets advertising Peace Corps service possibilities caught my eye – and held it when I noticed the titles. "An Exceptional Opportunity for Latinos," one read. "An Exceptional Opportunity for African Americans," said another. "The Business of Helping Others Help Themselves." "Use Your Talents to Help Others Grow."

As a postcolonial scholar, I was immediately intrigued and started rifling through the rack for a sample of each type to take home. My actions garnered an odd look from the recruiter. "What are you going to do with those?" she asked me after her guest had left.

"Study them," I replied.

"I see." She looked vaguely anxious. "What department are you from again?"

"Communication," I answered. "I'm interested in how these represent race and gender."

She visibly relaxed. "Oh! Well, obviously each minority group has their own pamphlet, and both men and women are pictured in all of them."

For many organizations, representations of diversity are enough to warrant pride in the organization, as if images are in and of themselves an accomplishment of equality (Ahmed, 2006a). Although 24% of current Peace Corps volunteers are minorities (Peace Corps, 2013b), and the Peace Corps "actively recruits people with a variety of backgrounds and experiences" (Peace Corps, 2013d), the recruitment materials still reflect a certain understanding of who the normative volunteer – and representation of the U.S. – is and should be.

In this essay, I explore Peace Corps recruitment pamphlets as a case study that illustrates the necessity of considering the intersections of whiteness and postcolonial theories in critical analyses of international volunteer organizations. Specifically, I describe how the images and text in these pamphlets portray the volunteer of color as an oddity who needs to be persuaded and rewarded to join the Peace Corps, as opposed to the white prospective volunteers who have the privilege of choosing to "*give* two years of their lives" (Peace Corps, 2013c; emphasis added), and the interpenetration of these racializations with neocolonialism. As a communication scholar, I focus on the way communication constitutes organizational processes (Ashcraft, Kuhn, & Cooren, 2009) by examining how the recruitment pamphlets reconstruct ideas of the normative U.S. volunteer.

I first explore the ways in which communication scholarship can supplement Critical Management Studies and argue that it is especially valuable for considering international organizations. Then, after introducing intersectionality, I make the case that international volunteer organizations should be analyzed through a lens that is sensitive to both whiteness and postcolonial dynamics. Next, I contextualize the specific volunteer organization that I examine within recent work on international aid organizations writ large. In the following case study of Peace Corps recruitment pamphlets, I display ways communication scholarship can support critical management work and the importance of considering intersections of race and nation in international scholarship. Finally, I conclude with a short discussion and implications.

Communication and Critical Management Studies

Although organizational communication scholars often refer to management literature, the relationship is not reciprocal (Mumby & Stohl, 1996). However, multiple scholars have argued that organizational communication can contribute to Critical Management Studies (Ashcraft, Kuhn & Cooren, 2009; Mumby & Stohl, 1996; Taylor & Robichaud, 2004). For one, organizational communication claims that communication is constitutive of organizational processes (Ashcraft, Kuhn & Cooren, 2009; Putnam & Nicotera, 2008), which can assist management scholars in deconstructing power relations that are built into organizational structures. Second, a focus on communication reveals how text and conversation are interrelated in the construction of organizational action (Taylor & Robichaud, 2004), allowing the discursive to be connected to the material (Ashcraft, Kuhn & Cooren, 2009). Third, organizational communication offers a means to challenge the dominance of the managerial voice (Mumby & Stohl, 1996), a central concern of critical management scholars as well. Finally, organizational communication problematizes universal knowledge claims and rationalities (Mumby & Stohl, 1996) and presents experimental methods of destabilizing such rationalities (Broadfoot & Munshi, 2007).

However, organizational communication is not the only subfield of communication studies that relates to Critical Management Studies. The usefulness of communication writ large has been established (Ashcraft, Kuhn & Cooren, 2009), but often critical management scholars refer only to *organizational* communication texts. I argue that intercultural communication work can also be beneficial. Specifically, a focus on critical intercultural communication has recently emerged (Nakayama & Halualani, 2010) and has prompted calls for work overlapping with critical organizational studies (Allen, 2010). As Critical Management Studies moves toward analyses of transnational organizations (Connell & Wood, 2005; Hearn, 2004), examination of global processes (Baines, 2010; Gopal & Gopal, 2003) and postcolonial approaches to research (Jack, Westwood, Srinivas & Sardar, 2011; A. Prasad, 2003; Prasad, 2012), critical intercultural communication has much to offer.

For one, critical intercultural communication highlights the importance of connecting the micro to the macro level. As Nakayama and Halualani (2010) explain, the field is "best suited to pay close attention to and follow how macro conditions and structures of power . . . play into and share microacts/processes of communication between/among cultural groups/members" (p. 5). Through this specific focus on micro/macro connections, they note that "critical intercultural scholars can . . . craft timely responses and strategies for how to interrupt dominant conditions and constructions of power" (p. 5). Thus, "there are limitless possibilities for what

385

critical intercultural communication studies can shed light on in terms of intracultural and intercultural relations on local-global levels" (Nakayama & Halualani, 2010: 5). Finally, critical intercultural communication is often explicitly intersectional in orientation (Allen, 2010; Moon, 2010; Nakayama & Halualani, 2010).

Intersectionality

Although critical management scholars are beginning to make headway in intersectional studies, the complexity of contemporary power relations requires a more attentive focus. Intersectionality recognizes that "it is ultimately futile to attempt to disrupt one system [of power] without simultaneously disrupting others" (Fellows & Razack, 1998: 337). Scholars often recognize multiple fields of power; however, "[i]n the field of organization studies and organizational change there is little evidence that the importance of these intersections is acknowledged" (Holvino, 2010: 249).

Intersectionality has been richly theorized at a variety of methodological levels. West & Fenstermaker (2002), for instance, look at the embodied performance of difference. By examining how a person 'does difference,' they consider gender, race and class as intersecting performances. On the other end of the spectrum, McCall (2001) interrogates organizational processes at the macro level by studying systems and quantifiable markers of inequality. Acker (2006) is situated somewhere between, theorizing what she terms "inequality regimes" and how they function to maintain hierarchical power relations within a particular organization. Thus, her theory operates on an organizational level, rather than addressing either individual performance or systemic relations.

The preceding authors have created a solid foundation for intersectional studies in organizational work, but Holvino (2010) adds dimensions to intersectional theory that have been lacking. First, she suggests "a reconceptualization of gender, class and race as simultaneous processes of identity, institutional and social practice" (p. 262) and thus creates a connection between the disparate analytical lenses of Acker (2006), McCall (2001) and West and Fenstermaker (2002). Second, she claims that "the simultaneity of race, class and gender . . . be expanded to include ethnicity, sexuality and nation in organizational analyses for . . . the explanatory value of these categories in today's organizations can no longer be ignored" (p. 262). Thus, Holvino builds the basis for the following case study by pointing out the necessity under current global conditions to account for nation as well as race and gender and by creating a theoretical link between micro and macro processes in intersectional intercultural work.

In the following section, I use Holvino's (2010) interventions as a starting point for arguing that postcolonial and whiteness theory should be used in conjunction to perform more complex intersectional analyses of international aid – and particularly international volunteer – organizations. Scholars have argued for the importance of incorporating postcolonial theory into intersectional analyses (Baines, 2010; Leonard, 2010); however, in intranational work, dynamics of nation are often unexamined. Simultaneously, though nation takes the foreground in international work, it sometimes obscures the importance of race. By attending to intersectionality, "we are more likely to observe how power and privilege may play out in intercultural interactions" (Moon, 2010: 41), both intranationally and internationally.

Intersections of race and nation

Although race is often discussed in critical analyses of international aid, it usually refers to the race of the people being aided (Balaji, 2011; Bell, 2011), rather than that of the Western aid workers, or in the way that racial hierarchies are constructed in the aid organization itself. Those being aided are often placed at one end of a black/white dichotomy, while the Western organization is considered simply white. A thorough analysis of the way race interacts with colonization *within the aid organization itself* rarely occurs. Thus, Western international power is often equated with white dominance in a way that obscures the complex work that is necessary within the organization in order to construct and put forth such a monolithic racial projection. On the other hand, work that is not internationally focused often fails to recognize the ways in which "bodies are shaped by histories of colonialism" (Ahmed, 2006b: 111) and that scholars should not try to "understand race and racism on their own terms, without discussing colonialism as integral to them" (Ono, 2009: 14). In the U.S. Peace Corps, the racial cannot be separated from the colonial; in fact, in order to perform an analysis that takes into account the ways that these aspects affect one another, I turn to an intersectional analysis that is informed by postcolonial theory and whiteness studies.

Postcolonial theory

Postcolonial theory and criticism is a radical perspective that de-centers Western rationalities, methods, and ways of being. Postcolonialism "represents an attempt to investigate the complex and deeply fraught dynamics of modern Western colonialism and anticolonial resistance, and the ongoing significance of the colonial encounter for people's lives both in the West and non-West" (A. Prasad, 2003: 5). Thus, postcolonial theory interrogates not only the foundational remnants of colonialism in continued global life but also neocolonial representations, actions and resistances. In Critical Management Studies, postcolonialism seeks to highlight that organizational processes maintain national and cultural hierarchies as well as gender and racial hierarchies.

Even though postcolonialism is "uniquely productive and highly heterogeneous" (Prasad, 2012: 15), it still occupies a marginal position within organization studies writ large (Prasad, 2012). In fact, even within other critical fields such as feminist studies and critical race studies, postcolonial theory is not often addressed (Holvino, 2010; Ono, 2009). When considering international aid organizations, postcolonial theory cannot be overlooked. In the pamphlets that I analyze in the following case, volunteers are often pictured with Host Country Nationals,[1] and thus the relationship is presented as foundational to what makes this person an authentic Peace Corps volunteer. If an analysis were to ignore the colonial aspects of such representations, vital understandings would be missed.

Whiteness theory

Whiteness is not simply the state of having a white body but rather a socially constructed ideology that is inherently oppressive and without any biological basis, yet having material consequences (Roediger, 1991). Whiteness oppresses by façade; it is a racial identity that masquerades as non-racial, universal and 'normal' (Frankenburg, 1994). It holds a silent power, for it claims to be 'just the way things are.' Yet, at the same time, it is not monolithic and stable but changes form depending on the current social moment (Omi & Winant, 1994) or interpersonal situation (Nakayama & Krizek, 1995). In fact, whiteness is so slippery that in some situations, "[a]ntiracism even becomes a discourse of white pride" (Ahmed, 2012: 170). When whiteness is accepted as an invisible norm, differences are ignored, and "white people, their assumptions, and ways are empowered" (Grimes, 2002: 382); thus it is important to bring such invisible norms to light, that they might be dismantled.

However, there is a dearth of research in organization studies with this specific focus (Ashcraft & Allen, 2003; Grimes, 2002; Nkomo, 1992), even though scholars have argued that race has been incompletely addressed in the field (Nkomo, 1992) and that organizational communication in particular is underwritten in racially problematic ways (Alley-Young, 2008; Ashcraft & Allen, 2003). At the same time, some organizational scholars have recognized the importance of considering whiteness in cross-cultural work (Leonard, 2010). Similarly, in critical intercultural communication, the links between whiteness and (inter-)national power dynamics have begun to emerge in fruitful ways (Moon, 2010; Moon & Flores, 2000; Shome, 2000; Steyn, 2010).

Intersections

These two theoretical perspectives must be brought into communication with one another, in order to deal with the complex dynamics of international volunteer organizations. Alley-Young (2008) specifically takes the relationship between postcolonial studies and whiteness studies as the focal point of his piece. He examines the two theoretical perspectives' intersections and divergences, finding that both can supplement the other in meaningful ways, arguing that "[j]uxtaposing postcolonial and whiteness perspectives allows for an exploration of the myriad ways in which the body is inscribed, displaced, replaced, and obscured with meaning" (p. 318). Clearly, whiteness is an important facet to consider in postcolonial power relations. As Shome (2000) explains, whiteness is inseparable from global imperialism as it "secures its hegemony in a highly racialized global system" (p. 368). Thus, whiteness is important for any postcolonial project to take into account.

However, the postcolonial aspect is also invaluable. Moon and Flores (2000) raise concern that whiteness, when interrogated on its own as a single dimension of power, may serve to reinscribe *other* dimensions of power such as colonialism, patriarchy and heteronormativity. As part of an explicitly intersectional project, postcolonial theory can help to interrogate whiteness in a way that counteracts the ability to obscure itself. By connecting postcolonial theory and whiteness studies, scholars may examine how "[c]olonialism makes the world 'white,' which is of course a world 'ready' for certain kinds of bodies" (Ahmed, 2006b: 111), as well as the way that "there continue to be close ties . . . between constructions of whiteness and of Westernness" (Frankenburg, 1994: 16). Peace Corps recruitment pamphlets offer an excellent text in which to display the necessity of drawing postcolonial theory together with whiteness theory in intersectional analyses.

The U.S. Peace Corps and international aid organizations

Before turning to the case study, it is important to first contextualize the Peace Corps within current studies of international aid and assistance. Within Critical Management Studies, the international volunteer organization is relatively under-theorized. Transnational organization studies examine large corporations (Connell & Wood, 2005; Elias, 2008; Hearn, 2004) or international nonprofits (Dempsey, 2007, 2009; Ganesh, 2003; Ganesh, Zoller & Cheney, 2005), but the international volunteer organization is rarely interrogated. The Peace Corps specifically has been addressed by only a few scholars within social sciences (Hall, 2007; Milligan, 2000). Thus, to many, the Peace Corps still "symbolizes an ideal form of American altruism" (Hall citing Cobbs Hoffman, 2007: 53). This speaks to why the Peace Corps often escapes the critical scholarly gaze that is levied against many other international aid organizations.

The efficacy, necessity and ethicality of international aid campaigns are widely debated (Richey & Ponte, 2011). As aid campaigns themselves gained notoriety and popularity in the early 2000s, so did scholarly work on the topics. Particularly, new forms of celebrity aid (Dieter & Rajiv, 2008; Repo & Yrjölä, 2011; Yrjölä, 2009) and brand aid (Richey & Ponte, 2008, 2011) caught the attention of critical scholars. By connecting celebrity popularity and capitalistic consumption to international aid, these campaigns and ads displayed the interrelations between global capitalism, poverty and disease in a much more explicit fashion than had previously been noted.

However, few scholars – in any field – have examined the contemporary manifestations of the Peace Corps or other international volunteer organizations. Although international volunteer organizations may hold similar goals to other aid organizations, the method of offering assistance to communities is very different. By offering a *person* as the means of help, rather than money or goods, the volunteer takes on a focal position. The volunteer becomes not only the means for people to help themselves, thus assuming a sort of savior role, but also a representation of the nation by which the volunteer is sent. Thus, international volunteer organizations invoke power dynamics in vastly different ways than traditional aid and make it imperative to consider the intersections of racism and colonialism in embodied form.

The Peace Corps was created in 1961 by President John F. Kennedy at a time "when popular faith . . . in the value of American ideals and the possibility of their translation into official policy was being shaken to its core" (Hall, 2007: 53). After World War II, the world felt as if it had lost its moral compass, and the U.S. felt it had lost "the frontier" (Cobbs Hoffman, 1998). In the wake of *The Ugly American*, which gave form to "a damning image of American foreign policy in the Third World" (Hall, 2007: 55) and a fear that the Soviet Union seemed more attractive to newly decolonized nations, the Peace Corps served to bridge the gap between a national desire to "believe in the fundamental goodness of America" (Hall, 2007: 55) and a feeling of the "moral ambiguity of Cold War policy" (Hall, 2007: 53). Additionally, the Peace Corps attempted to elide the tension "between a foreign policy of self-aggrandizement and a foreign policy that promote[d] the values of democracy and peace" (Cobbs-Hoffman, 1998: 4) internationally.

The following case study analyzes Peace Corps recruitment pamphlets from an intersectional position, concerned particularly with relationships between nation and race but also gender and class. By engaging in postcolonial whiteness analysis of these Peace Corps brochures, I examine the connections between U.S. Americans and white bodies, how those relate to U.S. Americentricism, and the discursive construction of the volunteer in relation to the Host Country National. In showing how the discourse equates the normative U.S. American with whiteness and reinforces U.S. American global dominance, I present a case for the importance of considering the intersections of postcolonial and whiteness theory in analyses of international volunteer organizations.

Peace Corps recruitment pamphlets: A case study

The Peace Corps is an independent U.S. government organization that has sent more than 215,000 Americans to serve in 139 countries over the past 50 years (Peace Corps, 2013b). On the website under the heading "Who Volunteers?" it states:

> One of the goals of the Peace Corps is to help the people of other countries gain a better understanding of Americans and our multicultural society. The agency actively recruits people with a variety of backgrounds and experiences to best share our nation's greatest resource – its people – with the communities where Volunteers serve around the globe.
>
> *(Peace Corps, 2013d)*

The description of the Peace Corps as "multicultural" and recruiting a "variety" of people is notable and seems to be sensitive to issues of race and gender. However, as Ahmed (2006a) has written about in institutions of higher education, the *marketing* of diversity does not necessarily correspond to diverse *organizations*. In fact, she claims that such strategies can serve to conceal underlying, persistent inequalities and even construct new forms of racism through the initiative itself (Ahmed, 2012). When diversity is represented in recruitment pamphlets for an international volunteer organization, an organization where people become the face of one nation to another, racial and neocolonial dynamics intertwine in important ways.

At the university where my research took place, the recruitment pamphlets are prominently displayed in the Peace Corps office, directly to the right of the visitor seating. Portable and intriguing, they offer easy informational access. Nine different eight-panel pamphlets are available, each folded from a single piece of glossed paper. Each pamphlet has both color and black-and-white sections, with action shots of volunteers in the field as well as formal headshots of individuals augmented with written text. Every pamphlet has a plain white back page with a mailing address, Peace Corps logo, and tagline: "Life is calling. How far will you go?" Also similar in each brochure are the immediate center pages, with a box in the top right corner describing the "Mission of the Peace Corps" and the left-hand page with the same general information regarding the Peace Corps in each pamphlet. However, the surrounding pictures are different in each pamphlet. Although the remainder of the layout is similar, the text, pictures and focus differ greatly from one pamphlet to another.

Five pamphlets focus on a specific type of work that can be done as a Peace Corps volunteer. I will refer to these as Work pamphlets. They are entitled, respectively:

- "Community Development Through Mentoring and Teaching" (Education)
- "The Business of Helping Others Help Themselves" (Business)
- "Use Your Talents to Help Others Grow" (Agriculture)
- "A Journey of Hope" (HIV/AIDS)
- "Opportunities in Health and HIV/AIDS" (Health)

The other four pamphlets focus on the "opportunity" present for specific ethnic groups. These I will refer to as Worker pamphlets. They are entitled, respectively:

- "An Exceptional Opportunity for African Americans"
- "An Exceptional Opportunity for Asian Americans"
- "An Exceptional Opportunity for American Indians and Alaskan Natives"
- "An Exceptional Opportunity for Latinos"

By analyzing the ways that text and images work together in these brochures and the differences between Worker pamphlets, as well as across the Work and Worker pamphlets, I argue that these brochures serve to reinscribe whiteness as normative and normalize a neocolonial U.S. Americentric perspective.

Case 1: The work pamphlets

The pictures in these brochures are unlabeled. The supplemental quotes and other text do not refer to the pictures themselves but rather lend a certain air to the brochure as a whole. Since the images picture both volunteers and Host Country Nationals, who is the volunteer, and how is that made clear? One of the first things that struck me in the Work pamphlets is that volunteers of color are rarely pictured alone or with similarly aged peers. I began to see that in every picture featuring a volunteer of color, there is a clue present to alert the reader to who the volunteer is. However, white volunteers are often pictured alone or with similarly aged peers. This implies that the volunteer of color must be given legitimacy of some sort but that the white volunteer is already legitimate simply because of his white body.

Clue 1: The volunteer of color is shown with children.

Volunteers of color are often pictured teaching or holding children. On the cover page of the Health brochure, a Black woman whom we are led to assume is the volunteer is shown holding a baby. In two different pictures of the Business pamphlet, two volunteers of color – one woman and one man – are shown standing over a group of students who are sitting at a table. The Education pamphlet cover shows a female volunteer of color standing and instructing a classroom full of sitting children. In all of these images, the 'volunteer' of color is placed in conjunction with those who can automatically be ruled out as prospective 'volunteers'; the children cannot possibly be volunteers because of their age.

Clue 2: The volunteer of color is pictured with technology.

Working with technology can also be seen as a clue. Two volunteers of color are shown working with a computer, which, when read through the colonial discourse of "industrialization as synonymous with Westernization" (Frankenburg, 1994: 200), serves to legitimize the people of color as volunteers. The text of the pamphlet reinforces this interpretation, stating that "[i]n response to the changing needs of a global economy and the expansion of computer use in developing nations, the number of business and information technology volunteers continues to grow." Thus, these pictures can be read as additional clues; the volunteer of color is shown working with technology in order to make up for the lack of a white body and still be seen as a legitimate volunteer.

Of course, this connection of the U.S. American volunteer to technology and the representation of the Host Country National in opposition as needing technological assistance, is not apolitical. From a postcolonial perspective, it is important to note that information and computer technology (ICT) can serve a neocolonialist function (Gopal, Willis & Gopal, 2003). In fact, Gopal, Willis and Gopal (2003) go so far as to say that "far from being emancipatory, as the elites of both core and peripheral societies would have us believe, ICTs might actually represent the most potentially effective means of continuing the project of dominance inaugurated during colonial times" (p. 239).

Clue 3: The volunteer of color watches as the Host Country Nationals work.

In the Business pamphlet, one woman of color is sitting on the outside of a circle of women who are sewing. The outside woman simply sits, watching. The obvious separation from the group, as well as her hands-off, aloof demeanor reveals a difference from the other women. That difference can be read as 'volunteer.' Thus, watching as Host Country Nationals work is another way the volunteer of color can be authenticated.

Obviously, the Western volunteer – who is ostensibly there to serve and is represented as sitting back and watching as the Host Country Nationals do domestic work – has gendered as well as neocolonial implications. It reaffirms the 'place' of the (female) Westerner in the host country – there to help with teaching, technological or other 'advanced' work that places her in a position of authority over the Host Country Nationals and yet 'charmed' to learn about the 'quaint' work of the natives. This representation is reminiscent of Prasad's (2003) ethnographic imagination, where "identities and relationships that are vividly reminiscent of colonial dynamics" (p. 150) are reproduced out of nostalgia for the ethnographic adventurers of old, displaying a neocolonial desire.

Clue 4: The volunteer of color is branded with Peace Corps insignia.

If all else fails, the volunteer of color is simply shown wearing Peace Corps insignia. The Peace Corps branding is an obvious volunteer designation, which leaves no doubt as to the volunteer's legitimacy. This last resort is used in the Education and Business pamphlets and often in conjunction with other clues.

No clues necessary: The white volunteer stands out/alone.

When the volunteer is a person of color, there are 'clues' that reveal who the volunteer is. However, for the white volunteer, no clues are necessary. In multiple pamphlets, white volunteers are pictured interacting with peers: an older, female volunteer talking with an older woman at the market, a male volunteer at a table of what appear to be businessmen, a male volunteer teaching with an assumed Host Country National peer, a female volunteer shaking the hand of a Host Country National farmer. The reader does not need to be clued in to who the volunteer is in these pictures; whiteness itself is enough of a designation. This not only normalizes that the volunteer is housed in a white body but that the normative U.S. American is white. The racial conceptualization of the 'volunteer' in the context of Peace Corps is inextricably tied to the nation.

Furthermore, white volunteers, unlike volunteers of color, are pictured alone. One man is shown on a computer, another holding a farming implement of some sort. In a third picture, a white man and a white woman stand in front of a chalkboard, the suggestion being that they are teaching, though no students are shown. The Host Country Nationals do not need to be shown in these pictures because the whiteness of the body is enough for the volunteer to be recognized.

Additionally, these images imply that the Host Country National is a person of color. Though Peace Corps works in Eastern European countries and in other places with predominantly white populations, few pamphlets display images of such peoples. Even the three images present are small and hidden in corners. Compared to the large, full-panel pictures of Host Country Nationals of color, the implication is that the normative Host Country National is of color, just as the normative volunteer is white.

Case 2: The worker pamphlets

As mentioned, four Peace Corps pamphlets are designed to appeal to prospective volunteers of certain races/ethnicities: African-Americans, Asian-Americans, American Indians/Alaskan Natives and Latinos. There is no one pamphlet specifically for the white would-be volunteer. The sheer fact that these pamphlets exist, combined with the fact that a white one does not, has racial implications: that the volunteer of color needs to be enticed into Peace Corps service, while the white volunteer does not. Thus, the white volunteer is considered to be of a certain, privileged class that can *choose* to serve overseas, whereas the lower-class volunteer of color must be *persuaded*.

For instance, the Worker pamphlets are titled: "An Exceptional Opportunity for . . .," implying not only that Peace Corps work is something that will benefit the non-white volunteer but that it is also out of the ordinary – an exception to the rule. This can be taken in more than one way: the experience of volunteering is outside of the norm for people of color or that people of color are outside of the normal embodiment of 'the volunteer.' I argue that both readings are active, serving to reinforce a perception of the volunteer of color as low-class and the normative volunteer as white.

The word 'opportunity' is also worth discussing. When used in the Work pamphlets, 'opportunity' refers to how the volunteer *creates* opportunities for the Host Country National rather than how the volunteer himself is *given* opportunities. Instead, the word 'service' is used to describe Peace Corps volunteer work in the Work pamphlets. These two different framings of Peace Corps as 'opportunity' or 'service' reveal the different class conceptualizations attached to white and non-white volunteers, as well as a hidden paternalism. The white volunteer is assumed to be of middle-class background, to have the economic privilege to decide to spend two years 'helping others' and doing 'service,' while the non-white worker is assumed to be low-class, not having the privilege to decide to help others, as she must help herself. Thus, the Peace Corps is framed as an 'opportunity,' and the reader is given examples of what she will gain from Peace Corps work. The low-class worker of color must be given incentive in order to serve.

This assumption of privilege in the normalized white worker also reveals a paternalism in the action of 'serving.' The volunteer is the one who serves, and it is the *white* volunteer who serves. Here, whiteness becomes conflated with being U.S. American. It is implied that the white volunteer has more knowledge and skill than the Host Country National and is thus able to 'help' or 'serve.' In a neocolonialist fashion, the Host Country National is relegated to a passive role, that of 'being helped.' Yet the Host County National is not alone in this; the work of the volunteer of color is rarely presented as 'service.' Instead, it is an 'opportunity,' an 'exceptional' offer, revealing not only a neocolonial paternalism but also a racist paternalism.

Of the four Worker pamphlets, the one designated for Latinos is of particular interest. Unlike the other pamphlets of its type, this racial (or ethnic) group is not expressed as a type of 'American' (as opposed to African-*American*, *American*-Indian, etc.). It seems to dissociate the Latino from a U.S. American identity. In fact, Latinos are described as in a constant state of immigration, having only just arrived in this country that is not yet their home.

This is especially clear in the quotes chosen in the pamphlet. Keeping in mind that these quotes are "filtered through Peace Corps logic" and "chosen as 'appropriate' by Peace Corps editors" (Polonijo-King, 2004), they say more about what Peace Corps designates Latinos to be than what they declare themselves. I would like to focus on one specific quote, important enough to fill an entire pamphlet segment:

> When my daughter told me she wanted to join the Peace Corps – ouch! – she almost killed me. At the time, she was helping me pay the house bills. But then I started thinking that she would be helping my people, and she would see, with her own eyes, the scenes that I told my children about. The decision she made was right. Her experience in the Peace Corps has been very good for her.

This is the only quote used in any of the pamphlets from the parent of a returned volunteer rather than the volunteer herself. As the intended reader of this pamphlet is a prospective Latina/o volunteer, the implication of this quote's inclusion is that it will assuage fears Latinas/os have of leaving their family for two years. The use of a parent reflects a perceived need for family approval in the Latina/o home, a need that is not reflected in any of the other pamphlets. That this ovation to family approval is found in the Latino pamphlet alone implies that family approval is not something that the normative white worker needs to consider or that the normative U.S. American needs to consider.

The focus on family approval only in the Latino pamphlet implies a deviation from the norm: that of white independence. This, then, ties back into the lack of explicit recognition of the Latina/o's U.S. Americanness in the title of the pamphlet. The ideal of U.S. Americans as independent is reinforced by separating the family-dependent Latina/o from the normative U.S. American. This separation is furthered by the mother's use of the term "my people" in reference to those Host Country Nationals her daughter went to serve. Together, these moves serve to alienize the Latina/o in a similar manner to the way Mexican immigrants were constructed in the 1930s "as outside of the national body" (Flores, 2003: 373) through a "rhetorical border" (Flores, 2003: 378) between Mexican 'aliens' and 'real' U.S. Americans. In a similar manner, the Latina/o here is presented as a perpetually just-arrived immigrant, renormalizing the 'real' U.S. American as white.

Discussion and conclusion

Even ostensibly 'positive' representations can reproduce colonial and racial power structures (Said, 1993), and work that "highlight[s] the best of human empathy and compassion" can have colonizing implications (Balaji, 2011: 50). The Peace Corps, though it attempts to represent both the humanity of its mission and the diversity of U.S. Americans in these pamphlets, ends up reinscribing both neocolonialism and whiteness. The way that the normative volunteer is constructed as white through text and image reinforces an idea of the white man's burden: that the entirety of the globe is the white man's responsibility because only he has the necessary knowledge, skills and privilege to care for it (Balaji, 2011; Cloud, 2004; Mohanty, 1991). The Peace Corps recruitment pamphlets thus construct a white volunteer who is privileged enough to *choose* to serve others and who has the necessary skills that Host Country Nationals lack. However, by being offered this "exceptional opportunity" – however paternalistically – U.S. Americans of color are invited to take part in the white man's service to the developing world. This reveals a tension in the discourse: from one side, it seems as if this burden of world service is primarily a racial ideology, and from another it seems to stem primarily from nation. Only through the simultaneous analysis of race and nation can the critic explain this complex interaction between whiteness and neocolonialism.

Whiteness is slippery and may change form in order to maintain power (Nakayama & Krizek, 1995; Omi & Winant, 1994), at times supporting racial hierarchies, yet also obscuring them in order to reinforce U.S. global dominance. These discourses work to simultaneously accept and reject the volunteer of color as U.S. American and continually recode the ideological basis of the white man's burden, switching between race and nation where the need arises. Through this case study of an international volunteer organization, it is clear that critical management scholars need to consider postcolonial and whiteness theory as interwoven (Alley-Young, 2008). Examining physical embodiment as representative of a particular nation or people requires a more nuanced analysis of intersecting power dynamics.

This case study also demonstrates what communication studies – both organizational and intercultural – has to offer Critical Management Studies. Through a communicative analysis of the way the normative volunteer is constructed, in both image and text, a basis emerges for future organizational analyses of both the Peace Corps and other international volunteer organizations. By tying the micro discourses of the organization to macro discourses of U.S. American culture, the analysis adheres not only to critical intercultural communication standards (Nakayama & Halualani, 2010) but to critical management ideals as well (Alvesson & Karreman, 2000). This chapter offers not only a call but an invitation for future partnerships between critical communication and Critical Management Studies: each field has much to help the other in reaching our mutual emancipatory goals.

The Peace Corps itself poses an interesting problem for the critical scholar. Is the Peace Corps a national institution that should be maintained? What might shifts in its discourse enable? Hall

(2007) and Cobbs Hoffman (1998) argue that the Peace Corps serves to mitigate tensions in the national imaginary through myths that give "coherence to the nation state" (Cobbs Hoffman, 1998: 6). Of course, this coherence comes through an emphasis on "individual idealism as a way to rise above glaring contradictions in domestic and foreign policy" (Hall, 2007: 56). If, as Hall (2007) argues, the Peace Corps largely affects the U.S. American perspective on themselves, then the reinforcement of whiteness and neocolonialism affects not only intercultural relations but also U.S. American cultural imaginaries. Thus, the Peace Corps as an institution simultaneously enables political progress within the nation and reinforces hegemonic ideals within the national imaginary.

Given this complexity and the work at hand, I would like to suggest three directions for future scholarship addressing the U.S. Peace Corps. First, future scholarship should examine how the national imaginaries about what Peace Corps volunteering is (or will be) affect volunteer work and intercultural relationships in the field. How do these recruitment materials create an expectation of work for the Peace Corps volunteer, and how does this expectation partially constitute the volunteer's actions and experiences in another country? Second, researchers should explore the experience of minority Peace Corps volunteers. If the normative volunteer is implicitly constructed as white, how does this affect the experience of volunteers of color? Finally, scholars should engage with management relationships in the Peace Corps. Volunteers on the ground are often geographically and communicatively separated from their Peace Corps overseers but have local, Host Country National supervisors. What are the relational dynamics among the distant organization, local supervisor and intercultural volunteer? "Because of its deep appeal to the country's imagination" (Cobbs Hoffman, 1998: 4), examining the Peace Corps allows the researcher access to fundamental tensions in U.S. culture and international relations. Ultimately, I hope that future research will help to address the question of how one might recognize the problematic aspects of the Peace Corps while still embracing the desire for intercultural partnership.

Note

1 'Host Country National' is the preferred Peace Corps term to refer to citizens of the countries to which Peace Corps volunteers are sent.

References

Acker, J. (2006). Inequality regimes: Gender, class, and race in organizations. *Gender & Society, 20*(4): 441–464 [doi:10.1177/0891243206289499].
Ahmed, S. (2006a). The nonperformativity of antiracism. *Meridians: Feminism, race, transnationalism, 7*(1): 104–126.
Ahmed, S. (2006b). The Orient and other others. In S. Ahmed, *Queer phenomenology: Orientations, objects, others*: 111–154. Durham, NC: Duke University Press.
Ahmed, S. (2012). Speaking about racism. In S. Ahmed, *On being included: Racism and diversity in institutional life*: 141–215. Durham, NC: Duke University Press.
Allen, B. J. (2010). A proposal for concerted collaboration between critical scholars of intercultural and organizational communication. In T. K. Nakayama and R. T. Halualani (Eds.), *The handbook of critical intercultural communication*: 585–592. Oxford: Blackwell.
Alley-Young, G. (2008). Articulating identity: Refining postcolonial and whiteness perspectives on race within communication studies. *The Review of Communication, 8*(3): 307–21 [doi: 10.1080/15358590701845311].
Ashcraft, K. L., & Allen, B. J. (2003). The racial foundation of organizational communication. *Communication Theory, 13*(1): 5–38 [doi: 10.1111/j.1468–2885.2003.tb00280.x].
Ashcraft, K. L., Kuhn, T. R., & Cooren, F. (2009). Constitutional amendments: "Materializing" organizational communication. *The Academy of Management Annals, 3*(1): 1–64 [doi: 10.1080/19416520903047186].
Baines, D. (2010). Gender mainstreaming in a development project: Intersectionality in a post-colonial un-doing? *Gender, Work and Organization, 17*(2): 119–149 [doi: 10.1111/j.1468- 0432.2009.00454.x].

Balaji, M. (2011). Racializing pity: The Haiti earthquake and the plight of "others." *Critical Studies in Media Communication, 28*(1): 50–67 [doi: 10.1080/15295036.2010.545703].

Broadfoot, K. J., & Munshi, D. (2007). Diverse voices and alternative rationalities: Imagining forms of postcolonial organizational communication. *Management Communication Quarterly, 21*(2): 249–267 [doi: 10.1177/0893318907306037].

Cloud, D. (2004). 'To veil the threat of terror': Afghan women and the 'clash of civilizations' in the imagery of the U.S. war on terrorism. *Quarterly Journal of Speech, 90*(3): 285–306 [doi: 10.1080/0033563042000270726].

Cobbs Hoffman, E. (1998). *All you need is love: The Peace Corps and the spirit of the 1960s.* Cambridge, MA: Harvard University Press.

Connell, R. W., & Wood, J. (2005). Globalization and business masculinities. *Men and Masculinities, 7*(4): 347–364 [doi: 10.1177/1097184X03260969].

Dempsey, S. E. (2007). Negotiating accountability within international contexts: The role of bounded voice. *Communication Monographs, 74*(3): 311–332 [doi: 10.1080/03637750701543485].

Dempsey, S. E. (2009). NGOs, communicative labor, and the work of grassroots representation. *Communication and Critical/Cultural Studies, 6*(4): 328–345 [doi: 10.1080/14791420903348625].

Dieter, H., & Rajiv, K. (2008). The downside of celebrity diplomacy: The neglected complexity of development. *Global Governance: A Review of Multilateralism and International Organizations, 14*(3): 259–264.

Elias, J. (2008). Hegemonic masculinities, the multinational corporation, and the developmental state constructing gender in "progressive" firms. *Men and Masculinities, 10*(4): 405–421 [doi: 10.1177/1097184X07306747].

Fellows, M. L., & Razack, S. (1998). The race to innocence: Confronting hierarchical relations among women. *The Journal of Gender, Race & Justice, 33*(5): 335–352.

Flores, L. A. (2003). Constructing rhetorical borders: Peons, illegal aliens, and competing narratives of immigration. *Critical Studies in Media Communication, 20*(4): 362–387 [doi: 10.1080/0739318032000142025].

Frankenburg, R. (1994). *The social construction of whiteness: White women, race matters.* Minneapolis: University of Minnesota Press.

Ganesh, S. (2003). Organizational narcissism: Technology, legitimacy, and identity in an Indian NGO. *Management Communication Quarterly, 16*(4): 558–594 [doi: 10.1177/0893318903252539].

Ganesh, S., Zoller, H., & Cheney, G. (2005). Transforming resistance, broadening our boundaries: Critical organizational communication meets globalization from below. *Communication Monographs, 72*(2): 169–191 [doi: 10.1080/03637750500111872].

Gopal, A., Willis, R., & Gopal, Y. (2003). From the colonial enterprise to enterprise systems: Parallels between colonization and globalization. In A. Prasad (Ed.), *Postcolonial theory and organizational analysis: A critical engagement.* New York: Palgrave Macmillan.

Grimes, D. S. (2002). Challenging the status quo? Whiteness in the diversity management literature. *Management Communication Quarterly, 15*(3): 381–409 [doi: 10.1177/0893318902153003].

Hall, M. R. (2007). The impact of the U.S. Peace Corps at home and abroad. *Journal of Third World Studies, 24*(1): 53–57.

Hearn, J. (2004). Tracking 'the transnational': Studying transnational organizations and managements, and the management of cohesion. *Culture and Organization, 10*(4): 273–90 [doi: 10.1080/1475955042000313722].

Holvino, E. (2008). Intersections: The simultaneity of race, gender and class in organization studies. *Gender, Work & Organization, 17*(3): 248–277 [doi: 10.1111/j.1468-0432.2008.00400.x].

Jack, G., Westwood, R., Srinivas, N., & Sardar, Z. (2011). Deepening, broadening, and re-asserting a postcolonial interrogative space in organization studies. *Organization, 18*(3): 275–302 [doi: 10.1177/1350508411398996].

Leonard, P. (2010). Organizing whiteness: Gender, nationality and subjectivity in postcolonial Hong Kong. *Gender, Work and Organization, 17*(3): 340–358 [doi: 10.1111/j.1468-0432.2008.00407.x].

McCall, L. (2001). *Complex inequality: Gender, class, and race in the new economy.* New York: Routledge.

Milligan, J. A. (2000). Neocolonialism and Peace Corps teaching in the Philippines. *Philippine Studies, 48*(1): 109–120.

Mohanty, C. T. (1991). Under Western eyes: Feminist scholarship and colonial discourses. In C. T. Mohanty, A. Russo & L. Torres (Eds.), *Third World women and the politics of feminism*: 51–80. Bloomington: Indiana University Press.

Moon, D. G. (2010). Critical reflections on cultural and critical intercultural communication. In T. K. Nakayama and R. T. Halualani (Eds.), *The handbook of critical intercultural communication*: 34–52. Oxford: Blackwell.

Moon, D., & Flores, L. A. (2000). Antiracism and the abolition of whiteness: Rhetorical strategies of domination among "race traitors." *Communication Studies*, *51*(2): 97–115 [doi: 10.1080/10510970009388512].

Mumby, D. K., & Stohl, C. (1996). Disciplining organizational communication studies. *Management Communication Quarterly*, *10*(1): 50–72 [doi: 10.1177/0893318996010001004].

Nakayama, T. K., & Halualani, R. T. (Eds.). (2010). *The handbook of critical intercultural communication*. Oxford: Blackwell.

Nakayama, T. K., & Krizek, R. L. (1995). Whiteness: A strategic rhetoric. *Quarterly Journal of Speech*, *81*(3): 291–309 [doi: 10.1080/00335639509384117].

Nkomo, S. M. (1992). The emperor has no clothes: Rewriting "race in organizations." *Academy of Management Review*, *17*(3): 487–513 [doi: 10.5465/AMR.1992.4281987].

Omi, M., & Winant, H. (1994). *Racial formation in the United States from the 1960s to the 1990s*. New York: Routledge.

Ono, K. A. (2009). *Contemporary media culture and the remnants of a colonial past*. New York: Peter Lang.

Peace Corps. (2013a). About us. *Peace Corps*, November 21. Retrieved from http://www.peacecorps.gov/about/.

Peace Corps. (2013b). Fast Facts. *Peace Corps*, November 20. Retrieved from http://www.peacecorps.gov/about/fastfacts/.

Peace Corps. (2013c). Remarks of Senator John F. Kennedy. *Peace Corps*, November 20. Retrieved from http://www.peacecorps.gov/about/history/speech/.

Peace Corps. (2013d). Who volunteers? *Peace Corps*, November 25. Retrieved from http://www.peacecorps.gov/learn/whovol/.

Polonijo-King, I. (2004). In whose words? Narrative analysis of international volunteer stories from an anthropological perspective. *Croatian Journal of Ethnology and Folklore Research*, *41*(1): 103–123.

Prasad, Anshuman. (2003). The gaze of the other: Postcolonial theory and organizational analysis. In Anshuman Prasad (Ed.), *Postcolonial theory and organizational analysis: A critical engagement*: 3–43. New York: Palgrave Macmillan.

Prasad, Anshuman. (2012). Working against the grain: Beyond Eurocentrism in organization studies. In Anshuman Prasad (Ed.), *Against the grain: Advances in postcolonial organization studies*: 13–31. Frederiksberg, Denmark: Copenhagen Business School Press.

Prasad, Anshuman., & Prasad, P. (2003). The empire of organizations and the organization of empires: Postcolonial considerations on theorizing workplace resistance. In Anshuman Prasad (Ed.), *Postcolonial theory and organizational analysis: A critical engagement*: 95–119. New York: Palgrave Macmillan.

Prasad, P. (2003). The return of the native: Organizational discourses and the legacy of the ethnographic imagination. In Anshuman Prasad (Ed.), *Postcolonial theory and organizational analysis: A critical engagement*: 149–170. New York: Palgrave Macmillan.

Putnam, L. L., & Nicotera, A. M. (Eds.). (2008). *Building theories of organization: The constitutive role of communication*. New York: Routledge.

Repo, J., & Yrjölä, R. (2011). The gender politics of celebrity humanitarianism in Africa. *International Feminist Journal of Politics*, *13*(1): 44–62 [doi: 10.1080/14616742.2011.534661].

Richey, L. A., & Ponte, S. (2008). Better (Red)™ than dead? Celebrities, consumption and international aid. *Third World Quarterly*, *29*(4): 711–729 [doi: 10.1080/01436590802052649].

Richey, L. A., & Ponte, S. (2011). *Brand aid: Shopping well to save the world*. Minneapolis: University of Minnesota Press.

Roediger, D. R. (1991). *The wages of whiteness: Race and the making of the American working class*. New York: Verso.

Said, E. W. (1993). *Culture and imperialism*. New York: Vintage Books.

Shome, R. (2000). Outing whiteness. *Critical Studies in Media Communication*, *17*(3): 366–371 [doi: 10.1080/15295030009388402].

Steyn, M. (2010). "The creed of the white kid": A diss-apology. In Nakayama and Halualani (Eds.), *The handbook of critical intercultural communication*: 534–548. Oxford: Blackwell Publishing Ltd.

Taylor, J. R., & Robichaud, D. (2004). Finding the organization in communication: Discourse as action and sensemaking. *Organization*, *11*(3): 395–413 [doi: 10.1177/1350508404041999].

West, C., & Fenstermaker, S. (2002). Doing difference. In S. Fenstermaker & C. West (Eds.), *Doing gender, doing difference: Inequality, power, and institutional change*: 55–79. New York: Routledge.

Yrjölä, R. (2009). The invisible violence of celebrity humanitarianism: Soft images and hard words in the making and unmaking of Africa. *World Political Science Review*, *5*(1): 279- 292 [doi: 10.2202/1935–6226.1072].

24

American soft imperialism and management education in Brazil

A postcolonial critique

Rafael Alcadipani

I begin this chapter by highlighting a point made by Prasad (2003) that I fully agree with: "[t]he long history of Western colonialism, its global reach, and the uniqueness of many of its constitutive practices and structures imply that Western colonialism and non-Western resistance to such colonialism have played a significant role in shaping the contours of the world as we know it today" (p. 5). Scholars have long argued that (neo-)colonialism has affected management thought and education (Jack, Westwood, Srinivas & Sardar, 2011; Özakzanç-Pan, 2008; Prasad, 2003, 2012). These scholars' concern with investigating the consequences of colonialism has opened up the discipline of management and organizations studies to the postcolonialist approach. The roots of this approach may be found in the 1950s and 1960s and even earlier. However, the presence of postcolonial theoretic ideas in the social sciences seems to have been increasing especially since the early 1980s. The key focus of postcolonialism is to critically examine various aspects of modern Western colonialism and neocolonialism (Prasad, 2012). For Jack, Westwood, Srinivas and Sardar (2011: 277), the approach "is a broad rubric for examining a range of social, cultural, political, ethical and philosophical questions that recognize the salience of the colonial experience and its persisting aftermath."

One of the precursors of postcolonialism is Aimé Césaire (1955) who critiques the colonialist mind-set that seeks to impose Western logics over the people under Western rule. His work has played an important role in that of Fanon (1961), another important postcolonialist thinker, who highlights colonization as a violent process that suppresses the humanity of the colonized and imposes an inauthentic identity on them. Edward Said and Homi Bhabha are other key thinkers of the postcolonial tradition. Said (1978), for instance, discusses how over the years the West has constructed a distorted version of the Orient, portraying its inhabitants and their modes of living as barbaric and uncivilized. Such "Orientalist" discourses played an important role in legitimizing colonial activities and attitudes. Homi Bhabha (1994) defends "the third space" or "in between" as a way to highlight hybridism and to fight dualist (e.g., West/East) modes of representation that usually reinforce exclusion. Thinking of a third space is a way to avoid an essentialist mode of building meaning.

Whereas postcolonialist perspectives are varied, they generally tend to censure Western epistemology as a system for the exclusion of non-Western realities and forms of knowledge (Prasad & Prasad, 2001). Postcolonial approaches critique the notions of "progress" and "modernity" as defined in the West. From such a perspective, there is a tendency in the West to emphasize economic conditions and to depict access to and the progress of science and technology as imperatives for the "development" of certain regions of the world while others remain undeveloped. "Development" within the parameters of the Western culture or wealthy nations concludes by categorizing people and cultures of non-Western nations as "undeveloped" or "primitive," which leads to the exclusion of their knowledge, values and cultures (Prasad, 2012).

In short, postcolonial thinkers recognize a tendency in the West to regard economic well-being as the main goal that all nations should strive for and to see science and technology as the best pathway toward reaching it. Further, this discourse produces a hierarchy between 'developed' (mainly Western) and 'underdeveloped' or even 'primitive' (mainly non-Western) countries. The problem, however, with this kind of thinking, according to postcolonialism, is that an entire gamut of values and knowledge belonging to the so-called underdeveloped world is in danger of being disregarded and eventually lost.

Postcolonial critiques of such ethnocentric tendencies are many and varied and have joined with other detractors of imperialism such as Harvey (2003) who warn of a new imperial order produced through a regime of global government led by the West that is in pursuit of wealth accumulation through world domination. Writers like Harvey (2003) and Hardt and Negri (2001) trace this new imperialism to the actions taken by the U.S. and its Western allies after World War II to facilitate the spread of a Western-style capitalism and culture across the world.

This chapter contends that in trying to understand these newer forms of imperialism, the notion of *soft power* is likely to be useful. The idea of soft power was developed by Joseph Nye (1990, 2004) to suggest one way in which U.S. influence in world affairs could be achieved without the direct use of force. Soft power is exercised through cooperation and the forces of cultural attraction rather than through military muscle. For Nye (1990), factors such as technology, education and economic growth become key elements of international soft power. As he observes, "While military force remains the ultimate form of power in a self-help system, the use of force has become more costly for modern great powers. Other instruments such as communications, organizational and institutional skills and manipulation of interdependence have become more important" (Nye, 1990: 158). Soft power refers to the capacity for effective communication, as well as the development and utilization of multilateral institutions to one's own advantage. At the core of soft power is the deployment of ideologies that promote favorable images of a dominant nation.

This chapter sees soft power as a occupying a crucial place in the new imperial order. While traditional imperialism relied primarily on hard power mechanisms such as military might, the new imperialism is much more dependent on soft power. I am therefore putting forward the notion of *soft imperialism* as a strategy for achieving global dominance. Soft imperialism draws attention to the presence of soft power in today's imperial order. This chapter examines management education in Brazil as an important case of soft imperialism. The role of education as a powerful weapon in the service of U.S. and Western imperialism has already been noted by other scholars (Tikly, 2004). In this chapter, I will be drawing on these ideas as I look at the interventionist actions taken by the U.S. to shape Brazilian management education in such a way as to reflect American business values and practices. I will also be discussing how these efforts serve wider U.S. interests in Latin America.

U.S. soft imperialism in Brazil

The 'discovery' of Brazil was the outcome of European colonial expansion in the Americas, Africa and Asia in the 15th century. The name 'Brazil' was given to the South American country by the Portuguese colonial power due to the large amount of Brazilwood (*Pau-Brasil*) to be found

in the 'new' land. Brazilwood was the first product extracted from Brazilian soil by the colonizers to be sold in the European market. As such, Western exploitation of Brazil became ironically
marked in the nation's very name (Calligaris, 1993). In the Americas, Mignolo (2008) points out
that the Mayans, Incas and Aztecs were not even aware of the existence of other civilizations.
They thought they were the world's only inhabitants. As such, 'America' was not expecting to 'be
discovered', but it became an invention for the European colonial powers who were expanding
their territories and disseminating 'modernization' all over the world. As a consequence, stories,
practices and knowledge of the inhabitants of the Americas were pushed to one side and, on most
occasions, contested. Thus, the region the Europeans called the Americas started being managed
and transformed through the lens of metropolitan perspectives and for the benefit of the European metropolis (Mignolo, 2008).

The colonization process was legitimized under the banner of bringing 'civilization', religion and 'modernity' to the local people, who were seen as 'natives.' The civilizations in all of
the 'Americas' became subject to European control. Such control was exercised over the local
people's economy, politics, gender relations, epistemology and subjectivity (see Mignolo, 2008).

Not all 'America' was colonized in the same manner. Most of what we call today the U.S. followed a model of settler colonialism, which means that entire families moved from the metropolis
to the new land to reproduce the metropolitan model (Belich, 2009). Unlike the U.S., Brazil
faced a model of exploitative colonialism, which means that the country's economic production
and local population were exploited to profit the European colonizer, to generate wealth only
for the European nation.

As discussed by Fanon (1961), colonialism leaves deep roots within the colonized mind. Brazil's model of exploitative colonization and the constant friction between Brazil and the different
colonial powers that attempted to exploit the country left in the Brazilian mind-set a wish to follow a superior foreign role model fostered by the feeling that whatever originates from the West
is always superior to anything Brazilian (Caldas, 1997). In seeking to become modern, the Latin
American elite reinforced the colonial logic in the region (Mignolo, 2008). This was the context
within which U.S. imperialism at a later date flourished in Brazil.

The roots of U.S. imperialism in Latin America in general and in Brazil specifically can be
traced back to the Monroe Doctrine. This doctrine was created during the term of President
James Monroe in 1823 and stated that further European efforts to colonize or interfere in South
or North America would be taken as an act of aggression against the U.S. and would require U.S.
intervention (see Perkins, 1927). The principle of such a doctrine was 'America for the Americans.' For Chomsky (2004), the Monroe Doctrine was the first act of U.S. hegemonic will in
the region, and it marks the start of a U.S. foreign policy that aimed to put the entire American
continent decisively under U.S. influence. For Mignolo (2008), the imperial ambitions of the U.S.
were already present in the early 19th century.

Alcadipani and Caldas (2012) argue that during Herbert Hoover's term in office (1929–1933),
the idea of bringing the U.S. and Latin America closer together became more explicit. This was
manifested in the idea of pan-Americanism that drove the continent's economic and political
union, with the aim of defending and developing the region. It was the time of the Good Neighbor Policy. Latin America was perceived by the U.S. as a major consumer market, and it had very
significant strategic importance in the period preceding World War II. The success of Hoover's
policy toward Latin America, however, was unclear (for an overview of the influence of the U.S.
in Latin America, see Accioly, 1945; Ianni, 1979).

During President Franklin Delano Roosevelt's terms (1933–1945), new attempts to establish
stronger relations between the U.S. and Latin America were made. It was during this administration that it was decided to carry out an orchestrated Americanization of Brazil (Tota, 2000).

According to Tota (2000), in the period before WWII, it was clear to the U.S. that the country's security relied on good relationships with other nations in the Americas. In attempting to create such relations, a plan was devised that included political and economic exchanges, the aim being to increase the links between the U.S. and Latin America. The covert aim of such a plan was to prevent the influence of Nazi Germany and Fascist Italy in the region, as well as to overcome the anti-Americanism that was prevalent, especially in left-wing groups.

According to Tota (2000), to implement such a project, the Office of the Coordinator of Inter-American Affairs (OCIAA) was created. The strategy of the OCIAA was to systematically export U.S. cultural and economic values in order to make the U.S. an important role model for the southern part of the Americas. Brazil was chosen as the key target due to its size and relevance to Latin America. Specifically, the OCIAA aimed to foster the implementation of U.S. economic policies in Brazil and attempted to keep the region politically stable in the defense of the U.S.'s values in opposition to the Axis Powers. The OCIAA also aimed to enhance and protect U.S. investments on the South American continent (see Tota, 2000).

For Tota (2000), the OCIAA employed several strategies to achieve its aims. First, there was the dissemination of information that created a positive image of the U.S. in Brazil. Media campaigns were very important for achieving such an aim. Major companies, such as GE and Ford, were per-suaded to advertise their products through positive associations with the American way of life. The idea that was underlined was that the American way of life promised a modern and happy future for all. Moreover, the culture industry was also used to achieve the aims of the OCIAA. Cartoon characters like Los tres Caballeros and Ze Carioca emerged as friends of Donald Duck in cartoons that were shown on Latin American TVs. American movies were filmed in Rio de Janeiro with Hollywood depicting Rio de Janeiro in line with U.S. propaganda (Freire-Medeiros, 2005). Car-men Miranda, the alluring woman in a hat covered with fruit, achieved remarkable success singing Brazilian songs in the U.S. Tota (2000) also argues that several technical and scientific programs were designed to stimulate cooperation between Brazil and the U.S. There were exchange programs for students and teachers, incentives for English language teaching and the dissemination of U.S. culture, technical qualifications and support missions, technological modernization programs and economic assistance and financing programs associated with industrial development. In addition, special funds were set up to reduce poverty and to foster the implementation of democratic institu-tions in Brazil. In brief, the OCIAA became a U.S. ideology factory for Brazil (Tota, 2000).

The U.S. ideology promotes the liberal state, democracy, the need for economic progress, utilitarianism, market economy and mass society. When WWII was about to end, Brazil's devel-opment was entirely dependent on U.S. resources (Tota, 2000). The end of WWII marked the rise of the U.S. as a global superpower and its growing tension with the other emerged superpower, the Soviet Union. In the aftermath of WWII, the U.S. took responsibility for the welfare of the world's capitalist system as a way of protecting capitalist superpowers' own interests. Members of the U.S. government attempted to actively remodel the world to fit the U.S.'s needs, since they considered the country's security and prosperity depended upon establishing a peaceful and stable world. U.S. government agents also aimed to have a strong international economy, thus allowing the country to have access to raw materials and markets.

During the Cold War, Brazil continued to receive attention from the U.S. government (Tota, 2000; Alcadipani & Caldas, 2012). For Haines (1989: ix), in Brazil "US policymakers worked to preserve and expand US influence. They strove to maintain the area as an important market for U.S. surplus industrial production and private investments. To exploit its vast reserves of raw materials, and to keep international communism out."

In doing so, according to Haines (1989), the Cold War diplomacy of the U.S. continued to focus on the Americanization of Brazil from 1945 to 1954. During Truman's and Eisenhower's terms in office, the U.S. maintained similar policies toward Brazil by opposing economic nationalism and state control of economic life by attempting to maintain a favorable environment for U.S. business and private investment in the country and to make Brazilian natural resources, specially oil and minerals, accessible to American companies. Specifically, the U.S. tried "to control, influence, and mold Brazil's progress toward modernization" (Haines, 1989: xi). Washington paid particular attention to fostering private enterprise, exploiting strategic resources, promoting U.S. business practices and fighting communism (Haines, 1989).

For Haines (1989), the North Americans were channeling Brazilian development toward areas that were beneficial to the U.S. and to maintaining Washington's power and influence in the region. In practical terms, U.S. policy-makers were nurturing a democratic political system and opposing communism by closely watching and bringing influence to bear against the Brazilian communist party in Brazil. Moreover, U.S. government officials cultivated the military as an ally for fighting communism by supporting military forces with training and supplying Brazil with American military equipment. Furthermore, the U.S. government continued to finance Brazilian development by offering special conditional loans to the country and making U.S. companies invest in Brazil.

In terms of development, the American model was positioned as a blueprint for Brazilian economic success. U.S. private capital was defended as the best way to exploit Brazilian natural resources, and North American technical aid and economic assistance were deployed to help in developing infrastructure in Brazil. In terms of industrial development, Washington aimed to protect U.S. company interests as much as it could. In cultural terms, U.S. officials promoted the culture and values of the U.S. and also tried to diminish the strong French influence in the Brazilian cultural scene (see Haines, 1989). This was done by

> drawing on the World War II experience of the OCIAA. Policy makers instituted a massive cultural and information program designed to win over the Brazilian population. They used both traditional cultural exchange methods and, increasingly, the mass media to influence Brazilians. A steady flow of U.S. visitors, information, and educational materials flooded Brazil. All proclaimed the advantages of the free way of life, of the American way.
>
> *(Haines, 1989: 175)*

In doing so, the tactics deployed by the OCIAA of selling U.S. ideology in order to keep the U.S. as a role model for Brazilians were still being used as a form of soft power (Nye, 2004). For Alcadipani and Caldas (2012), the culture of U.S. dependency of the 1950s and 1960s led to the intensive incorporation of U.S. technology and capital, as well as social, esthetic and consumption habits. Supported by a strong institutional system and efficient cultural mobilization machinery, the U.S. was able to foster this influence in subsequent years, encouraging the consumption, dissemination and social reproduction of references to the U.S. (Ianni, 1979). The U.S. role model was fundamental to the local elite, which considered the foreign way of life as "superior" and "modern" (Tota, 2000). Imitating U.S. models was a way for the elite to differentiate itself from the other local social groups and helped establish its control over Brazilian society (Alcadipani & Caldas, 2012).

As discussed here, the U.S. acted in a different manner from the traditional European colonial metropolis when dealing with Brazil. In Brazil, the U.S. mostly employed ideological and cultural dimensions in its attempt to shape points of view and to direct national policies to the benefit of the U.S. government's aims. The U.S. as an empire did not want to establish full command and control of regions of the world. The key idea was to generate a dependency that would allow for the U.S. influence. The U.S. empire is different from the traditional European empires (Hardt &

Negri, 2001). From what I have presented in this section, the notion of soft power (Nye, 2004) seems a more appropriate way of describing the actions of the U.S. in Brazil. I prefer to use the notion of soft imperialism as its highlights the imperial dimensions of soft power. Brazil has been under soft U.S. imperialism for a long time. In the next section, I will discuss how management was interwoven with soft U.S. imperialism.

Management education as an instrument of soft imperialism

Management education began in Europe at the end of the 19th century in commercial schools in France and Germany (Üsdiken, 2004). In these institutions, professionals used to share their experiences with people interested in learning the 'tricks of the management trade.' The French model was very influential in Italy, Spain and Turkey (Kipping, Üsdiken & Puig, 2004), at the same time that the Germans had a distinct influence on Nordic countries (Engwall, 2004). There was no reference to U.S. management education in Europe before World War II (Kieser, 2004). Management education was also present in places such as Latin America, where textbooks written by Spanish authors were prevalent in Argentina during the 1920s (Gantman & Rodrigues, 2008). However, this scenario changed profoundly after WWII and the beginning of the Cold War.

The U.S. fight against communism was a crucial element in the Cold War that had an impact on science within the U.S. when the country's military apparatus started to play a decisive role in the research and development agendas of universities and corporations. This war had an important catalytic effect on the creation of a military-industrial-academic complex (Leslie, 1993). In particular, the Cold War affected management because it occurred between 1946 and 1989, a crucial period for the development and consolidation of management thinking and for the establishment of important theoretical sources in the U.S., among which are the Human Relations Theory, the Systems Theory and the Socio-Technical Theory (Kelly, Mills & Cooke, 2006). The Cold War offered a grand narrative, in which management was an integral element. In broad terms, the Cold War culture conceived the limits of what management could deal with and the form and type of management that it should preach (Cooke, Mills & Kelly, 2005; Kelly, Mills & Cooke, 2006; Landau, 2006). According to Cooke, Mills & Kelly (2005), the Cold War culture was characterized by a few central elements, among which were an idealization of the American way of life and a consequent demonization of everything un-American.

In the context of the Cold War, management education traveled from the U.S. to other parts of the world (Alcadipani & Rosa, 2011). The U.S. began to strongly influence management education worldwide due to some specific conditions after WWII when the country consolidated its presence as a global power and took action to fight against the spread of communism. According to Westwood & Jack (2008), the growth of U.S. transnational companies in particular and of U.S. business in general meant that multinationals needed to have U.S.-trained managers in foreign countries and to deal with different cultures and different economic and social conditions. Moreover, as noted in the previous section, development initiatives involving U.S. aid were important for containing the 'communist threat.' In addition, Westwood and Jack (2008) also argue that the recent independence of some African and Asian countries affected the emergence of management as a global phenomenon. This was so because the U.S. feared these countries could turn to communism in an attempt to organize and reconstruct their recently decolonized countries, especially as most of the newly independent states had been under European control and after decolonialization wanted to avoid the influence of their former rulers (see Westwood & Jack, 2008).

Europe was one of the first places to be affected by the Americanization of management education. The first step in that direction was through training within industries. This type of education was provided as a package for the reconstruction of European industry at the end of the 1940s and beginning of the 1950s (Leavitt, 1957). Moreover, the Marshall Plan also had a catalytic effect by encouraging management higher education to adopt curricula based on U.S. educational institutions (Kieser, 2004). In addition, European companies were able to take loans from the U.S., providing they adopted U.S. management principles and methods (Kieser, 2004). Thus, the reconstruction of Europe after WWII had important consequences in terms of the dissemination of U.S. management ideas and practices on the continent (see Leavitt, 1957).

U.S. management education also spread outside Europe. One instrument used by the U.S. to Americanize Latin America was economic aid – providing that U.S. productivity models (e.g., Taylorism) were adopted by companies and public organizations in the region (see Tota, 2000). During the 1960s, management graduate courses were implemented in Latin America following U.S. management knowledge and practices, as happened in Argentina, for example (Gantman & Rodrigues, 2008). U.S. management education was sent to the East (see Neal & Finlay, 2008) via 'American' universities, such as the Lebanese American University. Such educational institutions were also present in Israel (Frenkel & Shenhav, 2003). A similar movement took place in India (Mir, Mir & Srinivas, 2004). Specifically, foundations like Ford and Rockefeller played a significant part in disseminating American values. Such foundations have been accused of exercising cultural imperialism (see Alcadipani & Cooke, 2012).

According to Alcadipani and Rosa (2011), the prevalence of the U.S. in the field of management education is far from coincidental. It is rather the result of a long process in which U.S. government agencies and nongovernmental organizations had a major involvement (see also Vernon, 1994). It was during the Cold War that business schools were established and consolidated in the U.S., Europe and other countries. These institutions followed the model of the management schools that were becoming increasingly preeminent in North America. Different mechanisms were used to send U.S. management education abroad, such as U.S. academic delegations being sent to other countries, academics from other countries taking post-graduate courses in the U.S., the export of U.S. syllabi and the translation of textbooks (Kipping, Üsdiken & Puig, 2004; Leavitt, 1957; Srinivas, 2009; Üsdiken, 2004). It is significant that U.S. foundations, such as the Ford Foundation, played a crucial role in the process and in supporting Cold War culture (Parmar, 2002).

In doing so, management consolidated itself within a U.S. commercial-military-political agenda (Westwood & Jack, 2008) and was affected and constituted within the Cold War's grand narrative (Cooke & Mills, 2008; Cooke, Mills & Kelly, 2005). It can be understood as a phenomenon sparked by the Cold War (Kelly, Mills & Cooke, 2006), which spread across the world (Alcadipani & Rosa, 2011) with the purpose of protecting the so-called free world from the communist threat; management education played a central role in that respect. As discussed in the previous section, the U.S. tried to influence societies by offering a new ideology, which was strongly associated with the discourse of modernization. Management ideas and initiatives were usually sold as a way of fostering development and creating modernization (see Westwood & Jack, 2008). Americanization is synonymous with modernization (Alcadipani & Caldas, 2012), a key theme challenged by postcolonial approaches (Prasad, 2012). However, on some occasions modernization meant that management served as a tool for supporting torture and murder. As such, management education can be seen as an "historical outcome of U.S. foreign and domestic policy and part of the grand narrative of the Cold War" (Westwood & Jack, 2008: 383). Management education is not only a U.S. institution (Khurana, 2007); it can also be perceived as an instrument of soft U.S. imperialism. In the next section, I will use the case of management education in Brazil to argue that it was an instrument of soft imperialism.

U.S. soft imperialism: Management education in Brazil

As discussed in the first section, the U.S. used soft imperialistic mechanisms in Brazil to foster its interests. Management education had been developed in Brazil since the late 1800s (Barros, 2011); however, it was only during the 1950s, when the Americanization of Brazil was under way, that it surfaced in dedicated courses and in dedicated schools and departments. Before the 1950s, there was no presence of U.S. ideas in management education in Brazil.

The first Brazilian school of management, Escola Superior de Negócios (ESAN), was started in the late 1940s by a Jesuit priest. He used the Harvard Business School as a model (Bertero, 2006), but there was no direct U.S. state involvement. The importance of ESAN was overshadowed by the creation of the São Paulo School of Management (FGV-EAESP) in 1954. The school was created by the Getulio Vargas Foundation (FGV), a foundation that had been set up in 1944 with the aim of modernizing public service in the country and that had created a public management school in Rio de Janeiro in the 1940s. The FGV-EAESP was designed to be a business school and was set up by an agreement between the Brazilian government, the U.S. government, the Getulio Vargas Foundation and Michigan State University, the last-named as the educational institution responsible for implementing the enterprise.

At the beginning, the FGV's aim of creating a business school was enthusiastically sponsored by a Brazilian tycoon, Earl Matarazzo. Matarazzo, who was born in Italy and had immigrated to Brazil, was the richest man in the country in the 1950s. He offered substantial financial support to the FGV to create a business school, and he wanted it to follow the Italian Bocconi management school as a role model, at the same time wanting to have little U.S. influence in the project. The U.S. government was simultaneously offering to provide the FGV with full support in creating a business school on the condition that a U.S. business education style was fully adopted. The FGV decided to accept the support offered by the U.S. government and rejected the influence of Matarazzo. The U.S. provided the Brazilians with a mission of U.S. academics who would set up the school, gave financial support and also had Brazilian academics trained in the U.S. (see Alcadipani & Bertero, 2012; Alcadipani & Caldas, 2012). The case indicates that the U.S. government used its influence for displacing European-inspired (i.e., Italian) management education in Brazil. Later, the Ford Foundation also helped in the school's development (see Alcadipani & Cooke, 2012).

FGV-EAESP offered active support for starting two other management schools in Brazil. One in the south (the management school of Rio Grande do Sul Federal University) and one in the northeast of Brazil (the management school of Bahia Federal University). The U.S. mission that created FGV-EAESP also inspired changes in the production engineering course at São Paulo University. The aim of the U.S. government was to spread U.S.-style management education to different parts of Brazil. The U.S. government considered FGV-EAESP as a successful case of international aid (Alcadipani & Bertero, 2012).

After the role played by FGV-EAESP, the U.S. model of management education became prevalent in Brazil after 1960. The effect of this was to spread notions of scientific management, human relations, systems theory, strategy, marketing and finance (see Alcadipani & Caldas, 2012), all content that reinforces elements of 'Americanist' ideology (Tota, 2000). If management theory is an ideology (Tragtenberg, 1971), it is an 'Americanist' ideology. There were studies of the influence of the U.S. on management education in Brazil in the 1950s and 1960s (e.g., Alcadipani & Bertero, 2012; Alcadipani & Caldas, 2012; Alcadipani & Cooke, 2012; Barros, 2011). However, there has been very little discussion about the influence of the U.S. on current management education in Brazil.

Management education in Brazil is impressive in its scope. It is the undergraduate course with the largest number of students (about 1 million students enroll in such courses every year), and there are about 60 research degree programs in the country. Brazil has almost 70 journals in the academic field of management, and the number of executive MBA courses has not been calculated, but there are quite probably more than 3000 such programs in the country. It is also important to note that Brazil is one of the countries with a high level of inequality.

The setting up of management education under U.S. auspices in the 1950s left profound legacies for the evolution of subsequent education in the country. Today, most of the textbooks used in management courses in Brazil are either direct translations of U.S. textbooks or are produced by Brazilian authors who draw heavily on U.S. material. Academic production in management in Brazil is, to some extent, an ill equipped copy of U.S. theories and perspectives. Some degree of originality is present in only a few areas, such as organization theory.

In an unequal country such as Brazil, management education institutions are divided by the social classes of the students they attract. In Brazil, the bachelor's degree is considered the most important academic degree, and the reputation of academic institutions is usually based on the quality of their management education at the undergraduate level. The best management schools are usually regarded as being the ones attached to state universities, such as UFRGS, UFBA and USP. Academics in these institutions are full-time and are meant to carry out research, even though a considerable number of the professors also earn money from consultancy work and executive education. Such schools are still heavily influenced by U.S. teaching and academic materials.

The presence of U.S. influence is even stronger in the 'top market' non-state business schools, which can be perceived from the glamour attached to AACSB accreditation. FGV-EAESP is regarded as the top management school in the country, and the U.S. presence is noted in the requirements the school has to follow in order to keep its AACSB accreditation. FGV-EAESP, however, has a long tradition of fostering Brazilian critical thinking, which is to a large extent critical of the U.S. (Alcadipani & Bertero, 2012). Other 'top market' academic business institutions, such as Insper, a private institution owned by a Brazilian banker, follow a harder U.S. line in terms of management education and research. A considerable number of Insper's academics obtained their PhDs in the U.S. and tend to advocate a neo-liberal agenda in Brazil (Lazzarini, 2011). By following a more hard-line, U.S. view of management education and research, Insper has much less local embeddedness. It resembles INSEAD in France, a kind of Euro-Disney that is associated with the French intellectual scene and French local practices and concerns.

Executive education is also heavily influenced by ideas originating in the U.S. Both the FGV and Insper have a strong presence in executive education, in which U.S. influence is felt in all sorts of teaching materials. The first course at FGV-EAESP back in the 1950s was an executive education course ironically called CIA, which is the Portuguese acronym for Intensive Course in Management. There is also the Dom Cabral Foundation, which is one of the leading providers of management education for top executives in Brazil and which also follows the lead of the U.S. in terms of teaching material and academic research. Dom Cabral is listed as one of the top eight providers of executive education in Brazil in the *Financial Times* ranking. They all seek to have exchange programs with U.S.-type business schools as a positive asset.

The influence of the U.S. is also felt in academic production in the management field. Brazil has a large academia in management, with academic journals published in Portuguese, PhD programs and book publishers. Different analyses of academic production in Brazil have shown the prevalence of Anglo-Saxon references among the work of Brazilian academics. Moreover, the studies conducted in Brazil in the field of management, in general terms, tend to be a poor copy of Western thinking. It is quite common to have papers published in Portuguese with most of the references coming from the U.S. (see Alcadipani & Caldas, 2012). To have a PhD from the U.S. or an Anglo-Saxon country is perceived as a signal of prestige and status. Ibarra-Colado (2006) explores how scholars who obtain PhDs from the U.S. return to Latin American countries preaching an Americanist ideology.

U.S. management is also taught in Brazil today via companies that promote global gurus and content from U.S. 'pop' management books and articles. For example, H.S.M. promotes seminars around Brazil with U.S. management gurus, such as Michael Porter and Tom Peters. Such seminars are commonly presented in huge theaters, usually packed with executives eager to assimilate the latest U.S. management fashion. H.S.M. also has a magazine and a publishing house that produces books and articles from popular U.S. management thinkers. The management fashion industry is quite expansive in Brazil (see Paula & Wood, 2009). U.S. professional bodies, such as the Project Management Institute (PMI), are very much in evidence in Brazil, doling out professional course qualification certificates to Brazilians regardless of whether or not the content of such courses is appropriate to the Brazilian environment. In general terms, management knowledge and teaching materials that originate in the U.S. are perceived as 'modern' and 'top knowledge' that tend to be followed blindly in Brazil. Since management teaching is heavily based on U.S. ideas, which preach an 'Americanist' ideology, it will still act as an instrument of soft U.S. imperialism in Brazil as long as it continues to be accepted without question in most academic institutions in the country. The U.S. created the foundations in the 1950s, and until today their influence has been felt in management education practice. Colonial practices leave strong ties in the minds of those who have been colonized (Fanon, 1961).

During the 1960s, the U.S. was involved in an attempt to dismantle the critical content of secondary education in Brazil. Chauí (1985) argues that public schools had to start producing individuals to serve as cheap labor for the country's industries. The aim was to create low-cost, value-added, poorly qualified labor, intended to serve as manpower for the multinational organizations that were setting up in Brazil (Alcadipani & Caldas, 2012). The provision of poor-quality management education can be perceived as another façade of the U.S. influence on management education in Brazil. This is particularly relevant for universities that have management graduates aiming to enter the low end of the market. Since the 1990s, a whole host of new, low-cost universities have been set up in Brazil. Such institutions are highly profit-oriented and care little about the rigor and content of their courses. This movement has been called the 'McDonaldization' of higher education in Brazil (see Alcadipani & Bresler, 1999).

Ritzer (2008) contends that the world has faced a process of McDonaldization, which means the tendency of society to accept and sponsor organizations that resemble McDonalds. It is a new version of Weber's iron cage. In terms of higher education in Brazil, McDonaldization means the creation and development of educational institutions that are concerned solely with maximizing profits with the minimum input and a lack of interest in producing students that are able to think. Anhanguera Educacional is the archetypical "McDonald's university." It has almost 500,000 students with branches all over Brazil. Teachers have no right to choose what to teach and have to follow a very standardized teaching content, which even includes the PowerPoint presentations that should be used in each lecture. The institution is traded on the Brazilian stock market, and education is measured in terms of profits for its shareholders. The management degree attracts the most students, and it is an inexpensive course to set up and run. The McDonaldization process is associated with Americanization (Ritzer, 2008) and is arguably a façade of U.S. soft imperialism. Here, the influence of the U.S. on Brazilian management education is again evident in terms of providing the particular logic of imparting knowledge and producing desired subjects.

407

Discussion

This chapter has engaged in a fine-grained examination of specific manifestations of American soft imperialism in Brazil in the management education sector. At one level, the extraordinary influence of U.S. business education models in Latin America in general can be understood as yet another case of institutional isomorphism. However, as this chapter shows, there is more to this than mindless organizational mimicry. The postcolonial lens adopted here helps us see some of these imitative tendencies in a different light – as also emerging out of conscious strategic moves on the part of the United States that are intended to take care of its geopolitical interests in the region.

The notion of soft imperialism is particularly useful here as it draws our attention to the power of American cultural imperialism as a driving force behind the widespread adoption of U.S. business education models in Brazil. The chapter also stresses the effects of its isomorphism in producing large numbers of 'educated' managers who have internalized ideas about the superiority of American business practices, and who are consequently less likely to be critical of the U.S. corporatization of Brazil. While this chapter focuses exclusively on the Brazilian case, it suggests that similar inquiries into soft imperial practices by the U.S. in other countries might yield insights of interest to critical management researchers.

References

Accioly, H. (1945). *O Reconhecimento do Brasil pelos Estados Unidos da América*. São Paulo: Companhia Editora Nacional.

Alcadipani, R., & Bertero, C. (2012). A Guerra Fria e o Ensino do Management no Brasil. O caso da FGV-EAESP. *RAE*, *52*: 84–299.

Alcadipani, R., & Bresler, R. (1999). A McDonaldização do Ensino. *Carta Capital*, May 10.

Alcadipani, R., & Caldas, M. (2012). Americanizing Brazilian management. *Critical Perspectives on International Business*, *8*: 37–55.

Alcadipani, R., & Cooke, B. (2012). The Ford Foundation's "mess" in Brazil: A counter-deterministic account of US philanthropy and management education. Paper presented at the European Group of Organization Analysis Colloquium, Helsinki.

Alcadipani, R., & Rosa, A. R. (2011). From grobal management to glocal management: Latin American perspectives as a counter-dominant management epistemology. *Canadian Journal of the Administrative Sciences*, *28*: 453–466.

Barros, A. (2011). O Desenvolvimento das Escolas Superiores de Administração: os saberes administrativos brasileiros no contexto de hegemonia estadunidense. Paper presented at XXXV Enanpad, Rio de Janeiro.

Belich, J. (2009). *Replenishing the earth: The settler revolution and the rise of the Anglo-world, 1783–1939*. Oxford: Oxford University Press.

Bertero, C. (2006). *Ensino e Pesquisa em Administração*. São Paulo: Thomson Learning.

Bhabha, H. (1994). *The location of culture*. London: Routledge.

Caldas, M. (1997). Santo de casa não faz milagre: condicionamentos nacionais e implicações organizacionais pela figura do 'estrangeiro'. In F. C. Prestes Motta & M. Caldas, *Cultura organizacional e cultura brasileira* (pp. 44–56). São Paulo: Atlas.

Calligaris. C. (1993). *Hello Brazil!* São Paulo: Escuta.

Césaire, A. (1955). *Discourse on colonialism*. New York: Monthly Review Press.

Chauí, M. (1985). *A crise no ensino Brasileiro*, São Paulo: Série Depoimentos, FFLCH-USP.

Chomsky, N. (2004). *Hegemony or survival*. New York: Henry Holt.

Cooke, B., & Mills, A. (2008). Management as a Cold War phenomenon? *Human Relations*, *59*: 603–610.

Engwall, L. (2004). The Americanization of Nordic management education. *Journal of Management Inquiry*, *13*: 109–117.

Fanon, F. (1961). *The wretched of the earth*. New York: Grove Weidenfeld.

Freire-Medeiros, B. (2005). *O Rio de Janeiro que Hollywood inventou*. Rio de Janeiro: Jorge ZahLar Editor.

Frenkel, T., & Shenhav, Y. (2003). From Americanization to colonization: The diffusion of productivity models revisited. *Organization Studies, 2*(4): 1537–1561.

Gantman, E., & Rodrigues, C. (2008). Notas sobre la evolución del conocimiento administrativo em la República Argentina y su comparación con el caso español (1913–2007). *Cadernos EBAPE.br., 06*: 2–22.

Haines, G. (1989). *The Americanization of Brazil: A study of U.S. Cold War diplomacy in the Third World.* Wilmington, DE: Scholarly Resources.

Hardt, M., & Negri, A. (2001). *Empire.* Boston: Harvard University Press

Harvey, D. (2003). *The new imperialism.* Oxford: Oxford University Press.

Ianni, O. (1979). *Imperialismo e Cultura.* Petrópolis, Brazil: Editora Vozes.

Ibarra-Colado, E. (2006). Organization studies and epistemic coloniality in Latin America: Thinking otherness from the margins. *Organization, 13*: 463–488.

Jack, G., Westwood, R., Srinivas, N., & Sardar, Z. (2011). Deepening, broadening and re-asserting a postcolonial interrogative space in organization studies. *Organization, 18*: 275–302.

Kelly, E., Mills, A., & Cooke, B. (2006). Management as a Cold War phenomenon? *Human Relations, 59*: 603–610.

Khurana, R., (2007). *From higher aims to hired hands: The social transformation of American business schools and the unfulfilled promise of management as a profession.* Princeton, NJ: Princeton University Press.

Kieser, A. (2004). The Americanization of academic management education in Germany. *Journal of Management Inquiry, 13*: 90–97.

Kipping, M., Üsdiken, B., & Puig, N. (2004). Imitation, tension, and hybridization: Multiple "Americanizations" of management education. *Journal of Management Inquiry, 13*: 98–108.

Landau, O. (2006). Cold War political culture and the return of system rationality. *Human Relations, 59*: 637–663.

Lazzarini, S. (2011). *Capitalismo de laços: Os donos do Brasil e suas conexões.* Rio de Janeiro: Elsevier.

Leavitt, H. (1957). On the export of American management education. *The Journal of Business, 30*: 153–161.

Leslie, S. (1993). *The Cold War and the American science.* New York: Columbia University Press

Mignolo, W. (2000). *Local histories/global designs: Coloniality, subaltern knowledges, and border thinking.* Princeton, NJ: Princeton University Press.

Mignolo, W. (2008). *The idea of Latin America.* London: Blackwell.

Mir, R., Mir, A., & Srinivas, N. (2004). Managerial knowledge as property: The role of universities. *Organization Management Knowledge, L*: 126–137.

Neal, M., & Finlay, J. (2008). American hegemony and business education in the Arab world. *Journal of Management Education* February, *32*: 38–83.

Nye, J. S. (1990). Soft power and American foreign policy. *Political Science Quarterly, 119*.

Nye, J., Jr. (2004). *Soft power: The means to success in world politics.* New York: Public Affairs.

Parmar, I (2002). American foundations and the development of international knowledge networks. *Global Networks, 2*: 13–30.

Paula, A.P.P. de, & Wood, T., Jr. (2009). Management: Tales of passion, power and profit. *International Journal of Organization Theory and Behavior, 12*: 595–617.

Perkins, D. (1927). *The Monroe Doctrine, 1823–1826.* Cambridge, MA: Harvard University Press.

Prasad, A. (Ed.). (2003). The gaze of the other: Postcolonial theory and organizational analysis. In A. Prasad (Ed.), *Postcolonial theory and organizational analysis: A critical engagement*: 3–44. London: Palgrave.

Prasad, A. (Ed.). (2012). *Against the grain: Advances in postcolonial organization studies.* Copenhagen: Copenhagen Business School Press.

Prasad, A., & Prasad, P. (2001). Otherness at large: Identity and difference in the new globalized organizational landscape. In A. Mills & I. Marjosa, *Gender, identity and culture of organizations* (pp. 57–71). London: Routledge.

Ritzer, G. (2008). *The McDonaldization of society.* Los Angeles: Pine Forge Press.

Said, E. (1978). *Orientalism.* New York: Viking.

Said, E. (1993). *Culture and imperialism.* New York: Vintage.

Srinivas, I. (2009). Mimicry and revival: The transfer and transformation of management knowledge in India, 1959–1990. *Studies of Management & Organization, 38*: 38–58.

Tikly, L. (2004). Education and the new imperialism. *Comparative Education, 40*: 173–198.

Tota, A. (2000). *O Imperialismo Sedutor – A Americanização do Brasil na Época da Segunda Guerra.* São Paulo: Cia das Letras.

Tragtenberg, M. (1971). A Teoria Geral da Administração é uma Ideologia? *RAE, 11*: 77–21.

Üsdiken, B. (2004). Americanization of European management education in historical and comparative perspective: A symposium. *Journal of Management Inquiry, 13*: 87–89.

Vernon, J. R. (1994). World War II fiscal policies and the end of the Great Depression. *The Journal of Economic History, 54*: 850–868.

Westwood, R., & Jack, G. (2008). The US commercial-military-political complex and the emergence of international business and management studies. *Critical Perspectives on International Business, 4*: 367–388.

Wyrick, D., & Beasley, J. (1997). Postcolonial Journal. *Jouveret, 1*.

Index

Note: Italicized page numbers indicate a figure on the corresponding page. Page numbers in bold indicate a table on the corresponding page.